Communities
of Discourse

Communities
of Discourse

*Ideology and Social Structure
in the Reformation, the Enlightenment,
and European Socialism*

Robert Wuthnow

*Harvard University Press
Cambridge, Massachusetts
London, England 1989*

This book is printed on acid-free paper, and its binding materials
have been chosen for strength and durability.

Library of Congress Cataloging-in-Publication Data

Wuthnow, Robert.
  Communities of discourse.
  Bibliography: p.
  Includes indexes.
    1. Social History—Modern, 1500–   . 2. Ideology.
  3. Reformation. 4. Enlightenment. 5. Capitalism—
  Europe—History. 6. Socialism—Europe—History.
  I. Title.
HN13. W88 1989   303.3'72   88-35792
ISBN 0-674-15164-X (alk. paper)

For Sally

Acknowledgments

A BOOK OF THIS scope takes many years to write. During that time I have drawn from the work of hundreds of scholars whose knowledge of particular subjects was deeper than mine. I have acknowledged many of these debts in the accompanying notes and citations. I was able to initiate the project largely because of an honorific fellowship from Princeton University, made possible by a grant from the William Paterson Foundation, which provided a stipend and released time from teaching. The project also received support through a number of grants from the Committee on Research in the Humanities and Social Sciences of Princeton University. Research assistance was provided by Laura Mason and James Wald, who at the time were advanced graduate students in the Department of History at Princeton. Lisa Frodsham and Clara Kim helped me prepare the reference material and index. Opportunities to test out preliminary versions of parts of the book were made available by the Comparative Historical Section of the American Sociological Association, the Church History Society in conjunction with the American Historical Association, the Conference Internationale de Sociologie des Religions, the Russell Sage Foundation, the Association for Religious Studies in Tokyo, the Volkswagen Foundation, Jagiellonian University, the University of Edinburgh, Harvard University, UCLA, and the University of Notre Dame, among others. I received valuable advice on early drafts of some of the chapters from Geoff Eley, Leonard Hochberg, Albert Hirschman, John Elliott, and John Sutton. Many conversations with Robert Liebman during his years at Princeton helped shape the project. Theda Skocpol's faith in the venture was another sustaining force. Wendy Griswold, Robert Liebman, John Meyer, and Charles Tilly read the entire manuscript and gave me valuable suggestions for cutting and revising. Michael Aronson of Harvard University Press deserves special thanks for his patience and encouragement. Finally, I owe a great debt to my family for standing with me through the entire process.

Contents

Communities
of Discourse

Introduction ᕙ᷍ᕗ
The Problem of Articulation

O N MARCH 6, 1522, after nearly a year of enforced seclusion
and study at the Wartburg castle, Martin Luther returned to
Wittenberg. His decision to return, despite obvious risks to his own
safety, was prompted by a desire to quell the social unrest that had
erupted in the wake of his disciples' preaching. Three days later, on
Invocavit Sunday, he mounted the pulpit of the parish church and
delivered what many still consider one of his most powerful sermons.
No controversy remained untouched: purification of the mass, images, instruction in partaking of the Eucharist, monastic vows, fasting,
civil insurrection. On all these issues Luther counseled a bold attitude
of faith tempered with love. Faith without love, he said, "is not faith
at all, but a counterfeit faith, just as a face seen in a mirror is not a
face but merely the reflection of one."[1]

Luther's Invocavit sermon, together with seven additional sermons preached the following week, constitutes a decisive turning
point in the religious struggles of the period. With masterly rhetoric
Luther recaptured the leadership of the reform movement, quieted
the simmering social unrest at Wittenberg, and turned the movement
in a peaceful direction by emphasizing individual freedom and responsibility. He asserted the authority of Scripture against those who
sought radical reforms based on personal revelations of divine guidance, and yet he admonished his followers to examine their own
hearts and let the divine Word be the instrument of reform rather

than violence or coercion. Contemporaries were particularly impressed with the power of Luther's discourse. A student in the crowd wrote: "[Luther] drives home his points, like nails, into the minds of his hearers." Another member of the audience wrote to a friend: "All week long Luther did nothing but set up what had been knocked down and took us all severely to task."[2]

At the moment of Luther's exposition, Wittenberg was awash with the broader economic currents then transforming life in central and northern Europe. Trade, mining, and other commercial activities were beginning to alter traditional social arrangements. The leading religious reformers were at odds with one another, so much so that their cause seemed endangered unless an authoritative voice could be found. Frederick, elector of Saxony, had begun to supply military protection and offered personal encouragement to the reformers but was also pressing them to avoid saying anything that might promote civil insurrection. The religious reforms that were taking place, now in the fifth year of their Lutheran phase, were producing actions and reactions that played back into the narratives of their own spokesmen. During the preceding six months clerical celibacy had been abandoned, monastic begging disallowed, private masses abolished; both the bread and the chalice were being distributed during the Eucharist; preaching was conducted in German; and since January several episodes of image breaking had erupted. With even further unrest on the horizon, the city council appealed to Luther to return in hopes of restoring order to the movement. At the center of it all, legitimating its own role as a producer of ideas, was an assembly of writers and theologians, preachers and laity—a community of discourse. We cannot coerce, Luther told his followers, but "we have the right to speak."[3]

The sermon at Wittenberg on Invocavit Sunday was followed over the next half century by thousands of sermons (more than 3,000 preached by Luther himself), by a huge proliferation of tracts and pamphlets, and by countless disputations, letters, and colloquies. Between 1517 and 1550 approximately 150,000 new books, with combined sales of 60 million copies, were published—at least four times as many as had appeared during the entire fifteenth century.[4] In Wittenberg alone some 600 different works appeared between 1517 and 1523, and during the same period an estimated tenfold increase in the number of tracts published by German printers took place: according to one inventory, nearly 400 printers, 125 places

of publication, and approximately 900 authors were involved.[5] Together these sermons, tracts, and disputations constituted what came
to be known as the Protestant Reformation. Each sermon, each tract,
each disputation was produced in a specific social setting. Each setting
was in turn connected with broader social, economic, political, and
cultural forces. These forces constituted an environment, more conducive in some areas to be sure than in others, in which the Reformation could emerge as a concrete collective movement. The
opportunities and limitations facing the reformers came from this
environment. The reformers could advance their ideas only by securing resources from it. Some ideas gained the necessary resources
and became part of the institutional arrangements of European society itself; others failed or succeeded only on a modest scale. The
ideas that made up the Reformation were thus contingent to a certain
extent on their relation to the social environment. And yet, had they
been contingent only on that environment, it seems doubtful that
they would have gained the lasting place in Western culture that they
did.

The problem of articulation is particularly enigmatic in the case
Great works of art and literature, philosophy and social criticism,
like great sermons, always relate in an enigmatic fashion to their
social environment. They draw resources, insights, and inspiration
from that environment: they reflect it, speak to it, and make themselves relevant to it. And yet they also remain autonomous enough
from their social environment to acquire a broader, even universal
and timeless appeal. This is the problem of articulation: if cultural
products do not articulate closely enough with their social settings,
they are likely to be regarded by the potential audiences of which
these settings are composed as irrelevant, unrealistic, artificial, and
overly abstract, or worse, their producers will be unlikely to receive
the support necessary to carry on their work; but if cultural products
articulate too closely with the specific social environment in which
they are produced, they are likely to be thought of as esoteric, parochial, time bound, and fail to attract a wider and more lasting
audience. The process of articulation is thus characterized by a delicate balance between the products of culture and the social environment in which they are produced.

The problem of articulation is particularly enigmatic in the case
of discourse that specifically challenges the status quo. The Reformation provides a vivid example. Its success depended on securing
the resources necessary to organize a vast social movement. In ad-

dition to raising the more obscure points of doctrine that aroused the passions of theologians, it became a social movement that required finances, buildings, training centers, legislation, political patronage, and eventually the sword. Its discourse did not occur in a social vacuum: tax systems, property rights, and political regimes were all at stake. Somehow the reformers' ideas won the support of large segments of late medieval society at the same time that these ideas were undermining the very basis of that society. Was it that the social environment had already begun to change and the ideas merely reflected these changes? Certainly it makes good sense to suspect that something was happening to provide the reformers with new resources and new possibilities for advancing their ideas. But surely this is not the whole story. If it is, it gives little strength to the reformers' ideas themselves. Did these ideas not feed back into the social settings in which the Reformation took place, opening up new horizons and creating turbulence that was itself unsettling for many decades to come? And perhaps even more important, how was it that these ideas came to have a more dramatic and lasting effect than even their proponents expected? Perhaps the reformers were shortsighted and simply unaware of the deeper shifts at work in the societal substrata. And yet, putting it this way shifts all the power to blind features of the social environment. Can the power of discourse be so readily dismissed? What was it about the ideas themselves that allowed them to transcend their immediate circumstances?

The irony is that the Reformation's success required it to articulate with its social environment and to disarticulate from this environment at the same time. The Reformation spoke to the needs and longings of men and women living in sixteenth-century towns and villages. It seemed relevant enough to persons in power to gain their protection. It frightened others so deeply that they took up arms to stamp out the new ideas. At the same time, the reformers somehow protected themselves from merely doing the bidding of their supporters. They set the terms of their own debates rather than simply providing legitimation for those in power or for those aspiring to power. Once set in motion, their formulations created the conditions ensuring their own perpetuation. They provided moral meanings that cut across broad segments of European society and outlasted the sixteenth century. Ideas came into being that related to the concrete struggles of the sixteenth century but also dealt with lasting questions of freedom, responsibility, will, faith, righteousness, in-

dividual discipline, and civic order. The social scientist who studies
the Reformation, therefore, must not only ask about the social conditions that shaped its ideology but also inquire into the reasons why
these conditions did not shape it more.

This is a study, in the broadest sense, of the problem of articulation. Its aim is to shed light on the ways in which ideas are shaped
by their social situations and yet manage to disengage from these
situations. The relations to be examined come from the three episodes of cultural production that have probably challenged the status
quo, in terms of culture itself, more than any others in the development of modern societies: the Protestant Reformation, the Enlightenment, and the rise of Marxist socialism. It is a study of the
ways in which social conditions in each period made cultural innovation possible, of variations in the extent to which each movement
(as a carrier of its own distinctive ideology) became institutionalized
in different societies, and of the ways in which the resulting ideologies
were shaped by and yet succeeded in transcending their specific
environments of origin.

The kinds of questions to be addressed, although at a broader
and more comparative level, are suggested by Luther's Invocavit
sermon. If the German states were in fact witnessing economic
changes at the start of the sixteenth century, what effect, if any, did
these changes have on the reformers' chances of making their voices
heard? What political circumstances made it possible for Elector
Frederick and others to aid the reformers? Why, if civil insurrection
was a real possibility, were Luther and the other reformers given
pulpits in towns like Wittenberg? What prevented them from gaining
a sympathetic hearing in other towns? How did the genres of their
own discourse affect its reception? Did specific social circumstances
become objects of the reformers' discourse? And if so, how did this
discourse come to incorporate more general appeals as well?

Much evidence has accumulated, even within the past few years,
with which to address questions such as these. No longer can broad
theories of cultural change be advanced without close attention being
paid to this evidence. Much sifting and augmentation of the historical
record has taken place. This study draws extensively on these efforts.
It is, however, not principally historical but sociological: the soci-
ologist's task is to sift and reconstruct, but in a different way. Its aim
is to compare, to bring societies and time periods into conjunction
with one another, to draw diverse literatures together, and to assess

the results with theoretical issues in mind. It is not, in the present case, to unearth new facts about Wittenberg but to bring what is known about Wittenberg together with what is known about London and Stockholm, to bring together the evidence accumulated by students of economic history with that yielded by studies of the church, and to compare the results, first across regions in the sixteenth century, and then with similar developments in the eighteenth century and the nineteenth century. For each period attention must be given not only to the places where new ideologies were successfully institutionalized but also to those places where ideological innovations failed to take root. Systematic comparisons of the various regions and nation-states in each period provide the evidence necessary to assess the weight of alternative arguments about the role of economic change, social classes, cultural precedents, and political arrangements. Understanding the social contexts of each ideological movement then provides a basis from which to examine the internal structure of each ideology itself in order to illuminate the processes of articulation and disarticulation.

There is also an implicit theoretical scaffold on which this reconstruction depends, and an explicit aim of the substantive comparisons that follow is to examine the validity and utility of this theoretical framework. It is in fact a scaffold more than it is either a foundation or an inner system of girders and beams. It provides a loose-fitting framework from which an edifice of many particular details and architectural refinements can be constructed. It can be torn away so that the empirical contours of this edifice can be seen unobstructed. It does, however, affect the way in which these contours are arranged. Therefore, something of its composition needs to be known from the outset.

In examining the social conditions in which Protestantism, the Enlightenment, and socialism came into being, a distinction of the most general kind is drawn between environmental conditions, institutional contexts, and action sequences.

Environmental conditions refer to the most general social, cultural, political, and economic contours of the period under consideration. Knowing whether a particular society in a given period is subject to increases or decreases in population, whether the economy is expanding or contracting, whether the larger political climate is characterized by war or peace, and whether the society is religiously unified or divided is usually a relevant place to begin. Considering the rise of new ideological systems makes it especially important to know how these broader environmental conditions may be changing. Changes in the social environment are likely to provide the resources necessary to bring into being an innovative cultural movement.

Institutional contexts are the more immediate settings in which these resources are molded. They are the organizational situations in which ideology is actually created and disseminated, and are likely to include the arrangements of power, economic supplies, personnel, and legitimation that directly affect the creation and dissemination of an ideology. Of relevance here are schools and universities, churches, reading societies, scientific academies, newspapers, governing agencies, and political parties. Within these contexts the producers of culture gain access to necessary resources, come into contact with their audiences, and confront the limitations posed by competitors and persons in authority.

Action sequences happen within institutional contexts. They refer to the behavior of culture producers and consumers and the decisions of patrons, censors, political leaders, and others who affect the behavior of culture producers and their audiences. These actions often remain shrouded in the historical record, or are too idiosyncratic to be amenable to systematization. Yet the very concept of action sequences serves as an important placeholder: it reminds us of the importance of human agency, even if that agency occurs within the constraints of institutional structures, and it reminds us that cultural innovations do not emerge full-blown all at once but are the result of years and decades, and for this reason have a sequential effect on their own development.

Together, then, these three conceptual categories help to focus the analysis of the social environment in which cultural action takes place: first, the broad terrain from which resources derive; second, the immediate institutional contexts in which these resources are arranged and distributed; and third, the specific actions involved in producing cultural objects.

Particular attention is given to features of the social environment that are associated with the development of capitalism. Indeed the three episodes of cultural change that are at issue provide opportunities to consider the relations between ideology and social structure in three of the most formative periods of capitalist development. An early phase of capital accumulation occurred in the sixteenth century in conjunction with the rapid commercial expansion and price inflation of the period; the eighteenth century witnessed the high point of mercantile capitalism; and in the nineteenth century industrialization transformed capitalism. The ideological movements of each period could scarcely have been unaffected in some way by these far-reaching economic transitions. What the effects were and how they were mediated by institutional contexts are questions that will occupy much attention in the following chapters.

The institutional contexts that receive special emphasis include not only the organizations (churches, salons, and so on) that produce culture but also agencies of the state that channel resources to these organizations. These three episodes of cultural change provide glimpses into the ideological activities of the state at distinct phases in its development. During the Reformation the major territorial regimes, and many localized regimes as well, manifested the tensions associated with efforts to secure greater fiscal and administrative autonomy from the landed elite. The modern state as such had not yet come into being: states consisted largely of the household bureaucracies of strong territorial princes whose lands often remained scattered and whose dynastic claims often remained tenuous; they also consisted of magisterial councils in semiautonomous imperial cities; and in a few instances they consisted of emerging, but by no means absolute, centralized monarchies. The eighteenth-century state exhibited strong growth in central bureaucracies, but it was also fraught with an increasing variety of internal divisions. During the latter half of the nineteenth century mass political parties and tensions between aristocratic-monarchic factions and liberal-republican factions dominated many of the European states. In all three periods, then, the emphasis is inevitably less on standard attributes of state building, such as centralization and national integration, and more on the internal struggles that characterize ruling elites and organized agencies of the state.

Much of what follows will constitute an argument about the relations between the broader social environments and the immediate institutional contexts in which the Reformation, the Enlightenment, and socialism developed. I shall argue against theories that have associated these cultural developments with social unrest, dislocation, unsettled lives, anxiety, anomie, and the like. I shall also argue against interpretations that privilege the role of new social classes and the presumed need for class legitimation that gives rise to new ideologies. The interpretation that best fits the evidence, in my view, is one that emphasizes the available supply of economic and political resources. Each of these episodes of cultural innovation, as I shall try to demonstrate, occurred during a period of exceptional economic growth in western Europe; moreover, those areas that experienced the greatest growth generally led in cultural developments as well.

My argument is not, however, yet another attempt to discover the roots of ideological change in simple economic conditions. I do not suggest that economic growth shaped these cultural movements directly, either by altering the outlook of culture producers or by changing the interests of culture consumers. Instead, I emphasize the ways in which economic expansion interacted with institutional arrangements to restructure the contexts in which producers and their audiences came together. Economic expansion alone did not create new opportunities for new ideas to emerge; rather, it resulted—in some areas—in new alignments among segments of the ruling elite (who themselves played active roles in furthering certain kinds of economic expansion). Generally speaking, the new political alignments that accompanied each period of economic expansion included (a) an overall increase in the size and functional responsibilities of central regimes; (b) heightened diversity, tension, and cleavages within the ruling elite; and (c) a somewhat enlarged set of actors and issues relevant to the collective decision-making process. These changes, in turn, typically resulted in an expansion of the immediate organizational settings in which cultural production could take place, as well as a restructuring of the relations between culture producers and the state and a rise of new concerns about definitions of individual and collective responsibilities. An important part of my argument, then, is that the Reformation, the Enlightenment, and European socialism were social movements whose development (temporally and geographically) depended on a conjuncture of economic expansion and realignment among ruling elites.

Also at issue in each of the three periods, somewhat more specifically, is the relation between social circumstances and a temporally associated form of ideology: the way in which the two articulate with each other. This is a process of mutual influence, adjustment, accommodation. Process is the key. And there is also a conceptual scaffold from which to consider the complex interactions that constitute this process. Here a conceptual distinction is drawn among three analytically separable processes that together constitute the overall process of articulation.

One can be referred to simply as *production*. Ideas are formulated, sermons are preached, discourse is initiated, books and pamphlets are written, courses are taught, newspapers are published. Cultural artifacts come into being, often in great profusion. Questions can be asked about the resources making possible this productivity and the uncertainties motivating it.

Then there is the process of *selection*. Once a profusion of cultural products has come into being a selective process is also likely to become evident. Writers choose some genres and neglect others; preachers adopt certain rhetorical styles over others; certain schools of thought become dominant in place of others; the ideas and influence of certain leaders flourish more than others; new forms of thought replace older forms; some of these variations seem to gain more favorable hearings in certain social contexts than in others. The factors that account for these selective processes may be different from those that account for the sheer act of production in the first place. Particular resources flow to particular forms of ideology; certain genres adapt to new environments better than others; in general, a degree of "fit" or articulation begins to become evident between modes of discourse and the contexts in which they occur.

Finally, one can speak of *institutionalization* as an analytically distinct process. Routinized mechanisms for the production and dissemination of particular modes of discourse come into being. Writers become known for a certain literary style; this style gains expression in a particular literary community; an ecclesiastical structure is modified to ensure the survival of a particular creed or doctrine; the very forms in which an ideology is communicated become more familiar; journals and publishing operations are set in motion; the organizations in which culture is produced gain greater control over their own access to resources and become more autonomous in setting up their own systems of rewards and expectations. The net result is that not only is a particular ideology produced, and not only does it compete with alternative ideologies, but it becomes a relatively stable feature of the institutional structure of a given society.

The purpose served by these conceptual distinctions is to guide the task of relating the otherwise crude and largely unmanageable notions of social structure and ideology to each other. Specifying environmental conditions, institutional contexts, and action sequences points to the importance of determining precisely what it is about social structure that may affect ideology. Distinguishing these three categories of the broader social milieu gives a more precise indication of where the process of articulation may be taking place. Similarly, one can say somewhat more precisely how social conditions influence ideological outcomes by separating these outcomes into analytically discrete processes.

Distinguishing production, selection, and institutionalization permits me to develop a number of subarguments about the ways in which social conditions and particular ideologies came to articulate with one another. One dimension of each of these periods of cultural change, as the Wittenberg example has already illustrated, was a sheer increase in the overall volume of books, pamphlets, sermons, political tracts, and other formalized modes of cultural production. It is thus important to ask at some level—without much regard for the actual content of these artifacts—what conditions facilitated these increases in productivity. In general, I argue that these increases were greatly facilitated in each instance by an expansion in various forms of political patronage and by changes within the state that restrained the hand of censors and restricted the voice of established cultural authorities. A significant aspect of this argument, moreover, is that the resultant increases in productivity were also characterized by a fairly wide range of substantive and formal diversity. In short, competing schools of thought emerged, which in turn motivated higher levels of productivity. Rather than attempting to thematize the Reformation, the Enlightenment, and socialism, as many students of the history of these ideas have sought to do, it is thus important to emphasize the conditions under which diversity itself was able to develop. I show how these competing schools were to some degree rooted in localized and regional variations in the institutional contexts from which they emerged. I also show that these contexts "selected for" certain genres, styles, and themes over time and "selected against" others.

In this context it also proves useful to separate the question of institutionalization from questions of production and selection. Stable access to resources, communication networks, established organizations, autonomy, and control over processes of evaluation and debate are all important features of institutionalization. In each of the three cases I present systematic comparisons to show how culture producers' relations to the state influenced their capacity to institutionalize new forms of ideology. To an important extent institutionalization depended on stable political arrangements that supplied material resources. But institutionalization also involved culture producers' maintaining a degree of autonomy from their patrons. Part of the balance was achieved tacitly through structural arrangements—again often resulting from changing alliances within the state and the ruling elite. Part of it was also achieved actively through the ways in which ideas articulated with these structural arrangements.

It remains to consider, then, what became articulated. For this purpose a final set of conceptual distinctions comes into play. Never is there a complete fit between an ideology and its social milieu: never does one in all its raw complexity simply provide a model for the other; and never does one simply mirror the other in every respect. Moreover, the very idea of articulation, as I have suggested, points to a relation that is partial. Articulation always implies disarticulation. Some features of an ideology resonate closely with the social context in which they appear; others point toward context-free concepts and generalizations. It is not enough, then, to account for as much variation in ideologies as one can with reference to the social environment—and grudgingly credit the rest to idiosyncrasies of individual genius, creativity, or serendipity. Rather, the search for features of ideology that resemble features of the social milieu must also include an account of the ways in which an ideology becomes at least partially free of contextual determination.

The scaffolding that guides this aspect of the analysis distinguishes among social horizons, discursive fields, and figural action (or figural actors).

The *social horizon* refers to features of the real, experienced social context in which ideology is produced, selected, and institutionalized. These features exist as both contexts of ideology and elements of the texts of which ideology consists. The unrest in Wittenberg in 1522 provided the context for Luther's Invocavit sermon; it also became a feature of Luther's discourse. Luther spoke about iconoclasm, about the conflicts between the reformers and the church, about himself and his struggles with the pope. In other instances, struggles between social classes, among factions within the state, or between political parties may provide the immediate occasion for the production of ideology—ideology which in turn presents an image of these struggles. The experienced world becomes, as it were, incorporated into the text. But the process of incorporation, of textualization, is itself selective and transformative. The social world of the text and the social world in which the text is produced will resemble each other only partially. Struggles between social classes in the experienced world and the narrative or theoretical representation of these struggles will differ by virtue of the constraints imposed by narrative and theoretical construction itself. The two will articulate but remain disarticulated as well.

The *discursive field* refers to a symbolic space or structure within the ideology itself. In the ideologies to be considered here a relatively simple discursive field defined by some fundamental opposition of binary concepts is often evident, but more complex discursive structures are sometimes evident as well. In Luther's discourse a recurrent theme consists of the opposition between the received authority of the church on the one hand and the authority of the Word of God on the other hand. Admonishing his followers in Wittenberg, he equated the one with mere externalities, the other with internal conviction. The received authority of the church was a matter of coercion, of chains and imprisonment, a structure that would "come falling down by itself," part of "Satan's plan": he likened those who focused on these externalities to "those disgraceful people [described in Deuteronomy 23:12] who fouled the camp of Israel."[6] The Word of God, in contrast, offered freedom, liberty; it was the "new wine" that worked effectively in the hearts of believers. On the one hand were "dangerous abuses," "superstitions," "endless, innumerable, un-Christian and damnable tyrannical diminutions," "burdens," and "blasphemies"; on the other hand was the true gospel, "the liberation of holy Christendom."[7] These oppositions define a basic polarity that gives structure and organization to Luther's reforming ideology. Many of his observations about specific social or theological issues are mapped onto this basic discursive field.[8] They give it objectivity; it in turn organizes the relations among them, thereby shaping the manner in which they are interpreted. A discursive field of this kind provides the fundamental categories in which thinking can take place. It establishes the limits of discussion and defines the range of problems that can be addressed. The question of articulation at this level becomes a question of specific features of the social horizon being incorporated into the discursive field as symbolic acts and events, or of parallel formations in one being superimposed on the other. In the simplest case, conflict between two factions in the social world may dramatize the basic opposition around which ideological statements are organized. The question of disarticulation becomes one of identifying ways in which the discursive field provides contrasts with features of the social horizon itself, thereby evoking a conceptual space in which creative reflection can take place. Luther's discourse drew on conflicts present in his own social context, but the basic axes of his polemics abstracted features of these conflicts and set them in a more general framework. In this way he identified theoretical issues of more lasting and universal significance.

Figural action refers to representative behaviors, modes of thinking, or characters that occupy space within a discursive field and are defined by the structural features of that field. Faith and love in Luther's Invocavit sermon are examples of such representative behaviors. They take on significance within the broader polarities around which Luther's discourse is organized. If discursive fields define the range of problems that can be considered, figural action provides, as it were, a representative range of solutions to these problems. Figural action defines a course of behavior that makes sense, given the problems and possibilities that have been identified. Faith tempered with love offered to Luther and his audience on Invocavit Sunday a model for behavior that avoided both the extremes of conforming to a corrupt ecclesiastical system and over-zealous purification of that system. "It is enough," he counseled, "that each one do that right thing which is appropriate to himself and incumbent upon him."[9] It will be seen that a number of other representative actions and actors—the righteous magistrate, the prototypical bourgeois, the valorized proletarian—are also framed in this manner. They are figural characters, abstracted from concrete social situations, but framed within a more general pattern of discourse that permits them to transcend their immediate situations. Here again, the question of articulation becomes one of identifying features of the social horizon that are incorporated directly into the depiction of figural action, or that limit the ways in which that action can be depicted. And the question of disarticulation is a matter of determining the ways in which figural action is indeed representative and confined within more abstract conceptual fields rather than being limited to specific actors or actions in the immediate social horizon. For figural action to provide an effective model for behavior it must demonstrate both concreteness, which comes from exemplars found within the immediate social horizon, and generality and openness, which come from being cast within a less situationally restricted ideological framework.

My arguments about social horizons, discursive fields, and figural action are both theoretical and substantive. At the theoretical level

I attempt to show the transformative power of these tropological elements: they help us understand the relations between social conditions and ideologies by specifying some of the ways in which social conditions are themselves textualized, structured by basic conceptual distinctions, and turned into figural elements that have metonymic functions.[10] Substantively, I argue that Luther, Voltaire, Marx, and their respective compatriots were able to formulate critical ideological discourse by thematizing certain features of their social environments, setting them in opposition to alternative visions of cultural authority, concretizing both by drawing on conflicts evident in the societies in which they wrote, and supplying figurations of behavior that mediated between present and idealized realities. Changing social circumstances that produced new cleavages within the ruling elite were thus important, not only in providing institutional space in which to create ideology but also in creating the conceptual space of which new ideologies were themselves constructed. Furthermore, the diversity of situations in which each of these ideological movements emerged precluded any simple or concrete program of behavior from being workable and thus encouraged the formulation of more abstract, representative, figural notions of behavior that were able to transcend immediate situations more effectively.[11]

All of these conceptual distinctions remain in the background throughout the substantive analyses that follow in order to allow the substantive patterns themselves to be emphasized. Only in the final theoretical section do they again become the focus of discussion. It should be evident even with this brief introduction, however, that the present approach places the concept of culture itself in a distinct light. Culture is understood here not as some subjective or idealized world view that is to be distinguished from behavior but as a form of behavior itself and as the tangible results of that behavior. In the present context it is distinguished largely on empirical grounds relevant to the historical cases under consideration: as religious discourse, sermons, theological writings, instruction in the ways of worshiping, literature, plays, newspapers, philosophical treatises, political tracts, party platforms, and propaganda. For other purposes different distinctions could well be drawn between culture and the social structures to which it is to be related. The important point is that culture, as conceived here, is explicitly produced rather than simply being implicitly embedded in, or constitutive of, social arrangements.[12]

To a significant degree, culture in the present sense can be observed in the activities and artifacts of its producers. Moreover, it exists within the dynamic contexts in which it is produced and disseminated rather than being abstracted from these concrete settings. It is for this reason that the image of a community of discourse is invoked. Discourse subsumes the written as well as the verbal, the formal as well as the informal, the gestural or ritual as well as the conceptual. It occurs, however, within communities in the broadest sense of the word: communities of competing producers, of interpreters and critics, of audiences and consumers, and of patrons and other significant actors who become the subjects of discourse itself. It is only in these concrete living and breathing communities that discourse becomes meaningful.

The term *ideology* is also used in a special sense. It refers in the present context to an identifiable constellation of discourse that in fact stands in some degree of articulation with its social context. All ideology, by this definition, bears some relation with its social environment. The extent to which this relation is characterized by a high or low degree of articulation, and the processes by which that degree of articulation comes into being, are empirical questions. In this usage, then, ideology is also an analytic feature of a community of discourse. It is that aspect of discourse that pertains in some special way to its social surroundings. To analyze ideology is to focus on the question of articulation. To do so, however, does not preclude other kinds of questions—philosophic, aesthetic, critical. Nor does the analysis of ideology in this sense imply questions of legitimation, distortion, or false consciousness. Ideology is neither assumed to be an accurate reflection of reality nor accused of distorting reality, only of bearing a relation to the specific social context in which it appears.

Emphasizing the problem of articulation draws an explicit contrast with two alternative approaches to the relation between ideology and social structure. One is the rather prosaic but common view that ideology somehow reflects social structure: for example, that an authoritarian ideology is likely to mirror a highly centralized, vertical distribution of political and economic power; or that an ideology of professional competence reflects the actual asymmetry of status and rewards between professionals and their clients. The other is the view, held perhaps even more widely, that ideology can essentially be understood in terms of the legitimating role it plays in relation to social structure, either in the sense of promoting passive acceptance of social conditions by presenting a distorted image of them, or in the sense of motivating a more active acceptance of certain courses of behavior through an ideological connection between them and higher legitimating values. Although the second perspective grants ideology a more influential role in social relations than the first, both remain limited insofar as they depict the relation between ideology and social structure in relatively simplistic and unmediated terms. Social structure tends to be taken largely as a given, or as something basically unaffected by ideology, and it then shapes ideology or nurtures an ideology that plays a relatively circumscribed role.

There is no reason to suppose that ideology plays an entirely passive role in relation to social structure, or if not a passive role, that it merely legitimates what is going on anyway. Nor is there any reason to suppose that the relation between ideology and social structure is as simple, direct, and undifferentiated as either of these views implies. To suggest that Luther's Invocavit sermon merely reflected or legitimated the social circumstances under which it was given is as farfetched as it is inimical to a deeper understanding of the relations between ideology and social structure. The issue of articulation, by contrast, points simply to the fact that in many cases an apparent fit seems to develop between an ideology and its social context; that the two intermingle. How this situation comes about becomes the central question. But the question's answer is relatively more complicated than is suggested either by the simple causality implicit in the reflection approach or by the functional reasoning evident in the legitimation approach. It requires paying greater empirical attention to the environmental resources used in ideological production, to the ways in which the producers of ideology and these resources come to be organized, and to the ways in which the ideology itself is internally structured.

In examining these questions the role of the state and its relations with ideology will occupy an important place, as they do in nearly all studies of ideology. It is, however, not so much the issue of ideology legitimating the state that assumes prominence here, as that of the state as a context in which different kinds of ideological production can be legitimated. The holders of authoritative positions within the state make decisions with respect to culture producers that greatly enhance or impede the work of these producers. These decisions, however, need not conform (either consciously or tacitly) with some grand requirement for state legitimacy. They are more likely to be made with near-term solutions to immediate problems in mind and within the constraints imposed by institutional arrangements themselves. It is, therefore, especially important to examine the state's relations to ideological production within the broader framework of environmental conditions, institutional contexts, and action sequences that has just been described.

The substantive inquiries that make up this study take up in sequence the Reformation, the Enlightenment, and the rise of Marxist socialism. In each case the analysis proceeds from an initial consideration of the social environment at the start of the period to a comparative examination of the contexts in which the new ideology became or failed to become institutionalized, and concludes with a discussion of the internal structure of the resulting ideology and the degree to which this structure articulated with the social conditions under which it emerged. Accounting for cultural change requires having a clear sense of the ways in which the established producers of culture are institutionalized: of the ways in which these institutions extract resources from their environment, of their role in dramatizing and maintaining status relations, and of the status groups most likely to come to their defense. Accounting for cultural change also requires an understanding of broader changes in the social environment that may generate new kinds of resources—changes in population, national wealth, modes of production, trade, colonies, military commitments. From these broader changes may come the specific alterations in institutional contexts that make cultural innovations possible. And yet, changes of this kind are never monolithic. They are channeled by previous institutional arrangements and by differences in natural resources, locations, religious traditions, military strength, and a region's competitive position in larger networks of trade and diplomacy. These differences come into sharp relief when systematic comparisons are made, region by region or country by country. Such comparisons illuminate the differences in environmental conditions and institutional contexts that become decisive in facilitating or deterring the development of new cultural forms. Once these factors have been examined, it becomes possible to narrow the question of how ideology gains articulation with its social contexts. Some aspects of the social environment turn out to be more closely related than others to the production of ideology in specific historical instances. These particular contexts can then be examined in conjunction with the content of ideology itself to identify the processes of production, selection, and institutionalization that are involved. Finally, the question of articulation necessitates paying attention to the discursive fields of which each ideology is composed, the figural action defined within these discursive fields, and the ways in which these fields are dramatized and objectified within concrete social horizons.

The discussion of the Reformation focuses on the period from 1519 to 1559, the period bounded at the start by the crowning of Charles V of Spain as Holy Roman emperor and ending with the Treaty of Cateau-Cambrésis (which formalized the relations between France, Spain, and the Holy Roman Empire for decades to come), the murder of Henry II in France, and the publication of the definitive edition of John Calvin's *Institutes.* It was during this brief interval, spanning only four decades, that the Reformation gained identity as an international movement, became fully institutionalized on a wide scale, and effected a permanent split within Christendom. These were years in which social factors played an important role in channeling the Reformation: both its content and its geographic distribution were decisively affected. At the start of the period much of the intellectual groundwork for the movement had already been laid. Doctrinal ferment had been brewing in the monasteries and seminaries of Europe for at least a century; Luther had already, two years previously, posted his famous theses on the church door in Wittenberg. The events that were to unfold in the coming decades influenced the further specification of the Reformation's central doctrines, the institutionalization of the Reformation in local pulpits and in official government pronouncements, and the ways in which the Reformation would respond to its own successes; but these were not the years in which the initial creative sparks began to appear in individual hearts and minds. Those are probably obscured from the historical record and in any case raise questions quite different from the problem of articulation that is at issue here. At the start of the period Charles V had just been crowned Holy Roman emperor, Luther was engaged in his famous disputation with Johann Eck in Leipzig, most of the monarchs and princes who were to play an important role in the Reformation already occupied their positions, and the broader social changes that were to influence the Reformation were clearly under way. At the close of the period Luther was dead, Calvin was firmly established in Geneva, Charles V's reign had ended in bankruptcy, Henry VIII had imposed the Reformation on England, large sections of central and northern Europe had adopted the reformers' teachings, equally large sections of Europe including France and Spain had set in motion strong opposition to the religious reforms, and the stage was set for a century of religious wars that would radically alter the social conditions under which different religious teachings could be advanced. By comparison with later periods, the first half of the sixteenth century was relatively peaceful. Changes in economic circumstances and shifts in the balance of power among ruling elites played the decisive role in shaping the outcome of religious reforms, rather than violence, war, persecution, and bloodshed. During these early decades the Reformation nevertheless became officially institutionalized in several large sectors of Europe and elicited firm resistance in others. Comparing these regions' economic conditions, class structures, and political systems provides a basis for examining the ways in which religious ideology gained articulation with its social surroundings.

Examining the social conditions under which the Enlightenment became institutionalized yields an opportunity to consider what was similar and what had changed with respect to cultural innovation in the century and a half after the Reformation. The discussion of the Enlightenment focuses on the years between 1715 and 1789, the period defined by the death of Louis XIV and the French Revolution. As in the case of the Reformation, the intellectual antecedents of the Enlightenment were already well in place by the start of this period. The great discoveries of Newton and other scientists of the seventeenth century had already been made, and Locke's great political treatises were already being widely disseminated. Yet it is the eighteenth century that is generally associated with the high Enlightenment itself. These were the years of Voltaire and Montesquieu, Addison and Steele, Richardson and Defoe, Rousseau, Adam Smith and the Scottish moralists. It was also the period in which the Enlightenment gained identity as an international movement; the period in which new ideas ceased to be enunciated by isolated writers and came to be the collective focus of salons and academies; the period in which university reforms were made, new publishing ventures initiated, and reading societies founded in large numbers. These activities turned the Enlightenment into an institutional arrangement and rendered it vulnerable to the shaping influences of its surrounding social environment. Like the Reformation, it prospered in some parts of Europe and made only modest headway in others, thereby rendering possible comparisons of the similarities and differences in these conditions. Up to the French Revolution, one can discern the effects of tradition on the one hand and of modest change on the other in shaping the progress of the Enlightenment. Once the revolution came, of course, these dynamics all changed. War and political instability more generally, financial crises, fears of insurrection, repression, and wild hopes of democratic freedoms became the dominant forces shaping the further progress of Enlightenment thought. Thus it is for strategic as well as historic reasons that the comparisons to be made focus on the central decades of the Enlightenment itself rather than the years after the French Revolution.

The discussion of the rise of Marxist socialism focuses on the years between 1864 and 1914, the period bounded by the founding of the First International and the outbreak of the First World War. In relation to the longer trajectory of socialist ideology, this period corresponds most closely with the periods under consideration for the Reformation and the Enlightenment. It witnessed the development of Marxist socialism into an international movement and its institutionalization in collective entities, most important the various social-democratic parties that spread throughout Europe in the decades preceding the war. The basic intellectual antecedents of the movement were already in place at the start of the period. The ensuing developments brought these ideas into a more direct relation with their social contexts, forcing them to articulate with these contexts and yet giving impetus to ideals that were to transcend these immediate contexts. These were years of relative peace, in which the impact of industrialization, the rise of the proletariat, and the effects of alternative political arrangements could play a prominent role in shaping the reception of socialist ideology. With the outbreak of the war and then with the Russian Revolution, the dynamics of the movement again became subject to quite different forces.[13]

These, of course, are not simply three cases chosen at random to reveal something generalizable to a broader population of similar episodes. They are in fact the three intellectual movements, as movements, that scholars have most often credited with importance in the shaping of modern culture. Individual contributions, scientific discoveries, technical inventions, and political upheavals in other periods may actually outweigh the significance of these movements in accounting for specific intellectual developments. But it would be difficult to find other periods in which the force of ideas alone came to be identified with such collectively influential developments. This means too that the sequence of the three episodes is important. Each contributed to the foundations on which the next was built. The continuity was often more implicit than explicit; indeed, it was broken by the unsettled periods that intervened. But there is a successive dimension to the episodes that is important in its own right. The political and economic conditions under which the Enlightenment developed were markedly different from those of the Reformation, and the conditions under which Marxist socialism arose differed from either of the former. Comparing the three, then, provides a way of seeing what was similar and what was different.

In the largest sense, this is an inquiry into the ways in which the growth of capitalism in Europe since the sixteenth century, and the accompanying development of political institutions, has shaped the categories in which formal thinking about ourselves has often taken place. In understanding the social conditions under which the Reformation, the Enlightenment, and socialism arose, we can hope to gain a greater realization of the ways in which these cultural episodes have contributed to the shaping of modern society. These were periods in which the horizons of thought did seem to expand. And yet the direction of that thought was not the result of some inner dynamic within the mind alone. It was also a function of institutional arrangements and the selective interaction of ideas with these arrangements. Tracing these relations can provide insight not only into the past but also into the ways in which our own ideas articulate with our social experience.

PART I

The Protestant Reformation

1   Contexts and Perspectives

*L*IFE IN EUROPE AT the time of the Reformation was overwhelmingly rural. Upwards of 85 percent of the population
lived on the land itself, and most of the remainder earned their
livelihood from the land.[1] The principal mode of social organization
was the rural village and manor. Urban life was relatively uncommon
and even sizable cities seldom had populations of more than fifty
thousand. The vast majority of goods were produced from the land
for direct consumption, and many of the commodities that were
produced for sale, such as grain and wool, also came from the land.
Consequently the landed sector, and principally the wealthier landlords, were in a position to exercise great influence over society,
including both church and state. Fernand Braudel writes: "Everywhere the creation of the state . . . had to contend with those owners
of fiefs, lords over village, field and road, custodians of the immense
rural population."[2] Similarly, Perez Zagorin observes: "Above all,
the political system was a symbiosis between crown and nobilities;
and speaking generally, it was especially nobilities and aristocracies
that . . . constituted the dominant and governing class . . . in the early
modern states."[3] Thus, it would appear that efforts to understand
the social history of the Reformation should begin with the landed
sector, for it was here that the church's roots were deeply planted.
And it was here that the power lay to oppose any sweeping ideological
reforms in the church.

The official records from which the history of late medieval religion has been reconstructed scarcely reveal the thoughts and habits of the common person. The task of describing rural religion at the popular level is, however, not as hopeless as one might at first suppose. Historians have been sufficiently interested in the problem that some insightful descriptions have been pieced together. From church manuals and the writings of clergy a picture has developed of the manner in which marriages, baptisms, funerals, and other rites were carried out. Records from manors and parishes provide detailed portraits of day-to-day life in a number of villages, especially in England and France. Occasional glimpses into the thoughts and behavior of the people themselves were captured in testimonies taken by the Inquisition. And in Spain the government conducted a fairly rigorous survey for its time asking questions about religious conduct in a number of parishes.

The Moral Economy of Agrarian Religion

The picture that has emerged from these inquiries shows clearly that at the close of the Middle Ages European religion was an integral feature of rural life and drew its primary strength from the dominant position of the landed sector in European societies. Religion existed not only as a matter of individual belief and formal theology but as an important dimension of the moral economy of rural life, a collective practice that expressed the moral obligations of peasants to one another and the bonds between peasants and landlords. To the modern mind, trained to think of religion in terms of individual piety, sincerity of intentions, and private devotion, religion in this period consisted to a much greater degree of liturgy, officially organized and sanctioned by the church, which united the entire community in corporate participation.[4]

In collective ritual, and in the symbols associated with these rituals, the church mirrored the social relations of agrarian society. It reminded peasants of their dependence on landlords and landlords of their elevated social status compared with peasants. Marriage rituals, held in the church building and solemnized by the priest, imposed order on social relations, not the least of which were property and inheritance rights. They also ceremonialized the patriarchal hierarchy of village life.[5] The wedding rite itself, in a manner less characteristic of its modern counterpart, symbolized the joining together of two entire kin groups within the village, not just the bride and groom.[6] Baptisms performed a similar function.[7] Practiced much as they had been since the thirteenth century, baptisms formalized bonds of responsibility among parents, sponsors, and godparents, often purposefully chosen to include members of the upper stratum.[8] On behalf of the infant, godparents made vows that bound the two families together for mutual physical and spiritual protection.[9] Having an infant baptized was, in fact, no small occasion in the routine of village life. The event brought godparents and kin together in such numbers that the church sometimes had to impose restrictions on the number of sponsors involved in order to retain control over these rites.[10]

Rituals commemorating devotion to the saints also dramatized the relations between peasants and landlords.[11] In the first place, saints were disproportionately selected from the landlords' ancestors. The relation of peasants to the saints also served as a model of the client-patron relations presumed to exist between peasants and landlords. Peasants in the Champagne area, for example, "approached the saints, these exemplars of humanity, in the same way that the poor approached their betters. They offered prayer in exchange for patronage and favor."[12] In Poland stories about the saints, often enacted during festivals, advised peasants "to discharge their duties conscientiously, to be pious and charitable, to fill up their time with work and prayer [and placed emphasis] on obedience to their masters, on conscientious and willing fulfillment of their instructions."[13] Nor was the practice of venerating saints merely an expression of grassroots folk piety, as some have suggested. It was systematically encouraged by the ecclesiastical hierarchy as well. Many well-known theologians published treatises on the saints, assigning them to various spheres of life, and instruction booklets told parish clergy how to encourage participation in rituals devoted to the saints.[14] Other rituals, especially the widely practiced festival of Corpus Christi, provided an occasion to act out and ritually resolve the tensions that were invariably present among the different social strata.[15]

In more straightforward ways the relations between peasants and landlords were also clearly dramatized in the life and practice of late medieval religion. The physical arrangement of the church itself reflected the class structure of rural society. In many parts of Europe members of the nobility had pews in the front section of the church; peasants stood in back. In England the number of pews in public churches was allocated in proportion to the amount of land owned in the parish by each family. Other churches in England were owned entirely by the landlord on whose land they were located and were sometimes physically joined to the manor house. Everywhere the churches and graveyards contained memorials commemorating the wealth and benevolence of the nobility. In the confessional, which was often held publicly rather than in private as in more recent times, priests resolved disputes between landlords and peasants and encouraged the latter to be loyal and hardworking. On feast days processions organized the landowners and peasants into their respective ranks. Burial plots were arranged by social standing. And church records, ownership of pews, and testimony by the clergy were often required in order to certify noble standing.[16]

Church practices and status relations, augmented by fears of death and anxieties about sin, also came together in the last testaments and wills of the rich: servants, tenants, and paupers were asked to pray for the souls of their patrons and in return received promises, sometimes of material rewards, but more commonly of spiritual blessings. Thus the lower strata extended their services to the rich even beyond the grave.[17]

In addition to its other functions in the status hierarchy of the rural community, the church provided a way for noble persons of privilege and power to demonstrate their virtue, their honor, their magnanimity. Serving the church became tantamount to demonstrating one's moral virtue. Magnanimity meant valor, spirituality, thinking big, or, in the words of a sixteenth-century writer, "loftiness, grandeur, and nobility of courage, which makes a man brave as a lion and of great enterprise."[18]

Lucien Febvre provides a graphic summary of the deep extent to which religion in this period was embedded in the routines and status hierarchies of village life:

> All men's actions from birth to death were permanently controlled by religion; it regulated the smallest details of one's work, one's leisure, what one ate and how one lived; as surely as the church bells rang to signal prayers and offices, religion regulated the rhythms of human life. The Church was the center to which men rallied in times of danger and in times of joy. Every Sunday and every feast day saw the whole community assembled together, in hierarchical order. The men of the cloth were in the choir. In the

seigneurial pew way up front, were the gentry, milord with his dogs, his wife, and his children. The magistrates stiffened with peasant dignity sat just behind them, then the laborers, and finally the humble folk, the valets, servants, children, and animals which were just as much at ease in the church as anywhere else.[19]

In addition to ceremonializing the relative status of peasants and landlords, the church also served as a storehouse of public goods from which both peasants and landlords could draw as need arose. Although peasants' incomes were in some instances on the rise during the half century preceding the Reformation, the majority still lived sufficiently close to subsistence that periodic crop failures, illnesses, and fluctuations in the market induced severe hardship.[20] These short-term crises and periodic fluctuations, happening from one year to the next, as opposed to the long term upward trends in prices and wages, were the harsh realities that forced peasants to depend on one another, on the landlords, and on the church for subsistence. The personal bonds between vassals and lords that had functioned in the past to shield peasants from subsistence crises were, however, giving way in many parts of Europe to rentier capitalism involving money payments to absentee landlords. Consequently, peasants were forced to rely increasingly on one another and on the church for emergency relief.

To meet this need, parishes generally maintained charity funds, almshouses, and hospitals, and distributed food to qualifying members of the community.[21] Local priests sometimes enjoyed sufficiently comfortable incomes that they were able to serve as creditors to their parishioners.[22] The monastic houses also operated on a large enough scale to allow supplies to be stockpiled for just such emergencies. Although the amount allocated for charity and relief represented only a small fraction of the monasteries' wealth, these supplies were often quite substantial in absolute terms.[23] Even the sale of indulgences, against which so much of the reformers' wrath was to be vented, sometimes played a role in augmenting public goods. After a disastrous flood in 1515, for example, a three-year indulgence was offered to anyone in Holland and Flanders who contributed to restoring the dikes.[24]

The church also encouraged moral obligations among the peasants themselves, counteracting tendencies toward competition and creating a basis for mutual assistance in times of crisis.[25] Parish boundaries generally coincided with those of the village, or with the estates owned by a single landlord, and were small enough to promote firsthand relations.[26] Usually no more than three hundred to four hundred people lived in each parish, and the distance from each dwelling to the church could easily be traversed on foot.[27] Oaths of mutual responsibility, which bound the community together in an almost quasilegal bond of commitment, were formalized in vows to the saints and were sworn publicly before the local priest.[28] Church buildings served as places for community gatherings, church bells signaled meetings and important events, religious holidays imposed uniformity on the rhythms of work, and church treasuries provided funds for community defense.[29]

Less tangible contributions to the material well-being of peasant life were often evident as well. The folk beliefs that for centuries had given the common man and woman solace in the face of evil, fortitude with which to confront discouragement, and hope against the harsh realities of daily life were closely integrated into the round of more official religious practices. Magical expectations were as much a part of community life as they were of individuals' beliefs. Participation in sacred rituals was a way of promoting the collective good just as it was of attaining private security. For example, magical healing was believed to result as the community gathered on Easter morning to view the crucifix being raised from the Holy Sepulcher. At the liturgy on Palm Sunday palms were sanctified for use not only in the service but also to protect dwellings from summer storms. On the feast of the Assumption of the Virgin (August 15) herbs were blessed for medicinal uses, as talismans, and for the protection of livestock. Animals were also believed to be kept healthy by being led to the village church to receive holy water after the services, and crops and cattle were protected by communal processionals in which prayers and Scripture were recited around the perimeters of fields. Sacred objects of numerous kinds as well as liturgies, exorcisms, and special dedication rituals imparted healing and restoration. There was, one author observes, an "economy of the sacred," an economy in which relations with the divine were "ordered through a patterned sequence of human action."[30]

More generally, this economy of the sacred was closely intertwined with the calendrical rhythms of rural life, marking the seasons and placing them in the context of divine imagery. In many areas the feast of Purification marked the halfway point between winter

and spring, denoting the lengthening seasonal light as well as re-
minding people of the greater light brought into the world by the
purity of the Virgin. Other feast days, celebrated in memory of the
various saints, told villagers when spring planting could begin, when
pruning of vines should cease, and when sheep should be mated,
and provided occasions for bringing into collective memory the
health of their animals, prayers for good weather, and hopes for an
abundant harvest. In these festivals disorder was removed from the
world—sickness, rodents, locusts, worms—and the holy, sanctifying
offices of the church were invoked to create a sacred order of protection and reassurance. On special occasions exorcisms were also
performed, following carefully prescribed liturgical procedures, to
rid the community or an individual of extraordinary danger. Private
conjurations supplemented the collective rituals with prayers and
supplications in the name of Christ, the cross, and all the saints.
Divine anger was thereby allayed and the natural order purified and
renewed.[31] All these practices, so deeply embedded in village life,
gave the church an institutional base that could not be subverted
easily, not even by the reformers' zealous preaching against the superstitions of "idolatrous" and "magical" rituals.[32]

     In return for performing these various functions the church
derived the resources necessary for its very survival. Peasants contributed their tithes, offered up their loyalty, and participated in
religious rituals.[33] Landlords set aside space on their estates for parish
buildings, contributed to the construction and upkeep of these facilities, and donated directly to parish salaries. They remembered
the church in their wills, and in cases of uprising lent their arms to
the church's defense.[34]

     The church's interests were also served by recruiting the younger
sons of the nobility into the clergy. Members of this stratum had the
requisite skills for administering the church's vast estates and other
temporal affairs. Their connections with secular power were not
unimportant either. Indeed it was sometimes better, Thomas Aquinas
had written, to take "the less saintly and learned man . . . on account
of his secular power or experience."[35] As early as the fifth century,
arguments had begun to appear defending noble recruitment into
the clergy. The nobility not only brought power and experience; they
gave the priesthood honor and dignity. Where serfdom prevailed,
recruiting clergy exclusively from noble ranks also protected the
church from accusations that it was stealing bond laborers.[36] The

practice of recruiting from the nobility had the further consequence of solidifying important social relations. Kin ties between nobility and clergy were especially close. A study of more than two thousand persons from twenty-seven noble dynasties in German territories, for example, has shown that 28 percent of these persons became ecclesiastical celibates.[37] Another study concludes: "An upper-class family would not have been upper-class if it had not had a shrewd appreciation of the accessories to political power. The church was such an accessory, at least where it was well established. The occupation of the local bishopric by a younger brother made at least for a smooth partnership."[38]

The church's theological disposition may have been, as Max Weber thought, otherworldly. But the church survived because it was able to secure resources of a very tangible kind. "In the case of pre-Reformation Europe," Mary Douglas observes, "when the clergy were prevailing on the landlords, knights, and merchants to part with lands, cash, and booty, the clergy themselves were behaving in a notably this-worldly fashion as far as their own interests were concerned."[39]

For their part, the landlords had struck a felicitous bargain with the church as the condition for their patronage. Not only did the church contribute in symbolic ways to their sense of well-being; it was also a material contributor to the maintenance of the landlords' class position. In the first instance it functioned as part of a regressive tax system that channeled revenue indirectly from the poor to the rich. Of the tithes collected by the church a significant proportion went to the state, which in turn exempted the landed nobility from taxation. In Spain one-third of the revenue from tithes, as well as income from the sale of indulgences, went to the crown, contributing at least a quarter of its total revenue, while the nobility were exempted from the major types of royal taxation.[40] In England the crown received a tenth of the annual revenue from all clerical benefices and a sum equal to the first year's income of every newly appointed bishop.[41] In other areas forced loans from the church reduced pressures on the state to increase its revenues by taxing the nobility.[42]

Beyond these purely financial contributions, the church also assisted in maintaining the landlords' privileges by expressing the landlords' interest in ecclesiastical administration and by using its influence in the political arena. From the local priest to the highest levels of ecclesiastical bureaucracy, appointees to church offices were closely linked to the landed elite, most generally by blood or else by patronage. Everywhere members of the clergy were recruited disproportionately from noble families and held their appointments at the favor of the most powerful landlords in each parish. Through the clergy landlords exercised political influence at both the local and regional levels. In central Europe the landed elite largely succeeded in making the church, in the words of one writer, "feudally subject" to its own interests, appointing bishops and priests, making inspections of monasteries, and imposing taxes on church lands.[43] In the absence of a strong centralized regime, the local nobility in this part of Europe often ruled through the titles and offices of the church, from which many of their fiefs had been acquired through grants in perpetuity.[44] In Poland, according to Marceli Kosman, "the gentry did not . . . forgo the opportunity of subordinating to themselves such an important element of village life as the local level of church administration."[45] In France and England members of the clergy were not only linked to the nobility at the local level but also significantly represented in parliaments and assemblies. The church, therefore, constituted a political bloc with interests that were generally allied directly with those of the landowners or, as an important landowner in its own right, was likely to have interests that coincided closely with those of the landowners.[46]

In many areas the church was in fact owner of extensive landholdings and was able to employ these holdings to ensure the loyalty of local elites. In addition to providing symbolic gratifications the church was able to supply local notables with actual fiefdoms on favorable terms. Landowners were able to extend their own holdings through these arrangements. The church received rents, and military service was sometimes required as a condition of holding fiefs as well. Landowners in return were given roles in the episcopal officialdom as judges and bailiffs, held title to feudal rights over serfs on their lands, and enriched themselves through the sale of agricultural products. In areas in which agricultural markets were expanding, the church was able to increase its position both directly and indirectly by these arrangements.[47]

Another aspect of rural life that was often conducive to maintaining the church's strength was a relatively underdeveloped, unorganized system of secular government. In many areas the only institutions of community government were informal village assemblies. In areas with strong feudal traditions the seigneur was likely to preside over these assemblies; in other areas the assemblies consisted of gatherings of local family heads who collectively selected representatives and settled on matters of taxation and communal property. Priests generally did not attend these meetings, but the assemblies provided an additional connection between the church and the structure of village life. The same meetings that decided on community activities often settled on matters of parish finance; boundaries of parishes and seigneuries coincided; and vestries and assemblies comprised the same people. Barring other social divisions, therefore, it was unlikely that patterns of governance in the villages would be turned against the church.[48]

The relations between landowners and peasants at the beginning of the sixteenth century varied widely, of course, from one part of Europe to another.[49] And religious patterns reflected these variations, again demonstrating the close relations that existed between the church and agrarian social structure.[50] Monastic establishments, the majority of which had been founded prior to the fourteenth century, were most common in the rural villages of thickly populated arable farming regions in Castile, southern England, north central and southeastern France, Saxony, and the vicinities of Cologne and Strasbourg.[51] In comparison, these establishments were less common in the grassland regions of Spain and Scotland, in woodland areas of the Baltic, and on the large estates in recently settled territories of eastern Europe. Generally speaking, the areas in which monastic establishments were most common were also those in which long traditions of feudalism had resulted in an accumulation of property that could be bequeathed to the church. These areas, with several exceptions, also had the highest concentrations of ecclesiastical wealth. Estimates of the extent of church lands, while at best crude approximations in most instances, customarily include figures that range from 10 to 15 percent for Poland, Holland, and sections of France and Germany with traditions of free tenancy and smallholding; to 20 percent for other parts of France, Friesland, and Sweden; to 30 percent for England and Utrecht; to as much as 50 percent for Spain.[52]

The character of parish organization also reflected differences in the social relations of agrarian life. France and Spain, with more numerous and smaller estates, were organized into parishes averaging 15 to 25 square kilometers in size, while sections of eastern Europe with vast grain-growing estates had parishes ranging in size from 50 square kilometers in Poland to 350 square kilometers in Lithuania.[53] In England, where manorial holdings were farmed by tenants and where newly cleared lands were often under freehold, parish government tended to be relatively more democratic, as was also true in smallholding regions of northern Europe. In contrast, sections of Spain, Poland, and France with strong seigneurial traditions had ecclesiastical patterns that typically exhibited strict hierarchical control over parish affairs.[54]

Some other aspects of religious practice also followed these regional variations in agrarian patterns. Worship of patron saints was less common in Scandinavia, the Low Countries, and the British Isles than it was in Spain, France, and eastern Europe.[55] It has also been suggested that folk religions, superstition, and mysticism continued to be practiced with greater vitality in those sections of Europe— the mountainous or woodland regions—in which the relations between peasants and landlords were weaker.[56]

These variations give further indication of the close relations that existed between agrarian class structures and religion at the beginning of the sixteenth century. More important than the variations, however, were the constant features of these relations. In nearly every area the late medieval church was an integral dimension of rural life. Religious rituals solemnized the moral order of the peasant village and reaffirmed the obligations of peasants and landlords to each other. The church created public goods for distribution to loyal parishioners and played a central role in the process of redistributing wealth from peasant producers to the landowning elite. In return, the church received loyalty and protection as well as the financial contributions necessary to sustain itself.[57]

To summarize briefly, the moral obligations on which rural life depended were deeply reinforced, both ritually and ideologically, by prevailing religious practices. In nearly every area of Europe the landowning class gave its strong support to the church's defense. In return, the landed elite generally derived material and symbolic rewards from the church. Yet economic changes were to come about that would create resources that could be used, principally by agents of the state, to extricate religious policy at least temporarily from the grip of the landowning class. These resources were to provide a basis for the production and institutionalization of religious reforms.

Patterns of Economic Expansion

During the second half of the fifteenth century Europe began to experience an intensification of economic activity that was to have profound effects on the balance of power between the landowning classes and governing regimes. As a result of population pressures, exploration, and other social changes, a dramatic upsurge of commercial activity occurred. New trading routes were opened, markets expanded to encompass larger geographic areas, the total volume of trade multiplied, and new commodities were brought into production for the market. Local and regional markets grew significantly in volume and in the types of commodities traded. Long-distance trade, spanning the length and breadth of the Continent, grew in proportion to the thriving transoceanic trade. As it did, local and regional markets gradually became integrated with one another: markets that had previously been isolated were now linked, creating what could be described with increasing accuracy as a single European economy.

There had been active trading of a number of commodities within the Mediterranean region since at least the thirteenth century, but the Mediterranean and other regional markets now became integrated into a larger network of commerce that included eastern, central, northern, and western Europe. Venice and Naples imported grain in exchange for wine, salt, oil, and cloth. Along the Rhône valley an especially vigorous trade developed, turning cities such as Lyons and Geneva into commercial centers. To the north, Antwerp became a hub of trade and cloth production and an international financial center. Raw wool traveled from Spain to Antwerp and was traded for finished cloth. Wine, grain, spices, and metalware flowed down the Rhine and then to Antwerp, while cloth went from Antwerp by sea to England and the Baltic. Other trades also flourished. Italy became a supplier of alum, glassware, and spices to England and the Low Countries. Copper flowed from the mining areas of the Tyrol, Thuringia, and Hungary through Venice to the Levant and India in payment for spices. Grain, textiles, and metalware produced a steady increase in the trade between Flanders and southern Germany, and linens from southern Germany were traded in Italy while those from northern Germany were traded in Spain. Cattle shipments, which tripled during the first half of the sixteenth century, went from Denmark to the cities of Holland and the Rhineland. From the Baltic also came shipments of timber for masts as well as copper and iron. Eastern Europe supplied wheat, rye, and cattle in growing volume. And shipments of bullion from the New World multiplied several times. The first half of the sixteenth century—the period in which the Reformation was to occur—was on the whole, therefore, characterized by a high rate of economic expansion.[58]

The reasons behind the timing and magnitude of this expansion remain at least partially obscure. Rising population, however, looms as one of the important explanations. Since the thirteenth century the population of Europe had generally declined, chiefly as a result of war and a series of devastating plagues. Toward the end of the fifteenth century this trend was finally reversed, and during the sixteenth century population grew by as much as 100 percent in some parts of Europe. In France the rate of growth was fairly low—around 20 percent—although some sections of France grew at a much more rapid pace. The rate was also fairly low in Switzerland (approximately 30 percent). In contrast, Castile and Aragon, England, Poland, Denmark, and Sweden all grew between 40 and 60 percent. The rates in Hesse, the Tyrol, and Holland were even higher, ranging from 80 to 100 percent. Not surprisingly, the cities grew more rapidly than the countryside. Towns such as Zurich, Gdansk, Antwerp, Seville, and London—all principal centers of trade—grew between 200 and 400 percent during the century. Overall, the population of Europe increased from about 80 million in 1500 to nearly 110 million in 1600, growth that had been virtually unknown during the previous century and a half. This increase, among other things, appears to have stimulated trade by heightening demand for essentials such as food and clothing. The growing cities especially came to depend to a greater extent on food and clothing produced in other areas.[59]

The other primary factor that contributed to the commercial expansion of this period was a rapid rise in the level of prices. The extent of this inflation has, in fact, been calculated with considerable precision: over the course of the sixteenth century grain prices rose 424 percent in England, 379 percent in France, 651 percent in the Low Countries, 318 percent in Germany, and 335 percent in Poland. Meat prices rose an average of 250 percent, while the price of wine, construction materials, hemp, wool, and finished textiles rose nearly as sharply. The source of these dramatic price increases appears to have been twofold: on the one hand, rising population drove up demand, giving sellers an opportunity to raise prices; on the other hand, the total supply of money was expanding, chiefly because of bullion imports from America, and the velocity with which money circulated was rising because of the increased volume of trade. Both should have driven up prices. But whatever the reasons, the price inflation appears to have had a significant positive effect on trade. In the first place, rising prices led merchants to seek supplies anywhere in Europe where prices might be lower, thereby causing markets to expand geographically. Furthermore, as the unit price of any commodity increased, the relative cost of transporting it decreased, since shipping costs remained relatively stable. As a result, it became economically feasible to import or export goods over longer distances. Finally, because of fixed contract agreements, merchants were able to prevent wages from rising as rapidly as the prices they charged for commodities. And declining real wages for laborers meant rising profit margins for employers. Thus, more money became available to the wealthy for purchasing the luxury goods that were being shipped over long distances. And more investment capital became available to merchants for use in expanding their enterprises.[60]

Interpretations of Social Influences on the Reformation

It has been argued in some of the literature on the Reformation that the commercial expansion of the sixteenth century had a direct effect on individuals' religious beliefs. According to this interpretation, individuals could not help noticing that the environment in which they lived was changing. "A sense of urgency, a longing for something new—for change—pervaded every area of life during the decades preceding the Reformation," one writer observes.[61] Everything was in flux—new cities, new prices, more people, more trade. And so, individuals must have reasoned, why not a new religion as well? If circumstances were in transition, if opportunities were expanding and horizons broadening, then religious beliefs need not be static either. World views needed to change with the times. And the reformers' teachings offered liberation, a greater sense of individual efficacy in matters of the spirit, a chance to seize control of one's faith and adapt it to the new environment. In short, a direct connection has been seen between environmental change and ideological innovation—a connection rooted in individuals' perceptions of their world.

One variant of this argument is illustrated by a leading British historian who has recently tried to demonstrate that the whole tenor of English history in the sixteenth century can be understood in terms of a kind of "paranoid style" that developed in response to rapid economic, social, and political change. She writes: "Everywhere the venerable signposts, the historic methods, and the ancient loyalties were being corrupted by newer political and economic alignments and obligations . . . All had become unhinged, and change was on the march in raucous and atrocity-committing battalions unimaginable in the past . . . There was excitement, curiosity, and dynamism aplenty [and] there was much to fear and to grieve."[62] Anxiety, in this writer's view, led people to "expect the worst" and thereby caused the religious ideas to which they gravitated to emphasize as no other religious tradition had "sinfulness," "a sense of panic," and "extreme emergency."[63]

But this interpretation of the Reformation is clearly an oversimplification. It imposes the modern view of religion on the sixteenth century, a view in which religion is nothing more than the private beliefs of individuals. It assumes that individuals, as individuals, freely and voluntarily adapt their beliefs to conform to their sense of the economic environment. It fails to consider the intervening social processes that mediate between the economic environment and changes in individual religious practices.[64] It fails to recognize the institutional contexts in which religious discourse is embedded—its organizational structure, its dependence on the procurement of resources, and its relations to the distribution of wealth and power. This view also denies the institutional complexity of economic change itself, failing to consider its impact on elites and governments and the extent to which it is conditioned by local subcultures and traditions. As a result, this interpretation attributes too much significance to the direct effects of the commercial revolution on individual perceptions while it probes too little into the social mechanisms by which the commercial revolution may have affected ideological change. It generates an individualistic view of religion that reveals nothing of the collective character of public discourse. Nor does this view give an account of the widely differing patterns of adoption that the Reformation experienced. In assuming that individuals everywhere were simply influenced by their awareness of change in the wider world, it fails to explain why the Reformation was adopted so readily in some parts of Europe and why it failed so miserably in others.[65]

As it happened, the commercial expansion of the sixteenth century contributed less directly than indirectly to bringing about the Reformation. Rather than directly changing the outlook of individuals, the commercial revolution influenced the Reformation through a fairly complex conjuncture of social processes. It operated more through institutions than among masses of disaggregated individuals. And this should not be surprising, for the vast majority of persons living in Europe at the time of the Reformation did not experience a fundamental disruption of their lives as a result of the expansion of trade or the price revolution. They continued, as they always had, living off the land, securing their livelihood from direct production and from the sale of surplus items. The expansion of markets gave some of these individuals greater opportunities to sell their commodities. For many others it simply brought competition, which made it more difficult to sell their products. The inflation of prices benefited some whose goods were now worth more. Others found their rents and taxes rising at higher rates than the income from their produce. As the value of land increased, some of the landowners became rentier capitalists, living off the rents of vast estates. Others tightened control over their tenants in order to keep production at peak levels without purchasing additional estates at inflated prices. And even though some of the rural population was being affected by the commercial revolution, these changes seem not to have altered significantly the institutional contexts in which their religious practices were embedded. The moral dependence between landlords and peasants remained essentially intact. Peasants remained tied to landlords for land and supplies; landlords obtained their livelihood through the labor of peasants. And the religious practices that were embedded in these relations were not greatly challenged, at least not by any radical disruption in the relations between peasants and landlords.[66]

The rural parishes in the Lyonnaise area provide a vivid example of how resilient rural religion tended to be in the face of economic change. Because of their proximity to a major trading city, many of the 750 parishes in this region experienced the effects of economic expansion during the first half of the sixteenth century to a significant degree. Peasants increasingly earned their living by harvesting flax, spinning thread, and weaving linen for the Lyons market and by supplying food for the growing number of townspeople. Although some lives remained unchanged, large numbers of peasants experienced rising standards of living, became increasingly involved in artisanal work, and found themselves living in villages in which the principal economic factor was cash sales of marketable commodities such as grain, wine, flax, and cloth. Yet, despite these changes, the church remained quite strong. Even at the height of the Reformation in Lyons itself, very few among the rural population converted to Protestantism. Despite rising economic fortunes, most of the rural population were still native born, were heavily steeped in the local traditions, and remained in close contact with parish clergy, who were also native born and often interrelated with the local population. Not only were the clergy kinsmen of the villagers; they were also godparents to many of the children, dressed and behaved more like peasants than priests, and spoke French but could not read Latin, which left them unfamiliar with the larger debates going on in theological circles. As in other rural areas, the customary rituals offered by the church forged strong bonds between priests and laity. Rather than consisting of large, formal ceremonies, these rituals tended to be personal and informal. Babies were christened, new mothers blessed, and baptismal banquets held. Whole segments of the villages recited confession in unison and received absolution collectively. Holy Communion itself was often a festive event. At Easter, for example, members of the community supplied wine (unconsecrated) to help wash down the host. Marriages and funerals also brought religious elements together with village ceremonies. Processionals, fairs, special invocations for crops and rain, and other religious practices "bound man to man, placated God, gave expression to joy, sorrow, and anger, . . . helped each participant overcome crises in his life, [and] instilled and perpetuated local values and traditions."[67]

The effects of the commercial revolution on the Reformation were mediated to an important extent not by the rural manors and villages but by the towns. For it was in the towns that population growth, new wealth, changing price levels, and the different kinds of work made possible by the expansion of trade became most prominently concentrated. It was also the towns that gave the Reformation its decisive imprint. Towns such as Zurich and Geneva provided the pulpits from which the reformers' ideas were disseminated. And at the popular level, Protestantism's greatest appeal was in the towns. This was as much the case in Poland and France, even in Spain, as it was in the German and Swiss territories or in England. Evangelical teachings spread along trade routes from city to city, from Geneva to Lyons, from Antwerp to London and Seville, from Lübeck to

Copenhagen and Gdansk. Everywhere the new doctrines were carried by merchants and traders and by the preachers who followed in their path. Those who were attracted to the movement included a broad variety of urban residents ranging from the merchant oligarchy to craftsmen, skilled artisans, and vagabonds.

Various features of urban life contributed to the movement's appeal. It was in the towns that literacy and the desire for vernacular religious teaching were generally highest. It was also here that the church's procedures for administering poor relief, for collecting tithes, and for appointing and supervising clergy fell subject to the greatest pressures from rapid social change. In some towns the percentage of persons needing some kind of poor relief ranged from 25 to 50 percent. Church supplies, great as they were, were generally ill equipped to meet such needs. Other towns grew too rapidly and developed new industries on too large a scale for the traditional parish and guild organizations to function effectively as moral communities. The church's economic role in the towns was also considerably less influential than it was in the countryside. Direct ownership by the church of urban properties other than houses of worship was generally quite modest. Even in towns with the strongest ecclesiastical structures no more than a small proportion of the town itself was likely to be owned by the church, and these holdings were usually residences occupied by clergy or rented to sextons, churchwardens, or other tenants. Loans by the church could sometimes be used for political and economic leverage in the towns. But as trade increased, the relative importance of these transactions tended to decrease. Indeed, the chance to repudiate long-standing debts to the church sometimes provided added appeal to the demands for religious reform.

The cities' growth also held potential for religious reform because of changes in the status of the poor. As urban populations grew, the character of the poor—to which the church had long given attention—begin to shift. Already in the fifteenth century, some evidence suggests, the poor were coming to be feared—not only because of their desperate physical condition but also because they were increasingly an anonymous category.[68] The effect of their removal from villages and estates was to break down the firsthand relations that had typically characterized the giving of alms. Not only did the poor appear more threatening as a result, but they also came to be dealt with as a nameless category. Religious attitudes still generated sympathetic feelings toward the poor, and wills continued to channel relief to them, but increasingly this relief was directed toward charitable *institutions* rather than individual recipients. In Lyons, for example, 25 percent of all wills left bequests directly to hospitals and other charitable institutions; in Paris and Toulouse the proportion was nearly 60 percent.[69] The institutionalization of charity often provided a more effective way of dealing with the growing numbers of urban poor. As charity became institutionalized and therefore more formalized and visible, however, it also became a more significant item of political controversy. Questions were raised about the church's effectiveness in managing these institutions and about the apparent contrasts in life styles between those in charge and those to whom help was to be given. Where revenues were more than sufficient to cover the costs, town councils saw prospects of turning these surpluses to their own ends. And where revenues were deficient, magistrates worried about finding more effective solutions lest the poor become a threat to domestic tranquillity.

These concerns inevitably multiplied in direct proportion to the rising numbers of urban poor. Indeed by the beginning of the sixteenth century the system of administering public relief to the poor was in crisis in many areas. Especially in towns where the church's revenues still depended heavily on a declining rural economy while the demand for relief depended both on flight from the countryside and economic fluctuations in trade, the situation was severe.[70] For many town councils, therefore, the problem of charity was rapidly becoming a source of friction between themselves and the established religious hierarchy.[71] In some instances religious officials, realizing their own inadequacy in the face of deteriorating conditions, actively turned to the civil authorities for help, thereby voluntarily giving up some of their own autonomy; in other cases Protestant teachings provided an opportunity for civil authorities to seize the initiative.

The organizational structure of the church in urban areas also enhanced the likelihood that reforming sentiments would be especially attractive to the rising merchant and artisan classes in towns undergoing rapid economic expansion. At the diocesan level the most powerful segment of the ecclesiastical structure was likely to be the cathedral chapter, itself influenced by the kind of ties existing between its members and families of local importance. The clergy associated with the cathedrals and wealthier collegiate churches in the towns were generally separated by rank of birth from the lower strata and led ostentatious lives that evoked resentment from persons of lesser means, who were forced to pay tithes and other assessments to the church. Next in importance were the religious orders, generally populated by sons and daughters of the nobility and often only marginally under the supervision of the bishop or archbishop. Depending on the balance of power in the cathedral chapter, the orders often made a ready target for secularizing tendencies since they held wealth of their own and sometimes presented a challenge to the hierarchical authority of the church. Lower parish priests were less likely to have family ties to the nobility and were most exposed to lay influences both at the popular level and through the municipal elite. Wherever the civic elite was also segmented from the nobility, the parish clergy could provide a point of leverage for reforming activities within the church. Through its control of benefices, the civic elite was often able to exercise influence over the appointment and discipline of clergy at this level. Parish clergy, however, were likely to be recruited almost exclusively from local families, while in rapidly growing towns a large segment of the population consisted of recent immigrants and itinerant laborers. The parish clergy often appeared reluctant to welcome these outsiders, had few effective means of bringing them easily under the umbrella of parish activities, and in the crises over labor surpluses that broke out periodically generally sided with the more established residents. In stagnant economies the clergy could serve usefully in supporting the guild restrictions that aimed at limiting labor supplies. But in expanding economies their attachment to established residents was more likely to work against the demand for larger supplies of labor, thereby pitting them against merchant employers and the masses of itinerant laborers. In rapidly expanding trades involving high rates of literacy and close ties with artisans in other towns, such as printing, these tensions were especially likely to erupt into demands for religious reforms.

In some cities the dynamics of ecclesiastical reform were also conditioned by an excess supply of clergy in lower ranks whose career aspirations placed them at odds with the upper clergy. Although they were sometimes better educated and more familiar with new ideas than their superiors, these clergy generally earned a meager income and could entertain only modest hopes of rising in the ecclesiastical hierarchy unless reforms were implemented. Sensitive from firsthand experience to corruption among the upper clergy, they sometimes became enthusiasts for reform doctrines. And when other pressures for reform in the cities mounted, they provided a supply of trained personnel with which to fill evangelical pulpits.

The cities themselves were creations of trade and expanding labor; thus, the growth of Protestantism in these settings was in some sense a product of the commercial and demographic expansion of the period. This expansion in the broader environment affected the institutional contexts in which religious practices were embedded. It created new opportunities for many merchants and artisans. At the same time, it created pressures to which the church could not easily respond, thereby enhancing the likelihood of municipal councils' throwing their weight behind ecclesiastical reforms.

Still, the cities were not islands of self-determination capable of deciding their response to the Reformation solely on the basis of popular demand. They functioned as institutional crucibles of religious ferment. But the resources needed to turn this ferment into the heady wine of reform seldom fell exclusively within their own jurisdiction. In varying degrees the cities remained in close dependency with the surrounding countryside, where traditional religious practices were firmly implanted. It required the full resources of the central regime—or where that was lacking of territorial regimes, or of exceptionally strong municipal regimes—to bring the Reformation to fruition as an institutionalized ideology.

The Role of Regime Structures

The state's role has scarcely been ignored in previous accounts of the Reformation. Most overviews of the period in fact portray political development, along with population increase and urbanization, as one of the contextual factors to be reckoned with in understanding the full importance of religious reform. Such accounts typically depict the fifteenth and early sixteenth centuries as a formative period culminating in the centralized, absolutist regimes of the late seventeenth century. Thus the dominant tendencies to be observed include the rise of standing armies, "domestication" of the feudal nobility, a nascent central bureaucracy of fiscal and administrative agents loyal to the crown, and closer fiscal supervision (if not exploitation) of the peasantry. These developments are said to have been a destabilizing force in western Europe generally, giving rise to more innovative political and theological speculation, unsettling the populace, making it more difficult for the church to carry out its functions in the traditional manner, and serving as a kind of catalyst for social conflict of all kinds. The effect of political development on the Reformation, therefore, is pictured as a kind of general, continentwide conditioning factor.

Where more direct links between regime structures and religious reform have been sought, the most common arguments have drawn a connection between reform and a relative *absence* of political centralization. The Reformation is said to have begun in the German territories because they were being squeezed by the growth of absolutism in France and Spain but lacked a domestic regime strong enough to quash dissent or implement more gradual reforms. In this interpretation the origins of the Reformation, as with many other kinds of collective behavior, are attributed to social strains. The subsequent adoption of the Reformation in England, with its centralized regime, is explained as a matter of expediency; that is, once developed, the reformers' ideas could be exploited by powerful monarchs. The Reformation's spread into Scandinavia is attributed to the same causes, or is laid to the work of German-speaking traders, and much emphasis is placed on the otherwise relatively minor encroachments of reform teachings on eastern European soil because it too lacked a strong centralized regime.

These arguments, however, founder on the rocks of more detailed considerations of the various regimes and their relation to other powerful groups in each society. Absolutism was still well in the future; the nobility had scarcely been domesticated in many parts of Europe; and peasant life was not as unsettled as has generally been portrayed. Moreover, the regimes that seem on the surface to resemble one another most closely by virtue of formal structure or military strength actually differed in terms of the institutional bases on which their power rested. Nor was there simply a power vacuum in the German territories, and the institutionalization of the Reformation in other areas requires more complex explanations than those based simply on expediency or cultural diffusion.

In what follows I will argue that the effects of the commercial revolution on the Reformation were mediated primarily by a special type of institutional change that affected some of the towns and some of the major governing bodies of Europe. For both, commercial expansion appears to have created pools of exploitable resources— resources that would be essential to the success of the Reformation. Revenues from customs, duties, and tolls gave some municipal and territorial governments an opportunity to expand their budgets without raising taxes on the land.[72] These resources, unlike most of the traditional concessions that monarchs had claimed, generally did not require negotiation with recalcitrant parliaments or quid pro quo negotiations with the rural elite. Royal monopolies on mining and control over the coinage and valuation of money, shipping, and imports of precious metals and spices served a similar purpose. Revenues from these sources went directly to royal coffers for use in maintaining the royal household, expanding its professional administrative staff, paying for military campaigns, or bestowing offices and titles on royal favorites.

As the cities grew in population and prosperity, their councils were also in a position to benefit. Revenues from municipal guilds, taxes, and commercial investment permitted many of the larger cities to strengthen their fortifications, purchase surrounding catchment areas on which food and supplies depended, develop alliances with other cities, and heighten their influence in larger political bodies. In turn, the cities provided another source of revenue for governments that might fall in need of ready cash or short-term loans. Their influence in political assemblies could also be courted as ballast against the aristocratic and ecclesiastical estates.

These new kinds of resources, and the institutional changes to which they contributed, were important because of the close relations that existed between established religion and rural society. As we have seen, religious customs were deeply embedded in the social relations of rural life, and the powerful elites that dominated rural life were, barring other social disruptions, deeply committed to defending these customs. For the Reformation to be successful, some form of institutional leverage was needed to effect change despite the resistance of these elites. The social effect of the commercial revolution, in brief, was to create resources that cities and states could deploy in order to gain autonomy from the powerful landed interests that continued to dominate so much of European society. Or, framed in more general terms, changes in the broader social environment produced resources that in some cases altered the balance of power between central governing agencies and the rural elite. Where this alteration occurred, central governing agencies gained autonomy that allowed them to function positively as part of the institutional context in which innovative religious discourse could be produced and disseminated.

Incentives for municipal and state agencies to encourage innovative religious discourse were present nearly everywhere: direct windfalls from the appropriation of church lands and properties, tighter control over ecclesiastical appointments, independence from Rome in formulating domestic and foreign policies, greater freedom in the conduct of trade, appeasement of popular unrest in many of the towns, legitimation of secular authority. In those areas of Europe where the governing bodies had gained relative autonomy from the landed sector, the Reformation found political sponsorship and generally succeeded in becoming institutionalized. Local, regional, and national political units that had gained fiscal and administrative autonomy as a result of the commercial expansion of the period were in an advantageous position to pursue policies toward the religious unrest that would also further their own ends. In areas lacking this kind of political autonomy the outcome was generally quite different. States that remained subordinate to the financial, administrative, or military power of the landed upper strata found their options toward the Reformation greatly restricted. Thus, popular religious dissent in the towns became official doctrine and succeeded in spreading to the entire region in some areas, while in others the same dissent failed to gain the adherence of more than a minority.

What does it mean, though, to say that cities and states gained "autonomy"? The notion of autonomy, and specifically relative autonomy, has acquired much currency in the social science literature. It has emerged, chiefly in Marxist theories, as a phrase used to describe the fact that states seem *not*, at least in many cases, to act simply as agents of the ruling capitalist class.[73] In other words, states (or more accurately state managers) appear to act in accordance with their own interests rather than simply reflecting the interests of some broader ruling class. The difficulty with this formulation is that the interests of the state are not easily separated from those of the ruling class. What appears good for the ruling class may also be in the immediate interests of the state. Or, what appears on the surface to be an act of self-preservation on the part of a particular regime may also accrue in some indirect way to the ruling class.

In view of this problem, several alternative approaches to the idea of relative autonomy have been proposed. Some argue that the state enjoys *apparent* autonomy only because (or when) there are divisions within the ruling class. Thus, the state may appear to be acting against a segment of the ruling class, although its actions may well be in the best interests of the ruling class as a whole. Others claim that states are always to some degree at odds with the ruling class because the latter, since early in the development of capitalism itself, have had economic interests transcending the boundaries of particular states. Still others regard the state as a powerful vested interest in its own right, jealous of its prerogatives, and oriented toward the preservation, if not the expansion, of its bureaucratic apparatus and resources.[74] This last view is the one that seems most applicable to the present case. Relative autonomy, however, need not be considered exclusively from the standpoint of interests.

It can also be considered more explicitly as a function of the flows of resources and obligations between the governing agencies of the state and any powerful sector of the society. The governing apparatus may extract resources from the ruling class in the form of taxes but in return grant the ruling class power to approve or disapprove of changes in the rate of taxation. The state thereby sacrifices some of the fiscal autonomy it gains from tax revenues. Or the state may build up its bureaucratic staff by offering lucrative appointments to members of the ruling class. But if these members retain their loyalties to the ruling class, the state's autonomy is likely to be impaired. In these examples it is the level of actual constraint over the activities of the state by the ruling class that determines how high or low the state's relative autonomy is. States with high autonomy are ones with ample social and economic resources over which the ruling class does not exercise control. States with low autonomy may also have resources, but these resources have strings attached to them. Under either condition the state may pursue policies that benefit the ruling class. But states with higher relative autonomy conceivably have a greater variety of policy options available to them.

In the present case the relations at issue occur principally between the state—or in some instances municipalities functioning as states—and the landowning upper stratum. The principal means by which the landowning sector maintained control over the state prior to and during the sixteenth century included fiscal subjection and administrative subjection. Fiscal subjection was accomplished through direct loans to the state, grants of monetary concessions or powers of taxation in return for parliamentary representation or special privileges such as exemption from direct taxation, and payments in kind such as the provisioning of troops or staffing of armies. Administrative power generally went hand in hand with financial control and included strategies such as influence over parliamentary assemblies, control over the staffing of government offices at the local level where the administration of justice was carried out, or staffing of central administrative posts through venality of office or voluntary service. States were able to attain relative autonomy from the landed elite to the extent that they managed to weaken these bonds of dependency. This was the importance of the commercial revolution, for it gave the states access to fiscal and administrative resources not under the control of the landed elite.

So conceived, the idea of relative autonomy represents an aspect of the state that has for the most part not been featured in discussions of the sixteenth century. Accounts of this period have instead concentrated on the distinction between weak and strong states. Spain and France, with large armies, massive central bureaucracies, and large budgets, serve as examples of strong states. England and the territorial principalities of central Europe, having smaller armies, smaller bureaucracies, and smaller budgets, exemplify weak states. Yet analyses of the effects of having strong or weak states lead to the anomalous conclusion that weak states were often more desirable than strong states. And this conclusion has raised further questions about the appropriateness of labels such as "strong" and "weak" in the first place.[75] The idea of relative autonomy, focusing as it does on a more specific type of relation between the state and the landed elite, circumvents some of these problems.

The relative autonomy of states and municipalities from the landowning sector varied widely from one region of Europe to the next. Although the commercial revolution was a phenomenon that affected every region of the Continent to one degree or another, its effects were experienced differently depending on preexisting geographic, social, and political differences among the various regions. The commodities produced for export in different regions varied according to climate and other conditions. These variations, in turn, meant that different social strata were most likely to benefit from the profits of expanding trade. Geography placed some areas in the heartland of trade, others on its periphery. In addition, the capacity of states, municipalities, and landowners to profit from changing conditions depended on regional differences in land tenure provisions, in the administration of cities, in the size and military strength of the nobility, and in the size and degree of unification of territorial jurisdictions. The degree to which various states attained institutional autonomy from the landowning class as a result of commercial expansion therefore depended on a complex interaction between this expansion and these local conditions. The outcomes of these interactions were to affect greatly the manner in which different regimes and municipalities eventually responded to the Reformation.

In addition to altering the balance of power among the various fractions of the ruling elite, of course the economic and demographic trends of the period also directly affected the church as an institution. Increases in population, for example, made it necessary for large numbers of recruits to be brought into the clergy in order to maintain the same ratio of priests to parishioners. Any significant drop in this ratio could well have weakened the church's capacity to withstand the onslaught of zealous reformers.

Studies of the direct effects of such changes on the church, however, reveal no simple relationships that might permit an explanation to be advanced without regard to the changes in state autonomy. In England, for example, detailed records of ordinations from the thirteenth to the sixteenth centuries reveal that the clergy actually grew *faster* than the general population during the century preceding the Reformation. Rising economic prosperity may have been one of the factors behind this increase, for many of the newly recruited clergy were paid by wealthy elites to conduct private masses and to perform pastoral functions on their estates. Some speculation exists as to whether the rapid increase in clergy may have been accomplished at the price of having to reduce educational standards. And this possibility has been linked to the Reformation as a potential source of the dissatisfaction that laity began to express toward clergy. Other evidence, however, suggests that schools to provide training for larger numbers of clergy were probably being established at a sufficiently rapid rate to maintain educational standards.

Evidence from other parts of Europe also casts doubt on the idea that clergy were either less numerous relative to the rest of the population or less qualified on the eve of the Reformation than in previous centuries.[76] In this way at least, then, there appears to be little support for the idea that the Reformation was furthered by direct economic changes in the church. It was, as I shall attempt to show in the next chapter, the *indirect* effects of economic change on the relations between states and the landed segment of the ruling class that provided an institutional context conducive to the adoption of the Reformation.

2

State Autonomy
and the Reformation

CENTRAL EUROPE, extending from Lorraine on the west to
the Elbe valley on the east, and from the Swiss Confederation
on the south to the Low Countries on the north, was the seedbed
of religious reform on the Continent. Giving birth to Lutheranism
in the German principalities and to Zwinglianism and Calvinism first
in the Swiss cantons and later in the Low Countries, this region was
the "dorsal spine" of the Reformation as much as it was of the Continent's geography.

Two other locations also provide settings in which to examine
the environmental conditions and institutional contexts in which the
Reformation was nurtured. Northern Europe, particularly Denmark
and Sweden, adopted the Lutheran reforms and institutionalized
them as an official ideology. And England initiated the Henrician
Reformation, which resulted in the establishment of the Anglican
Church.

The specific theological content of the reforms in these various
areas was shaped by differences in language, local customs, and mental outlooks. The substance of Reformation teachings can scarcely
be understood apart from these cultural preconditions. But an understanding of the economic, political, and social resources needed
to make the Reformation an accepted mode of religious discourse
requires a consideration of the roles played by those municipalities
and states that acquired the institutional autonomy necessary to give
backing to the reforms.

Institutional Contexts of the Continental Reformation

The spread of evangelical teachings in central Europe was conditioned by many factors, including ease of travel, the relative prosperity of the German universities, conflicts within the clergy, literacy, and urban growth. Ease of travel along trading routes and among neighboring towns encouraged personal contact—formally at diets and disputations, as well as informally—between Luther, Bucer, Capito, Erasmus, Zwingli, and other leading intellectuals of the Reformation. The rise of the German universities and the relative freedom they enjoyed from papal censure was clearly another contributing factor. A deepening split within the clergy between those under monastic vows (generally sons of landed nobility) and those in the secular clergy (including a growing number from commercial and artisan backgrounds) was also an important factor. Throughout central Europe literacy rates were also relatively high in the towns, providing an audience capable of reading the Scripture translations and pamphlets of the reformers.[1] In all of this the towns played an especially prominent role, producing young men whose backgrounds and loyalties differed from those of their counterparts in the monasteries, promoting the growth of prestigious universities, and later providing civil protection for preachers under condemnation by the church.

Indeed, reformed teachings had broad appeal in the towns, especially among merchant traders, artisans, and the poor. Actual counts of the religious affiliation of persons in Antwerp, Strasbourg, Nuremberg, and several other cities show that merchants, especially those of moderate wealth and without family connections with the nobility, disproportionately adopted Protestantism.[2] Among members of the lower strata, artisans and skilled craftsmen were generally more likely to adopt the new ideas than local shopkeepers or part-time laborers from the countryside.[3] In some of the towns unemployed workers and poor people were also particularly susceptible to the reformed teachings, especially to variants of Anabaptism that offered mutual support in tight-knit religious communities.[4]

The new doctrines were capable of attracting the various strata in the towns for a number of reasons. In effect, the reformers' teachings reincorporated religion into the collective life of the towns, ending legal and political disputes which came about as a result of the church's dual position as an institution of the town with loyalties and responsibilities extending well beyond the towns. In this respect the Reformation also embodied the principle of *corpus Christianuum,* which had long been an explicit conception of the city in political theory. Towns that adopted the reforms were also quick to vest control of clergy appointments in the city councils, to subject the clergy to taxation, to seize ecclesiastical lands and properties, and to transfer legal jurisdiction from ecclesiastical to municipal courts.[5] As one writer suggests, the religious reforms "ought to be seen less as inevitable products of individual politicians' conversions than as actions of urban governments, which, pushed from below by their commons and harangued by the preachers, came to see that the new gospel offered welcome solutions to nagging old problems."[6]

For artisans and craftsmen the Reformation offered vernacular worship, access to the sacraments and Scripture, and a greater sense of participation in religious services. The Reformation also held appeal for the magistracy and the poor: the former generally used the reforms as an occasion to seize control over the administration of poor relief and to redirect church funds into common chests for this purpose; the latter benefited materially from these reforms. These changes were initiated in Wittenberg, Leisnig, and Nuremberg soon after Luther's break with Rome and spread quickly to other cities such as Basel, Berlin, Leipzig, and Strasbourg.[7] A number of towns also adopted reformed teachings in the face of urban unrest. Fluctuations in the urban economy were closely associated with outbreaks of iconoclasm, and city magistrates in a number of towns appear to have responded to the unrest by declaring themselves in favor of the new doctrines in order to release funds for the needy and to protect their jurisdictions from external intervention.[8]

The response to the reformers' views was considerably less enthusiastic in the surrounding countryside in the German and Swiss lands and in the Low Countries than it was in the towns. Despite the potentially disintegrating effects of rising absentee ownership, free tenancy, a curtailing of common usage rights, and the decline of the lesser nobility, peasant villages in these areas remained intact and served both as a protective moral economy for their residents and as a base of support for traditional religious practices.[9] The widespread unrest that broke out among the peasants in 1525 was itself in some cases testimony to the organizational capacity of the peasant village and largely took the form of political protest against the towns and princes rather than religious reform.[10] In its aftermath Anabaptism appealed to some of its more displaced elements, but these sects attracted only a minute fraction of the peasantry.[11] Indeed, many of the same peasants who participated in the revolt of 1525 appear to have been much opposed to the religious reforms being accomplished in the cities. Less than six months prior to the revolts near Mühlhausen, for example, peasants in that area had denounced evangelicals' efforts in the city to install a reform-minded town council and had withheld pledges to the new council, charged the guilds with "unchristian insubordination," and assisted the conservative council members in ousting the reform preachers from the city.[12]

The German, Swiss, and Dutch landowners, whether living in the countryside or residing in the towns, remained dependent on the stability of rural class relations and, therefore, predictably supported the religious practices that had long undergirded these relations. The principal exception to this pattern was in Bohemia, where the Hussite Wars and grievances against the monarchs gave cause for conversion among the nobility.[13]

But the success of the Reformation on the Continent was not a function simply of its popular support in the towns relative to that in the countryside. It was to a considerable extent a function of the towns' growing political independence. This independence provided the latitude necessary for town councils—acting as semiautonomous regimes—to institute religious reforms without fear of strong internal dissent or of reprisals from the outside. And these institutional capacities were in turn contingent on the great expansion of commerce that overtook central Europe during this period.

Central Europe was ideally situated to benefit from the growth in commerce. This was the region across which the trade between northern Europe and the Mediterranean had to pass. As trading in spices, wine, grain, and textiles increased, this area became its major conduit. The Rhine, and to a lesser extent the Danube, served as major arteries of transportation. It was here too that the overland trade in cattle and grain between east and west had to pass. Rich in mineral deposits, central Europe also became a chief supplier of precious metals and a major source of arms for Spain, Italy, and Flanders. By the end of the sixteenth century the economic decline of the Mediterranean and concentration of trade between England and Amsterdam would undercut the prosperity of this region. But in the meantime central Europe was clearly the hub of the Continent's expanding trade.

As trade increased, a number of cities in central Europe became major commercial centers: Antwerp, Amsterdam, Strasbourg, Nuremberg, Augsburg, Magdeburg, Cologne, Ghent, Vienna. By the start of the sixteenth century all of these cities had populations of at least 25,000. Most of them were linked commercially with one another and with cities as far away as London and Seville. The larger merchant houses maintained envoys in all the major cities and sent messages back and forth by horseback or boat concerning contracts, economic conditions, and other news. There were also a number of smaller cities, such as Aachen, Colmar, Geneva, Leipzig, and Heidelberg, which served as regional centers of trade or as sources of brassware, metals, and other artisan crafts. The south German landscape along the upper Rhine, Danube, Neckar, and Lech rivers was especially prominent for its growing towns. A contemporary wrote, for example: "Augsburg in particular has grown unbelievably rich through the Portuguese monopoly. Ulm has not so much private wealth as Augsburg, though it has greater public wealth and a larger territory. Then comes, if a step lower, Frankfurt am Main. Nuremberg also belongs, of course, to the big cities . . . On the other side [of the Rhine] lies Strasbourg, whose power, though formerly greater than now, is not despised. Metz in Lorraine still recognizes its Imperial status and is mightier than all other free cities, except for Nuremberg."[14] In the mining areas of southern Germany and Bohemia "boomtowns" sometimes appeared within the space of a few years. Joachimstal in Bohemia, for example, grew from one thousand to fourteen thousand residents in little more than a decade. Overall, no more than about 3 percent of the total population of the region lived in these cities, but the affluence of these communities and their importance as centers of commerce gave them a disproportionate share of political influence.

The effects of commercial growth on the social structure of central Europe were also mediated by the fact that this area was not politically centralized. Formally it was roughly coterminous with the Holy Roman Empire and thus was largely under the official jurisdiction of the Spanish and Austrian Hapsburgs. In practice, central Europe was actually a patchwork of more than two hundred quasi-independent principalities, duchies, bishoprics, archbishoprics, and imperial cities. Of these, forty-five dynastic principalities were the most powerful, controlling 80 percent of the land and population.[15] Many of the major cities also had long traditions of political autonomy which they had purchased or won through military ventures. This autonomy was jealously guarded. Among the territorial princes there were also fierce rivalries as each struggled with the others to control contested territory, exploit trading routes, and gain favors with the sovereigns of France, England, Spain, Scandinavia, or the papal states. None had succeeded in unifying the region, but several had built up considerable strength. These duchies, imperial cities, and territorial principalities were the primary political units or states, albeit by no means the unified national states of later periods, whose autonomy or lack of autonomy from the landed elite would constitute a decisive factor in the progress of the Reformation.

Commercial growth served mainly to enhance the political autonomy of the imperial cities and territorial princes. Artisan manufacturing, mining, commercial investments, and tolls provided new sources of revenue. Cities used these revenues to further their financial and military independence in a number of ways. They built better fortifications, paid for mercenaries when needed, and established protective alliances with other cities or with the territorial princes. They purchased surrounding areas on which food supplies depended and guarded themselves against labor unrest that might invite outside intervention in municipal affairs by setting up poor-relief services. They enacted legislation aimed at furthering commerce and restricting excess labor. They also attracted members of the nobility into the ranks of merchants both through the prospect of handsome profits and by extending rights of *embourgeoisment* which often gave greater legal protection and civic standing than the title of nobility itself.[16]

Territorial princes also gained greater independence from the local landed interests. In Württemberg, for example, the duke had by the beginning of the sixteenth century effectively reduced the nobility as a class to virtual nonexistence. Much of the land was owned by the duke himself and was leased directly to peasants on inheritable tenure arrangements that involved high levels of taxation. Rapid economic expansion in this region was accompanied by greater integration of the local economy into larger trading networks, by rising urban prosperity, and by an enlarged central bureaucracy of tax collectors and other officials.[17] Princes such as the duke of Saxony and the landgrave of Hesse, two of the most powerful sovereigns in the region, built up armies and bureaucratic staffs and expanded their overall revenues by drawing on the earnings of mines under their concession, securing loans from the urban patriciate, enforcing legislation against the lesser nobility, and receiving income from tolls and customs in return for their protection of transportation routes.[18]

The growing economic significance of trade in the region also encouraged closer alliances between the cities and territorial princes. The cities depended on the princes to protect trade and transportation militarily, to maintain favorable tax and customs policies, and above all to defend them against the intermittent efforts of the Hapsburgs to impose greater control over the areas to which they claimed title by dynastic right. In return the princes derived a number of benefits from the cities, including tax revenues, loans, and income from the sale of metalwares and other commodities. The princes and towns also shared a common cadre of professional administrators. By 1500 many of the princes and towns were already linked through an elite of bourgeois jurists who had become indispensable to the princes as administrative councilors.[19]

Unlike the territorial princes in many other areas of Europe, the princes here also found it in their interest to pass legislation which encouraged the concentration of industry in the cities rather than allowing it to diffuse among the rural population. The princes in Saxony, Hesse, Bavaria, Mecklenburg, and Schleswig-Holstein all established what was known as the "mile zone" around cities in their territories—a zone reserved for urban craftsmen, while in the countryside no artisan work was permitted except that needed for farming.[20]

In other ways the interests of the towns and those of the princes sometimes failed to coincide, of course, and not all of the princes developed a stake in the expanding commerce of the towns. Open conflict among the various factions erupted intermittently. The towns and many of the princes, however, gained greater autonomy from the rural interests by collaborating against them.

As for the landlords, their position had gradually diminished over the previous century and was further eroded during the early decades of the sixteenth century. In several areas, particularly Saxony and Thuringia, patterns of free tenancy and smallholding had arisen during the fourteenth century, thereby restricting the influence of the nobility.[21] In other areas the profits of merchants grew more rapidly than those of the nobility. And as land values increased, it was the merchants who were best able to purchase land and use it as a source of collateral for riskier investments. An examination of estate records and taxes paid by the leading merchants of Antwerp around the middle of the sixteenth century reveals, for example, that these merchants invested a large share of their profits in rural holdings, obtaining collateral for loans as well as stable sources of revenue that could be used as a hedge against ventures in shipping or commercial speculation. These investments were most often made during prosperous years when extra profits were available and proved especially valuable during lean years when commerce was contracting.[22] Another study indicates that about 70 percent of the land surrounding Strasbourg was owned by residents of the city. Many of these parcels had been acquired through forfeitures on loans, and of the remaining 30 percent of the land, a good share appears to have been mortgaged to urban creditors.[23] During the same period the lower nobility generally declined, joining the ranks of yeoman farmers or becoming salaried overseers for absentee landlords.[24]

The net effect of these changes was to alter the balance of power among the various elites in central Europe. Most of the population continued to live in small villages in the countryside. But an increasing share of the land was owned directly by small cultivators or fell into the hands of absentee landlords in the cities whose principal interests were in trade. The cities' prosperity stemmed from trade and was sufficient for them to guard the political autonomy they had gradually acquired. Their relations with the knights and peasantry in surrounding areas were often less than peaceful. Indeed, the status differentials between urban and rural elites in many parts of central Europe had reduced the latter to petty brigands who preyed on merchants and travelers. And peasant uprisings were not infrequent in those areas in which the cities and nobles struggled to exert hegemony. But the cities generally commanded the resources necessary to deal with these threats from the countryside. On several occasions leagues were established among neighboring towns to retaliate against noble brigands, to track down the worst predators, and to burn out their castles.[25] Among the territorial princes, many of course remained dependent on revenue from their own estates and on the support of Hapsburg rule, but others gained economic strength and political autonomy from their involvement, both directly and as allies of the cities, in the growing commercial activity of the period.

Several indications point clearly to the significance of the towns' political autonomy for the progress of the Reformation in central Europe. One is that the imperial cities, distinguished by having a strong tradition of self-government, led the way in supporting the

Reformation. More than fifty of the sixty-five imperial cities in central Europe officially accepted the Reformation.[26] Of the thirty-four imperial cities in southwestern Germany, only three were unaffected by it.[27] Another indication is the prominence of Reformation activity in the larger trading cities—those cities where the landed elite had a weaker voice than in the smaller towns.[28] In southwestern Germany a linear relation existed between city size and speed of adopting the Reformation.[29]

Regional comparisons also indicate the importance of state autonomy vis-à-vis the landed elite. In the Low Countries the Reformation spread most quickly in Holland, Friesland, and Groningen. Here the nobility was weak and the town councils were better able to protect the reformers. Groningen was in an especially favorable position to encourage religious innovation because it was also far from the royal capital in Brussels and contained no royal garrison.[30] By comparison, seigneurial power was stronger in Utrecht and Flanders and was more closely allied with the church.[31] In these areas seigneurial power inhibited the growth of Protestantism except in the larger cities.

Regional comparisons among the Swiss cantons point to similar relations. The Swiss Reformation began in Zurich and spread quickly to Berne, Basel, Strasbourg, and Geneva, all of which were virtually autonomous city-states.[32] Basel, for instance, was a town of about ten thousand inhabitants by the beginning of the sixteenth century and had enjoyed a tradition of autonomous municipal government for more than a century. In 1499, Emperor Maximilian I had tried unsuccessfully to force Basel into a closer association with the empire, and in 1501 it joined the Swiss Confederation, further securing its military autonomy in relation to the empire. Economic growth during the fifteenth century had increased the city's financial strength sufficiently that by 1521 it was able to exclude the episcopacy from exercising temporal power and forbade citizens from taking an oath to the bishop. During the same period the nobles and patricians had lost influence in the town relative to a new merchant elite of bankers, textile manufacturers, wine merchants, and tradesmen. On the eve of the Reformation, the city council was composed almost entirely of this elite's repesentatives.[33] In contrast, the Reformation did not succeed in Zug, Lucerne, Schwyz, Uri, and Fribourg, where the landed nobility was more firmly entrenched and posed strong resistance to the reformers.[34]

Case histories of particular cities also demonstrate the importance of city councils in fostering and defending the Reformation when their autonomy was strong. Cities were better able to support the Reformation when the nobility's involvement in civic affairs was weak, and members of city councils often appear to have seen the Reformation as a means of augmenting their own autonomy. Nuremberg's city council, relying on the town's considerable economic strength as a major trading city and its autonomy as an imperial city, strongly resisted pressures from the emperor to repress Protestantism.[35] Members of the council defended the reformers as much from concern for their city's right to determine its own religious policy as from personal conviction. As a corporate entity, its chronicler observes, "it pursued only one aim in its religious policy, the enhancement of the city's freedom of action."[36] Strasbourg's magistrates, acting to preserve the city's defenses and peace, also firmly supported the reformers.[37] Here the city's elite included members of the nobility who resisted the reforms, but representatives of the merchant oligarchy ultimately prevailed. Ever mindful that "Charles V might invoke his imperial authority and step in to pacify the city at the ruling families' expense," the magistrates followed a course of moderate reform: they swept away the church courts, subjected the clergy to civil law, assumed responsibility for nominating pastors and maintaining relief chests for the poor, and satisfied popular demands for reforms in worship, but sternly opposed iconoclasm and the more radical demands of the Anabaptists.[38] In Geneva the reformers' strongest support came from the newer merchant families who were not bound by familial ties to the landed nobility.[39] A similar situation prevailed in Antwerp.[40] Deventer, in contrast, failed to institute the reforms effectively, largely because of resistance from the landed elite.[41] Erfurt, Ulm, and Basel all enjoyed greater independence from the nobility and were able to adopt the Reformation.[42] In most of these instances reformed teachings were initiated by the populace rather than the governing bodies themselves.[43] But the latter provided the protection and official sanctioning without which the reforms would likely not have succeeded. One writer concludes: "The process of gaining government sanction was an integral part of the development pattern and of the final content of the Reformation; magisterial consolidation is an essential part . . . of the Reformation."[44]

The cities' autonomy, rooted in commercial expansion, gave

them an opportunity to pursue the Reformation; threats to their autonomy provided an added incentive. These threats, at least the ones that were new, were also rooted in the broader economic and political changes of the period. One was the growing Hapsburg influence in the region. Whereas the Austrian Hapsburgs had long been too weak militarily and too much in debt to the cities financially to pose much of a danger, the Spanish Hapsburgs under the reign of Charles V now commanded a more imposing presence. This, together with the continuing incursions of the Ottomans to the east, placed central Europe squarely in the path of the two most powerful imperial regimes. And the cities' wealth appeared to the Hapsburgs to be the most promising source of revenue with which to finance their campaigns against the Turks. As it happened, the Imperial Diet of Worms in 1521—the diet at which Charles first made a personal appearance before his German subjects and which became famous for Luther's confrontation with Charles—was the occasion for a major tax reform that threatened to increase substantially the apportionment assessed against the towns. In subsequent diets the rate of taxation was shifted even more inequitably from the nobility to the towns.[45]

As evangelical teachings began to spread among the urban populations, the emperor's religious policies also came to pose a distinct threat to the towns' autonomy. The emperor demanded that town councils simply ban all further instances of heretical practice. In virtually all of the major towns the magistrates temporized, however. Their appeals testified to the fact that their greatest fear was not reprisal if they did not comply but the danger of popular insurrection if they did. Fearing for their own positions, especially in towns with some degree of elected representation, and for the increased vulnerability to surrounding powers that internal dissension would create, the magistrates for the most part chose a cautious policy of passive support or tolerance toward the reforms rather than risking attempts to eradicate them.

Faced with the same threats from the outside, or with internal needs to strengthen their military or financial position, towns without the requisite autonomy from local landed elites were, however, less free to initiate religious reforms, or even to protect reformers with substantial support from below. The town of Münster provides a case in point. Rising deficits between 1538 and 1548 caused the bishop of Münster to consider secularizing church lands. A decade earlier radical reformers and Lutherans had held power in the town. Yet in neither situation were reforming sentiments able to gain full or lasting institutionalization. In 1535 the reformers had been overthrown by surrounding armies, and over the following decade secularization of church lands was prevented from being accomplished by the distribution of local authority. During the fifteenth century the most influential members of the town council had been merchants. But during the first half of the sixteenth century the merchant elite found itself in a declining competitive position within the cloth and grain trades of the Hansa, and were forced to turn increasingly to investments in land. They also became increasingly dependent on loans from the surrounding landed nobility. The nobility remained firm supporters of the church throughout the Reformation period. Many of their younger sons found employment in the priesthood. And the urban elite were often intermarried with members of the nobility who had close ties to the church, in addition to being economically interdependent with them. According to one study of the town: "By the sixteenth century, the non-patrician urban elites were . . . increasingly sinking investment in land. Both magisterial and leading guild families bought up farms, pastures, and gardens around Münster. The pursuit of landownership inevitably brought the urban elite into contact with the Church, and it is in landholding that the pattern of interpenetration between segments of urban society and the rural clerical regime is most visible."[46] In contrast to the towns in which the magisterial elite had greater autonomy from the land, in Münster the elite made many of the critical decisions during the 1530s that prevented the Reformation from taking hold.

Freiburg in the vicinity of the upper Rhine provides another comparison that demonstrates the same general pattern. With little land of its own and a precarious position in relation to larger trading networks, its economy depended heavily on the good will of the neighboring nobility. Food, animal products, wool, and other basic raw materials all came from the surrounding countryside, while most of the town's surplus crafts and entrepôt goods were purchased by the same peasants and landowners. Despite recurrent shortages of revenue, the town council did not attempt to raise taxes from its hinterland for fear that the nobles would order their subjects to boycott its commodities.[47] Although there were a considerable number of skilled artisans in the town, the fate of political and religious issues depended primarily on the interests of the countryside. Lacking sufficient revenue to purchase its autonomy, the town was forced to rely chiefly on the Austrian Hapsburgs for military and political protection. When the reformers' teachings began to be heard in 1521, some popular support, fueled by nascent anticlericalism, was voiced. In 1522 a petition was drawn up by a group of burghers to receive the Eucharist in both kinds.[48] From the beginning, however, Archduke Ferdinand pressed for a suppression of the reforms, and the town council readily complied. House to house searches were conducted to confiscate evangelical books, and persons suspected of evangelical sympathies were arrested. The failure of the reforming movement was thus a result of the town council's dependence both locally and regionally on political actors whose interests ran in favor of established religious practices.[49]

The other main group that had gained political autonomy as a result of the commercial expansion in central Europe—the territorial princes—also played a significant role in defending the Reformation. Geoffrey Elton suggests that they "preserved the Reformation [and] without them it could almost certainly not have been preserved."[50] In part their motivation came from the towns whose interests were closely related to their own. It also stemmed increasingly from relations with the Hapsburgs. Although the princes' economic position had improved substantially as a result of growth in trade and mining, their lands were increasingly subject to impositions of imperial taxes, requisitions of troops for the imperial army, and efforts by the emperor to legislate greater uniformity in religious practices.[51] The strongest of the princes, including Saxony, Brandenburg, and Hesse, banded together to resist these impositions, while a number of the weaker ones came increasingly into the Hapsburgs' orbit of influence.

At a minimum, the ambivalent relationship between many of the territorial princes and the emperor created a situation in which passive restraint toward the religious reformers became the operative policy. The imperial Council of Regency in Nuremberg, formed in 1521, was the highest governing body whenever the emperor was absent from the region. It was to this body that papal nuncios repeatedly appealed to enforce the Edict of Worms against Luther and his followers. Several conditions, however, weakened the council's willingness—and its capacity—to comply with these wishes. One was that the council was internally divided by the various dynastic and territorial claims represented and therefore was relatively ineffective in enforcing any decrees. A second was that the uncertainty of whether support of or opposition to the reformers would be most threatening to domestic peace kept the councilors in a "wait and see" attitude rather than pushing them into decisive action. A third was the council's reluctance, because of its regional interests, merely to do the bidding of the emperor or of the emperor's ally, the pope. A fourth was that the imperial cities were able to weaken the council's authority by playing it and the emperor against each other. Finally, the emperor himself was sufficiently ambivalent toward the potential power of the council, as a rival to his own, to undercut the kind of financial and legal authority that would have been necessary for it to become an active force in religious affairs. As it was, the council managed through inaction to let the Reformation spread at its own pace during the critical period until 1523, after which the council was temporarily disbanded and eventually reorganized on Austrian territory.[52]

As elsewhere, the territorial princes also tended to be inclined in some cases toward the Reformation because of the opportunity it posed for arrogating church lands to themselves. In consequence, those who had attained a degree of fiscal and administrative autonomy often threw their weight behind the reformers.[53] Saxony, with a strong centralized administrative staff—among the members of which were Luther's friend Spalatin and for a short time another confidant of Luther's, John Bugenhagen—and close economic ties with commerce and mining, played the most visible role in protecting the reformers.[54] Hesse, with growing commercial revenues and a centralized bureaucracy, also lent strong support.[55] Over the following decade others—Württemberg, Pomerania, Nassau, Brandenburg—followed suit.[56] And by the 1550s the Electoral Palatinate was becoming an increasingly powerful supporter of the Reformation.[57] Here the nobility objected strongly to the reforming process because they regarded it as undermining their power in the villages.[58] The elector's administrators and jurists, however, were recruited mainly from bourgeois circles in the southwestern German imperial cities and from families involved in mining and finance.[59]

Opportunism played a role in the princes' overtures toward the towns as well. As early as 1526 the princes of Saxony and Hesse approached the major towns in which evangelical stirrings were evident with an offer of military protection. The peasant uprisings of the previous year had drawn Luther to regard the princes with higher esteem and had illustrated at least one of the common interests of the princes and towns. Suspicious of sacrificing any of their autonomy to these territorial lords, however, the towns rejected the idea. By the end of the decade the towns had become more receptive. Religious unrest had grown more serious, and efforts to promote a unified urban front, while successful at first, had foundered on the rocks of regional differences and theological disputes. When the Smalkaldic League was proposed in 1531, with the princes again offering military protection, many of the Protestant towns joined. The principal deterrent to the princes' actions, as to that of the cities, was the threat of military reprisal from the emperor.[60] Virtually absent was any sense of effective resistance from the landed nobility.

And if the principal deterrent was the emperor, even his power was constrained by the broader economic and political forces operating across the Continent at the time. Despite the size of his dynastic possessions and the strength of his armies, Charles V was in a position to give only weak opposition to the Reformation in central Europe. Only three weeks after Luther's famous declaration "Ich kann nicht anders" at the Diet of Worms, Charles signed a warrant for his arrest and declared it an act of treason as well as blasphemy to give Luther aid and comfort. Charles's ability to enforce this edict, however, was uncharacteristically weak and was to remain so during the next critical decade of the Reformation's development. His own expanding dynastic possessions were rivaled by the economic and military expansion of all his major competitors, especially the kings of France and England and the territorial princes who controlled German lands. The latter had been especially effective in gaining concessions for themselves. Indeed, Charles had bargained away many of the rights that might have given him the capacity to quash the reformers two years previously in return for his election as emperor. In addition to making monetary and linguistic concessions, he had promised not to station Spanish troops on German soil, pledged that only Germans would be appointed to imperial posts, and restored the Council of Regency to govern in his absence. With friction also brewing between himself and the pope, and with severe financial constraints and impending war with the Turks, he was able to do little more than levy threats at the reformers from a distance.[61]

The effects of broad changes in the social environment, namely the commercial revolution, then, were mediated in central Europe by the specific institutional contexts provided by the towns and some of the more powerful territorial princes. The nature of economic expansion in this region was such that the towns and princes derived added resources, whereas the landed nobility generally declined. With the nobility's capacity to protect established religious practices temporarily weakened, the merchant oligarchies and their princely allies were in a stronger position to support religious reform. Sometimes the incentives for reform were sufficient to generate active support; in other instances pressures from above and below were sufficiently complex that the reforms progressed more from inaction on the part of governing bodies than from active support. On balance, however, the capacity of the various parties involved to bring pressure on town councils and territorial administrators was a decisive factor in settling religious disputes.

Scandinavia: Contrasts and Similarities

In northern Europe the situation was similar in many respects to that in central Europe. This region also experienced a sharp increase in trade during the first half of the sixteenth century. Large quantities of wood were exported to England and Holland for shipbuilding and other types of construction. Exports of Swedish iron doubled during this period. Copper was mined in increasing volume. Flax and hemp were exported to Russia. And much of the wheat and rye exported from eastern Europe to the west had to pass through this region. By midcentury more than two thousand ships annually passed through the Danish Sound. Along trading routes cities such as Copenhagen, Malmö, Stockholm, Revel, and Riga grew in population and importance. Copenhagen, for instance, accounted for 11 percent of the entire Danish population by 1500. The chief difference relative to central Europe was that here the region was less fragmented politically. Although territorial claims continued to be contested, the monarchs of Denmark and Sweden were clearly the dominant powers.[62]

The effects of commercial growth, both in Denmark and in Sweden, were to strengthen the autonomy of the central regime relative to the landed elite. In both countries the landowners had been the dominant class during the fifteenth century. Less of the land was owned by the nobility (perhaps no more than a fifth) and smallholding was more common than in many other areas of Europe. Nevertheless, the nobility enjoyed broad political and economic prerogatives. In Denmark the nobles controlled most of the smaller towns and through legislation prevented members of the bourgeoisie from purchasing land. In Sweden they dominated the council of state, resisted all efforts at centralization and taxation, and had succeeded in creating a de facto aristocratic republic prior to the rise of Gustav Vasa in 1523. Commerce and industry were mainly limited to the larger trading cities along the coast and mining regions. This, together with the fact that merchants were excluded from owning rural estates, meant that the effects of commercial expansion affected the structure of rural life less directly than it did in central Europe. The main effect was to give the monarchs vastly increased financial resources in their struggles against the nobility.

Tolls from the ships that passed through the Danish Sound in growing numbers went directly to the crown. These revenues gave it the resources necessary to impose a uniform system of centralized administration, pay for military campaigns against Norway, and expand crown lands. During this period it also actively encouraged mercantile interests and sought to cultivate them as a political counterforce to the nobility. By the end of the century the Danish crown was taking in four times as much revenue as Poland, with only a tenth of Poland's population. The structure of its revenues, moreover, gave it virtual independence from the landed elite: 50 percent came from royal domains, 35 percent from tolls, and only 15 percent from taxes.[63] In Sweden the crown increased its revenues primarily through monopolies over the production of silver and copper and to a lesser extent through customs and tolls. The loyalties of Stockholm and the Bergslag mining district were cultivated and given strong political representation. The crown also received direct support, both economically and militarily, from Lübeck and Gdansk in return for granting favorable trading concessions to these cities.

When the Reformation came, these regimes played a major role in initiating and defending it. The Reformation spread quickly to northern Europe as a result of its proximity to northern Germany. It gained ground particularly in the leading trade centers in Copenhagen, Malmö, Stockholm, and Lübeck, all of which were commercially linked with central Europe.[64] As a politically autonomous merchant oligarchy, Lübeck was especially important in spreading the Reformation, just as the imperial cities in central Europe were.[65]

But it was the crown that became the strongest advocate of the reforms. Conflict between crown and nobility, coupled with a visible alliance between the nobility and clergy, provided the incentive for reform; the crown's rising fiscal and administrative autonomy from the nobility gave it the opportunity. Christian II of Denmark actively supported humanistic reforms within the established church and courted the merchant class to the point that a temporary uprising among alienated segments of the nobility forced him to flee the country in 1523. A year later he converted to Lutheranism. His successor, Frederick I, took an oath to suppress the Lutheran heresies under pressure from the nobility, but in practice promoted them within his own district of Schleswig and after 1527 permitted evangelical preaching wherever there was support for it. In the same year ties with Rome were effectively broken and religion was declared a matter of conscience. The following year a printing press was set up in Vyborg to promote evangelical teachings, and reformers acquired many of the prominent pulpits in Copenhagen. Before Frederick's death in 1533 the secularization of church lands was well under way. This process was pursued vigorously by his successor, Christian III, who issued a decree at the start of his reign in 1536 requiring all his subjects to become Lutherans and oversaw the chartering of Lutheranism as the state church in 1539. Evangelical clergy were brought in from Wittenberg and elsewhere or were promoted to positions of power within the Danish church, and reforms of the University of Copenhagen, visitations, confiscations of church property, and other programs were carried out.[66] Most of the revenue from church lands as well as from the tithe went directly to the crown. As a result, its income increased by approximately 300 percent.[67]

The Reformation in Norway proceeded at about the same pace as in Denmark. Here the secularization of church lands gained momentum after 1528 and was completed over the next decade and a half. Lutheranism was imposed by royal edict in 1536. Norway was under jurisdiction of the Danish sovereign, so the reforms were carried out primarily at his initiative. This meant, however, that they also encountered greater resistance than in Denmark simply because of negative sentiment among the Norwegians toward Danish intervention in their affairs. It has been suggested that this was one reason for the more limited success of the Reformation in Norway than in Denmark. Catholic customs continued to be associated with the call for Norwegian independence long after Lutheranism became the official faith.[68]

In Sweden and Finland the Reformation was sponsored by Gustav Vasa, who became king of Sweden in 1523.[69] Vasa enjoyed a relatively high degree of fiscal and administrative autonomy relative to the nobility. To repay debts to Lübeck Vasa took forced loans from the church, incurring some dissent among the nobility and peasants.[70] But this dissent was weak and ineffective. He also diverted part of the tithe for military payments and appointed clergy favorable to his views. At about this time the ideas of Luther were being introduced in Stockholm by merchants from Germany and by students from German universities. Vasa saw arguments in the new teachings that would be of value in his drive to consolidate power. In 1527 he dissolved the monasteries, using the occasion to secure loyalty from a segment of the nobility by selling them at favorable terms. Most of the monastic lands were retained by the crown, however; accordingly, crown lands quadrupled as a result of the Reformation, while those of the nobility stayed roughly the same.[71] Over the next fifteen years Lutheran-style worship was gradually introduced and royal supremacy was extended over the church. As was to be the case in England, these reforms took place at the higher levels of church bureaucracy, while many aspects of popular religious practice remained unaffected.[72] In short, the Reformation in northern Europe proceeded not so much from popular demand but "as a thing imposed from above."[73]

In both central and northern Europe, then, expanding trade appears to have interacted with preexisting local conditions to enhance the autonomy of the governing elites. Geography and natural resources shaped the manner in which these areas participated in the European economy. Both had commodities for export and were located across major arteries of trade. But the relative weakness of the nobility in the countryside, traditions of urban self-determination, and territorial regimes capable of exploiting mineral resources and tolls while for the most part avoiding expensive military encounters with other regimes determined how the commercial revolution would influence the social structure in each area. In central Europe the new profits to be made from commerce increased the options available to the municipalities and princes in a variety of policy areas, among which were their policies toward the Reformation. The resources gained were divided among the numerous regimes represented within the Holy Roman Empire. No single regime gained sufficiently more than the others to impose its rule over the entire region—a fact that would also shape the outcome of the Reformation.

But the nobility in each area was effectively weakened to the point that the towns and princes no longer had to fear strong resistance from that quarter. In northern Europe the outcome was similar, with the exception that the Swedish and Danish kings were the prime beneficiaries.

The Tudor State and the English Reformation

In England it was also the crown's relative autonomy from the land-owning elite that provided the decisive opportunity for the Reformation to succeed. Some demand for religious reform had long been present in England, most notably in the form of Lollardy. Luther soon came to be a household name among the merchants and artisans of London as well. Nevertheless, the decisive action that shaped the English Reformation came from the top, from a regime that had acquired the capability to pursue an independent course of religious reform, more than it did from any groundswell of popular demand. As in Scandinavia, the Reformation in England was a "revolution from above," imposed by the state and only gradually accepted by the society.

Virtually all accounts of the changes that were initiated in England emphasize the state's role. For example, Geoffrey Elton observes: "England's march away from Rome was led by the government for reasons which had little to do with religion or faith."[74] In a similar vein, T. M. Parker asserts: "It is probably true to say that only the English monarchy could have carried through the English Reformation without destroying the country; no other contemporary autocracy could have accomplished such a *tour de force*."[75] Claire Cross echoes the same sentiment in declaring: "The Henrician Reformation must still be seen as a naked act of the state, the imposition of the will of one man, the Monarch, upon an entire nation."[76]

In many respects the English state was militarily and bureaucratically underdeveloped in comparison with its counterparts in France and Spain (as will be seen in the following chapter). But the English state achieved a relatively high, if temporary, degree of autonomy from the landed elite during the first half of the sixteenth century as a result of the economic and social changes that accompanied England's role in the commercial revolution.

England's commercial expansion depended, as elsewhere, at least partly on rising demand from a growing population. Though not spectacular, this growth was steady, giving the country a population about 50 percent higher at the end of the century than at the beginning.[77] Yet, with a population only half that of Spain, one-third that of Germany, and one-sixth that of France, England was in an economic position as closely associated with foreign trade as with the growth of its domestic market.

England's foreign trade tripled during the last half of the fifteenth century and multiplied several times during the sixteenth.[78] Along with Flanders, England became a principal source of manufactured cloth. The value of these exports quadrupled between 1500 and 1550.[79] Under both Henry VII and Henry VIII the crown actively promoted the trade in cloth and other commodities. Treaties were initiated with Denmark and the Baltic cities; commercial relations were reestablished with the Low Countries; restrictions on trade with France were removed; commercial pacts with Spain and the Mediterranean states were negotiated; and sizable loans were granted to the merchants of London.[80]

Although Dutch and Hanseatic cooperation was involved, England's export trade was consciously concentrated in the hands of its own merchants rather than being allowed to slip into foreign hands as in Poland and Spain. Accordingly, London became a prosperous commercial center, multiplying in population by more than 350 percent during the century.[81] By 1500 London had already become a powerful lobby to whose interests the crown paid close attention. As loans and treaties stimulated commerce, the crown gained both financially and politically. Financially it prospered from the sizable increase in customs revenues that accompanied rising exports. Politically, in the words of one observer, "the revival of commerce was helping the rise of new men who could be used by the crown as a counterpoise to what was left of the old aristocracy."[82] As the London merchant community prospered, the crown also gained a powerful political ally. "Closely linked together by their wealth, their family ties, and their membership [in] the great livery companies, the rulers of London were a cohesive and united group, devoted to the interests of their own community and invariably loyal to the crown."[83]

By the beginning of the sixteenth century the crown had once again become solvent as a result of rising customs revenues, better management of its estates, and a policy of frugality in military affairs and in the administration of the royal household.[84] But more important, the *structure* of crown revenues gave the state a degree of

fiscal autonomy from the landed sector that was virtually unparalleled
at the time. According to estimates at the beginning of the reign of
Henry VIII, 35 percent of the crown's revenues came from customs,
another 35 percent came directly from the earnings of crown lands,
and an additional 20 percent came from special sources such as revenues from the royal mint.[85] Thus, only 10 percent was left to be
raised from direct taxes on land or other properties.

Administratively the state also succeeded in emancipating itself
in large measure from the control of the landed elite. The Tudors,
unlike their counterparts in France and Spain, practiced a deliberate
policy of restricting the nobility's access to high appointive office,
preferring instead to make appointments selectively and with provisions that guaranteed officials' loyalty to the crown. They also
avoided selling offices to the nobility merely to raise supplemental
revenue. Instead officeholders at the top levels of government were
selected from the royal family itself, from merchant and professional
families, from gentry whose fortunes depended on the crown, and
from the lower strata. As a result the king's top advisory councils
and ad hoc commissions were largely independent of noble connections.[86]

Like representative bodies in every other European country at
the time, the English Parliament continued to reflect the vested interests of men of wealth, among whom were the landowners. But
by the reign of Henry VIII the influence of this elite in Parliament
had been greatly reduced. Through a series of strategic moves the
crown had gradually increased the representation in Parliament of
merchants and city officials, members of the clergy, and royal officeholders—all of whom were in some manner loyal to the crown
or dependent on its network of patronage.[87] Thus, the Parliament
of Henry VIII—the Parliament that was to assist at every turn in
advancing the English Reformation—was an ally on whom he could
generally depend, rather than a foe ready to defend the landowners'
interests.[88]

In the House of Commons the Parliament of 1529 consisted of
74 knights of the shire and 236 burgesses. The former were landowners, and all but a few had stronger ties to the landed elite than
to the crown. The burgesses, in contrast, were residents of the towns,
and most were engaged in commerce of some type. Indeed the majority were engaged in some aspect of the cloth trade: drapers, hab-
erdashers, cloth exporters, shipowners, financiers. Among the

remainder were local officeholders or professional people such as lawyers and surveyors with close connections to the crown. Thus, the landed interests were outnumbered by a margin of as many as three to one. This was a highly unusual situation both in comparison with other countries and in comparison with the strength that land-owners had held in England during the previous century. It was also exceptional in comparison with the strength that the landed elite would again enjoy before the end of the century.[89]

In the same year the House of Lords was also a strong ally of the crown. Nearly half its members were representatives of the church—a surprising fact in view of the ecclesiastical reforms they were to approve. But ecclesiastical appointments had for some time been made by the crown. And representatives who opposed royal policy were likely to find the seats they vacated filled by appointees with more pliable views. Among the temporal lords, many were longtime servants of the crown and held peerages created by the king in return for their services, while others were members of the royal household itself. The crown also held traditional prerogatives that gave it considerable influence over the Lords. It could command opponents not to attend, or at least intimidate them. It could threaten the positions of ecclesiastical and royal officials. And it appointed its own chancellor and other nonnoble servants of the House. Overall, its influence over the Lords was probably as great as, if not greater than, its influence over the Commons. Contrary to the often-voiced supposition that England represented a democratic state in which royal power was balanced by Parliament, therefore, it is probably more appropriate to conclude, as one author does, that Parliament had still "not established itself as an effective and sufficient vehicle for the expression of opposition and for the resolution of political conflict."[90]

The means by which the state administered local justice were also symptomatic of the crown's capacity to rule in a manner that was largely autonomous from the landed elite. Under the Tudors the collection of local taxes did remain either directly or indirectly under the influence of the local landed elite. But the total amount of these collections was by no means the centerpiece of crown fi-nances as it was in France and Spain. Nor were the local clergy, who remained closely allied with the landowners, utilized to any significant extent in the administration of local justice—certainly not to the extent that they were in France. Gradually their role was modified

toward becoming little more than hortatory in function. Justices of
the peace were the primary officials concerned with local administration, and, although they were in effect selected by the local landlords, they were increasingly subject to the authority of royal lords-
lieutenant. In addition, courtier justices and crown lawyers played
an increasing role in local government.[91]

Special commissions were also used to administer the crown's
policies without giving the landlords an opportunity to consolidate
political influence. Usually these commissions included some members of the local gentry. But they were closely supervised by royal
agents and were used as a counterbalance to the more traditional
political forces in the countryside. Since these commissions were
temporary, they provided a means of conducting royal business without establishing a permanent bureaucracy in areas that could become
co-opted by the local landowners.[92]

Finally, the Tudor state had also reduced the influence of the
landowners over its policies through sheer force and intimidation.
The fortunes of leading families were unmade by royally instigated
lawsuits contesting their inheritance rights; those who fell from favor
might be systematically excluded from holding even minor offices
in local government or transferred to out-of-the-way military charges;
and in other instances the crown's capacity to dispense land and other
favors was used to move members of the gentry to new areas where
their influence was minimal.[93] Charges of treason against members
of the nobility and royal officials alike, such as the duke of Buck-
ingham, Thomas Cromwell, and the duke of Norfolk, served as show
trials demonstrating the crown's commitment to the use of force to
preserve its sovereignty.[94] In all, 883 charges of treason were levied
between 1532 and 1540 alone, and of those persons brought to trial,
fewer than 10 percent were acquitted.[95]

None of these policies was sufficient to strip the landed aristocracy entirely of its power; nor was it in the Tudors' interest to do
so. Their success lay primarily in placing themselves at the center of
a vast network of officials and gentry whose power and wealth ultimately depended on the crown. Family names were made and unmade by the granting of titles and offices and by dismissals and
charges of treason; incomes depended to a large extent on royally
conferred prerogatives; checks and balances among competing families kept officeholders from rising too high on the basis of their own
patronage networks; and periodic transfers of officials from region

to region weakened local ties still further. Increasingly, those who rose to power in the countryside did so more on the basis of their ties to London than because of the religiously legitimated moral economy of rural life itself. These arrangements were not always effective, but the Tudors were aided in their cause both by the relative independence of their own finances and by the devastation to which many of the leading families had been subjected as a result of the long civil wars of the previous century.[96]

Henry's desire to divorce Catherine of Aragon was the immediate stimulus to the Reformation without which, as Elton suggests, "there would have been no Reformation."[97] Catherine's failure to produce male offspring left the Tudor succession in jeopardy, and the main barrier standing in the way of a solution to the problem—divorce and remarriage—was the church, or more specifically the pope. While there were means available in canon law for an annulment to be granted, and such practices were not rare, the pope was at the time constrained by none other than Charles V of Spain, who was Catherine's nephew. Charles stood to gain the English crown for himself or his successors if the Tudor line failed, so he was unwilling to see the pope grant an annulment. In 1529, when Spain defeated France and concluded the Peace of Cambrai, Henry's hopes of gaining his ends through papal concessions died. Thus, the fate of his regime itself was endangered by the imperial strength of the Hapsburgs and more proximately by the influence of the church.

With the customary means of seeking papal support blocked, Henry embarked on a course of legal reforms which, over the next five years, consistently increased his control over the church. In 1533 a secret marriage with Anne Boleyn was concluded, and in the following year the king was proclaimed head of the Church of England. This act placed the entire jurisdiction of ecclesiastical affairs in England under the state's authority. In one of the first acts of the new ecclesiastical hierarchy, Thomas Cranmer, named archbishop of Canterbury, declared the marriage with Catherine void and publicly married Henry and Anne. A year later a general investigation of the monasteries was launched, culminating in a series of dissolutions that by 1539 included virtually all monastic lands. In 1540 all wealth and property of the church was declared vested in the crown. Thus, by the time of Henry's death in 1547 the official character of English religion and its relation to the state were markedly different from what they had been only two decades before.

The receptive soil that England provided for the Reformation under the sponsorship of Henry VIII has most often been attributed to the personal needs and religious leanings of the king himself instead of the larger institutional framework in which royal decisions were made. Had it not been for the divorce issue, Henry would certainly have been less interested in initiating religious reform. That the initiative was furthered more by institutional circumstances than by the king's own religious convictions, however, seems clear. Henry was well schooled in Catholic theology, having been destined for the priesthood before the death of his elder brother. When Luther's *Babylonian Captivity* began to circulate in England, Henry wrote a strong attack on it (published in 1521) that was much admired in Rome and secured for him the coveted title "defender of the faith." Over the next five years the rift between Henry VIII and the Lutheran reformers continued to widen. Luther wrote polemical tracts against the king and Cardinal Wolsey; Henry paid his leading theologians to rebut Luther, brought in Thomas More to defend the orthodox position, and oversaw the proscription and burning of Lutheran books. On the very eve of the first intimation of his desire to divorce Catherine, in fact, Henry was busy negotiating with the merchant council in Antwerp to stem the tide of heretical religious writings being smuggled into England and was commissioning an even more vigorous round of theological treatises against the reformers. Ironically, the later commissioning of tracts and sermons in defense of the divorce and his own ecclesiastical reforms may actually have been modeled on these earlier attempts to shape sentiment through the conscious mobilization of polemical discourse.[98]

The importance of the state to the actual production of Reformation ideology, moreover, went beyond the mere initiation of ecclesiastical reforms. Its support of and control over the book trade was also of considerable consequence. Books that received the royal stamp of approval, such as prayer books, official editions of the Bible, and favored volumes of sermons, were protected by royal monopoly, easing the risk that printers took in devoting resources to projects that otherwise might have been copied by clandestine presses. Officially authorized books were often printed under government orders that permitted labor and equipment to be commandeered. They were assured of circulation by royal decrees requiring them to be read in the churches in conjunction with worship services. And, following laws enacted in 1539, they were further protected by prohibitions against printing books outside London. Approved books often contained royal coats of arms or other insignia that conferred prestige on them.[99]

Prior to the Reformation writers had generally relied on members of the aristocracy for patronage to cover their living expenses and the costs of publishing.[100] With the advent of Thomas Cromwell as chief minister, however, Protestant writers were taken into the court's company and paid to write books. Cromwell specifically saw the need to cultivate support for religious reform through the printed word. Consequently, books that defended the royal supremacy and focused on the church's wealth as a source of its spiritual weakness were especially favored.[101]

Many of the specific religious reforms enacted by the crown had been called for during the previous century by adherents of the Lollard movement. By the beginning of the sixteenth century this movement retained only a modicum of its former strength, but with the birth of Lutheran and Zwinglian teachings it experienced a revival, particularly in the towns of southeastern England, which were most exposed to influences from the Continent. The Lollards' influence was strongest among weavers and other cloth workers in the towns and may have served as a crucible for the anticlericalism that was to erupt periodically in other forms in these areas. But Lollardy's appeal to the upper strata was generally negligible, and there is little evidence of its having been a significant factor in the Henrician reforms.[102]

The strongest assistance given the crown as it initiated religious reform was from Parliament. As the previous discussion has indicated, Parliament had largely ceased to function as a political voice for the landlords, unlike its counterparts elsewhere. Rather, it was for the time being dominated by a coalition of cloth merchants, burgesses, and royal officials who were closely allied with the crown. In 1529 the so-called Reformation Parliament canceled the king's debts, giving him more freedom to maneuver in negotiations with the pope. It was also through acts of Parliament that the main reforms of the church were actually accomplished. In 1531 Parliament imposed an indictment on the clergy and fined them for acting without respect for the king's rights. In 1532 it forced the clergy to surrender ecclesiastical law to the jurisdiction of the crown and forbade the granting of papal annates. In 1533 the Act in Restraint of Appeals to Rome prohibited appeals from domestic courts to courts outside the realm. And in 1534 the Act of Supremacy named the king supreme head of the Church of England.[103]

Merchants and burgesses played a significant role in the Reformation Parliament's religious actions.[104] Since they had benefited greatly from the crown's efforts to promote trade, they may have been inclined to support its religious policies for this reason alone. But there were also religious reasons for their actions. At least several burgesses in Parliament were devout Protestants, and a number were familiar with Protestantism through commercial contacts with the Continent and through Lutheran preachers in the towns. Some of the merchants' economic grievances were also directed against the church. Among these were sentiments that the church inhibited commerce through its own economic establishments, its foreign policy, and its attitudes toward usury; that church courts charged excessive fees; that the church failed to provide adequately for the public welfare in London and other towns; and that the church's monastic houses engaged in unfair economic practices which took business away from the merchants.[105]

More generally, it was in the towns that the reforms had their greatest appeal. Provincial towns that were relatively isolated from the expanding Continental trade, such as Worcester, tended to deviate from this pattern, but London and other towns in the southeast were notable centers of reforming activity.[106] Anticlericalism was particularly strong in London, but the same spirit was evident in other towns as well. Sandwich, closely linked with London and the Low Countries by trade, was involved in violence against the papal vicar in 1535. In Canterbury the town council was strongly in favor of religious reform and in its parliamentary election of 1536 voted in a slate of candidates who firmly reflected this position.[107] Coventry, which had been influenced by Lollardy in the previous century, became a center of Protestant teaching from the Continent early in the sixteenth century.[108] Sussex showed much the same pattern, with Protestantism making its greatest inroads in towns such as Brighton, Hastings, and Lewes.[109] Thus, it was not surprising, as one scholar has observed, that the "two interest groups who were most influential and inveterately opposed to clerical privilege [were] the common lawyers and the city lobby in the House of Commons."[110]

The influence of the towns in Parliament, then, was one source of support that the crown could count on in its policy of religious reform. But the stronger partner in this alliance was always the crown.

The towns' representatives were personally beholden to the crown for trading privileges and for the crown's promotion of favorable foreign relations. In addition, the crown had cultivated loyalty among its ecclesiastical appointees, royal officials, and the temporal lords. These, together with the crown's strong financial condition during this period, gave it a high degree of maneuverability in dealing with the church and its supporters among the nobility.[111]

Resistance to the reforms came, predictably, from the landed elite, whose wealth and power remained most firmly embedded in the religiously sanctioned status relations of rural life. Increasingly the old forms of worship became, as one writer remarks, "the property of an embattled gentry minority, sheltering as best they could a few humbler folk."[112] The English Reformation was clearly a triumph for the central regime over the decentralized, provincial power of the landowners and was recognized as such by the latter, as the uprisings in Lincolnshire and York in 1536 and the Cornish rebellion in 1549 revealed.[113] These developed at least partly in response to the crown's religious policies. Although other grievances were involved as well, nothing symbolized the crown's growing influence in the countryside more than the sight of local religious treasures being loaded onto royal carts for shipment to London.[114] Indeed, such transfers were so inflammatory in some instances that precious relics and images were shipped away secretly and under cover of darkness. Using the organizational resources of the church, the landowners were sometimes able to muster and provision local armies of peasants against these incursions. What they accomplished through these uprisings and the threat of others was to diminish the impact of the reforms at the local level. For fear of provoking further resistance the crown practiced a calculated policy of gradualism and restraint in implementing its reforms. Studies of Lincolnshire, Kent, Shropshire, and Essex all indicate that the Henrician reforms had little impact on popular religious practices in rural areas.[115] Not until the reign of Elizabeth I did the reforms begin to have general acceptance. In the interim ecclesiastical authority remained largely unaffected except at the highest levels of church government. As for the rebellions themselves, the crown was able to draw on a wide variety of resources to crush them before they could pose any serious threat to royal authority: "Enough of the regionally powerful families had been made loyal to the crown through offices and intermarriage that the rebels were unable to call on them for support. The king's troops were strong enough that the rebels seem to have never seriously considered accomplishing more than simply a minor reform of royal policy."[116]

Thus, the crown remained clearly in control of the religious reforms. Although the church was deeply integrated into English rural life, as it was on the Continent, the state's virtual independence from the rural sector in the realm of finances, its alliance with the expanding commercial sector in the towns, and its control over local jurisdiction and the military gave it a strong hand in institutionalizing the Reformation.

Common Patterns: The Contexts of Reform

Overall, each of the three major regions in which the Reformation proved successful—central Europe, northern Europe, and England—demonstrate the crucial importance of the state in initiating and defending the reforms. Town councils, territorial princes, and centralized monarchies were as yet far from being able to exercise the full range of functions that were to be arrogated by the state over the next century and a half. Personal rule, small representative bodies, privy councils, chambers of account, titled retainers, and a few professional advisers characterized agencies of government, rather than extensive functionally differentiated bureaus. These agencies nevertheless held control of many of the resources on which the fate of religious reforms depended: influence over the selection and payment of clergy, power to mandate certain styles of public worship, military force or financial leverage capable of intimidating interested parties from the outside and quashing popular upheaval from below, legal authority to convene religious councils and disputations, oversight of publishing and book distribution, and responsibility for doling out public assistance. Where social conditions made it possible for ruling bodies to exercise these functions at their own discretion, their role cast a decisive imprint on the Reformation. An expanding economy and population provided the broad environmental conditions from which resources necessary for the successful execution of the Reformation could be extracted. These resources, however, had to be channeled before they could influence the course of the Reformation. This channeling took place within the institutional contexts provided by the various municipal and territorial regimes. Popular acceptance of evangelical teachings, particularly in the towns, became transmuted into official doctrine in these areas largely under the sponsorship of regimes that could risk initiating such actions because they were relatively independent of control from the landowners. In central Europe this freedom was enjoyed by the imperial cities with a tradition of self-government and revenues from trade which made it possible to exercise these prerogatives, and by several of the more powerful territorial princes who had close relations to the cities. In northern Europe the monarchs of Denmark and Sweden had extricated themselves to a significant, if temporary, degree from the nobility's control by promoting trade and mining, drawing revenues from tolls, and cultivating alliances with the cities. England's crown derived autonomy from the nobility in much the same manner. In all three areas the local landowners remained steadfastly opposed to the Reformation. Their very livelihoods were indebted to the established church, both as a vehicle for stabilizing their relations with the peasantry and as a source of power and prestige. But their resistance was ineffective against the policies of the territorial sovereigns. In other sections of Europe, where the balance of power was less conducive to autonomous state action, the Reformation took a decidedly different turn.

3

The Failure of Reformation

THE SIGNIFICANCE of the institutional contexts in which
Reformation ideology was nurtured, particularly the state's
autonomy relative to the landed nobility, is equally apparent from
the ways in which the absence of this context militated against the
Reformation in other parts of Europe. Eastern Europe, France, and
to a lesser extent Spain all experienced some of the reforming fervor
that fundamentally altered the church in other sections of Europe
and furthered the production of a new mode of religious discourse.
As in those sections, the grassroots appeal of reformed teachings in
these areas was also most prominent in the cities. Neither the cities
nor the state, however, was capable of instituting policies of religious
reform without paying close attention to the landowners' interests.
Economic expansion was by no means absent in the larger social
environment in the sections of Europe where the Reformation failed.
But this expansion did more to strengthen the landed elites than it
did to extricate the municipal or territorial regimes from their control. Consequently, the landed interests were able to play a critical
role in determining the fate of the Reformation. Other factors were
involved as well. But it was not simply the church in isolation that
thwarted the reformers; it was also the broader institutional web in
which policies were made and enforced.

Parliamentary Sovereignty and the Reformation in Eastern Europe

Eastern Europe did not escape the influx of reformed teachings from the west. Lutheran ideas spread from Germany to Gdansk, Elblag, and Toruń, all with sizable German-speaking minorities who were linked to the west by trade. By 1526 popular uprisings had occurred in twenty-seven Polish and east Prussian towns, all with visible Protestant activity.[1] As in central Europe those who were attracted to Lutheranism at this stage were mostly merchants, artisans, and the urban poor. Neither the gentry nor the peasantry showed much interest in the new doctrines.[2] Nevertheless, the number of immigrants carrying Protestant ideas grew. Some patronage for the new form of worship was obtained (the most notable example being that of Duke Albert in East Prussia). And after 1547 Calvinism began to make some headway among politically alienated segments of the population in southwestern Poland and Lithuania.[3] At its peak, Protestantism numbered approximately five hundred congregations, including about one-sixth of the landed gentry, although in Great Poland the figure was no more than a tenth.[4]

Several factors encouraged the growth of Protestantism in eastern Europe. One was the presence of a German-speaking minority with strong ties to the west. From the twelfth century there had been eastward movement among people from the west, such that by the sixteenth century, sections of northern and western Poland were predominantly German in origin.[5] Among those who populated the larger towns, such as Gdansk, Elblag, and Königsberg, many were connected by trade with Protestant areas in Germany, Denmark, and the Netherlands. Moreover, these areas remained only partially and uneasily assimilated into any centralized political structure. Royal Prussia had been officially incorporated into Poland only in 1466, for example, and ducal Prussia did not submit to Polish suzerainty until 1525.[6] A second factor was a general scarcity of labor in Poland which motivated landlords to encourage immigration especially during the early and middle parts of the century when the demand for agricultural exports was growing more rapidly than the indigenous population.[7] Protestants fleeing persecution in southern Germany and Bohemia were a ready answer to these needs. Third, Catholicism was not yet deeply integrated into the pattern of rural life in the more recently settled regions of eastern Europe, giving landlords who wished to Christianize their lands but were fearful of interference from as centrally organized a religion as Catholicism an incentive to adopt Protestantism.[8] Finally, anti-Hapsburg sentiment appears to have been a factor promoting dissatisfaction with Catholicism, and therefore attraction to Protestantism, in southwestern Poland and other areas where the advances of the Hapsburgs in nearby Bohemia and Hungary were particularly evident.[9]

The dominant response to the Reformation in eastern Europe, however, ranged from indifference to repression. The uprisings in Gdansk and other northern cities in the first decade of the Reformation were forcibly repressed by armies under the nobility. Royal edicts forbade the sale and distribution of Lutheran books. Not until the 1540s did any appreciable numbers of the gentry appear interested in Protestant doctrines; even then only a small minority actually converted; and those who did appear not to have significantly altered their life styles or adopted new attitudes toward the peasantry.[10] Among the peasantry itself, one authority writes, "only a minute proportion . . . adhered to the Reformation."[11]

In order to understand why the Reformation was relatively unsuccessful in eastern Europe, the particular character of this region's economic and political structure must be considered. Here climate and geography largely favored the raising of grain and cattle.[12] As the population of western Europe grew, increasing the demand for food, terms of trade for grain and cattle became increasingly favorable, and producers in eastern Europe were finding it ever more attractive to enter the export market. Although much of the grain and cattle raised east of the Elbe continued to be consumed domestically, the remainder was exported at a high profit margin, and efforts were made to expand the volume of these exports. Accordingly, exports to the west multiplied three- to fourfold between 1460 and 1500, and doubled or perhaps tripled again by 1565.[13] Imports, particularly of English and Dutch textiles and various luxury items, also rose dramatically. But the rise in exports was sufficiently greater, exceeding imports by 30 to 40 percent, to require net cash payments from the west.[14] Approximately 70 percent of eastern Europe's exports flowed through Gdansk, Poland's largest port, much of it headed for reexport from Amsterdam.[15] Shipments of Polish grain and Hungarian cattle also passed overland directly to Germany and Switzerland. The political unification of the territories of Poland and eastern Pomerania during the fifteenth century played an important role in opening these areas as export producers.

Domestic demand also increased rapidly in eastern Europe as a result of population growth. This growth appears to have been as great as in many parts of western Europe. Poland's population grew by approximately 40 percent during the sixteenth century, compared with rates of 20 to 25 percent in some of the neighboring areas west of the Elbe.[16] Both in domestic consumption and in trade, therefore, eastern Europe experienced an expanding economy. But neither the towns nor the central regimes gained political autonomy from this expansion as they did in central and northern Europe.

It was the landed nobility whose economic and political position was enhanced.[17] Since at least the twelfth century the nobles in Poland and Hungary had ruled as virtually unrivaled overlords in their own territories. Not until the sixteenth century were some of these territories brought under the jurisdiction of the state. And even then the nobility maintained its monopoly over economic power. In Poland virtually all of the export trade was concentrated in the hands of the wealthiest landowners.[18] In Hungary an elite of sixty families owned over half the land and dominated the trade in grain and cattle.[19] As the price of grain and cattle mushroomed, landlords' profits rose dramatically, encouraging them to expand their demesnes and giving them the economic clout to impose strict controls over peasant labor.[20] Thus, the position of supremacy they had long enjoyed was simply magnified by the growth of commerce.

By midcentury the "second serfdom" was well under way. Peasants were reduced to the status of serfs. Legally tied to the landlord's estate, they were unable even to leave the estate without the landlord's permission. Whole villages belonged to a single landlord, who held a monopoly over mills, fisheries, bakeries, distilleries, and grazing lands. Landlords alone were responsible for the administration of local justice, tax collection, and the drafting of soldiers.[21] Moreover, peasants were required to spend an increasing share of their time cultivating the landlord's demesne in addition to their own parcels, which they rented from the landlord. As many as three to five days a week were typically required. Thus, by the second half of the century over half the landlords' income was from direct production of the demesne rather than from rents.[22] With each prolonged rise in the price of grain, the amount of land placed in the demesne tended to increase. Since the peasants' own plots were gradually reduced in size, their capacity to save in good years or to develop their own supplies for collective distribution during times of emergency was greatly diminished. Even though the local village structure of the peasantry remained largely intact, they thus came increasingly to depend solely on the landlord's provisions for subsistence during poor harvests, times of plague, or other emergencies. Out of necessity the moral economy between peasants and landlords was retained and strengthened. As Witold Kula concludes: "The peasant assumed more often than one might believe the attitude expressed in the formula: 'I belong to Your Lordship, let Your Lordship feed me.' "[23]

The state in eastern Europe developed along lines reflecting the growing influence of the landed elite. The Polish dynasty prior to the sixteenth century was in one writer's words "one of the most powerful in Europe, competing with the Hapsburgs for primacy in the eastern half of the continent."[24] But during the sixteenth century the landlords subjected it almost totally to their interests. Parliament was the key to landed influence over the state. Its prerogatives in comparison with those of the crown were exceptionally broad. Under its jurisdiction fell complete control over taxation, the right to elect the monarch, and the power to convene itself without royal summons.[25] Parliament was dominated by the nobility, who used its offices at every turn to their own advantage. They exempted themselves from taxes on production and, unlike in other areas of Europe, on consumption as well. They kept river transportation free of tariffs for the goods they exported, arranged favorable terms for themselves as lessees of crown lands, influenced foreign policy, and restricted the activities of merchants.[26] Not surprisingly, Poland came to be regarded by contemporaries as the "republic of nobles."

The state's central bureaucracy fell captive to noble influence both financially and administratively. Rather than attempting to tax the nobility, the crown sought to exist from the revenues from its own lands; but these were poorly managed and left the crown with constant financial shortages. The crown did maintain its own bureaucratic staff, a fact that has led some observers to suggest that the state did not decline relative to the nobility.[27] This was a "power elite" of officials and magnates whose power depended on favors from the crown. The composition of this group, however, was highly unstable and subject to familial and territorial cross-loyalties, and therefore failed to be effective in exercising power.[28]

Nor was the nobles' influence over the state the kind that required them to assimilate into the central bureaucracy. Nobles retained their local and provincial ties and continued to exercise authority at these levels: "The most peculiar characteristic of the Polish and Lithuanian senatorial magnates was their provincialism which contrasted strongly with the aspirations of the great nobles in more centralized monarchies. Unlike the latter, a Polish magnate's power did not depend on residence in the capital or with the king."[29] Indeed the nobility arrogated to itself most of the state's administrative and juridical functions at the local level. Matters concerning peasants were gradually shifted to village courts, giving the landlords virtual sovereignty in the jurisdiction of manorial affairs.[30]

In contrast with the situation in central and northern Europe the state was also denied an ally among the bourgeoisie because of the nobility's systematic efforts to thwart the bourgeoisie's development. During the fourteenth and fifteenth centuries the towns in eastern Europe had developed in much the same manner as those to the west. Cities such as Krakow, Poznan, Warsaw, and Lvov were similar to, and in certain respects consciously patterned after, cities such as Nuremberg, Strasbourg, and Antwerp, particularly as far as fortifications, religious practices, town government, and civic organization were concerned.[31] But by the beginning of the sixteenth century these similarities had begun to disappear. Unlike in the Rhineland, where members of the bourgeoisie enjoyed distinct political and legal privileges, in eastern Europe they were subjected to severe legal restrictions and systematically excluded from positions of power. They were denied the right to hold office in parliamentary councils, forbidden to purchase land, and restricted from lending money to the crown.[32] The nobility increasingly sought to undercut their economic position as well. Preference in trade and industry was given to foreign merchants, and nobles who were engaged in grain exporting dealt directly with foreign brokers.[33] They also sought to monopolize local markets, requiring purchases of vital commodities to be made on the manor itself. In addition, the concentration of profits in the nobility's hands gradually eroded the competitive position of the Polish merchants. Costs were high, raw materials were in short supply, and foreign competition was severe. As a result, merchant capital gradually became divested from productive activities.[34] One historian summarizes: "The burghers were pushed aside and condemned to the fringes of political life by a dominant nobility, which emerged as the most active, aware and internally cohesive social group within the country. Bourgeois losses were more than just political—they were also economic and social."[35]

The overall effect of commercial expansion on eastern Europe, therefore, was nearly the opposite of that in central and northern Europe. Eastern Europe's participation in the expanding economic activity of the period consisted primarily of direct agricultural production rather than transport brokerage, finance, artisan manufacture, or mining. In consequence, the nobility's position was strengthened while that of the cities and merchants diminished. Far from gaining fiscal or administrative autonomy, the state became increasingly subject to the economic and political interests of the nobility.

With the exception of towns such as Gdansk, where rivalries between the merchants and surrounding landlords ran deep and privileges of religious freedom were eventually acquired by outright purchase, or Königsberg, which received protection from Duke Albert of Prussia, little support for the Reformation developed among the bourgeoisie, unlike in central Europe.[36] Most of the towns had only a weak indigenous merchant class, owning to the economic power of the landlords; the larger cities were almost entirely dependent on trade initiated by the landlords; and the majority of smaller towns were under the private jurisdiction of local landlords. Nor did the urban patriciate have a strong incentive to support Reformation ideas when these happened to be favored by a member of the neighboring gentry, since these reforms promised mainly to invite further intervention in urban affairs by the landlords.[37]

With the growth of refeudalization, the little support that the Reformation had achieved gradually eroded. By 1600 the number of Protestant congregations had declined by 30 to 40 percent, and by 1650 less than 20 percent of the original number remained. In Lithuania the decline was less severe, but there was a steady downward trend which accelerated in the first half of the seventeenth century.[38]

As elsewhere, the church was an attractive prize for any regime that might be able to seize control of it. Church lands accounted for a smaller share of the countryside than in England, Denmark, Spain, or France, but these estates occupied the most desirable land and were concentrated in attractively large units. Had the state been in a position to seize these lands, as in England or Denmark, it could either have become the most prosperous landholder in eastern Europe or granted them to royal favorites as a counterpoise to the nobility. The crown did in fact cultivate patronage among the clergy in hopes of controlling the nobility but did not have the power to risk outright subjection of the clergy as in England. The state was simply unable to exploit these opportunities because it was dominated by the nobility.

Indeed the nobility gradually increased its control over the church as well. Just as it acquired a strong position in relation to the towns and the state, so it acquired growing privileges in the realm of religion. By virtue of its unchallenged influence over the state, it was able to legislate a number of acts which subjected the church increasingly to its control. Offices in the church came to be limited to members of noble families. Parish clergy had to be nominated by the local landlords. After midcentury the church's power to bring suit against landlords for nonpayment of the tithe was severely restricted. Clergy were required to pay taxes and the church became subject to levies required for the country's defense. Later, the Conference of Warsaw granted gentry freedom to practice religion as they chose and forbade the crown from persecuting anyone for religious convictions. The landlords also succeeded in preventing the Hapsburg candidate from acquiring the crown and restrained the clergy from expanding military offensives against the Turks. As the century progressed, the landlords enjoyed sufficient control over the church that they had little incentive to turn toward Protestantism. In short, eastern Europe dramatized the difficulties the Reformation was to experience when the state's autonomy relative to the landed elite was weak.

France: The Effects of Seigneurial Preeminence

These difficulties were also evident in France. The Reformation gained enough support in France that the second half of the sixteenth century was characterized by religious wars between Protestants and Catholics. But in the end France remained firmly within the Catholic tradition. Protestant inroads were relatively late in developing, and as one historian notes, even "in its hour of greatest success and stoutest resistance, French Protestantism was unable to escape from being the creed of a minority."[39]

The church was an integral feature of peasant-landlord relations and its institutional manifestations were evident at every level of French society. Reformers' attempts to introduce new ideas and practices into the church held their usual appeal for artisans and merchants in the cities. But the reformers were unable to evoke either the uniform support from municipal councils that they enjoyed in many of the towns in central Europe or gain official sponsorship from the state as in England and Scandinavia. Catholicism was too much a part of agrarian class relations, and the nobility were too much in control of the state, for the Reformation to succeed.[40]

Like the rest of the Continent, France participated in the general economic expansion of the period. After more than a century of war, which had badly depopulated the country, ample signs of demographic recovery developed during the last two decades of the fifteenth century and first half of the sixteenth century. Demand for food and other necessities rose, stimulating more vigorous trade in local markets and providing incentives for an expansion of agricultural production. Coastal trading cities such as Bordeaux, Nantes, and Rouen as well as regional trading centers such as Lyons grew at a rapid pace. By 1550 Bordeaux had grown to 20,000; Nantes to 25,000, Rouen to 71,000, and Lyons to 58,000.[41] Generally, however, the topography of France did not lend itself to as widespread or as intensive an involvement in commerce as did that of areas such as the Rhine valley or the Low Countries. Approximately nine of every ten persons remained closely tied to the land. The majority of France's landed elite had few opportunities for a more prosperous livelihood in the cities.[42] For the most part they remained in the countryside, strengthened the traditional seigneurial system, and succeeded in limiting the power of the bourgeoisie.[43] This retrenchment was to have profound political and religious implications. Indeed, Marc Bloch has described it as "the most decisive event in French social history."[44]

Serfdom had been practiced in France since at least the tenth century, but by the end of the fifteenth century it had declined substantially. Expansion of local markets generated outlets for cash crops and home-crafted goods, yielding revenue with which serfs could purchase their freedom. Landlords were often eager to promote these transactions, since they provided lump sums for paying taxes or legal fees in arrears. But the displacement of serfdom with heritable tenancy did not loosen the bonds between landlords and peasants in a way that might, by itself, have been conducive to radical religious change within the rural population. Instead the relations between the two appear to have remained strong, wedded in mutual economic and cultural dependence.[45] Gradually the landlords acquired a stronger claim over the proprietorship of common lands, often by promising to forgive peasants' debts in return for these concessions. Peasants who might otherwise have been free to cultivate their own parcels thus found themselves at the landlords' mercy for grazing privileges and access to timber. These practices were sometimes opposed by royal officials whose job it was to protect the king's basis of taxation within the peasantry. But in most cases the officials appear to have been swayed more by the landlords' influence than by the desires of the king.

As for the French state, it was clearly not, contrary to some characterizations, the epitome of centralized absolutism.[46] This may be an apt characterization of Louis XIV's rule in the seventeenth century. But it does not apply to the regime of Francis I. Although the royal administration had arrogated certain powers to itself such as extending the taxatory powers of the crown and expanding venality of offices, the French state bore a resemblance to that of Poland in its relations with the landed elite.[47] Rather than being particularly strong, centralized, or capable of taking autonomous action, the French state appears to have been, in one prominent historian's words, "inherently weak, not strong." Its monarchs, to quote the same source, "accepted the decentralization of the state and made little effort to centralize it."[48] Some professional "technicians of power" were employed in the royal councils, but the wealthy titled nobility still predominated. And during the first half of the sixteenth century the ability of persons from aristocratic backgrounds to rise in the royal hierarchy appears to have increased. In addition, the number of councilors in the Parlement of Paris, also selected overwhelmingly from the nobility, grew rapidly at the start of the century. And at the local level the administration of justice remained largely in the hands of the seigneurs. As in Poland, separate provinces retained their distinctive prerogatives in administering local justice. The landed elites in the provinces cultivated their own patronage networks, opposed centralization of tax administration, kept a rein on venality of office, objected to the garrisoning of troops, and retained regulatory control over the grain trade.[49] The central bureaucracy was understaffed and ineffective in implementing royal policy. Military strength remained almost exclusively in the hands of wealthier nobles, as their private armies were to demonstrate during the period of religious wars.[50] The Treasury, created in 1523, remained little more than an agglomeration of private funds. And the financial condition of the crown steadily deteriorated, from the fiscal crisis of 1522 to its eventual bankruptcy in 1559.[51]

It was the landed nobility who retained a high degree of control over the state. This control had grown to the point "where the crown had become the archpatron and a number of powerful noble factions had created networks of their own influence."[52] They continued to dominate the parlements and provincial governorships. Reforms had been made in these institutions, to be sure, but these reforms were "satisfactory to the nobility. The great still participated, the middle nobility were happy to escape the trouble and expense of personal attendance, and the seigneurs who had previously been largely ignored now received a voice through their deputies. Indeed, the new mode of holding the Estates General provided further indication of the rising importance of this class."[53] At the local level village autonomy declined despite royal efforts to preserve it and jurisdiction continued to be indirectly in the hands of the landowners, who appointed professional jurists.[54] Financially, the landowners also held close rein over the royal budget. Already at the start of the sixteenth century only one-fifth of the king's revenue was supplied by crown lands, the remaining four-fifths having to be raised from taxation and borrowing.[55] As far as taxation was concerned, the nobility claimed broad prerogatives for itself, including exemption from major taxes and control over the officials who supervised the administration of local taxes.[56] And taxes alone failed to be adequate for the king's needs. Intermittent wars with the Hapsburgs, including Francis I's defeat, capture, and ransom in 1525, required extensive borrowing. Between 1522 and 1547 this borrowing tripled. And most of it came from the larger landowners who held provincial offices, either in the form of payments for office or direct loans.[57]

In the end, therefore, the landed elite in France was able to exercise strong control over local, regional, and national affairs. "The most powerful class was the nobles, seigneurs, and gentlemen who possessed a great portion of the rural properties, and still had fortified castles. They were wholly employed either at court or in war, or held appointments as governors of provinces and captains of strongholds. The nobles alone constituted the regular companies of cavalry, that is to say, the dominant element of the army. This class was therefore of influence in the state and the most material force in society."[58] Or as a more recent study of French class structure concludes: "Aristocratic control of such key institutions as the church, provincial estates, Parlement, and royal council were never challenged, nor was the social and seigneurial regime on which noble preeminence rested significantly modified."[59]

From its inception in France (which occurred within a year or two of Luther's break with Rome), the Reformation was greeted with official repression and unofficial hostility.[60] In 1521 an official condemnation of Luther was issued, and Lutheran writings were banned by ordinance of the Parlement of Paris. Soon after, heresy trials were initiated and the first executions were carried out. At first these occurred independently of royal involvement. But by the 1530s they were being initiated by the king himself. The next two decades, particularly with the advent of Calvinism in the 1540s, witnessed an intensification of anti-Protestant activities, including book burnings, executions, and forced oaths of allegiance.

Much of the active resistance to reform teachings came from the Faculty of Theology at the University of Paris, the so-called Sorbonne. Its members spoke with divine authority against the heretical doctrines that were endangering the church. By unanimous vote in 1521 it condemned Luther's writings and on five more occasions between 1523 and 1536 issued rulings against the reformers. These rulings included a ban on all books favorable to Luther and a plan to send out preachers to speak against the reformers. The Sorbonne was not, however, simply the mouthpiece of the pope nor a voice uttered from the throat of the church alone. Twice in fact, once in 1502 and again in 1505, it had issued statements that challenged the pope's authority, and in general it upheld the principles of conciliarism against those of papal supremacy. Like the church itself, it was closely tied to other segments of the ruling French elite. Following a period of faculty and student unrest in the middle of the fifteenth century, the university had been placed under the jurisdiction of the Parlement of Paris. Graduates of the university, as might be expected, given the high costs of attending, also tended to reflect close ties with this body and with the aristocracy more generally. Data on seventy-two graduates of the Faculty of Theology between 1500 and 1536, for example, reveal that 80 percent either were of noble origin or had family connections with the Parlement of Paris. For more than a century the university had also been in direct conflict with the crown. Thus it was not surprising that the Faculty of Theology pitted itself against the crown's efforts to promote political centralization. The Sorbonne became a voice for stability and traditionalism in general, including the religious customs on which traditionalism rested.[61]

The minority who became identified with Lutheranism or Calvinism in France during the first three decades of the Reformation was concentrated, as it was elsewhere on the Continent, almost entirely in the cities. In the north Protestant adherents were mostly concentrated in the Seine valley, especially in the city of Rouen, a center of textile production and a way station for imports and exports passing along the Seine to and from Paris. Rouen's industries were based primarily on imported materials, and the city had close commercial ties with England and the Low Countries and indirect ties with Lyons and Geneva. As with many other cities, this involvement in international trade exposed Rouen to Protestant influences from central Europe and gave its merchants an incentive to experiment with the new doctrines. By 1560 perhaps as much as one-third of its population was Protestant.[62] To the east in Ile-de-France Protestants were most likely to be found in Paris, Meaux, Beauvais, Senlis, Soissons, and other towns, while the rural areas remained solidly Catholic. In Meaux, for example, reforming activities were evident as early as 1516, including preaching in the vernacular, lay emphasis on the study of Scripture, and removal of images from the churches; and by 1523 close ties had been established between the town and the leading German and Swiss reformers.[63] In none of these towns did the population turn overwhelmingly toward reform teachings, but in Paris perhaps as many as one-fourth converted.[64] In Champagne the Reformation was centered at Troyes, a regional crossroads in both trade and ideas.[65] In Brittany it was the port of Nantes that generated assemblies of Protestants. To the south Lyons, with commercial ties to Switzerland and a booming trade in textiles, printing, and banking, was by far the most important center of Protestantism—perhaps the most important center in all of France. By midcentury about one-third of its sixty thousand residents had turned to Protestantism.[66] Montpellier and Nîmes were also focal points of the Calvinist movement in southern France.[67] In central France as a whole Protestant activity was less common than in the outlying districts to the north and south, but there was some reformed teaching in towns such as Issoire, Saint-Etienne, and Clermont-Ferrand. Thus, the popular appeal of the Reformation in France was largely an urban phenomenon, just as it was in Germany, the Low Countries, England, Denmark, and Sweden.

Within the towns the largest number of Protestant converts appear to have been artisans—partly because artisans made up a large segment of the towns' total population. Nevertheless, some trades were more attracted to Protestantism than others. In Lyons the artisans employed in publishing and printing were particularly likely to become Protestants, while butchers, bakers, and vintners were less likely to adopt the new faith. Textile workers were also among the most involved in Amiens.[68] Carders and weavers in the woolens industry were the most frequent converts in Montpellier.[69] Merchants made up a numerically smaller segment of the Protestant bodies because there were fewer of them in total. But generally merchants were disproportionately involved in the new Protestant churches. This was as true in Paris and Rouen as in Lyons and Montpellier or in Troyes and Reims. In contrast, members of local and regional parlements, lawyers, royal officials, and members of noble families living in the towns were generally unrepresented among the Protestants. Nor was there much support for the new teachings among the ranks of unskilled workers, day laborers, independent craftsmen, peasants living temporarily in the cities, or vagrants and beggars.

Several interpretations can be adduced to account for these patterns. One is that literacy was the decisive factor in furthering the Protestant cause: merchants, textile workers, and certainly printers were among the more literate segments of the towns.[70] Another is that religious convictions corresponded closely with occupational interests: printing and Protestantism, fishmongering and Catholicism.[71] A third is that the more skilled trades gave artisans a greater sense of efficacy, motivating them to adopt a more individualistic religion. Perhaps all these factors played a role.

But the expansion of commerce in the cities, integrating merchants and artisans into expanding markets beyond local communities, is also a factor that should not be overlooked. Textile workers, printers, goldsmiths, and merchants were all involved in trades that depended on materials from external sources and on distribution beyond local markets. The majority of artisans and craftsmen in these industries were not themselves independent as far as wages or working conditions were concerned. Indeed, they were probably less free

to organize their own work than were neighboring butchers and
bakers. In other words, the role of expanding commerce was scarcely
to create independent workers who might have been attracted to a
more individualistic religion such as Protestantism. Rather, artisans
and craftsmen shared a common economic fate with their masters or
merchant industrialists, and for the most part their well-being depended directly on their capacity to compete for goods and markets
in the expanding regional and foreign trade of the period. Thus, their
industrial organization, their position in the marketplace, served as
the basis of their relations with one another and with those in authority in the workplace. Local regulations, taxes, customs, traditional
guilds, and devotion to patron saints were, if anything, likely to
restrict their freedom to participate in the larger marketplace. They
had, in effect, an incentive to adopt a religious style that freed them
from these local, traditional restrictions.

Yet the Reformation did not gain as much support in the towns
in France as it did in central Europe. Nowhere did it succeed more
than temporarily in becoming the official creed of entire towns, and
at the popular level large segments of the urban elite remained devoted to Catholicism. Wealthier merchants feared to sympathize with
Protestantism because of royal ordinances against it. Others in the
urban elite had strong ties to the land or family connections with the
nobility, or held offices that depended on the favor of the nobility.

The Reformation failed to gain widespread support in the cities
to a large extent because of the power of the landowning elite over
the cities and the closeness of its relation to the state. What Protestantism depended on in France, as in other areas, was sponsorship
from the state or from municipalities with sufficient autonomy from
the landed elite to risk such actions. But generally such autonomy
was lacking in France. Where it was at least partially present, as in
Lyons, Protestantism experienced a degree of success. Elsewhere the
presence of local and regional governments under the control of the
nobility served as an ominous threat to the growth of Protestantism:
"Most of the greatest Huguenot strongholds—LaRochelle, Montau-
ban, Nîmes—were situated far from the watchful eyes of the local
parlement, while those cities which housed high courts proved almost
uniformly to be less heavily Protestant than other major towns in
their *ressort*."[72] Bordeaux was perhaps the chief example of the dampening effect of provincial government under the tutelage of the nobility. Despite its importance as a commercial center, Protestantism

was virtually absent. Toulouse and Paris also appear to have witnessed less reforming activity than other towns because of the influence of provincial governing bodies under the nobility's control.

In those cities that did have substantial numbers of Protestants the dampening effects of the nobility through local and regional governments was also in evidence. Protestants were generally not well represented among members of the provincial parlements or among magistrates and lawyers or other high officials, all of whom wielded a strong influence over municipal affairs. The religious allegiances of these elites appear to have been influenced more by ties with the countryside than by association with merchants and artisans.

In Rouen, for example, the parlementaires were largely of rural landowning stock, even though they maintained residences in the city. Most of them had extensive land-holdings, and the largest share of their incomes came from these holdings. Since their estates tended to be scattered and were at some distance from the town itself, most of their time was actually spent away from Rouen. Evidence also suggests that these elites lent money to, and on occasion borrowed from, the crown, thus exercising some degree of financial influence over the state; but their financial ties with the local bourgeoisie were relatively weak.[73] In other words, it was primarily the land that determined the economic well-being of the parlementaires. Their interest was more likely to be served by maintaining stability in the countryside rather than by siding with religious dissidents in the city. Thus, when religious violence broke out in Rouen, they immediately expressed their hostility toward it and with the assistance of neighboring landlords soon suppressed it.

A similar uprising at about the same time in Lyons was also forcibly suppressed and soon after Protestantism became virtually extinct. In Reims and Troyes the town councils were similarly influenced by neighboring landowners, and only a few of these "notables" were converted.[74] The same was true in Aix, where the municipal council was dominated by enfiefed nobles and gentlemen and only weakly representative of the bourgeoisie.[75]

In Toulouse the influence of Protestantism, which had been increasing steadily, was effectively eliminated in 1562 after a bloody insurrection in which more than two hundred Protestants were killed and another two hundred were executed. The difficulties that evangelical teachings had faced in gaining an institutional base well before the uprising itself had been aggravated by the fact that authority in the city was divided between two bodies: the municipal council and the royal parlement. The former enjoyed a high degree of autonomy and functioned much in the same manner as the representative magisterial bodies governing imperial cities in central Europe. It included some members of the aristocracy but was dominated by merchants and professionals who tended to express sympathy toward the Protestant cause. The parlement, in contrast, was the exclusive preserve of the aristocracy. It oversaw the king's interest in the region and kept close ties with the ecclesiastical establishment of the city and the province. In the months preceding the insurrection the municipal council moved strongly in the direction of seizing ecclesiastical property, supporting greater religious diversity, and imposing curbs on the power of the clergy. The parlement, however, kept a suspicious eye on these policies and maneuvered to impose stronger restrictions on the Protestants. When conflict finally broke out, the council was too weak to prevent violence against the Protestant minority in the city, and the parlement proved unwilling to take any action against the violence.[76]

These examples point to the continuing importance of the landed elite in municipal and provincial governing bodies as a deterrent to the Reformation. The landed elite also exercised a direct role in many of the urban churches, influencing the clergy to side against the reformers and their dissident followings among the indigenous townspeople. In Lyons, for example, the most influential churches were controlled by the nobility, while the merchant elite dominated only a few of the local parish churches. The clergy associated with the cathedral were required to prove that they were descendants of at least four generations of nobility. They were also expected to make a large contribution to the cathedral's endowment upon assuming their post, thus assuring the likelihood of their being descended from not only titled but also wealthy noble families. Many of the cathedral clergy had extensive land-holdings themselves, and almost all were related to a number of wealthy landowners. The nobility also dominated the three largest and wealthiest collegiate churches in the city.[77]

The Lyons case also illustrates how the churches' ties to the rural economy could pit them against the merchant and artisan classes, thereby encouraging reform sentiments among the latter while reinforcing resistance to these sentiments among the more powerful ecclesiastical officials. For example, one of the hottest disputes in

Lyons emerged over the merchants' attempts to tax wine and grain that passed through the town. Because much of the wine and grain raised in the vicinity came from church lands or from the lands of nobility related to the clergy, the church strongly opposed these attempts.[78]

Another group that secured power primarily from the land and played an important role in containing the spread of Protestantism was the provincial governors. Their position in relation to the crown had oscillated from dominance to subordination during the fourteenth and fifteenth centuries. But during the early part of the sixteenth century their strength appears to have grown decisively, giving them "the opportunity to exploit their enormous influence and authority to the full and act as sovereigns in their own provinces."[79] It was the governors whose influence orchestrated the relations between the landed elite in local areas and the central regime. By virtue of their vast estates, their prominence in military affairs, and their capacity to bestow patronage on allies they were able to build up strong power blocs among the landed elite. Just as the relations between peasants and landlords were governed by principles of clientage, so the relations between landlords and governors involved diffuse expectations based on reciprocal trust and obligation:

> Fidelité was based on the mutual expectations of patrons and clients rather than on one-for-one exchange at the same point in time as in a business transaction. Clients performed services for patrons who were morally bound to reciprocate, but the time and exact nature of the reciprocation were not specified in advance. Obligations were indefinite because the goods and services exchanged were putatively philanthropic. To appearances, the affective dimension of the relationship prevailed over the materialistic side. Years or decades of service, often at the client's great expense, might be necessary before the hoped-for reciprocation was forthcoming, and in the interim there were only effusions of total loyalty and boundless love.[80]

Shared religion provided one of the visible arenas in which these loyalties were enacted. The governors, rather than the crown, were in practice in charge of most high ecclesiastical offices and used them as a means of garnering loyalty among the landowners in their territories. The landowners in return gave deference to the governors in religious ceremonies and generally supported them in their campaigns to rid the country of religious heresy.

Whether Protestantism succeeded in becoming institutionalized even temporarily in the cities depended greatly on the support or opposition it received from the local nobility and the provincial governors. As the cases of Rouen and Lyons suggest, the presence of a predominantly landowning segment among the urban elite kept Protestantism from dominating the local power structure in the cities and made it vulnerable to internal or external repression. Some of the nobility, however, did lend support to the Reformation, particularly during the 1560s. In most of these instances there were unusual combinations of circumstances which gave them sufficient autonomy from established rural class relations to break with religious tradition, and often there were political incentives for supporting Protestantism. In some instances the nobility who supported the Protestant cause were independently wealthy and thereby less dependent on maintaining good relations with tenants than their less prosperous neighbors; in other instances they were residents of forested regions where the seigneurial system was virtually absent; in still other instances political factions within the nobility itself became a factor in deciding religious loyalties.[81] Generally, however, the governors and nobility who supported Protestantism were regionally more isolated and had less solid support from the landowning class within their territories than those who defended Catholicism. In consequence, they were incapable of imposing their religious views on the rest of the country by force.[82] Catholicism was deeply embedded in rural life, and the majority of the landed elite remained loyal to it. Land and wealth, wealth and power, power and social order were linked together as part of a matrix in which the services of the church were an integral feature.

At the national level the church was also closely allied with the state, which derived both political and economic advantages from it. Since France was at the time the most effective check on the expanding temporal power of the Hapsburgs, the papacy supported France at the same time that it sought peaceful relations with Spain. Gallican tradition gave the king considerable control over religious affairs, including the nomination of cardinals.[83] The Concordat of Bologna in 1516 extended these privileges, giving the king the right to nominate candidates for high ecclesiastical office. Materially the king also benefited both from regular receipts from his share of the tithe and from special loans from the church.[84]

But the Reformation's failure in France stemmed less from the interests of the crown itself than from the interests of the landed elite which operated upon the state. It was the landed elite whose economic condition steadily improved during the first half of the sixteenth century and whose influence over both the church and the crown played the most decisive role in maintaining the church and inhibiting Protestantism. They, rather than the king, were the prime beneficiaries of the Concordat of 1516. Of the 129 appointments to ecclesiastical office that were made between 1516 and 1547 as a result of this agreement, for example, 123 were members of the nobility. "The military and political power of these families was still significant. Francis I hoped that by granting their members financial inducements in the form of administrative offices and benefices he could obtain, in return, their loyalty and thus ensure political stability."[85] Instead, the growing strength of the landed elite developed virtually unchecked to the point where the crown was reduced to serving as their patron while they created vast networks of regional influence. By midcentury virtually all appointments to high ecclesiastical office were under the control of the powerful Guise faction. In the local and provincial assemblies the nobles and seigneurs had also managed to bring the clergy more completely under their control by securing appointments to these assemblies for the middle-level clergy while excluding members of the upper clergy.[86]

As the financial resources of the crown deteriorated, the state was left with little opportunity to oppose the landlords' increasing dominance of the church or to defend the Protestants against the church and its allies. Thus, the situation in France was not greatly dissimilar to that in eastern Europe. Protestantism penetrated both regions to some extent, particularly in the cities and among alienated segments of the rural elite. But the landed sector remained sufficiently powerful that neither the cities nor the central regime was able to lend effective support to the reforms.[87]

Imperial Expansion and Aristocratic Power in Spain

Like France, Spain also failed to develop any sustained support for the Reformation. Indeed, Protestantism penetrated the Iberian peninsula to far less of an extent than it did in either France or eastern Europe. The religious climate was not wholly unconducive to reform, and some were in fact made. Nor was the state wholly without incentive for encouraging the Reformation. Yet the political economy of Spain was such that modern observers have difficulty even imag-

ining what might have been necessary for it to have sponsored religious innovation of the type practiced in England or Denmark.

The Reformation came to Spain in 1520 with the arrival of
Lutheran books and missionaries in several of its port cities. Soon
after, Protestant preaching was observed in a number of towns. As
in other parts of Europe, merchants and artisans showed the greatest
attraction to the new ideas. There was also an indigenous movement
toward reform of the church which stemmed from the influence of
humanism in the Spanish universities and, indirectly, from the Spanish Low Countries. This movement exhibited a high degree of interest in the teachings of Erasmus and included devotees among the
royal council.[88] Spain was, in many respects, the cultural as well as
the political center of Europe at the time. Its universities were well
endowed; literacy was relatively high; and its cities were connected
with centers of religious ferment across the Continent. On these
grounds it would not have been unthinkable for reformed ideas to
have gained a popular hearing. Indeed, some inroads were actually
made within the royal family itself; for example, Charles's sister Maria
was widely regarded as a supporter of the new evangelical teachings,
and Luther himself saw her as a sufficiently promising ally that he
dedicated one of his pamphlets to her.

On balance, however, neither Lutheranism nor humanism was
able to penetrate the Spanish church. With the exception of several
small nuclei in Seville and Valladolid, reformed teachings failed to
take root.[89] The Inquisition acted immediately to confiscate all Lutheran books and to suppress missionary activity. After 1530 the
same pressures were applied to the Erasmian movement. As the
century progressed, both the Inquisition and the church became all
the more powerful, and Spain led the movement to reverse the entire
course of the Reformation in Europe.

Some have argued that the Reformation failed in Spain simply
because there was no need for it. One version of this argument holds
that the Spanish church had managed to reform itself: "The fact that
the Spanish church had already undertaken to reform itself, deprived
Protestantism of much of the reforming justification it claimed in
northern and central Europe and helped to make Spain less accessible
than other countries to Protestant propaganda."[90] Another version
is that the state had no incentive to advance reforms. Being such a
powerful political force, it had struck a bargain with the pope that
was much to its advantage.[91] For example, it claimed the right to

nominate bishops and archbishops, to impose fines and admonishments on the clergy, and to take its share of the tithe.[92] Still another variant suggests that the Spanish state was essentially an empire, drawing the bulk of its resources from dynastic possessions in central Europe and the New World.[93] The church legitimated these claims and thus received support from the state.

These arguments contain some truth, but they do not reveal the whole story. Whether the church in Spain was any less in need of reforming than the church in England appears doubtful. The Spanish Inquisition was both disliked and subject to abuse; higher officials in the church held office more from family connections than from exemplary spirituality; lower clergy often existed in near destitute conditions; and popular religion was no less filled with superstition than elsewhere. Nor does the evidence from England or other countries that participated in the Reformation indicate that the motivation for reform was necessarily or even primarily to rid the church of its abuses. The Spanish crown, to be sure, derived important concessions from the church. But these were by no means as sweeping as those imposed by Henry VIII in England or by Gustav Vasa in Sweden. Even the revenues Charles V derived from his share of the tithe amounted to a pittance compared with the vast wealth he might have acquired by seizing church lands—and he was always sorely in need of additional income.

The argument about the church's importance to Spain's imperial policy is perhaps the most compelling of the various ideas, for many of Spain's military ventures were concerned with keeping its possessions—and, apparently, with keeping them free of heresy. Yet those who have emphasized the importance of Spain's larger possessions have tended to neglect the fact that its real base of economic strength was not central Europe or the New World but Castile.[94] And in any case it is difficult, in the face of Spain's costly wars in central Europe and with England and Italy, to maintain that it derived more from these possessions than it cost to protect them. Had Spain been the religious ally of the German princes, the Dutch magnates, and England, it is possible to imagine that its position in Europe over the following century would have remained much stronger than it actually did.[95] Indeed, Charles's own ambassador in Rome advised him that siding with Luther might be the most politically beneficial course.[96] But even to imagine this possibility reveals that the Spanish crown, as powerful as it was, was not in a position simply to choose.

It was constrained on all sides by the institutional structure of which it was a part.

As elsewhere, population growth in Spain stimulated the economy, particularly by increasing demand for food and clothing. According to two censuses of exceptional thoroughness for the period, the population of Castile grew from 4.4 million in 1530 to 6.6 million in 1590, an increase of fifty percent in little more than fifty years.[97] Other sections of Spain grew more slowly, but Castile accounted for three-quarters of the Spanish population and dominated economically and politically. The city of Seville grew from 50,000 to 150,000 over the same period. The growth in population caused land values and rents to increase. As a result, previously unused acreage came increasingly under cultivation. Imports of grain, mainly from the Baltic and Sicily, also increased. In industry, too, there was noticeable expansion. The production of iron, copper, lead, marine salt, forest products, arms, and ships all experienced unprecedented growth. Had it not been for the restrictive policies of the guilds many of these industries would likely have expanded even further.

The most distinctive feature of the Spanish economy was the tremendous expansion it underwent as a result of the discoveries in the New World. Pierre Chaunu in his magisterial treatment of the Atlantic trade estimates that the total tonnage of ships entering or leaving Andalusian ports grew from around 15,000 tons during the first decade of the sixteenth century to more than 100,000 tons by midcentury.[98] Gold from Guinea and silver from Mexico and Peru poured into the ports of Cádiz and Seville. Spices were also imported in increasing quantities first from the Mediterranean and then from the Indies for reexport to northern and central Europe, where there was rising demand for luxury items of all kinds. In addition, Spain produced a number of domestic commodities for export. Raw wool was produced in large volume under royal prerogative by the Mesta and shipped to Italy and Flanders for manufacture. Exports of olive oil, leather goods, and wine also increased steadily during the first half of the century.[99]

Yet, despite its burgeoning commerce, Spain failed to develop a prosperous or powerful indigenous bourgeoisie. Detailed studies of the leading port cities of Cádiz and Seville reveal that trade was concentrated almost exclusively in the hands of foreign merchants, principally the Genoese. Ruth Pike's research on Seville shows that the Genoese merchant community doubled in size during the last half of the fifteenth century and largely dominated the Atlantic trade.[100] These merchants also functioned as creditors to the Spanish crown, a tradition that had been established in the fourteenth century and continued to grow until 1575, when Philip II was forced to declare bankruptcy.[101] Correlatively, indigenous sources of merchant capital and finance remained so weak by the second half of the century that the king found his domestic bankers lacking in funds, without the networks necessary to raise capital, and deficient of sound financial practices. The same situation prevailed in commerce more generally. Although some businessmen made substantial fortunes from the burgeoning Atlantic trade, these ventures were sufficiently risky and so thoroughly dependent on the whims of government policy that Castilian men of wealth left the field largely to foreign entrepreneurs or withdrew to the security of landed rents and government office.

The chief beneficiary of Spain's expanding commerce was the state. As in Denmark and Sweden, the Spanish trade was of the type that could be monopolized by the crown, and the crown was sufficiently powerful to seize the opportunity. The Spanish trade consisted of precious metals that could be directly appropriated by the crown, exports and imports that could easily be controlled for purposes of taxation, and special industries maintained as royal monopolies. The revenues obtained by the crown from these sources were unparalleled and unprecedented by any European state. During the last quarter of the fifteenth century Spain experienced a *thirtyfold* increase in royal income.[102] Much of this income was used for the conquest of Granada and for vigorous overseas exploration, setting the stage for further economic gains during the following century. In the sixteenth century 40 percent of all American bullion flowed into the royal treasury. This revenue grew from less than 400,000 ducats during the first decade of the century to 2.8 million ducats during the middle decades, and then mushroomed to 18 million ducats by the last decade of the century.[103]

By the beginning of the sixteenth century the state's power in relation to other interest groups had also begun to be evident. Aragon and Castile were united, royal patrimony was extended, and an improved tax collection system was put into place. Increasingly the administrative functions of the state were also centralized under the crown. Pierre Vilar writes: "In the political sphere, the Catholic kings had crushed the turbulence of the great nobles and begun to domesticate them, they had started to channel the adventurous spirit of the lesser nobility towards the army, taken over control of the Military Orders, and converted the local forces of order . . . into state police. They had introduced their *corregidores* into the major municipalities, been sparing in the convocation of the Cortes . . . and turned the *procurador* of these assemblies into a type of civil servant."[104] By the reign of Charles V, Spain's vast economic resources had given it the capacity to create a far-flung empire which many contemporaries feared capable of bringing the entire Continent under its jurisdiction.

Yet, for all its commercial revenues and dynastic territory, the Spanish state did not succeed in extricating itself from the grip of the landed elite. The lack of an indigenous bourgeoisie left the state without one of its principal sources of leverage in this process. Rather than serving as a source of autonomy from the landed elite, the commercial sector gradually declined in Spain, just as it did in Poland. A "schema of dependence" developed which prevented Spanish merchants from competing favorably in the international market: "With all the foreign markets, and hence all the bulk overseas trade, in the hands of capital interests based abroad, a Spanish merchant could never hope to compete favorably."[105] Or, as Immanuel Wallerstein concludes, "Charles V, Castile, Antwerp, the Fuggers were all imbricated in a huge creation of credit laid upon credit, cards built upon cards, the lure of profits based on hope and optimism."[106] Instead of the state's being able to build on the strength of a rising bourgeoisie in order to enhance its own autonomy, relations with the bourgeoisie all ran the other way: government finance was so heavily dependent on trade that its needs sapped away the commercial sector's vitality, reducing it to a stunted appendage of the larger economy. As the century progressed, the structural weaknesses of the bourgeoisie left the state increasingly at the mercy of the rural elite.

By the beginning of the sixteenth century the state had, in fact, managed to reduce the political influence of the landed nobility to some extent. Apart from several regional exceptions, feudal power residing in locally independent overlords was generally weaker on the Iberian peninsula than in many other parts of Europe. The privileges of the nobility were to a greater extent, therefore, received as concessions from the crown, rather than being prerogatives imposed on the crown. Among these concessions were freedom in testation, primogeniture, exemption from seizure for debts, grants of office, and above all immunity from taxation.[107]

Nevertheless, the nobility maintained its position as the dominant social and economic force in Spain, controlling approximately half of all the land and dominating the royal household. Jaime Vicens Vives concludes that "behind the facade of monarchic authoritarianism, behind their apparent political submission to the crown, the nobles made themselves the great dominating force in the country."[108] Another study concludes that the reign of Charles V was faced with the strong and continuous influence of the nobility.[109]

Much of the nobility's influence lay in the fact that it held the key to the state's financial condition. Although the state derived large sums from its ventures in the New World, its financial needs were even greater because of the tremendous costs involved in claiming and defending the Hapsburgs' many dynastic territories.[110] Thus, even at the height of Spain's transoceanic trade, the state continued to depend heavily on taxes and loans from the landed sector. The extent of this dependence is clearly revealed by the fact that toward the end of Charles V's reign no more than 10 to 15 percent of the crown's income came from the American connection, whereas by comparison approximately half came from taxes on the landed sector and much of the remainder came from loans from the nobility.[111] Another estimate suggests that the crown received five times as much from Castilian taxes as it did from America.[112] Although members of the nobility were exempted from the *servicio*, this tax accounted for no more than 15 percent of royal income during this period, and its value steadily declined as a result of inflation. More important was the *alcabala*—the sales tax—which accounted for more than half of the crown's receipts and fell on nobility and nonnobility alike.[113] Loans from the landed elite were the most available source of supplemental revenue to pay for Spain's rising military expenditures. Among these were the *juros de resguardo*, which were restricted to Castilian subjects. Altogether about four-fifths of the crown's loans came from the Castilian nobility.[114] Between 1504 and 1550 the value of these loans quadrupled, multiplying again nearly sixfold by century's end.[115] As a result the crown contracted an increasingly heavy load of interest indebtedness to the nobility. At midcentury interest on these debts alone amounted to about half the annual earnings from bullion imports.[116]

The crown's financial dependence also left it administratively dependent on the nobility. High officials of the realm had to be recruited exclusively from the nobility. Taxes and supplemental revenue measures had to be voted on by the nobility-controlled Cortes.

Municipal affairs in all but the largest towns were firmly under the control of the nobility.[117] Legal codes were upheld which permitted the nobility to maintain its property despite the changing economic circumstances. The Mesta's powerful position in the wool trade was firmly defended.[118] And maintenance of domestic order as well as the success of military campaigns depended on armies under the nobility's command. The sovereignty of the Spanish state, in short, while clearly royal, was scarcely absolute. As in France it remained to a very serious degree limited—limited, as J. H. Elliott has observed, by "seigneurial power."[119]

On the eve of the Reformation, then, the Spanish state was deeply in debt to the nobility as a result of its exorbitant military expenditures. It depended on them indirectly to supply a large share of its revenues by enforcing a system of taxation that fell heavily on the peasantry, and it gave them a strong voice in policy matters by granting royal offices exclusively to the nobility and by leaving local and regional jurisdictions largely in their hands.[120] Landowners remained the most powerful political and economic force in Spain, and the state functioned effectively by enlisting their support. Indeed, Braudel goes further, suggesting that it governed only with the consent and cooperation of the nobility: "It relied on the nobles for the maintenance of peace and public order, for the defence of the regions in which they owned estates or castles, for levying and commanding the ban . . . for the siege of Perpignan . . . the war of Granada . . . the invasion of Portugal . . . The king would keep prominent nobles constantly informed of his intentions, orders and important news; he would ask their advice and oblige them to lend him large sums of money . . . The advantages granted in return . . . were by no means negligible."[121] In short, the state's religious policy, like its policy in military affairs and its stance toward the bourgeoisie, was inevitably to be constrained by the interests of the nobility.

The church was, above all, part of the institutional structure on which the landowners relied to maintain their social and economic position. It supplied lucrative posts to members of noble families, channeled relief to the dispossessed, administered the *hermandades* which functioned as a police force and local judiciary, settled legal disputes, and even kept family records or gave testimony that was required in order to claim the title of nobility.[122] Indirectly the church served as a mechanism of regressive taxation, channeling money from peasants to the state through its share of the tithe, which in return allowed the nobility to claim exemption from some forms of taxation.[123] In less tangible ways the church also maintained the social position of the nobility, dramatizing their power in village ceremonies, securing from commoners prayers for their souls, and giving a unified structure of ritual and symbol to the rural community. As Spain's economic position in the broader European market began to decline, especially during the second half of the sixteenth century, the church became increasingly important to the nobility, supplying many of their less fortunate members with stable incomes through ecclesiastical offices.[124]

The nobility, therefore, had ample reason to shield the church from any reforms that might disrupt its power or alter its tradition. In areas of Europe where the state (or municipalities) seized church lands and instituted reforms the consequence of these changes was always to strengthen the state or the cities in relation to the landlords, weakening them economically or else making them more dependent on the state and giving opportunities for "new men" with loyalties to the state to enter and dilute their ranks. In Spain the nobility's economic position and its importance to the state were too significant to allow this to happen. As long as the nobility retained its position, religious reforms of the kind initiated in central and northern Europe or in England were unthinkable. The state's means of governance remained too heavily dependent on them to entertain any notions of religious reform that would undo the relations between the nobility and the church.

To situate Hapsburg religious policy in the context of nobility-state relations is to suggest, of course, that religious affairs were not simply a function of the church alone. In some views neither the nobility nor the state need be given particular attention because the church itself was a sufficiently powerful social institution to guard against any unsettling incursions from the Protestant reformers. The two sources of ecclesiastical power most commonly identified in these views are the pope and the Inquisition. A closer inspection of the facts, however, reveals that neither the pope nor the Inquisition provides an adequate explanation for the fate of the Reformation in Spain.

Noting the crown's symbolic and economic benefits from the title "defender of the faith," some have argued that Spain's lack of support for the Reformation stemmed from the fact that the monarchy remained too heavily dependent on Rome. Yet the fact of the matter was that the king enjoyed a considerable degree of autonomy from the pope. In 1486 Ferdinand and Isabella had obtained rights of patronage to all major ecclesiastical appointments in conquered Granada. They also nominated Spanish bishops. They prevented appeals from Spanish courts to Rome. And they imposed taxes on the clergy. Thus, it cannot be claimed persuasively that the Spanish crown was unable to resist papal influences.

There is, as I have mentioned previously, the opposing argument, which suggests that the Spanish crown actually controlled the pope and therefore had no need to seek reform of the church by other means. The tax revenues and patronage received by the crown from the church, for example, would seem to support this argument. Comparison with other regimes that favored the Reformation, however, casts this argument into doubt. In England the pope's right to provide ecclesiastical benefices was struck down in 1351 and again in 1390. Appeals beyond the king's court to the pope were forbidden by statutes in 1353 and 1393. Rights of sanctuary in religious buildings and clerical immunity were struck down during the reign of Henry VII. In German territories control over ecclesiastical appointments had also been wrested from the pope and placed in secular hands, and many of the imperial cities had begun to exercise control over local religious affairs. Nor was the situation in France marked by significantly greater or lesser degrees of control over the papacy than in the Protestant areas or Spain. By the conciliar reforms known as the Pragmatic Sanction of Bourges (1438) the pope had been deprived of rights of appointment, jurisdiction, and taxation in France. These comparisons, therefore, suggest that an understanding of the various regimes' position toward the reformers cannot be attained simply by focusing on the bilateral relations between rulers and the pope. At times, nearly every ruler ran into conflict with the pope, especially so, it appears, in the late fifteenth century and early sixteenth century, with the expansion of trade and the simultaneous increase in military conflict over contested territory. When policies toward the religious reformers were framed, it was not only the state's relations with the pope that mattered but a considerably more complex set of power relations within the ruling elite itself.

As for the Spanish Inquisition, its role in combating heresy is well documented. Recent studies, however, cast new light on the Inquisition by showing that it, too, was rooted in broader institutional contexts rather than operating strictly as an entity unto itself. Two points in particular stand out from this research. First, the Inquisition was, as one authority has put it, "a bureaucracy not of the Church but of the State."[125] That is, by background, training, and interests the inquisitors were jurists rather than clergy or theologians; they focused on legal more than on theological issues; and the most common line of career advancement ran from inquisitor to office in the high courts of the realm rather than to ecclesiastical office. Were this all that was known about the inquisitors, then, it would be apparent that efforts to understand its religious policies need to be directed at the state rather than toward the church alone. The second feature of the Inquisition that bears on the present discussion, however, is that it functioned in close connection with the nobility. This connection was established only in part through the relatively elite backgrounds from which jurists and inquisitors tended to be recruited. It was effected most directly by the offices of familiars and comisarios. Because of the sparsity of tribunals and the limited number of inquisitors, the Inquisition was forced to rely on members of the public to fill these offices. Essentially, the familiars were lay servants of the Holy Office who performed duties for the tribunal, were allowed to bear arms to protect the inquisitors, and enjoyed many of the material and symbolic privileges of the inquisitors. During the sixteenth century, a high proportion of familiars were nobles and titled persons. Thus the Inquisition was scarcely an isolated organization, set apart from the society and operating strictly from ecclesiastical dictates. Like the church itself, it was integrally related to the broader status relations of Spanish society. Indeed, much of its effectiveness lay in the fact, as Henry Kamen observes, that it "was able to attach to its interests a large and possibly influential section of the local population."[126] Given the close-knit bonds on which most of the rural communities in Spain were established, it would have been exceedingly difficult for inquisitors from the outside to function with any degree of effectiveness. Having the familiars positioned within local communities tended to resolve this problem. Moreover, the landed elite readily offered their services as familiars because, as Kamen notes, this position "protected them from secular jurisdiction and gave them privileges of freedom from some types of taxation."[127]

Also relevant to an understanding of the role of the Inquisition in Spanish society is the fact that it failed to amass a strong economic or political base of its own. Despite its considerable legal powers, especially its ability to confiscate wealth, the Inquisition appears to have served more as a conduit to the landed elites who controlled it than as an organization with control over its own resources. Some of its resources went to the crown. But as early as the 1540s it appears that the crown was in a dependent position relative to the Inquisition, just as both were to the nobility. Especially when the king was absent, the inquisitors and familiars effectively withheld confiscations from the royal treasury and forged religious policies on their own. To this extent the Inquisition was in fact one of the reasons for the Reformation's failure in Spain. But its capacity to play this role must be understood in the context of the crown's continuing dependence on other segments of the ruling elite and in conjunction with its own embeddedness in the status structure of the aristocracy.

Environmental Conditions and Institutional Contexts

In each of these three major areas of Europe in which the Reformation failed, then, we see the obverse of those factors that contributed to its becoming institutionalized in other sections of Europe. It was more the specific institutional contexts in which economic and political resources were shaped than it was the broad environmental conditions that determined these different outcomes. Eastern Europe, France, and Spain all experienced a great deal of economic growth during the period just preceding, as well as during, the Reformation. This growth contributed the resources necessary for some segments of the ruling elite to enhance their social position. But in each case it was not the kind of growth that could easily be used by municipal or territorial regimes to extricate themselves from the financial and administrative dominance of the landed elite. In eastern Europe the economic growth of the period accrued mainly to the aristocracy itself, who in turn solidified their control not only over the peasantry but also over the bourgeoisie and the state. In France the opportunities for all segments of the elite to benefit from economic growth were more restricted. Some centers of commercial and artisanal activity grew in strength, just as they did in the Rhineland and the Low Countries. Nevertheless, the manner in which most towns were governed demonstrates a more integral connection with the rural aristocracy. And the aristocracy, in turn, used its influence at both the local level and in relation to the crown to restrict demands for ideological reform of the kind called for by evangelical and Protestant leaders. Spain was in some ways in the strongest position to turn its revenues from trade, mining, and exploration into a more autonomous, centralized mode of state administration. The Hapsburgs' inexhaustible need for resources to defend their vast dynastic possessions, their military role in combating the advances of the Ottoman empire in the east, and the continuing embeddedness of the courts, the military, and the Inquisition in the aristocracy, however, all contributed to a more constrained religious policy than might otherwise have been the case.

The broad economic expansion that constituted the environment of the Reformation, therefore, became channeled by various institutional frameworks in ways that were to have quite different implications for the success or failure of the Reformation. In nearly every part of Europe some evidence of the reformers' activity was apparent in the cities and towns, among merchants and artisans, and at high levels of the state. Greater ease of communication, augmented by the increased rate of trade and by the broader integration of local and regional markets into a single European economy, ensured that the new humanistic and evangelical ideas were widely diffused. And, apart from the rural communities in which the traditional religious customs remained an integral feature of the local moral economy, incentives of various kinds ensured some degree of attraction to the new ideas. Whether these incentives derived from the more cosmopolitan outlook of merchants and traders, or the higher levels of literacy among some sections of the artisan population, the strains on public relief chests that were felt in many rapidly growing towns, the attraction of hearing sermons preached in the vernacular, or the opportunity to seize church lands and wrest control of both juridical and ecclesiastical decision making from the church, the incentives to initiate religious reforms were abundant. Whether the new ideas were "selected for" or "selected against," however, depended to a considerable extent on the relative balance of power among the various elites that made up the institutional settings in which major policy decisions were made. Except in rare instances, the aristocratic elite that had as its principal power base the agrarian economy defended the traditional religious customs that were deeply ingrained in the social structure of rural villages and manors. Representatives of the towns often had greater interest in supporting religious reform. But the capacity of these representatives to initiate reforms varied greatly, depending on how closely connected the towns were with members of the surrounding rural elite. Central and territorial regimes were potentially in the most opportune position to make decisions affecting the fate of religious reforms in their jurisdictions. And yet, the heads of these regimes were by no means free simply to follow their conscience in matters of religious ideology. Only in those settings in which the central regimes obtained a substantial degree of financial and administrative autonomy from the landed elite was it possible for Reformation ideas to gain active and decisive support.

The institutional context in which the ideological reforms associated with the Protestant Reformation were decided, therefore, was a context that brought the producers and disseminators of Reformation ideology into direct contact with the heads of municipal, territorial, and central regimes. These settings imposed, as it were, the institutional constraints in relation to which options determining the course of the Reformation were chosen. It remains to consider in greater detail the nature of these constraints, the action sequences that occurred within these contexts, and the ways in which the content of Reformation discourse itself became articulated with these institutional settings.

4 🙚🙙

Social Conditions and
Reformation Discourse

*T*HE REFORMATION was directed primarily at religious rather than political concerns. But in an age when states and religion were so closely intertwined, the Reformation necessarily carried broad political implications and could survive only by receiving some sort of official sanction. Conceptions of religious authority held immediate ramifications for control over ecclesiastical wealth, for the administration of ecclesiastical offices which in turn overlapped with civil authority, and for the ritual sacralization of moral obligations in local communities. Changes in these conceptions created fundamental opportunities, or threats, to which governments inevitably felt compelled to respond.

The commercial expansion of the European economy during this period contributed to, but by no means determined, the social patterns of the Reformation. This expansion created new sources of wealth and power which broadened the opportunities available to regimes. Nevertheless, preexisting differences in social and political structure and in geographic location and climate influenced the type of commercial activity that was to develop in the various regions of Europe. Moreover, the increasing integration of European markets during this period accentuated predispositions toward certain types of production, creating a sharper degree of specialization among the various regions. Increasingly, eastern Europe and Spain, and to a lesser extent France, specialized in the production of agricultural commodities, while England, northern Europe, the Low Countries, and for a brief time the German principalities specialized in manu- factured goods, shipping, and trade. The differences, in turn, left the former regions' regimes heavily dependent on the landowning class, while furthering the kings', princes', and cities' ability in the latter to emancipate themselves from the landed interests.

The much-debated effects of early capitalism on the Reforma- tion, therefore, can be said to have operated strongly through the institutional mechanism of the state. Nowhere did the nascent de- velopment of mercantile capitalism during this period effect such sweeping changes in local culture that the Reformation succeeded on the basis of popular appeal alone— not in Lyons, not in Augsburg, not even in Amsterdam or London. In each case the decisive effect of capitalism was to alter the balance of power between the central governing agencies and the landowning class to the point that the former were able to become a supportive institutional crucible for the Reformation. Religion was not the prime concern of merchant capitalists, nor did they particularly need it to legitimate their en- deavors, as some interpretations have argued. If they accepted re- formed religious teachings it was for personal reasons that undoubtedly bore as much relation to their spiritual interests as to any other part of their lives. But religion was always a central concern of those vested with formal power. As governments responded to pressures for reform, they drew on the various resources at their disposal. And these resources were in part conditioned by the emer- gence of capitalism in European commerce.

At the very minimum, the state established the institutional limits within which the reformers were compelled to work. Official declarations made it safe in some cases to advance reformed teach- ings, dangerous in others. The state's legal and military apparatus protected the reformers in some areas from violence that erupted against them among peasants, nobles, and unsympathetic segments of the urban population; in other areas it was unable or unwilling to provide such protection.

But governing officials played a more direct role in channeling vital resources to the reformers as well. In those areas that granted tolerance to reformed teachings the state became a major supplier of the resources necessary for these teachings to become institu- tionalized. For instance, the state often played a vital role in supplying Bibles. The Reformation is typically portrayed as a substitution of priestly religion with religion of the book. And it was, by all indications, facilitated by the invention of printing and rising literacy levels. But the general population was not, for the most part, the main purchaser of Bibles and other religious books. The cost was still prohibitive for most of the people. Nor was as much emphasis placed by the reformed churches on owning and reading the Bible as on learning the various catechisms and attending preaching services. The largest purchaser of Bibles was the state. Either public funds were channeled through the churches to buy Bibles for impecunious clergy to use or authorities made their own purchases and distributions. In Brandenburg, for example, the government mandated all towns to supply their pastors with Bibles, while in Saxony the princes bought up Bibles themselves in large quantities and distributed them. In other areas the state also became the principal means of disseminating new religious ideas. Clergy were the mouthpiece, but the authorities backed them up. Swedish officials, albeit with little effectiveness until later, passed acts requiring citizens to learn the catechism. And English officials supervised the preparation of prayer books and made sure they were available throughout the land.[1]

Selection and Institutionalization

If the geographic patterning of the Reformation was affected by the relative autonomy of state officials from the wider landed elite, the manner in which the Reformation was actually carried out was in some ways also a function of the institutional relations existing between states and the landed classes. A process of *social selection* was at work, linking different Reformation beliefs and practices with specific configurations of institutional resources. States' capacities to implement the reforms differed greatly from one region to the next. However great the various regimes' resources may have been in particular cases, their autonomy was always relative. In initiating religious reform they were compelled not to ignore the interests of the landlords entirely. Thus, the Reformation tended to be carried out more quickly and completely in those areas where the landlords' influence was weakest. The degree to which specific doctrines were accepted depended mostly on differences in culture and language. But the availability of alternative doctrines from which to select in the first place was itself partly a function of political relations. In addition, the degree to which countermovements developed in opposition both to the mainstream of Reformation doctrines and to the church was conditioned by the relations existing between regimes and the countryside.

The political autonomy of many of the cities in central Europe allowed the reforms to be accomplished with thoroughness and speed. Once it became evident that popular demand for reform had reached a point where it was unlikely to subside easily, city councils were able to decree sweeping changes and carry them out within the space of several months or years. The insurgents fomenting popular uprisings were permitted to engage in anticlerical demonstrations and even occasional outbreaks of iconoclasm; monasteries were closed and their lands sold; new clergy were brought in; parish boundaries were reorganized; new styles of worship and preaching were imposed; the mass was abolished and its abolition rigidly enforced; religious instruction was initiated; and in some areas new meeting places were erected. In the cities these changes could be initiated with relatively strong popular support, since parish boundaries generally corresponded with the city's own boundaries, while the religious practices of peasants and nobles in the countryside could remain unchanged. The weakness of the nobility's influence over urban and regional politics left them with little recourse but to tolerate the reforms being made in the cities.

In contrast, the Reformation in England and in northern Europe was carried out more gradually for fear of mobilizing political opposition in the countryside. The Reformation in these societies was advanced in relation to those practices of the church that least affected the common person and only later penetrated into popular religious practice itself. Monastic lands were the first to be seized, and high church officials were the first to be replaced. These changes could be accomplished with little impact on the manner in which local communities actually enacted their faith, and a portion of the spoils was generally used to secure compliance from distrustful members of the nobility. Later, valuables from the churches themselves were appropriated, resulting in widespread dissent and, in England and Sweden, several instances of armed rebellion. Only later, with the passing of generations, were new clergy installed, instruction in new doctrines instituted, and rigorous efforts made to abolish the old customs of worship. Parish boundaries were generally left unchanged; church buildings were kept intact, memorializing the status relations between landlords and peasants in seating arrangements and graveyards; many clergy retained their positions; and some elements of the traditional service remained. One English writer observes: "The new church that rose upon the ashes of the old remained Catholic and orthodox in every particular save one—it was English and Henrician, not Roman and papal."[2]

In many of the areas on the Continent that were officially brought into the Lutheran fold through territorial settlements actual changes in religious practice were also difficult to impose. The embeddedness of traditional religious customs in rural areas made it impossible to effect more than superficial changes in these areas, especially where the nobility retained its influence in local affairs. Guidelines for Lutheran worship accordingly fell back on the view that anything not specifically listed as an abuse could be continued. By the end of the sixteenth century many of the old ways were in fact unchallenged. Like their Catholic counterparts, Lutheran clergy heard confessions before communion and kept records of the sins confessed. Many services continued to be said in Latin; most of the old holidays were retained; and crucifixes and vestments, as well as other adornments in places of worship, continued to be used.[3] Only in the towns, with largely literate populations and territory under close supervision of secular as well as ecclesiastical authorities, were the reformers' dreams put into practice with a high degree of consistency.

The regions in which the Reformation was institutionalized also came to differ in religious diversity. Although many of the cities and territorial princes in central Europe had attained a high degree of autonomy relative to the nobility, their jurisdictions covered only limited geographic areas. Central Europe remained politically fragmented. The religious reforms that developed, therefore, also assumed a wide variety of forms, including the pronounced differences between Lutheranism and Calvinism, as well as more subtle distinctions such as those between the adherents of Luther and Carlstadt or Bucer, or between Zwingli and Calvin. Various reformers were allowed to develop their ideas and followings in different cities, and no centralized regime existed to impose religious uniformity on the entire region. Had it not been for the sincere efforts of many of the leading reformers to reach agreement on important doctrinal issues, these diversities might have been even greater. The fact that the reformers had a common religious enemy (the pope) and a common political foe (the emperor) probably also contributed to the unity of the Reformation in central Europe. Certainly it forced the various municipalities and duchies to ally themselves with one another for purposes of defense.[4] Nevertheless, the Reformation's diversity in central Europe persisted and, during the second half of the sixteenth century, proved to be one of the weaknesses that counter-reformers were able to exploit to their advantage.[5] By comparison, the centralized monarchies of England, Denmark, and Sweden were able to form monolithic state churches whose leaders only gradually and reluctantly came to tolerate religious diversity.

The diminished influence of the nobility in central Europe, together with the overall fragmentation of authority in this region, also contributed to the rise of separate reform movements among the dispossessed in rural areas—movements that ran parallel to the Lutheran and Calvinist reforms but which also formed in mutual opposition to them. These were the various Anabaptist sects. They recruited members from all strata of society, but generally it was the dispossessed, the poor and unemployed or unskilled workers, who were attracted in largest numbers, while merchants, patricians, and nobles were relatively exceptional among their recruits. These movements were not uncommon in the towns, including followings in England and northern Europe as well as in central Europe. But their greatest appeal was in the countryside among the peasants—a fact that is all the more striking because of the tendency observed nearly everywhere for peasants to have resisted the reforms.[6]

Central and southern Germany as well as the Low Countries were the most productive recruiting grounds for the Anabaptist movements. It was here that the nobility was weakest and the moral economy of village life least intact. Many of these areas had been cleared and colonized only in the fourteenth century and were characterized by smallholding and free tenure rather than demesne farming or large estates. These were also the areas where, for a number of reasons, the great Peasants' War broke out in 1525. Scholars disagree about the nature of direct linkages between the Peasants' War and subsequent Anabaptist movements. But one of the indisputable results of the Peasants' War and the violent means by which it was repressed was considerable disruption of peasant communities.[7] Many were left homeless and without families; others were banished or became fugitives; still others experienced a gradual erosion of their lands and means of subsistence. At the same time, the lesser nobility, who had formerly played a critical function in maintaining a kind of patron-client system of social order in rural communities, was rapidly disappearing, leaving a wide gap in vertical social relations between the dynastic princes and municipal landholders on the one hand and the peasants on the other. This gap created the social space in which the Anabaptist movements could appear. Overall they attracted a fairly minute proportion of the total peasant population, perhaps no more than 1 percent, according to an estimate based on extensive research.[8] The majority of peasants found refuge in safer pursuits, such as adherence to the traditional faith and membership in village communities. But for the few who did not find these avenues satisfactory, the Anabaptist groups provided a new source of community which recreated a sense of moral order among their members.[9]

Beyond the sheer diversity of Reformation practices in different regions, and the severity of the reforms, specific teachings and liturgical innovations were also subject to the wider selective processes set in motion by the institutional contexts in which the Reformation developed. The Reformation was, after all, a constellation of reforms, chosen from a much larger menu of possible reforms, rather than a single revision of belief and practice. It is possible, at least with the advantage of hindsight, to see how some of the reforms chosen fit neatly with the interests of those who did the choosing. And it is possible to see how these reforms contributed positively to the larger progress of the Reformation itself.

At the local level, the institutional arrangements that reinforced the selection of some reforms at the expense of others were often much in evidence. In Basel, for instance, demands for secularization of the monasteries were carried out quickly and completely at least in part because both the artisans and the town council recognized the monasteries as an economic threat that could be disposed of without much resistance. Vernacular preaching, reformed administration of the sacraments, and removal of icons from the churches were also accomplished under the pressures of strong popular demand. Proposals for a council of presbyters, independent of the town council, to rule in matters of church discipline were, however, uniformly rejected by the council. Such proposals threatened to restrict the powers of the council, which retained total control over the churches, and these proposals were not unanimously agreed on by the clergy and laity and were not easy to establish. Popular demands for changes in municipal government along the lines of greater constitutional democracy were also rejected. They received the support of neither the town council nor the clergy, who recognized a need to maintain firm authority over the people.[10]

In Strasbourg the initial wave of reforming zeal in the early 1520s included a bewildering array of proposals and counterproposals: doing away with church courts, subjecting the clergy to civil law, letting priests marry, destroying religious paintings and sacred statues, banning all taxes on peasants except those of the emperor, refusing to take oaths, limiting the church to gatherings of committed believers ready to withdraw from secular society, as well as advancing spiritualist arguments that denied the validity of all doctrinal quarrels and humanist orientations that sought only to infuse the established church with stronger moral and intellectual vitality. By the end of the 1530s the town magistrates had taken control of doctrinal matters, questions of discipline, and church organization. They supported the conservative evangelical reformers who advocated a strong role for the secular authorities and took harsh measures against other reformers who envisioned a more revolutionary transformation of the social order. In the process certain ideological themes gained reinforcement and became institutionalized: a more secular concept of the enforcement of morality, a sharpening of the distinction between the purely hortatory role of the clergy and the coercive powers of civil government, rationalized methods of selecting clergy and conducting church business, a more centralized and hierarchical conception of the church, a narrower and more closely supervised understanding of what was appropriate to print, an emphasis on citywide oaths and religious uniformity that masked underlying divisions, and a commitment on the part of the magistrates to use whatever means necessary to protect the city against heresy and maintain domestic order. Many of the other ideas that had initially been proposed gradually ceased to be regarded as legitimate doctrines. Iconoclasm appeared to represent too sweeping a challenge to domestic tranquillity to be tolerated, especially in view of the fact that the images being smashed had been given in commemoration of the ancestors of the city's wealthy elite. Refusals to take oaths and pay taxes undermined the city's legal and financial base to such a degree that these proposals were also dealt with sternly. And the more extreme teachings of the Anabaptists and others who attracted followings among the city's lower strata came to be defined as dangerously divisive and disrespectful.[11]

The direct role of the secular authorities in selecting certain religious patterns rather than others can also be seen in England. Having placed itself at the head of the church, the crown also took deliberate action to *control* the spread of Protestant ideas, especially among the lower strata, lest heresy lead to popular uprisings. Among the acts passed in 1543, for example, were laws limiting to the upper strata the reading of Scripture. Nobles and merchants were permitted to read the Bible; artisans, journeymen, servants, and laborers were permitted to read only royally inspired primers rather than the Bible itself.[12] Church courts, and secular courts in especially important cases, were relied on to bring to trial heretics who departed from the official reforms. The result was that the relatively moderate character of the English Reformation was preserved.

The reason why the Reformation in England resulted in as uniform a set of teachings as it did, and why separate sects or churches did not become institutionalized, was not that competing ideas were lacking. Evidence from heresy trials of the period reveals that a wide variety of doctrines and interpretations were advanced. Some resembled the views of earlier English reformers, such as Wycliffe and Tyndale; others followed closely the teachings of Erasmus or Luther; still others seemed closer to Zwingli, Carlstadt, or the Anabaptists; and many of the statements revealed self-conscious picking and choosing of ideas from several sources, as well as attempts to innovate and defend new arguments. Views of the Eucharist, the uses of Scripture, and the authority of priestly offices and ecclesiastical positions were especially subject to wide variations in interpretation. Some argued that the Eucharist was purely a symbolic, "commemorative" act, that preaching of the Bible took precedence over ecclesiastical authority, and that anyone could preach; others took less extreme perspectives on one or more of these topics.

The forces selecting against many of these ideas and leading to greater ideological consensus in England reflected the institutional context in which the English Reformation developed. Once ideas about change began to compete with one another, the weight of maintaining some institutional control over these changes exercised pressure in favor of some proposals and against others. The idea that anyone with something to say should be allowed to preach, for example, presented a radical challenge not only to the established church but also to the authority of the reformers. This idea was sternly and summarily, although not always easily, suppressed. In contrast, wide support was given to the idea that religious practice should be rooted in understanding. Pilgrimages and icons, for example, were opposed on grounds that these practices merely reflected tradition rather than a deep understanding of the Christian faith. Arguments for lengthier sermons in the vernacular took the same form. The message was to inquire more deeply, to learn what the reformers were teaching. It was quite different from being told to depend on one's private intuitions about faith or to seek direct revelations of the divine. Thus, the Reformation could be advanced, but under the watchful eye of the English church.

In other ways, the reforms that were selected in England also contributed effectively to the institutional commitment that would ensure their own survival. They transformed public discourse into collective discourse and embedded this discourse into the rituals and informal social relations of the church itself. Cranmer's reforms of the liturgy, promulgated in the prayer book of 1549, quite explicitly sought to reduce the distance separating clergy and laity and involved the latter symbolically in the church as a community. The book of "common prayer" was, in fact, so named because clergy and laity were to join together in lifting their voices to God. Clergy were required to face the audience while administering the sacrament. Sermons were given a more prominent role in the service and were to be enunciated clearly, loudly, and in a plain manner capable of being understood by everyone. Clerical vestments were made plainer, as were the altar cloths and utensils used in serving the communion elements. Communicants took the elements "in both kinds." And all citizens of the realm were required by law to attend services regularly. Parishioners were also admonished to make a deeper commitment to the church, participating with "hearts and minds" rather than with ears only. They were to think of themselves as "co-laborers" with the clergy and were to contribute freely to prevent pastors from having to seek financial support outside of the local congregation.[13]

The institutional context in which the Calvinist wing of the Reformation developed was in many respects quite different from that in England. It is possible nevertheless to identify some of the same kinds of selective processes at work. Perhaps the most crucial aspect of life in Geneva during Calvin's stay there was its virtually continuous state of siege. Relatively small and weak economically as well as militarily, Geneva was constantly threatened by its more powerful neighbors, particularly the dukes of Savoy and the neighboring canton of Fribourg (both of which were Catholic powers with designs of forcing Geneva back into the arms of the church) and Bern, Geneva's chief Protestant ally but one with designs of imposing its own hegemony on the town. Geneva maintained its political autonomy by carefully balancing these forces against one another, but not without letting its domestic life be affected by a siege mentality. Its walls were always guarded; citizens were required to keep weapons and participate in the militia; swords were presented at elections as insignia of citizenship; and a strict curfew was enforced. A show of unity was essential to the town's security as well, even though the magistracy was deeply factionalized. Above all, religious divisions had to be managed carefully because all the neighboring powers were eager to exploit these divisions to their advantage. Given these situational constraints, it is perhaps not surprising that Calvin's attention would be drawn to questions of moral discipline and the corporate regulation of religious practice.

Several themes took on increasing prominence in Calvin's writings during his time in Geneva. He became more preoccupied with the visible church. Laws and discipline became more important as features of the visible church. And clergy and magistrates were portrayed in a closer and more distinctly cooperative relationship, working together to reinforce piety, discipline, and a sense of collective responsibility among the faithful. These ideas were not simply a reflection of the new social context in which Calvin found himself. But they do show the marks of his having to confront more seriously than before the concrete tasks of forging ideas into institutional realities. It was in fact during this time that Calvin and the other ministers in Geneva drew up ordinances governing religious practice and presented them to the town council for approval, established procedures for administering the sacraments, encouraged more frequent participation in communion, defined strict sanctions for moral and doctrinal deviations, and instructed the population in their duties toward the clergy and civil magistrates.[14]

The selective role played in Calvin's thinking by Geneva's political structure was perhaps less straightforward but equally important. Although Geneva was governed in a representative style by a set of councils that were to a degree elective during Calvin's lifetime, there appears to have been no simple relation between this structure and Calvin's political ideas. Rather than simply building a defense of republicanism or democracy into his theology, Calvin appears to have dealt rather gingerly and ambiguously with politics. More decisive than the general political structure, it appears, was Calvin's own experience with Genevan power. His fate, as a mere *habitant* (until 1559, when he was granted citizenship), was contingent on the political strength at any moment of different factions in the electorate. His expulsion from the city in 1538, the subsequent invitation to return in 1541, his harassment from the late 1540s until 1555, and his eventual ascendancy thereafter were all contingent on swings in the power of different factions. Faced with an unreliable political climate of this kind, Calvin perhaps not surprisingly was slow to develop straightforward teachings about the role of magistrates or to address his writings to them in particular. Instead he specifically advocated that church leaders should be governed primarily by a spirit of cooperation with whatever form of civil government they might find established. There is, over time, relatively clear evidence that his personal preferences leaned increasingly away from monarchy and toward a mixed or "estates" form of government not unlike that which he had witnessed at Strasbourg and in Geneva. But these preferences were always subordinated to his more general view that in matters of civil government, whatever is is right. He was well aware of the problems that could be present under any system of government, but still maintained his conviction in the divinely instituted nature of government—of all kinds—by distinguishing sharply the offices from the persons occupying these offices. His efforts, consequently, focused more on the internal discipline of the person and on church government than on secular government. Both were differentiated sufficiently from political ideas to render them somewhat durable amidst changing political circumstances. It is understandable, therefore, that subsequent generations of his followers were able to derive quite varied political doctrines from his work.

In all these examples, the evidence points toward specific doctrines and religious practices being selected from a wider array of possible alternatives. Selective processes were set in motion by such practical considerations as the need to maintain secular and clerical authority over the reform movement, by the mix of secular and clerical authority to which the leading reformers themselves were subject, and by the need to evoke collective commitment from the movement's followers. In some cases a greater range of acceptable practices was retained than in others. But everywhere, the range of possible reforms available for consideration greatly exceeded the number that were actually adopted.

The mechanisms operating to select for some reforms and to

reject others were sometimes blind, functioning simply as the unforeseen outcomes of numerous near-term decisions. But in many
cases the process of selection involved explicit competition among
the various reformers. Having arisen in different locations and with
different traditions, training, and interests as part of their institutional
contexts, the reformers constituted a single movement mainly by
virtue of their common opposition to established practices. Beyond
that, they functioned as competitors, the most ambitious of whom
increasingly came to be at war with one another, struggling to assert
the priority of their own ideas and to see these ideas adopted in
wider segments of the larger movement. The image of war is indeed
apt, for one sees all the tactical maneuvers, skirmishes, and escalation
of conflict usually associated with physical battle. Among the leading
reformers, letters and tracts were exchanged with increasing frequency in efforts to gain allies, stake out rhetorical positions, launch
attacks, and engage in counterattacks. Although the substance of
argumentative claims was clearly at stake, personal attacks, appeals
to secular authority, and contests over the more practical aspects of
reform were also clearly in evidence. One is impressed with both
the intensity and subtlety of argument on which these struggles were
waged. Yet the image of war is only partially correct because the
debates were seldom limited to bilateral conflict; they involved as
many as half a dozen or more major contestants, each defending a
distinct version of the truth.

To a significant extent, the major writings that constituted the
extraordinary level of productivity associated with the Reformation
represented moves and countermoves stimulated most directly by
competition among the reformers themselves. Evidence indicates
repeatedly that the sheer volume of output was, in fact, greatly augmented by the need writers felt to refute one another. In Luther's
case, for example, occasion after occasion reveals that his energies
were turned toward writing yet another treatise, despite other interests and demands, by an attack written by one of his competitors
in which an implicit or explicit challenge to reply was included. The
titles of many of his treatises demonstrate these intentions. To remain
silent was tantamount to conceding the authority of a competitor's
position—a tacit admission to those who followed these debates with
more than passing interest that one did not know how to respond
or had grown weary of providing leadership to the movement. Often
these occasions provided the stimulus necessary to sharpen previous

arguments, to disseminate them to a new audience, or to work out seeming inconsistencies within the writers' own oeuvre of positions on other topics.

In this respect, competition also proved to be an important impetus toward the "rationalization" or internal coherence of Reformation theology. Sometimes the result was a notable increase in the subtlety, sophistication, and sheer attention accorded specific issues. For example, the controversy concerning a proper interpretation of the Lord's Supper that broke into the open among Luther, Carlstadt, the Bohemian Brethren, Speratus, Zwingli, Schwenkfeld, Krautwald, and Oecolampadius in 1525 and 1526 consumed enormous energies on the part of all its major protagonists and produced most of the central interpretations that were to predominate among Protestant bodies for the next several centuries. In absolute volume, the controversy generated thousands of pages of tightly argued text.

Controversies such as this also played an important role in giving Reformation discourse a distinct internal structure. Complex and often subtle theological arguments tended to be identified with their leading advocates. For example, the main positions regarding the character of the Eucharist came to be identified in this way. Preachers labeled themselves and their teachings accordingly. And in disputations or heresy trials these labels served as markers of acceptable or unacceptable practice. Books also served this purpose. In addition to disseminating ideas, they provided markers with which to identify friends and enemies. Mere ownership of certain books evoked suspicion of harboring certain beliefs. In these ways, sharper distinctions could be drawn among the various branches of the Reformation. And on the basis of these distinctions, selective processes could be set in motion to reinforce the likelihood of particular ideas becoming institutionalized in particular settings.

Public Discourse and the Problem of Articulation

There were, then, a number of ways in which the institutional contexts in which the Reformation took place—the relations among the heads of state, the landed elites, the church, and the broader society—influenced the content and direction of the Reformation. The severity of the reforms, the scale on which they were instituted, and the diversity of competing reforms were all affected by the relations of power with which the reformers had to contend. But the content of the Reformation was not shaped simply by these contextual factors. It owed its character to the creative acts of the reformers themselves. It was a mode of public discourse that came to have a distinct internal structure of its own. And this structure represented not only a response to broad social conditions but also the influences of the movement itself. Reformation ideology was composed of active discourse—discourse that took shape within the changing contours of the movement's own activities. Out of this sequence of actions, responses, and adjustments, Reformation discourse gained both a distinct relation with its social context and a quality that allowed it to survive well beyond that immediate context.

The specific sequence of events by which the Reformation was introduced varied considerably from one locality to another, a fact that is itself consistent with the foregoing emphasis on the relative autonomy of municipal and territorial decisionmakers. Having at least some autonomy from the social conditions in which traditional religious patterns were embedded, decisionmakers were able to initiate their own courses of action in response to the Reformation. Some actively supported it, some pressed for even stronger reforms, others temporized. The specific sequences of events were often shaped most directly by the internal unfolding of the reforms themselves and by the larger institutional pressures to which decisionmakers remained subject. A full accounting of these events generally requires consideration of the strength of popular demand, the role of reform clergy, relative political strengths among the secular authorities and the nobility, the various factions' influence over different segments of the ecclesiastical hierarchy, and external factors such as the threat of imperial intervention, participation in urban alliances, and peasant uprisings. Nevertheless, within these general contexts, some common activities and modes of discourse inherent to the Reformation itself can be identified.

In most of the towns that became centers of reforming activity, grassroots dissent was initiated to an important degree, as the German historian Peter Blickle has recently emphasized, by the sermon.[15] Sermons that attacked the papacy and the position of the established clergy and monastic orders and asserted in their place the authority of the "pure" gospel quickly earned the label of being "Lutheran," "evangelical," or "reformed." They were readily distinguishable by their content. But apart from content, the fact that the genre of choice was the sermon—as opposed to the philosophical treatise, novel, or epic poem, for example—was significant in itself. Much of the closeness between Reformation discourse and its social context can in fact be attributed to the distinctive qualities of the sermon (and to related genres such as the commentary and the polemical tract).

The sermon contributed in several important ways to the articulation of Reformation discourse with its social setting. For one, the sermon was a public act from which a clear identification between narrator and narrative—and thereby between the narrator's social role and the discourse uttered—could be established. Rather than it being possible (as was to be the case during the Enlightenment, for example) for utterances to be purveyed through the written text under pseudonyms or anonymously, speakers immediately acquired a public identity in connection with the stance taken in their own discourse. Second, the existence of so strong an identification between the preacher's public role and his text, together with strong suppositions of "sincerity" as part of the preacher's illocutionary style, meant that the likelihood of any clear demarcation of the private person from public roles was diminished. In contrast with the pattern that was to become evident in the Enlightenment, questions concerning self-identity and the relations between selves and social roles were therefore less likely to arise. This, as we shall see, permitted speakers to identify themselves as figural actors in which both the private aspects of religious piety and the public manifestations of religious service were brought together. Third, the public character of the sermon, dependent as it was on the immediate and direct response of a physically proximate audience, meant that questions of authority and legitimacy necessarily required central and effective attention. Asserting their own right to articulate statements, especially when these statements challenged the very institutional underpinnings of the preaching role itself, the reformers had to make constant reference to some higher-order legitimating principles. This requirement for authority, in fact, became particularly significant as a constraint shaping Reformation ideology.

Attacks on the hierarchical authority of the church, coupled with assertions about scriptural authority, necessarily set up a strong opposition between categories of power. Within this framework, ideology came to be formulated in terms of strict conceptions of allegiance. To have faith meant that one was to be *faithful* in the sense of giving oneself over fully to the authority of Scripture and its pastoral defenders. There was, moreover, high compatibility between this conception of the Word and the immediate social contexts in which preaching took place. The right to preach generally remained vested as much in the hands of secular authorities as in ecclesiastical hands. Thus, the relative weight of various ruling factions in defining the outcomes of municipal and territorial deliberations was, as we have seen, decisive. In the process, however, it was difficult to avoid an identification being established between the contestants in these political struggles and the polarities of authoritative affirmation built into the religious discourse itself. Consequently, entire regimes came to be closely identified with the "Protestant cause" (or with its opponents), and their actions took on significance as test cases in a more cosmic arena of spiritual warfare.

From a different angle, the Reformation's emphasis on authority, together with its routine institutional manifestation in urban pulpits, also gave it practical significance that secular authorities could scarcely afford to ignore. On the reformers' side, questions concerning the right to preach immediately imposed a relation between appeals to scripture and appeals to magisterial arbitrators. On the magistrates' side, appeals for rulings on the right to preach could be backed up by the reformers in threats or actualized in instances of popular violence, withholding of contributions for public charities, and acts of iconoclasm. The Reformation, therefore, quickly evoked political conflicts on which the reformers were forced to take a stand. These stands, in turn, effected direct ideological connections between the more abstract tenets of reform doctrine and the immediate events associated with the movement itself.

Another factor that wedded ideological production to concrete action sequences was that the reformers were as keenly interested in practice as they were in doctrinal theory. This goes, perhaps, without saying; yet the fact that their work took place within an institutional context and was devoted to reform meant that a host of institutional practices had to be addressed. By 1521, for example, Luther had written major treatises on confession, the mass, celibacy, and monastic vows, and all of these were composed amidst the heat of controversy being generated by priests' actually abandoning and challenging the conventional practices. In seclusion at Wartburg castle Luther enjoyed the freedom from these activities necessary for study and writing; but an active correspondence with colleagues closer to the front lines of parish reform kept him abreast of the matters at hand, and his writings convey a pastoral concern that goes well beyond the purely theoretical. Thus, it might be said, as Marxists would argue in a later period, that the power of Luther's pen depended on the more practical risks being taken by the foot soldiers of the movement. And yet, it was also the fact of the church's deep involvement with ordinary life, as institutionalized both in ritual practices and clerical roles, that gave the reformers this opportunity to unite theory and practice.

The reformers' own efforts to relate scriptural authority to the practical matters at hand, moreover, brought ideology into closer articulation with its social surroundings by drawing models from preexisting repertoires of popular discourse. These repertoires not only corresponded to the identities of specific communities but also included quite specific references to their own situations and local histories. From abstract conceptions of social order to concrete oaths of citizenship and civic responsibility, these models provided templates against which to assess the propriety of specific political acts.[16] An illustration of the ways in which these models welded discourse with concrete circumstances can be found in city councils' appeals to restore tranquillity in the wake of religious dissension. As I have suggested, the desire to maintain political autonomy vis-à-vis surrounding regimes provided a strong incentive to deal with religious unrest in an expedient manner. The desirability of maintaining domestic peace, however, was not simply an implicit feature of the social context but was built explicitly into the language of public discourse. Hans-Christoph Rublack provides two examples, one from Nördlingen, the other from Nuremberg.[17] The Nördlingen case is taken from an address to the city council in 1525, when the town was confronted with an assembly of peasant insurgents gathering some five kilometers east of the city. Among the appeals advanced in the address was the following: "Even those with the least understanding appreciate that no empire, principality, territory or city can endure without peaceful unity. The weak and the small are raised through peace and unity, the great decay through lack of peace." The Nuremberg case comes from a tract written by the town clerk early in the sixteenth century and articulates a similar argument: "As we see through daily experience peace and harmony can raise little things and cause them to develop. But large things, an entire community and government can come to nought and completely pass away through disunity and lack of peace." In both cases, the arguments about peace draw inspiration from biblical examples and utilize language recognizable from scriptural sources (such as Matthew 12:25) as well as pointing toward examples from social experience in which peace or disunity had the alleged effects. "Peace" itself became a slogan, an actual element of discourse that guided the connection between ideology and practice. Like the norm of civic unity, it became explicitly validated in common catchphrases, and these, once rendered, could be adapted to a variety of circumstances.

Even with the opportunity that concrete reforms provided for linking Reformation ideology with its institutional setting, there is nevertheless a feature of this linkage that cannot be understood apart from the specific genre of Reformation discourse itself. Luther's writing displays a nearly continuous interplay between references, on the one hand, to the events, actors, and actions of which his own social milieu was constructed and, on the other, to scriptural injunctions and biblical characters who provide alternative models of behavior. Against the institutionalized religious practices of his day he established Scripture as an even more powerful authority. Neither abstract nor merely the written word, Scripture became in Luther's discourse an active agent expressed in tangible and graphic imagery.[18] "One must wield God's Word like a bared blade and let it powerfully cut down all opponents and errors," he wrote in a treatise dedicated to the knight Franz von Sickingen in 1521. Scripture, he insisted in another treatise, "intends to exercise either all authority or none at all."[19] In setting institutional authority and scriptural authority in opposition to each other, Luther constructed an ideology that was inherently articulated with practical circumstances and yet capable of casting these circumstances in a critical light. He created, as it were, a *discursive field* in which to bring together in imaginative ways the practical realities of institutional life on the one hand and the ideals evident in Scripture on the other.

To the basic polarity that defined this discursive field, Luther attached a large number of contrasting pairs, the starkness and consistency of which tended to reinforce the underlying distance across which the discursive field itself was measured: heaven-earth, iron-brass, God-emperor, divine affairs–human hands, spirit-devil, strength-fatigue, innocence-guilt, Word-sword, sheep-wolves, Christians-papists. These were not presented as mere rhetorical conventions (although they were that too), or as the backdrop for a convenient dialectical synthesis, but as diametrically opposed features of reality. "There is no middle kingdom," Luther instructed Erasmus, "between the kingdom of God and the kingdom of Satan, which are mutually and utterly in contradiction to one another."[20] Eventually the actors in Luther's own environment who supported or opposed the reforms also became attached to the same polarity. Thus, the Wittenberg councilors and Elector Frederick came to stand against the Archbishop of Mainz, the emperor, and of course the pope. His friends, such as Spalatin and Lazarus Spengler, symbolized the life of faith, enemies such as John Eck and Duke George the treachery of religious custom: they become, in Luther's graphic depictions, "flatterers of the pope," "enemies of Christ," "liars," "tricksters," "raving madmen," "blasphemers," "dreamers," and "plain fools."

Peasants, for whatever reasons, even prior to the great insurrections of 1525, were generally depicted less as friends than as foes or at best hindrances to the cause. Superstitious, deeply attached to the traditional rituals, illiterate, and largely incapable of understanding the reformers' arguments, they threatened to inhibit the evangelical cause by subverting its higher aims for their own material ends. Godliness and virtue were portrayed in opposition to the peasants' superstitions, and the peaceable effects of preaching the Word were contrasted with the violence of peasant insurrections. Landlords on the whole fared little better in Luther's depictions than peasants. Even when they were not the subject of direct attack, they provided models with which to associate the worst of institutional authorities. The trouble with popes, he told an audience in Wittenberg, is that they "lounge around on cushions and act like landed gentry, laying burdens on us such as they themselves would never touch."[21] And by the end of the Peasants' War his wrath toward the landlords was even more pointed. Calling them "lawless and robbing nobles" and accusing them of "fuming and raving" like "devils," he held forth little hope of their ability to maintain peace were it not for the restraining hand of God.

In all of this Luther depicted himself as a kind of embattled intermediary. He identified himself with Jeremiah and the other biblical prophets, and yet he also wrote of himself in disparaging and self-effacing ways—which the layperson could identify with—calling himself a "barbarian" and a "miserable and fragile little vessel." His pen he likened to a spark that the winds of divine will would fan into a flame, which in turn would transform the earthen vessel of religious practice into a golden treasure. As translator, writer, and interpreter, "Luther" was, then, as much a construction of the ideological field itself as he was the producer of this field.

The symbols that anchored the two ends of the polarity around which the reformers' discourse was organized were readily available in the contexts in which this discourse was enunciated. Tensions between the common people and the clergy had typically found symbolic expression in complaints about the immorality of the priests. Accusations of insobriety, drunkenness, debauchery, and scandalous activities of all kinds were not uncommon, especially in the towns in which broader social changes were widening the cleavages separating priests and people. Whether or not these accusations were well founded, they became the discursive vehicles by which grievances of all kinds could be expressed. Instances were frequently recorded of townspeople shouting accusations at priests they particularly disliked, calling them hypocrites, condemning them for acts of immorality and incorrigibility, and defaming them ritually with effigies and mock processionals. The ideal standards of conduct that were supposed to elevate priests to a higher level than parishioners provided ready contrasts with the actual behavior in which priests were said to be engaged. These contrasts, pitting the pollution of institutional behavior against the purity of spiritual ideals, provided ready imagery on which the reformers could draw in enunciating their own appeals. And, once enunciated, these appeals meshed in a familiar way with the informal language already in use among those to whom the reformers' sermons were addressed.

At a popular level, acts of violence against the clergy, iconoclasm, and, more generally, the mere violation of taboos associated with the sacraments added to the symbolism of institutional negation. Often the first acts of institutional negation included breaking Lenten rules, disrupting religious processionals, and violating dietary restrictions. Initially these tended to consist primarily of negative acts, rather than positive affirmations of reform teachings, but were highly visible violations of the church's authority. The reformers themselves generally did not call for iconoclasm, and for the most part urged restraint rather than condoning it. But there was a relation between their teachings and these acts. In the decade prior to 1520 hardly any image breaking was evident; during the early 1520s it erupted in a number of towns where Luther, Bucer, Carlstadt, Zwingli, and others were having an influence. The reformers preached against the

saints as a false mode of godliness; their followers took these teachings literally and attacked the images themselves. Those who engaged
in these acts dramatized the weakness of supposedly sacred practices.
In separating themselves from these practices, they reinforced the
discursive polarity betwen the traditional and the spiritual.[22]

Once public acts of institutional negation were committed, those
in authority were typically forced into a position of having to make
some response. And in responding, the various factions involved in
making public decisions came to be identified with the negative and
positive positions expressed in the reformers' public discourse. In
Basel, for example, violations of sacramental regulations were quickly
condemned by the higher clergy, especially those associated with the
cathedral, and by many of the wealthier patricians. Support was registered by the lower parish clergy and by many of the artisans.[23] In
Lyons the following incident was recorded, which also shows how
quickly the various agents of authority were identified with one end
or the other of the reformers' discursive polarity: "At the entry
parade of Archbishop d'Este in 1540, a fight broke out between the
city youth and the priests representing the churches of Lyon. The
youths disrupted the clergy's parade order and roughed up some of
the priests so severely that they had to be taken to the hospital. A
few of the injured clergymen were hurt so badly that the cathedral
and collegiate churches took up a collection on their behalf. In addition, the churches decided to sue the city government, since the
city youth apparently acted under the council's auspices."[24] Whether
the council had actually encouraged the youths is impossible to determine. The broader institutional conflicts that existed between the
churches and the council, nevertheless, immediately set the two in
opposition when an event of this kind occurred.

There was, however, no sense in which preexisting social cleavages can be said to have predetermined the fundamental polarities
that constituted the discursive fields enunciated by Luther and the
other reformers. Here, perhaps more clearly than in any other way,
the invention of printing, and the effect of this invention in making
Scripture available in tangible form, may be understood as an objective source of the polarity in Lutheran ideology between Scripture
and institution. But even this should not be overemphasized relative
to the importance of Luther's own visionary recognition of the reforming value of Scripture set in opposition to established practices.
Against this ideological polarity, the rising divisions that were be-

coming evident in the social environment between town and country and between state officials and aristocracies served mainly as political and economic resources—sources of support and opposition—that became mapped onto the ideological field itself. Serving as a "model for" social relations, to borrow Clifford Geertz's language, the ideological field had an existence independent of its social environment.[25] But the divisions in the social environment, themselves the result of forces antecedent to the Reformation and initially independent of it, provided tangible reinforcement to the articulation of this discursive field and in supporting or opposing the Reformation served as a dramaturgic "model of" the basic symbolic polarities as well.

The role of a clear discursive field such as that enunciated by the reformers was to alter the framework in which specific conflicts and grievances were expressed. Often there was a clear relation between some specific complaint about clerical abuse and the more general attacks of the reformers on institutional deviations from Scripture. But the latter permitted the former to be discussed as instances of a general category of complaints. In this sense, the terms of debate, if not the perception of grievances themselves, were altered. And it was in opposition to the scriptural that the negative aspects of the religious institution became most clearly evident. Thus, the whole structure of the discursive field figured into the terms of religious discourse, turning specific events into mere instances or exemplars of broader conceptions.[26]

Working back and forth between the poles of institutional reality and scriptural ideals, Luther and the other reformers commented authoritatively on proper and desired courses of action. They drew principles from Scripture and applied them to the exigencies of daily life as it unfolded through the events of the church in its relations with the larger society. Commenting on Scripture provided the occasion for stating practical lessons about the believer's conduct. Indeed, the "commentary" became a much-utilized genre of collective discourse.

Patterned after a well established form of theological reflection, yet similar enough to the verbally uttered sermon to be understood by lay readers, the commentary provided opportunities to make creative connections between passages of Scripture and the practical affairs of individual and collective life. It not only functioned well by virtue of being easily recognized in terms of familiar patterns of theological discourse but also offered a suitable means of reinforcing the Reformation's main tenets. It did so largely on the basis of its discrete, separable format. Commenting on passages verse by verse and chapter by chapter provided the reformers with ample opportunity to be redundant, thereby driving home certain central tenets of their ideology.[27] And the specific lessons that could be drawn from particular passages appear to have been relatively fluid, providing opportunity to reflect on current events rather than being constrained by canons of systematic dogma.

In commenting on the Magnificat, for example, Luther turned the statement "He has put down the mighty from their thrones, and exalted those of low degree" into an opportunity to caution present rulers against perpetuating evil lest God punish them and transfer power to another source. In the same commentary, he found occasion to lecture the "pope and his herd" against demanding their rights and went on to present David as a model of someone who "often looked the other way" if an assertion of rights would bring undue harm to others.[28] There was, in these and other instances, a wedding of the immediate with the timeless, a clear sense of "this-worldly" relevance and yet a temporal specificity couched in the more enduring framework of scriptural truth.

Although systematic theology was by no means absent from the Reformation, much of its writing consisted of passage-by-passage reflections that varied from topic to topic as the occasion dictated. Thus, to find remarks on topics as different as temporal authorities and auricular confession, as one does in Luther's treatise on the Magnificat, was by no means unusual. The commentary, like the sermon, appears to have been an especially suitable genre of discourse for enhancing this kind of situational flexibility. Checking the tendency toward inconsistency that might be associated with this flexibility, however, was the redundancy of the commentary.[29] Reformation leaders seized on particular principles (*sola fide,* for example) and, as much as inventing whole systems of thought organized around these principles, repeated them over and over again in commenting on various passages. They believed in an intertextual consistency within Scripture and thus were not embarrassed to hammer away at the same theses whenever the occasion arose. This repetition not only gave added emphasis to dominant themes but also permitted the meanings of these themes to be defined more precisely as they were applied to successive situations.[30]

Once the Reformation began to unfold, producing the events that became the subjects of its own discourse, a secondary level of discourse also began to appear: commentaries and testaments written by minor participants and bystanders who came to recognize themselves as witnesses to a great history-making spectacle.[31] The reflexivity involved in these commentaries contributed not only to the possibilities for later generations of historians to preserve the Reformation as a decisive episode in the evolution of modern culture but also to the degree of articulation between ideas and events as they were perceived by contemporaries. The reformers' ideas became part of an ongoing narrative that included their own exploits and adventures. The validity of Luther's arguments with Müntzer and Carlstadt gained appeal in the sympathetic retelling of these encounters by his followers in a way that transcended recondite theological hair splitting. These narratives, moreover, situated ideas in an institutional context that, although a discursive reconstruction itself, evoked the appropriate conditions under which particular arguments could be regarded as plausible.[32]

Second only to the commentary, in which an exigetical style prevailed, was the disputation, carried out either in verbal debate or in an exchange of letters and treatises, and generally characterized by a polemical style.[33] Disputations provided additional opportunities to repeat, clarify, and elaborate major theses and, quite at odds with the intentions of the Reformation's opponents, set in motion a kind of audible feedback that quickly multiplied its volume and intensity. As a mode of argumentation, disputations were contingent not only on the fact that opponents and proponents of the Reformation were clearly pitted against each other but also on the fact that the Reformation itself was divided into numerous factions, themselves supported by various regimes in different localities. If one asks why the Reformation witnessed such an intense level of verbal and written ideological productivity, therefore, one has to look at least partly to the internal competition among the different strands of the Reformation.[34]

Figural Action

On the whole, the political and economic heterogeneity of the broader European environment contributed to the emergence of a more variegated religious culture. And this culture, as is frequently observed, also credited the individual with greater discretion in making religious choices. Both the diversity and the individualism of Reformation discourse appear, in retrospect, to have enhanced its capacity to adapt to changing circumstances. As the Reformation became institutionalized, however, its teachings did not become simply more closely aligned with the social contexts in which they appeared. The discursive field which pitted the reformers' conception of scriptural authority against their view of institutional realities was more accurately the context in which the Reformation's more lasting cultural contributions were made. This dimension of Reformation ideology is particularly evident with respect to the reformers' seminal contribution to the creation of modern individualism itself—the so-called "Protestant ethic" on which Max Weber and others have focused so much attention.

Luther's image of the individual is both symptomatic of the polarity that provided the discursive field in which his ideology was constructed and revelatory of the writer's own image of himself. Unlike the later writers of the Enlightenment, who struggled with divisions internal to the self, Luther saw the individual as an essential, inseparable whole. God, as the highest in a single hierarchy of authority, was the source of each individual's personality. Yet there was an internal struggle within the soul of every individual by virtue of living, suspended as it were, within the symbolic polarity of Scripture, heaven, and godliness above and the actual, earthly, corrupted environment below. Just as ideology more generally was constructed by forging together elements from both of these poles, so the individual was conceived as a unity despite the tensions pulling in different directions. Do two souls dwell in the same breast? No, Luther contended, there is but one soul, torn between heaven and earth, spirit and flesh.

The tensions pulling the individual in different directions nevertheless received graphic expression in Luther's discourse. These tensions demonstrated that the individual of which he spoke was not merely an actual person, modeled directly after the individuals with whom Luther was acquainted. Luther's individual was an ideological construction that depended on the discursive field in which this construction was placed.[35] Each of the extreme poles that defined the basic axis of Luther's discourse bore a distinct relation with the individual. To the institutional authority of the church that defined the negative pole of Luther's discourse the individual was attached by outward conformity: the church imposed law on the individual, set in motion a relation of force, and required conformity to norms of good and evil; the individual responded with "external churchliness," of which good works and superstitious performances of religious rites ("prattle") were the hallmarks. To the divine word of God that defined the positive pole of Luther's discourse the individual was attached by inward faith: from the Word the individual received gentle leading, support, mercy, and refuge; in return, the individual cultivated an inner attitude of faith and prayer.

It is the individual's suspended state between earth and heaven that provides, perhaps curiously, the basis for Luther's distinctive—and, in Weber's view, ethically powerful—formulation of individual freedom and responsibility. Realizing both the dangers and the practical impossibility of doing away entirely with the despised forms of worship—of effecting a pure reconciliation of heaven and earth—Luther turned increasingly to an argument stressing the active role of the individual. It is not so much whether one participates in the mass or whether one has images in places of worship, he argued, but how one views these practices and objects. Ultimately the struggle between good and evil must be fought in one's heart. Thus, the individual enjoys freedom with respect to the circumstances of daily life—a fact that allowed Luther to reconcile his teachings with a variety of local constraints and to admonish his followers against actions that might prove politically unsettling. In freedom the movement gained adaptability to its environment. At the same time, each believer acquired the burden of responsibility for articulating his or her own vision of life in such a way that upheld the principle of faith as a heavenly standard and yet demonstrated love in the realm of earthly relations. The individual's "calling" in this framework was not so much a matter strictly of vocational choice but involved the more general duty of right understanding and proper conduct. It was, nevertheless, practically speaking, "this-worldly" from the very beginning, for the individual was constrained until death to live actively within the symbolic space between earth and heaven, between surroundings and the Word.

Insofar as an ideology of ethical individualism emanates from the Reformation, as has generally been argued, then, it is an ideology not so much of invention—for precursors of ethical individualism can be found much earlier—but of articulation; that is, of explicit instruction in reconciling theoretical truth to a social environment in which idealism remains out of the question. Although there may well have been strong latent sentiments favoring greater individual freedom and responsibility, the reformers objectified these sentiments by expressing them within the context of specific questions concerning the nature of religious worship. Sacraments and vows provided issues of collective concern; tracts and sermons addressed these issues publicly. Individuals received instruction in taking responsibility for their own attitudes and actions in relation to priests, icons, and other religious matters. Moreover, this instruction specifically provided for its own legitimation, for once the individual's responsibility was defined, its need for tutelage and pastoral instruction was also observed. Thus, the creation of the private individual was by a paradoxical construction the product of a fundamentally public ideology.

The same kind of discursive field formed the structure of Luther's major contributions to the theory of the state and its relations to the church. Promulgated most clearly in his treatise *On Temporal Authority: To What Extent It Should Be Obeyed,* published in 1523, Luther's theory was framed by a fundamental opposition between the "two kingdoms" perceived to be operative within the world: temporal governance and spiritual governance. As with Luther's other oppositions of this kind, the distinction between temporal and spiritual authority arose within the context of an observed institutional arrangement—namely, bishops governing castles, cities, lands, and tenants—that Luther criticized in terms of an alternative model perceived in Scripture. By creating a polarity between the two realms, he drew a conceptual distinction that had become blurred in practice. The either-or he established between the temporal and spiritual, however, did not serve simply as a characterization of improper and proper conduct but as an analytic device with which to frame the discussion of improper and proper conduct. Having established this opposition as a basic categorical division, he used the two poles, as in other cases, to affix oppositions of other kinds as well. Thus, faith was assigned to the realm of spirituality, function to the temporal realm, and freedom was associated with faith, while external order was associated with function.[36]

The purpose of these assignments, again, was not to force choices between one and the other but to create a discursive space in which elements from both poles could be selectively combined and coordinated. Luther placed squarely within this space two prototypical actors upon whom, in keeping with his more general image of the individual, were bestowed the opportunity and responsibility of making decisions: the Christian citizen and the Christian ruler. Both were to be oriented simultaneously toward each pole of the discursive field: toward their common life as temporal creatures and toward principles of scripturally guided conscience as spiritual beings. From the common life came principles of justice, order, and charity; from the spiritual life came standards of forgiveness, sacrifice, and endurance. Always the individual citizen was to balance these principles against one another, living in the world but being guided by norms transcending it. Always the ruler was to look simultaneously to the nonviolent voice of the Word and to the law-enforcing powers of government, to freedom of conscience and restraint of evil at the same time. Neither the individual nor the collectivity could divide life into two separate compartments. Thus, responsible and active discretion was always mandated to bring the two together in a way that constituted doing the will of God.

To this end, Luther's admonitions, even those dealing with practical matters, took the form of "counsels of the heart" rather than abstract formulas. His purpose was to provide guidelines for responsible decision processes, rather than prescriptions that would constitute decisions themselves. To Christian rulers, for example, he counseled confidence in God, a commitment to Christian service, untrammeled reason and unfettered judgment, and restrained firmness toward evildoers. Here, as in the case of questions about ecclesiastical practice, then, Luther articulated an image of the individual in which persistent, dutiful exercise of the will was required, but he also set up clearly defined limits in relation to which the will was to be exercised. The intent of these limits was to guide action in concrete situations. The formulas presented, however, derived from a discursive field created by opposing situational and conceptual categories each to the other.

As the Reformation unfolded, providing its own models of faith in practice, more ample opportunities became available for articulating the figural action identified in theory with cases of actual practice. Models of church order that had proven effective, such as those at Altenburg and Leisnig, were taken as examples from which more general theoretical conclusions could be derived. The growing need for trained pastors, church discipline, care of the poor, and resolutions to other practical matters also led the reformers to borrow models from secular sources. Especially in matters of governance, models were borrowed from the experience of secular authorities. For example, Luther legitimated arguments permitting the authorities to press labor into service for constructing and repairing church buildings by observing that secular rulers made the same claims for the maintenance of roads and bridges. Similarly, secular rulers were admonished to promote religious instruction, discipline among the young, and care of the poor in the same way they looked after the public good when negotiating treaties or waging war. Reformation discourse came to be articulated with its immediate social circumstances in this way. But the specific actions that were held up as exemplary models of behavior remained figural. They served as exemplars, not as prescriptions to be followed exactly or literally. They could be treated as figural action, thereby transcending their specific situations, because they were framed within the context of the reformers' discursive polarity between the spiritual and temporal.

Luther's separation of the spiritual and temporal realms, along with similar oppositions expressed by other leading reformers, has often been taken as contributing to the process of "institutional differentiation," which social scientists associate with the transition from premodern to modern societies. In distinguishing the spiritual from the temporal, the reformers presumably paved the way for a clearer separation of the functions assigned to the institutions of church and state. Yet it must be seen that this outcome emerged neither from the complex social circumstances in which the Reformation took place nor from inherent features of reform thought itself but from a creative juxtaposition of the two. Fundamental to the symbolic disaggregation of the two institutions was the prior opposition that the reformers drew between Scripture and religious convention. Moreover, the mode of symbolic differentiation involved less the construction of two distinct categories in which discrete forms of action could take place than a conceptual polarity that could never be separated in practice and always had to be mediated by responsible individuals. The construction of institutional differentiation, therefore, remained entirely contingent on the simultaneous construction of the autonomous individual.

Calvin, like Luther, also established the possibilities for theological argument within a well-defined discursive field bounded at one end by the materiality of conventional institutions and at the other by the spirituality commended in Scripture. To these opposing poles Calvin attached the basic objectifications that served as a framework for the more subtle aspects of his discourse about religious conduct: man versus God, false worship versus true, the finite versus the infinite, fleshly devotion versus the "entirely other."[37] Even the sources of his words and the rhythms of his sentences often underscored these basic oppositions.[38]

Like Luther's, the basis for Calvin's oppositions lay in part in the realization of an actual contrast between the institutional life of established religious practice and the idealized image of religious practice depicted in Scripture. Whereas Luther's polarities operated primarily as negative and positive nodes, respectively, which needed to be brought together in a creative act of unity, however, Calvin's discursive field was a step further removed from actual experience and therefore required an intermediate stage in producing arguments that articulated with religious practice. Calvin's polarities consisted less purely of negative and positive valences and more of analytic abstractions concerning the essential characteristics of reality. Both the finite and the infinite, the material and the spiritual, were inevitable features of existence, and they were always forced to relate to each other. It was in the improper mixing of the two that Calvin depicted a strong negative valence, and this valence set up the basis from which his own arguments could serve as a positive resolution. His critique of Catholic "idolatry," for example, focused on a condemnation of the improper mixing of the spiritual and material in worship. He perceived idolatry as a fundamental evil because it mixed the sacred and the profane, thereby domesticating God and robbing the divine of its wholly other, transcendent quality.

Calvin's argument, on the surface, resembles a Durkheimian analysis of primitive taboo, namely, that the sacred and profane must be kept radically apart, and any blurring of the boundary separating the two becomes an instance of extreme pollution.[39] The frequent usage of pollution concepts in Calvin's rhetoric in fact reinforces this interpretation.[40] Calvin, however, was no dualist who believed in strictly separating the material from the spiritual. The two always come together, not only as a matter of ordinary existence but also—especially—in worship. Thus worship becomes the centerpiece of Calvin's theology and the focus of his greatest reforming efforts. The structure of his discursive field, in effect, first poses a contrast between the material and the spiritual but then draws an inevitable connection between the two, and it is this seam—this discursive intersection—that acquires exceptional power, either as a locus of supreme evil or as a source of ultimate good. It is in fact the necessity of this connection that gives rise to the most forceful of Calvin's polemical arguments. Whereas Luther is often able to recommend compromise or a position of moderation by bringing together the two facets of practicality and scripturality, Calvin associates inherent evil or good with the very manner in which this mixing takes place.

The method by which Calvin's ideology becomes articulated with socially contextualized action, therefore, differs in at least one potentially significant respect from the same process in Luther. Whereas Luther's discursive field requires proper action to be distanced from the relatively stylized negative valence attached to the concrete institutional religious practices of the past, Calvin's places the believer in a constantly tension-ridden zone of potential danger from an improper mixing of the material and the spiritual. Luther's actor can resolve the question of proper behavior within a fairly wide realm of discretionary practice, thereby conforming to Luther's more general emphasis on individuality and freedom. Calvin's actor lives with perpetual uncertainty, perhaps less so because of the inherent uncertainty of predestination that Weber emphasized than because of the more complex location of evil itself in Calvinist discourse. Faced with the possibility of improperly mixing the material and the spiritual, the Calvinist actor, like Luther's, must exercise responsibility in the actual world, but must do so with greater care. This degree of care must come partially from within but also requires to a considerable extent the care of the religious community. Thus Calvin's own writings and the work of his followers are to an important degree concerned with providing instruction in the form of specified ethical guidelines, with "regulative" standards of worship, and with the more collective aspects of religious community.

Calvin's emphasis on discipline—the systematic ascetic ethical life that interested Weber—can perhaps be understood best as a joint construction of his distinctive discursive field and the social circumstances with which the Reformation was faced by the time Calvin's leadership began to emerge.[41] Sensing the danger of idolatry from an improper fusion of the material and spiritual, he was able to argue not only against the religious practices of the Catholic church but also against those who sought compromise and fellow reformers who favored different styles of worship. In relation to both the latter groups, Calvin's framework encouraged a stronger level of commitment among his followers to the tenets of his segment of the reforming movement. In response to moderate Catholic theologians and humanists who accused the Protestants of perpetuating disputes over trivial issues, his arguments elevated the question of acceptable patterns of worship to the highest level of priority. The proper exercise of one's worshipful actions toward God ceased to be a matter of discretion and became a duty:

> "There is nothing to which all men should pay more attention, nothing in which God wishes us to exhibit a more intense eagerness than in endeavoring that the glory of his name may remain undiminished, his kingdom be advanced, and the pure doctrine, which alone can guide us to true worship, flourish in full strength."[42]

The very choice of language suggests the intensity of activity that the believer is enjoined to demonstrate in avoiding idolatry and in pursuing the good: "pay more attention," "intense eagerness," "endeavoring," "be advanced," "flourish in full strength."

The motivational element in Calvin's discourse rests, however, not on an appeal to duty alone but on developing an additional vertical polarity in which to situate his call for action. Whereas the initial polarity that establishes the basis for his discussion of the improper mixing of the sacred and the profane takes place primarily on the horizontal plane of human existence, the vertical axis in which his motivational arguments are situated focuses on the distinction between those things that weight one down and the higher truths that pull one up. On the lower level are the props associated with false worship, carnal conceptions of God, futile aspirations, and confusion in searching along misguided avenues for God. On the higher level is God himself, glorious and awe inspiring, calling the faithful to enter into a covenant relationship, and raising the believer's heart above the world. From the higher end of the vertical axis come two kinds of divine initiative: the "calling" that compels the chosen, both individually and collectively (as a covenant people), to seek the will of God; and God's commandments, a source of specific guidance and encouragement. Both, as it were, draw the faithful up the ladder toward God and away from the false pursuits of the unregenerate. As motivation, then, Calvin's imagery provides resources from above that can be used to sustain action of a pure and more zealous variety.

Built into this imagery is an inducement to respond as well. Calvin establishes an exchange relationship between the person and

God along his vertical axis. On the one hand, God provides gifts of both a general (divine law) and a specific (the calling) kind. On the other hand, God expects a worshipful response in return. Especially for those who have been called, and therefore given the possibility to elevate themselves above the folly of ordinary life, this response must be active and obedient. God's gifts derive from an inscrutable, providential hand; in the same manner, the regenerate person should respond without holding anything back. Once again, then, Calvin's discourse calls for an intense level of commitment among the faithful.

As one considers the structure of Reformation ideology, it becomes evident, therefore, that the institutional contexts in which this ideology was produced did not determine its content. Yet the ideology did articulate meaningfully with its institutional contexts at the same time that it transcended these contexts. The political autonomy attained by certain segments of the municipal and territorial ruling elite provided resources crucial to the advancement of the Reformation: military protection, financial aid, personal patronage, certification. These allies figured into the reformers' depictions of the good, just as the landowners, peasants, and representatives of the church figured into their portrayals of evil. In the most direct sense, the ecclesiastical order and its broad social underpinnings served as a negative valence in the reformers' construction of their own discursive field. The positive end of this discursive axis, however, was a more inventive phenomenon. Although it depended heavily on advances in literacy, demands for preaching in the vernacular, and the revival of biblical scholarship, insofar as Scripture was its most tangible symbol, it was also the reformers' most creative contribution. In pitting the godly, spiritual, and scriptural against the temporal world of institutional practice, they opened up an ideological space, as it were, in which to pose alternative forms of conduct and thought.

The reformers' role cannot be understood simply as one of negating the established social order, or even of formulating a vision of an alternative to this order, however. As the foregoing has shown, the reformers' discursive fields served mainly as a symbolic framework in which to situate the religious actor. Within this framework, the actor was then credited with certain moral obligations, including those of exercising discretion, acting responsibly, serving godly ends within the temporal world, and following proper regulative standards in worship and in ethical conduct. The reformers provided neither strict prescriptions for all avenues of personal and collective conduct nor a purely idealized vision of a perfect life to be struggled for in a vain hope of actually succeeding. They offered a framework that concretized the various forces, both negative and positive, in relation to which the individual was likely to function. And within this framework, they constructed the necessary resources—including freedom of will, hope of forgiveness, and divine guidance—for the individual to function as a morally responsible actor.

The discursive fields invented by the reformers played a central role in articulating Reformation ideology with its social contexts. On the one hand, the contexts in which these fields were produced provided symbolic material from which the basic discursive polarities were defined. The moral actors who became, in a sense, figural representatives of the ways in which to function within these symbolic frameworks were sufficiently realistic, even complex, to generate identification.[43] Moreover, the genres chosen by the reformers— sermons, commentaries, disputations—reinforced the opportunities to link theoretical discourse with concrete, collectively recognizable episodes, and encouraged a great deal of repetition of basic themes. On the other hand, the integrity of the reformers' own discursive fields transcended the immediate concerns presented by specific social situations. And the figural role played by the moral actors within these fields was sufficiently open ended to speak to individuals long after these situations themselves had changed.

Reformation Outcomes: Costs and Benefits

And what of the Reformation's immediate social and political consequences? Those states having enough autonomy to encourage religious reforms generally acquired quite tangible rewards for their efforts. Revenue from church lands filled government coffers, providing resources with which to repay loans, build up military forces and fortifications, and expand bureaucracies, all with minimal indebtedness to the nobility.

Geneva's public revenues rose sixfold during the quarter century following the seizure of ecclesiastical property and played an important role in maintaining the city's independence against Hapsburg advances in the area by improving its fortifications and establishing diplomatic relations with Protestant allies.[44] Basel and Strasbourg used their newfound wealth for similar purposes.[45] Erfurt's magistrates manipulated religious policy both to enlarge their control over urban affairs and to reduce the city's debts.[46] Strasbourg, Nuremberg, Antwerp, and Amsterdam used the occasion of the Reformation to seize control of hospitals and relief chests, impose vagrancy laws, and restrict begging, thereby gaining greater control over the labor market.[47] Hesse secularized approximately fifty monasteries in its territories, using approximately 60 percent of the proceeds to establish hospitals and poorhouses for the needy and directing the remaining 40 percent to the court itself.[48] In the Palatine Frederick II extracted approximately 100,000 florins from the church upon declaring himself in support of the Reformation.[49] In Sweden Gustav Vasa used the revenues from church lands to pay German mercenaries and build up a large standing army free of noble control and to repay debts to Lübeck. The crown's land holdings also expanded to the point that more than two-thirds of the entire country was under royal control by 1560.[50] Denmark's revenues from church lands and tithes caused royal income to triple, permitting the state to reduce mortgages on crown lands, employ mercenaries, and build up the royal fleet.[51] Revenues also tripled in England as a result of the dissolution, providing resources to cover a substantial share of the king's rapidly rising expenses.[52] Another consequence of the sale of church lands in England was that a new kind of landowner came into prominence, including wealthy merchants from neighboring towns or from London with liquid capital for making improvements, or bankers and moneylenders who acquired an indirect stake in the land through mortgages. Whereas the monastic houses had used surpluses from marketable products to expand the number of monks and nuns they supported, the new secular owners turned surpluses toward capital improvements, pursued reclamation and drainage schemes more aggressively, increased productivity, and imposed shorter-term escalating leases on tenants.[53]

In northern Europe and England church lands were also used to solidify patronage systems. Lands were sold or leased to families with political connections, including members of the court, professionals, merchants, and financiers, rather than the wealthier and more powerful nobility.[54] In the Low Countries merchant oligarchies used the Reformation to tighten control over city councils, suppress seigneurial rights, and acquire land.[55] The Reformation also fostered mutual defense leagues which became instrumental in protecting central and northern Europe from Hapsburg efforts to consolidate and expand the empire, among which were the Schmalkaldic League and various alliances among Denmark, Sweden, England, Hesse, and Saxony.[56] Wealthier and more powerful members of these alliances supported weaker members financially and militarily.[57]

The Protestant heresies also weighed heavily on the Hapsburg empire. Taking the defense of universal Christian faith under the church as its raison d'être, it was forced to increase taxes, sell off imperial lands, and raise levels of indebtedness in the Netherlands in order to execute its vast military policies against the Protestants.[58] On top of Spain's conflicts in Italy, with France, and against the Turks, the Protestants added a tremendous administrative burden which contributed in no small measure to its gradual economic decline. Most important, the Hapsburgs were unable to unify Europe under a single imperial regime, a fact, it has been suggested, that contributed greatly to the political conditions necessary for capitalism to emerge and flourish in Europe.[59] With the passage of time, merchants, artisans, and other refugees fled from Catholic sections of Europe, and England, the Netherlands, and Scandinavia became the dominant economic forces in the entire region.

There were, perhaps, enough economic and political gains to be derived from the Reformation that the regimes supporting it had little need to examine closely the actual content of its ideas. Nevertheless, these ideas were highly compatible with the states' interests. What made them especially so was their tendency to *desacralize* existing religious authority, thereby giving the states an opportunity to exercise greater control over religious affairs. During the Lutheran, Zwinglian, and early Calvinist phases of the Reformation, desacralization was, as we have seen, a prominent theme in evangelical teachings.[60] The mass was desacralized, rituals and sacraments that bound people to the church were attacked, priestly authority was denied, and in its place the authority of faith and conscience was substituted. These teachings consisted not only of abstract doctrine but also and more tangibly of practices that radically altered the relations between believers and the church. All of the leading reformers recognized the importance of this fact and devoted as much of their efforts to stripping the church of its sacred authority as they did to developing new conceptions of religious authority. As one writer has observed recently in discussing Luther: "The longer the perspective, the easier it is to interpret his career as an ascending series of rejections— beginning with paternal authority and going on to canonist tradition, papal supremacy, the old sacramental system and finally the Emperor himself."[61]

The Reformation drew upon, consolidated, and significantly added to a rich legacy of religious symbolism in its bid to desacralize the church. The figure of the Antichrist, applied to the papacy, played a prominent role in reformed preaching, as did woodcuts of the Harlot Rome, collective acts of iconoclasm in conjunction with feast days and carnivals, mock processionals, satires of the mass, book burnings, and desecrations of religious objects.[62] At the grassroots level Protestant teaching had the effect of desacralizing the patron-client relations which existed directly between priests and laity and correlatively between landowners and peasants. Whereas the customary duties of the late medieval priest created moral bonds of service and obligation with the laity, including public confession, administration of the sacraments, and attendance on the sick, the reformers' emphasis on scripturalism and the doctrine of *sola fide* reduced these relations primarily to that of preaching and hearing.[63] Distinctions between laity and clergy were minimized, mutual obligations among the laity themselves were emphasized, and the universal nature of religious truth and salvation was stressed.[64]

Natalie Zemon Davis's suggestion that popular religious practice among the Protestants in Lyons resembled a "loose network" is a particularly insightful metaphor to describe the type of moral order implicit in evangelical teachings.[65] Protestantism dissociated religious practice from particular establishments, shrines, places, and objects. It rejected fixed statuses in the community and permanent membership in traditional organizations. Instead it taught acceptance toward newcomers and openness toward fellow travelers. Rather than undergirding hierarchical patron-client relations with religious ritual, it taught mutuality in charitable service and moral responsibility based on voluntary commitment. It was, as Proudhon later pointed out, "the germ of dissolution which was to enable people to pass imperceptibly from the moral rule of fear to the moral rule of liberty."[66] In a word, the Reformation stressed freedom—freedom which enhanced the options of both the rising merchant class, as Davis observes, and the autonomous magisterial, princely, and monarchical regimes. And yet, this freedom was conditioned by a clear sense of authority, both political and within the community of religious discourse.

With the exception of the widely persecuted Anabaptist sects, the reformers acknowledged the authority of civil government over the church and looked to it to settle religious disputes.[67] In other words, the reformers needed the secular authority of the state in their struggle against ecclesiastical tradition and were willing to grant it considerable legitimacy in their teachings in return for its cooperation. In practice this meant the sacrifice of a number of ecclesiastical prerogatives to the state, including the selection of bishops, appointment of preachers to vacant parishes, and payment of clergy salaries. The reformers also turned to the state to issue decrees and for aid in eliminating the mass, protection from ecclesiastical persecution, and guidance in dealing with heretics.[68] Only later, with the repression of the Huguenot movement in France, the revolt in the Netherlands, and the Scottish Reformation under John Knox, did the reformers adopt an explicitly militant stance that challenged the state's authority. Only then did they seek to weld religious minorities into disciplined cadres oriented toward the seizure of power. During its initial phases, the Reformation primarily reinforced the decision-making power of the regimes that supported it, rather than posing ideas that challenged the state.

Most of the immediate, tangible economic gains that regimes acquired from the Reformation were, however, to prove transient. Protestant areas did in fact develop at a more rapid pace economically than did most of the Catholic areas. But these differences were already becoming apparent at the outset of the Reformation and, according to most economic historians, were probably only an indirect consequence of the Reformation, if they were affected by it at all. Nor did the Reformation ensure that states would remain financially and administratively autonomous from the landed elite. The commercial expansion that contributed to the autonomy of particular regimes during this period brought vast increases in wealth to the landed sector in many areas as well in the form of rising grain and wool prices, increased land values, and higher rents—wealth that the landlords could use to repurchase political influence. Then during the second half of the sixteenth century, partly as a result of the religious divisions produced by the Reformation and partly because of the declining economic positions of Spain and the Mediterranean, military conflicts increased, severely taxing the financial resources of most European states and forcing them into renewed dependence on the landowners. Antwerp, Strasbourg, and many of the towns in southern Germany were unable to maintain their municipal autonomy against the military power of the Hapsburgs and were eventually reclaimed for the church. In the northern Low Countries the struggle for independence proved successful in the end, but not without creating divisions between the magistrates, landlords, and the stadt-holder which were to play an important role in Dutch politics over the course of the following century. After 1560 the nobility in both Denmark and Sweden began to regain their former control over the state; relations with Lübeck once again worsened, and conflict be-tween the two countries left both financially weakened. In England the nobility recovered sufficiently to encourage a Catholic revival, and conflict between court and country gradually deepened to the point of civil war. Even by the end of the reign of Henry VIII debts and military expenditures had largely wiped out the temporary gains from the secularization of church wealth. As Geoffrey Elton remarks: "If the dissolution was undertaken to secure the financial independ-ence of the Crown, it failed."[69]

Nevertheless, the short-term inducements offered by the Ref-ormation had been sufficient to gain for it the support of a number of Europe's leading regimes and thereby to ensure its impact on the evolution of modern religion in particular and modern culture more generally. Most apparently, the Reformation expanded the array of official doctrines and practices encompassed within Christianity, ren-dering them more adaptable to the increasingly heterogeneous social environment of early modern Europe. From a highly centralized, uniform set of doctrines whose legitimacy depended greatly on claims of universality, Western religion was transformed into a diverse set of geographically and institutionally segmented practices patterned to conform with different political and economic configurations. Above all, the Reformation severed the link between the ideal of Christian universalism and Hapsburg efforts to implement this idea in the form of a politically unified empire. From that point onward the evolution of Western religion came to depend less on the fortunes of any single political entity than on the economic and political strength of Europe as a whole.

The Reformation also succeeded in maintaining much of the religious rationality that had developed within the church since the high Middle Ages, while reinfusing Christianity with legitimacy de-rived from Scripture and faith. The fact that a considerable degree of rationality was retained during this process was in no small measure itself a function of the Reformation's relation to the state. Those branches of the Reformation that denied the state any legitimate role in religious affairs—the so-called radical Reformation—showed the strongest propensity to splinter into purely localized practices that relied on the charismatic authority of particular leaders. They also emphasized direct divine revelation as opposed to codified scriptural or institutional authority and frequently deemphasized the need for standardized rules or procedures for the conduct of ecclesiastical affairs. In comparison, accounts of the Lutheran, Calvinist, and Anglican branches of the Reformation indicate that reliance on civil governments for such tasks as the establishment of churches, prosecution of heresy, and settlement of religious disputes necessitated standards of rationality that the state had begun to implement in codifying its own statutes and laws and in developing decision-making procedures.[70] These included standards of consistency in treating similar cases and in establishing juridicial precedent, standards of universalism in dealing with matters within the state's jurisdiction, and standards of procedural rationality in preparing and presenting cases concerning doctrinal disputes.

In view of the significant role played by the state in initiating and defending religious reforms, it appears difficult to sustain the argument that the Reformation led directly to greater institutional separation between religion and state, except perhaps conceptually, as I have noted. In the long run the leading states of western Europe found that close relations with particularistic religious traditions were a liability in dealing with domestic conflicts and in maintaining stable international relations and as a result gradually opted for a hands-off policy in the area of religion that was tantamount to institutional differentiation between religion and the state. But these developments were long in coming. In the interim the immediate patterns of the Reformation depended heavily on the states' involvement in religious affairs.

PART II

The Enlightenment

5

Mercantilism and
the House of Learning

THE ENLIGHTENMENT is often compared with the Protestant Reformation in terms of its significance for the subsequent development of modern culture. If one attempts to see the Enlightenment as it was experienced by contemporaries, rather than viewing it through the lens of history, however, its significance is not as immediately apparent as that of the Reformation. In contrast to the part played by the Reformation, the Enlightenment's role in mobilizing large segments of the European population was quite limited. It did not initiate new systems of worship or overturn the hierarchies governing ecclesiastical institutions. In no direct or immediate fashion was it responsible for peasant uprisings, revolts, or wholesale land reforms. Its effects among contemporaries were restricted largely to limited circles of courtiers, artists, scientists, pamphleteers, playwrights, and intellectuals. The leading books, plays, performances, and theories it produced failed to attract an audience much beyond these limited circles.[1] And even the content of the Enlightenment depended heavily on the received wisdom of the past.

Yet the circles in which the Enlightenment flourished included many individuals in positions of power, many with disproportionate stocks of wealth, and many with access to the most influential channels of communication. The Enlightenment sank its roots deeply into these circles. It became established in more than the ephemeral moods of intellectual opinion and artistic taste. It took root in informal gatherings and in university lecture halls, in scientific academies and in state bureaucracies. Beginning in the seventeenth century as a correlate of mercantilist policies, greater and more important shares of cultural production became concentrated in the state and among the influential ruling factions surrounding the state. The arena constituted by these ruling elites gradually expanded and became transformed during the eighteenth century into a public sphere. It was here that the Enlightenment secured the necessary resources and gained an appropriate level of autonomy to grow and to supplant the more traditional institutions of cultural production.

Religious Conflict and the General Crisis

To the extent that economic and political resources were, as we saw in Part I, essential to the production and dissemination of a new ideological orientation, some attention must be given at the outset to the turmoil that occupied these resources for most of the period from the middle of the sixteenth century to the middle of the seventeenth century. This turmoil had much to do with the timing of the Enlightenment. Starting with the religious wars that dominated much of central Europe, France, and the Low Countries during the second half of the sixteenth century, and culminating in the Thirty Years' War and the English Civil War, this period was relatively devoid of the secure and generally prosperous conditions that later were to provide the basis for the Enlightenment. New ideologies and more extreme variants of older ideologies were produced in abundance. But the institutionalization of a fundamentally altered world view that would significantly supplant the religious tensions born of the Reformation was an outcome that had to await the cessation of this turmoil.

In contrast to the commercial, agricultural, and demographic expansion that had characterized the early part of the sixteenth century, and that would again become evident by the start of the eighteenth century, most of the intervening years were characterized by recession and stagnation. Population failed to expand significantly and in some areas actually declined as a result of war, emigration, and declining birth rates.[2] Major crop failures occurred in 1629 and 1630, in 1636 and 1637, in the period between 1648 and 1651, and again between 1660 and 1662. Temporary increases in grain prices accompanied each of these failures, but over the longer run, prices for agricultural commodities, rents, and peasant incomes all fell. In Spain, a general decline in economic fortunes, coupled with continuing military expenditures, forced the crown to declare bankruptcy approximately every twenty years between 1557 and 1647.[3] In the Low Countries the economic expansion that had returned following the religious and political struggles of the second half of the sixteenth century came to a halt around 1648 and did not return until the 1680s. In France some growth in population was evident, but most indicators of economic strength remained stagnant until late in the seventeenth century: silver imports from the New World essentially collapsed during the first half of the century; grain prices declined, leaving peasants with smaller incomes; textile production peaked around 1635; and the Baltic trade gradually diminished. Only in England was the general stagnation of the period mixed with some significant signs of growth, especially in foreign trade and the woolens industry. The common denominator in most sections of Europe is more aptly characterized as one of retrenchment, in which a series of "slumps, bankruptcies and shocks" dominated the Contintent while Europe "in effect prepared for a new phase in the long continuity of economic history."[4]

Under these circumstances, the various factions of the ruling elite struggled with one another for scarce resources and imposed tighter restrictions on the populations that were subordinate to them. Members of the landed aristocracy continued to oppose factions of the elite who were more closely aligned with the court and the state bureaucracy. With the overall contraction of economic opportunities, monarchs and state officials found it more difficult to resist the demands of these factions. Increasingly, the role of the central bureaucracy became that of arbitrating competing demands—a role that periodically devolved into forcible repression and that often resulted in the interests of the lower classes being sacrificed to those capable of pressing their demands more forcefully. Peasants suffered from the general squeeze of declining grain prices and from constant, if not increasing, tax rates. In addition, systems of *intendants* and justices of the peace extended the watchful eye of the state more effectively into the routine activities of local villages, and religious reforms in the Catholic church and among the various Protestant churches sought to impose greater doctrinal and ritualistic conformity on the population.[5]

The broader social environment in these years was also conditioned by a recurrence of violent uprisings, changes in regime, and wars among the major European powers. During the four decades preceding the reign of Louis XIV, for example, France was shaken by three major revolts among the aristocracy, seven years of religious war, two major rebellions, two changes in the monarchy, and a series of peasant uprisings. England sustained major regime changes throughout the century as a result of the continuing battle for supremacy between Parliament and the crown, and more generally between "court and country." Between 1640 and 1710 it was engaged in war almost continuously, sustaining more casualties than during the entire following century, including those resulting from wars with the United States and France.[6] In 1650 a palace revolution created a new form of government in the United Provinces of the Netherlands, and in 1672 another abrupt change in regime occurred following the murder of Johan de Witt. Other revolts included those in Catalonia in 1640 and in Portugal in the same year, unrest in Andalusia the following year, and the uprisings in Naples and Sicily in 1647. Among the major societies, international tension was also a predominant characteristic of the period: in only one year between 1600 and 1667 were the major powers not at war with one another.[7]

The Mercantilist Equilibrium

After the middle of the seventeenth century, a more stable pattern of international relations increasingly became evident among the major European powers, and this pattern was to provide the specific context in which the cultural antecedents of the Enlightenment were to appear. Military conflict among the major powers did not cease, but domestic upheaval gradually subsided, central governments became stronger, and the principles on which trade and diplomacy were based appear to have become clearer. Mercantilism as a concept was not applied to this system until later, but as an operational system it was evident in the ways in which states conducted themselves in relation to one another and their own populations. The Enlightenment's leading contributors were to challenge the assumptions on which this system functioned, calling, for example, for greater freedom in economic policies and less intervention by the state. Nevertheless, it was this system that provided the economic and political expansion from which the Enlightenment grew.

Mercantilism was above all a method of generating income for the state. It functioned as a system of state planning and state encouragement of trade and other economic activities. Merchants and investors were granted charters and monopoly rights by the state. In return, they loaned money to the state and brought in taxable revenues. From these receipts, the state paid interest on its loans, protected shipping routes, and engaged in military activities when necessary to protect markets.

During the second half of the seventeenth century, France and England increasingly became the dominant mercantilist powers. The Dutch Republic rivaled France and England in economic strength but relied on free trade to a greater extent than on protectionism to maintain its position in the international economy. Increasingly, Prussia and the smaller German states, Sweden, Spain, and Russia were also drawn into the mercantilist system. Its functioning was in fact contingent on the relative balance that existed among the principal mercantilist countries. Military campaigns, accordingly, tested the relative strength of these countries periodically, and capital flowed across state boundaries as taxes and prices fluctuated. These conflicts were intensified by the presupposition that the overall amount of resources for which each country could compete was relatively fixed.[8] The system also presupposed a relatively stable population, or at least one that grew more slowly than the supply of food, for if the demand for food increased too rapidly, food prices would increase, turning the terms of trade in an unfavorable direction, and giving the landed interests a stronger hand in formulating state policies. The most reliable outlet for excess population growth was colonization. And colonies played an increasingly important role in supplying raw materials, cheap labor, and markets for the goods produced by, and reexported from, the core states. Each state sought to avoid having to export bullion. Consequently, much effort was devoted to obtaining favorable terms of trade, finding inexpensive materials, keeping shipping costs down, preventing taxes and labor costs from driving up prices above competitive levels, reducing imports of food and clothing, and maintaining protective monopolies over colonial markets.

Mercantilism was thus a highly regulated form of economic activity in which the state played a central role. Offices were established to supervise exports and imports. Trading companies were given monopoly rights by the state to open colonial and long-distance markets, and these companies relied heavily on the state's prestige and underwriting to raise loans. The state also passed laws that created protective tariffs around domestic markets. It chartered shipping companies and gave them naval protection. It used military force to obtain colonies. And it enforced trade embargoes when necessary to keep commerce under its control.

The relations among mercantile states, therefore, were characterized primarily by competition. Each state operated along similar lines to those of its competitors, adopting different policies primarily because of differences in domestic resources, but always for the same ends. To the extent that mercantilism constituted a single system, it was a system that depended on this similarity of action, more than it did on cooperation or overt agreements. Indeed, the underlying principles on which it operated reinforced the antagonisms that states displayed toward one another. As Klaus Knorr observes: "The salient feature of this international system . . . was the existence of antagonistic drives coupled with the almost total lack of any common and, hence, unifying, interest."[9]

If mercantilism perpetuated war as a result of this antagonism, it nevertheless solidified the domestic power of the state by drawing a significant cross-section of the ruling elite into a dominant coalition. Monarchs, aristocrats, merchants, and state bureaucrats all benefited from the revenues that mercantilism generated. Though the states differed in backgrounds and in specific interests, their role increasingly drew them into a common framework. It made them dependent on collective action and presented them with policies that affected their collective well-being. It necessitated an expanding array of agencies and bureaus and made them responsible for an increasingly complex set of policies and regulations. Rarely, one historian has written, have the resulting laws and edicts "been more complex."[10] The state's validity seems not to have been questioned, at least for a time, even when it failed. Mercantilism gave the state reason to penetrate into all realms of social, economic, political—and, increasingly, cultural—life.[11]

Cultural Production and the State

Along with the other activities in which the mercantilist state became involved, cultural production became an object of increasing interest. Technical and utilitarian motives played an important role in focusing some of this interest. Experimentation was encouraged with ways of increasing crop yields, with further refinements in navigation and ballistics, and in metallurgy and the manufacture of pumps, optics, and dyes. But cultural production was also promoted for ceremonial reasons. Each of the major powers was locked in head-to-head competition with the others. Mercantilist theory dictated that such competition was inevitable and that the equilibrium of the entire system depended on it. Rulers who governed responsibly needed to consider all policies in terms of their contribution to the overall wealth and power of their domains. Cultural production was one of the ways in which wealth and power could be demonstrated. By sponsoring cultural activities, rulers could show their strength to their competitors.

Rulers had of course patronized cultural activities for centuries. The work of great architects, artists, musicians, and writers supplied the artifacts with which sovereigns displayed their glory. During the sixteenth century, with the development of stronger state bureaucracies, the state's role in patronizing the arts and literature had become increasingly common, and this tendency was accentuated further in the seventeenth century.[12] Except for the occasional largesse of a particularly wealthy and powerful regime, however, these opportunities embraced a relatively small number of cultural producers. For the most part, the institutional locations in which writers, artists, musicians, and intellectuals had been supported were the religious hierarchies and the universities.

Except for the privileged few who were able to secure patronage from the court, learning remained firmly under the monopoly of religious authorities and university officials. And in some instances the training received in these settings was excellent. The Collège de Clermont, for example, provided an entire generation of intellectual leaders in France—among them Voltaire—with a solid academic foundation. Rather than merely inculcating basic technical skills or reinforcing the piety of their students, these institutions, like the academies that succeeded them, were designed to mold their students into cultivated men of taste, and to this end, training was given in a wide range of classical philosophy, in literature, and in the dramatic arts. Yet these institutions were also limited in the opportunities they provided for intellectual innovation. Professors and curricula generally faced close supervision by ecclesiastical authorities. The main focus of training was on ancient wisdom rather than contemporary customs and issues. Training in mathematics was often sparse. And insufficient economic resources generally imposed severe restrictions on the number of new recruits who could find employment in these institutions.

The growth of the mercantilist state, and its increasing role as a patron of cultural production, therefore, constituted an important opportunity to broaden and vitalize the institutional contexts in which cultural producers typically functioned. As the leading practitioner of mercantilist policies, the French state under Louis XIV led the way in actively promoting cultural production. Following the Fronde, which ended in 1653, the great nobles were increasingly made dependent on the king for financial support and began to settle in Paris and live at court. Their physical proximity, along with common standards of taste and decorum, combined to promote participation in the salons that soon began to appear in Paris and encouraged them to attend royally sponsored dramatic and musical events.[13] After 1662, under Colbert's supervision, the royal treasury achieved a surplus; industry was encouraged; communication was improved; and the entire population came under closer economic, legal, and military supervision. The same tendencies affected literature, science, and the arts. Academies were founded for literature, sculpture, science, and architecture; and beyond the mere act of founding these academies, the government also exercised close control over their appointments and routine business. Incentives were provided in the form of pensions and royal subscriptions on the one hand, while on the other hand controls were imposed in the form of censorship, arrest, exile, and imprisonment.

In all of this the increasing awareness of national identity, and the growing sense of national competition, that accompanied the rise of mercantilism played an important role in stimulating the founding of academies and the state's encouragement of scholarship more generally. One indication of these tendencies was the initiation of academies specifically concerned with the promotion of national languages. Between the Italian Renaissance and the seventeenth century various fraternities and informal groups of scholars had advanced the use of vernacular language, had promoted its purity and elegance, and had fostered its territorial diffusion. With the growth of the mercantilist state in the seventeenth century these activities took on added significance, serving as mechanisms of national integration and therefore receiving official support. Most notable was Richelieu's Académie Française, begun in 1635, but an even earlier example was the Fruchtbringende Gesellschaft in Saxony, founded in 1617.[14]

Shortly after the founding of the Académie Française, a proposal, unsuccessful as it turned out, was also put forward to initiate a similar venture in England.[15]

Each of the major European powers promoted its own language and sponsored its own distinctive forms of cultural activity. But they also imitated one another, often adopting the same standards of fashion, architecture, music, and art in a seeming effort to demonstrate their membership in elite society and their commitment to common European norms. Typically the influence of the Italian Renaissance remained strong, but increasingly France set the standards in cultural tastes just as it provided leadership in mercantilist economic and political activities. Especially for the smaller and weaker states and principalities, imitating France provided a way of demonstrating national standing, and this imitation in turn encouraged the diffusion and production of new cultural styles.[16]

Science became the particular beneficiary of the mercantilist state. Because of its supposed potential for stimulating technological innovation, and perhaps because of its sheer novelty as well, science came to be one of the ceremonial activities that nearly all regimes felt compelled to support as a way of dramatizing their strength and sophistication. Through state-sponsored academies scientists received patronage, support for equipment, publishing rights, and respectability. The rising competition among states for their services gave them additional opportunities for employment, and sometimes reinforced the personal rivalries that resulted in scientific discoveries, criticism, and the formulation of alternative theories.[17] It also provided them with leverage that could be put to good advantage against overbearing patrons: alternative sources of employment, models to cite when bargaining for equipment and support, and in the final instance a refuge when political winds shifted and forced them into exile. With the domestic and international turmoil that characterized much of the seventeenth century, the migration of scholars and technicians across national boundaries did in fact play a significant role in broadening the locations in which scientific activity took place.[18] The increases in diplomacy and trade that mercantilism fostered also meant that scientists found it easier to forge communication networks across national boundaries and to benefit from philosophical and technical developments throughout the Continent.[19]

In addition to the relations that increasingly became evident between the state and science, an important connection between the state and the expressive arts was strengthened in these years. Court musicians and painters formed part of this connection, as I have already noted. Increasingly, writers were also drawn into a closer relation with the state. Some were given patronage as bibliographers and diplomatic secretaries, much in the same way that scientists were employed in these roles. In addition, the growing popularity of the royal stage became an important source of employment. It was in fact this employment that solidified the reputations of the period's greatest writers and gave them access to fortune and high society. Molière, for example, rose to prominence as the greatest French writer of the latter half of the seventeenth century after having spent thirteen years in penury with a traveling theater company in the provinces. His fortune suddenly changed in 1658, when he was asked to present a performance for Louis XIV at the Louvre. Until his death fifteen years later, nearly all his plays were written for royal audiences.[20]

If the state was already becoming a prominent aspect of the institutional contexts in which cultural production was located, it nevertheless provided a fairly precarious base of operation. Patronage was as yet far from being institutionalized on any secure or consistent footing. Changes in regimes, in regimes' financial well-being, or in the whims of rulers and their advisers could spell an almost instant termination to the good fortune that writers, artists, and scientists enjoyed. Even the most prominent writers' livelihoods fluctuated wildly, depending on rulers' whims and audiences' reactions to their works. Despite his prestige as a writer, for example, Molière found royal favor highly capricious; he was intermittently in trouble with the authorities, and the receipts of his theater company varied tremendously from season to season.

More generally, the evidence of prosperity in scholarship and the arts that had been witnessed in the 1660s and 1670s was interrupted by the economic and political difficulties that spread across Europe during the last decades of the century. By the 1680s, signs of stagnation were already appearing, especially in France. In 1683 the royal budget was faced with a sizable deficit, and in 1689, with the outbreak of the War of the League of Augsburg, the government defaulted on all the pensions on which men of science and literature depended. By the end of the war in 1697, government receipts were running only slightly more than a third of government expenditures. Over the next decade, poverty and famine resulted in bread riots

which occupied the authorities' attention, and the religious intoler-
ance that had surfaced in the revocation of the Edict of Nantes in
1685 intensified, leaving a much-reduced range of appropriate topics
for literary and philosophical speculation.[21]

Intellectual Antecedents

For all its difficulties and uncertainties, the scholarship produced
during the latter half of the seventeenth century did provide some
of the intellectual groundwork on which the Enlightenment writers
were able to build. New genres of literature and drama were experimented with. Science provided an intellectual framework in
which to think about broader philosophical and political issues. The
works of specific writers came to have a kind of symbolic significance
for those who were to become the leaders of the Enlightenment
itself. It was also possible to trace these intellectual currents into
concrete social networks that were to provide a basis for more fully
institutionalized modes of cultural production.

One of the intellectual developments of the seventeenth century
that was to play an indirect but powerful role in shaping the Enlightenment grew out of the religious conflicts, and particularly the sectarianism, that had been left in the wake of the Reformation.
Controversies between the various interpretations of Lutheran, Calvinist, and Anabaptist doctrine had played a significant role in the
political conflicts on the Continent during the preceding century.
Catholics and Protestants still found themselves at odds on many
issues. The controversies in England among Puritans, Anglicans,
Catholics, and members of smaller dissenting groups had also been
especially pronounced.

In France outright sectarianism in the form of separatist religious
movements did not break the church into distinct organizations, as
it did in England, but a serious cleavage did emerge within the church.
This cleavage came about as a result of the Jansenist movement and
the mutual antagonism that developed between it and the Jesuits.
The Jansenists emerged as a distinct movement only in the 1640s
after the publication of a book by Cornelius Jansen, bishop of Ypres.
The book was immediately denounced by the Jesuits, but over the
next half century its disciples attracted a large and influential following. Broadly speaking, the Jesuits had come to a theological position
that accommodated itself to the more secular spirit of the times by

stressing the goodness of human nature, free will, divine mercy, and moral leniency. The Jansenists, in contrast, wanted a return to the primitive church, believed that salvation must come from a conversion experience, held that strict penance should be observed in order for the believer to be admitted to the sacraments, and advanced doctrines of God and of the elect that were in many ways reminiscent of the teachings of Calvin. Jansenism gained ground as an opposition movement as a result of its appeal to Gallican opponents of papal authority and because of its attraction to anti-Jesuit and antiroyalist members of the nobility, especially in the Parlement of Paris. The significance of the Jesuit-Jansenist controversy for the later development of the Enlightenment lay primarily in the fact that by the end of the seventeenth century each faction had gained a firm institutional base and was thereby able to advance its views with some degree of freedom from official pronouncements aimed at imposing orthodoxy. Both sides had founded a number of colleges, and the Jesuits, for their part, took pride in providing a more broadly liberal curriculum than the Jansenists. This division, as we shall see in the next chapter, effectively weakened the religious authorities' capacity to restrict intellectual currents that ran counter to established traditions. On the Jesuit side, it also provided some legitimacy for a more tolerant orientation toward secular knowledge.[22] And it figured as part of the firsthand experience from which Enlightenment writers were prompted to denounce religious dogmatism and religious disputes.

The fact that Enlightenment writers wrote for—and were able to focus their efforts on—a highly restricted audience is also an important matter to understand in order to appreciate the kinds of intellectual genres on which they were able to draw. The literary genres chosen by the leading contributors to the Enlightenment were to a large degree already well known to the limited segment of the public that constituted the Enlightenment's audience. An epic poem such as *La Henriade* had a far more limited audience than a sermon, a religious tract, or even an allegory such as *Pilgrim's Progress*. It required some exposure to the kind of higher education that gave readers an appreciation of the classics and of literary style. In this respect, the Enlightenment was facilitated by the fact that higher education had been expanding in many places since the middle of the seventeenth century. Fueled initially by the demand for better-trained clergy on the part of both Protestant and Catholic bodies and then by the rising demand for a cultured civil service, this expansion added measurably to the ranks of elite readers who could appreciate the literary styles adopted by Enlightenment writers. There was, however, a more profound sense in which these styles were limited to a small elite. Even the most obscure theological treatises bore some connection to the broader mass population because they were assumed to have implications for religious practice. This connection could at least be visualized because of the vast institutional infrastructure linking people together in common modes of worship. The genres of literature on which the Enlightenment was founded, in contrast, grew out of the more limited contexts of courtly and aristocratic leisure. These contexts had always been the protected preserve of the elite, largely invisible to the general population. As the social environment changed in the eighteenth century, a larger number of people found it possible to participate in these pleasures. They remained pleasures, nevertheless, that were largely unavailable to the mass population. Rather than having to worry about the broader social consequences of their ideas, therefore, the philosophers who forged the Enlightenment were able to work in a relatively privileged environment. Their greatest restrictions came, on one side, from religious authorities who feared that their ideas *did* have broader consequences, and on the other side, from technically minded officials who hoped their ideas might have practical economic consequences. In between was a broad zone that could be devoted to the pursuit of entertainment and speculation. Some of the variation in the content of the Enlightenment from one city or country to another can in fact be understood as a function of the breadth of this zone. In England and France, for example, where the connections between the literary community and the state were relatively loose and informal, we find a high degree of philosophical speculation, fiction, poetry, and other kinds of literature written for elite entertainment. In Prussia and Scotland, by contrast, the linkages between literature and the state bureaucracy were usually tighter, involving membership on university faculties or in academies with technical concerns, and here we find a somewhat more restrained, practical, and of course utilitarian strand in the writings produced. What shines through in all these contexts, however, is the fact that the literary genres in which the Enlightenment writers worked, and the elite audiences for whom they worked, reinforced one another and shaped the subsequent directions in which Enlightenment discourse developed.

The strides that had been made in science during the seventeenth century are generally considered to have provided another important intellectual antecedent of the Enlightenment. It has been suggested, for example, that the Newtonian synthesis provided an image of cosmic order and harmony that gave writers in the eighteenth century the confidence to advocate greater freedom for the individual and to place greater faith in the free operation of the marketplace.[23] It has also been suggested that the pursuit of science, even apart from the content of scientific discoveries, came to symbolize reason and moderation as opposed to sectarianism, dogma, and ideological conflict. Science was something on which reasonable people could apparently agree and work together for the public good. To support science, even as an amateur, could thereby be conceived of as an act of public service. As the Enlightenment unfolded, therefore, it was not uncommon to find the terminology of science and reason used in broader arguments about the public good.[24] At this point in its development, science was not yet highly professionalized or strictly set apart by disciplinary boundaries. Thus, it was relatively common for scientific ideas to filter into other kinds of academic and artistic discourse.[25] Many of the Enlightenment's leading writers had in fact worked with scientific ideas or had engaged in scientific experimentation at some point in their careers. Montesquieu, for instance, began his career writing treatises on physics and physiology for the Academy of Bordeaux. Rousseau studied astronomy, medicine, and mathematics. Condillac, Condorcet, and Turgot were all familiar with the important works of their day in chemistry, natural history, and physics. Thus, there were often direct institutional and even personal linkages between science and the Enlightenment, as well as more general intellectual currents that were simply available in the culture at large.

Also at this relatively concrete level, the growth of science in the seventeenth century was to a significant extent responsible for setting a precedent for thinking of innovative intellectual endeavors in close connection with the state. As scholarship in the eighteenth century expanded into new areas of inquiry, it did so from an institutional base that was already centered on the state and its officials.[26] In addition to shaping the resources that were to be made available for intellectual pursuits, this institutional location became a constitutive element of so-called enlightened discourse itself. From the beginning, questions of the public good, the relations of political issues to the scholarly life, and the relevance of knowledge to the state were to play an important role in the Enlightenment.

Apart from these broader intellectual antecedents, the role of one writer in particular needs to be singled out: John Locke. The influence of his work on the Enlightenment, especially his ideas on knowledge, the mind, religion, tolerance, civil government, and political dissent, have of course been the focus of much debate. Not all of the similarities between his ideas and those of the major writers of the eighteenth century can be attributed to his work alone, nor were his ideas accepted uncritically. Nevertheless, certain features of the social context in which he wrote made him and his ideas particularly attractive to many of the writers who followed in his footsteps.

The immediate social context from which Locke's most important intellectual contributions emanated was the admixture of religious and political conflict that, as we have already seen, dominated the middle decades of the seventeenth century. Indeed, this conflict continued to be a decisive feature of English society during the Restoration period and only gained some degree of resolution in the Glorious Revolution of 1688. The turmoil in which Locke became involved began in 1670 with the highly secretive Treaty of Dover, an agreement between Charles II and Louis XIV in which the former promised to declare his adherence to the Catholic religion in return for an annuity and provision of troops from the French that would have rendered the English crown largely free from parliamentary restrictions. As word of this agreement began to leak out, staunch defenders of Protestantism who relied on parliamentary action to protect their interests became duly alarmed. Among the leaders of the parliamentary opposition that ensued was Anthony Ashley Cooper, the first earl of Shaftesbury, with whom Locke was intimately acquainted. From 1672 Locke became increasingly involved in Shaftesbury's political activities, conducting research, writing speeches, screening clerical appointments, maintaining a parliamentary journal, and performing secretarial duties in connection with Shaftesbury's trading and colonial interests.[27]

Between 1673 and 1675 Shaftesbury's opposition became increasingly strident, eventually provoking a sufficiently strong reaction from the crown that Locke sought voluntary exile in France and Shaftesbury himself was imprisoned. Locke's travels in France between 1675 and 1679 were in retrospect fortuitous for the French Enlightenment, for they sharpened many of the criticisms of religious and political absolutism that were later to find their way into his writings and were to prove attractive to the younger French dissidents who became leaders of the Enlightenment. During these travels Locke also operated as a spy on the French government, a role that may also have later enhanced his image among the French dissidents. In any event, the role that Locke was to play in English politics over the next decade provided him with ample opportunities to reflect both on the nature of political dissent and on government more generally.

By 1679 a relatively well organized group of dissidents had gathered around Shaftesbury, and during the next two years this group became increasingly active in pressing for the Exclusion Bill, which, had it been successful, would have excluded the Catholic heir, James II, from succeeding to the throne. When this strategy was defeated, the group around Shaftesbury, it now appears, became active members of the Rye House conspiracy, one aim of which was to assassinate Charles II. When these plans were discovered in 1683, Shaftesbury and most of his associates, including Locke, fled to Holland. For the next six years, Locke lived quietly in Holland and Utrecht, but evidence suggests that he was closely associated with the exiles who planned the unsuccessful Monmouth Rebellion in 1685, perhaps serving even as a financial conduit for the conspirators.[28]

Locke's *Two Treatises of Government*, composed in 1681 but not published until 1689, bore a decisive imprint of the public debates that had surrounded the Exclusion Bill. Although these treatises contained arguments that were distinctly his own, they also reflected the views that were evident at the time in political speeches, tracts, and sermons. Tolerance, the nature and sources of knowledge, questions about authority and the people, and issues of rights all had specific meanings in the context from which they emerged in addition to the more general uses to which they would be put by later generations of political theorists.

The impact of Locke's thinking on the Enlightenment was of course greatest in England. There it articulated closely with the particular communities of discourse with which Locke himself was associated; it drew on slogans made familiar in sermons and tracts; and it came to be regarded as a set of principles that legitimated the Glorious Revolution. The Scottish Enlightenment, which remained relatively distinct from the literary renaissance centered in London, also had direct institutional connections with the Lockean heritage. William Castares, who played a major role in reforming higher education in Scotland as principal at the University of Edinburgh, had been one of Locke's and Shaftesbury's coconspirators in the 1680s.[29] And it was Castares's nephew, Charles Mackie, who became the first professor of civil history at Edinburgh, and was an active member of one of the clubs at which the leaders of the Scottish Enlightenment gathered.[30]

Locke's influence was also particularly apparent in France. Voltaire was to serve as the principal intermediary, drawing heavily on Locke's ideas in his *Philosophical Letters*. Again, there were social connections to buttress mere intellectual affinities. How Voltaire came to be aware of Locke's work is generally attributed to his stay in England from 1726 to 1729 as a political exile. During this period Voltaire was in contact with John Gay, Alexander Pope, and Jonathan Swift, and he wrote *La Henriade* and began work on the *Philosophical Letters*. His decisive encounter with Locke's ideas had come some three years earlier, however, as a result of a visit to Viscount Bolingbroke, who was himself living in exile on the outskirts of Orléans, in December 1722. After this visit and some subsequent correspondence in which Bolingbroke recommended Locke's *Essay Concerning Human Understanding*, Voltaire's work began to move decidedly in the direction of Locke's ideas and showed increasing signs of deism and positivism.[31]

Historians have attributed Voltaire's attraction to Locke to an affinity of intellectual presuppositions: dissatisfaction with Cartesian philosophy, an interest in Newtonian science, a commitment to empirical philosophy. There were, however, less abstract aspects of Locke's biography that made him particularly suitable as a hero for the network of dissident young French intellectuals with whom Voltaire associated. A man who had run afoul of the authorities and been forced into exile was likely to hold some appeal to Voltaire in view of his own experience in the Bastille and his subsequent exile. Bolingbroke and Shaftesbury, as well as Shaftesbury's other close associate Alexander Pope, also shared this attraction for Voltaire. The French philosophe could also appreciate Locke's emphasis on religious toleration, having already run up against the harsh injunctions of the church. In addition, Locke's and Shaftesbury's anti-Catholicism, their leadership as opponents of monarchical absolutism, and their role in countering the French court's influence in England disposed them toward a favorable reception from Voltaire and his peers. Furthermore, Locke's association with Shaftesbury's coterie of artisans and merchants and the prominent position Locke had attained as a government adviser were not likely to be missed by someone who was himself from an artisan background and who aspired to a diplomatic career. In sum, Locke's social position and his role in the radical political unrest of the 1670s and 1680s made him a likely symbol of intellectual dissent that a new generation of Enlightenment leaders could draw upon for inspiration. It was not as if they had to depend strictly on the logical strength of differing philosophical arguments to arrive at their intellectual presuppositions. The figure of Locke fairly sprang out at them for a whole variety of contextual reasons as well.

Other ideological precedents for the Enlightenment also existed, just as surely as they did for the Reformation. During the seventeenth century pockets of freethinking poets who championed atheism and sexual promiscuity, for example, are known to have existed in France, Italy, and England. Their work, although never popular with a very wide audience, was familiar to most of the writers who became leaders of the Enlightenment.[32] Before the end of the seventeenth century, experiments with new forms of writing and with novel political ideas could be found. And at a more general level, the rediscovery of the classics during the Renaissance, the religious skepticism that had been initiated by the Reformation, and the progressive rationalism that had been advanced in both the Protestant and Catholic traditions all provided antecedents on which the Enlightenment writers could draw. The question, therefore, is not so much how or why the Enlightenment invented entirely new genres of discourse, for the appearance of invention was at least partly one of synthesis and adaptation from these earlier antecedents. The essential question rather concerns the conditions that permitted this kind of ideology to be produced on a much-expanded scale and the ways in which this ideology articulated with those conditions.

Economic Expansion: The Role of the Bourgeoisie

The broader social environment in which the Enlightenment developed, like that of the Protestant Reformation, was not static. The eighteenth century witnessed renewed growth in trade, in domestic production, in overseas colonization, and in population on a scale unknown since the first half of the sixteenth century.[33] Population estimates for Europe as a whole indicate an increase of only 10 percent during the seventeenth century, after a figure of 28 percent for the sixteenth century; but during the eighteenth century population rose by a dramatic 65 percent.[34] Agricultural productivity, after a long period of stagnation, increased in most areas at a rate faster than the growth in population. Correlatively, famine became less frequent, and food generally became more available, permitting the dominant powers such as England and France to reduce grain imports and in some years even to export agricultural goods, thereby reducing the likelihood of incurring an unfavorable balance of payments. Industrial production and trade also expanded. The number of colonies claimed by European powers increased by approximately 20 percent during the eighteenth century, prior to the losses sustained by the American War of Independence, and increasing proportions of overall trade flowed to and from the colonies. In France industrial production doubled, trade tripled, and colonial trade multiplied fivefold.[35] The population of England's colonies grew from less than a quarter of a million at the start of the seventeenth century to more than five million by the end of the century.[36] And British exports doubled between 1720 and 1763 alone.[37]

This expansion was perhaps unspectacular by standards that became commonplace in the nineteenth and twentieth centuries. But it was a notable contrast to the essentially static assumptions on which the mercantile system was built. Having predicated many of their policies during the second half of the seventeenth century on the supposition that each country could expand its wealth and power only at the expense of another, the major powers and many of the secondary powers discovered in the eighteenth century that expansion of a different sort was also possible. Extending themselves into the lucrative colonial trades was the most obvious means of generating economic growth. But increasingly, discovering cheaper and more mechanized means of producing goods also became a way of promoting economic expansion.

The most decisive feature of this expansion, according to the retrospective accounts that have dominated the social sciences during the last century, was the rise of the bourgeoisie. Members of the landed nobility increasingly found it possible to enlarge their resources by exploiting the timber, coal, or iron deposits on their land or to invest excess funds in commercial ventures. A growing segment of the elite invested in joint-stock companies, in commercial schemes sponsored by the state, and in the sugar, coffee, and rum trades. The bourgeoisie also grew in proportion as the number of families that were drawn directly into the professions, shipping, banking, and industry increased.

As the bourgeoisie expanded, it created a new market for cultural objects. Literate, for the most part, and wealthy enough to devote a share of its resources to nonessential expenditures, the bourgeoisie apparently made possible the development of newspapers and literary periodicals, an expansion of the book trade, greater opportunities for playwrights and composers, and a heightened interest in science, technology, and formal education in general.[38] In creating this demand, the bourgeoisie also presumably shaped the content of the major cultural innovations of the period. Increasingly, bourgeois tastes replaced the traditional styles favored by the aristocracy and the court, and the bourgeoisie's needs for legitimacy influenced the kinds of intellectual currents that gained popularity.[39]

If the analysis of the Reformation in Part I is any indication, however, the ideological changes that constituted the Enlightenment did not come into prominence simply because more individuals belonged to the bourgeoisie than in the past. The effects of broader changes in the social environment were mediated by the institutional contexts in which writers and artists performed their tasks. And, as the foregoing has suggested, these contexts were by the end of the seventeenth century closely associated with the state. It is, therefore, not only to the bourgeoisie but also to changes in the structure of the state that we must look to understand the ways in which the Enlightenment came to be institutionalized—or, in other cases, failed to be institutionalized.

I shall argue, based on comparisons of the nine leading societies in Europe at the time of the Enlightenment, that the institutional setting in which the Enlightenment was best able to flourish consisted of a conjuncture of two critical conditions: an enlarged state bureaucratic apparatus and a heterarchic division of authority within this apparatus. Growth in the central bureaucracy and other agencies of the state provided resources—patronage, academies and salons, printing facilities, titles and offices, and a concentrated audience—for Enlightenment writers and prompted discussion of core collective values. Shifting and cross-cutting cleavages and alliances among those who constituted this political center gave writers the relative autonomy they needed to produce abstract and innovative philosophical reflections. Together these conditions formed the "public sphere" in which Enlightenment thought emerged. The character of this public sphere, and writers' relation to it, I shall also argue, conditioned the form and content of Enlightenment discourse. Particularly important was the division that emerged in this period between private selves and public roles.

6

Cultural Production
in France and England

A N INESCAPABLE, but often neglected, feature of the French Enlightenment is its close proximity to the state. Everywhere one follows the philosophes—from the academies to the salons, in the workplace and the publishing houses—the imprint of the state is clearly evident. The eighteenth century was to a very large extent the product of developments beginning in the latter half of the seventeenth century, and these included the tight connection that had been created between the state and science under Colbert and Louis XIV. That connection now extended to encompass nearly all the institutional settings in which the Enlightenment writers pursued their craft.

The position of the church was still sufficiently strong that few writers could escape its influence, but over the course of the century this position underwent a marked decline. In most of the rural provinces the church remained the dominant cultural institution, controlling as much as one-tenth of the land, including the wealthiest and most powerful members of the community within its hierarchy, and supplying as many as six priests for every hundred residents.[1] The church produced books and sermons, controlled local education, dispensed poor relief, and used its voice in the courts, all of which contributed to the shaping of public opinion. In the country at large the ecclesiastical population, estimated at around 130,000, would have likely outnumbered the serious philosophes by at least 100 to

1. Yet most authorities agree that the eighteenth century was a period of slippage for the French church, especially in matters of lay participation in Paris and other cities, political control, revenue, and recruitment into religious orders.[2] In addition, the conflict between Jesuits and Jansenists, which reached new heights in the 1730s and 1740s, appears to have been a significant factor both in promoting dissatisfaction with the church and in preventing the church from applying its censorship powers more vigorously to attack the philosophes.[3]

Closely allied with the church, colleges and universities also experienced a relative decline as centers of intellectual activity during this period. Until at least the middle of the century French universities displayed little interest in the new ideas beginning to emerge in science, natural history, mathematics, and literature.[4] Most remained dedicated to the training of students for ecclesiastical service: only one of Paris's institutions offered a full year in the study of mathematics.[5] In medicine an even more radical failure to adapt to changing conditions was evident: the number of universities with active faculties of medicine dropped from twenty-two to five over the course of the century. One of the principal factors in this decline was a drop in royal patronage as a result of the monarchy's growing aversion to the religious teachings prevailing in the universities.[6] At the secondary level, colleges also remained firmly in the hands of Jesuits, Jansenists, and Oratorians, but here greater change was evident owing to the intervention of state officials.

The State as Context

Most of the growth in new institutions of learning took place at the secondary level, and since charters from the state were required for the founding of new colleges, officials were able to impose requirements for instruction in science, history, geography, and politics.[7] The expulsion of the Jesuits in 1762, which resulted in more than a third of the country's 350 colleges falling under the supervision of secular administrative boards, also gave the state a significant opportunity to initiate reforms.[8]

Of greater significance than the state's reforms of college instruction, however, was its role in initiating academies for the conduct of scientific and intellectual work. The Académie Française, founded in 1635 as a royal corporation with legal privileges and rights of addressing the king, established the pattern on which dozens of other academies were modeled over the following century. The more prominent of these included the Académie des Sciences (1666), the Académie Royale d'Architecture (1671), the Académie des Inscriptions et Belles-Lettres (1716), the Ecole Royale du Genie de Mezieres (1748), the Ecole Royale Militaire de Paris (1751), and the Académie Royale de Marine (1752). These institutions in effect short-circuited the universities' authority over intellectual affairs by placing such matters under direct supervision of the state.[9] They performed valuable services for the state, disseminating the French language, historical studies, scientific experiments, advice on patents, and training in architecture, engineering, and military science.[10] In return, scholars fortunate enough to be associated with these agencies received stipends and pensions, recognition, legal protection, access to research and publishing facilities, and opportunities to establish contact with private patrons.[11] During the same period, provincial academies were also founded in virtually all towns of moderate size, increasing from nine in 1710 to thirty-five by 1789.[12] Through their connections with Paris and local officials these academies served as important conduits for channeling promising young scholars from the provinces into the intellectual world of the metropolis.[13] Raynal, Montesquieu, and Rousseau were but a few of the prominent writers whose careers were nurtured by these academies.

The academies played a particularly valuable role in fostering the work of writers associated with the Enlightenment. On the side of natural philosophy the Académie des Sciences continued the work it had initiated during the seventeenth century, serving as the most generously financed scientific society of the eighteenth century and providing facilities, pensions, and publication outlets as well as valuable communication with scientists in other countries. Its membership expanded from fewer than 60 in 1699 to an average of 153 for the eighteenth century, the greatest growth occurring between 1746 and 1760.[14] On the literary side the Académie Française served as a focal point for Enlightenment scholarship particularly during the latter part of the century. Between 1760 and 1770 the philosophes waged a concerted battle to seize control of this prestigious academy. At the start of the decade only four of their number were included among its membership; by 1772 nine more had been added and d'Alembert succeeded to the post of secretary. Although nothing of specific literary value was accomplished by these maneuvers, the philosophes gained prestige by their association with the academy, reduced the platform from which critics could launch attacks, and secured dominance in French intellectual life.[15]

Besides the academies, the context in which the Enlightenment was fostered—indeed, with which it came to be almost synonymous—was that of the Paris salons. Unlike the academies, the salons had no official connection with the state, but it is inconceivable that the salons could have acquired the importance they had without close associations with the subculture of official life.[16] Among the notable writers who frequented these salons were d'Alembert, Voltaire, Diderot, Grimm, and Rousseau. The salons increasingly took the place of universities as centers of open philosophical inquiry and complemented the academies with an informal atmosphere conducive to the exchange of ideas. These were the supportive contexts in which ideas that may well have been unacceptable in broader public settings could be developed.[17] Nevertheless, they also drew writers into the circles of wealth and power from which patronage and influence derived. Here were opportunities to discuss political theory and current events with nobility and members of the court and to mix with ministers in high office such as Turgot and Necker, as well as to place oneself in line for private patronage or government office.[18]

Patronage was itself an important tie between scholars and the state, as was government employment; indeed, the boundary separating patronage and employment was often quite tenuous, rendering difficult the distinction between sinecures and actual service to the state. Well established as a source of support for leading literary figures in the seventeenth century, patronage became even more prominent in the eighteenth century as the supply available directly from the court was supplemented through the salons and high officials.[19]

Many writers lived scarcely above starvation level, as research on the lower literary life of Paris has shown, but those with talent or sufficient good fortune to rise to the top could anticipate rich rewards from the state.[20] Election to the Académie Française or the Académie des Sciences generally brought lucrative fees in addition to regular stipends; others received posts at the Faculté de Médecine or the College de France or were employed at the court as physicians, diplomats, or advisers, or were simply granted patronage from wealthy individuals who fancied their ideas. Still others found employment from individual officials who secured their writing skills for political purposes.[21]

In the case of scientists the role of patronage and government employment appears to have been even more pronounced. According to one estimate only 17 percent of the French scientists who reached adulthood prior to the Revolution earned their living in education; most worked as civil servants or were independently wealthy.[22] Even more compelling evidence of the state's role comes from a study of scientists affiliated with the Académie des Sciences which reveals a preponderance of government officials, inspectors, royal architects, lawyers, and military engineers. The study's author concludes: "Our data support the possibility that the man of science, before his research was valued per se by universities or for its potential profitability by industries, first carved a social niche for himself by providing *the administrative service and expertise required for the expanding interests of central government.*"[23]

The supply of patronage and government positions was sufficient to yield truly handsome incomes for a few and to permit those with inherited wealth to expand their holdings into vast fortunes. Suard, Morellet, and Marmontel all received subsidies valued at more than 20,000 livres annually; Diderot had an estate valued at more than 200,000 francs; d'Holbach's fortunes expanded to include rents of at least 60,000 livres annually; and Helvétius' estate was valued at more than 4 million livres.[24] Sizable as they were, these sums nevertheless constituted a relatively small drain on the royal treasury; indeed, they may have been a wise investment if only for the sake of drawing talent into the state bureaucracy.[25]

Other than easing the life style of a privileged few, patronage also functioned as a direct catalyst to the production of Enlightenment culture. Not without significance was the state's role in the advancement of publishing.[26] In some instances the state's role was quite explicit, as in the publication of Buffon's forty-four volumes of natural history, all of which were printed on royal presses at state expense.[27] Usually, though, the state's role was less direct, albeit no less important. The publishing industry was itself a product of the state's omnipresent expansion. Publishers frequently owed their success to the state's growing demand for reports, almanacs, statistical summaries, and biographies. A particularly noteworthy example was LeBreton, publisher of Diderot's *Encyclopédie,* whose capital equipment and personal fortune had been won printing the *Almanach royal.*[28] Because of the state's demand, publishing houses were in existence whose incomes were no longer tied closely to the church and whose social relations, like those of the philosophes, were intimately connected with the royal bureaucracy.

More generally, the existence of a literate elite oriented toward reading and thus providing an additional outlet for the publishing industry appears to have been in some measure a by-product of the state. According to one estimate, adult male literacy rose from 16 percent in 1600 to 29 percent in 1720 and then to 47 percent in 1788.[29] Along with these changes, increases also appeared in purchases of books and journals. According to an examination of household inventories in western France, the proportion containing books increased from approximately 25 percent in 1700 to 40 percent in 1780.[30] By midcentury Paris had 130 public libraries totaling more than one million books.[31] The number of periodicals in Paris grew from six or seven in 1730 to more than twenty in 1770, and for France as a whole the number of official periodicals increased from one in 1700 to about two dozen in 1725 to nearly four dozen by 1750.[32] Popular journals such as the *Journal de Trevoux* and the *Journal des savants* reviewed the activities of literary and scientific academies and the publication of scholarly works; new periodicals such as the *Journal étranger* and *L'Europe savante* covered scholarly developments across the Continent; and specialty journals provided translations of literature from England, Holland, Germany, and Italy.

Had it not been for a literate public these developments would undoubtedly have been delayed. Yet, more careful analyses of the effects of literacy on literary production suggest only a loose relation. Robert Darnton's investigation of sales patterns for the *Encyclopédie,* for example, suggests no relation between sheer literacy and the Enlightenment.[33] Instead, the market for the *Encyclopédie* appears to have been concentrated in areas in which the state had created a special clientele for such literature; that is, among notables, officials, and professionals in cities hosting provincial parlements and academies. The same conclusion is drawn by Daniel Roche, who suggests that the growth of the state, demanding a professionalized hierarchy of officials, was one of the chief sources of expansion in the educated public and in the availability of books and booksellers, both in Paris and in the provincial capitals.[34]

The state's importance to the literary world was also manifested acutely in questions of censorship. Writing was of necessity associated with the state because of the fact that the state claimed exclusive control over all publishing. On numerous occasions the weight of state censorship fell against Enlightenment writers, forcing them to patronize the flourishing industry in clandestine publishing which was carried out along the borders of France in Switzerland and the

Dutch Republic.[35] The very fact that this industry could flourish as it did, however, attests to the casualness with which state censors carried out their tasks.[36] Censorship had become an obligation to which the state remained formally committed but which it took too lightly to apply either consistently or effectively.[37] In certain instances the state even intervened to save writers who had experienced the misfortune of offending the censors. This was particularly true under the ministries of the duc de Choiseul and Turgot, both of whom had close personal associations with the philosophes and held their work in high regard.

The most familiar instance in which state intervention played an active part in furthering the Enlightenment was the case of Helvétius, whose *De l'esprit* (1758) caused such an outcry from the church and from the Parlement of Paris that the book's distribution was suspended and its author forced to retract the work on three separate occasions. Helvétius escaped imprisonment only because of the intervention of Choiseul and Mme. de Pompadour.[38] The state's role was not always this positive, and other writers wrote under pseudonyms or voluntarily suppressed their more controversial works to escape censorship.[39] Yet the fact that censorship resided in the state rather than in the church or the more traditionally minded provincial courts was itself a positive factor, given the ties that existed between many writers and the bureaucracy at other levels; indeed, one authority on the French Enlightenment suggests that the state's control over censorship played a critical role in promoting the early writings of the philosophes.[40]

In virtually every area in which social resources were required for the production of culture, therefore, the state was clearly visible: restricting, regulating, and circumventing the church's role in education; sponsoring scientific and literary academies, research, and training in engineering and the arts; directing patronage to aspiring writers through the unofficial channels of the salons and the official channels of sinecures and government offices; promoting, expanding, and protecting the publishing industry and its market. In one way or another nearly all of the important means of cultural production were under the state's control. Book publishing was in the hands of privileged guild corporations whose charters were granted by the state; censorship was the task of state appointed officers; and the most respected professional societies—the Académie Française, Comedie-Française, Académie Royale de Musique, Académie de Peinture et de Sculpture, as well as the Académie des Sciences and Société Royale de Médecine—were royal bodies deriving legitimacy and patronage from the state.

The philosophes themselves were by and large either supported directly by the state or associated closely enough with officers of the state to be aware of and interested in the affairs of practical politics. Montesquieu served as councilor and then as president of the parlement of Bordeaux; Rousseau functioned as secretary to the ambassador in Venice; Helvétius was a farmer-general; Mably worked on treaties and foreign negotiations; Grimm hired himself to German courts as a Parisian agent; Turgot held offices as intendant of Limoges and then as minister; D'Argenson served as councilor and minister of foreign affairs; Voltaire was an avid reader of periodicals on political economy and wrote commentaries on most of the important political issues of the day; others either dabbled in politics as pamphleteers or attended salons where they rubbed shoulders with members of the court.[41] If the philosophes, as Tocqueville suggested, "toyed" with political issues, they also, again, in his words, "all took notice of them in one way or another."[42]

The Broader Social Environment

How was it possible for the state to command the conditions of cultural production to such an extent? Modern scholars, having grown used to government grants and tax supported institutions, are likely to miss the significance of this relationship. The fact that the state had so much to do with scholarly activities was relatively new in the eighteenth century. Not that the state had ever been divorced from cultural production; but the sphere in which the state was able to exert its influence greatly expanded during this period, creating a new supply of resources, as it were, which to a significant degree made possible the intellectual work that subsequently became known as the Enlightenment. The role that the state played in fostering the Enlightenment constituted only a fraction of the state's activities, and in many respects this role was neither conscious nor deliberate. It was rather an integral feature of the broader forms of expansion to which the French state was subject. In order to understand how it was possible for the French Enlightenment to develop when it did, therefore, one must consider the nature of the state and the broader social forces affecting its development.

Perhaps the simplest way of suggesting the relevance of broader developments in French society to the Enlightenment is to say that these developments led to an expanded repertoire of social resources that became located in the state, and these resources then made possible the specific resources that were of strategic value to the philosophes. The crucial points in this argument include a consideration of the economic growth which permitted the French state to expand its sphere of activities, the manner in which these activities in fact expanded, and the particular nature of the state's responsibilities which led to its involvement in cultural production in the ways already considered.

Contrary to an earlier view, recent economic history demonstrates that the eighteenth century was one of marked economic growth in France.[43] Following a "prolonged standstill" from about 1600 to 1690 and a severe depression from 1689 to 1697 during the War of the League of Augsburg, the French economy underwent a period of general expansion not unlike that of the early sixteenth century.[44] Between 1710 and 1789 gross physical product increased from 1.5 billion francs to 4 billion francs, with particularly rapid growth in metallurgy, cotton fabrics, and silk manufacture.[45] Population rose from 19.2 million to 26.6 million, lending an important stimulus to agriculture, which grew even more rapidly.[46] The greatest area of growth, however, was in foreign trade, where a fivefold expansion took place between 1715 and 1789, causing trade to rise as a proportion of total product from 7 percent to 25 percent.[47] The colonial trade, rising tenfold and accounting for nearly 40 percent of all foreign trade, was particularly important.[48] Overall comparisons indicate that growth rates in agriculture, trade, and physical output were all higher in France than in England for this period.[49]

In straightforward terms the significance of this economic growth for the state was that it made possible an extremely rapid rate of expansion in state expenditures. From a low of 60 million francs in 1660 to 104 million francs in 1733, total state expenditures rose to 237 million francs in 1758, 400 million francs in 1774, and 620 million francs in 1781.[50] Not only did the tax base itself increase, but new taxes were levied and a more efficient, centralized system of tax collection was imposed.[51] The state's rising expenditures were also financed from direct investment in government annuities which attracted investors from a broad cross-section of the wealthier strata.[52] These expenditures ultimately represented even more than the broader economy could support, however, and after 1775 a series of financial setbacks coupled with the rising costs associated with the American war left the state in such desperate straits that many historians now credit the French Revolution in some measure to the fiscal crisis that preceded it. Nevertheless, for more than sixty years prior to the Revolution the French economy supported an unprecedented array of progressive state programs.

Until quite recently the eighteenth century was portrayed as a period of retrogression for the French state. Compared negatively with the earlier advances of Louis XIV and with the developments following the Revolution, it was characterized as a period of "aristocratic reaction" in which the nobility succeeded in recovering much of the power it had lost during the reign of Louis XIV and thereby prevented the crown from initiating reforms or ruling effectively, with the eventual outcome being the Revolution, which was presumably needed for any genuine progress to take place. This view is belied, however, by the fact that its estimation of Louis XIV's power in relation to the nobility appears exaggerated, and more important, by the considerable growth in state-building activity that actually characterized the eighteenth century. If absolutism in the form of personal rule was not as spectacular under Louis XV as under Louis XIV, the latter period nevertheless witnessed much growth in bureaucratic administration.

The basic structure of administration developed by Louis XIV consisted of the king, a chancellor who kept the royal seal, a controller general in charge of finance, several ministers of state without portfolio, and about forty administrators divided into four councils with only advisory powers to the king.[53] In the eighteenth century this structure was revised and repeatedly expanded to handle the growing need for efficient professional administration. The Royal Council was reorganized along functional lines into five major divisions, and each expanded its authority in formulating and implementing policies. The number of top officials increased from 40 to 125, including many professional civil servants from families previously without connections to the state; a system of promotion based on merit was instituted, as were finer gradations in the hierarchy; and increasingly after the 1730s a host of subordinate bureaus and ad hoc commissions was created to handle the rising amount of business in which the state was involved, including road construction and canals, mail service, printing and book selling, tax collection, military provisions, and general matters of trade.[54] Counting barristers, clerks, officials of Parlement, and other functionaries who earned their living in conjunction with the state but not as employees of the state, the number of bureaucrats and related officials is estimated to have ranged in the thousands.[55]

The most direct linkages between the mercantile state and the kinds of activities that fostered enlightened culture were in the areas of science, engineering, and technical administration. In these efforts the developments of the eighteenth century represented merely an extension of initiatives begun during the previous half century. Frederick Artz notes in his study of the development of technical education during the late seventeenth century that "to make the state strong in a military and naval way, to improve the quality and amount of its manufactures so that they would command both domestic and foreign markets were the steady aims of statesmen. Unless this is clearly grasped, the efforts to improve technical education cannot be understood."[56] In the eighteenth century scholars with talent and imagination continued to be enlisted in the service of the state, and the state's enlarged capacity to finance academies and bureaucratic agencies dramatically increased the demand for such talent. Many of these connections reached new heights during the ministry of Turgot: Lavoisier's talents were deployed in work on munitions, Condorcet's at the mint, d'Alembert's on technical aspects of canal construction; and other members of the Académie des Sciences contributed to diverse programs ranging from the standardization of weights and measures to the investigation of cattle epidemics.[57] Even prior to Turgot, however, periodic censuses of the population were conducted, better records were kept on trade and material wealth, and growing efforts were made to develop an officer corps trained in the latest discoveries from science and the world of learning.

Although the model still in use for applying technical skills to the economy was that of seventeenth-century mercantilism, the paradoxical result for the state was that as the economy grew, it became less feasible to maintain close administrative control over it. French mercantilism was characterized by a meticulous code of regulations which had gradually been extended during the seventeenth century to virtually all crafts, industries, and types of trade. These regulations were rigidly enforced through state supervision of local guilds and national codes specifying quality standards, dimensions, and other features of goods produced. Between the 1660s and 1730s these regulations were administered in ever increasing detail by a growing army of state officials.[58] But the economic growth that characterized the eighteenth century increasingly created contingencies that the established system of mercantilist regulations was ill prepared to handle. Technological innovation led to new products and modes of production that rendered many of the existing codes archaic and inequitable. Potential markets for inexpensive goods were also opened by the expanding colonial trade, but these markets could not be exploited effectively as long as the mercantilist codes which had been designed to create high-quality goods at high prices for the Continental market remained in effect.[59] With expanding colonial trade, military and naval provisions for protecting colonies and shipping routes also had to be figured into the calculus of state intervention as well; mercantilism had to pay for the rising costs of its own defense.[60]

One way in which the state adapted to these challenges was to incorporate a broader array of economic interests into the governing apparatus itself. As early as 1700, a Council of Commerce was established to give merchants involved in the Atlantic trade a greater voice in determining economic policies. This step was apparently taken because evidence was already available that the existing bureaucratic structure was becoming ineffective in the face of growing trade. According to Lionel Rothkrug: "The situation which caused the government to call this body into existence was above all created by the fragmentation of bureaucratic control. A major expansion in the Atlantic trade since the last year or so of the war, and the need to reexamine the principles which were to govern France's future foreign trade, helped to complicate the direction of economic matters to the point where they could no longer be effectively centralized under one man. The task of economic regulation was parcelled out among several agencies."[61]

As a result of these newly represented interests a greater variety of views with respect to the proper nature of the state became integrated into the state bureaucracy itself. Harold Parker writes: "Changing conditions and new theories gave rise to debate among industrialists, administrative civil servants, and *controleurs general*. They debated, along with other issues, the role the government should play in the economy, and specifically, the necessity for guild regulations."[62] In this context ideas began to circulate based on quite different suppositions than those on which the mercantilist system was built. In place of a static, nonexpanding economy, it came to be assumed, technology and colonialism could serve as bases for continuous economic growth; agriculture was perceived, particularly in the writings of Quesnay and his disciples, as being amenable to improvements that would greatly enhance production; and new theories of the market suggested that market competition could substitute effectively for guild regulations as a means of maintaining quality in production.

The debate that emerged had the earmarks of an ideological conflict between the rising bourgeoisie and representatives of an outmoded aristocratic form of government. It was, however, neither this simple nor framed in such purely ideological terms. It came rather to be institutionalized within the state itself among the various bureaus concerned with promoting and regulating commerce. Ministers adopted different views depending on training and constituencies, and the debate over mercantilism spread to other agencies and to members of the broader informed public.

The expansion of French commerce under the mercantilist system was thus associated, first, with an expansion of the state bureaucracy whose responsibility it was to supervise the economy, and second, with tensions concerning the nature of the state's involvement in the economy as a result of the differing interests and opinions represented in the bureaucracy. For scientists and technicians, as well as the broader scholarly community that had grown up in conjunction with the state, the effect of these developments was also twofold. The growing array of agencies and interests was associated with an absolute increase in the number of positions open to scholars. Ministers charged with the responsibility of formulating economic policies were fully aware that changing circumstances obviated the possibility of simply implementing the doctrines of Colbert and others of their predecessors. The division of interests and opinions among their staffs as well as the merchants, industrialists, and landowners affected by government policies was readily apparent.[63] Under these conditions it was of utmost importance for ministers desiring to retain their offices to acquire information about the perceptions and needs of different constituencies. Accordingly, in-house commissions were created to supply such information, and even the pamphlets and periodicals of the broader intellectual community came to serve a vital purpose. To the more narrowly defined ranks of officers and commissioners a layer of functionaries was added to provide administrative expertise as well. The first assistants who occupied the highest of these positions enjoyed a high degree of autonomy in making decisions, often developing the basic policies that were merely ratified by their superiors, but they were required to have extensive training and to be knowledgeable on a wide variety of public issues.[64] In addition, the debates that arose over the proper role of the state in relation to the economy contributed, as we shall see, to the diversity and openness that characterized Enlightenment thought more generally.

The growth of the French state provides a partial explanation for the positions and stipends that were available to scholars during the Enlightenment, but the fact that scholars attained sufficient freedom to contribute in ways other than meeting the sheer technical demands of the state warrants additional consideration. Writers of the French Enlightenment appear to have been relatively unintimidated by the closeness of their association with the state. By no means were they apologists who gave uniform support to the state's policies. Yet at the same time they were scarcely as aligned in opposition to the state as historians reading backwards from the Revolution have sometimes made them out to be. What characterized the writings of the leading figures of the period more than any uniformity of orientation was their sheer diversity, and hence, their enormously varied complexity.

The Bases of Intellectual Diversity

Evidence of the intellectual diversity of Enlightenment figures is readily apparent from comparisons of such varied personalities as Montesquieu and Voltaire or Diderot and Rousseau. Not only did the various writers who dominated the intellectual scene in eighteenth century Paris reflect different interests, backgrounds, personality predispositions, and literary styles in their writings; they also took different sides on political, religious, and economic issues and frequently infuriated one another by their obstinacy in defending these points of view. Even individual writers of the period seldom lend themselves to easy characterization. Voltaire alone has been described as a radical, a liberal, a conservative, an advocate of enlightened despotism, a monarchist, a constitutionalist, and a champion of the nobility. Some of these descriptions are perhaps more accurate than others, but the truth is that Voltaire, like most of his compatriots, evidenced little in the way of orthodoxy, either in support of or in opposition to prevailing norms and institutions. As one student of the Enlightenment suggests: "The *philosophes* were in frequent disagreement, changed their minds, and in spite of their concern with language and definition, were not at all clear about some of the important ideas they professed. As a result, we can find *philosophes* who argued both sides of almost any question."[65]

On the whole, differences of opinion probably contributed positively to the intellectual creativity that characterized the French Enlightenment, and yet these differences were sufficiently divisive that several historians suggest the importance of projects such as the *Encyclopédie* which helped to forge greater unity among the philosophes.[66] The informal settings provided by some of the salons may also have contributed to the creation of a more cohesive spirit; for example, d'Holbach's circle of friends appears to have sustained both internal diversity and close friendships. Within the more formal establishments, however, diversity and factionalism seem to have been more in evidence than any uniformity of ideological commitment. Roger Hahn's depiction of the Académie des Sciences is particularly revealing:

> Outside the bi-weekly meetings lasting two hours each, occasional committee gatherings, a yearly mass celebrated at the Oratoire, and two public assemblies, there were no collegial activities to bind them together. So far as is known, they did not act as a large group socially. On the contrary, the annals of the Académie are replete with evidence of bitter cleavages. Factionalism was rampant and manifested itself ferociously on the occasion of elections, and this divisiveness was further aggravated by political differences... There were cliques and schools ... and these subgroups were generally reinforced by ties of patronage.[67]

The diversity of Enlightenment scholarship was in no small measure a function of the varied backgrounds and interests of its leading contributors, as well as a result of the fact that individual scholars were in competition with one another for recognition and support and thus were obliged to differentiate their work from that of even their closest competitors.[68] These conditions notwithstanding, there were aspects of the social milieu in which scholars worked that also facilitated their ability to display such diversity.

Much of the actual growth that added to the personnel, activities, and expenditures of the state took place, as we have seen, in the executive bureaucracy. Growth of this sort was closely linked with the expanding responsibilities confronting mercantilist states as the realms of commerce and industry became enlarged, and this growth introduced significant new dimensions into discussions of social order, law, authority, and privilege. But in France one of the reasons why these discussions carried the weight they did was that the executive bureaucracy did not grow unopposed.

After the death of Louis XIV the position of the Parlement of Paris was greatly enhanced, and over the following half century it functioned as a significant locus of opposition to the expanding powers of the bureaucracy.[69] The interplay between these bodies created, as it were, a basic polarity in French government which affected the work of most scholars whose interests were concerned with public affairs. Olwen Hufton suggests that each body actually represented a fairly well defined constituency and spoke for one of the two prevailing modes of authority concurrently competing for legitimacy. On the one hand, there was "a centralizing force composed of the king and an impressive range of councils and ministers concentrated in Versailles and in close contact with the intendants in the localities"; ranged against them, on the other hand, was "the older decentralizing force of provincial estates, *parlements*, *baillages* and *senechaussées* which asserted older rights and sought to restrain monarchical encroachments upon local powers and privileges."[70] Although the bureaucracy usually served as the closest source of support for Enlightenment scholars, the presence of Parlement and its allies as a counterforce provided a liberating source of ballast. As Norman Hampson explains: "The disgruntled *parlements* . . . weakened the authority of the state and offered at least the possibility that critical writers might find protectors amongst their disunited opponents."[71]

The kind of freedom created by this polarity in government may have been mainly symbolic (one finds few instances of Parlement actually defending the philosophes), but it was nevertheless real. Conflict between royal administrators and Parlement raised legal and theoretical issues which not only expanded the work load of the bureaucracy but also stimulated theoretical debate over the nature and responsibilities of government.[72] Each party oriented its actions toward resistance to the other, thus creating a basis of government by debate rather than autocratic rule. Whether the two branches of government were in substantial agreement or not, the expectation was that some show of opposition would be made. William Doyle suggests: "Resistance, in fact, was a matter of not obstructing the government while appearing to; government was a matter of ignoring resistance while appearing not to."[73] A climate of symbolic opposition was thus created by the copresence of the royal councils and parlements which in a sense provided the kind of political atmosphere in which the critical observations of the philosophes came to be tolerated if not actually valued.

Nearly all observers of the French state emphasize the importance of both the Parlement of Paris and the provincial parlements as a check on royal administration during this period. Betty Behrens writes, for example: "The parlements had a power to obstruct the royal wishes which in the eighteenth century was without parallel in the other European autocracies; for they not only possessed a long tradition of opposing the Crown, which even Louis XIV had been unable to destroy; they were corporations with a strong espirit de corps fostered by their being continuously in session for a large part of the year."[74] The powers vested in the Parlement of Paris were particularly extensive, rendering it far more than merely one of many provincial courts. It held supremacy in judicial matters over large sections of central and northern France; heard cases involving crimes of violence, seigneurial rights, appeals from ecclesiastical courts, royal prerogatives in certain economic affairs, peerages, public welfare and sanitation, guilds, and censorship; and above all claimed the right of remonstrance, which could be particularly effective in matters of taxation.[75]

Yet, a portrayal of the state during this period as an essentially polarized entity fails to be totally accurate; nor does it correspond very well with the more diverse character of the Enlightenment. Had the political climate of the period been subject to a single deep polarity, we would expect to find a rather uniform alignment between the philosophes and the royal bureaucracy, given the support they received from it. But in fact this was not the case, nor were the basic constituencies so clearly defined. The view that polarity was present is partially accurate, but historians appear to have been led to overemphasize this polarity in seeking to locate antecedent causes of the Revolution, such as the kind of administrative stalemate implied by this polarity. Matters were in fact more complex.

The administrative bureaucracy was itself riven with several kinds of competing interests. The sheer expansion that the bureaucracy had undergone since the last half of the seventeenth century made it, to quote one writer, "an amalgam for older and new families with varying degrees of noble lineage and varying periods in judicial and administrative office."[76] In the course of waging war and administering the economy according to mercantilist principles, the bureaucracy had taken on many new functions that were potentially disruptive of traditional privileges. In addition to the tensions already noted between centralizing forces and agents of decentralization, these changes also resulted in complicated divisions within the various agencies of the central bureaucracy itself, for the changes taking place were never initiated with strict consistency over time or advocated without hesitation and reversals by the king. As a result, differences of opinion were endemic among the various ministers and counselors who sought to articulate alternative policies and to persuade the king of their desirability.

Particularly prominent were debates over the need for tax reform versus the need to maintain the loyalty of privileged orders affected by such reforms, debates over justice administered according to traditional property rights versus the need to mobilize new resources for the public good, and debates over the need to enhance efficiency in government agencies versus the desire to maintain established agencies.[77] In the area of commerce officials were subject to an additional set of cross-pressures: generating revenue for the crown often conflicted with the promotion of private commerce, and the latter goal involved intermittent conflicts between advocates of foreign trade and those of local industry.[78]

All of these issues were compounded by several structural features of the bureaucracy itself: first, a continuing tension between the royal household and the professional bureaucracy which, despite gains being made by the latter, left the two in a sufficiently precarious balance that "at any time personalism could overtake rationalization";[79] second, the divide-and-conquer strategy to which Louis XV subjected his chief ministers in order to retain personal control over the regime rather than being dominated by his first minister;[80] and third, the existence of a dual recruitment mechanism for higher offices—one through the lower ranks of the bureaucracy itself and the other through office in the Parlement of Paris—which tied officials into different personal networks and added yet another axis to the delicate geometry of public affairs.

The complexity of interests represented in the bureaucracy was partly a reflection of the fact that France's economic growth during the eighteenth century was fairly well balanced; thus, a broad set of interest groups was able to exert claims on at least some segment of the bureaucracy. The nobility was scarcely declining in an absolute sense: French agriculture showed fairly steady increases in profits at least through the third quarter of the century, and, perhaps more important, the nobility was deeply integrated into the world of commerce and finance.[81] On the whole, the nobility was relatively open because there was no law of primogeniture and titles could be purchased easily. Behrens writes: "It included people so different in point of wealth, lineage, and occupation . . . that one might fairly say that one nobleman had nothing necessarily in common with another except the legal rights which belonged to nobles as such."[82]

The numerous members of landed noble families who spent time in Paris and frequented the literary salons in their abundant leisure time were by no means allied, as some have suggested, with the parlements against the king, for the parlements were their champions only in matters of taxation and local justice, whereas the king, acting through the various commercial commissions and intendants, was responsible for a series of favorable acts that reduced tolls on grain, encouraged free trade, and gave landowners access to larger profits.[83] Even within the bureaucracy, many of the nobility were directly involved as a result of the high degree of recruitment of nobility into the ranks of provincial intendants who, in turn, were an important source of recruits to the central bureaucracy.[84] After midcentury, the nobility's influence also increased significantly as a result of its renewed dominance in the military officer corps.[85]

At the same time, the expanding bureaucracy provided numerous opportunities for incorporating new families with different interests and ideas from the realms of commerce, finance, and office holding itself.[86] During the seventeenth century the essence of mercantilism had been economic policies carefully orchestrated by the state and carried out largely by state-owned monopolies; now with the increasing intensity of economic competition mercantilism necessitated a partnership between the merchant community and state agencies, thereby supplying the bourgeoisie with greater opportunities to influence government activities.[87] Yet the merchant community was itself divided between those who benefited from the state's intervention in the economy, and who therefore favored strong royalist policies, and those who were already in a favorable position to survive in the international market under conditions of unrestricted free trade. In this the War of the League of Augsburg appears to represent a watershed; for after this date, although the influence of the bourgeoisie continued to increase in French policy, the unity of interest between merchants and the state began to erode, particualarly on issues of war, tariffs, and taxation.[88]

In addition to this internal division, the state also represented a resource about which the bourgeoisie could genuinely manifest ambivalence. On the one hand, state expansion came to represent the kind of stability that any merchant could favor insofar as it meant the capacity to maintain domestic peace and external security; on the other hand, state expansion also conjured up fears of despotism that ran counter to provincial traditions and the pursuit of private privilege.[89] To the extent that diverse orientations were evident within the bureaucracy, therefore, these orientations were likely to reflect some of the conflicting sentiments prevailing in the ruling class more broadly.

Apart from the bureaucracy, the parlements were also subject to many of the same kinds of internal divisions. Summarizing the activities of the provincial parlements prior to the Revolution, Doyle writes: "Diversity and disunity therefore characterized the reactions of the parlements as a whole . . . There was certainly no united and sustained opposition to the government's policies."[90] At the provincial level some of the diversity evident during these years was a reflection of local interests and their differing positions in the larger economy. But the Parlement of Paris also exemplified many of the cross-cutting loyalties that gave diversity to the state. As persons of wealth who frequently owned vast landed estates, its members shared interests with the more traditional segments of the nobility in areas of taxation and economic policy; yet the authority and prestige of this body came chiefly from its role in upholding the law. Consequently, the parlementaires jealously protected the sanctity of the law even against incursions by the nobility and cooperated in enforcing it with the king, on whom their authority also depended. There was thus a division of interests which, though not exactly similar to the alleged cleavage between sword and robe, nevertheless served to prevent the parlementaires from becoming strictly the representatives of aristocracy against the king or of king against aristocracy.[91] Despite the fact that the Parlement of Paris often raised opposition to the king, its loyalties were sufficiently complex that its opposition could easily shade over into actual compliance.[92] Other divisions also tended to reinforce this complexity, particularly the close relations in terms of career mobility that continued to characterize the intendants and parlementaires, and splits between the upper and lower chambers along lines of age and personal outlook, as well as the complex relations between Parlement and the various factions of the clergy.[93]

Beginning in the 1740s and deepening seriously in the 1770s, the growing fiscal problems of the state added a further dimension to the internal divisions that characterized all branches of the state. The rising costs associated with administering the mercantilist system in the face of ever widening colonial empires left the state with mounting debts, military expenditures, and interest payments. After entering the War of the Austrian Succession in 1741 it was never solvent, and the devastating outcome of the Seven Years' War, together with France's commitments during the American War of Independence, finally forced the state to declare bankruptcy in 1788.[94] France had yet to organize an efficient national banking system for the administration of state credit and was thus compelled to seek additional revenue through the dual strategy of widespread borrowing from the wealthiest classes and an increasingly more universalistic series of tax measures aimed at tapping the privileged as well as the underprivileged.[95] Both of these tactics had the effect of tightening, as it were, the relations between the state and the privileged classes, thereby altering in two substantial ways the diverse character of the public sector in which many of the discussions over public policy were taking place.

One consequence was to reassert gradually the polarity between the bureaucracy and the privileged classes that had otherwise been muted by the numerous cross-pressures.[96] This polarization does not appear to have crystalized until the very eve of the Revolution, and thus lies outside of the present discussion, but the fact that this polarity was being reasserted during the 1770s and 1780s serves in part to distinguish the period from roughly 1715 to 1760 as the high point of cross-cutting divisions within the state and thereby to associate these divisions somewhat more narrowly with the temporal zenith of the Enlightenment.[97] Second, the fiscal crisis appears to have added to the debate over the legitimacy of the state in its various functions and agencies which had become increasingly prominent over the preceding half century.[98] As the state was drawn deeper into a relation of financial dependency on the privileged sector, this sector lost some of its character as a loose aggregation of separate interests and came increasingly to be a collectivity whose corporate interests were bound together by the state. In turn, the failure of the state to perform as effectively as all of the parties associated with it would have liked raised genuine questions about the correctness of its structure and procedures.

The picture of the French state during the years of the high Enlightenment, then, is scarcely that of an absolutist bureaucracy employing a growing cadre of scholars to enhance the efficiency of its administration; it is rather an agglomeration of interests and agencies whose relations with one another remain tenuously defined as a result of the transitional character of the larger society, but which are fraught at best with numerous overlapping and fluctuating cross-pressures. Although the bureaucracy on the one hand and the parlements on the other represented a basic polarity in the state, other issues and organizational divisions prevented a sharp crystalization around this polarity until the last decade before the Revolution. The state remained divided along multiple, cross-cutting fissures, and these divisions took different shapes at various times depending on the issues under consideration.

The Emergence of a Public Sphere

The literary figures and scientists of the Enlightenment were bound to the state rather loosely as a result of these diverse factions. In addition to supplying many of the tangible resources necessary for scholarly and literary work, the state constituted a public sphere in which issues not only could be debated but had to be debated for effective decision making to occur. In the absence of a tightly knit bureaucratic structure, informal discourse in the salons and academies and in the emerging periodical press provided an invaluable means of connecting agencies, bureaus, and interest groups. It is, in fact, instructive that this was the period in which the term *publicist* shifted in connotation from someone professionally concerned with handling legal matters to include the broader range of professional writers, journalists, and pamphleteers who addressed public issues. The charters and official *lettres-patentes* of the new academies also explicitly recognized that their purpose was to promote the "public good" by bringing intellectual discussion to bear on political and administrative problems.[99] More generally, the self-identity of the philosophes, in contrast with that of the seventeenth-century *honnête homme,* appears to have included a much stronger orientation toward the idea of the public good. The earlier figure was generally a noble courtier of some wealth who displayed a personal interest in cultivated, cosmopolitan, intellectual activities. The philosophes sought to turn these interests to public use. Critical reason and autonomy were more strongly valued in order to transcend narrow political and customary constraints, and the aim of their gatherings was to convey social information and encourage the formation of collective opinion.[100] This was also the period in which official pronouncements shifted away from the view that the king alone could determine what was in the public interest toward the position that open discussion on the part of the informed public was the best way to arrive at effective policies. The latter position was of course compatible with the differentiation that was distributing governmental functions into administratively separate bureaus.[101]

The effect of this loosely coupled structure was to enhance freedom for writers and scholars, both from formal censorship and from informal orthodoxy, thereby encouraging scholarship to take an innovative turn. Alan Kors's conclusion from examining the activities of the philosophes associated with d'Holbach's salon is worth quoting in full in this regard because it expresses with exceptional clarity the importance of the cross-pressures that characterized the state:

> [In] a society so divided by political questions and jurisdictional disputes there was no way to achieve a unified or concerted effort to impose intellectual order. The same parlement that Joly de Fleury or Seguier could move to condemn a philosophical work was itself at odds with a police administration under royal authority that sought to suppress the circulation of the parlement's own remonstrances. The same Assemblée du Clergé that demanded censure of and vigorous enforcement against books impugning the dignity of the Church would itself contest the authority of a parlement it viewed as sympathetic to the Jansenists. The crown, at odds with both, did not appreciate interference with its jurisdictions in any area, including that of defense of the faith in the realms of police and administration of the *librairie*. In the end, thus, the task of implementing the laws concerning books and authors was given to the royal bureaucracy alone, an intellectually diverse body of

men who thrived on protection, patronage, formal (if insincere) statements of obedience, and informal, mutual accommodations among respectable persons—all modes of operation advantageous to the philosophes.[102]

An additional consequence of these overlapping and fluid cross-pressures was to motivate the kind of scholarship that wrestled with redefining the ambiguous relations that were everywhere evident within the public sphere. Thus it is not surprising that many of the treatises dealing with monarchical, constitutional, democratic, and republican government in ways that continue to be of interest were produced in this context. As Peter Gay has observed, the eighteenth century was fraught with genuine ambivalence toward the functions of monarchy as opposed to the parlements and other bodies capable of providing a check on monarchical power.[103] On the one hand, monarchy represented the single most powerful force capable of implementing economic reform and defending France's interests in the European sphere; but on the other hand, monarchy threatened to devolve into despotism serving only its own interests. Different writers therefore took different positions, and their debates formed a critical axis of Enlightenment literature. For instance, during the debate over tax reform in the 1750s, Voltaire wrote pamphlets supportive of the king, Montesquieu argued chiefly for limitations on royal prerogatives, and Diderot sought to express a position that mixed absolutist and representative views.

It is difficult, as literary critics have noted, to find anything in the way of close connections between the work of particular writers and their social backgrounds or positions during this period in French history. There are some notable exceptions, of course; for example, Raynal was closely associated with a faction in the bureaucracy that was oriented toward economic reform, and many of his treatises emphasize the merits of free trade; Morellet and Galiani appear to have been linked to a different faction, and their works include treatises against free trade. But generally the philosophes were able to explore a wide range of themes and ideas because of the fluidity of their environment. These topics of course ranged well beyond immediate political issues, including poetry, fiction, drama, and music. The role of the state was not to circumscribe the literary activities that were pursued but to provide a focal point for scholarly work through the concentration of resources in a central location.

The fact that this location was also situated temporally in a relatively prosperous period of French history meant that both the state and private patrons were able to engage in a fairly high degree of luxury consumption that included the arts as well as more practical modes of scholarship.[104] The French Enlightenment was largely contained within this privileged context, rather than having to attract a mass constituency in order to become institutionalized.[105] This, too, was probably a condition that promoted its diversity.

On the whole, little of the available evidence supports the widely contended idea that the French Enlightenment owed a special debt to the rise of the bourgeoisie. Although this view can be found in both Tocqueville and Marx, as well as in some recent discussions, it fades increasingly into the recesses of the imagination as questions are addressed concerning the actual mechanisms by which such a relation might have occurred. Inquiries into the class origins of individual writers provide little support for the idea that Enlightenment writers were subjected to bourgeois ideals through early socialization. Darnton's study of the occupational origins of contributors to the *Encyclopédie,* for example, reveals that only 4 percent were from backgrounds in commerce or manufacturing.[106] The same study demonstrates virtually no connection between the bourgeoisie and Enlightenment literature in terms of readers and purchasers of the *Encyclopédie:* manufacturers and merchants showed remarkably little interest in it, or indeed in literature of any kind; for the most part, subscribers were royal officials, parlementaires, provincial administrators, lawyers, professionals, and others of wealth.[107] Similarly, Roche's work on the membership of learned societies concludes that merchants were relatively uninvolved both in the provincial academies and in Paris.[108] Out of some 6,000 members of these academies in all, merchants and men of business numbered fewer than 160. And other measures suggest similarly low levels of representation: fewer than 5 percent of the subscribers to the *Mercure de France* were commercial men; only 3 percent of the subscribers to the *Dictionnaire d'Expilly* were from the merchant class; studies of letters to writers such as Diderot, Montesquieu, and Voltaire show that under 5 percent came from the bourgeoisie; and records from estate inventories reveal that only one merchant in six left books as part of his estate, compared with a majority of the estates of government officers such as members of parlement and nobles at court. In some instances, such as the academies, the bourgeoisie was consciously excluded, or membership was limited only to the wealthiest of merchants. More generally, it appears, men of commerce were uninterested in the circles in which the new ideas of the Enlightenment were being produced.[109]

If the bourgeoisie had any significant impact on the Enlightenment, therefore, it must have been an indirect effect. But even at this level, research suggests caution in attributing too much to the bourgeoisie, for its rise now appears to have been neither as dramatic nor as distinctly separable from other classes as once supposed. By the end of the old regime only about 20 percent of private wealth in France was industrial or commercial wealth, whereas 80 percent was in land, urban properties, annuities, or investments in venal office. In Paris the wealthy elite consisted not so much of merchants and industrialists but lawyers, officials of the courts, tax collectors, and royal administrators; outside Paris the bourgeoisie was virtually nonexistent except for a few of the major port cities. Among the new men who were being integrated into the state, again little evidence points toward any strong input from the commercial bourgeoisie: most of the new recruits were descendents of officeholders; fewer than 10 percent were sons of businessmen.[110]

Doubt about the connections between the Enlightenment and the bourgeoisie has also been raised by studies of the nobility. Regional differences and ambiguities in identifying important distinctions within the nobility have rendered firm conclusions difficult, but many of the stereotypes suggesting that the Enlightenment played a clear ideological role in the rivalry between nobility and bourgeoisie now appear to be at best debatable. The upper nobility that was associated with the court had the wealth and leisure to serve, as we have seen, as patrons of the arts, science, and the literary salons. Not only did they participate in the culture of the Enlightenment, but they also helped to elaborate it. New members of the nobility, especially after 1760, were increasingly given recognition by the state for their practical knowledge in scientific, technical, and administrative activities. At the same time, it cannot be argued simply that the nobility was undergoing a process of bourgeoisification. Relatively few of the upper nobility participated in commerce or industry; the largest shares of nonlanded wealth came from annuities, court pensions and gifts, and matrimonial ties to financiers. The newer nobility appear not to have constituted an effective point of integration between the nobility and the upper bourgeoisie. And, while acquiring

Enlightenment themes in its discourse, the nobility did not in principle abandon its claims to honorific privileges, nor did it in practice move significantly away from feudal economic patterns.[111]

To the extent that the Enlightenment can be associated with the bourgeoisie at all, it is not with a commercial or industrial bourgeoisie but a bourgeoisie of professional bureaucrats and officeholders whose ranks and personal interactions were closely associated with the nobility and with men of finance and power and whose common identity consisted mainly of being part of the expanding yet highly diverse administrative structures of the state. These structures continued to provide the resources for scientific and technical work, but their internal diversity also proved conducive to the broader literary production that became known as the Enlightenment. Where these conditions were approximated elsewhere, similar modes of cultural production were also evident.

Cultural Production in Hanoverian England

The Enlightenment in England has been described as a "historical paradox": so diffuse that the term itself seems somewhat anomalous when associated with England, yet clearly of lasting significance in the history of ideas.[112] In contrast with its French counterpart, the English Enlightenment had neither the distinct identity of that provided by the philosophes nor the strident anticlericalism that aroused passions against it.[113] The scholars who became its spokesmen, from Locke to Burke, spanned a relatively longer period of time and were for the most part deemed less radical than the philosophes, if only because their ideas were adopted more immediately and on a broader scale. As E. P. Thompson has remarked: "The Enlightenment proceeded in Britain, not like one of those flood-tides massing against a crumbling dyke, but like the tide which seeps into the eroded shores, mudflats and creeks of an estuary whose declivities are ready to receive it."[114]

But if the Enlightenment in England seems somehow less prominent than its counterpart in France, it was nevertheless a source of inspiration to the philosophes themselves, serving both as their guide in scientific advances and as their model for the justification of political and cultural demands. Writers everywhere looked to England as the country that had produced Newton and Locke and that continued to provide a haven of freedom for intellectual inquiry and the expression of diverse views. English deism provided the inspiration for rationalistic critiques of religion. English political tracts—and the political system described in them—served as ideals for treatises on political theory throughout the Continent. English science inspired hope that the application of reason to empirical evidence would produce similar breakthroughs in fields such as medicine, law, history, and ethics. And English publishing, both of literary tomes and of periodical commentary, was widely envied and imitated.

As in France, the Enlightenment in England represented an upswing in cultural production that went well beyond the work of a few particularly prominent writers. Gregory King's estimate at the end of the seventeenth century of some 75,000 persons in the "sciences and liberal arts," although it includes occupations ranging from architecture to pharmacy, gives an indication that the production and use of intellectual work was already gaining in social importance.[115] So do statistics on publishing and periodicals: in 1688 only twenty printing houses were in operation; by 1724 there were seventy in London alone and another twenty-six outside London.[116] Between 1700 and 1750 the number of regular periodicals published in London increased from two to fifty.[117] And newspapers became a mode of publishing in England which excelled to an even greater extent than in France. In 1702 the *Daily Courant* became London's first daily newspaper. By 1771 more than fifty newspapers circulated in London, and at least forty-four provincial newspapers were being published on a regular basis.[118] Estimates suggest that total sales had reached 200,000 by 1760, with a combined readership of at least several times this number.[119] Newspapers not only reported the news but also printed political commentary and literary criticism of generally high quality. Among the writers who worked as journalists at one time or another were Samuel Johnson, Daniel Defoe, Henry Fielding, Tobias Smollett, Oliver Goldsmith, James Boswell, and of course Joseph Addison and Richard Steele.

Beyond these media, cultural production of a wider variety also flourished. Drama in England did not experience the same success as in Paris, where royal sponsorship gave it a decided financial edge. But the reign of George I (1714-1727) brought renewed interest to the London stage, and gradual increases became evident in the number of plays produced and in the size of audiences.[120] Between 1700 and 1750, 1,095 new plays were produced; during the next fifty years this number climbed to 2,117.[121]

Over the course of the century a similar increase in attention to the visual arts was also evident. Already flourishing in Hanoverian London, the visual arts were given a substantial boost in 1769 by the founding of the Royal Academy, a deliberate effort to encourage native talent at the expense of French, Dutch, and German rivals.[122] The period was also noted for a rapid rate of cultural diffusion from London to the countryside involving the construction of concert halls, theaters, museums, and libraries.[123]

In science, nothing rivaled the achievements Newton had made during the last decades of the seventeenth century. But the eighteenth century witnessed scientific growth with a firmer institutional base. Apart from the publication of Newton's *Principia* in 1687, the last quarter of the seventeenth century had been, as one historian has suggested, "the bleakest" in the history of the Royal Society.[124] In contrast, this body's progress was much more substantial during the first quarter of the eighteenth century. Newton's long term as president gave its activities international eminence. Major advances were made in the classification of plant and animal life. Progress was also evident in attempts to understand human physiology, in pneumatics and optics, and in the development of chemistry and astronomy.[125] As in France, these advances in science deeply influenced the thinking of writers more generally. And these writers, in turn, helped popularize scientists' discoveries and theories.[126]

Another notable parallel between England and France lay in the fact that intellectual inquiries began to be conducted to an increasing extent outside the established universities. Oxford and Cambridge were still England's leading universities. But their activities remained carefully supervised by the church. Both institutions had experienced a steady, and dramatic, slump in enrollments and in intellectual quality during the seventeenth century. Neither provided incentives for innovative scholarship.[127] As Roy Porter observes: "The great scholars of Georgian England—the law reformer Jeremy Bentham, historians such as Edward Gibbon, Archdeacon Coxe, and Charles Burney, and scientists such as Joseph Priestly and Henry Cavendish—were not dons."[128] Or, as another historian notes, about half the leading writers of the eighteenth century had received training at Cambridge or Oxford, but hardly any of these writers went on to occupy positions at Cambridge or Oxford.[129]

The focal point of London's intellectual life was its coffee houses. The first of these had been established, as far as is known, in 1652.

By 1739 there were more than 550. Approximately 400 were located in Westminster alone, where political events provided ongoing topics for discussion.[130] London's coffee houses functioned similarly to Paris's salons. Both provided informal locations for the exchange of ideas. During the latter half of the eighteenth century, salons also came increasingly into existence in London. They were consciously modeled after their Parisian counterparts. Unlike the coffee houses, they provided women as well as men of the upper strata exposure to literature and the arts.

Another significant development in the institutionalization of innovative cultural discourse was the founding of formal debating societies. The first of these was organized in London in 1747.[131] In the following decades debating societies became increasingly popular. Their members included many prominent writers as well as political leaders and aristocrats. Unlike the scientific academies, in which topics of discourse were narrowly restricted, these societies focused deliberately on controversial political and religious issues of the day. More formally organized literary and philosophical societies, many of which grew out of less formal coffee house gatherings, also showed a notable increase. These included the Philosophical Societies in Bristol (1670), Spalding (1712), Peterborough (1730), Manchester (1781), and Derby (1783).[132]

Explanations for this efflorescence of cultural activity in England have typically emphasized changes in class relations. Perhaps to an even greater extent than the French Enlightenment, the cultural advances in England at the end of the seventeenth century and during the first half of the eighteenth century have been attributed to the rise of the bourgeoisie. According to this argument, the period dating from the Glorious Revolution and extending on through the eighteenth century witnessed the coming to power of a commercial and protoindustrial bourgeoisie. This community of upwardly mobile elites constituted a distinct social class which, in turn, produced its own distinctive style of self-legitimating discourse. C. H. George has expressed the essence of this view in his essay on the history of the bourgeoisie in England: "The English bourgeoisie have never felt more full of themselves and sure of their revolutionary mission than in the climactic generations following the Glorious Revolution. The moralizing of Addison, Steele, Pope, and above all, Defoe is the proof that the English bourgeoisie not only existed, but fairly vibrated with power and histrionic glory to match the great moments of past elites."[133] Another writer asserts that the bourgeoisie secured "its political hegemony" after 1688, and by 1720 "had established one of the world's great class dictatorships."[134] In this writer's view, the English Enlightenment was strictly the work of the bourgeoisie: "As a class, the bourgeoisie bought and controlled the press, censored the theatre, and supported such incidental expenses of a capitalist society as the minister and the teacher."[135] Other writers, focusing on more specific dimensions of the English Enlightenment, have suggested that the novel, for example, was "the bourgeois literary form *par excellence*," and that science was one of the "main battering rams used by the bourgeoisie in the late eighteenth century to destroy the aristocratic edifice."[136]

But, as in the French case, this argument proves difficult to substantiate. Strictly defined, the "bourgeoisie"—merchants, traders, businessmen, financiers—scarcely dominated English society. Even in London they continued to be outnumbered by a ratio of four to one by wealthy members of the landed aristocracy.[137] Nor was the bourgeoisie a distinct class. In kinship, marriage, and investments it remained closely integrated with the landed aristocracy.[138]

The close proximity between London's literary centers and its commercial and financial centers, of course, left its mark on English literature. Writers such as Defoe and Steele, for example, celebrated the expansion of industry. They saw in this expansion beneficial consequences for the nation's military and economic strength. Yet it could scarcely be said that the Enlightenment bore anything but loose connections with the process of embourgeoisment.

The members of philosophical societies continued to be drawn chiefly from the aristocracy rather than the bourgeoisie. Scientific academies, touted by some historians as agents of industry and technology, were founded in areas scarcely affected by industry. And the leading residents in some of the most heavily industrialized areas showed little interest in science. Private patrons from the landed elite, as well as patrons with semiofficial ties to the governing establishment, constituted the immediate social context in which many intellectual contributions were produced. Standards of taste, as well as many of the specific subjects which were written about, reflected the interests of the governing elite more closely than those of the merchants. And this was true even for writers who were critical of the state.

Nor were the expanding markets that facilitated the publication of a greater number of books as closely linked to the bourgeoisie as they were to the state.[139] The "inescapable conclusion," one of the leading literary historians of this period observes, is that

> "for *belles-lettres* . . . the market was still dominated by the traditional 'bookish' classes. All considerable subscriptions are headed by aristocrats (often with a tinge of royalty), ministers, MPs, government placemen, prominent churchmen, university dignitaries, professional men, and such like . . . Except in very special cases, the new men of commerce and industry have receded almost out of sight."[140]

The Role of Economic and Political Expansion

If direct links between the bourgeoisie and literary or scientific production in England prove difficult to establish, the broader role of economic and political developments were nevertheless significant. Like France, eighteenth-century England underwent a great deal of expansion in important sectors of the economy. The functions and personnel associated with the state bureaucracy also expanded considerably. These developments were, in fact, sufficiently similar to those taking place simultaneously in France that similar kinds of institutional resources for the production of culture became available. At the same time, relations between the state and the economy were different enough in England that its version of the Enlightenment took on characteristic features not evident in France. In neither case was the state's role in any way determinative of the ideas produced. But in both cases the state's expansion contributed immeasurably to the resources utilized in cultural production.

The economic growth that characterized this period in England was by no means universal enough to support the thesis that cultural production grew simply in an environment of generalized affluence. Economic growth was limited to particular areas. Indeed, it was limited mostly to those areas in which the state was actively involved. Overall growth had been relatively strong between 1660 and 1700 but then stagnated from about 1720 to 1750, after which it resumed a somewhat more rapid pace.[141] Some indicators continued to show growth even during the decades of stagnation, but the general pattern suggests that economic expansion was greatest at the beginning of the Enlightenment period rather than during its peak.[142] Indeed, the relative stagnation in principal industries such as woolens and linens during this period was a matter of sufficient concern to prompt several significant attempts at state intervention, including legislation to promote exports and the formation of joint-stock companies to improve production.

In comparison with the sluggish condition of the economy at large, the metal trades showed relatively steady expansion. They constituted one of the areas in which state policies, particularly in encouraging the colonial trade with Africa, were having a positive effect. Iron production also expanded as a result of the state's encouragement. It depended on political intervention to exclude Swedish exports, and mines remained largely under royal monopoly. In other areas the state's role was also an important factor. Roads and canals were built with public subsidies. The building industry expanded mainly because of the state's efforts to rebuild London. The paper industry showed mixed growth and decline, but also depended heavily on the state's actions because protectionism and war seemed to be the main ingredients involved in its recapture of the domestic market from the French.

The general area in which state policy had the greatest success in stimulating trade was in exports, especially to the American colonies. Between 1700 and 1750, export industries grew in output by 76 percent while domestic industries increased by only 7 percent. From 1750 to 1770, export production grew another 80 percent while domestic output grew only 7 percent again.[143] Over the same period, colonial trade increased as a proportion of total trade from 15 percent to 30 percent. Moreover, the rising importance of trade was evident in naval growth during this period: from 100,000 tons of shipping in 1685 to 325,000 tons in 1760; an increase from approximately 3,000 vessels to more than 9,000 vessels.[144]

As a result of this growth in exports and in some sectors of the domestic economy, the state's revenues showed a dramatic increase. Overall, the state's receipts grew from £32.8 million annually between 1688 and 1697 to £65.9 million between 1739 and 1748, and then to £141.9 million annually between 1776 and 1783.[145] Between 1700 and 1770, tax revenues increased even more rapidly than the economy, rising 123 percent at constant prices, compared with a 55 percent increase in national income. The state's growing role in the economy was thus evidenced by the fact that taxes constituted an increasing share of national income, rising by one estimate from 9.1 percent in 1700 to 13.1 percent in 1770.[146]

During none of these years, however, were tax revenues alone sufficient to meet government expenditures. Largely because of increasing military costs, state expenditures rose from £49.3 million annually between 1688 and 1697 to £236.5 million a year annually during the war with the American colonies. Accordingly, annual deficits ranged from £20 million to £90 million. Government spending, as a percent of national product, rose from approximately 7 percent in 1715 to 16 percent in 1783, and then to 27 percent in 1801, producing a staggering increase in the total national debt: from £14.2 million in 1700 to £130 million in 1763 to £456 million in 1800.[147]

The crucial difference in public finance between England and France was that in England the state had considerably greater capacity to raise money from loans than in France. Total revenues from loans grew from £16.6 million annually in the period 1688-1697 to £94.6 million annually between 1776 and 1783.[148] This capacity to borrow came about in part as a result of trade dislocations during the war years, when investments had to be channeled into other outlets. But the government's capacity to borrow also reflected the fact that investments in the state were good business, earning steady returns.[149] Lacking productive outlets for investments in industry, men of wealth turned to the state. And the state's extensive borrowing, in turn, proved to be an important stimulus to the growth of London as a financial and commercial center.[150] By 1750, when the national debt stood at £77 million, more than 60,000 persons held government investments, with almost £40 million concentrated in the hands of 5,000 to 6,000 London financiers.[151]

The combination of an effective revenue-generating mechanism and the continuation of mercantilist policies of state intervention in the economy—together with the added incentive provided by England's escalating military involvements—resulted in a considerable increase in the size of the state's administrative apparatus. The number of civil servants employed full time rose from approximately 10,000 at the turn of the century to 12,000 in 1720 and 16,000 in 1759.[152] In addition, about 1,000 persons were employed as retainers of the royal household, approximately 500 persons held high judicial positions, at least 10,000 earned their livings in the practice of law, and about the same number held commissions as naval and military officers.[153]

The two administrative functions that appear to have been most responsible for this growth in the state bureaucracy were fiscal and military affairs. Tax farming had been eliminated in 1684. In its place, tax collection was centralized under a single administrative hierarchy which was to grow both in size and importance.[154] The number of revenue boards increased from three in 1693 to nine in 1711. By 1714 there were 113 head commissioners in charge of 18 major departments. Customs alone employed 561 officials in London and another 1,000 in the provinces. On the whole, J. H. Plumb observes: "The number of men employed by the government grew faster between 1689 and 1715 than in any previous period of English history, and perhaps at a rate not to be equalled again until the nineteenth century."[155] In a similar vein, Roy Porter writes that the bureaucracy "was snowballing" as a result of "more contracts and concessions" and "new openings in the colonies and the excise, the expansion of Treasury, clerkships, cashierships, and controllerships, and the setting-up of the Board of Trade—all carrying jobs in the Government's pocket."[156]

These increases were partly attributable to the growing amount of foreign trade in which England was involved. They were also a product of the state's expanding mercantilist policies—policies aimed at generating increased revenues and protecting domestic commerce. As one writer, who otherwise diminishes the role of the state during this period, acknowledges: "Protectionism, with the consequent elaborate and confusing codes of fiscal control, gave more power to government and contributed greater numbers to its establishment than any other realm of government affairs."[157] In addition, the growth of trade was closely associated with increasing naval and military needs, especially in response to the rising costs of French privateering.[158] The period of warfare that ensued between 1689 and 1712 appears to have been a particularly decisive factor in the growth of the state. By the end, England had a fleet of 200 ships and approximately 120,000 men under arms, all of which required unprecedented efforts simply to coordinate, let alone to maintain through raising and dispensing public finances.[159]

The connections between intellectual activity and the expanding state apparatus in England were close, just as they were in France. Perhaps the similarities should not be overemphasized, for writers in London were probably freer on the whole from having to take roles in the bureaucracy than their counterparts were in Paris.[160] Nevertheless, much of the patronage that allowed scholars to function was channeled to them by wealthy members of the governing elite or by the state bureaucracy itself. This relation between writers and the state was in fact one of the more significant features of the period. As Leslie Stephen notes: "The relation between the political and the literary class was at this time closer than it had ever been. The alliance between them marks, in fact, a most conspicuous characteristic of the time. It was the one period . . . in which literary merit was recognized by the distributors of state patronage."[161] Or as another writer has remarked: "Literature had been brought out of the monkish cell and the market-place. Now it could aspire to courtly virtues."[162]

Virtually every writer of eminence became the recipient of patronage in generous proportions. John Gay received housing and living expenses from the duke of Queensberry, Johnson and Smollett from the earl of Bute, Boswell from the earl of Eglington, and Addison from Lord Halifax.[163] Alexander Pope complained that he was "the only scribbler of my time, of any degree of distinction, who never received any places from the Establishment, any pension from the Court, or any presents from a Ministry."[164] Yet his housing and living expenses were paid by the earl of Oxford. Many of Pope's contemporaries did, in fact, receive pensions, sinecures, and offices as well. John Gay was made commissioner of the state lottery and Edward Gibbon became lord of trade (for which he received the handsome pension of £800 a year).[165] Defoe and Swift each earned about £1,000 annually from various minor offices; Steele served in a number of posts, including commissioner of stamps and commissioner for forfeited estates, earning about £2,000 a year; and Addison became a commissioner of appeals in the Excise and then under secretary of state, receiving an annual income of £10,000.[166]

Less is known from the standpoint of the donors about the total cost of these expenditures to the state. But in the case of Walpole, one of the leading patrons, it has been estimated that he spent more than £50,000 from public funds during the 1730s alone on writers and printers.

These sums help put into a clearer perspective the earnings writers received from selling their works on the open market. Although such earnings were sometimes considerable, they seldom rivaled the amounts writers received from pensions and offices. Even successful writers earned relatively small sums from the open market. Addison and Steele, for example, split £1,000 for the first four volumes of the *Spectator*. Fielding received £600 for *Tom Jones*. And Swift earned only £200 pounds for *Gulliver's Travels*.[167] Probably the most successful publication during this period was Pope's translation of Homer, the total income from which amounted to £11,000. Most successful publishing ventures, however, paid only a few hundred pounds, and average earnings appear to have amounted to less than £100.[168]

These figures do not support the idea that the Enlightenment in England might have been made possible by the sheer expansion of a commercial publishing market. Instead, direct patronage from official and semiofficial sources was by far the most significant financial resource on which writers could rely. Geoffrey Holmes has remarked: "Very few poets, dramatists or writers of serious pretension could hope to live prosperously by their literary work alone . . . in the overwhelming majority of cases, influence, sponsorship or patronage of some kind was necessary to secure an aspirant his first foothold in this new profession."[169] It has even been suggested that the rise in commercial book publishing (typically associated with the second half of the eighteenth century) may have had a *negative* effect on literary careers—and certainly was perceived so by contemporaries—because it was accompanied by declining levels of personal patronage.[170]

Still, the role of direct patronage should not be exaggerated. London had its share of starving writers, just as did Paris.[171] But patronage was not something bestowed only on eminent writers who had already made their mark, rather than in the more critical stages of their careers. Of more than twenty eminent writers who received patronage from official sources during the first half of the eighteenth century, for example, only two appear to have received this support as a result of their literary distinction. All of the remainder received patronage at a time and in amounts that contributed to their later success.[172]

Although many of the arrangements by which patronage was given were idiosyncratic, the patronage system was more elaborate than any of the foregoing might suggest. At least five distinct mechanisms by which patronage was disseminated can be distinguished. First, a number of state offices were created specifically for the advancement of literature: poet laureate, historiographer, master of the revels, inspector of plays, Latin secretary, gazette writer, and royal librarian, to name a few. Second, offices not intrinsically concerned with literature or the arts were frequently granted to writers. Some of the departments in which offices were so occupied, for example, were ordnance, the treasury, the mint, wine licensing, customs, excise, and the post office. Third, private patronage was often given by leaders of state, some of whom have already been mentioned. Fourth, the government press, which was generally underwritten by ministers and party leaders from special funds for the purpose of propaganda, provided valuable revenue for newspapers, salaries for authors, and fees for specific publications. Finally, and of increasing importance, was the system of underwriting publishing costs by soliciting subscriptions from wealthy patrons, many of whom (although by no means all) were government functionaries. The author of this taxonomy concludes: "The patronage system, in its limited way, was surprisingly workable. It benefited relatively few writers, but the endurance of so many varieties of patronage during the century shows that a free market for literary property had not yet fully developed."[173]

How much the broader expansion of the state bureaucracy may have contributed to the development of literary patronage is difficult to establish except in the context of comparisons with countries in which this growth was not evident. It nevertheless appears that the expanded size and prosperity of the bureaucracy in the eighteenth century was one of the reasons why patronage was more readily available than it had been during the second half of the seventeenth. Michael Foss observes, for example, that despite the favor with which artists and writers were viewed during the Restoration, the fiscal problems facing Charles II prevented much attention being given to the arts.[174] Furthermore, the shift away from personal rule toward a more bureaucratized mode of government created a more elaborate system of personal linkages in which patronage, not just of writers, but of colleagues and subordinates in general, became an expected norm. To quote Leslie Stephen again: "The new race of statesmen were coming to depend upon parliamentary influence instead of court favour. They were . . . able to dispose of public appointments; places on the various commissions which had been founded as parliament took control of the financial system—such as commissions for the wine-duties, for licensing hackney coaches, excise duties, and so forth—besides some of the other places which had formerly been the perquisites of the courtier. They could reward personal dependents at the cost of the public; which was convenient for both parties."[175]

As this observation suggests, the state was not simply a rationally organized bureaucracy that incorporated writers into its formal structure. To a significant degree, the English Enlightenment took place within an institutional context that was not confined to the formal governmental bureaucracy as such. The context in which cultural production took place consisted, instead, of a loosely integrated ruling oligarchy bound together by complex webs of patronage and indebtedness. The state's influence on literature and science, moreover, was not restricted to that associated with direct patronage. The state served as an organizing vehicle. It facilitated the concentration of private resources. And it contributed to the creation in England, as in France, of a public sphere in which private interests took on a corporate identity. Understanding the nature and functioning of this public sphere appears to be the key to grasping the relation between writers and the state.

The Public Sphere

The public sphere that developed during this period should not be confused with the "electorate" in its modern sense. Although some have sought to portray the Enlightenment in England as a product of electoral politics, this view is difficult to sustain in light of what was actually happening to the electorate. Electoral politics were in fact contracting rather than expanding. After 1716 the frequency of general elections was cut in half. Between 1705 and 1747 the proportion of contested seats in electoral contests dropped from 65 percent to 8 percent. And over the same period the total electorate, which consisted of less than 1 percent of the population until well into the nineteenth century, grew by less than half the rate of growth in population, with some areas experiencing a reduction in eligible voters by as much as 50 percent.[176] Most of the state's activities were not subject to scrutiny by a broad electorate or "public," but were still controlled by a relatively small community of elites which, though scarcely tight knit, was nevertheless closed to outsiders. Few writers were privy to the circles in which information about political affairs flowed.[177] The privileged few among the literary elite who had access to these circles were, therefore, not so much the representatives of a diffuse public mind, for no such phenomenon existed as yet, as the cultural embellishment of a political oligarchy.

Nor was the public sphere simply a segment of the bourgeoisie that exercised rule behind the scenes. The ruling oligarchy included both bourgeois and aristocratic elements: merchants and industrialists but also landowners and rentiers. Revenue from customs on foreign trade made merchants an important ally of the state, which in return provided naval protection and favorable tariffs. The merchant oligarchy's role in financing public loans also brought it into a position of potentially stronger influence, and merchants frequently held important government positions.[178] Nevertheless, the landowners' position vis-à-vis the state remained strong and may actually have increased in strength during this period. Tax revenues were divided almost equally among land taxes, customs, and excise. Landowners were vital to the expansion of foreign trade, since woolens accounted for about half of all exports. And a growing number of the aristocracy received positions as diplomats, judges, party officials, and military personnel.[179]

Much debate has focused on the relative weight of the landed classes and the commercial classes in English political affairs during the eighteenth century. But the important fact as far as the production of literary discourse is concerned appears to be the degree to which the state was involved in the interests of both. Common interests necessitated collective action which thus drew the elite into a sphere of discussion centering on the state.

The public sphere was an adjunct of the growth of bureaucracy and patronage, just as it was in France. It was the product of an interdependent set of governing bodies that were not yet organized along strictly hierarchical lines of authority.[180] Power was formally divided. The crown appointed leading ministers and courtiers. Parliament operated under constitutional authority as the guarantor of liberty and privilege. Ministers, who functioned as heads of civil bureaus, could also exercise a great deal of influence in practical affairs. None of these entities, however, operated with much efficiency or in clearly articulated roles. Absenteeism, favoritism, promotion based on seniority rather than merit, ambiguous lines of responsibility, and an inadequate division of labor all compounded the problems facing the major governmental departments.[181]

Under these conditions the crucial ingredient for wielding effective power was patronage. As J. B. Owen suggests: "In an era of mixed government, before well-disciplined and nationally organized parties had emerged, and when the royal Closet was still on a higher political level than any Cabinet, nominal or efficient, the most basic ingredient promoting harmony between the king and his ministers on the one hand and the Commons on the other was of necessity the complicated nexus of interests created by the web of patronage."[182]

Ministers served at the pleasure of the king, but their actions were subject to criticism and censure by Parliament and the courts, and they were at the mercy of shifts in royal outlook. Ministers were able to provide a steady and powerful hand to the governing process only as long as the opinion of the various networks of patronage was on their side. And the experience of many eighteenth-century administrators demonstrated how quickly these opinions could change.[183] Not surprisingly, therefore, ministers included writers, publicists, and satirists within their patronage networks in an effort to shape public attitudes. This involvement worked to the material advantage of many who could command an audience with their publications, as we have seen. And yet, few writers appear to have been linked so closely with their patrons as to have lost the capacity to function in ways other than as propagandists.

The patronage systems in which English writers were integrated were neither rigid nor unchanging. These networks were products of the overlapping, diverse, and highly fluid coalitions and counter-coalitions that characterized the state in England perhaps to an even greater degree than in France. Roy Porter's description aptly portrays the situation: "Whig and Tory, Low and High Church, landed and moneyed property, pro- and anti-war, pro- and anti-Hanoverian factions tore at each other's throats like fighting cocks. Factions factionalized, and affected all arenas of life within the political nation."[184]

The divisions characterizing the public sphere in England in the eighteenth century had a long history: some dated to the Civil War, others originated as far back as the Reformation. Vestiges of the division between "court and country" continued to be evident in the crown's relations with Parliament, just as the various divisions between Anglicans and Nonconformists or Roman Catholics continued to affect domestic policies.[185] Other carryovers from the Restoration period, such as divisions in the London financial community between overseas and domestic traders and between family networks in the landed gentry, also made their presence felt on particular issues.

As the eighteenth century unfolded, two further bases of opposition emerged: one of relatively short-term duration, the other of longer-range significance. The first revolved around the conflict that developed between the new ministers of the Georgian court and those who had been loyal to Anne. The second was the relatively unstable, and for that reason all the more significant, set of shifting alliances and cleavages between the two factions that gradually became known as Whig and Tory.[186]

The polarization that eventually produced the labels Whig and Tory developed during the last decade of the seventeenth century and the first decade of the eighteenth century as a result of controversies surrounding royal succession, the church, and England's role in the War of the Spanish Succession. Tories generally opposed parliamentary monarchy, championed the church, and begrudged the financial burden of the war. Whigs welcomed the Protestant succession, protected Dissenters, and accepted the war.[187]

Despite the existence of these factions, though, neither group nor any of the interests to which party labels became attached was able to command the loyalty of a large bloc of officials for any length of time. A study of members of Commons, as constituted in 1742, for example, shows that the royal ministry and treasury commanded the allegiance of only 100 of the 550 members involved and that most of the remainder had no permanent ties to either of the major parties.[188] There was relative parity between the two parties and still sufficient independence for other factions to command allegiance. As late as the 1750s, neither party had an effective organizational structure of the kind that characterizes modern parties.

Ideology, therefore, became all the more important for cultivating party "principles."[189] Contemporaries readily ascribed ideological positions to the two parties and used these labels to categorize friends and foes. In the absence of party organization these labels served—apparently with considerable effectiveness—to generate voting along party lines on major issues of the day.[190] Ideology also appears to have legitimated the allegiances that party positions did command, for loyalty to "party" as such was still regarded with suspicion, whereas commitment to ideological positions could be defended as "principle."

Paralleling but in some ways also cutting across party divisions were the prevailing tensions between landed and commercial factions of the ruling class. Lawrence Stone has characterized this division as a fundamental conflict between "the landed interest which had traditionally held a virtual monopoly of political power, and the rapidly growing monied interest of the Bank, the East India Company, and the City."[191] After 1714 this conflict appears to have subsided somewhat because of increasing investments on the part of landowners in the Bank of England, intermarriage, and common interests being served by the state's colonial policies. Nevertheless, the tensions were by no means fully resolved. Each side still played a fundamentally different role in the economy, and for this reason held divergent political views on many questions. Naval and military preparations and war, in particular, were always divisive issues, because tax requirements for the military invariably fell heaviest on the land, while financiers and contractors typically prospered.[192]

Cutting across both partisan and class factional divisions was yet another fundamental cleavage which, though rooted in historical differences, was exacerbated by the growth of the administrative bureaucracy. The tension between bureaucratic or centralizing tendencies and the decentralizing tendencies of privileged groups, as we have already seen in the case of France, had been endemic in the conflict between court and country in England during the seventeenth century. During the early years of the eighteenth century this division generally occupied a background position relative to that between Whigs and Tories, but in subsequent decades it surfaced repeatedly. On one side were leading courtiers and political managers who were personally indebted to the monarch and who believed in stronger royal authority as the best means of promoting social order. On the other side were members of Parliament who had kept themselves free of obligations to the crown, objected to the corruption they perceived in royal patronage, and desired to limit the crown's exercise of power. The two sides found themselves at odds on numerous issues, such as the crown's right to maintain a standing army, the land tax, national debt, and changes in ministries and revenue departments.[193] What was especially important about this conflict was the degree to which it came to be regarded as an important source of balance to be preserved within the government.[194] This notion came into being only gradually, following more than a half century of disequilibrium with first Parliament and then the crown attempting to assert hegemony.

The fact that these contending factions negotiated their differences through the established state structures also constitutes a notable feature of the eighteenth century. Virtually all conflicts were fought out within the framework of parliamentary elections, through parliamentary debate, in the courts, and within the administrative departments, rather than evoking extraconstitutional solutions.

Moreover, they were contained in ways that kept them from precipitating direct action on the part of the broader populace. This was important in England, as it was in France, because it allowed political discourse to be located principally among the elite, rather than being turned toward mass mobilization.[195]

The clearest relation between factionalism in political life and the English literary world lies in the freedom and diversity that typified the literary community during this period. If patronage resulted in certain affinities between writers and their patrons, patronage networks were nevertheless sufficiently fragmented to support writers with highly diverse opinions.[196] Swift, Pope, and Gay, for example, were all friends of Bolingbroke and lent their talents to opposing the Walpole administration. Far from enunciating any form of bourgeois apologetics, they wrote from a perspective that was generally more in sympathy with aristocratic values than with commerce and high finance.[197] Steele and Congreve, in contrast, served as principal propagandists for the Whigs, and received generous stipends for their services. Samuel Johnson's intimate ties with the London business community, to take another example, were reflected in many of his essays on mercantilism; yet his views were also clearly distinguishable from those of a more radical defender of trade such as Mandeville.[198]

Writers concerned with popular topics could perhaps be expected to do little other than reflect the fragmented state of public affairs. But even in more technical fields, such as medicine, the different patronage networks to which practitioners were tied seem to have made a distinct impact. Physicians were not above conforming to the wishes of their patrons either in matters of style or in theoretical orientations. A student of the period writes: "In the absence of academic or professional criteria, patients recruited their practitioners by means of personal selection in the context of primary social interaction. Thus physicians were enjoined to adopt the stereotyped lifestyle of their genteel clients whilst simultaneously advertising their services by means of individual display. This peculiar amalgam of social conformity and personal eccentricity, when translated into intellectual activity, led to the creation of a profusion of competing theories."[199] In medical theory as in literary taste, the diversity of output was in some measure associated with the fact that resources were not yet concentrated in any single interest group capable of imposing its own orthodoxy. However much the pressure toward conformity may have accompanied patronage, the sources of patronage were still divided among contending political factions.

The heterogeneity of the public sphere also played a more active role in stimulating cultural production. To the extent that the different factions were engaged in a struggle among themselves for control over important state activities, they generated controversy, often willfully. And writers played a skillful hand in shaping these controversies. Lawrence Stone has suggested that the emerging cleavages between Whigs and Tories, which were in his view particularly intense from 1689 until about 1721, contributed greatly to the growth of popular literature.[200]

The pamphleteering that was initiated and paid for directly by contending ministerial factions was, of course, a product of these cleavages. But so were the coffee houses and debating clubs in which many fledgling writers became involved. Serving as headquarters for political candidates who needed some convenient mechanism for interacting with their constituents, the various coffee houses, taverns, and clubs came to be identified with different political orientations. Among the better-known gathering places, the Kit-Cat Club was a Whig stronghold which brought together such writers as Addison and Steele with men of influence such as the publisher Jacob Tonson and patrons such as the dukes of Newcastle, Somerset, Devonshire, Manchester, Dorset, and Montagu, and the earls of Lincoln, Bath, Wilmington, Carbery, Carlisle, Berkeley, and Halifax. The Brothers Club (later the Scriblerus Club), in contrast, was a Tory creation frequented by leading party members such as Harley and Bolingbroke and propagandists such as Swift, Gay, Pope, and Arbuthnot.[201] At first the clubs functioned mainly to bring writers and patrons together; but as time went on many of them also became sources of publications, and a few had professional writers directly in their employ.[202]

During much of the period from about 1700 to 1750 the division between Whigs and Tories appears to have overshadowed other political cleavages, or coincided so closely with them that it resulted in a relatively bipolar political climate. This division was not wholly beneficial to the production of scholarship. Although it does appear to have stimulated discussion and patronage, it nevertheless focused attention on specific issues that became the subject of topical pamphleteering. Thus it earned for the literature of the period a reputation of being somewhat more practical, if also superficial, and of less theoretical importance than its French counterpart.

Whether this reputation withstands scrutiny is a matter of debate. The evidence, however, does suggest a somewhat greater degree of involvement in partisan pamphleteering among leading writers in England than in France. The political situation in France appears to have been both more dynamic and ambiguous, giving writers the opportunity to engage in higher levels of abstraction and to struggle perhaps more deeply with creative alternatives in the fields of political and ethical inquiry. In England writers appear to have identified somewhat more readily with one faction or another and to have devoted their energies toward the defense of partisan positions. Insofar as the political climate remained polarized, intellectual diversity was sustained within the broader literary community, but individual writers may have succumbed more easily to the pressures associated with patronage. As Michael Foss notes: "At the end, political patronage and the alliance between the arts and politics appeared a destructive chimera—an invitation to bad work for the artist . . . The best wits perceived this and, angry at their prison that they helped to build, struck out at their gaolers."[203]

The best writers not only recognized the dangers inherent in patronage but also sought to rise above the factionalism they perceived within the public sphere. Depending on their vocations and interests, they sought to accomplish this feat in different ways, all of which nevertheless colored the output of their work. The self-imposed rule against engaging in political or religious discussion which members of the Royal Society had initiated at its founding continued to be observed during the eighteenth century, with the result that science came to be regarded as a form of truth above any petty squabbles of the day.[204] A similar attitude pervaded the work of some who wrote on political issues as well. Championing the virtues of reason, they used the very existence of partisan divisions as evidence for the need to pay greater heed to their form of dispassionate analysis.[205] A related response was to objectify the nature of political factionalism itself, making it a subject of scholarly inquiry. The shifting alliances and cleavages that characterized English politics were in fact a topic of considerable fascination to writers who sought both to depict the origins of these cleavages and to determine their implications for the future.

The division that appears to have stimulated the greatest share of literary reflection was that between monarchical and representative aspects of government. Limited constitutional monarchy existed in principle, but it remained a precarious institution. Writers devoted a great deal of energy to debating its strengths and weaknesses. Although the chances of royal patronage being used to subvert the constitutional framework appear in retrospect to have been exaggerated, contemporaries feared that the crown's power could be corrupted by self-interested ministers. Most feared was the revival of a despotic system in which parliamentary powers would be reduced to ineffectiveness. Writers with such diverse views as Gibbon, Swift, and Gay argued against any arbitrary extension of ministerial power. At the same time, the threat of an overweening House of Commons with powers to block efficient and effective central decision-making was also recognized. Writers suggested that the crown's ministers needed to create strong patronage networks in order to counterbalance other interests and to create coalitions around mutually beneficial policies. Hume and Mandeville, among others, joined the debate on the side of patronage and material interests as guarantors of constitutional liberty.[206]

The existence of an increasingly powerful administrative bureaucracy arrayed against a strong constitutional Parliament gave substance to these discussions. An apologetic literature emerged on both sides. But an increasingly important literature which reflected the genuine ambivalence of the situation, and which argued for *balance* as the ideal resolution, also emerged. The concept of sovereignty itself came to be redefined to include a balance of authority among the crown, ministers, and Parliament. It was in this context that the authority of reason and arguments relating to the laws of nature, as advanced in Locke's *Two Treatises of Government,* took on special importance. In a sense, perhaps as real as its dependence on political patronage and protection, the fate of Enlightenment discourse thus became tied to the state, for the success of the state tended to vindicate the arguments from reason on which a balanced conception of sovereignty was defended.

Balanced sovereignty was regarded as inherently precarious, despite the fact that it was deemed most beneficial to the preservation of social order in the long run. In the face of multiple contending factions it was not surprising, therefore, to find specific events being debated in relation to this broader conception of the public good.[207] Any and all policy questions became occasions on which to dramatize concern for the public good. Differences in the wealth of urban and rural elites were popularly perceived as one source of potential disequilibrium, as were the king's choice of ministers, laws protecting private property, celebrated court cases, religious differences, and accusations of "corruption" within the state's many bureaus. Teetering always on the brink of a potentially disastrous imbalance, the state generated continuous discussion that extended beyond political theory itself into theology, law, and ethics. For the balance required was sufficiently precarious to require all the reasoned virtue that could be mustered.

The public sphere in England was thus an arena, not unlike that evident in France at the same time, in which rational reflection on public affairs acquired vast importance. It was an amalgam of contending factions whose interests were welded together by the expanding central agencies of the state. And the exact balance among these contending interests was widely held to be a delicate equilibrium susceptible to any number of disruptive forces. The state's expanding resources supplied not only the patronage on which writers' fortunes depended but also an ambivalent political atmosphere in which scholars enjoyed the freedom—and the compulsion—to argue the seemingly endless issues of public propriety and civic virtue.

7

Enlightenment Developments in Prussia and Scotland

*T*HE ENLIGHTENMENT in the German states did not peak until late in the eighteenth century and was therefore in a position to reflect borrowings from both the French and English literary revivals.[1] It nevertheless included a number of important native contributions and came to be institutionalized as a major cultural phenomenon, particularly in Prussia, which at the time dominated the other German states by virtue of its power and size.[2] Following the work of Leibniz and the Berlin Academy, which had been founded at the start of the century, writers such as Lessing, Mendelssohn, Nicolai, and Kant brought international luminosity to German literature. Through their work, and the important institutional foundations that were laid in Prussia more generally, the principles of the Enlightenment came to be firmly planted, or as one observer has asserted, "imprinted more deeply in Prussia than anywhere else."[3] The other country that became known for its own Enlightment was Scotland. Here, too, the contributions of prominent individuals stand out: Hume, Smith, Robertson, Reid, among others. But the Scottish Enlightenment was also typified by a broader upsurge of scholarly production and by its institutionalization in social activities. The Scottish and German cases provide two additional contexts in which to observe the interplay of conditions that were to prove conducive to cultural innovation.

Cultural Expansion in the German States

Indicators of cultural activity uniformly portray the eighteenth century as a period of dramatic growth in German literature. The total number of books listed in catalogs of the Frankfurt book fairs between 1701 and 1710 was 1,213; by the last decade of the century this number had climbed to 3,529. Over the same period the proportion of books on the lists that were printed in German rose from 58 percent to 89 percent.[4] Leipzig, which was the center of the German publishing industry, revealed an even steeper rate of growth in its book catalogs, particularly between 1760 and the end of the century. The number of books listed remained about constant between 1700 and 1720 (978 and 979, respectively), then rose to 1,326 in 1740, dropped slightly to 1,198 in 1760, then increased to 2,642 in 1780, and grew to 4,012 in 1800.[5] Further evidence from the categories in which books were classified also points to the broadening of intellectual activity that is typically associated with the Enlightenment. Between 1740 and 1800 the number of books dealing with religion and theology declined from 436 to 241; over the same period works on politics, history, and geography increased from 221 to 631; and works on philosophy, science, and mathematics increased from 334 to 1,590. Several estimates suggest that by 1773 there were approximately 3,000 full-time professional writers in the German states, and by 1787 this number had increased to approximately 6,000.[6] Given the increased number of writers, a growing number of publishers, and gradually expanding print runs, it has been estimated that the overall number of copies of books printed during the last two decades before the French revolution may have been as high as 50 million.[7]

The periodical press in Germany also demonstrated rapid growth during the eighteenth century. From the beginning the popular press fed off the Enlightenment, profiting from the intellectual controversies it generated, earning a foothold in the cultural market by disseminating new ideas to the educated public, and utilizing the doctrines of tolerance and reason to gain freedom for itself.[8] The first daily newspaper (called the *Vossische*) appeared in Berlin in 1721 and articles containing political commentary were soon openly encouraged by the court.[9] After 1740 philosophical and learned discussions also began to be included in the newspapers.[10] Between

1741 and 1765 approximately 700 newspapers were founded in the German states and about another 1,000 were established by 1780.[11] Another estimate shows that approximately 250 new periodicals of all kinds were founded between 1766 and 1769 alone, that over 700 were established in the 1770s, and that more than 1,200 came into being during the 1780s.[12] Altogether, the number of readers of these periodicals and newspapers probably reached 1 million by 1750 and some 3 million shortly after the French Revolution.[13]

Science was another area in which the German states evidenced signs of significant advancement. The number of eminent scientists living in German states multiplied four times between 1700 and 1800, rising to a level that rivaled that of England in absolute numbers and that within another fifty years would exceed that of either England or France. Closer inspection of these figures reveals that Prussia alone accounted for nearly half the German scientists of the eighteenth century, far exceeding the number in any of the other German states, of which only Saxony, Hanover, and Bavaria accounted for more than a few eminent scholars. As in England, the institutionalization of scientific research on any significant scale within the universities did not come about until the first part of the nineteenth century.[14] Nevertheless, it is generally recognized that the eighteenth century played a critical role in laying the foundation for these later developments. By midcentury the ideas of Newton appear to have been widely in vogue among German intellectuals, popularized especially by Maupertius and Euler, and were adopted at least to some extent by Kant.[15] Toward the end of the century chemistry also registered particularly rapid advances as the number of salaried positions in this field rose from eighteen in 1750 to forty-eight in 1800.[16]

As in France and England, a major locus of growth for the new forms of scholarship was found in the reading clubs, salons, and academies of the period. A leading center of Enlightenment thought was the Monday Club, founded in Berlin in 1755; another was the Society of Friends of the Natural Sciences, patronized by Frederick II. So-called "Wednesday Clubs," similar to the salons in Paris, also sprang up in Berlin during the first half of the century, drawing leading officials, civil servants, and teachers into their circles, as well as writers and philosophers.[17] Similar clubs are known to have existed in Hamburg, Wittenberg, Lüneberg, Halberstadt, Mainz, Ulm, Frankfurt-am-Main, and Erlangen.[18] These clubs were followed during the second half of the century by the more broadly diffused reading societies (lesegesellschaften), which rose in number from only five in 1760 to more than two hundred by 1789.[19] Over the course of the century at least a dozen scientific and philosophical societies of a more formal kind were also founded, including the prominent Societas Scientiarum (1700), the Nouvelle Société Littéraire (1742), and the Académie des Sciences (1744), all in Berlin, and such regional centers of intellectual work as the Nuremberg Cosmological Society (1748), the Royal Scientific Society in Göttingen (1752), and the Munich Academy of Sciences (1759). These academies played an important role in the initiation and dissemination of Enlightenment ideas by drawing scholars together, providing research facilities, and sponsoring essay competitions to stimulate interest among younger writers.[20] As R. Stephen Turner notes in his study of Prussian culture: "At the peak of their confidence and vigor by 1750, the academies had not only become centers for the promulgation of Enlightenment ideas, but had also replaced the universities as the undisputed leaders of scholarly inquiry into such fields as science, mathematics, and history."[21]

Although the intellectual activity that was centered in the academies eclipsed in some respects that of the universities for its innovativeness, the universities nevertheless underwent a transition that made them important contributors to the Enlightenment as well. Unlike their counterparts in France and England, the German universities had already begun to show some signs of liberalization during the seventeenth century in theological and philosophical orientations, which provided the groundwork for subsequent developments in the eighteenth century.[22] By the 1720s philosophy had clearly begun to overtake theology in importance, and ideas about natural law and historical criticism were beginning to penetrate discussions of the state.[23] Prompted by mercantilist policies, cameralism and the science of the state *(Statistik)* were also appearing in university curricula.[24] Universities in both Protestant and Catholic areas were to a larger extent than in France or England under secular control, giving faculty somewhat greater latitude in dealing with religious issues.[25] By 1700 there were twenty-eight universities in all, the largest of which were Cologne, Leipzig, Wittenberg, and Halle. The next half century witnessed both advance and decline, depending on the institution at issue. Cologne, Strasbourg, and Trier ceased operations entirely, while newer institutions such as Halle (1694),

Breslau (1702), Göttingen (1737), and Erlangen (1742) grew in size and scholarly significance. The newer institutions were well funded, downplayed theological disputes, emphasized science and philosophy, and drew leading scholars as well as students from across Europe.[26] Enrollment figures appear to have climbed only until 1750, after which they receded relative to the larger population; but the universities continued to have a cumulative impact on intellectual activity, becoming in the nineteenth century models of graduate education in scientific and technical specialties.[27]

The political context in which the German Enlightenment was nurtured differed to a significant degree from that of either France or England in that the German states had not yet been unified under a single regime but retained the distinction of being "a collection of virtually independent states."[28] Leaving aside the Austrian lands (which will be considered in the next chapter), authority in the German territories remained divided among 94 spiritual and lay princes, 102 courts, 40 prelates, and 51 imperial cities. Moreover, many of these territories comprised noncontiguous tracts or were internally divided, so that as many as 2,000 administrative units existed in all.[29] Prussia and Saxony, each with populations of approximately 2.5 million in 1700, were the largest of these units, but together they accounted for only about a third of the total German population. Other territories of significant size included Bavaria, Hanover, and the Palatinate.

One of the positive consequences that scholars have generally perceived in this lack of political unity is an enlarged number of sponsors for the production of scholarly work. After the Thirty Years' War the numerous German courts had become leaders in patronizing the arts, opera companies, and theater groups.[30] Competition to outdo one another in the symbolic dimensions of princely splendor appears to have been one of the factors leading to generous increases in levels of patronage.[31] In the eighteenth century some of this competition remained evident in the manner in which universities were supported. In sheer numbers the fact that twenty-eight universities existed in a population smaller than that of France was itself tribute to the fact that every major sovereign and prelate felt it necessary to sponsor at least one institution of higher learning.

In more direct ways the reforms that brought new life to some of the leading universities were also to a degree influenced by the competitive nature of German politics. The most notable example was the founding of the University of Göttingen under the patronage of the Hanoverian kings, allegedly in response to the success that Halle had achieved under Prussian tutelage.[32] According to Charles E. McClelland, Göttingen appears to have "interested the culturally distinguished Elector George II less for itself than for the prestige it would give him in his bitter rivalry with the king of Prussia."[33] The university at Erlangen was initiated with similar goals to those of Göttingen and Halle, but failed to succeed to the same extent because of the comparative lack of resources available from the Franconian principalities of Ansbach and Bayreuth. Toward the second half of the century rivalry between the Protestant north and Catholic south served to initiate further academic development. One writer observes: "As the Catholic princes of the *Reich* sought to emulate their Protestant colleagues in transforming their territories into states, so did their need for properly trained administrators, educators and priests prompt them to remodel the universities which could supply them."[34] Also benefiting from these political rivalries, although probably to no greater a degree than the provincial academies in France, were the scientific and philosophical societies. The Society of Sciences in Göttingen appears to have been established in 1742 in direct response to its Prussian rivals.[35] In subsequent decades the Erfurt Academy of Useful Sciences (1754), with patronage from the elector of Mainz; the Bavarian Academy of Sciences (1759), under the sponsorship of Elector Maximilian II; and the Electoral Academy of Mannheim (1763), with generous patronage from Elector Carl Theodore, all were initiated with apparently similar intentions.

If prestige was a principal factor in the sponsorship of learning, some writers have suggested that mercantilist policies, with not wholly beneficial consequences for scholarship, were also involved. The role of the provincial university was to keep young men and their wealth within the state while, it was hoped, drawing foreign students as well. During the reign of Frederick the Great, these aims were reinforced by laws that prevented Prussian youth from studying abroad and by university policies that prohibited professors from resigning their Prussian posts in order to accept positions elsewhere.[36] These injunctions gradually fell into disuse during the eighteenth century, as Prussian universities became more competitive in terms of curricula and salaries.

Probably the most positive consequence of the divided German political system was the freedom it afforded scholars who ran afoul of censorship laws or university trustee boards. The presence of numerous jurisdictions, most with a university or academy, meant that scholars could find autonomy by migrating from one jurisdiction to another. Much like the role of contending factions among French and English patrons, multiple jurisdictions—all within a common language zone—reduced the force with which restrictions on novel ideas could be applied. The most famous case in which this condition was actually utilized to a writer's advantage was that of Christian Wolff whose eminent career at Halle was cut short in 1723 when he fell into disfavor with the trustees and was expelled. Like others in similar situations, Wolff escaped more severe repercussions from his work by moving to Saxony, where he remained until 1740.[37] The advantages of contending political jurisdictions can also be seen in the career of Gotthold Ephraim Lessing. At the age of nineteen Lessing managed to escape repaying a substantial debt in Leipzig by fleeing to Berlin. For more than a decade he frequented both cities, and then (in 1765) accepted a position in Hamburg after falling out of favor with the court in Berlin. Five years later, after failing to secure the financial support he needed in Hamburg, Lessing settled in Wolfenbüttel under the patronage of the duke of Brunswick. For others in less severe circumstances migration itself was perhaps not as crucial as the knowledge that an escape could be made if necessary. As Fichte, reflecting on the eighteenth century, wrote in 1808: "A truth that could not be uttered at one place, could at another . . . and so in spite of much one-sidedness and narrowness, a higher degree of freedom of enquiry and expression was possible in Germany as a whole than in any other state before."[38]

Growth in the Prussian Bureaucracy

Apart from this lack of political unity, the same tendencies that were apparent in the state-building activity of France and England were also apparent in German areas, most notably in Prussia. The Prussian bureaucracy began to expand rapidly during the second half of the seventeenth century in response to changing demands and opportunities. The "general crisis" that beset the central European economy with particular severity during the first half of the seventeenth century had resulted in serious reversals for the agrarian aristocracy—the Junkers—who had dominated Prussian politics, thus creating an opportunity for the Hohenzollern dynasty to play a stronger centralizing role in the region.[39]

Rising involvement in European military affairs, together with growing efforts to apply mercantilist policies to Prussian finances, led to further bureaucratic expansion. According to W. H. Bruford: "From about 1660 there were commissaries in every corner of the land to negotiate in matters of excise, taxation, billeting and so forth with the local authorities, the beginnings in fact of an anti-feudal bureaucracy."[40] By the beginning of the eighteenth century additional offices had been created to deal with the management of crown land, rents, and other economic matters, and new departments were added for trade and industry, customs, mines, forests, and military administration. Functions arrogated by the state included not only the administration of royal estates and military affairs but also closer supervision of religious matters, controls over trade and industry, the regulation of pricing and promotion of exports, and the overseeing of conditions affecting labor and agriculture, competition among companies, and features of the social infrastructure such as crime and health conditions.

To accommodate these growing functions the bureaucracy developed from a relatively small set of committees administered by the Privy Council to a highly complex structure of approximately thirty functionally differentiated departments, cabinets, and commissions with responsibilities ranging from tax collection to the administration of justice, to diplomatic relations, to the formulation of economic policies.[41] At the top, officials in the various departments met regularly to coordinate affairs of state; at lower levels, their authority extended into the provinces through an elaborate system of deputy ministers, not unlike the staffs of the French intendants, who collected taxes, provisioned troops, built roads, and inspected mines.[42]

During the eighteenth century the bureaucracy continued to expand in the face of even broader responsibilities. A Supreme Appeal Court was founded in 1703, and a General Finance Directory was added in 1713; in the same year the *Landrate* was reformed to reduce provincial control over its revenue collection functions; a year later the General Auditor's Office brought treasury functions under one head; compulsory primary education was introduced in 1717; and throughout this period the army grew under the administration of the General War Commissary, rising from 39,000 men in 1713 to 78,000 in 1740, and then to 200,000 in 1789.[43]

At the center of this growth were the state officials or *Beamtentum,* which became the most dynamic segment of Prussian society during the eighteenth century. Concentrated largely in Berlin, which grew in population from only 6,500 in 1661 to 60,000 in 1721 and then to 150,000 by 1795, this class of state officials and their dependents is estimated to have increased at least fourfold in number during the eighteenth century, comprising as much as one-third of Berlin's entire population by 1783, and reaching a high point that was not exceeded even in the following century.[44]

It is no less difficult than in the cases of England and France to conceive of this growth taking place except for the rapid rate of economic expansion that also characterized Prussia during much of the late seventeenth and eighteenth centuries. Trade, industry, and population had declined during the seventeenth century as a result of the Thirty Years' War and the shift of Europe's economic axis toward the Atlantic seaboard. The eighteenth century witnessed a dramatic reversal of these trends, as trade once again grew, new industries developed, and population increased.

To an even greater extent than in France or England, these developments were the result of deliberate mercantilist efforts by the state rather than simply exogenous conditions from which the state happened to derive benefits. Beginning in the seventeenth century the leading princes in Prussia, Hanover, Saxony, and Bavaria had begun to take over the role that wealthy merchant families such as the Fuggers and Weslers had played in promoting international trade and finance, and the residential cities of the princes, such as Berlin and Munich, gradually replaced the imperial free cities as centers of power and urban growth. Prussia's adoption of mercantilist policies appears to have been initiated principally as a means of generating sufficient revenue to sustain itself militarily. To achieve this objective the commercial policies of Holland were actively imitated, including the establishment of new industries, the levying of protective tariffs, the use of military purchases to stimulate growth in domestic textile production, the suppression of guilds, and the issuing of incentives to encourage technological innovation. In 1709 an internal customs system was established; between 1718 and 1723 a series of tariffs and import restrictions on cloth was imposed to protect the emerging textile industry; from 1732 to 1735 craft guilds were reorganized to encourage domestic industrial development; and over the following two decades the state supplied credit to new firms, created monopolistic companies, and founded factories.[45]

Despite some successes achieved by these measures, agriculture remained the mainstay of the Prussian economy, and it was to this sector that the state made its most notable contributions. New lands were brought under cultivation on a large scale; imports of foreign grain were prohibited and a vast grain storage program was initiated; measures were taken to encourage increases in productivity; and efforts were made to equalize the tax burden and provide greater legal protection for the peasantry.[46] The greatest need in the area of agricultural policy, however, was to increase the labor supply. Its population having undergone first the Thirty Years' War, then the Swedish-Polish War, and then the plague of 1709, in which an estimated one-third of the population died, Prussia was left with a population-to-land ratio only a quarter that of France and a third that of England.[47]

To encourage population growth the government pursued a vigorous policy of internal colonies created at state expense to attract refugees and other immigrants. Thus during the 1740s and 1750s close to 50 million thalers was spent in draining approximately 500,000 acres of land, and inducements were given to attract approximately 285,000 immigrants. Natural increase also continued at such a rapid pace during this period that by 1793 population density stood at 30 per square kilometer compared to only 18.7 in 1740.[48]

In addition, the state deployed its military strength to add substantially to its teritories, drawing in East Pomerania, Silesia, the area around Magdeburg, and scattered possessions in the north, central, and southern parts of the empire. The acquisition of Silesia in particular added significantly to Prussia's economic base, since Silesia was already one of the most prosperous agricultural districts in central Europe and included valuable linen, pottery, and glass industries, which together nearly doubled Prussia's exports, as well as rich mining areas.[49]

During the 1760s Prussian agricultural exports received an added boost because of rising grain prices in western Europe, and after the Seven Years' War industrial exports began to make a stronger showing as well.[50] Thus, by the time of the French Revolution, Prussia's overall trade yielded an annual surplus of 3 million thalers, compared with sizable deficits prior to 1740; population stood at 5.8 million, compared with 2.2 million at the beginning of the century; annual state revenues had increased at least fourfold; and the treasury boasted a surplus of 55 million thalers in place of a net deficit at the beginning of the century.[51]

Although the state's initiatives succeeded by the end of the century in promoting growth in commerce and industry as well as in agriculture, little evidence suggests that anything resembling a "bourgeois revolution" took place in Prussian society or that the state was to any significant degree dominated by a commercial or industrial bourgeoisie. By all estimates the bourgeoisie remained comparatively underdeveloped. Even in relatively commercialized cities such as Magdeburg and Halle, estimates of wealth and occupation suggest that less than 3 percent of the labor force were merchants, industrialists, owners of capital, or wealthy professionals.[52] Although the number of privately owned trading houses and industrial firms rose steadily, relatively more of the economy was controlled by the state than in many other areas, and economic initiatives were more likely to come from the state than from the bourgeoisie.[53]

Nor could the central bureaucracy itself be considered in any straightforward sense a product of the bourgeoisie; if anything, the bourgeoisie lost influence in the bureaucracy as the century progressed. At the beginning of the eighteenth century only about a quarter of the top officials came from the aristocracy, the remainder apparently stemming from a bourgeois background of one kind or another; by midcentury a majority were nobles and many of the remainder were sons of clergy and professional bureaucrats or jurists; and by the end of the century three-fifths of all ministers and high officials were of noble background.[54] Leonard Krieger remarks: "The officials of burgher origin . . . not only remained numerically inferior to the nobles in state service but they tended themselves to be absorbed into the aristocracy."[55]

Initially the centralization of state power itself had come about at the expense of the nobility, but the state's continuing dependence on the agricultural sector for its financial and military needs forced it to make numerous concessions to the nobility, thus giving the Prussian state, again in Krieger's words, "a more definite aristocratic character" than its counterparts elsewhere.[56] As Alfred Cobban has suggested, the Prussian state "purchased autocracy by guaranteeing and even increasing the social and economic privileges of the nobility."[57]

The State, Patronage, and Culture

As far as the cultural sphere was concerned, it was clearly the state rather than the commercial or industrial bourgeoisie in any larger sense that provided the bulk of resources that permitted significant growth in this sphere to occur. One of the most visible ways in which the expanding state affected German scholarship was in breaking the monopoly of the traditional learned professions over the definition of legitimate knowledge. Prior to the 1740s the faculties of theology, law, and medicine held almost exclusive control over the universities, exercising guildlike power in the credentialing of members of the educated elite on the basis of learned knowledge rather than practical skills. With the growth of state agencies having increased authority over the universities and a greater need for practical skills, this monopoly was gradually broken. New universities such as Halle were established under state jurisdiction to provide training for the civil bureaucracy, including courses in modern languages, geography and history, mathematics, science, and methods of practical administration.[58] The students attracted to the newer universities came not from the commercial bourgeoisie but overwhelmingly from the bureaucratic and aristocratic classes.[59]

Another avenue by which the state enhanced its role in the universities was the examination system. Although examination procedures were also put into place in France and England, the Prussian system was uniquely direct and comprehensive. As early as 1725, physicians were required to pass an examination before the Medical Collegium in Berlin. Twelve years later a similar edict mandated that all councilors and judges sustain a three-day examination before the High Court of Appeal, and by 1740 evangelical clergy were normally subjected to some form of examination before being allowed to accept a call to serve in a local church. Since all of these examinations demanded as a prerequisite at least two years' attendance at a Prussian university, the state's licensing procedures proved to be an effective means not only of imposing standards on the traditional professions but also of indirectly putting pressure on the universities to adapt their curricula in such a way as to prepare students to pass the required examinations. It was in fact through the examination system that the state gradually pressed the professions and their counterparts in the universities away from the traditional model of erudition, rhetoric, and classical scholarship toward innovative standards of technical competence.[60]

The state's relation to the church played a prominent role in initiating further reforms in the universities. The highest levels of church administration had been supervised directly by the state since the Reformation, giving secular officials wide latitude in appointing ecclesiastical officials favorable to the state's policies. This role, together with the presence since the end of the Thirty Years' War of a relatively strong representation of all three major religious groups (Lutherans, Calvinists, and Roman Catholics), permitted the heads of state to exercise a powerful hand in deciding religious cases in the courts and controlling activities in the realm of education.[61] During the first half of the eighteenth century, violent disputes within the theological faculties among orthodox Lutherans, rationalists, and Pietists gave the state an opportunity to intervene further in the universities. In 1742 the University Commission was created as a separate department to oversee reorganizing the universities, taking over this function from the Spiritual Department, which had formerly been responsible for the universities. This reorganization took the appointment of professors out of the hands of the religious interests and permitted the state to promote secular learning.[62] Official encouragement was given to the ideas of Christian Wolff, who sought a synthesis between the Enlightenment emphasis on reason and traditional Lutheran theology, and university curricula were modified to enable students of theology to study mathematics, science, and philosophy, and for students of law to give greater attention to natural philosophy and less to theology.[63]

In 1756 the state again increased its control over the universities and learned professions by securing rights to inspect the universities, to require reports from professors, to certify requirements for matriculation and graduation, to approve the selection of pastors and teachers in the provinces, and to control entrance into such professions as law and medicine. Under these conditions learning and scholarship became closely linked to the state and were allowed to proceed only in the direction that the bureaucracy deemed desirable. As one writer concludes: "Caught in the web of the judiciary, the student embarked upon a course of study determined by the state, obtained a position with the sponsorship of the state, and could never escape the conclusion that he was a quasi bureaucrat."[64]

Beyond the universities, the state's role was also particularly evident in the academies. At the more formal level there had already been a build-up of state activity around the turn of the century aimed at promoting natural philosophy and technological experimentation. In addition to the University of Halle and new colleges of medicine and beaux arts, the Societas Scientiarum was established in Berlin with Leibniz at the helm. An observatory and an anatomical laboratory were also constructed; nevertheless, except for these contributions, little more was accomplished until the 1740s. The state's allocation of resources was sporadic, meager, and structured to permit scholars little freedom to pursue independent interests. The accession of Frederick II in 1740 represented a genuine turning point. The Societas Scientiarum was disbanded in 1744; two years later the new Berlin Academy was inaugurated, modeled after the Académie des Sciences in Paris, and given a broad mandate to regulate its own affairs; and two internationally prominent scientists, Maupertius from France and Euler from Russia, were brought in to head its activities.[65] It has also been suggested that the administration's sponsorship of its own academies during this period was a calculated act aimed at transferring some of the state's resources into channels, other than the universities, in which the state's influence could be applied with fewer restrictions.

Less formally, the growth of voluntary reading clubs and philosophical societies also appears to have owed something to the growth of the state, to judge from the fact that members of these societies and subscribers to their journals were drawn chiefly from the burgeoning ranks of the bureaucracy.[66] The lesegesellschaften, as the smallest, most informal, and most geographically diffused of these organizations, were probably least affected by the state. But even they demonstrated the imprint of the political context in which they arose: the core of their membership was drawn from officers, professors, physicians, pastors, and the service nobility, all members of the rising elite that depended on the central and regional bureaucracies; the periodicals and books held by these associations contained a large proportion of material on politics, technical information, and discussions of current events; and their very existence was contingent on forbearance by the authorities, as evidenced by the fact that the numbers of these associations declined rapidly under the more restrictive conditions that followed in the early decades of the nineteenth century.[67] Out of these circles, particularly during the last quarter of the century, came much of the impetus for vocational training, schools of trade and commerce, and the system of universal primary education that was put into practice prior to the 1830s.[68]

Other forms of patronage, such as those common in England between private sponsors and individual writers, appear to have been relatively less characteristic of the Prussian Enlightenment. Insofar as private patronage was recorded, it appears to have come mainly from the court. Frederick II, a great admirer of the philosophes, invited Voltaire to live at court for several years and gave Rousseau protection during his exile from France. Pufendorf and Thomasius both received patronage from the court, as did August Hermann Francke, the architect of Prussian popular education. Through the founding of the Berlin Opera, the Royal Library, and the Comedy Theater, as well as the king's household itself, which employed a retinue of approximately sixty musicians and actors, the arts more generally received cultivation.

Few of the higher aristocracy in the rural provinces and few among the commercial or industrial bourgeoisie appear to have shown any interest in the arts and literature until relatively late in the eighteenth century.[69] There does, however, appear to have been a clientele for these forms of culture among the ranks of the bureaucracy. The numerous newspapers and journals that appeared during the last third of the century catered mainly to diplomats, officers, and civil servants, who, like their counterparts in France and England, were hungry for news and political commentary.[70] Their patronage and subscriptions also appear to have been crucial to the publishing industry, especially since the lack of uniform copyright laws in the German territories until 1871 made it virtually impossible for writers and printers to recover costs simply from sales on the open market.[71] In the absence of copyright protection, a strictly commercial market for books and periodicals was in fact slow to develop. Until well into the eighteenth century, publishers exchanged books sheet-for-sheet at annual publishing fairs rather than pricing them for commercial transactions.[72] Printers' most dependable sources of income continued to be government contracts. And those who formed reading libraries and lending libraries tended to be associated with the professions that government service encouraged. Although the number of publishing houses increased on the whole, and they became more geographically scattered by the end of the century, their relations to the government remained evident in the fact that a disproportionate number were concentrated in towns with government residences, such as Berlin, Dresden, Gotha, Weimar, and Mannheim.[73]

If private patronage on the whole was not as extensive as in France or England, this gap was nevertheless more than compensated for by the abundance of positions for scholars within the bureaucracy itself. The Prussian bureaucracy did not evolve in a vacuum but expanded its functions at the expense of other agencies whose power was rooted in more limited and localized interest groups. These competitors consisted chiefly of the old Regierungen and other high judicial courts, the structure of which continued to reflect aristocratic interests and posed strong resistance to the centralizing tendencies of the state.[74] During the first half of the eighteenth century the bureaucracy waged a steady war of attrition against these courts in order to acquire greater control over judicial affairs. Among the tactics that proved most effective in this campaign was the substitution of uniform standards administered by educationally prepared and professionally competent functionaries in the place of an older system based on unsalaried clients of local patrons, discretionary fees, and bribery. The state thus developed a strong interest in the advancement of professional knowledge and in associating new ideas with its personnel not only for strictly aesthetic reasons but as a tactic in the state-building process itself. Accordingly, many scholars were given positions in the bureaucracy or moved back and forth from university to government positions. Thomasius, Wolff, Goethe, Wieland, Martini, Sonnenfels, Riegger, and Jacobi were but a few of the eminent scholars who held administrative posts at one time or another. On the whole it was, as one writer notes, "the academically trained authors active in government, university, and religious life, who provided the majority of material for the new literary market."[75] Indeed, it was probably this connection with the bureaucracy (either directly, in the case of government officials, or indirectly, in the case of professors and clergy) that gave the Prussian Enlightenment much of its distinctive character. As T. W. Blanning observes: "More than anything else, it was this academic-bureaucratic predominance which distinguished German culture in the eighteenth century. Nowhere else in Europe did the literate classes have so many thousands of opportunities for state employment."[76]

Care must be taken not to credit the social environment with too much of a role in shaping the Prussian Enlightenment beyond that of supplying it with vital resources; nevertheless, most writers have also seen in the Prussian bureaucracy the source of some of the distinctive features of the scholarly developments associated with it. For example, the fact that science and philosophy retained a fairly integral relation with each other, perhaps more so than in France or England, has been attributed partly to the fact that the state's control over the universities provided a common location for both activities to be pursued, thus preventing the kind of fragmentation of literary and scientific sponsorship that may have been associated with less formal academies or salons.[77] A somewhat stronger case has been made for the state's role in inhibiting the radical or revolutionary intellectual tradition that seems to have developed in France, or at least which made French writers view Prussian scholarship as a more conservative variety. In part, the availability of government and academic posts to Prussian writers may have inhibited the development of a "Grub Street" literary proletariat with which much of the radical rhetoric of the "low Enlightenment" in Paris and London was associated. In addition, the concept of liberty itself came to a greater degree in Prussia to be associated positively with the state's authority and with freedom from external domination rather than being viewed as contradictory to a strong state.[78] Another notable feature of the Prussian Enlightenment that may have reflected the state's predominance, especially in relation to the ecclesiastical hierarchy, was its relative absence of anticlerical rhetoric and its concern with metaphysical and ethical questions.[79]

The high degree to which rationality was sought to inform the ethical sphere also appears to have been related to the prevalence of bureaucratic development. Among the ideological pronouncements produced in an attempt to structure the administration of the state at the level of moral commitment were detailed codes of official conduct promulgated by the state for its administrators. These *reglemènts* set forth the norms which were to govern the daily conduct of officials in the performance of their duties, the standards by which they were to be evaluated, and the moral virtues they were expected to display in personal and public conduct. The areas of behavior covered by these codes were far-reaching, extending not only to the minute details of the occupation itself, such as proscriptions concerning luncheons and rest periods, but also covering a general set of expectations concerning the official's character, the exercise of conscience, and the application of ascetic discipline. Although these highly rationalized codes ran at odds with the actual compromises on which the state was obliged to function to such a degree that they were seldom strictly enforced, they nevertheless reflected the growing influence of rational learning and served as a model which other treatises of less official character tended to emulate.[80]

On questions of policy the Prussian Enlightenment also exhibited perspectives that corresponded with the manner in which the state ruled, particularly with heavy involvement from the nobility and comparatively weak involvement from the bourgeoisie. Certain economic doctrines such as cameralism and eventually the doctrines of free trade that Prussian scholars were borrowing from England fit well with the nobility's role as exporters of agricultural products and in turn corresponded with the state's interest in expanding its revenues from taxes on these commodities. The predominantly agrarian base of Prussian society militated, however, against ideas espousing greater freedom for the peasantry, universal suffrage, and peasant property rights, and also limited the extent to which ideas favoring commerce and industry could be advanced.[81]

Although some writers have continued to attribute the Prussian Enlightenment chiefly to the rise of the bourgeoisie, evidence indicates that the bourgeoisie gave little support to the new forms of learning and that scholars associated with these centers of learning seldom produced arguments favorable to the bourgeoisie.[82] To the contrary, the new literary circles were outspokenly disappointed with the bourgeoisie's taste for luxury consumption as opposed to intellectual pursuits and lent their support to the state's efforts to impose a new series of sumptuary laws; they supported the state's campaign against coffee and tea despite the bourgeoisie's interest in importing these commodities; and they supported the military as an important consumer of research and training despite the bourgeoisie's opposition.[83] On the whole, the Prussian Enlightenment tended to emphasize the philosophical and technical issues facing an aristocratic state rather than the broader array of ideas that eventually came to legitimate bourgeois or democratic reforms.[84]

Heterogeneity and the Public Sphere

If the Prussian Enlightenment was thus influenced to a considerable degree by its association with a highly centralized state bureaucracy, this bureaucracy was nevertheless sufficiently heterogeneous to foster intellectual debate reflecting opposing points of view. The degree to which the various functions of government were organized under a single hierarchy of administration was higher than it was in either France or England, but diverse interests and bases of power were nevertheless accommodated within this structure. Internal divisions persisted throughout the eighteenth century based on regional traditions, on ambiguities in the interrelation of royal and aristocratic privileges, and on firmly established constitutional limits on monarchical power.[85]

The Prussian state, contrary to earlier views that characterized it as an absolutist system under a monolithic bureaucracy, was neither absolute nor monolithic. As one study concludes: "Neither rule by an absolute despot nor rule by a monolithic bureaucracy existed in Prussia between 1740 and 1786."[86] The Prussian state was characterized in practice as well as in theory by two features that distinguished it from a purely despotic system: a judiciary independent of royal power, and intermediate consultative bodies which mediated the sovereign's decisions and translated the special interests of local and regional groups into policy.[87] In both the judiciary and the administrative bodies authority was further divided between firmly entrenched institutions representing decentralized interests and the newer centralized agencies of the crown. Judicial authority was divided, much as in France, into what amounted to a "dual system of law": public law emanating from the crown, administered by central executive agencies, and identified with public or collective needs; and private law stemming from tradition, administered by the courts, and associated with private interests. The latter were sufficiently powerful to pose genuine limitations on the crown; as Hans Rosenberg notes: "In spite of the rigorous 'police' character of the Hohenzollern state, the range of administrative centralization and hence of bureaucratic *étatisme* was more restricted than in the French absolute monarchy."[88] Within the administrative agencies the same kind of dual and therefore self-limiting structure was evident. The new service bureaucracy supported by the king seriously challenged the older system of *officiers;* yet the *officiers* enjoyed the support of the Junker aristocracy and held claim to such traditional rights that even after several generations of attrition their authority had not been severely eroded. These divisions and the balance of power between them constituted, as in England, areas of continuing debate within the knowledgeable public.[89]

The rapid expansion of state functions that occurred chiefly between 1740 and 1786 as a result of economic growth, conquest, and "great power" foreign relations also imposed a diverse structure on the bureaucracy that had not been as keenly apparent before. Hubert C. Johnson writes: "No single bureaucratic system existed after 1740, and functions were not divided up logically and assigned to persons placed in a bureaucratic hierarchy. The Prussian government obviously became more and more decentralized; it was divided into mutually antagonistic parts as it evolved after 1740."[90] Overlaid in an ambiguous, semiautonomous manner onto the preexisting executive departments were at least four new loosely structured bureaucracies: one for the conquered areas of Silesia, a second composed of diplomats and foreign advisers, the third an entrepreneurial bureaucracy of mercantilist financiers and industrialists, and fourth a judicial bureaucracy for supervising the churches and schools.

The increasing decentralization of the bureaucracy contributed directly to the growth of intellectual activity during the second half of the century. A certain type of secular rationalism rooted in Wolffian philosophy was encouraged in the universities by the judicial bureaucracy. The bureaucracies controlled by foreign advisers and entrepreneurs, in contrast, found little favor in Wolffian philosophy, but became channels for the transmission of new ideas from England and the rest of the Continent as well as mercantilist and antimercantilist doctrines that had failed to penetrate the universities. The courts served as yet another locus of intellectual activity, especially the literary and aesthetic arts which were less attractive to other parts of the bureaucracy.[91] In the short term, then, the growing division of labor within the bureaucracy encouraged intellectual diversity beyond that which might have developed within a more rigidly centralized system.[92] In the longer term this structure also provided the basis for one of the distinctive features of German learning in the nineteenth century, namely, the differentiation of *technische Hochschule,* specializing in engineering studies and administered by the new technical departments of the bureaucracy, from the universities, which remained under the supervision of the judiciary.

In addition to the more rationally ordered decentralization which characterized the bureaucracy was another kind of internal diversity that stemmed chiefly from the persistence of older structures, a diversity that made the bureaucracy, in Hans Rosenberg's words, "an untidy and disjointed amalgamation of the new merit system with the old 'spoils system.' "[93] The Prussian bureaucracy was created not from scratch but as a compromise with previous structures, including those representing the aristocracy. Patronage networks, old wealth, and family lineage continued to dominate the circles in which professional bureaucrats attempted to carry out their growing responsibilities. Dependence on patronage networks kept open the way for idiosyncratic influences based on personal ties and personality differences. Nevertheless, there was also a growing tendency for training and specialization to be included among the prerequisites of office and for criteria of efficiency and administrative effectiveness to be imposed as standards of evaluation.

The upshot of this transitional situation was to generate a high degree of ambiguity with respect to the criteria by which performance of administrative duties was to be governed. Not only was there ambiguity at the subjective level (officers' personal standards of conduct and self-appraisal), but also the grounds on which co-workers related to one another were left open: different standards were applied according to expediency or in some cases on what must have appeared to be a purely capricious basis. Under these circumstances it is not surprising to find that an exceptional degree of importance came to be attached to discussions about the nature of the state, the moral obligations of those in leadership positions, and the bases of establishing mutual respect and solidarity. As in England, accusations of corruption in high places served poignantly to dramatize many of these concerns. In the absence of a semiautonomous literary culture with support from an established opposition party, such accusations did not attain the level of articulation they attained in England. Yet they functioned in much the same manner, raising to public consciousness the question of civic virtue. Moreover, writers were able to capitalize on the more general climate of normative ambiguity by serving as propagandists for various decisions. Lacking a well-institutionalized set of procedures with which to legitimate decisions, the state depended to an important extent on the literary elite to interpret and justify its actions.

The Broader German Context

Added perspective on the special circumstances promoting cultural production in Prussia can be gained by comparing the Prussian situation briefly with that in several of the other German states for which information is available. As a rule the Enlightenment received relatively little support from the ecclesiastical principalities such as Cologne, Trier, and Westphalia, the reason cited most often being that the Catholic church was antagonistic toward the new doctrines of reason and secular philosophy. It bears observing, however, that many of these principalities were also ruled by representative aristocratic assemblies that militated against the development of powerful centralized bureaucracies.[94] These assemblies gave the nobility a strong voice in determining political affairs; indeed, one can say that the nobility in these areas functioned as an independent class with few of the dependent relations that bound the aristocracies in France, England, and Prussia to the central bureaucracy. Compounding this fact was the custom in ecclesiastical principalities that the ruler was denied the right of dynastic succession, thus reducing the likelihood of a strong regime being imposed on the estates. The state was thereby constrained in initiating its own cultural reforms, not by the authority of the church alone but by its almost totally decentralized, aristocratic structure. The nobility in these areas controlled decisions on taxation and used these powers to prevent the rise of either a standing army that might be used to centralize power or an expansive service bureaucracy oriented toward economic supervision. In the absence of an expansive bureaucracy or system of offices bestowed as patronage by the state, the only resources readily available for the production of ideology by persons directly dependent on the state were the private resources of the ruler himself.[95]

Mainz, the third-largest political entity in central Europe, with a population of 350,000, provides a valuable case for consideration. Although the area remained commercially underdeveloped at the end of the seventeenth century, mercantilist policies were adopted and the economy expanded greatly during the next fifty years. In this case the state played an active role in initiating economic development and exhibited some growth as a result. It also included an elective assembly capable of opposing the central executive—all conditions conducive to the development of a public sphere in which enlightened discourse could occur. Indeed, some efflorescence of cultural activity did take place, including patronage of the arts, literary discussions, and dialogue with French writers. Yet the central bureaucracy remained relatively small; an army only one-fiftieth the size of Prussia's could be mobilized; and no success was achieved in seizing control of educational facilities. As a result, subsequent developments in the literary and scholarly fields went unsupported, and the Enlightenment failed to make any significant impact. As one writer concludes: "It is simply impossible to discover any spontaneous secular literature in Mainz, apart from a few wretched eulogistical poems . . . to mark special occasions."[96]

The role played by noble estates in deterring the kind of centralized state expansion which facilitated cultural production was not limited to Catholic principalities. Württemberg is a particularly revealing example since it experienced the kind of economic growth that might have fostered the development of a strong centralized bureaucracy, yet its estates remained dominated by Protestant nobility. During the last sixty years of the eighteenth century its population rose by 50 percent, and increases in exports and agricultural productivity made it one of the more prosperous of the German territories. Despite this growth it nevertheless failed to develop either a stable state bureaucracy or a reputation for supporting scholarship. Except for a brief period of bureaucratic growth, the estates with the aid of surrounding princes managed to restrict the ruler's role in taxation, kept the bureaucracy in check, and prevented a large standing army from being created.[97] The irony of the situation as far as cultural production is concerned is that Württemberg was often touted by Enlightenment figures for its constitutional democracy; yet in the absence of a stable bureaucracy intellectual activity did not become institutionalized, remaining instead subject to the whims of individual rulers.[98] Indeed, innovative intellectual and social proposals often became the victims of harsh reactions by members of the estates who saw in them dangerous signs of administrative centralization.

Other than Prussia, the states most noted for their support of the Enlightenment were Brunswick and Hanover, both of which had developed a relatively powerful administrative center. During the last quarter of the eighteenth century, education in Brunswick was reformed, religious toleration granted, freedom extended to the press, and efforts made to attract scholars from Paris and Berlin. Hanover presented a somewhat different case, since it lacked a resident ruler; yet it was efficiently administered by a strong central bureaucracy that kept the nobility in check while advancing its own interests. Here as in Prussia the need for better-trained civil servants appears to have been an important stimulus to growth in higher learning. In 1737 the University of Göttingen was established at state expense and, in imitation of Halle, was closely administered by the central bureaucracy. Among the scholars who brought international distinction to Göttingen were Möser, Struve, and Stein.[99]

Saxony played a somewhat smaller role in the Enlightenment, serving as the location of the book trade in Leipzig, but giving less official support to the work of scholars themselves.[100] Other areas in which some support for the new ideas of the Enlightenment was found included Bavaria, Hesse-Darmstadt, Saxe-Weimar, Anhalt-Dessau, and Schaumburg-Lippe, all of which provided personal patronage to major literary figures such as Schiller, Goethe, and Herder. In most of these areas little was accomplished in institutionalizing the Enlightenment on a broader scale, however, at least partly because the aristocratic diets retained control over taxation, public finance, and high administrative posts, thus preventing the growth of a centralized bureaucracy with the capacity to seize control of the universities or create alternative centers of learning.[101]

The Scottish Enlightenment

The Enlightenment in Scotland is typified by such writers as David Hume, Adam Smith, William Robertson, Adam Ferguson, John Millar, Thomas Reid, and Dugald Stewart, all of whom contributed major works in the fields of moral philosophy and history. In addition to elaborating on the work of Locke, Newton, and Montesquieu, these writers brought to their investigations a distinctive sense of empirical argument that has generally been credited with laying the foundations for the subsequent development of the social sciences, including the deterministic historicism of Karl Marx.[102] By the middle of the eighteenth century Edinburgh, and to a lesser extent Glasgow, had gained international recognition as centers of learning, and by the end of the century Scottish achievements in the study of political economy, most notably Adam Smith's *Wealth of Nations,* and in science, including the discoveries of James Watt and Joseph Black, were among the most outstanding anywhere.[103] Writing in 1771, Benjamin Franklin could assert that Scotland possessed "a set of as truly great men, Professors of the Several Branches of Knowledge, as have ever appeared in any Age or Country."[104] In 1789 Thomas Jefferson echoed a similar sentiment about Scottish science, commenting that "no place in the world can pretend to a competition with Edinburgh."[105] More recent assessments have generally drawn the same conclusions.[106]

But the Scottish Enlightenment is not equivalent to the accomplishments only of its leading scholars; it was also a broader development involving the institutionalization of resources for scholarly activity. The Scottish universities, like those in Prussia, underwent significant changes in the eighteenth century which made them strong bases for the production and implementation of new ideas. Both at Edinburgh and at Glasgow chairs were added in mathematics, law, history, medicine, botany, and astronomy; and both universities were sufficiently prosperous and well organized to attract new professors who were highly qualified in their fields.[107] Salaries doubled during the first half of the century and again between 1750 and 1800, and professors were able to supplement their income from positions outside the universities.[108] As faculty and curricula expanded, enrollments also increased, rising at Edinburgh from 400 in 1700 to 1,100 in 1775, and at Glasgow from 250 to 650 over the same period.[109] Edinburgh in particular became internationally renowned both for its teaching and for the broader intellectual climate it fostered.[110] After the union with England in 1707 an increasing number of English students attended Edinburgh, with the result that more of the British scientists born during the eighteenth century came to be trained at Edinburgh than at any other institution.[111]

Scotland also conformed to the pattern seen in France, England, and Prussia of institutionalizing the Enlightenment in numerous clubs, academies, and literary societies. Beginning around the time of union and continuing through the first half of the century, a number of relatively informal literary clubs flourished in Edinburgh which were quite similar in membership and in the content of their discussions to the salons of Paris. Among these were such groups as the Easy Club, the Athenian Society, the Grotesque Club, and the Rankenian Club.[112] Frequented by students, professors, writers, and members of the Edinburgh political establishment, these clubs were instrumental in disseminating the writings of Locke, Newton, Shaftesbury, Butler, and others to the Scottish elite; they brought writers and potential patrons into contact with one another and provided settings in which common approaches and problems were identified for investigation; and through correspondence and foreign visitors they gave Edinburgh international visibility as a cultural center.[113] These were followed by more formal organizations in Edinburgh, Glasgow, and Aberdeen, among which were the Medical Society of Edinburgh (1731), the Edinburgh Philosophical Society (1737), the Political Economy Club of Glasgow (1743), the Glasgow Literary Society (1752), the Select Society of Edinburgh (1754), and the Aberdeen Philosophical Society (1758).

The founding of the Select Society in many ways symbolized

the institutionalization of the Enlightenment in Edinburgh. Led by Hume, Smith, and Robertson, it attracted well-born, affluent members from all the elite strata of the city, uniting them around themes of social improvement and intellectual interests in political economy, moral philosophy, science, medicine, and technology. Their discussions emphasized empirical evidence, lauded the contributions of Locke and Newton, paid close attention to scientific discoveries, emphasized experience over revelation in matters of religion, and employed historical comparisons in the search for social principles. At a practical level, the Society provided opportunities for members to sharpen their ideas against the consensus of the group and established networks which led to the creation of other organizations. In 1755 it gave rise to the Edinburgh Society for Arts and Manufactures, a practical arm of the Society that was devoted to the advancement of science in agriculture and industry through debates, essay contests, and subsidies for books and journals. In 1761 another related organization was founded to promote reading and speaking in English as a response to the growing demand in London for civil servants from Scotland. After the Select Society disbanded in 1764, many of its members continued to be active patrons of scholarship, and more than thirty of them published significant scholarly works themselves.[114]

Beyond the universities and voluntary societies, the growth of scholarly activity in Scotland was also manifested in the publishing industry. Starting with virtually nothing at the beginning of the century except for the example of pirated Dutch editions of expensive London books, it grew to the point of taking over much of the Dutch trade in cheap reprints from London and Paris and of operating a bustling export business to France and the American colonies. With a list of several thousand books in print, it thrived on the publication of legal and official documents in Edinburgh and serviced writers both from the university and surrounding community.[115] By 1763 the Edinburgh publishing industry included six printing houses which consumed 6,400 reams of paper annually; and by 1790, the number of printing houses had grown to sixteen, consuming 100,000 reams of paper and supporting approximately 20,000 workers.[116] Because of the high rate of literacy in Scotland, the publishing industry was also able to develop a flourishing market in periodicals, despite otherwise unfavorable conditions, including the *Northern Tatler* (1717) and the *Edinburgh Evening Courant* (1718), both modeled after London newspapers, and the *Scots Magazine* (1739) and *Edinburgh Review* (1755), both oriented toward literary and philosophical discussion.[117]

The Scottish Environment

The emergence of Scotland as one of the leaders of cultural renewal in the eighteenth century constitutes an extremely interesting case from the standpoint of sociological explanation. Ravished by a century of internal political conflict as well as dependence on England, Scotland was by the beginning of the eighteenth century the location of neither a progressive bourgeois economy nor an effective state bureaucracy. Although mercantilist policies had been pursued during the latter half of the seventeenth century, these were largely unsuccessful because they tended to set Scottish firms in direct competition with more powerful enterprises in England.[118] By English standards Scotland's economy thus remained exceptionally weak until the end of the seventeenth century: trade had not expanded in over a century; there were few signs of technological innovation; total exports and imports on a per capita basis remained only one-sixth the size of England's; tax revenues from customs and from agriculture calculated per capita were scarcely one-seventh of England's; per capita consumption of iron was one-fifth that in England; and wage rates ranged from one-third to one-half as high as in England.[119] Political development also remained "retarded," to use David Ogg's term.[120] Except for a brief period from 1637 to 1651, Scotland had been governed by England ever since 1603. In the king's absence administrative functions had been fulfilled by the Privy Council at Edinburgh, while the Scottish Parliament and judiciary remained nominally separate from English institutions. With the union in 1707, even the fate of these institutions appeared doubtful.

Yet the Act of Union accomplished for Scotland what had been achieved by other means in France and England. Although economic growth remained slow until the second quarter of the century, the overall results were scarcely short of spectacular. Between 1720 and 1770, total foreign trade more than tripled, imports of raw tobacco grew eightfold, linen production multiplied tenfold, and cattle shipments to England increased sevenfold.[121] The Act of Union was not the sole source of these developments, for the linen and cattle trades with England had already become so important to the Scottish economy that England was able to place considerable pressure on the Scots to accept the union by threatening to exclude these commodities.[122] Nor were the economic effects of union entirely positive for Scotland, since investments and profits subsequently flowed with greater ease toward London.[123] Nevertheless, political unification did contribute to Scottish economic growth in at least five major respects: first, by funneling increased investments of English capital to Scotland, particularly in view of the fact that interest rates in Scotland generally remained above those in England; second, by providing government grants for the development of such industries as woolens, linens, and fisheries; third, by giving Scottish ports access to the lucrative colonial trade in tobacco imports and linen imports; fourth, by further opening the English market for Scottish cattle; and fifth, by constructing roads and bridges and by enhancing the political stability of the region through military expenditures.[124]

The political consequences of union with England were equally profound insofar as the administration of Scotland underwent almost total reorganization, and much of the impetus toward economic development came about through active intervention by the British government. The initial result of the union appeared to be that of diminishing government activity in Scotland as a consequence of the absorption of the Scottish Parliament into the British Parliament and its transfer to London.[125] This effect was more than counterbalanced, however, by the increase in bureaucratic activity and patronage that came with the administrative reorganization. Although Scottish affairs formally resided with the secretary of state and the first lord of the treasury, these officials normally paid little attention to Scotland. Most administrative functions were in practice delegated to a powerful Scottish minister, who executed policies, distributed patronage, maintained cooperation among the Scottish representatives in Parliament, and represented the interests of Scottish merchants and landowners in London.[126] The main task in Scotland was to consolidate British power by creating a strong coalition of interests centered on the crown. This objective was accomplished largely through the dissemination of patronage on the one hand and the creation of a centralized bureaucracy on the other.

Patronage played a vital role in Scottish politics under British administration, perhaps even more so than in England. State "managers" such as the duke of Argyll exercised power by channeling resources created by British rule to local elites in return for loyalty to British policies. As David Kettler has noted in his study of Adam Ferguson: "To speak of 'politics' in eighteenth-century Scotland is to speak of access to the jobs, force, and favors at the disposal of the British Crown and the House of Commons."[127] The union had created a precarious political situation that was to produce armed protest on more than one occasion in the form of Jacobite uprisings. It was thus imperative to pacify potential opposition, and thereby close the "back door" (as it was called) to foreign invasion, through "the establishment of a single 'interest' in Scotland, supporting the Crown, providing orderly government through the judicious exercise of patronage."[128] Patronage was the device employed to cultivate a loyal centrist coalition in Scottish politics. The Scottish members of Parliament were particularly important to control, since they spoke as official representatives of Scottish interests, and for most of the eighteenth century it was commonly recognized that no Scottish nobleman could gain election without the official backing of the king's ministers.[129] London systematically played local factions against one another and drew major segments of the rural aristocracy, merchants, and professional classes into its network of influence. Rather than imposing a professional bureaucracy entirely from the outside, London drew local elites into the bureaucracy, thus creating a common interest in the state that counteracted private or sectional interests.[130] In one author's words: "The result was a large body of court supporters who would come to terms with anyone rather than be out in the cold."[131]

A central bureaucracy was created by adding new layers of officials to traditional institutions and vesting them with broad authority over financial, legal, and administrative functions. The groundwork for bureaucratic control was laid during the two decades following the Act of Union, in which a number of important legal reforms were imposed: guild restrictions were reduced or eliminated; forfeiture of estates provided opportunities to minimize resistance in the Highlands; banking was brought under royal control; and somewhat later the system of local sheriffdoms was reformed to bring it under central control.[132] Key agencies of the new bureaucracy included the Customs and Excise Boards, which employed approximately five hundred officials between them as well as a much larger number of persons in supportive positions. Other avenues of employment that the bureaucracy opened up included offices as collectors, comptrollers, and surveyors; salt officers, land waiters, and local inspectors; supervisors and trustees for industry, agriculture, fisheries, transportation, and poor relief; and sheriffs, sheriff clerks, and justices of the peace.

Edinburgh became the headquarters for many of these offices as well as the location of the major courts of Session, Justiciary, and Exchequer; the minor courts of Commissary and Admiralty; the General Assembly of the Church of Scotland; and the Convention of Royal Burghs.[133] In all, as much as £100,000 per year may have flowed into Edinburgh for salaries alone, an increase of three or four times over preunion levels.[134] In addition, the bureaucracy served as its own revenue-generating mechanism, taking in £160,000 on the eve of union, a figure that by the end of the century mushroomed to £1.8 million annually.[135]

Institutionalized Patronage and the Public Sphere

The growth of patronage and bureaucracy, concentrated as they were in Edinburgh, had important consequences for the production of scholarship. The union itself was not the decisive factor—certainly not in the sense of merely provoking an intellectual crisis which culminated in the Enlightenment. As Charles Camic notes, it was "several years before the oldest member of the Scottish Enlightenment was born, more than thirty years before he published a word, and nearly eighty years before the Enlightenment's last major work."[136] It was instead the changes in state structure that had begun prior to the Act of Union and continued over the whole course of the eighteenth century that altered the institutional conditions under which scholarship was produced. Integration into the broader intellectual and political world of England was itself decisive, introducing Scottish writers to broader questions, increasing the demand for instruction in English as opposed to Latin, and providing new outlets for promising Scottish writers in the wider literary world of London, to which the careers of Hume and Smith bore witness.[137] Yet it was chiefly in Scotland itself that the changes were most evident.

As elsewhere, Scottish writers depended on direct patronage for a considerable portion of their livelihood, and much of this patronage was linked to the expanding role of the British state. Even prior to union, the king had channeled patronage in large sums to the Scottish intellectual establishment as a means of garnering loyalty, stimulating economic development, and overriding traditional patterns of learning. In the final years prior to 1700, a Royal College of Physicians, an Advocates Library, and a Physic Garden were initiated in Edinburgh; the university was granted a new charter; and patronage was granted for work in medicine, cartography, mathematics, and engineering.[138] These innovations were often resisted by the guilds, local magistrates, and members of the clergy, but gradually control of the university and other intellectual activities fell into the hands of those whose loyalties resided with the crown.

As time went on, virtually all the leading figures of the Scottish Enlightenment benefited from official patronage. Lord Kames, the author of treatises on law, morality, and agriculture, was both the recipient of patronage, serving as lord of Session and later as lord of Justiciary, and an important distributor of patronage. Adam Smith, John Millar, and many other young writers were among the scholars on whom he bestowed patronage. The playwright John Home obtained a position as personal secretary to Lord Bute and served as tutor to the Prince of Wales, for which he received a handsome stipend; William Cullen, one of Edinburgh's leading professors of chemistry and medicine, was supported by the earl of Islay; David Hume and Adam Ferguson served successively as keeper of the Advocates Library; and William Robertson's appointments as principal at the University of Edinburgh and royal historiographer of Scotland owed much to the patronage of the current state manager, the earl of Bute.[139] Publishers were also greatly benefited both by direct patronage and by lucrative contracts for printing legal documents and government reports.[140]

In addition to providing support to writers in the form of direct patronage, the expanding bureaucracy drew the scattered factions of the Scottish elite into a more concerted form of action, creating an enlarged public sphere in which issues of common interest were discussed.[141] The aristocracy came by this route to play a prominent role in the intellectual life of Edinburgh. A study of Scottish scientists during this period, for example, stresses that "the landed classes and the prestigious lawyers, to whom they were related by birth and social standing, were indispensible as beneficent patrons of Edinburgh's cultural endeavors."[142] Evidence from the Philosophical Society of Edinburgh, which included approximately 20 percent of the town's educated elite, points to a similar conclusion, showing that the typical member was "an active professional man from the landed gentry who was politically involved and who held a patronage post which enhanced an income not wholly derived from rents."[143] The same study suggests that the merchant and business elite of Edinburgh was strikingly absent from the Philosophical Society's membership.

Scholarship in Edinburgh was similar to scholarship in Paris, London, and Berlin in that it was supported intellectually and financially not through the generosity of public-spirited individuals alone, but through the involvement of officials, lawyers, and professional writers whose very existence depended on the central bureaucracy and whose numbers were expanding with the growth of bureaucratic functions. This point is forcefully made by Roger Emerson, who writes in his study of the Scottish Enlightenment that "the civil administration was large enough to provide men through the century who could realistically consider practical problems of government as well as provide places for others like Adam Smith who did so."[144] Emerson's study of the 162 men who joined the Select Society of Edinburgh between 1754 and 1764 demonstrates clearly the preponderance of their attachments to the state bureaucracy: a majority (87) were by occupation members of the courts or the army or held public office; another fifth (29) were professionals and clergy; only one in nine (18) was a businessman or merchant. By background they originated overwhelmingly from "the political class of decision makers, patrons and beneficiaries of the status quo," and most had improved their wealth and prestige by obtaining offices or patronage. In all, at least 132 had held a significant position in the state or in the universities or ecclesiastical establishment, all of which were subject to the patronage system. Among the holders of these positions, fifteen (including Adam Smith) were in the customs service, twenty-five were members of Parliament, eighteen were appointive judges at the Court of Session, thirteen were sheriffs, and five were barons of the Exchequer.

Most of these positions required the incumbent to be in favor with the state managers currently in power, rather than being dispensed by family right or tradition. Others directly manifested the state's growing penetration of Scottish society: twelve were associated with the board of trustees for fisheries, arts, and manufactures; nine with the commission for annexed estates; six with the Edinburgh exchange; and four with the harbor improvement commission. Others had served as military officers or as directors of the royal bank and were large investors in government stocks. The influence of the British patronage system was, therefore, well in evidence.[145]

The state played a similarly important role among the members of the Edinburgh Philosophical Society. During the tenures of the duke of Argyll and Lord Milton as state managers of Scotland, the study of chemistry and its applications to the improvement of agriculture had received official encouragement with the result that in the 1740s the Philosophical Society became the focal point for vigorous discussions of science and social improvement. Chemists brought in by the various state bureaus concerned with industry and agriculture, along with professors from the university, physicians, and amateurs in high government posts, provided the nucleus for these discussions. During this period an increasing proportion of the intelligentsia appears to have been recruited from the ranks of professors, physicians, lawyers, and officials, and a growing number derived their income entirely from offices, fees, and salaries rather than inherited wealth or rents. The Philosophical Society, like the Select Society, was thus composed chiefly of men whose livelihood depended on the state. Through the regular gatherings of the Philosophical Society several scholars were brought into contact with individuals who subsidized their work; others gained posts at the university or in the state; some received stipends for lecture tours or equipment; and the body as a whole bestowed prestige and recognition on the work of its members.[146]

The transformation of the universities that occurred from about 1690 to 1740, turning them from "small schools teaching a decadent scholasticism in Latin" into internationally respected centers of learning, was the result of several factors, not least of which were features of university organization which allowed faculty to initiate changes.[147] These features would likely not have been sufficient to bring about the resultant changes, however, had it not been for the additional impetus from the governing bureaucracy. The patronage system was extended, just as it was in other realms of public service, to bring the universities into a more dependent relation to the state. At the beginning of the period fewer than 10 percent of faculty appointments were made by the crown; as time progressed this proportion increased to more than 30 percent. Students and student tastes, as we have seen, came increasingly to reflect the state's interests in promoting law, history, natural philosophy, medicine, and applied science. By the 1740s, approximately one student in four entered the civil service and another 12 percent went into teaching or medicine, thus bringing the demand for public employment up to approximately the same level as that for clergy and making this group more than twice the size of that entering occupations in industry or commerce.[148]

The state also used its legislative powers and extensive patronage system to undercut the traditional privileges of faculty guilds and to reduce the control of town councils and ecclesiastical authorities over the universities, thus creating opportunities and providing incentives for professors to engage in projects concerned with social improvement.[149] Professors were sufficiently integrated into the centers of power that they could scarcely be described as alienated intellectuals; they were instead moderate reformers who assisted with projects for improving society, helped the bureaucracy by filling government posts and serving on government commissions, and participated in voluntary organizations concerned with the application of knowledge to practical problems.[150] In short, their interests corresponded closely to those of their patrons in the state. Emerson again makes a point of this affinity, writing that the dispensers of patronage "were the country's improvers and enlightened men, so it is not surprising that their protégés in the colleges reflected their interests in economic developments, agricultural innovation, 'moderatism,' *belles lettres* and a curriculum that was useful, polite and career-oriented."[151]

Like its Enlightenment counterpart in Prussia, Scottish scholarship contained little that in the short run could be described as radical or revolutionary. If it generated ideas that were eventually to legitimate democratic claims in the American colonies or even later to serve as fountains of Marxian analysis, it was scarcely as conducive to the Grub Street style of critical writing as was that of London and Paris or even very likely to produce an alienated exile with the intellectual disposition of a Rousseau. Scottish writers were too well integrated into the British patronage system centered in Edinburgh to produce literature that intentionally threatened any of the foundations of this system. As Bruce Lenman suggests: "The leaders of Scottish intellectual life became spokesmen, overtly or tacitly, for the very conservative court or establishment Whiggism which was the prevailing ideology of Hanoverian Britain."[152]

But the Scottish Enlightenment was not a form of ideological production that simply mirrored the specific interests of its patrons. These interests were characteristically narrow, self-serving, and at odds with one another. Like the ruling elite in London of which it was a satellite, the dominant class in Scotland was fraught with divisions along party lines, lines of patronage, and lines of economic interest.[153] Divisions still prevailed between Highlanders and Lowlanders, between staunch supporters of the crown and those who reluctantly pledged their support, between officials of the bureaucracy and those whose power rested on informal patronage, and between landed aristocrats and men of commerce.

The state played a strong centralizing role in relation to these interests, but its structure was by no means monolithic. As in France, the judiciary remained relatively powerful and because of internal divisions within the administrative bureaucracy was able to maintain a high degree of professional autonomy, thus serving as a locus for independent political debate.[154] Rivalries within the state were compounded by the persistence of competing factions in the church and by different patronage networks organized around the powerful dukes of Hamilton, Queensberry, Atholl, and Argyll.[155] During the half century following union the nature of Scotland's incorporation into the broader national polity also continued to produce strife.[156]

Indeed, the strife that accompanied the period of union resulted in one of the principal debates of the Scottish Enlightenment. On one side, rooted in Presbyterian, Whig, aristocratic circles, was a deterministic strand of philosophy, exhibited in Hume and Smith, which favored union with England and conceived of progress and social order as inevitable products of virtuous and rational deliberation. On the other side, rooted in Episcopal, Jacobite, provincial circles was a "common sense" orientation that questioned philosophic determinism, asserted the value of free will, raised questions about the desirability of union, and recognized the role of political struggles in social affairs. The expression of these alternative perspectives was in some respects precipitated by the Act of Union and the debates that ensued for several decades following it.[157]

Yet the broader effect of union with England was not to polarize these positions but to add a new dimension to Scottish intellectual life. Union with England permanently altered the structure of Scottish politics by introducing into a set of provincial institutions, which otherwise remained intact, a centralizing network of political patronage. Once accomplished, the new political environment became a reality that different sides could favor or oppose but, more important, a reality with which all sides had to live. Just as the tension between bureaucratic and representative institutions in other countries stimulated serious reflection on the best manner in which to take advantage of this new reality, so the tension between centralizing and traditional institutions in Scotland was an accomplished reality that writers sought to mold into an amalgam beneficial to the growth and stability of Scottish society.[158] The public sphere in which Scottish elites participated (already divided by regional, religious, and economic differences) was subjected to additional complexity by the intrusion of the British bureaucracy. The leading figures of the Scottish Enlightenment, themselves dependent on British patronage and intimately associated with those in public life, were keenly aware of the tensions cross-cutting Scottish politics and sought in much of their work to reconcile these tensions for the betterment of Scottish society. The very complexity of the situation provided a certain degree of freedom for their work, for as one writer observes: "The Scots found that they were groping for an alternative to a political language which did not make sense of their own political predicament."[159]

The novelty of the political situation in Scotland naturally resulted in different writers offering different recommendations for social improvement. Writers such as Francis Hutcheson, James Steuart, David Hume, and Adam Smith all sought in different ways to formulate philosophical positions that would reconcile the opportunities for progress perceived to be available because of the English connection with the desire for social stability through provincial law, religion, and education. Thus views as different as those of Adam Ferguson, a Jacobite supporter, and Adam Smith, whose opinions generally corresponded closely with Whig ideology, came to be expressed, as did more synthetic views, such as Hume's, which favored a careful balance between commercial progress advanced by central government and enlightened discussion in provincial communities of the requisites for social order and personal happiness.[160]

Though relatively small and politically dependent in comparison with France, England, or Prussia, Scotland came to have many of the same features that promoted innovative ideological reflection in these societies. Both the economy and the state bureaucracy expanded dramatically over the course of the eighteenth century, thereby providing the overall resources that made it possible for universities to expand, informal clubs and academies to flourish within an enlarged society of public officials, and a network of periodicals and publishers to develop as economically solvent enterprises. In addition, the centralizing tendencies associated with the Act of Union with England drew the disparate factions of the ruling elite in Scotland into greater economic and political dependence on one another, with the result that public debate over matters of material improvement, social order, and political style became of greater common interest. The new reality of a centralizing regime imposed on the more traditional institutions in which social order and political interests had been expressed also raised broader questions about the character of government, society, and civic virtue which became the hallmarks of the Scottish Enlightenment.

8

The Enlightenment
in Decentralized Societies

*B*Y MOST INDICATIONS the Dutch Republic should also
have been a major contributor to the Enlightenment. During the seventeenth century, scholarship and the arts in the Dutch
Republic had flourished to such an extent that it became a serious
rival of France and England, just as it did in commerce and industry.
Amsterdam in particular provided a haven for scientists, philosophers, students, and religious refugees. Huygens, Leeuwenhoek,
Swammerdam, and Boerhaave achieved international recognition in
science. Rembrandt, de Witt, Vermeer, and Spinoza became celebrated figures in the arts and in philosophy. Some of the Enlightenment's leading forerunners, including Descartes, Locke, Bayle, and
Shaftesbury, took up residence in Holland as fugitives. Foreign students flocked to the universities of Leiden and Groningen, where
they found an atmosphere of freedom and intellectual ferment. The
Dutch publishing industry also flourished, perhaps more than anywhere else in Europe, because of the general climate of political
toleration. Furthermore, the broader social milieu of the Dutch Republic was characterized by two of the features that later scholars
have tended to associate with intellectual development during this
period, namely, a Protestant ethic and a powerful bourgeoisie. Thus,
the Dutch provinces were widely touted by writers and intellectuals
even in France and England as the *exemplum virtutis* in which tolerance and prosperity promoted wisdom.[1]

But the eighteenth century failed to generate anything in the Dutch provinces resembling in quality or quantity the Enlightenment in France or England or even in Prussia or Scotland. Indeed, the achievements of the seventeenth century were in no way rivaled by those of the eighteenth century. Historians are uniform in describing the eighteenth century as a period of decline in Dutch scholarship. E. H. Kossmann, comparing the eighteenth-century writers with Dutch scholars during Holland's "Golden Age" in the seventeenth century, asserts that the seventeenth-century scholars "had no successors whom we would be inclined to consider their equals."[2] J. L. Price concludes that after the seventeenth century the Dutch Republic "became a minor power culturally, very much under French influence, and with very little of its own to offer the rest of Europe."[3] He suggests that the decline in quality in both literature and the arts was even more apparent than the decline in quantity. C. H. Wilson makes a similar observation: "There are few great names in the visual or social arts after the 1670s. Even in the Dutch galleries and museums the visitors will search in vain for any Dutch artists of the eighteenth century to compare with Vermeer, Cuyp or Ruysdael."[4] Simon Schama notes simply that there was no "Dutch Enlightenment."[5] And I. L. Leeb observes with some interest that the great works of Voltaire, Rousseau, and other Enlightenment figures, despite being printed on Dutch presses to escape censorship laws elsewhere, seem to have had little impact on Dutch intellectual life and were not even translated until long after their original appearance.[6]

These observations tend to be supported by studies of the various institutions responsible for the production of Dutch scholarship. From the mid-1690s a noticeable decline appeared in enrollments at Dutch universities, and this decline deepened during the course of the following century.[7] A dramatic drop in foreign enrollments accounted for much of the overall decline. At Groningen, for example, only 22 percent of student enrollments between 1689 and 1808 were foreign, compared with 44 percent between 1614 and 1689.[8] The rising quality of German and Scottish universities appears to have been responsible for foreign students' declining interest in the Dutch universities. Protectionist policies in Prussia and France also made it increasingly difficult for students to enroll in foreign universities and largely prohibited faculty from accepting teaching posts abroad.

On the whole, the quality of instruction at Dutch universities also appears to have suffered an absolute decline, and curricula failed to keep pace with the new developments being institutionalized in Prussia and Scotland. Leiden and Groningen were already low on funds by the end of the seventeenth century, making it difficult to appoint new faculty, and existing faculty had begun to leave in order to escape heresy hunting and to find greater academic freedom.[9] Bernoulli was a particularly severe loss, leaving Groningen in 1705 to accept a position in Basel. Boerhaave stayed on at Leiden until his death in 1738, despite several more lucrative offers elsewhere, but the university was unable to find a replacement who could carry on his work.[10] The Medical Faculty thus fell increasingly behind its competition at the University of Edinburgh.[11] Some progress was made in introducing instruction in physics and chemistry, but even so by the end of the century Leiden lagged far behind in mathematics.[12] Schama concludes: "Leiden resembled Oxford or Cambridge much more closely than a Scottish university, its student population dwindling and spending more time hunting, duelling and whoring than in the lecture theatres."[13]

Nor did private salons, reading clubs, or professional academies develop as alternatives to the universities on a scale similar to that in France and England or Prussia and Scotland. The only formal academy that provided for discussion of a wide range of literary and philosophical issues was the Society of Dutch Literature in Leiden, not founded until 1766. With one exception, salons appear to have been virtually unknown, apparently because of a lack of interest among the wealthier merchants and aristocracy.[14] The exception was the Knights of Jubilation, organized in Leiden shortly after the turn of the century on the model of a French salon. It was also responsible for publishing a journal of some distinction for more than a decade.[15] The existence of this group can scarcely be regarded as evidence of any significant Dutch involvement in Enlightenment thought, however, for virtually the entire membership consisted of French refugees, and by the 1720s the group had already begun to turn away from scientific and philosophical pursuits toward Freemasonry. Reading societies, in contrast, did appear in the Dutch provinces in significant numbers, as they did elsewhere. Most of these were relatively late in forming, however, dating only from the 1770s, and functioned solely as consumers rather than producers of Enlightenment scholarship.[16]

The main contributions of Dutch scholarship to the Enlightenment were focused fairly narrowly, more along the lines of seventeenth-century inquiries, in the area of science, and even in this area the trajectory of developments showed some evidence of decline. Both the number of eminent scientists and the number of scientific discoveries declined between 1700 and 1800.[17] Most of the work carried out during this period consisted of experimentation, made possible by the skills of Dutch craftsmen in making scientific instruments, rather than theoretical innovation or developments in natural philosophy. The major achievements thus took place in microscopy, botany, and chemistry, while the primary theoretical ideas guiding these experiments continued to derive from England and France.[18] Numerous scientific academies concerned with discussing experimental results were founded during the second half of the century, but a central institution did not come into existence until 1777, when the Scientific Society of Holland was founded.[19] During this period the Dutch also lagged behind other countries in carrying out scientific expeditions, and even experimental science gradually lost some of its competitive edge as growing numbers of skilled craftsmen in hydraulics, engineering, optics, and glassmaking emigrated to England and Scotland in search of a higher standard of living.[20]

Why did the Dutch Republic, after being a notably strong center of cultural innovation in the seventeenth century, fail to keep pace with other countries in the eighteenth century? Price suggests that the decline in intellectual activity was simply part of the "general ossification" of Dutch life.[21] But this is too broad an answer to afford much insight into the actual process by which the decline occurred. An examination of the economic and political conditions that were seen to be associated with cultural production in France, England, Prussia, and Scotland is the most likely place to begin. These conditions, it appears, were in fact notably lacking in the Dutch Republic.

Institutional Factors in the Decline of Dutch Scholarship

Each of the countries in which the Enlightenment flourished experienced marked economic growth in the eighteenth century; the Dutch economy, in contrast, faltered. Population underwent a steady decline after about 1680; agriculture and grain prices were generally depressed, resulting in widespread rural poverty; and Dutch commerce, once the envy of every other country, fell increasingly behind its competitors. Between 1650 and 1750 the total value of Dutch trade declined from between 300 and 400 million florins to somewhere around 250 to 270 million florins and remained stagnant until the 1790s. An increasing share of the Baltic trade slipped into English hands, causing the Dutch share of shipping through the Danish Sound to fall from 53 percent in 1660 to 28 percent in 1770. Dutch trade with the Continent also declined, as did profits from the Dutch East India Company, and French protectionism resulted in an increasingly unfavorable import-export ratio with France.[22] The number of Dutch whalers fell from 260 in 1700 to 50 in 1775; exports of paper to England fell by four-fifths between 1710 and 1760; and the number of new ships constructed dropped from 306 in 1707 to 25 in 1770.[23] Another serious blow to the Dutch economy was the decline of the Leiden textile industry: from 139,000 pieces in 1671 to 85,000 in 1700, to 54,000 in 1750, and 29,000 in 1795.[24]

The impact of these conditions on Dutch scholarship was in some cases direct. The role of tight finances in causing the Dutch universities difficulty in adding and retaining faculty and in keeping up student enrollments has already been mentioned, as has the emigration of Dutch craftsmen to England and Scotland. The decline of the Leiden textile industry was also significant since it greatly affected the economic and social condition of the republic's leading university. Between 1672 and 1795 the city's population fell from 72,000 to 30,000, and chronic unemployment and pauperism became prominent features of the area.[25] The university thus ceased being the intellectual center of an attractive, flourishing community enlivened by the cultural ferment of immigrants and traders, and much of its local financial support was cut off.

Economic stagnation also interacted with the political system to inhibit the kind of state growth that contributed to the Enlightenment elsewhere. The country's financial condition hardly provided the basis on which to build a powerful, centralized state. Taxation was already at a higher level than in England or France, and most of the revenues obtained were needed to service the huge national debt, which had risen from 30 million guilders in 1688 to 148 million in 1713.[26] With agriculture faltering, farmers could not be expected to pay additional taxes, and any increases in customs and excises had to be balanced against the risks of driving the price of Dutch goods to noncompetitive levels on the international market. The only secure means of raising additional revenue was through an increase in trade and industry, but these were in decline. Yet the weak condition of the Dutch state hardly provided the means with which to stimulate the economy. Among the reasons for the decline of the Leiden textile industry, for example, was the state's unwillingness or inability to intervene in town politics; hence, the ruling patricians passed taxes on to the workers, necessitating increases in wages, thus driving up the price of goods, which resulted in Dutch textiles being undersold by foreign competitors.[27] Nor was the state able to build up the country's military strength in the same manner as Prussia or France; indeed, its military force declined from one hundred ships and 24,000 men in 1700 to seventeen ships and 3,000 men in 1780.[28] Thus the country gradually lost its status as a great power and became less and less able to dictate terms of foreign policy to its highly mercantilist neighbors.

In other areas of economic policy the state also proved largely ineffective at intervening to promote greater efficiency or growth. Unlike France it did little to assist or protect industries, instead leaving such matters to local authorities. Road building was also left to local authorities and thus gradually lagged behind that of other countries. Tariffs and customs duties were ineffectively administered, resulting in widespread smuggling, which was made possible by corruptible officials. The state, again in contrast with France or Prussia or England, also failed to prevent capital from leaving the country by providing a centralized banking system or serving as a source of stable investments and loans. Thus by 1782 an estimated 1.2 billion florins of Dutch capital had been invested abroad, the return on which amounted to approximately 40 percent of all privately earned wealth in the country.[29]

The Dutch state had been the subject of much acclaim during the seventeenth century because of its republican structure in comparison with the more absolutist structures elsewhere. But by the eighteenth century this structure had become less than effective. In part its decentralized character may have been ill suited to carry out some of the more massive economic mobilization schemes that increasingly contributed to the strength of more centralized systems such as those of France and Prussia and to some extent England. In other ways a type of centralization may in fact have occurred, but not of the kind conducive to effective administration.

Olwen Hufton argues that the republican structure of the Dutch state collapsed in on itself during the last part of the seventeenth century, resulting in a closed oligarchic system.[30] The regents in whose hands governmental responsibility was vested consisted of a tightly knit group of approximately forty families whose impressive marital and financial connections allowed them to retain a firm grip on power. In the absence of a powerful stadtholder, the office of which actually remained vacant from 1702 to 1747, the regents were able to protect their own, largely provincial interests at the expense of developing a more effective form of central administration. Not until 1748, when widespread tax protests broke out in the major cities, was the hegemony of the regents challenged by the new stadtholder, William III. His efforts to create a more efficient system of administration produced no decisive results, however. Patronage continued to favor family connections more than merit; tax reforms were not introduced; revenues still lagged behind the government's needs; and bold proposals for improving the economy were dealt mortal blows by the merchant aristocracy.[31]

Even at the height of its prosperity in the seventeenth century the Dutch Republic had not moved toward a bureaucratic system of administration such as that initiated in France and England. To the contrary, as E. N. Williams notes, "far from becoming streamlined and modern, her administration stayed cluttered up with rights and liberties dating from a bygone age."[32] As it evolved into the eighteenth century, the Dutch state actually consisted of little more than a designated time and place for representatives of the various towns and provinces to come together for the purpose of discussing common problems such as foreign policy and defense. Rather than consisting of a powerful central bureaucracy, it existed chiefly as a loose confederation of town councils whose obligations to one another remained so weak that any one of them could unilaterally disband its army against the wishes of the rest. It was, as another writer has characterized it, "a large number of almost sovereign political units, separated by trade barriers, mutually jealous, retaining separate fiscal and legal systems, and increasingly unable to agree on a common economic, financial or foreign policy."[33]

The Dutch state also lacked any clear sense of legitimation as a sovereign entity with a corporate existence over and above the parties forming it. Dutch political theory affirmed the separate interests of the provinces, especially Holland's, but denied arguments which subjected the provinces to broader conceptions of sovereignty or unification. The liberty of each locality was defended largely on the basis of special, particularistic claims without any concise or uniform definition of authority and representation. The state operated without any explicit legislative, executive, or judicial functions, and even the stadtholder lacked the legitimacy to impose corporate or central claims on the provinces. Thus, as I. L. Leeb states in his study of Dutch political ideology, there were "no historical rights confirmed in positive law, no natural rights from the nature of things or the people, no divine rights from God through any of the several available channels. There shines through only the immediate pragmatic and practical problem of organizing . . . a wide range of interests."[34]

By the end of the eighteenth century the Dutch state remained no more unified or capable of effective administration than it had been a century earlier. High offices were appointed on the basis of wealth rather than merit and were held for life rather than being subject to termination pending performance.[35] At the provincial level the authority of representative committees was weak and remained subject to competing local interest groups. Each province had a unique political system which functioned more at the bidding of its leading towns than at the provincial level itself. By all indications people identified more with their immediate localities than with the broader province; as a study of Holland suggests, they were "in the first place burghers of their own towns, and only after that Hollanders."[36] At the local level, government operated with little more effectiveness, being performed by various oligarchies of officials whose only responsibilities were to the wealthy interests with which they were most closely associated.[37] From the standpoint of having any centralized bureaucracy with legitimate authority the Dutch system, therefore, was virtually lacking; it continued to exist, in Kossmann's words, as "a chaos of rights, privileges, usurpations, and abuses."[38] With no center of authority capable of mobilizing the full resources of the state, decisions were made only when virtual consensus could be obtained from the various wielders of power—meaning that disagreements usually forestalled any effective collective action.[39]

In comparison with France, England, Prussia, and Scotland, the Dutch Republic had only one of the conditions which, when paired with other factors, appear to have proven favorable to Enlightenment scholarship, namely, competing and cross-cutting interest groups vying with one another in a situation of ambiguously divided authority. Leeb's study in particular stresses the presence of political factions in the Dutch Republic during the second half of the eighteenth century: Orangists, patriots, aristocrats, democrats, regents, burghers.[40] Had other conditions been more favorable to scholarship, the state apparently encompassed enough diversity in patronage networks and ideological orientations that scholarship would not likely have been subject to limitations on its freedom and would have found plenty of issues on which to focus.

What was lacking, however, was a sufficient sense of corporate identity to generate discussion about the public good. Unlike in Scotland, where the presence of the British state forced the various local interests to reconcile their competing claims with a broader sense of collective progress, the Dutch interests remained almost totally decentralized. It is partly for this reason that historians of Dutch culture have emphasized the fact that Dutch scholars in the eighteenth century seem to have paid very little attention to political issues, at least prior to the French Revolution, and as a result contributed little to the political theories of the Enlightenment. According to Price, for example, Dutch writers were generally complacent about political affairs and, when they did write on controversial topics, tended to frame their discussions narrowly in terms of the conflict between Orangists and republicans. There appears to have been no sense of a constitutional crisis that cut across old political divisions and required framing issues in new terms of discussion.[41] Kossmann suggests that Dutch intellectuals generally showed little evidence of any concern for the state as a corporate entity or for society as a collectivity until the "nationalist" writings of the 1790s.[42] Indeed, it is generally held that the first political tract to address the Netherlands as a corporate state was *An Address to the People of the Netherlands,* published anonymously in 1781.[43]

It has also been pointed out that the only groups that found the Enlightenment as such particularly attractive prior to the 1790s were those who supported a stronger central regime organized by the stadtholder. This faction was relatively small, however, and its political orientation deviated sharply from that of the merchant oligarchs. Consequently, to espouse Enlightenment doctrines was to identify oneself with an undesirable political minority.[44]

The other negative consequence that the lack of a stronger central bureaucracy had on Dutch scholarship was the unavailability of patronage, offices, and a corps of interested civil servants of the kind who supported the Enlightenment in France, England, Prussia, and

Scotland. A state that did not build roads or sponsor agricultural improvement projects, that did not administer its tax system effectively or establish boards to encourage industry, was not likely to set up organizations in which writers and scientists could earn secure livelihoods. The universities, therefore, were left largely to the mercy of local financial arrangements, and alternative institutions for the promotion of scholarship failed to develop. Even during the more prosperous years of the seventeenth century, when constraints on the budget should not have been an issue, the state played only a passive role in cultural affairs, neither regulating scholarly output through censorship and other restrictions nor encouraging it through the establishment of universities or academies.[45] The most eminent figures in Dutch intellectual life were thus compelled to find support from sources other than the state; for example, Leeuwenhoek was a self-educated merchant, Swammerdam supported his own research with an apothecary shop, and Spinoza earned a modest living grinding lenses. The eighteenth century was no different: among prominent writers one finds publishers, clerks, physicians, nobles, merchants' sons, and religious dissenters. Scarcely without exception there is no evidence of writers being supported directly or indirectly by the state.

Sweden in the Age of Liberty

Sweden also provides a comparison that in some respects resembles the example of the Dutch Republic. It too failed to provide a context that was conducive to the production of Enlightenment ideology despite several conditions that on the surface made it a promising candidate. It had experienced a period of university construction in the seventeenth century, which in conjunction with other developments gave it a respectable share of scientific activity that continued throughout the eighteenth century. It became widely envied for its political freedoms during the so-called age of liberty (1719 to 1772); indeed Montesquieu, Voltaire, and Rousseau all wrote in glowing terms about its liberty and praised its republican constitution.[46] Sweden was firmly committed to mercantilist principles of political economy which recognized the potential economic contributions of science. The religious climate was also favorable to Enlightenment scholarship, insofar as the Protestant ethic has been thought to facilitate such activity, because Scandinavia shared the heritage of the Reformation along with England, Scotland, and Prussia.

Yet, despite some notable achievements in science, Sweden did not develop a tradition of Enlightenment scholarship that in any way distinguished itself. As one authority on the Enlightenment has noted, comparing Scandinavia with Scotland: "Copenhagen and Stockholm with populations larger than those of Edinburgh and Glasgow could point to no cluster of men of comparable brilliance."[47] The same sentiment, with perhaps a less problematic ethnocentric bias, has been expressed by a Swedish scholar who observes, discussing the Enlightenment in Scandinavia, that it "never formed a truly coherent current of ideas or became a unified movement."[48]

At one level, scientific discoveries—especially ones that held potential for improvements in agriculture and industry—were eagerly sought. King Charles XI founded a chemical laboratory and a mechanical laboratory in Sweden prior to the end of the seventeeth century in order to promote practical experimentation. A voluntary association for the general advancement of science, the Collegium Curiosorum, was founded in 1711, but led an on-again, off-again existence until its demise in 1728. Other pioneering efforts included the formation of an informal scientific academy in Uppsala in 1719 and in 1728 the Societatis Regiae Scientiarum Uppsalansi, with small funds from the crown, of which Celsius and Linnaeus were members.[49]

The period's main accomplishment toward providing an institutional base for scientific inquiry was the founding of the Royal Swedish Academy of Sciences in 1739. Inspired largely by mercantilist ideas and initiated with the assistance of several top officials in the ruling party who were acquainted with Sweden's scientists, the academy provided a meeting place for scholars, received permission to publish its proceedings, and after 1747 was able to support itself because of a royal monopoly on almanacs and calendars. Its work led to several discoveries in chemistry, geology, and mechanics. Celsius and Linnaeus gained international recognition; several lesser-known scientists and mathematicians contributed locally to the advancement of their disciplines; and in absolute numbers Sweden may have had almost as many productive scientists by 1750 as Scotland.

But on the whole Swedish science made faltering progress. Most of the academy's resources were devoted to disseminating technical knowledge for limited utilitarian objectives; the universities were slow to provide positions in chemistry and physics; medical students still had to be trained abroad; and by the end of the century the number of productive scientists had begun to decline.[50]

Other forms of Enlightenment scholarship witnessed even fewer advances toward institutionalization. No independent circle of literary figures of the kind existing in France developed in Sweden, not even on a smaller scale. The universities supplied the only important centers of intellectual activity, and they remained subject to narrow restrictions imposed by the church and state, while internal conditions continued to reflect the dominance of theology and rationalism.[51] Writers did not escape the pressures of censorship and other political controls, nor did they show any inclination to raise broad constitutional and theoretical issues of the kind that enlivened the Enlightenment elsewhere.[52]

Numerous reasons can be adduced to explain the relative lack of Enlightenment scholarship in Sweden: language barriers, religious orthodoxy, geographic isolation, social unrest—all may have contributed to the difficulties of institutionalizing intellectual activity on a broader scale. But it is also important to consider the manner in which economic and political conditions combined to preclude the development of a public sphere in which such activity could germinate.

Economic affairs, in contrast to those in the Dutch Republic, were carefully orchestrated by the state, albeit without the kind of results that were sought. By the beginning of the eighteenth century, Sweden had initiated vigorous mercantilist policies aimed at stimulating economic growth and strengthening state power, especially to defend itself against hostile neighbors. Its policies were predicated largely on decades of almost uninterrupted war in Poland and with Russia. It initiated standard mercantilist tactics: closer regulation of guilds, subsidies for domestic industries, import restrictions, chartered monopolies, and innovations in agriculture.[53]

These policies were not demonstrably successful, however. Sweden did not have a domestic market sizable enough to create large-scale, efficient production on the basis of protected sales alone; it did not have a tax structure or rural market system sufficiently developed to stimulate a money economy; and it was not particularly strong in natural resources other than timber and iron.[54]

Sweden's iron exports had grown tenfold during the century following 1630. After 1730 these exports remained basically constant, however, making it increasingly difficult for Sweden to maintain a positive balance of payments. Textiles and handicraft industries grew only modestly despite strong encouragement from the state, and these industries virtually collapsed after 1760; the timber industry did not begin to expand until near the end of the century; fishing and shipping grew slowly; and copper exports, the mainstay of Swedish expansion during the seventeenth century, peaked in 1687 and declined thereafter. On the whole, total output and employment patterns in Swedish industry during the first three-quarters of the eighteenth century fluctuated widely, usually in synchronicity with cycles of inflation and deflation, but overall they remained relatively stagnant in real terms.[55] Despite concerted efforts to implement mercantilist policies along the same lines as in France or Prussia, then, the economic situation in Sweden demonstrated little of the growth achieved in these other countries. As Eli Hecksher has remarked, "Everything was tried and nothing achieved."[56]

By the 1770s Sweden was forced to accept an increasingly peripheral role in the larger European economy. Mercantilist policies were gradually abandoned as the industries and monopoly trading companies they were designed to protect collapsed against foreign competition. The principal sources of profit shifted increasingly toward exports of raw materials and the carrying trade, both of which were stimulated more by reciprocal tariff agreements guaranteeing open trade than by protectionism. As a carrier rather than a primary producer of industrial goods, Sweden also found it increasingly expedient to adopt a policy of neutrality in the frequent European wars that took place during the second half of the century instead of attempting to maintain a large military force.[57]

These shifts in policy had dramatic implications for the state. Not only was the trajectory of economic growth different than it was for mercantilist powers such as France and Prussia, but the shift away from mercantilism and military force stripped the state of two of its major bases of bureaucratic expansion. Without strong economic growth the state was not able to expand its administrative activities to effective levels; and even domestic peace was difficult to maintain because the state was unable to develop a sufficient tax base, administrative apparatus, or military force to impose political stability on its territory while it promoted commercial expansion. Indeed, the country's war efforts had virtually exhausted the state's financial resources by 1710 and depleted its credit with the Estates'

Bank.[58] The internal structure of the state and its relation to the ruling elite was at the same time a factor that inhibited economic growth and failed to produce the type of centralized public sphere with which the Enlightenment was associated elsewhere.

The aristocratic Riksdag retained privileges of representation and deliberation independent of the king, thereby inhibiting the growth of royal absolutism. Although the country had been governed by absolute monarchs for nearly forty years, this system came to an end with the assassination of Charles XII in 1718. Charles died without an heir, and the abuses that had been sustained during his reign left all the interest groups capable of reasserting their rights a powerful incentive to do so. The Vasa dynasty had built up a large and effective administrative structure during the last half of the seventeenth century, including bureaus for the collection of taxes and forced loans, conscription, and an exceptional army for the country's size.[59] Indeed the bureaucracy had expanded more than two and a half times in sheer numbers of officials.[60] Yet when the dynasty collapsed in 1718 this administrative apparatus collapsed with it, and government was carried out on a much more restricted scale in the hands of the Riksdag, which carefully avoided actions that might arouse opposition from either the aristocracy or trading classes.

Having lost many of its provincial possessions—a loss that reduced the crown's standing revenue by more than half—the crown was also subject to severe financial constraints. Moreover, the groups that sought to reassert their rights were sufficiently divided among themselves to prevent a stable government from being formed easily in the absence of a strong central leader. This Sweden did not have. From 1719 to 1720 the deceased king's younger sister, Ulrika Eleanora, functioned as nominal sovereign, but at the discretion of the Riksdag and without hereditary right. In 1720 her husband, Frederick of Hesse, was invited to take the crown. His role, however, was also primarily nominal. Effective power resided in the Riksdag. Like its counterparts elsewhere, the Riksdag had long been the preserve of the landed aristocracy. As a result of the years of absolutism, though, the older nobility and their traditional privileges had eroded considerably. In their place, the dominant force that now prevailed was a coalition of lesser nobility, professionals, and army officers. During this so-called age of liberty, the Swedish state consisted largely of a commercial-aristocratic oligarchy not unlike that governing the Dutch Republic.

Though scarcely a bourgeoisie in any strict sense of the word, the men who now found themselves in power in the Riksdag included at least one prominent faction that gave vociferous support to new industrial enterprises, enthusiastically backed the Swedish East India Company, and advocated mercantilist economic policies. These men also exhibited an optimistic faith in the role of science as a means of economic advancement, patronized the arts, and dispensed rewards to scholars and inventors. These progressive inclinations, however, foundered against the rocks of inadequate economic resources on the one hand and political factionalism on the other. Throughout the period, government finances operated with considerable deficits which were made up only by extensive borrowing from the French and British. Unlike its allies, Sweden was barely able to keep its civil bureaucracy intact, let alone pursue a policy of bureaucratic expansion. Even the military, which in other countries often constituted a strong and expanding component of the bureaucracy, was unable to grow.[61]

Members of the Riksdag jealously staffed administrative posts with their own allies from the aristocracy, limited the size and authority of the bureaucracy, and consistently interfered with the activities of the executive councilors and their staffs in order to prevent these bureaus from becoming staging grounds for rival claimants to power.[62] Thus by mid-century the total number of civil servants in a country of approximately 2 million residents numbered only about 300, a figure that was probably only a fifth the size of the bureaucracy in Scotland and less than one tenth as large as the bureaucracy in Prussia.[63]

Until the coup d'état of Gustav III in 1772 the Riksdag held virtual power, providing sufficient representation that Sweden's form of government during this period has been compared favorably with that of England.[64] Mercantile interests received consideration as state policy was used to regulate the monetary supply, to provide credit, and to control foreign exchange rates.[65] The oligarchy was nevertheless by no means monolithic in its representation or constituencies. Throughout the period it was instead characterized by "discord" and "factional strife."[66] Between 1720 and 1721 power resided largely in a Hessian party; from 1721 to 1726 in a Holstein party; between 1727 and 1738 it was balanced between the so-called Hat and Cap parties; and from 1738 to 1765, despite Hat dominance, continued to be subject to strong Cap opposition, particularly in the area of foreign policy.⁶⁷ These divisions, together with the flimsy economic base from which power was exercised, prevented the state from effectively extending its control over the country. Indeed the middle part of the century was plagued with unsuccessful coup d'états, incipient rebellion among the peasants, and growing intrigues within the Riksdag involving foreign powers.

The Riksdag functioned with only poor efficiency at least in part because it was divided into four estates and lacked an executive agency with authority to implement programs. It was also too large and unwieldy to take on the duties of a modern bureaucratic state. With more than 1,000 members from the nobility, approximately 100 bourgeoisie, 50 clergy, and more than 150 peasants, each group registering its vote separately, major policy questions were often tied up in stalemates and were always slow to be resolved. Even such simple matters as tallying votes and reading resolutions to so many representatives made governing slow and inefficient. Moreover, matters of routine policy administration were not delegated to executive agencies but were kept tightly under the auspices of the Riksdag itself, and many categories of officials who might have lent valuable expertise to these proceedings were excluded from membership. Professional lawyers, burgomasters, many substantial landowners, most forge owners, and a majority of the lower civil service were excluded, while those who were included often lacked the financial means to serve in office and therefore became frequent participants in corruption. Despite the fact that Sweden had a central administration of sorts, therefore, it is not surprising that this body failed to gain coherence or function in a way that would promote expansion in either the economic or cultural spheres.⁶⁸

Perhaps because of the precarious foundations on which its power rested and the intermittent dangers to which its very existence was exposed, the Swedish Riksdag jealously protected itself from the open debate that became characteristic of the public sphere elsewhere. Freedom of speech among representatives themselves was constrained by the fact that members voicing unpopular opinions could find themselves voted out of the house and disqualified for future election. There was a weekly periodical that functioned as a house organ for the dissemination of official views, but replies to these views were not welcomed. And if public debate was limited among the representatives themselves, it was denied entirely to the broader public. Until the 1760s, members of the Riksdag considered themselves above public opinion, protected from criticism, and happily infallible. They forbade all discussion of their own acts, or of the Constitution, on the ground that "ignorance is better than wrong ideas."[69] No public exposure of abuses was allowed, no public discussion of foreign policy was possible, and all printed publications were subject to censorship. A clandestine pamphlet literature apparently existed, but anyone caught disseminating these materials was subject to heavy fines and even punishment by death.[70]

In comparison with countries in which economic and political conditions favored the production of Enlightenment intellectual activity, therefore, Sweden was not in a particularly advantageous position. Economic stagnation, despite earlier growth, impeded the kind of university expansion that occurred in Prussia and Scotland and limited the growth of a state bureaucracy that might have channeled greater resources to scholars in the form of patronage or offices or that might have created a broader clientele for discussion of public issues. The state was sufficiently oriented toward mercantilist planning that efforts were made, with some success, to promote scientific experimentation and its application to technological development. But the political conditions that might have bridged the gap between scientific discovery and broader Enlightenment debate were largely absent. The combination of representative government and competing political factions would probably have been sufficient to encourage scholarly debate had it not been for the censorship imposed by the Riksdag. Yet in the absence of a strong bureaucracy the resources with which to support such scholarship remained limited; moreover, the sense of corporate identity that appears to have accompanied the growth of central bureaucracy in other areas appears to have been lacking, perhaps not to the same degree as in the Dutch Republic, but enough that factional interests seem to have overridden schemes for collective improvement. Nor was the constitutional crisis of the same magnitude in Sweden as in, say, Scotland, where the tension between bureaucratic and aristocratic government was a continuing topic of interest. Although the tension between monarchy and aristocratic government had been severe prior to 1718 and was again an issue after 1772, this tension was largely resolved to the satisfaction of the ruling oligarchy in the intervening period and was not subject to the newer concerns that bureaucratic government added.

Decentralization and Enlightened Despotism in Austria

Austria presents another case in which the Enlightenment failed to take root. But here the failure occurred despite the enthusiasm of two of Europe's best-known "enlightened despots," Maria Theresa and Joseph II. Both monarchs tried seriously to bring new ideas from France and England and to cultivate an indigenous community of scholars. Yet by the end of the eighteenth century, Austria had contributed virtually no notable scholars to the Enlightenment. The Austrian case, then, provides a context in which to probe in greater detail the kind of regime capable or incapable of providing sustenance to the Enlightenment.

In order to grasp the details of the Austrian context for scholarship and literature, the eighteenth century needs to be divided roughly in half: the period up to about 1749, when Maria Theresa began to institute governmental reforms, and the period from then until the eve of the French Revolution, during which Maria Theresa and Joseph II sought to create an enlightened despotism.

During the first half of the century Austria remained politically decentralized. Despite the presence of Charles VI as monarch from 1711 to 1740, effective power lay in the representative Estates, which served as a bastion of aristocratic influence. After the expulsion of the Turkish army from Vienna in 1683 a course of autocratic centralization had been attempted. A central treasury was established in 1705, and decision making by specialized committees was initiated to give greater efficiency to the governing process. In 1717 this structure was reorganized hierarchically to emphasize the financial priorities of the state, and in 1721 a cabinet form of administrative supervision was formally instituted. Yet the process of actually implementing an effective centralized bureaucracy was impeded by powerful resistance from the nobility.

Provincial government remained in the hands of the nobility and was well organized, thus posing a major obstacle to the process of centralization. In most areas provincial Estates retained the right to vote taxes and to collect them, often with conditions attached which prevented all but a small share of the revenues raised from reaching Vienna.[71] The army was sizable, a fact that contributed under different conditions to the growth of central bureaucracy in places such as Prussia and France; but in Austria the various regiments remained in effect the private armies of local nobility and seldom functioned as a single cohesive fighting unit. The nobility's strength had in fact increased as a result of Austria's military engagements during the latter half of the seventeenth century. Both the need for fighting units and the financial costs of war left the state deeply dependent on the nobility. Thus as late as the 1740s the Estates and nobility "were very nearly separate, locally autonomous units, jealous of their rights and privileges and prepared to resent any undue royal influence in their affairs. The exigencies of war and diplomacy had forced a royal retreat from provincial government of which the Estates gladly took advantage."[72]

The nobility held wealth and privileges by virtue of landownership, religious connections, and ancient guarantees in constitutional law, thus retaining strong local allegiances even when elected or appointed to royal offices. The church functioned in close cooperation with the nobility, as it had two centuries earlier in resisting the Reformation. It continued to resist taxation of its extensive holdings, and by imposing strict confessional requirements on citizenship prevented Protestant areas from being fully integrated into the nation.[73] With scattered territories ranging from Naples and Sardinia to Hungary and Transylvania to the Austrian Netherlands, regional autonomy thus remained sufficiently high that efforts at centralization were extremely difficult to implement, prompting one writer to ask: "What, in fact, did the term 'state' signify? In each country it represented an historical territory which possessed its own special institutions."[74]

As a result of all this, the central bureaucracy made little headway toward developing a professional bureaucratic staff free of local loyalties and dependent on the bureaucracy itself for career advancement. One manifestation of the resultant weakness at the center was that administrative functions remained largely confined to the royal household rather than being dispersed among semiautonomous ministries and bureaucratic agencies. Another indication of the state's bureaucratic underdevelopment was the difficulty that the king faced in attempting to weld the various agencies of the state together into a functioning body. Regional diversity and aristocratic prerogatives carried over to the court itself through the various interests it was forced to recognize, thus inducing discord sufficient to impede the implementation of a coherent domestic or foreign policy. In actuality the conduct of state affairs continued to reside in a number of geographically divided chancelleries, each of which oversaw virtually all governmental activities within its own region.[75]

The economic situation in Austria was closely linked to the twin deterrents of a regionally decentralized, aristocratic administration and an underdeveloped central bureaucracy. The Austrian territories produced a diverse mixture of agricultural products, including timber, grain, flax, hemp, fish, and livestock, and the richness of its mineral deposits gave it potential as a leader in mining, iron production, silver, copper, and metalwares. Like its neighbors to the north, Austria sought economic growth through mercantilist policies, including such efforts as establishing workshops on nobles' estates, organizing monopoly trading companies, and initiating foreign trade.[76] But the success of these measures was limited by international and domestic conditions. Competition with Prussia and France for limited markets in finished goods, tariff policies among the major powers aimed at limiting imports, and the predominance of northern Europe in seaborne trade all contributed to Austria's disadvantage in the broader European economy.[77] Among the domestic conditions that aggravated these problems were territorial divisions, urban weaknesses, and the financial condition of the state.

Political, ethnic, religious, linguistic, and geographical divisions all militated against the development of a single domestic market integrated by natural trade routes and economic interdependence. Symptomatic of these divisions was the fact that internal customs barriers remained in effect until the last quarter of the eighteenth century. The position of the towns in many ways merely reflected the political and economic preponderance of the nobility. During the period of economic recovery which lasted from about 1660 until 1700, the landed nobility had been the chief beneficiaries, transforming themselves from receivers of customary rents into demesne-farming entrepreneurs trading in grain, timber, livestock, and other commodities.[78] Long-distance trade fell into the hands of the nobility, who characteristically dealt directly with foreign merchants rather than contributing to the creation of a domestic bourgeoisie, and whose expenditures consisted chiefly of nonproductive luxury imports. As demesne farming took root, the peasantry became increasingly impoverished, thus depriving the state of an important source of tax revenues.

Faced with major military commitments against Turkish forces in the east and rival claimants to sections of its dynastic holdings as far west as Spain, the Austrian state was perpetually on the brink of financial ruin. Its authority over the provinces was so weak that it was unable to tax the nobility or even impose substantial increases on the peasantry without evoking rebellion. Hampered by an inefficient system of collecting taxes and managing finances, the state was frequently unable to borrow sufficient funds to complete its projects, was forced to mortgage its assets, and was thus unable to give adequate assistance to industry and commerce and often had to postpone expenditures on roads, schools, and other public facilities.

Despite its efforts, the state was unable to stimulate much economic growth prior to the 1780s, thereby finding few resources from which to increase its own revenues or administrative capacities. Indeed its financial base underwent a serious decline during the first half of the century from military losses alone: by 1743 only Lombardy and Tuscany remained under its rule in Italy; all lands south of the Danube had been ceded to the Turks; and Silesia had been lost to Prussia.

These years brought few achievements in the scholarly and literary activities that were associated with the Enlightenment elsewhere.[79] The church and members of the nobility served as the leading sources of patronage to the expressive arts, concentrating their attention chiefly on music, architecture, painting, and sculpture. A baroque style of musical and artistic taste emerged, strongly influenced by Italian composers and artists, serving as an "outward and visible sign of the union between a high-aristocratic society dedicated to every form of devotion and a Church no less hierarchic and very little less worldly."[80]

The royal household was also a source of patronage for the arts, and many projects were commissioned as "an elaborate 'programme' or allegory, not of the artist's invention, relating to the titles, achievements and functions claimed for the sovereign."[81] Nevertheless, even the arts sponsored by the court reflected the dominance of the nobility. As Victor Tapie has suggested, they were chiefly "seignioral" rather than imperial: "It was the seignioral system which provided the resources for the enterprises of art patrons and stimulated rivalry among the great noble families. Thus the seigniory, which was the real foundation of the social and political system, rather than the State, was also the determining factor in the flowering of the arts."[82]

But if the visual arts flourished under the benevolence of the nobility, the literary arts which served as the carriers of Enlightenment thought were almost totally neglected. Between 1670 and 1729, over three hundred original novels appeared in northern Germany, but not one was published in Austria. Literary weeklies were being published, as we have seen, on an increasing scale throughout Europe, but the first of these weeklies in Austria did not appear until 1762. Academies and literary societies were also virtually nonexistent in Austria: only in 1761 was one such group founded—by private individuals without government support—and it soon disappeared for lack of funds.

Universities, too, were largely neglected, resulting in an overall decline in both numbers and quality of faculty and numbers of students.[83] The ideas of Thomasius, Wolff, and others with less conservative views concerning the relation of philosophy to theology gradually began to find expression in the universities at Salzburg and Prague.[84] But these ideas reflected the interests only of scattered individuals rather than anything resembling a coherent intellectual movement with an institutional base.

Austria also remained for the most part cut off from the foreign influences associated with the spread of Enlightenment ideas from France and Germany. Thus Paul Bernard's characterization of the situation appears almost as applicable to the Austria of 1750 as to the Austria of 1700: "Southern Germany had, in the cultural sphere, lost touch with the north; . . . southern baroque culture tended to value the plastic arts and music more highly than the book; . . . important figures at the court . . . allowed themselves to be so dominated by their political animosity for the governments of France and of the Protestant states of Germany that they furthered Hispano-Italian cultural influences to the point that Austria was effectively cut off from what was, for better or worse, the mainstream of Western thought."[85]

This state of affairs did not change overnight with the advent of Maria Theresa; indeed, it was only in the last years of her reign and during the subsequent reign of Joseph II that an enlivened climate of literary production came into being, and even then the continuities in political and economic conditions were sufficient to impede the monarchs' desires. Following the substantial losses of territory that Austria suffered during the 1730s and 1740s, the need for administrative centralization became more apparent. An enlarged bureaucracy was created which took charge of tax collection and provisioning of the military; a standing army of more than 100,000 men was established; and a network of local agents was created to supervise cameralistic reforms. The nobility strongly resisted these initiatives, however, causing them to fail in many parts of the empire.

The Seven Years' War, an extremely costly and largely unsuccessful venture for Austria, proved that further reforms were needed. To this end the army was increased to 300,000, a Council of State was formed to better coordinate fiscal policies, and the right to tax clergy was obtained. Nevertheless, resistance from the nobility and clergy, together with the fact that the peasantry could not itself bear the burden of further taxation, left the state on the brink of bankruptcy and unable to implement successfully its programs of centralization.[86]

None of the central governing committees had sufficient control over their own affairs or access to necessary resources to carry out their tasks effectively. Nor did the central regime succeed in administering its policies in the provinces: imperial lieutenants were constrained by the provincial diets from exercising their responsibilities effectively, and all judicial and financial officials "were dependent upon the local Diet and hence served that before their prince."[87] The nobility's right to exemption from taxation was upheld, and regional interests continued to divide the nobility who staffed central agencies, thus limiting their effectiveness. Virtually no success was achieved toward bringing the Hungarian diets or the Italian and Belgian chancellories under closer supervision, and even in Austria itself the reforms attempted consisted mainly of cosmetic reorganizations of standing committees.

By the end of Joseph II's reign only the army had been effectively reorganized and brought under more centralized control.[88] Olwen Hufton's characterization of the Austrian state provides an apt summary of the situation: "The uniqueness of the Habsburg monarchy was that it was only a political entity in the most tenuous sense and that the forces tugging it apart were far more apparent than the forces which held it together."[89]

The efforts of Maria Theresa and Joseph II to create a more centralized administrative structure were accompanied by some of the same kinds of intellectual developments that were associated with the Enlightenment elsewhere. But the partial and largely ineffective implementation of these reforms in the state, given its centrifugal tendencies and the weakness of its financial base, was also reflected in the realm of scientific and literary production.

In the 1760s some voluntary interest in wider literary developments began to appear among the Viennese elite who were associated with the state; for example, a group of writers and scholars founded the German Society to read and discuss works imported from Prussia.[90] The state also took some direct actions to improve its educational and technical base, particularly in military affairs, where Austria's weaknesses in comparison with Prussia were in vivid evidence. These actions were limited largely to the military itself but also included some broader reforms such as efforts to break the Jesuits' control of the universities and censorship.[91] The central agencies of the state did, as elsewhere, provide a base of operations for several distinguished writers and intellectuals during this period as well, although these figures were relatively exceptional cases.[92]

The most significant consequence of the reforms in the 1760s was to exacerbate the tension between crown and nobility, thus creating the same kind of intellectual debate, if on a much more modest scale, that had developed in France under similar conditions. The central bureaucracy's rising demands on the nobility in the areas of taxation and military expenditures necessitated new arguments with which to justify these demands. Maria Theresa appears to have been quite conscious of the need for such arguments with which to combat the counterclaims of the nobility and clergy. According to Ernst Wangermann: "It was precisely this need which prompted Maria Theresa to establish chairs of natural law in Austrian universities, for it was only with the aid of arguments drawn from natural law that some of the opposition's claims based on positive law and time-honored practice could effectively be countered."[93] It was in this context that the few Austrian intellectuals whose names became associated with the Enlightenment, writers like Sonnenfels and Blanc, did their work, contributing not to the justification of royal policy alone but to broader discussions of political theory.[94]

The figure who perhaps more than any other associates Austria with the Enlightenment is the "enlightened despot" Joseph II. Inspired by a desire to transform Austria into a powerful state resembling France or Prussia, Joseph set out to reform the society in ways that on the surface appeared to reflect the ideals of the French Enlightenment. Among the reforms attempted were modifications of provincial government, attacks on the seigneurial system of exploiting serf labor, impositions of financial obligations on the church, and regulations aimed at promoting domestic industry. Joseph was sufficiently schooled in the writings of the philosophes to recognize the importance of their arguments for the reforms he sought to initiate. Some efforts were made to liberalize the censorship laws so that political pamphlets could be distributed reflecting Enlightenment ideas, and the universities were pressed to put greater emphasis on mathematics and political theory.

But these reforms, like the innovation in scholarship elsewhere, were scarcely the accomplishments of a single far-sighted ruler. They were made possible by broader changes taking place in the state. According to Wangermann, the reforms in Austrian scholarly life were generally initiated by members of the civil service who had come to have an interest that was somewhat autonomous from the nobility.[95]

The broader changes were made timidly and piecemeal, however, and the state's relation to scholarship tended to reflect these limitations. Joseph rejected proposals for copyright laws that would have made publishing a more viable economic enterprise; unlike his contemporaries in France and Prussia, he bestowed no pensions, honors, or sinecures on authors; nor did he pursue the long-standing proposal to establish an academy of sciences in Vienna; and the universities atrophied badly during his rule.[96] Wangermann observes: "The money which might have been used for patronage of learning and letters remained in the coffers of the state."[97]

The larger political reforms that might have created conditions more favorable to the production of Enlightenment culture posed such violations to the interests of the nobility that with few exceptions they proved unworkable. Even the reforms that had promoted cultural inquiry for a while proved short-lived, as Isser Woloch notes: "Instead of consolidating the liberal cultural environment of the 1780s, Austria's government slipped back into its old authoritarian style in Joseph's last days."[98] Royal laws to the contrary, serfdom continued largely intact; members of the nobility clung tenaciously to the reins of provincial government, economic growth was slow; and the bureaucracy lacked sufficient resources to expand in scope or effectiveness. The emperor's own self-composed epitaph spoke tellingly of the limited effects of his reforms: "Here lies Joseph II, who was unfortunate in all his enterprises."[99]

The Effects of Decentralization

In each of these three cases—the Dutch Republic, Sweden, and Austria—the effects of political decentralization, then, were to dampen the institutionalization of Enlightenment scholarship and literary activity. Each of these cases manifested some of the political heterogeneity that gave autonomy to writers and intellectuals in France, England, Prussia, and Scotland. Towns, aristocrats, parliamentary representatives, civil servants, and royalty all contended with one another for authority. No single entity was capable of imposing its will unobstructed on the literary community. But political decentralization also worked against the formation of a literary community in the first place.

In the countries in which Enlightenment scholarship gained early support, a strong central bureaucracy contributed importantly to this support. But the Dutch Republic, Sweden, and Austria lacked a strong central bureaucracy capable of playing this role. Mercantilist aspirations notwithstanding, an effective administrative agency failed to develop. Strong local and regional interests, geographic and linguistic diversity, military reversals, aristocratic influence, and disadvantageous positions in the international economy all contributed to this failure. In the absence of a strong central bureaucracy, economic and cultural expansion alike proved difficult to promote.

Without the institutional sources of patronage and the center of public gravity that a strong bureaucratic state provided, scholars and writers were scarcely able to benefit from the freedom that political decentralization might otherwise have permitted. Indeed, this freedom itself was sometimes limited by the fact that local patrons were able to exercise closer control over the creative minds in their employ than was the case where a central bureaucracy provided ballast against these purely local networks. Above all, though, the weak development of Enlightenment culture in these settings testifies to the importance of expanding political and economic resources for growth in the intellectual sphere.

9 🙙🙚

Autocracy and the Limits of Enlightenment

*I*F THE PRINCIPAL contrast between the Dutch Republic, Sweden, and Austria on the one hand and those countries in which the Enlightenment prevailed on the other was the greater degree of decentralization which prevented the consolidation of a resourceful central bureaucracy, the contrast provided by Russia and Spain is not one of weak bureaucracy but of a bureaucracy without the kinds of cross-cutting pressures that promoted a public sphere in which scholarly debate could take place. The Russian and Spanish states did not succeed during the eighteenth century in becoming full-blown autocracies; but they came close—close enough that central bureaucracies were established which, despite limited resources, contributed to the development of academies, patronage, and university reform. Yet the triumph of autocracy also meant the demise of autonomous forces such as the nobility, estates, courts, or parliaments that created an institutional tension in which theoretical reflection was inspired.

Russia: Bureaucratic Expansion and Technical Knowledge

The growth of bureaucratic centralization in Russia came at the start of the eighteenth century under the rule of Peter I and was inspired largely by military demands. The war with Sweden from 1700 to

1709, along with simultaneous threats from Turkish armies, demonstrated the need for an administrative apparatus capable of mobilizing military resources on a more complete scale.[1] The bureaucracy that evolved was not dissimilar to that in Prussia; indeed, it was modeled after the Prussian system of boards or colleges which were differentiated by function. In 1711 the Senate, or "council of nine," was created with authority to execute all imperial policies, including the collection of taxes, distribution of revenue, allocation of offices, and the promotion of industry and trade. Seven years later, after consulting western advisers (notably Leibniz), Peter expanded the bureaucracy again, allocating administrative duties to nine boards or colleges, each with a distinct area of responsibility, such as foreign policy, war, tax collection, commerce, and justice.[2]

The construction of a centralized bureaucracy was accompanied by systematic suppression of other institutions from which challenges to autocratic rule might have been launched. During the seventeenth century the tsars had largely succeeded in undermining the Boiar Duma as an independent governing body.[3] By the end of the seventeenth century the courts were also reduced from having rights as autonomous institutions to being appendages of the central bureaucracy. Provincial courts other than those appointed by the state were abolished; judgeships were handed out to royal favorites, the largest category of whom were retired military officers; and inquisitorial tactics were introduced which subjected legal procedure to the demands of the state.[4]

The expanding bureaucracy under Peter's rule provided the means to curb opposition even further by drawing the nobility into a position of dependence.[5] To meet the demands for an enlarged military, mandatory service to the state was made a lifetime obligation of the nobility; greater care was given to drawing the children of nobility into state service; and harsh penalties were meted out to nobles who shirked their responsibilities or who registered dissent. A "service nobility" thus came into being whose wealth and prestige depended on service to the state and attainment of rank within the bureaucracy through meritocratic performance of prescribed duties.[6] In the absence of independent estates, the nobility's subservience to the bureaucracy gave the Russian state a distinctly autocratic character. As one historian notes: "This creation of distinct social groups at the behest of the State differed radically from the western European pattern of autonomous Estates based upon birth, privileges and legal traditions, conscious of their ancient political rights and special local status."[7]

Relatively early in the eighteenth century, then, Russia had, at least in formal terms, created one of the institutions most significantly related to the production of Enlightenment scholarship in western Europe. The bureaucracy employed approximately two thousand persons, more than one hundred of whom were in senior posts; and its revenues had tripled since the 1680s.[8] The service nobility, of which the bureaucracy was composed, was subject to a new set of expectations regarding the skills with which duties were performed, especially in areas in which technical competence was of clear value, such as navigation, artillery, and military engineering. More generally, a strong tendency toward rationalization was evident in the Russian state which carried significant implications for the relations between the tsar and the bureaucracy. Personal subservience to the tsar gradually gave way to a more formalized system of ranks and responsibilities, thus creating an administrative organization with which even the tsar had to deal as an objective entity operating according to its own norms and built-in procedures.[9] This normative change was itself an important accomplishment, as Barbara Meehan-Waters suggests: "For all the apparent whims, the blatant favoritism to court 'pets,' and the advantages given to the old nobility, the Petrine reforms had both worked and become the norms of the Russian state. A modernized nobility served a centralized state; a network of favorites, patrons, and kin served both sovereign and servitor."[10]

Thus by many indications the bureaucracy was ripe for promoting a new kind of secular, technical knowledge similar to that emerging in western Europe. This in fact was what Peter attempted to do in introducing his famous program of westernization. International communication was intentionally cultivated through a program of sending young nobles to study abroad in England, Holland, and France at state expense. A number of domestic academies were also founded to encourage research, instruction, and the application of technical knowledge to practical problems: artillery schools in 1701, 1712, and 1721; navigation schools in 1701 and 1715; engineering schools in 1709 and 1719; and a school for army surgeons in 1707.[11] Special efforts were made to upgrade medicine. Libraries, a national history museum, and schools devoted to agriculture (1701) and mining (1716) constituted other aspects of the state's westernization program.[12] Seven new publishing operations were initiated, all under direct control of the government, and as a result the total number of books in circulation began to increase significantly.[13] In addition to Peter's personal encouragement all these new enterprises appear to have had the backing of key officials in the bureaucracy and were selected with specific technological, economic, and military objectives in mind.[14]

The capstone of these initiatives was the St. Petersburg Academy of Sciences founded in 1724 and opened in 1725. Mandated in its charter was a full range of studies from mathematics and physics to the humanities, including history, law, and political theory. With its chemical laboratories, botanical gardens, anatomical theater, library, and salaried staff, all backed with the tsar's personal support, the academy promised to be a significant base for scholarly work.[15] Prior to this time intellectual activity had been concentrated almost exclusively in religious institutions. The new centers of learning promised to break this monopoly, giving scholars whose interests lay in topics other than theology and ecclesiology an opportunity to produce knowledge deemed of value to the state.[16]

But if the bureaucracy provided resources for scholarship, it also imposed strict limitations on the nature of this work. As long as the state held a virtual monopoly over the production of secular culture, a pragmatic or utilitarian orientation emphasizing the attainment and responsible use of practical skills prevailed. Along with positions and facilities came enforceable expectations concerning the roles scholars were to perform for the state. Academic training and inquiry focused heavily on applications to military and naval problems. Mathematics, ballistics, military engineering, and navigation, all with a highly technical orientation, were especially valued.[17] Two-thirds of the works published during this period consisted of laws, manifestos, regulations, and official notices, or focused on military affairs; only 3 percent fell into the categories of history, science, philosophy, and literature.[18]

Broader strands of political and philosophical work, as exemplified by Grotius, Pufendorf, and Locke, were familiar to some segments of the elite. But it was not until later, during the succession crisis in 1730, that these ideas gained more than abstract intellectual interest, and even then no institutional base existed from which to give these ideas expression as guidelines for political practice.[19] In the absence of other institutional bases from which to challenge autocratic rule neither the freedom nor the incentive existed for broader discussions of this type to develop. Even the more technically oriented St. Petersburg Academy found its work impeded by too exclusive a relation to the bureaucracy. Its activities were frequently interrupted by court intrigues and demands from the bureaucracy, the effect of which was not only to impede research but also to damage the academy's reputation and its capacity to attract foreign talent.[20]

As long as the bureaucracy was in a position to supply resources, the more technical aspects of scholarship and training progressed. But until the 1760s these resources were sufficiently limited and the condition of the bureaucracy itself was sufficiently precarious that cultural production of even the most technical kinds tended to falter. During the reign of Peter II (1727-1730) the Academy of Sciences fell low on the bureaucracy's list of priorities, forcing its activities to be seriously curtailed. Anne (1730-1740) devoted greater personal attention to the academy, but also restricted its members' freedom by placing them under closer bureaucratic supervision. J. L. Black suggests that the entire period between Peter I and Catherine II witnessed little in the way of support for the Enlightenment beyond personal encouragement: "Government-directed programmes of serious assistance to scholars, translators, and educators went into near abeyance."[21] These years also demonstrated the academy's continuing dependence on foreign talent: only three of its members during its first fifteen years were Russians.[22]

During the next two decades the academy's work continued, but still on a relatively modest scale and subject to much external interference. Little progress was made toward disseminating scientific ideas to a wider audience: enrollments in the academy declined steadily after the initial graduating class, and despite efforts to upgrade the general education levels of the bureaucracy, only one-third of the top officials had any formal training at all and fewer than one in ten had advanced instruction.[23]

Language barriers, cultural isolation, religious tradition, and indifference to formal education all contributed to the difficulties that technical advancement faced during the first half of the eighteenth century in Russia. These problems were compounded, however, by the fact that the principal resource supporting technical advancement—the bureaucracy—was also on shaky foundations. Despite the formal initiatives to institute a more functionally rational mode of bureaucratic organization, these initiatives largely failed to produce an effective administrative organization.[24] Corruption, incompetence, and suspicion combined to undermine the bureaucracy's operations, leaving the actual business of government in the hands of a closed network of secret agents or *fiskals* who were personally loyal to the tsar and who ruled through intimidation and intrigue.[25] The bureaucracy's problems were also compounded by a persistent shortage of revenue. Nearly two-thirds of the state's entire budget was consumed by the military, the size of which doubled between 1709 and 1745.[26]

At the end of Peter I's reign the number of bureaucrats in state service had to be cut in half, and for the next half century many failed to receive regular salaries.[27] Under these conditions it became increasingly difficult to attract qualified persons to staff positions, let alone to supply funds for research, schools, and other improvement programs. Publishing operations consistently ran at a deficit; huge stocks of books remained unsold; and without subsidies from the government, many of the presses that Peter had founded had to be dismantled.[28] Overall, the number of titles published during the thirty-year interval from 1725 to 1755 was approximately a third less than the number published during the preceding twenty-five years.[29] After the death of Peter I the bureaucracy also fell victim to an unstable succession of palace revolutions which produced regimes lasting on average only about six years. Bureaucrats increasingly cultivated their own careers with the expectation of short-term rewards, while little attention was given to the systematic long-term needs of the bureaucracy itself. The nobility also managed to perpetuate itself within the bureaucracy, using its authority to implement policies favorable to aristocratic interests, such as the exclusive right to own land and serfs, exemption from direct taxation, protection of the indivisibility of estates, and virtually untrammeled freedom in matters of local taxation.[30]

The bureaucracy's mixed, transitional, and yet to be fully realized internal characteristics—autocratic but weak, centralized but inefficient, rational but ineffective—were also evident in its relations to the economy. Many aspects of the economy remained unyielding to the state's efforts to stimulate growth: foundaries, shipyards, and cloth mills produced disappointing results; the three-field system established during the Middle Ages still prevailed in most agricultural areas; fertilizers and fallow-land farming were virtually unknown, and landlords did little to encourage capital improvements; farming was also disrupted in many areas by the mass conscription of peasants into the army.

Still, enough growth did occur to facilitate bureaucratic development. Rising demand for agricultural products in western Europe resulted in a tripling of Russian exports between 1726 and 1762, and even though imports also multiplied, the balance was such as to yield a net income of more than 4 million rubles annually.[31] Although much of the profit from foreign trade went directly to the nobility and was spent on luxury consumption, the state's earnings from state-owned lands were considerable. A rise in population of nearly 5 million also contributed to the state's base for taxation.[32]

The Catherinian Reforms and Enlightened Despotism

Under Catherine II (1762-1796) the bureaucracy underwent a period of renewed expansion and rationalization. The system of executive colleges was further divided into functionally distinct departments, and greater centralization was imposed on provincial administrators.[33] The number of civil servants at the central and provincial levels grew to more than sixteen thousand, roughly equal in size to the Prussian bureaucracy, and the bureaucratic elite gradually acquired sufficient independence from the crown to exercise power on its own behalf. In a modest degree the bureaucratic "ranks" were set free, coming to resemble estates capable of articulating separate interests within the state.[34] Exports tripled during this period, state-run industries registered a fivefold increase in output, and population grew steadily, all contributing to increases of approximately 200 percent in state revenues and expenditures. Still, the bureaucracy chalked up periodic deficits, was forced to borrow from Holland and Italy, withheld salaries from officials, and imposed austere limits on its own outlays.[35]

But the most important development, as far as conditions affecting cultural production were concerned, was an alteration in the relations between the state and the nobility. Measures were still in effect which bound the nobility to the state; for example, laws prohibited the nobility from taking an active role in commerce.[36] Coercion and mutuality of interest also combined to prevent opposition from arising within the nobility.[37] Nevertheless, a variety of evidence points to the conclusion that the nobility and the bureaucracy were becoming increasingly differentiated from each other. In 1762 royal initiatives "emancipated" the nobility from state service, recognized the legality of their property claims, and granted certain other civil liberties.

The consequences of these initiatives alone should not be over-emphasized, but they mark a turning point in the internal structure of the ruling elite. After this date, as Marc Raeff notes, "a division began to take place between the nobility—who served only for a short while or not at all and who were shifting their potential cultural and social role in the country—and the bureaucracy—a new class of career officials . . . who served in state offices."[38] The distinction between hereditary landowners and career civil servants became institutionalized both in practice and in terminology; corporate assemblies which functioned similarly to western Estates were permitted to come into being, giving landlords the right to vote on important issues; and in the absence of mandatory service from the nobility, the bureaucracy came to be staffed more by commoners, sons of clergy, and the bourgeoisie.

Despite the persistence of autocratic government in theory, the door was thus opened for a division of interests within the ruling class. As Richard Jones suggests: "The state and the nobles were aware that the two parties were currently set on different paths that would lead them farther and farther apart . . . the government of Catherine II and the rank and file of the nobility already had different interests and looked at the future of the nobility from two different points of view."[39] This division also provided a basis, however small, for critical opposition to be launched against the state, for as Hans Torke observes: "The nobility was now free either to become 'gentry' . . . or to develop a critical attitude toward the government, neither of which had been possible so long as every nobleman had been forced to serve and had been bound to the state."[40]

The bureaucracy also succeeded in becoming increasingly differentiated from the crown, both through actual concessions granting greater powers of self-determination and through the process of bureaucratic formalization which gradually reduced the monarch's ability to intervene directly in the day-to-day operations of the bureaucracy.[41] Catherine II was especially vulnerable to this process because she had seized power with the help of the bureaucracy and lacked dynastic legitimation. Although she remained very much in control of the state throughout her reign, she was sufficiently vulnerable to the demands of the bureaucracy to grant reforms and to cultivate loyalty from the nobility as a counterbalance.[42] While autocracy by no means ceased to characterize the overall system, a kind of dyarchy thus came into existence in which the bureaucracy and nobility both shared in the exercise of power.[43]

Under Catherine's reign, then, the conditions favoring Enlightenment scholarship were much stronger than they had been earlier in the century. Not only was Catherine herself favorably disposed toward the Enlightenment, but also the bureaucracy was in a better position to support scholarly work, and the internal divisions cutting across the ruling elite tempered the autocracy in a way that stimulated broader intellectual debate.[44] Limited resources, autocratic restrictions, and heavy demands on scholars to devote their attention to technical matters still impeded intellectual work, but some of the same developments that had taken place in western Europe now became evident.

In science Russia developed "a cadre of competent as well as professional scientists whose research activity was fully appreciated by the entire European scientific community."[45] Efforts to introduce science and mathematics into university curricula remained fairly unsuccessful, however, and attempts to reform education more generally met with resistance or indifference until the late 1780s.

These reforms also failed to reflect the ideals of liberal training advocated by Locke and Rousseau, instead favoring authoritarian methods of instruction and preservation of the status quo.[46] As the bureaucracy grew, however, an increasing number of educated professionals provided a concentrated audience for literary and artistic activities. The military, administrative, and even ecclesiastical elites were expected to have received formal training; elite schools and academies were expanded to meet this expectation; and more books were printed to stock these programs with instructional materials.[47] Theater and opera performances received subsidies from the court and were made available to members of the bureaucracy free of charge; orchestras and choirs also flourished as a result of court patronage. Literature underwent a more limited revival: Catherine demonstrated a personal fascination with the French Enlightenment and invited several of the philosophes to pay visits to the court; publishers' lists began to include books by French and German writers, yet there was little sense of deeper appreciation being given their work. According to Antony Lentin: "The fundamental ideas of the philosophes did not strike home. Their books were treated as fashionable gimcracks rather than stimulants to thought and action."[48]

The state's drive toward bureaucratization nevertheless stimulated literary production of a more general nature. The development of the secular press was almost totally a product of the state, albeit in an increasingly complex pattern of arrangements. Two of the first printing establishments were founded by the state in St. Petersburg, one for printing official documents, the other for publications by the Academy of Sciences. From these, periodicals and newspapers came to be produced, concentrating primarily at first on technical and bureaucratic matters, but eventually including satire, fiction, and other forms of literature oriented toward the leisure interests of the nobility and state officials. As other academies were founded, including Moscow University, the Naval Cadet Corps, and the Infantry Cadet Corps, additional presses were given official sanction. By 1774 eight new publishing operations had been initiated, four of which were associated with the state's elite training academies, and these presses together with the Academy of Sciences accounted for about three-quarters of all the books published.[49] Throughout this period rigid censorship was enforced by the state, and the first private printing houses were not permitted until 1783. Nevertheless, the effect of state sponsorship was to produce a fourfold increase in the number of books published annually between 1740 and 1770, with another threefold increase coming between 1770 and 1788 as a result of the advent of private publishing.[50]

Like other countries in which cross-cutting pressures within the state stimulated intellectual debate, Russia displayed greater diversity in its scholarship during the reign of Catherine II than at any time during the previous six decades. Although the autocratic nature of Catherine's regime still limited what could be said or written, the effect of greater differentiation among the bureaucracy, nobility, and crown was to prompt a more lively exchange of commentary and debate among leading writers.[51] Richard Pipes has noted particularly the importance of greater autonomy between the bureaucracy and the crown in this development, remarking that "a fissure thus appeared in the once solid patrimonial structure; literature became the first endeavor permitted to members of the tsarist service class that had nothing to do with promoting the sovereign's own interests."[52] Similarly, Marc Raeff has drawn an explicit connection between the rising autonomy of the nobility and a new mode of intellectual production, observing that there were "serious frictions between the autocracy and nobility—frictions that contributed to the emergence of the intelligentsia from among the ranks of the nobility."[53]

Political criticism as such was still unthinkable, but literature provided an outlet for reflection on the changing circumstances of power. Satire and drama served these purposes well. Writers began to use these media to explore problems within the bureaucracy, often judiciously winning support from the crown by praising it at the same time that they wrote against abuses in the bureaucracy.[54]

Although limited in scope, Walter Gleason's study of three prominent writers associated with the Catherinian Enlightenment (Fonvizin, Novikov, and Bogdanovich) demonstrates with exceptional clarity the impact of the changing relations between monarch and bureaucracy on intellectual work in this period.[55] All three writers were integrated into patronage networks within the bureaucracy and held positions as officials. When the bureaucracy began to be differentiated more clearly from the crown, the "political" character of these writers' work became increasingly evident. Not only was the work of all three writers increasingly identified with particular factions in the bureaucracy; it also became more self-consciously oriented to the theoretical issues associated with reconciling the disparities between different interests. Gleason also suggests that a gradual revision of the theoretical focus of these deliberations became evident. Constrained by the monarch's power to avoid ideas that threatened autocratic authority, all three writers turned increasingly toward an idealized, utopian form of political argument which framed discussion in abstract terms without explicit connections to the current regime. It was this set of abstractions, given more general applicability by their very abstractness, that came to figure prominently in the political debates of the following century in Russia.

Other scholars have also stressed the importance during this period of intellectual ferment arising from the tensions between the monarchy and nobility.[56] Although much of the elite ideology produced during the last third of the century consisted of conservative, apolitical literature for the amusement of the leisured class, a clear tendency was also evident toward the production of critical scholarship of the kind that later became identified with nationalist movements and democratic revolutions. Alexander Radishchev (1749-1802) became the hero and first martyr of a subsequent generation of intellectuals for his condemnations of serfdom and tyranny. Ivan Panin (1773-1805) utilized Lockean and Rousseauian precepts in developing a reformist critique of Russian society. Characteristic of the writing of this period, as most notably seen in Scotland, was a concern with the social bases of moral virtue, including a critique of the state for disrupting traditional patterns of moral obligation. Other writers focused on the reforming role of education, the need for moral development, and the relations between monarchy and social welfare.[57] Compared with writers in countries such as France and England, these scholars were less well institutionalized as members of whole networks of intellectuals with stable means of support. Nevertheless, they approximated in innovativeness and diversity some of the same themes that had developed elsewhere under similar conditions.

The threat of autocratic rule to the freedom of Russian scholarship was never far away, however. No sooner had the turmoil of 1789 broken out than tolerance for political and philosophical innovation quickly disappeared. Teaching in French was forbidden; plans for establishing more universities were abandoned; and rigid censorship was imposed to check the spread of books bearing ideas with western influences. Only the more technical and scientific disciplines continued to receive encouragement. The Enlightenment in Russia was thus of limited duration. The conditions that favored its development were not dissimilar from those in countries such as France and England. Despite limited resources, the bureaucracy provided support for scholarly activities that seemed amenable to mercantilist expansion. Yet the high degree of autocratic centralization that characterized the bureaucracy during most of the century limited the development of a broader public sphere conducive to the wider intellectual ferment associated with the Enlightenment.

Centralized Absolutism and the Enlightenment in Spain

The Spanish state under Philip V (1700-1746) and Ferdinand VI (1746-1759), and then particularly during the reign of Charles III (1759-1788), manifested tendencies remarkably similar to those in Russia. Despite immense differences in culture, tradition, and previous political involvements, Spain moved toward autocracy along much the same lines as Russia. Centralization characterized the main administrative reforms of the period; representative assemblies in the provinces were quashed; and the nobility were reduced in or excluded from power. As the Russian experience demonstrated, such measures were difficult to sustain over any extended period, for the nobility still occupied the predominant positions in the largest sectors of the economy. In Spain autocracy was achievable to an even lesser extent because of the continued existence of the nobility as a corporate order organized separately from the state. For this reason "centralized absolutism" is probably a more accurate phrase with which to describe the mode of government it achieved rather than autocracy. Nevertheless, the two countries bore sufficient similarities in state structure that the relations between the state and cultural production also turned out to be much the same.

Ironically, one of the preconditions that facilitated the accomplishment of centralized absolutism during the eighteenth century was the culmination toward the start of that period of Spain's long decline, a process that had been under way since the middle of the sixteenth century. By the treaties of 1713 and 1714 Spain lost its possessions in the Netherlands, Milan, Naples, and Sardinia to Austria, ceded Sicily to Savoy and Gibraltar to Britain, and renounced claims to the French throne. Thus for the first time in over a century Spain did not have to field vast armies to protect far-flung dynastic possessions. In the past, despite its considerable resources, the Spanish crown had always been forced to compromise with the nobility in order to raise even greater revenues as well as troops and officers required for its military campaigns. Now the state was able to take the upper hand, suppressing the representative institutions of the nobility and imposing a centralized mode of administration on the country. These reforms were, as one writer observes, far-reaching:

> From 1715 onwards Spanish monarchs began to view their territories as candidates for administrative reform very much along the lines adopted by Louis XIV in France some fifty years previously. Such reform was concerned above all with strengthening central control by reducing provincial boundaries and privileges: by making uniform the organs of provincial and municipal government: by superimposing a new royal official, the *intendente,* on a mass of hereditary and venal provincial offices to ensure the implementation of royal will: by abolishing or reducing the power of the erstwhile mighty *consejos,* the aristocratic councils which ran the provinces: and by creating what was to emerge as an unmistakable ministerial despotism.[58]

Despite considerable advances along these lines, one of the lingering barriers to achieving full autocratic absolutism was the de facto autonomy of many local jurisdictions. Although a number of programs were experimented with in order to bring these local jurisdictions more effectively under the central administrative apparatus, many towns and rural areas remained in practice dominated by members of the nobility. Full effectiveness in raising taxes and troops was always hampered by the presence of these remaining strongholds. Yet, as long as the state could prevent these areas from uniting in collective action and exclude them from direct participation in central administrative activities, the bureaucracy was able to develop and function largely according to its own dictates.

Within these constraints the administrative reforms of the Bourbon monarchy were for the most part effective. A uniform system of law was imposed on the diverse regions of the country, and specialized ministries conducted the actual business of the state. Under these ministries specialized commissions and boards were established, and a uniform system of provincial administrators was put into place. Functional division of labor within the bureaucracy was introduced in 1705 by a royal edict that divided top-level administration into five distinct secretaryships. Though subject to removal by the king, the holders of these offices were able to exercise considerable discretion in the conduct of their affairs.[59]

Accompanying this rise in formal bureaucracy was an increase in the use of professional civil servants for purposes of administration. Whereas the old regime had relied chiefly on personal favorites of the king to fill administrative roles, the new regime looked to trained, salaried officials for these functions. As the bureaucracy grew, its activities were delegated to nine major councils, each of which was responsible for supervising a number of committees and commissions. No estimates indicate the total number of persons that may have been involved, but to judge from the Council of Castile, which alone employed 140 officials and clerks, the number may well have exceeded 1,000[60]

In 1749 the bureaucracy was enlarged again through the creation of a system of provincial intendants, similar to that in France, for the purpose of organizing royal finances in the provinces.[61] Although their efficiency was hampered by a cumbersome and overlapping system of taxes that were difficult to assess, the intendants effectively carried out the suppression of local authority over taxation and brought it under the supervision of the central treasury.[62]

In 1753 another major obstacle to centralization was surmounted when the state obtained the right to nominate bishops, thus opening the path for a series of severe regulations and demands on the revenues of the church.[63] The overall result of these reforms is thus perhaps only slightly exaggerated by Richard Herr, who states that "the political centralization of Spain, never achieved by the Hapsburgs, was now an accomplished fact."[64]

The growth of a central bureaucratic structure, though nothing on the scale of that in France or England, was nevertheless achievable to a greater extent than in, say, Austria because of the fact (among other things) that Spain's economy recovered from its century-long stagnation and demonstrated notable expansion in some sectors during the eighteenth century. Mercantilist doctrines had been familiar in Spain during the seventeenth century, but they amounted in practice to little more than vain efforts to prevent Spanish bullion from flowing out of the country. Proposals for more concerted government efforts to encourage agriculture, industry, and commerce had generally fallen on deaf ears. During the last decades of the century and to an even greater extent during the eighteenth century, however, mercantilist reforms were initiated with greater zeal and effectiveness.

In 1679 the state created the Junta de Comercio to oversee policies involving trade, and later, mining, manufacturing, and minting as well. In 1728 the Réal Compania Guipuzocoano de Caracas was founded, a monopoly modeled after Dutch and French companies, to promote trade with Venezuela. Concerted efforts were made by state commissions to expand trade with the Americas in slaves, cotton, indigo, and tobacco; government-supported factories with monopolistic privileges for the production of woolens, tapestries, glass, porcelain, paper, pottery, and silk were created; and tariffs or prohibitions were passed against foreign goods that were in direct competition with fledgling domestic industries.[65]

These measures resulted in some direct successes: for example, the iron industry grew in direct proportion to iron exports to the American colonies; the number of silk looms in Valencia increased from 800 in 1718 to more than 3,000 in 1769; and over the same period the cotton industry expanded rapidly.[66] Until 1761 trade with France also increased dramatically, although the balance of imports and exports continued to yield net deficits. It was the American trade that contributed most: sugar production multiplied approximately thirteenfold during the century, as did the production of cocoa and leather; silver production recovered from its long decline, more than doubling after 1740; only the state monopoly over tobacco failed to live up to expected results.[67]

Broader shifts in price levels also worked to the state's advantage. After a period of falling prices between 1680 and 1700, prices began to stabilize between 1700 and 1750, after which there was a sharp increase. Overall, commodity prices rose by approximately 100 percent during the century, compared with wage increases of only 20 percent; thus dramatically higher profit margins were attained from which taxes and government loans could be drawn.[68]

Exact figures on the amount of revenue taken in by the state have proven difficult to estimate, but it is known that the state's overall financial condition improved greatly. Whereas it had been forced repeatedly to declare bankruptcy during the last years of the seventeenth century, the treasury had accumulated a net surplus of approximately 650 million réales by the end of the eighteenth century.[69]

At the same time that the state's revenues were increasing, the fortunes of its chief rival—the nobility—were declining. Despite steady population growth, rural areas remained underpopulated in proportion to the amount of labor required, and agricultural productivity continued to be relatively stagnant until sometime after 1765.[70] Grain prices were also relatively depressed until the last third of the century; with the exception of iron, mining tended mainly to regress; and the more traditional industries such as woolens and linens failed increasingly to compete in the international market.[71] In comparison with that of countries in which economic growth was relatively balanced across sectors, therefore, Spain's economic development tended to favor centralized bureaucratic expansion of a limited kind.

The growth in bureaucratic centralization was not of the magnitude to support machineries of cultural production like those in London and Paris. With a population of 150,000 in 1787, Madrid was more the size of Berlin than Paris or London, but without much of the dynamism that characterized the Prussian capital.[72] Nevertheless, the government managed by virtue of its nearly autocratic powers to initiate a number of reforms in the areas of science, literature, and education. Until the middle of the century little had been done to provide an institutional base for Enlightenment ideas. As Jaime Vicens Vives notes: "There was no college, no university institution, from which such impulses could arise. It was formed by reading, by travel, by informal conversations, by intellectual affinities."[73] Despite bans by the Inquisition against their books, Montesquieu, Buffon, Rousseau and others gradually became known to scholars in Spain. This familiarity stemmed in part, as it did elsewhere, from students attending foreign universities or making the proverbial "grand tour" of the Continent; it was also a function of Spain's diplomatic ties, which brought ambassadors into direct contact with writers such as Voltaire, Diderot, and d'Alembert.[74] It was not until the 1770s, however, that the impact of foreign writers on Spanish scholarship become particularly noticeable. During the first half of the century the only notable developments of an institutional kind were the formation of several official academies, including the Royal Spanish Society (1713), the Royal Academy of Medicine (1736), and the Academy of History (1738), and a somewhat larger number of official academies in the provinces and larger towns for discussing technical problems and economic concerns.[75]

The provincial academies were extended in subsequent decades, under both official and private auspices, but with close supervision by the state. They functioned as research agencies for the state, taking on a number of direct assignments for the government; their members were overwhelmingly government officials; and they received substantial sums for the support of their activities.[76] From these academies also developed during the last third of the century several larger academies which were directly monitored by the Council of Castile, such as the Royal Basque Patriotic Seminary, which offered courses in chemistry and metallurgy, and the Royal School of Metallurgy.[77]

During the 1750s and 1760s three observatories, a botanical garden, and a museum of natural history were established at royal expense. The first official academy for scientific work, the Sociedad Bascongada de los Amigos del Pais, was not founded until 1765 and received official endorsement three years later. In 1775 a similar academy was founded in Madrid, and Valencia's came a year later; the Barcelona city government prevented one from being established there until the nineteenth century. The focus of these academies was instruction in commercial arts and crafts, although they also promoted uniformity in the usage of language. In comparison with their counterparts in France and England, their content appears to have been restricted chiefly to technical applications of knowledge rather than broader philosophical debates concerning politics and morality.[78]

As in countries where the Enlightenment became more fully

institutionalized, the growth of a central bureaucracy also appears to have stimulated cultural production by enlarging the demand for secular literature. Studies of subscription lists have not reached the level of detail of such studies for France and England, but the available material suggests that an increasing number of subscribers came from the civil service and from related professions such as law and teaching. On the whole, an increase of more than fivefold occurred in the number of books published during the eighteenth century. By subject, the most dramatic change was the decline of religious books as a proportion of all books published, dropping from 52 percent of the total in 1730 to 27 percent in 1790. Over the same period the largest increases occurred in economics, history, geography, and science.[79] Part of the reason for these increases in publishing was also more favorable regulation by the state: in 1768 taxes were lowered on some of the essential ingredients of the printing industry; in 1778 taxes were abolished on domestic books, and copyright protection was extended to authors' heirs; and in 1780 taxes were reduced on paper. Not surprisingly, the state's policies were particularly favorable toward the writings of its own ministers, often subsidizing or publishing works regarded as being beneficial to agriculture or industry and encouraging treatises attacking ecclesiastical or aristocratic privileges.[80]

The universities in Spain had generally become deeply ingrown, making them unlikely candidates for the production of Enlightenment ideas. Faculty positions tended to be given only to those among a select group of the universities' own graduates whose social class and views promised to be unthreatening to the institution. Salaries and promotions were based strictly on seniority without consideration of talent or merit.[81] Efforts to introduce changes in curricula were usually resisted, and faculty were slow to adopt new methods of instruction. Enrollments had also declined steadily for nearly a century.[2] The state's intervention to reform hiring procedures, promotions, and curricula were thus of particular significance.

The expulsion of the Jesuits in 1767 gave government officials an opportunity to conduct a general housecleaning of the universities. In 1770 by proclamation of the Council of Castile universities were required to introduce more courses in mathematics, physics, and natural law. Greater disciplinary specialization was imposed, and salaries were not only increased but linked to scholarly contributions. A year later the San Isidro College of Royal Studies was opened by the state to provide specialized training in the sciences and law. Thus by the end of Charles III's reign in 1788 some noticeable progress had been made toward increasing the role of the colleges and universities in promoting new forms of learning.[83]

But the Enlightenment in Spain, as in Russia, differed chiefly from the Enlightenment in places such as France and Prussia in failing to generate broad theoretical discussions about politics, society, and morality. Having virtually unchecked power over a great many aspects of Spanish life, the state was also in a position to thwart those aspects of the Enlightenment that in any way appeared threatening or distasteful. At the same time that it was attempting to promote learning through the academies and universities, the Council of Castile took a position toward many of the more prominent writers of the Enlightenment in France and England which greatly restricted their influence in Spain. Especially after the Esquilache riots in 1766, the writings of Voltaire, Rousseau, and others who were perceived as sowing seeds of skepticism and discord were regarded as highly dangerous.

Unlike countries in which cross-cutting divisions of power within the state provided both motivation and protection for writers with diverse views, Spain presented a more uniform face to its writers. Institutions such as regionally representative assemblies and national courts, which elsewhere served as forums for the airing of diverse views, had been quashed in Spain.[84] Only the church retained powers that were not fully dependent on the state; but its interests in intellectual affairs ran closely parallel with those of the state. The church's role was not so much to suppress the Enlightenment as to channel it in a practical direction. Clerics lent active support to technical improvement projects and reforms in medicine and agriculture at the same time that they suppressed ideas resembling those of Hume or Voltaire.[85]

As in the case of Russia, therefore, autocratic control by the state appears to have resulted in a cautious, highly directed encouragement of cultural production quite unlike that which flourished in those countries where authority was divided between a strong central bureaucracy and other state institutions. The more practical, technical, utilitarian aspects of the Enlightenment were promoted by the central bureaucracy, not with the same success as in countries where the bureaucracy was larger and supported by greater economic prosperity, but still to a noticeable degree.[86] Yet the freedom to advance diverse ideas, the cross-cutting factions that shielded writers from the state's coercive force, and the constitutional crises that prompted reflection on the very nature of the state were largely absent. No notion of a social contract or of a natural order to which the state was subject appears to have emerged; only the practical skills that could promote the state's mercantilist policies were encouraged.[87]

10 ❧❧

Text and Context

THE DIFFERENCES in the extent to which the Enlightenment became institutionalized are, of course, relative. No country failed entirely to experience some growth in cultural production. Literacy expanded, publishing increased, new academies were founded, science and technical improvements were made, literature flourished. By the second half of the eighteenth century the Enlightenment was also fueling the fires of its own success as publishers vied to bring out cheap editions of Voltaire and Swift and writers tried to imitate Richardson and Defoe. Nevertheless, the various sections of Europe did differ significantly in the degree to which Enlightenment scholarship was able to establish itself as an active intellectual enterprise. France acquired international prominence as the leading contributor to the Enlightenment and retained that position to the end of the old regime; England had already gained attention for innovative scholarship through the contributions of Locke, among others, and in the eighteenth century pioneered advances in newspapers, political essays, science, and fiction on a wide scale; Prussia developed an Aufklärung of its own; and the Scottish moralists, historians, and political economists earned a reputation for innovative thinking that was unrivaled anywhere. In contrast, the picture of intellectual development in the Dutch Republic, Sweden, Austria, Russia, and Spain, though not lacking in merit, is largely one of smaller proportions, greater borrowing, and notable difficulties at the institutional level.

Language, population, location, and the intellectual advances made during the previous century all played a role in these differences, of course. More immediate factors also came to the fore, the most notable of which were the sheer differences in economic development. Generally speaking, the countries in which the Enlightenment flourished grew more rapidly and experienced progress in a wider variety of economic activities than the countries in which the Enlightenment did not flourish. Indeed, this connection has long been a commonplace among historians of the period. What the foregoing has suggested is the more specific manner in which economic expansion, or its absence, contributed to the production of Enlightenment culture.

The countries in which Enlightenment scholarship gained a firm foothold also tended to have a stronger bourgeoisie than those in which the Enlightenment was less prominent. Consequently, the bourgeoisie has often been pictured as the critical link between economic expansion and the new ideologies of the period. Some support for this interpretation has, in fact, been seen: men of commerce supplied a literate market for books and newspapers; the commercially minded joined reading clubs and improvement societies; some of the prominent writers of the period were themselves from the rising middle social strata; and so on. Other evidence, though, suggests caution in linking the Enlightenment too directly to the bourgeoisie: writers seldom supported themselves from sales to the reading public alone; merchants and industrialists made up a disproportionately small share of subscription lists; the same was true of memberships in the academies and salons; and writers frequently came from nonbourgeois backgrounds and wrote for an aristocratic clientele. Having a highly developed bourgeoisie was itself no guarantee that a society would become a center of Enlightenment activity, as the Dutch Republic illustrated. And even if credit is given the bourgeoisie for shaping tastes and promoting new interests, most of the questions about patronage, publishing, writing, and the specific settings in which scholars and their audiences came into contact remain unanswered.

The social stratum that contributed most directly to the Enlightenment consisted of public officials, administrators, parliamentary representatives, courtiers, lawyers, professionals, military officers, men and women of leisure, university faculty, and in some cases clergy associated with the hierarchies of state churches. This stratum included most of the prominent writers and intellectuals of the period, their patrons, and the larger audience for whom they wrote, and it provided the organizational settings in which economic and cultural resources for scholarly work became available, including the vital contacts among writers themselves, with publishers and patrons, and between the producers of culture and their audiences. It was a rising elite, distinguished by education and technical merit, and clearly oriented toward standards and customs different from those of the feudal or agrarian elites of the past. To this extent it was part of the rising bourgeoisie in the most general usage of the term. It was not, however, a bourgeoisie in any strict economic sense: not an elite distinguished by its ownership of the means of production, not a social stratum free of familial and economic ties with the aristocracy, not a class set apart from the land and identified directly with commerce and industry. If any single feature of this stratum stands out, it is the vital connection it had to the central governing agencies of its respective societies.

The relative levels of Enlightenment activity from country to country were closely associated with differences in the size and prosperity of the various governing agencies. France, England, Prussia, and Scotland all had sizable bureaucracies that grew significantly in personnel, revenues, and responsibilities. This growth provided opportunities for culture producers to secure employment within the administrative bureaus, enlarged the number of patrons with an interest in public issues, underwrote publishing activities, created a demand for higher education and technical skills, and concentrated writers and their audiences in places of close proximity to one another. In other parts of Europe the central bureaucracies were generally less sizable, or experienced less growth, and therefore provided a context less conducive to the production of Enlightenment culture.

The close relations that developed between culture producers and the state also adds perspective to the role played by economic expansion. The economy did not simply expand in some areas, as if responding to some hidden dynamic within its own soul, and then as an unforeseen consequence effect changes in ideas and life styles. The sequence of causation, to the extent that one can be identified, was less material and more political, less mechanical and more contingent. The government agencies that benefited from economic expansion also inspired it. They succeeded in promoting mercantilist policies, in stimulating trade, and in winning new territories through military conquest. The growth of their bureaucracies was as much a cause as it was a consequence of economic expansion. And the cultural activities associated with the state were promoted to further economic growth as much as they were responses to this growth.

It was, as the foregoing comparisons have suggested, necessary, but not sufficient, for an expanding state bureaucracy to serve as an institutional context for the production of Enlightenment culture. A heterarchic division of authority within this context also appears to have been necessary. Without a central bureaucracy, resources were generally lacking; without a division of authority, the freedom and motivation to think reflectively tended to be stifled. The Dutch Republic, Sweden, and Austria fell short on the first condition, Russia and Spain on the second. More specifically, France, England, Prussia, and Scotland all experienced significant levels of bureaucratic centralization: at least a doubling or tripling in the sheer size of the central bureaucracy, at least a threefold increase in government revenues, significant growth in the size of the military, a reorganization of the central bureaucracy along functional lines (which included a delegation of authority beyond the royal household itself), the implementation of an effective centralized tax collection system, and an increasing reliance on central judicial and policing agents at the local level. The Dutch Republic, Sweden, and Austria differed from the former in nearly all these respects. Russia and Spain did witness most of these centralizing tendencies, however. The countries in which the Enlightenment prospered were also characterized by certain centrifugal forces: an independent judicial system, a system of representative estates or parliament with power to curb the actions of the central administrative agencies, institutionalized channels for the articulation of religious and ethnic divisions, and multiple patronage networks at least partly autonomous from the crown. The Dutch Republic, Sweden, and Austria also manifested these traits. Russia and Spain did not.

It was the conjuncture of two sets of institutional forces, then, that distinguished the countries in which the Enlightenment gained its firmest footing. In the absence of one or the other, scholarship generally took a narrower, technical cast and failed to receive the impetus or the resources that led to a broader variety of philosophical and literary innovations. The specific forms of ideology that were produced, of course, varied from one context to another. But the political forces of which these contexts were composed played a significant role.

The Division between Selves and Social Roles

There is a kind of irony about the Enlightenment's relation to the state that also helps explain the peculiarities of its literary discourse. Although most of the Enlightenment's leading figures depended in one way or another on the state for support, they did not fit comfortably within the state bureaucracy. This was, as we have seen, less true in Prussia and Scotland than it was in France and England. But everywhere, the writers and intellectuals who formed the core of the Enlightenment appear to have retained at least some psychological distance from the state bureaucracies with which they were associated. Indeed many of them chafed at the strictures accompanying bureaucratic life, and most of the more prominent writers and scholars managed to obtain offices that provided them with some autonomy and flexibility. That they could do so was testimony to the fact that in most cases the bureaucracy itself was not yet fully routinized and the state retained caches of patronage that could be allocated for nonutilitarian purposes. The ambivalent relationship between writers and the bureaucracy nevertheless colored the style of their work in several significant and sometimes contradictory ways.

The relatively systematic and highly rationalized discourse in which matters of the state were conducted became a part of literary discourse as well. It did so especially in those instances when writers sought to present arguments in support of particular social or political programs. On these occasions ideology bore a close degree of articulation with its social milieu. Writers borrowed the style of discourse that was familiar to them from training in law or from functioning in bureaucratic roles. It has been said, for example, that Voltaire showed the marks of an excellent trial lawyer in the manner in which he marshaled and presented evidence.[1]

Yet writers criticized the rationalistic style of political discourse, extolled the freedoms of intellectual life, and created characters who manifested their own styles of deviant individuality. Being close to and yet in many ways on the fringes of the actual functioning of power, literary figures were in a position to be critical of it. To take Voltaire as an example again, his training as a lawyer was pursued reluctantly and only at the persistent urging of his father. He complained bitterly about the seemingly useless details he was forced to memorize and refused to accept an office as counselor to the parlement which his father offered to purchase for him.[2]

This kind of ambivalence toward the state was one source of

the tension that many of the Enlightenment writers felt between public and private life. As far as their public roles were concerned, they saw the constraints of organizational regimentation, and these roles differed dramatically from the more personal aspirations they entertained of pursuing literature and knowledge. There was in this polarity a tension between public responsibility and personal freedom, between duty and fulfillment, between role expectations and the self.

The ambivalence of the eighteenth-century writer toward his public roles can in fact be seen as an underlying dimension of much of the work of this period. One of the features that distinguishes this period from the Reformation, for example, is the greater diversity of literary genres that were developed and utilized by most of the leading Enlightenment writers. Their work demonstrates an almost schizophrenic tendency to fluctuate between the highly formalized polemic, essay, or treatise epitomized by *The Social Contract* and the more personal, fanciful, fictional style of *La nouvelle Héloise* and *Emile*. There is as well in the two genres a marked tension between the themes of responsible, self-sacrificing obligation to collective duties on the one hand and themes of revelry, introspection, and self-gratification, on the other. Political treatises are written in a style designed to persuade, whereas the poetry and fiction of the period is more often an act of self-indulgence.

In addition, the characters that frequent this literature are themselves positioned in the same ambivalent status as their authors. They are the foreign visitors of the *Persian Letters*, seeking to understand but demonstrating critical distance at the same time. They are the wealthy aesthetes, trying to find an appropriate balance between self-gratification and public service. And above all, they are the frail female characters caught up in a web of material and social obligations but also marginal to established society, and in their marginality they are more individual and have greater freedom than many of their contemporaries. In Richardson's *Pamela*, for example, the self is always defined in relation to the vortex of changing social circumstances with which it interacts. Pamela's very marginality, the ambiguity of her status, and her continuing dependence on others forces a separation between her inner self and her social roles that nevertheless makes the two contingent on each other.[3]

Another characteristic of the eighteenth-century social context that contributed to the separation of a purely private realm from public roles was a product largely of geography. The wedding of private lives and public roles in the Reformation was partly a function of the reformers' geographical separation from one another. With a few exceptions (such as Wittenberg and Basel), the reformers were scattered rather than being concentrated in single towns. The dangers involved in traveling, created by the political situation in Europe, and the reformers' tendency to assume pulpits in new locations to further the diffusion of the Reformation also increased their geographical separation. As a result, written correspondence rather than private conversation became the usual mode of communication. Their correspondence, however, could not be protected from the public eye as easily as it would be in later periods. One historian of the Reformation notes, for example, that "letters among the learned . . . were a form of press release. Publishers grabbed them up unscrupulously, with no intention of asking the writer's permission. They were copied by hand or printed and quickly reached those interested in literary controversy. Often such letters also fell into hands for whom they were not intended."[4] Knowing this, writers generally adopted a public style even in their private letters or grew accustomed to seeing their private ruminations become affixed to their public roles. During the Enlightenment, in contrast, writers not only enjoyed greater security in their written correspondence but also were less dependent on this mode of discourse itself by virtue of their physical proximity to one another in Paris, London, Berlin, and elsewhere. The growth of cities themselves, improvements in roads, and greater political stability all contributed to these writers' capacity to communicate privately. Their concentration within the major capital cities by virtue of their relations with the growing central state bureaucracies also looms, again, as an important factor.

The ease with which writers in the eighteenth century were able to assume false identities in public that did not correspond to their private identities, in fact, stands in sharp contrast to the integral connection that bound public and private together in the Reformation. In that period the reformers' discourse seemed not merely to rule out fictional identities but to draw the reformers toward identifying totally with their public constructions. Accounts of the final hours of Thomas Müntzer in May 1525, for instance, reveal that his demise was to a great extent due to this inescapable connection. Müntzer hid himself in an attic room, after the peasant army he had rallied broke up in mad flight, and pretended to be indigent and infirm. But his own creations belied his attempt to assume a false identity. Letters were found that gave him away. Torture, confession, and execution followed within days.[5]

In contrast, writers in the eighteenth century were able to shield, if not falsify outright, their private identities in connection with their public roles. Rousseau's disclosure of his private self in the *Confessions*, in notable contrast to the public roles he assumed, is sometimes cited as an example. In Voltaire the gulf between public and private was perhaps even more pronounced. The name by which he was known in public was, of course, not the name given him at birth. Except for the facts recorded on his baptismal certificate, little is known about the circumstances of his birth, for he tried throughout his life to shroud them in mystery. He even tried to pass as being older than he actually was.

Also instructive is the fact that so much privacy surrounded the writing of major works in the eighteenth century that historians have had difficulty establishing the exact year or month in which some of these works were written. Luther's pamphlets and treatises can be identified in nearly every case with the precise days or weeks during which they were written and can often be associated with the particular rooms in which they were drafted. Voltaire's *Philosophical Letters* and his *History of Charles II*, in contrast, remain shrouded in uncertainty.

Authors in the eighteenth century often wrote from private hideaways and restricted their comings and goings as well as their correspondence to the point that even close associates had little knowledge of the projects on which they were engaged. In some instances this style was a matter of personality, in others a calculated effort to avoid being anticipated by competitors. In either case the result was often the same. It sharpened authors' sensitivities to the objectivity of the very public institutions from which they were removed and heightened the separation of public roles from private selves.

More than many of his contemporaries, Rousseau appears to have been keenly sensitive to this separation of public and private. He wrote with an acute awareness of his own solitude and, indeed, exiled himself physically and mentally from the centers of Paris culture for long periods. It is, therefore, difficult to generalize about the sources of his differentiation between the public and private to those of writers who were more closely integrated into the cultural circles of the salons, academies, government bureaucracies, and universities. Yet there are aspects of Rousseau's marginality that bring into sharp relief, because of its very exaggeration, the manner in which private selves and public roles became divided in the Enlightenment.

Rousseau's marginality was more than simply a feeling of social distance or alienation (and more than the problem of gaining acceptance that some commentators have suggested predisposed him toward revolution). It was a social relationship characterized by partial integration into a community of scholars but based on integration of a particular social role rather than the self. And this mode of social integration was in turn a function of the social setting. As we have seen, the setting in which the Enlightenment writers worked was in a broad sense divided sharply into competing, cross-cutting factions, and these factions were insufficiently stable to provide a secure public identity with which individual writers could fully associate themselves. In addition, the immediate social context in which the leading figures of the French Enlightenment worked was sufficiently large, both in the number of writers and aspiring writers themselves and in the number of relevant patrons and government officials, to preclude intimate relationships of the kind that might have produced greater consensus about public identities (except for the small coteries and dyads that bound some of the major figures together). The complexity of the situation was compounded by several other factors as well: the broader urban environment in which the salons and academies were located, the fact that many who aspired to the literary life were migrants from the provinces or even men and women of more diverse origins and experience, and the normative uncertainties generated by the transitional character of the state and the broader economy.

In Rousseau's case the effects of this combination of circumstances are evident in the frequency with which questions of identity—including mistaken identity, false identity, true identity, and pretense—occupied his attention. It is instructive, for example, that the first interaction known to have taken place between Rousseau and Voltaire involved an episode of mistaken identity that to Rousseau at least seemed important enough to evoke a passionate letter of clarification. Even by this time Rousseau was no stranger to the subject of problematic identities, for his self-exile from Geneva as a youth of sixteen had forced him to assume a false identity whenever he returned to the city.

Rousseau's method of coping with the question of personal identity is also instructive to the degree that it involved a construction of an imaginary world in which the private self could reign. For Rousseau this imaginary world consisted of an idealization of republican Geneva. In it Rousseau regarded himself as a free citizen living in a state of tranquillity and peace, much in contrast with the more troublesome world of Paris and its environs.[6]

The problems of false, mistaken, or uncertain personal identity, and more generally of the self's separation from public roles, are also apparent in the lives of the fictional characters created by authors in the eighteenth century. The dispersed, overlapping, yet segmented character of social relations among persons occupying the public sphere often has an analogue in autobiographical fiction of the period. From the epistolary style of Montesquieu's *Persian Letters* to the almost wholly discrete letters of Richardson's *Pamela,* autobiographical fiction is itself segmented by virtue of its being presented as a series of contiguous records lacking the vantage point of a single omniscient voice. If representation is a way of organizing the self by exteriorizing experiences and binding them together to form a coherent memory, then this style of representation clearly leaves the self relatively disorganized. It can be portrayed flexibly, problematically, rather than having to be integrated by a single point of view. To the extent that the self is not only separated from but also a reflection of the public roles associated with the public sphere, it takes on the same fluid, segmented characteristics.

Like the writers themselves, fictional characters in this period also struggle with problems of false and mistaken identity. In some cases their private self is so fully hidden from public view that simply dressing in different garb allows them to fool their comrades into thinking they are someone else. But the problem of identity also goes deeper, causing characters trouble in maintaining their own sense of who they are. Dressed in different garb, characters sometimes have difficulty remembering their own past, or they take on simultaneous and even opposing identities. Moreover, the problem of identity is not simply one of clothing or circumstance; it is chiefly one of relationships. Characters feel their problems of knowing who they are are caused by other characters with whom they interact. Faced with a world of unstable and conflicting relationships, they discover the difficulty of establishing a firm sense of self. Public roles and private selves constitute two distinct arenas of concern, but the two also remain contingent on each other. The more fluid the public sphere becomes, the more the self becomes an object for reflection.

To the extent that the self is shaped by the interaction in which the person engages, it tends to be characterized in eighteenth-century fiction as vulnerable. Power ceases to be an attribute strictly of the will, or even of the person's occupancy of a dependable social status, but requires constant negotiation. Relationships are the key. And the secret to successful relationships is discourse. Thus, in perhaps a circuitous way, Enlightenment discourse constructs a vision of the self and its social relations in which discourse itself becomes especially valued.

The female character in eighteenth-century fiction often epitomizes the vulnerable self who must depend on relations and discourse. Her power is always relational, contingent on marriage or sexual alliances, dependent on someone else whose fortunes she cannot predict or control. Like the patroness of the salon, however, the female character commands a type of power that is based on orchestration and discourse. Always potentially subject to complete devastation, she manages artfully to hold chaos at bay by arranging alliances, by shifting identities, by engaging in deception, and by reversing the plot through skillful conversation. Words become the principal tools of her power.

As actors engage in discourse, they exhibit a certain degree of agency or selfhood. They express points of view, take political positions, and engage in physical and discursive action. In doing so, connections are drawn between their roles as persons and their public identities. Yet there is also a sense in which actors in this literature refuse to take responsibility as agents of their own action. Lacking easily distinguishable public roles, and facing difficulty in establishing stable self identities, they locate agency in social relations and structures other than themselves. Third person points of view and the passive voice, for example, are often used to separate agency from action. Circumstances are seen as constraints on behavior; vulnerability, again, is emphasized; and intentionality is subjugated to the role of broader historical or societal forces. Nothing would be more unusual in this context than the bold "Here I stand" of a Luther. Instead, selves claim no ground on which to stand but define themselves relationally and ground their claims in authorities other than that of their own voice.

Rather than taking up fixed positions and defending them, fictional characters tend to engage in verbal games that show their ability to challenge assumed meanings. Words are shown to have multiple meanings. By the clever turn of a phrase, arguments are shown to hide irony and paradox. Falsehoods are shown merely to be misrepresentations. Room for new interpretations is established by demonstrating the ambiguities of language. New discoveries, or revelations of obscure points of the past, open out onto new vistas of discussion. Indeterminacy becomes freedom. Nothing is settled, but in the process of exchanging indeterminate responses, freedom is dramatized.

As words lose the meanings that would otherwise be grounded in concrete social situations, it becomes necessary for actors to scrutinize the usage of words more closely. Cues about *sincerity* become problematic, and therefore more important to ascertain; that is, signals must be sought that convey a connection between what is said and who the speaker really is. And possibilities for deception are always present, for speakers can purposefully misrepresent themselves (showing they are "artful" rather than sincere). Through speech the self is turned into one thing or another. Speech, therefore, takes on power as a way of constructing reality itself.

Once it becomes subject to discursive construction, reality of course becomes problematic. No longer can a clear, simple demarcation be drawn between truth and fantasy. Even truth becomes, as it were, relational: one must examine it in relation to the words used to interpret it. Thus, room for creativity is made possible. Fluid social circumstances lead to blurred lines between representation and truth, which permit creative redefinitions of truth to be constructed.

For language truly to take on the power of reality construction it must, however, become autonomous to some degree from the self. That is, voices must become decentered, autonomous. This feat is again facilitated in the literature of the period by the self's lack of grounding in stable social situations. One's own roles can be disclaimed, allowing the products of one's discourse to be separated from their source. Speech thereby ceases to be action because the self is able to deny responsibility for its actions. Instead, the self becomes part of speech itself, and speech takes on the capacity to stand independently of the self and its public actions. With this independence, discourse can manipulate, blur, interchange, and redefine the categories of reality to the point where new differentiations can be made. Words, placed in new relations with one another, thereby take on added meanings.

In a sense, then, the opportunity to engage in innovative discourse—so vital to the Enlightenment generally—is enhanced by the separation perceived between selves and their public roles. The public sphere itself is sufficiently in flux to give writers and scholars opportunity to innovate. But the public sphere's very fluidity also generates a self that is set off from public roles and yet problematic because of its dependence on these roles. Lacking its own strong sense of inner authority, the self is defined as a product of its social relations, particularly discursive relations. Words become the key to power. And the ability to manipulate words, to objectify them and invent new meanings, becomes the hallmark of personal freedom.

Discursive Fields in Enlightenment Literature

Enlightenment discourse, as we have seen, was characterized by such diversity that virtually any attempt to offer generalizations about it can immediately be confronted with exceptions and counterexamples. Some of this diversity can be accounted for by the relative autonomy that writers experienced in interacting with the patrons and bureaus that supported them. Some of it also derived from the competitive and selective processes that arose in different national and regional contexts. Perspective on the diversity of Enlightenment discourse can also be gained by considering the more general discursive framework in which it was formulated. Like the Reformation, the Enlightenment developed a distinctive discursive field that grew out of its immediate institutional context but that also permitted it to gain critical distance from this context. Different writers expressed themselves differently within this framework. And the fact that they could do so was in some measure a function of the opportunities for symbolic formulations that this framework provided.

The discursive field of the Enlightenment, like that of the Reformation, was defined by a number of oppositional categories: passion and sobriety, tolerance and bigotry, freedom and confinement, critical reason and fanaticism. The new philosophy associated prevailing institutions with the negative pole of these oppositions, just as Reformation doctrine had done. Religion, law, aristocratic manners, conventional sexual standards, scholasticism, the established educational system—all came under attack. Or more precisely, they provided dramatizations of the negative concepts in relation to which the Enlightenment writers defined themselves, for these writers were by no means willing to abandon all affinity with the pretensions of aristocratic society.

Whereas the Protestant reformers had been able to anchor the positive end of their discursive field firmly in the tangible, authoritative text of divine Scripture, the Enlightenment writers were impelled to rely on a somewhat more difficult concept to define the positive pole of their discourse. This pole frequently received affirmation with reference to *nature*. But the book of nature was less easily cited than the book of Scripture. Despite considerable debates that had ensued concerning the proper interpretation of Scripture, the epistemological questions raised with reference to nature were far more complex and certainly more novel. Above all, nature required concretization in order to be a meaningful symbol of opposition to prevailing practices.

The manner in which nature was conceptualized, again like Scripture for the Protestant reformers, had to suggest an authoritative preference in relation to institutionalized knowledge and belief. All of the sources from which arguments about nature derived, accordingly, followed this pattern. Arguments were developed by extending the secret laws of nature that had been unearthed by the special techniques of scientific investigation and mathematical observation. Arguments were validated with reference to other societies, whether England, Holland, Switzerland, or Russia, in which social patterns presumably more in keeping with nature had emerged with apparent effectiveness in providing tranquillity and prosperity. Other arguments sought to extract nature from tradition by citing esoteric examples from the New World, India, the Orient, and primitive societies. Still others claimed superiority on the basis alone of being obvious, simple, and readily confirmed by common experience.

Philosophers were presumably in a position of advantage to serve as mediators of these new kinds of validation because they had the special understanding of science, mathematics, history, travel, and languages that was not part of the ordinary reader's experience. Yet the logic of nature was also supposed to be readily apparent to all. Thus the spokesmen of the Enlightenment reduced their esoteric wisdom to easily appreciated letters and narratives and appealed to universal sentiments such as love, self-interest, the common good, and above all the reasonableness of common sense.

The polarities between institutionalized beliefs and these arguments about nature provided the Enlightenment writers with a discursive space in which to develop their more refined and diverse analyses of social and personal life. The vantage point from nature gave them an opportunity to view critically the taken-for-granted characteristics of contemporary life. At the same time, spokesmen for the church, the state, and in many cases the universities contributed to the distance separating these polarities by sharply attacking arguments that appeared to elevate nature to a position of supremacy. These polarities also acquired objectivity in the life styles of the more bohemian members of the new literary elite, especially in well-publicized acts of adultery, promiscuity, religious nonconformity, and politically dangerous experimentation. From the beginning, Enlightenment literature also drew heavily on the classics, on scientific discoveries of the seventeenth century, and on the work of Shaftesbury, Bolingbroke, Locke, Bacon, and others with whom they shared intellectual affinities.

These cultural antecedents provided intellectual arguments and, perhaps more important, symbolic heroes with which to concretize the positive end of Enlightenment discourse in opposition to the authority of established institutions. As was the case for the Protestant reformers, however, various aspects of the social context in which the leading figures of the Enlightenment functioned also reinforced their discursive field. The distance they experienced between private lives and public roles was an important feature of this context. To the extent that writers themselves often occupied roles in the state bureaucracy or in ancillary institutions or, if not, were heavily dependent on these institutions for patronage and protection, it was not difficult for them to find examples of the authority of established institutions. Yet, as marginal members of these institutions, they could also portray this authority in a negative light. The increasing objectification and separation of private lives from public roles also provided a location, as it were, for their portrayals of the positive alternatives to traditional authority. Associated with private life were many of the tangible symbols of nature: freedom to live close to nature, experimentation with the life styles dictated by one's natural inclinations, the unobscured wisdom of common sense, and the inner perceptions available to those who would free their minds of institutional encumbrances.

In setting up a basic antinomy between established society and nature, Enlightenment writers needed to demonstrate that nature was sufficient, just as the Protestant reformers had argued that the

Bible was sufficient, to supply all that might be necessary for conducting a good and rewarding life. Knowledge, morality, and sentiments of sociability were the minimal components in these arguments, just as in the Reformation. Whereas it had earlier been argued that one could by reading and listening to sermons arrive at adequate knowledge, it was now argued that even a solitary, private individual in a state of nature could arrive at knowledge of self and the world. Especially in Locke, Helvétius, and Condillac, an empirical sensationalism provided the basis for this argument. And this emphasis on the senses as a source of knowledge generated many of the subsequent debates in which Voltaire, Diderot, and others engaged concerning the effects on experiential knowledge of sensory deprivations such as blindness and deafness. Questions concerning the adequacy of nature as a source of morality and sentiments of sociability also generated much discussion of the "innate" qualities of individuals and the character of their ties to one another.

It was perhaps inevitable that much of the discourse of the first generation of Enlightenment thinkers should have focused on these questions. Although a great deal of this work contributed to lasting lines of inquiry into such matters as the human senses, psychology, and sociology, it was of immediate importance primarily in defining nature (and related concepts) as an alternative to the received wisdom of established moral and political institutions. The context in which these contributions were made was itself highly polarized. The expanded economic and political contexts in which the new ideas of the Enlightenment were produced gave some degree of material support and freedom to their producers, but these writers remained subject to strict censorship laws and denunciations from scholars in the universities and religious institutions, and they had not yet acquired a firm institutional base or a clear identity as an intellectual movement. Only as the movement itself progressed and the bureaucracies, academies, and salons began to provide an institutional location did other ideas begin to supersede these initial polarities.

At the beginning of the eighteenth century, the polarity between negative and positive attributes that was evinced in moral arguments remained in the direct lineage of Reformation discourse. Increasingly, however, the specific content that was attached to this polarity ceased to be the simple vices and virtues of the Christian past and were no longer based on divine sanction. Characters who otherwise appear to have pure intentions become entrapped, comically or tragically, into committing acts that have ill effects upon friends and acquaintances. Others perform dutifully in public but conceal bad motives and self-interest. Thus, the growing separation of public and private becomes evident in the very depiction of good and evil.

As the century progressed, characters also became more realistic in the sense of combining both virtues and vices, of having to exercise discretion in the face of unclear alternatives, and of not always reaping the consequences of their own behavior. The lack of fit between actions and their consequences, which does much to erode the simple moral preachments of earlier discourse, is itself a reflection of the growing distance between individual selves and the public situations in which their actions have significance. Characters who display too straightforward a relation between themselves and their situations, or between their actions and standard moral principles, are increasingly regarded as naive, artificial, sentimental, and melodramatic.

In some individual cases the relations between these features of the social context and the discursive polarities formulated in Enlightenment texts was particularly evident. The polarity that formed the basis of Voltaire's discursive field, for example, had its counterpart in the polar communities to which he was exposed most deeply during his formative years. These were the Lycée Louis le Grand, in which he received instruction in Jesuit theology, and the Temple or residence of the duke of Vendôme in which he associated with the leading poets of his day. The former epitomized the rigorous, moralistic religion of the church, especially in the Jesuits' battle to define orthodoxy against their Jansenist competitors. The Temple concretely dramatized freethinking moral libertarianism, and an attitude of tolerance if not indifference toward religious orthodoxy. One carried the weight of established institutional authority, the other clearly held much of this authority in disrespect; over against church dogma and tradition, it championed freedom, a distant God who remained indifferent to fine points of moral conduct, and above all the expansive, alternative authority derived from conceptions of nature. The very fact that the latter depended on a flourishing clandestine manuscript market for both inspiration and dissemination of its ideas put it squarely in an antithetical relation with the former.[7]

Voltaire lived in both worlds to a sufficient extent for them to serve as anchors to his discourse. Indeed, his poetic writings, especially during the first decade of his literary career, demonstrate clearly his indebtedness to the rather structured classical style that he had learned from the Jesuits and the more free-form notions that filtered to him in the poetry of LaFare, Chaulieu, and others at the Temple. He generally attached more weight to his experience at the Temple than to his Jesuit teachers. Yet he was also sufficiently ambitious to desire greater prominence than could be attained within this small circle of freethinking poets. It was, therefore, midway along the axis of structure and freedom, tradition and deviation, that he chose to locate himself. And the virtues of reason and critical philosophy, as well as a distinctly realistic view of the inherent limitations within nature itself, became the instruments with which this location was created. Increasingly, Voltaire turned to the work of serious philosophers and scientists, especially Locke, Descartes, Malebranche, Huygens, and Newton, in this quest. His interest in their work, however, was greatly conditioned by the social and ideological polarity in which he found himself. Their contribution was to legitimate his own independence as a scholar rather than to provide preconceived formulas, and to suggest reasonable resolutions of the conflict between institutional authority and total freedom.

Despite its differences, the German context provided a basis for discursive reflections that were not unlike Voltaire's. At the negative end of its discursive field stood the evils of urban life, especially materialism, luxury, pretentiousness, hypocrisy, greed, and spite. An acquisitive spirit animated only by self interest was given a particularly negative connotation. The positive pole was defined in terms of intellect, cultivation, refinement, and a broader concern for public virtue. In the writing of Albrecht von Haller, for example, one sees what has sometimes been regarded as a highly conservative portrayal of society in which pride and selfishness are deeply criticized. It is, however, not only the aspiring commercial classes who are castigated but also the ruling elite and to some extent the urban poor as well. The discordant, "excessive" aspects of social life are in general lamented. And yet this negativity is always balanced by a more positive opposition framed in terms of enlightened ideals. Poverty is apotheosized in opposition to the follies of wealth; nature and rural life are championed against the disharmonies of commerce; and reason is pitted against the "artificiality" of customary social arrangements. In each case, the discursive field in which Haller's characters act and speak is clearly bounded at both extremes. Significantly, and more in keeping with the German context, the sole aspect of actual social life, other than an increasingly privatized conception of the family, that receives positive affirmation is salaried service to the state.[8]

As this example suggests, the conceptions that defined an underlying structure in Enlightenment discourse took on the coloration of their particular contexts. And, as the trajectory of Voltaire's writing indicates, the unfolding of Enlightenment thought itself contributed emendations to this structure. In Rousseau, for example, one sees the more complex structure of the mature Enlightenment, just as one does in contrasting the "second generation" Reformation discourse of Calvin with that of Luther.

Along the primary axis of Rousseau's discourse there still exists the polarity of tradition and nature, slavery and freedom, restraint and passion, society and the individual. Rousseau's arguments, however, do not take the form of essentially exhorting actors to move farther from one pole toward the other. To move in this manner is in one sense attractive, for it adds freedom and restores the individual to a refreshingly primitive relation to nature. But Rousseau recognizes the radical unworkability of these arguments for the larger social order. In his own withdrawal from society he realizes the impossibility of society itself being based on withdrawal. He is, in this respect, truly a representative of the mature Enlightenment— part of the generation of writers who are able to reflect on the implications of their own movement. Unlike Voltaire, who extolled the freedoms of the new philosophy, Rousseau speaks not from the vantage point of the new ideas themselves but as one who has objectified these ideas and gained distance from them. The new dimension evident in his discourse intersects the axis running from tradition to freedom. It suggests a perpendicular axis running from the private self to the collective good. The quest now becomes that of finding an appropriate location along this continuum at which self-fulfillment and social responsibility can both be maximized. At one end stands the artificial individual who is a product of history (tradition) and nature, and thereby unable to opt simply for one of these polarities over the other, and who is nevertheless in a state of unreflective, if not involuntary, dependence on fellow individuals. At the other end stand the political, the public, the general will, which calls forth from the individual a greater degree of self conscious, voluntary participation. Rather than superimposing the tradition-freedom distinction directly on the experienced separation of private lives and public roles, Rousseau objectifies the latter as a separate dimension, creating a more complex discursive space in which to formulate his moral and political arguments.

We see in Rousseau, therefore, the unfolding of the ideological process in a way that becomes a product of its own production. Being reflective on its internal development, the content of Enlightenment thought responds to the action sequences that occur as part of the production process itself. Early contributions make up acts that become the objects of subsequent writing. Here the process leads toward a fundamentally new dimension being added to the original polarity of the movement's discourse.

In making this emendation Rousseau did not rely simply on rebutting previous formulations. His success in defining a more elaborate discursive field lay in substantial measure in incorporating available categories and symbolic materials into his own schema. These fragments served as precedents that made his formulation more or less recognizable at the same time that the synthesis itself was decidedly new. Nature and freedom, for example, still occupied an important place although their role was redefined. Other precedents also gave contour to the schema. In the *Discourse on Inequality,* for instance, the basic axis running from the particular interests of individuals in their presocial state of nature to the general conditions under which individuals function as public creatures becomes concretized as "an immense space" by being equated with a historical process. Whereas the vertical axis of Calvin's discursive field had utilized the precedent of a hierarchical picture of the universe with God at the top and evil at the bottom, Rousseau's drew on the emerging conception of an evolutionary progression in time from lower forms of life to higher forms of society, from "ancient" to "modern," from primitive to contemporary, from the centuries of darkness to the century of light.[9]

The other formal similarity between Enlightenment and Reformation discourse is the identification of *figural actors* who model appropriate ways of behaving within the complex polarities of discourse itself. The creation of conceptual distance between the actual and the ideal in Enlightenment discourse provided the space in which a new set of public characters—prototypes of the ideal bourgeois—could be defined. These characters were not simply legitimated actors drawn from the commercial bourgeoisie itself. They were distinctly fictional, created from the symbolic axes of the discursive space in which they were situated, and then given flesh as statesmen, men of commerce, aristocrats, women in need, mothers, wives, and artisans. They provided a model for the expanding literate class to emulate.

A clear progression is evident in the way these figural actors are identified from the beginning of the eighteenth century to the end. At the beginning, characters are more likely to exemplify either the follies of too close an identification with the actual social environment or the pure, almost ethereal idealism associated with the classical age or with modern panaceas of natural innocence and freedom. By midcentury, the vast gap between these two kinds of characters is being filled with more realistic figures who combine elements of both extremes. Temptations, lowly origins, financial setbacks, and associations with the weak and corrupt still anchor characters to the negative pole of social life, but acts of virtue, high ethical standards, contacts with interesting people and fresh ideas, as well as an occasional tutor for the moral apprentice concretize a positive relationship with Enlightenment ideals.

The literary construction of the "bourgeois," therefore, was not simply an act of providing a new socioeconomic class with ideological legitimation. The bourgeois was a figural character that stood for something as yet unattained even by the rising middle segments of society. It was an exemplar to be striven toward, a model capable of guiding and inspiring ethical conduct, but also able to challenge the frailties of human behavior. Inevitably, the roles into which these characters were cast drew heavily from the emerging sectors of society rather than being taken from the familiar positions of the past. Emergent roles had a "not yet" quality that filled them with the same kinds of promise and potential for both good and evil that were implicit in Enlightenment ideals. Merchants and men of finance served as models, but so did members of the agrarian leisure classes, women of the city, foundlings, and bureaucrats. The "bourgeois" element that united all these characters was more their struggle to know their own potential and to triumph amidst the complexities of public life than it was any common class position. Only in the sense that they were defined in contrast with the vices of their "betters," and with those below, did they constitute a distinct cultural category.

It bears emphasis, then, that the bourgeoisie—including conceptions of bourgeois virtue and morality—was not simply a legitimating ideology that somehow came into existence because a new class needed legitimation. The evidence presented in the preceding chapters repeatedly cast into doubt the idea of any simple or direct connection between the bourgeoisie and the Enlightenment. Certainly the leading figures of the Enlightenment bore no special connections with the rising merchant elite, either as its natural offspring or its ideological clients. The context in which they worked was more clearly characterized by the expanding central bureaucracies of the state and by the complex public sphere that went along with this expansion. This context, however, did reinforce a particular kind of discursive field in which contrasts between tradition and nature, constraint and freedom, public roles and private selves rose to preeminence. It was this discursive field, rather than the direct effects of class relations, that constituted the space in which new conceptions of figural action could be formulated. The characters who typified this figural action were not themselves drawn from any distinct social class. But the virtues with which they were ascribed constituted a "model for" a new kind of social actor. As the bourgeoisie gradually rose in economic prominence and, after the French Revolution, to political importance, these figural actors in Enlightenment discourse supplied it with tangible cultural categories with whom to identify.

Notwithstanding the temporal distance separating the Enlightenment from the Reformation, then, the two movements served similar purposes insofar as both constructed an ideological context in which new forms of figural action could be identified. In the case of the Reformation, this process depended heavily on iconoclastic actions. Image breaking dramatized the separation between conventional and scriptural authority, helped to desacralize the former, and provided occasions for actual social actors to identify themselves with the movement or against it. Iconoclasm was also an important part of the Enlightenment.

Whereas the more extreme iconoclasm of the Reformation had consisted of violent acts against the church's images and relics, the Enlightenment's iconoclasm took extreme form in violations of courtly and aristocratic life styles. Voltaire's "Templars," for example, reveled in lives of drunkenness, gluttony, and sexual promiscuity. The less extreme forms of iconoclasm in the Enlightenment involved satire, polemics, and calculated literary desacralization of cherished symbols that were already beginning to fall into disrepute. There was, however, a connection between these acts of literary violence and the iconoclastic life styles of the extremists, just as there was between the moderate Protestants and the image breakers. This connection was sometimes direct, as in Voltaire's case, but also found expression in the link thought to exist between new ideas and social upheaval. Just as the earlier episodes of image smashing had done, the new ideas generated controversy and demanded a public response.

In both periods, iconoclasm was possible only because of broader conditions in the social environment. In the 1520s and 1530s it had been possible because of a stalemate between contending political factions. This stalemate prevented retaliation by Catholic forces and yet precluded any quick and effective implementation of Protestant reforms that might have rendered iconoclasm unnecessary. Iconoclasm was most pronounced in such areas as the Swiss, south German, and southern French towns in which this kind of stalemate existed. In the eighteenth century iconoclastic writing gained visibility under similar conditions. It was especially pronounced in France, where the church and the universities provided targets for writers' invectives but where the various factions in the state as well as in ecclesiastical circles prevented censorship and other kinds of legal intimidation from being implemented. In comparison, iconoclastic literature was much less common in places such as Edinburgh or Berlin, where the church was a less formidable institution relative to the state. The severity of the Enlightenment's critical discourse, therefore, must be understood not as a symptom of either the novelty of its ideas or the intransigence of the prevailing social order but as a consequence of the countervailing forces that characterized particular areas.

Like earlier episodes of iconoclasm, the Enlightenment's more controversial productions also evoked a mixture of responses from its leading figures. Some deplored the more radical statements issued by their contemporaries and called for moderation and compromise; others relished the attention that controversy elicited. Even among the more outspoken iconoclasts, however, efforts were often made to blunt the potential for legal reprisal, and these efforts shaped the character of Enlightenment literature itself. Pseudonyms were adopted, clandestine publishers were sought out, and fictional genres were adopted. Indeed a considerable share of the satirical prose, innuendo, and double meaning characteristic of the Enlightenment can be attributed to the need its writers felt to distance themselves from the more dangerous consequences of their own work. And this style of writing, as I have noted, increased the possibilities for producing an entirely fictional public identity that bore little correspondence to the private self of its producers.

Genre, Selection, and Articulation

To raise the question of articulation with reference to the Enlightenment is in some respects awkward, at least in comparison with the Reformation, for by many accounts the Enlightenment consisted chiefly of timeless philosophical generalizations, scientific theories, and literature designed only for the amusement of the leisured elite. Yet this view of the Enlightenment is clearly a lopsided picture that comes more from the fact that many of the Enlightenment's leading interpreters have been interested in philosophical questions than it does from the experience of the eighteenth century itself. As the foregoing has demonstrated, the writers who produced the Enlightenment were, with a few notable exceptions, intimately associated with the state or more generally with the network of roles and relations that made up the public sphere. Their work was, for reasons that have been partly explained, devoted in many instances to abstract theoretical questions. And yet, the more practical aspects of their work should not be neglected. Indeed, recent studies of the period have come increasingly to emphasize the deep interest in issues of the day that pervaded many of the works produced in the Enlightenment. Speaking of France, one literary historian concludes: "The *philosophes* directed their attention *primarily* to the social, political, and human problems of the day, and not to the entertainment of the many, or the aesthetic delight of the few."[10] And if this emphasis led them to address issues that grew out of their social milieu, it also imposed some urgency on the need to write in such a way that what was said found a receptive audience. As the same historian goes on to say: "They were aware of the fact that ideas are valid only in so far as they can be conveyed with vigour and vividness, for they knew that they had to convince and win readers over to their side."[11]

If this statement casts the matter too much in the direction of calculated effort on the part of writers themselves, it nevertheless poses clearly the question of articulation: whether consciously or in ways of which they themselves were not clearly aware, the eighteenth-century writers who generated the Enlightenment produced a kind of ideological oeuvre that bore a distinctive relation with the social circumstances under which it was produced. This relation did not happen all at once. Just as in the Reformation, writers responded to public events, and some of these responses themselves became public events of some importance. The process of articulation, therefore, was a product of action sequences that brought ideology and social circumstances together in a dialectic, interactive framework.

As they responded to public events, writers applied their arguments to concrete social circumstances and used these circumstances to draw retrospective lessons of a more general sort. The events thereby became figural occasions, exemplars of general interpretive frameworks. The Lisbon earthquake in 1755 provided the occasion for Voltaire to challenge the optimistic philosophies of Leibniz and Pope. The failed Jacobite uprising in 1745 gave William Robertson and Hugh Blair an opportunity to show the value of reading the historical record for signs of divine providence and of committing oneself to the civic community rather than succumbing to divisive passions. The conclusions drawn never corresponded simply to the facts of the event itself. Indeed others drew different conclusions. But often the same processes that determined the outcome of important events also "selected for" particular interpretations of these events. For example, the broader institutional resources that contributed to the failure of the Jacobite uprising also played a prominent role, as we have seen, in ensuring that the Hanoverian literati in Edinburgh would provide the dominant interpretation for this failure.

As in the Reformation, ideology seldom reflected social circumstances in a way that was this direct. But the broader social context in which the Enlightenment was produced did come into close articulation with the ideas that emanated from it. The contours of this articulation can be seen in some instances in the variations that emerged from one context to another and, more generally, in the factors that "selected for" certain genres at the expense of others. The distinction between private lives and public roles that underlay the discursive fields evident in Enlightenment literature also played a role in the country-by-country variations in literary style. Differences in religious conceptions of the roles of scholarship and education also reinforced these variations, but the basic structure of the public sphere in which writers functioned appears to have exercised an important influence.

As a rule, the most innovative literary genres became more prominent in settings in which a relatively loose level of formal coordination characterized the public sphere. Under these conditions writers functioned to a greater extent as private individuals, and less as occupants of public roles, even though their connections with the public sphere still encouraged them to address issues of common interest. Not only were the constraints less rigidly imposed in these circumstances but the conceptual distance between private selves and the public was also maximized. The latter especially appears to have been conducive to greater experimentation with genres that privileged the perceptual orientations of the private individual.

England provided the most extreme case of this kind of public sphere. Writers' attachments to the public sphere came less through offices involving formal responsibility to the state, universities, or the church than through informal patronage networks and commercial publishing ventures. France paralleled England to some extent, especially insofar as the need to publish anonymously forced some writers in France to effect distance between themselves and the public sphere. The negative pressures exercised by the church, as well as the greater degree of official patronage and direct integration into government circles, nevertheless mitigated some of the distance that writers experienced between their private lives and their public roles. Prussia and Scotland, in contrast, stand almost equally at the opposite end of the continuum. In both cases the growth of formal bureaucracy and the maintenance of close ties between the bureaucracy and the church on the one hand and the universities on the other meant that writers were more likely to occupy some official public role in addition to their own private roles.

Corresponding to these differences in social context, one sees the particularly prominent role of English writers in pioneering the novel, and the increasing importance of fictional biography and autobiography in both France and England. In contrast, greater continuity of moral philosophy and related genres, such as the fable, poetry, and the moral weekly, in which public standards of morality were imposed on the individual, remained evident in Prussia and Scotland.[12] Evidently the greater separation of public and private in some contexts was also conducive to a greater emphasis on the interior functioning of individual perceptual psychology. Once the private realm came to be regarded as an entity distinct from collectively defined realities, the role of perception and inner experience became more important—one might even say conceivable. From Locke's concern with the senses and mental capacities of the perceiver in *An Essay Concerning Human Understanding* (1690) to Berkeley's subjective idealism in *A Treatise Concerning the Principles of Human Knowledge* (1710), one sees an increasing fascination with the role of inner experience in shaping both the self and external reality. In fiction the same tendency is evident. Especially in the novel the narrator is able to disclose more fully than ever before the inner world that responds to, interprets, and essentially defines experienced events. "The reader," one commentator on the period says, "was allowed a perspective on reality which the novel suggested was the only meaningful perspective—the subjective and individual."[13]

The disjuncture between public and private also provided a context that reinforced the search for new, authenticating literary forms. Whereas the religious leaders of the Reformation period had generally spoken in the first person, drawing on their knowledge of the Bible and their activities as movement leaders for authentication, the Enlightenment writers found themselves increasingly unable to speak with authority from the sheer experience or knowledge that could be commanded by a single person. They could do so within the relatively limited circles of natural and moral philosophy in which the canons of knowledge and argumentation were relatively well defined. But for the broader audience of strangers who constituted the literate public, the match between the writers' private experiences and the issues and roles making up the public sphere was insufficient to authenticate discourse by itself. To gain an authoritative position in relation to this audience, writers increasingly turned to fiction.

Until around the middle of the eighteenth century the apocryphal autobiography was used extensively, after which the epistolary novel became the main form. The former allowed the author to assume the perspective of roles other than his own in real life, thereby assuming the authoritative identity of heroes, warriors, kings, or other prominent public figures, or else to occupy the position of more ordinary figures with whom the public could identify, such as merchant, artisan, or mistress. The apocryphal autobiography, in short, permitted the writer to develop as many varied roles in fiction as there were in the public sphere itself. And the capacity to do this effectively depended, of course, on some firsthand involvement with the actual occupants of these roles.

The epistolary novel added greater flexibility to this literary genre. Rather than having to adopt the single perspective necessitated by an autobiographical account, the author could now withdraw entirely into the background, letting the characters speak for themselves, much as they did in the theater, but now through their letters. Moreover, the relationships among multiple roles now became possible to emphasize through the exchange of letters. The fluidity of roles and role relations also became more easily portrayed because of the temporality of letters. In all of this, propaganda, philosophizing, and moral discourse continued to occupy a prominent place. Thus, the new fictional genres provided an instrument for developing articulation between ideological themes and the more complex roles that characterized the public sphere.

In contrast to the genres that came into greater use during the eighteenth century, the genres that were replaced appear to have been less readily suited to expressing these kinds of complex roles. Literary historians have observed, for example, that poetry dominated the output of many literary circles at the beginning of the eighteenth century, but as the century progressed, poetry gradually lost prominence. One of the reasons appears to be that in order to be understood and appreciated poetry required either a stronger commitment to established patterns or else a close community of readers. During the early part of the century poetry flourished, especially in France, where it remained the most certain way of gaining membership for its author in the French Academy. The training in classics that most members of the social elite had attained provided models for judging and appreciating poetry. Voltaire's *Henriade* was perhaps the most successful example, but numerous works incorporated the classical style. By the middle of the century, the audience for literature had become more diverse as a result of the growth and internal heterogeneity of the public sphere. Within this context, less could be taken for granted. More detail had to be devoted to character development, to the relations among characters, and to describing their social settings. Writers complained increasingly of the constraints imposed by the accepted canons of poetic construction. And a number of experiments with alternatives were tried. It was, however, the more elaborated forms of narrative prose that proved most successful in meeting the new demands.[14]

Some general differences in the way in which substantive matters were handled also suggest the effects of different linkages between the public and private. In France and England, writers tended to base the state and civil society in the perceptions and needs of individuals, for example, and therefore registered greater concern with the "artificiality" or independence of the state, and focused to a greater extent on the autonomous organization and regulation of the state. In Prussia and Scotland, one sees a closer integration of civil society and the state on the one hand and with the individual on the other hand through arguments about public morality and virtue. A greater sense of the historical continuities giving the state an organic existence is also evident. These differences were often muted, of course, by the degree of interchange that writers carried on across societal boundaries.

Without suggesting the existence of neat correspondences between social contexts and national styles, one can nevertheless understand some of the processes "selecting for" certain literary genres in general by considering the social contexts in which writers and their audiences interacted. The novel's capacity as a genre to elicit an identification between the lived experience of the reader and the narrated experience of fictional characters has, for example, been widely discussed. Its development depended greatly on a sufficiently large literate public with the wherewithal to spend money on books. Both conditions—literacy and income—were essential preconditions, but not sufficient in themselves, to account for the rise of the novel as a distinct genre. Literacy had already been prominent enough in many parts of Europe to have played a role in the Reformation, but reading the Bible and the development of the novel were temporally quite distinct. Economic means alone fail to account for the rising popularity of novels relative to theater and opera. Part of the novel's development may be attributable to the inner dynamic of literary taste and experimentation itself. Yet the fact of its growth in popularity suggests that broader social dynamics may have been involved as well. If it was in fact specially qualified as a mode of ideological articulation, then some of its popularity is likely to be illuminated by a deeper understanding of this relation.

Several features of the novel that were congruent with the broader social relations between private selves and public roles stand out. One is that the novel, unlike drama or opera, was written for private consumption. Like the weekly journals and daily newspapers, it could be read by an increasingly scattered array of private individuals who nevertheless held certain interests in common and thereby gained some insight into public affairs. More than the journal or news sheet, the novel also provided a glimpse into the private realities of other individuals, albeit fictional creations. The novel created greater distance between author and reader as well, thereby accentuating the author's own sense of the private self as opposed to public life, although in this respect the novel was no different from the allegory or epic poem.

The most distinctive feature of the novel, especially in comparison with the stage, was that it painted a visualized world within the reader's own mind. Unlike the stage, where the story was in fact a canvas "out there" to be visualized collectively, the novel presented the reader with words from which he or she had to create an internal visual experience. And in so doing, the reader increased his or her own sense of subjective involvement with the subjectivity of the story:

> By making thought visual—perceptions, reactions, and reflections—the novelist transposes this level more easily and fully into our imaginations, thus increasing our involvement with the character. The character's thoughts are described not in any abbreviated or condensed linguistic form but as he himself visually experiences them. Because thinking is visual, the character's thoughts pass into our own minds easily and readily without the necessity of our finding visual equivalents for them. Since our own thinking process is not fully activated, the character's ideas pass through our minds as our own visualizations. Of course, the images are conveyed in words and hence require that we fill them out from our own past visual experience. But such a process is not conscious and tends to personalize the images for us and even involve us more with the character.[15]

This is a particularly rich and important statement because it suggests there were actually some strategic advantages to the reader's having to develop a personalized visualization of the narrative. Rather than the novel merely being a poor substitute for seeing the story actually acted out on stage, it personalized the story in such a way that a stronger bond between subjective experience and the novel was created.

The subtle manner in which distance between public roles and private lives entered into the process of articulation is also evident in the period's increasing preference for "realism," whether in the novel or in nonfiction writing. To be realistic meant that literature somehow resonated closely with actual life. Or as an English writer of the period put it: "Imitations of life and character have been made [the novel's] principal object." The new literature appealed, he argued, because it placed persons in interesting situations "such as may actually occur in life."[16] As readers of the new literary forms sometimes acknowledged, it seemed possible to identify one's own experiences with those of characters in the stories. For example, a correspondent, signing herself "Philopamela," wrote to Samuel Richardson after the publication of *Pamela* in 1740: "I entirely agree with her in everything, sympathize in all her Distresses and Misfortunes, feel Pleasure or Pain only when Pamela does."[17]

On the surface it may appear obvious that novels such as *Pamela* depicted life so graphically as to evoke an almost instant identification with their readers. The problem of articulation was resolved, it might be argued, by the fact that literature merely described life. Consequently, the only significant question to be considered is that of who the actual readers were and how their lives resembled those of the characters portrayed. The fact that a growing percentage of readers were women, that they lived in cities, and that their livelihoods often remained precarious and at best were subject to the fortunes and misfortunes of male domination have, therefore, been advanced as plausible explanations for the growing appeal of novelistic realism.[18]

To say that literature itself was "realistic," however, largely begs the question of why it was perceived as such, for literature clearly did not simply "imitate" life. Nor was its appeal limited to an audience that had some straightforward similarity to the situations in which its characters were placed. Moreover, the ideological products of other times and places had also managed to articulate with their audiences, despite the fact that these products differed greatly from "realist" literature. In short, the question of articulation requires deeper probing beyond merely asserting that Enlightenment literature was somehow "realistic."

This is a question to which a number of literary historians have turned their attention. Microscopic analyses of the possible points of intersection between specific words and their audiences have suggested some valuable insights into the ways in which underlying forms may have enhanced receptivity.[19] The sense of "realism" that came with the growing popularity of the novel was in fact rooted in a particular way of defining reality. In spatial imagery it was as if the private individual had been forced to stand back a sufficient distance from the canvas of social life so that he or she could actually speak of viewing it and of adopting a distinct stance or angle of vision toward it. Separated as it were from the canvas under scrutiny and actually taking an active role in conceiving it, the individual became a matter of increasing interest, not simply as another object to be discussed from the outside but as a locus of subjectivity to be "gotten inside of." Philosophy and literature that failed to do this came under attack for not actually grappling with the essence of reality, whereas ideological forms that somehow created an identification between the subjective world of the reader and the subjective worlds of author, narrator, and character seemed more compelling. The point of articulation between ideology and experience became the sense that this kind of identification had been achieved.

In addition to the new fictional forms that were favorably selected, the historical narrative, historical poetry, and historical commentary provided useful genres with which to bring a distinct ideological perspective together with the lived world of experienced events. History was not simply a retelling of the past but a retelling within a particular interpretive framework. Works as different as Voltaire's *Henriade* and Robertson's *History of Scotland* gained a receptive audience by weaving together well known events from the not so distant past with explicit characterizations of key figures in ways that made them capable of appreciation by an eighteenth-century audience. Events such as civil conflict were portrayed as the unfortunate results of religious fanaticism, while developments that had become accomplished facts, such as the union of Scotland and England, could be heralded as major achievements.

The writing of history became in effect a means of resolving the dialectic tension that had been established in Enlightenment discourse between the negative pole of institutionalized realities and the positive pole of ideal reason and virtue. In giving a linear dimension to this polarity, history took away the artificiality of the positive ideal and replaced it with present and potential realities. As yet, no inevitable movement from the negative to the positive was a dominant theme. But events were capable of being arranged in such a way as to show the possibility of such movement.[20]

The peculiar view of history that many Enlightenment writers adopted had significant implications for the manner in which Enlightenment thought came to be articulated with actual social circumstances. Events and actors ceased largely to be regarded as being worthy of attention in their own right and if they were examined at all were treated as instances or types of more general kinds of processes and characters. In the *Discourse on Inequality*, for example, Rousseau apologized for neglecting times and places, arguing that what he had to say was directed toward the audience of "man in general" and therefore needed to be framed in a language suitable to all nations. In his contributions to the *Encyclopédie* Diderot em-

phasized inventions and technical achievements as evidence of the
general possibilities for progress and human advancement. Nearly
all of the Enlightenment's leaders "characterized" themselves as instances of genius in the lineage of great thinkers of the past. Even
much of their fiction consisted of allegory, moral tales, and stylized
characters such as the wealthy aesthete or victimized female who,
despite an increasing sense of earthy realism, still failed to resonate
closely with specific times and places.

It is imperative, therefore, to understand the precise sense in
which Enlightenment thought articulated with its social surroundings,
for this articulation did not include paying mind to the actual circumstances of its own creation. Certainly the period was marked less
by the specific appeals to concrete actors on the contemporary political horizon than was true of Luther or Calvin, and its thought was
marked by a thematization and universalism that was to contrast
sharply with the complex realism of literature in later periods. And
yet this very emphasis on generalization, if not abstraction, articulated
with the social circumstances of the Enlightenment and gave it much
of its identity as a distinct ideological movement. It was, first of all,
a style that bore a strong affinity with the character of scientific laws
that had gained attention during the second half of the seventeenth
century, namely, that nature is everywhere subject to the same laws
and therefore a reliable source of generalizations. It was also a style
that fit well with the increasing levels of communication, trade, and
diplomacy that were creating a stronger sense among educated elites
of Europe as a single, or potentially single, cultural zone. The same
awareness that foresaw greater cultural integration also decried the
conflictive tensions inherent in ethnic, local, and to some extent
national, but above all religious rivalries. In trumpeting the general
over the particular, writers from Locke to Rousseau were directing
strong criticism at the parochial passions that had caused much of
the seventeenth century to be dominated by war and were siding
with the voice of tolerance and peace.

There was as well a degree of articulation between the Enlightenment's penchant for generality and the social position of its leading
architects. Unlike Luther or Calvin, they were not the leaders of a
potentially disruptive mass movement. Their critics did of course
argue that the new emphasis on natural authority would undermine
the power of religiously sanctioned morality and contribute to the
demise of respect for political tradition. But, practically speaking,

the new ideas were known by relatively few. They did not augur changes in the daily patterns of religious worship, for example, as the Reformation had. Thus the Enlightenment writers could work at a level of generality that largely ignored the kinds of practical directives that the Protestant reformers were called upon to give. Nor were they in command of the reins of power, even though they often stood close to the seat of power. At the same time, their proximity to power, as we have seen particularly in the Scottish and Prussian cases, prompted an awareness of collective interests that transcended the pursuits of sheer private careerism or artistic pleasure. Thus the production of works characterized by a high level of generality was not so much a symptom of having escaped the bounds of social circumstances as it was the result of a particular constellation of social conditions that made this kind of orientation possible.

In considering the genres that characterized the Enlightenment, some attention must also be given to the fact that these genres seem, again in comparison with those of the Reformation, to include an infinitely greater variety: letters, memoirs, treatises, allegory, short verse, epic poems, chronicles, plays, narrative history, the novel. Whereas their predecessors had relied mainly on the sermon and polemical theological tracts, the reformers of the eighteenth century had at their disposal a far more varied repertoire of literary styles. And this variety was itself added to during the course of the eighteenth century. Indeed, it has been regarded as one of the ways in which eighteenth-century writers adapted to an increasingly complex social environment.

How the ideology of this period came to articulate with its social context was not, however, entirely dissimilar from that of the Reformation. As the foregoing has suggested, selective processes were at work which reduced some of the broader diversity in the Enlightenment just as in the Reformation, causing particular genres to be preferentially selected at the expense of others. Another striking similarity between the two periods is that both communities of discourse relied on literary genres that were well established and provided ready access to the desired audiences. The sermon offered a readily recognized mode of communication in the sixteenth century. By the second quarter of the eighteenth century, travelogues, allegories, fictionalized or at least sensationalized reportage of current events, and above all the quasipornographic serial or short novel had become readily available to the literate public in European cities.

The Enlightenment writers drew on these precedents, made use of their familiarity, and reached their intended audiences with narratives and satire that communicated more effectively than abstract philosophical tomes. An additional similarity to the Reformation's usage of sermons and tracts was that the Enlightenment's genres tended to be short, relatively disaggregated, and frequently revised. A fairly extensive compilation of English literature during the first three decades of the eighteenth century, for example, shows only a small proportion to be full-length treatises or long romances; most are short novellas, plays, and serialized fiction.[21] This type of literature was easily adaptable to current events, making it amenable to the process of ideological articulation in the same way that the sermon had been in the earlier period. Weightier contributions often shared certain features with this literature. Diderot's *Philosophical Letters* (1746) has generally been reputed to have been written over a single weekend. The epistolary style, more generally, permitted writers to set forth a variety of thoughts on a number of relatively discrete subjects without having to sustain a single, integrated argument. In this respect it shared much with the style of the verse-by-verse commentary adopted by the Protestant reformers. Even literature of a more integrated style often took its characters on excursions that by twentieth-century standards seem abrupt and poorly connected. The *Persian Letters*, *Candide*, and *Clarissa* all share this feature, roaming across a seemingly endless and bewildering range of subjects and introducing characters and situations almost at will. Just as the sermon and the commentary had done, these stylistic features permitted writers to address their ideas to a large number of contemporary issues. In addition, the relatively discrete character of this literature lent it easily to revision. Thus numerous examples exist of writers adding chapters to later editions of their work or sharpening their satire, and in other cases professing greater moderation, in response to the activities of censors and the reactions of other intellectual authorities.

The other feature of Enlightenment discourse that adds to its seeming discreteness and diversity, however, is the proclivity of its authors to adopt seemingly incongruous topics, genres, and levels of debate. Although some of the diversity within the oeuvre of single authors is also present in the Reformation, it stands out as a particular feature of the Enlightenment. We have a vivid example of this incongruity in Diderot, for instance, who in the same year (1748) produced the bizarre semipornographic *Les bijoux*, composed of allegory, wizardry, intrigue, and political satire, and the weighty *Mémoires sur différens sujets de mathématiques*, which took up questions of vibration, sound, atmospheric pressure, and pendulums. The same peculiar mixture of interests is evident in Voltaire, whose work ranged from a semipopular rendition of Newton's laws to papers on biology, to bawdy journalism.

That a single scholar could be capable of mastering such diverse subjects and styles has usually masked the more important question of what the consequences and inspirations of these interests were. The consequences were relatively straightforward: natural philosophy and science intermingled with the seamier fiction of the period, giving a kind of esoteric legitimacy to its claims, and became popularized in the process. The role of the Enlightenment in extending naturalistic and positivistic assumptions to other realms of human behavior has long been recognized. The temptation to try to work across the full range of scholarship from obscure mathematics to popular fiction, however, must be understood at least partly with reference to the social context in which many eighteenth-century writers found themselves.

They did, of course, have some basis for engaging in these diverse subjects by virtue of the less rigidly specialized education to which many of them had been exposed. But training provides only a partial explanation. They were also in the unique position of being close, but yet marginal, to the higher echelons of aristocratic society. Indeed their marginality, far from simply engendering a kind of subjective alienation, placed them tangibly between two kinds of audience on whom their livelihood and success depended. On the one hand were the increasingly large numbers of literate readers who purchased, or at least read, the seamier, popularized fiction that came streaming from their pens. On the other hand were the aristocratic, royal, and bureaucratic officials from whom patronage, recognition, and forbearance derived. A few held secure positions within the academies and bureaucracies of the latter, but very few began their careers with these amenities, and the number of aspiring writers always exceeded the positions available. Thus the most common tendency was to try to appeal to both audiences in some manner: writing bawdy fiction for the literate public, often satirizing the pretensions of the elite; composing learned mathematical, philosophical, and literary works in hopes of gaining prestige and elite approval.

The Enlightenment catered to both audiences, drew on both kinds of literary precedent, and in the process drew a closer connection between the assumptions of natural philosophy and the genres and issues of interest to the literate public.

The State, Factions, and Competition

If their relation to the state had some direct effects on the genres of discourse they produced, writers in the eighteenth century were also, as I have suggested in previous chapters, deeply affected by the factionalism that characterized most state bureaucracies during this period. We have seen some of the ways in which this factionalism figured into the more general cleavage between public roles and private lives that underlay much of Enlightenment discourse. Factionalism also played a significant role in reinforcing the competition among writers that lay behind some of the selective processes we have been examining.

In addition to merely providing a central location to which writers could gravitate, the state imposed a number of distinct social relations on the literary community, one of the most consequential of which was competition itself. Some of this competition, as we have seen, was directly linked to writers' involvement with competing political patronage networks. A more artificial form of competition was also superimposed on the literary community. In the case of the Reformation it was seen that public disputations pitting reformers against one another were often arranged by public officials to resolve theological controversies. These contests were usually conducted as face to face encounters, although briefs were sometimes required in advance, and they grew out of natural conflicts between well defined movements and factions. The contests of the eighteenth century had a more artificial character that made the state all the more important in conditioning the nature of the conflict. The typical mode of scholarly contest was no longer the disputation but the prize competition. Writers were invited to submit work on a specified topic to some agency of the state for judging in hopes of receiving a monetary prize, publication, and recognition. The origins of this idea can probably be traced to medieval jousts, artistic competitions sponsored by Renaissance patrons, or even the classical athletic tournaments, but the practice of sponsoring literary contests became increasingly prominent during the last half of the seventeenth century and early eighteenth century along with the growth of specialized bureaucratic agencies and the formation of philosophic, scientific, and literary academies.

Unlike the disputation, and in contrast to the courts or parliamentary bodies, literary contests were not promulgated as means of settling previously defined conflicts but were in a sense "games" that generated their own competition. As such, the contestants were not expected to take them seriously in the same way that they might engage in civil or legal disputes. Indeed the contestants played roles defined by the game itself that were to remain quite distinct from either their private selves or their other public roles. Thus one sees evidence of a kind of ambivalence toward these competitions. The poet Jean-Baptiste Rousseau, for example, cautioned talented poets against taking part in them lest they demean themselves. Voltaire, upon failing to win a competition sponsored by the French Academy in 1714, poked fun at not only the winner but the entire process. Jean-Jacques Rousseau, by contrast, regarded his early successes in the essay competitions he entered as a vital contribution to his subsequent rise to prominence. Even those who won, however, often submitted their work with some misgivings and embarrassment. The literary contest, in a sense, reinforced a degree of distance between self and the role of literary producer that was quite different from the close connections that were cultivated in the Protestant reformers' disputations.

Literary competitions also added a layer of conflict among writers themselves that often cut across other lines of intellectual disagreement. Though no defender of the ancients in debates over the validity of so-called modern as opposed to ancient knowledge, Voltaire attacked the modernist school with vicious satirical prose after losing the competition in 1714 to one of their rank. More generally, the contests encouraged writers to address one another, thereby adding to the overall stock of ideological production, much in the way that theological disputes had during the Reformation. Rather than simply writing for their own audiences, they addressed the ideas being produced by one another, giving the Enlightenment more of a communal character. In this respect their work began to articulate with that of the broader intellectual milieu in which they worked. Arguments were joined and rebutted. Fellow writers became not only the producers of literature but the objects of literary debate as well. Their work and their public images became part of an objectified collective identity, and this identity provided a social context in which to work as concrete as that of the academies and salons themselves.

The attacks that writers addressed to one another were in part engendered by the collective, competitive character of the literary community in which they worked. At this level, they articulated closely with the immediate institutional milieu in which they were produced. But at a different level, they took on an abstract, fictional, and often satirical cast that transcended these immediate contexts. It was possible to transcend the immediate institutional context, paradoxically, because literary autonomy was a feature of this context itself. The public sphere in which eighteenth-century writers worked provided, as we have seen, a high degree of autonomy, if only because it was relatively informal and unstable. In order for the kinds of scholarship the Enlightenment initiated to become fully institutionalized, it proved necessary for these conditions to be reproduced, usually within the autonomous contexts provided by the university or by the more informal distancing mechanisms that generated the same level of autonomy in bohemian and artistic communities. The cost of creating this kind of contextual *disarticulation*, however, was the disjuncture that appeared increasingly between private selves and public roles. To the extent that this disjuncture was also a feature of bourgeois, urban, and industrial life, the literature of the eighteenth century came to have a kind of lasting resonance with the problems of achieving authenticity in modern society. It was, nevertheless, a discursive style that was distinctive in the social location of its origins, and one that would necessitate its own replacement as these conditions became transformed during the following century.

PART III

European Socialism

Institutional and Intellectual Antecedents

MANY OF THE Enlightenment's supposed effects—effects that were widely accepted by writers in the nineteenth century—have long since been discounted. Doubts have been voiced about the Enlightenment's role in the French and American revolutions, its relevance for legitimating democracy and industrial capitalism, and its relations to the growth of scientific rationalism, the romantic reaction, and the secularization of the masses. Although some effects on all these developments remain uncontested, the singular influence of Enlightenment ideas has clearly been given more modest dimensions. The Enlightenment was, however, carried on to a significant degree in the main institutions of cultural production and dissemination that characterized the nineteenth century. Indeed, it is to these institutions that one must look in order to grasp the societal changes from which socialist ideology was to grow.

Established Cultural Institutions

Music and art, literature, science, the instruction given in colleges and universities, primary and secondary education, newspapers and other media for the expression of public opinion, and religion constituted the institutional arenas in which nearly all forms of deliberate cultural production took place in the nineteenth century. Most of these institutions had been transformed by the French Revolution, by Napoleon's administrative reforms, and by the broader changes in cultural style which these upheavals had initiated. Cultural production had also expanded in conjunction with the continuing growth experienced by state bureaucracies and the enlargement of the literate middle classes. Colleges and universities increasingly incorporated the historical, natural, and medical sciences that had been initiated during the Enlightenment and gradually evolved toward the style of graduate research training that came to dominate higher education in the twentieth century.[1] National systems of technical, secondary, and primary education were also established, significantly enlarging the share of the population to whom information, literacy skills, shared historical narratives, and other kinds of official discourse could be disseminated. Outside the employment provided by these institutions, many writers and artists still struggled to support their endeavors. But the market for books, periodicals, theatrical performances, and paintings steadily expanded, permitting the overall number of writers and artists to grow as well.[2]

In comparison with the growth evident in these cultural and educational institutions, established religion generally showed signs of decay. Hostile governments, more attractive career opportunities, and the general mood of anticlericalism which had found expression in the French Revolution all played a role in weakening the churches' popular appeal. And yet even the religious establishment showed many signs of continuity and renewed vitality. In France the end of the Napoleonic regime brought new freedom for religious activities; religious orders once again replenished their numbers and in many instances experienced growth; and new movements began to initiate revivalism, lay ministries, and doctrinal reforms. In the German states theological and liturgical conservatism—sometimes called a "New Lutheranism"—vigorously reasserted the importance of historical doctrines that had become the subject of scholarly criticism. Pietism continued to produce a sophisticated mixture of rationalism and faith. And a variety of free churches were created alongside the established denominations. Many of these developments were also evident in the Scandinavian countries and in the Netherlands. In England the established churches were far from healthy. But some signs of awakening and transformation were evident here as well. Movements within the Anglican church, such as the Pastoral Aid Society, the Oxford Movement, and a strong evangelical constituency oriented toward prayer and Bible study provided renewed vitality. After the repeal of the Test and Corporation Acts in 1828, Nonconformist bodies also experienced significant growth.

In most of the established institutions from which cultural objects were disseminated, therefore, the nineteenth century witnessed expansion, vigor, and vitality on a scale previously unknown. More producers and disseminators of culture were employed by these institutions than ever before, resources flowed to them on a more abundant scale, and the economic growth that had made their emergence possible in the eighteenth century continued to enlarge the audience to whom they appealed. The fact that these institutions were flourishing constituted an important feature of the broader social environment in which any new ideological movement or culture-bearing organization might emerge. Also significant was the place in the larger societal hierarchy that these institutions continued to occupy.

Despite the vast political upheavals that had occurred between 1789 and 1848, all of these culture-producing institutions remained directly or indirectly indebted to the state for legitimation and often for more tangible resources as well. Educational systems were particularly dependent on the state. Regarded by high officials as instruments for socializing potential state bureaucrats with necessary technical skills and personal tastes and as vehicles for the dissemination of nationally unifying outlooks and assumptions, schools tended to be closely supervised by the state. Teachers' training requirements underwent standardization; uniform curricula were imposed; in some places private schools were forbidden or discouraged; and attendance up to certain minimal levels became mandatory. For these systems to be effective, the state increasingly took responsibility for supplying most of the resources needed as well: teachers' training, salaries, administrative costs, school buildings, books.

Other means of cultural production and dissemination were generally tied less closely to the state than to the schools and universities, but good relations with the state were nevertheless essential to their functioning. Art and architecture were influenced mainly by the fact that the largest projects were still sponsored by the state, which in turn set guidelines for taste and initiated trends in dominant styles.[3] Newspapers were largely free of formal restrictions in England, but in France a highly effective system of warnings, suspension, and suppression was in operation, causing most newspapers to censor themselves, and in Prussia and Austria the press was closely controlled by the government. Despite some tendencies toward diversification and self-governance, the churches also drew resources mainly from public coffers and functioned at the discretion of state officials.

Producers and consumers of the cultural activities associated with these institutions also tended to represent the upper social strata to a much greater extent than the lower strata, just as they had in the previous century. Although a growing number of provisions were being made for education to be supplied equally to all social strata, the quantity and quality of schooling remained heavily skewed to favor those in the aristocracy and at the higher end of the bourgeoisie. Attendance at secondary schools generally required sacrifices of family income that few in the lower strata could afford. Adequate instruction was often limited to a relatively small number of secondary schools in the wealthier sections of the large cities or remained the preserve of private schools with high tuition fees. Entrance requirements at colleges and universities usually denied admission to all but the few whose family background had given them access to the best preparation, and even those who were admitted needed a handsome income to pay tuition and to support themselves.[4]

Efforts to disseminate the other culture-producing institutions of the upper strata to a larger segment of the general population were also largely ineffective. In England, for example, a bill was passed in 1850 to encourage the establishment of libraries and museums on a wider scale; but according to a study conducted eighteen years later, only fifty-two such facilities had been started. Newspapers were perhaps a more efficient means of reaching the masses, and as wages and literacy rates rose, newspaper circulation expanded enormously. Yet even the most popular newspapers failed to reach more than a small percentage of the larger population. In the 1850s, for instance, *The Times* in London had a circulation of only 55,000 copies in a city of nearly 3 million.[5]

As was true of the church on the eve of the Reformation, the dominant culture-producing institutions of the nineteenth century gained the resources they needed by mirroring, legitimating, and enacting the status relations of the larger social environment in which they were embedded. To be sure, some gains had been made in extending the resource base of these institutions into the bourgeoisie. No longer were the landed nobility in control of the churches or the leisured aristocracy of the court in control of the theaters and concert halls and the upper civil bureaucracy in control of the press. But the social location of most established cultural institutions was closely associated with the major centers of power and wealth.

In a certain sense the institutional locations of cultural production and dissemination in the nineteenth century predisposed them to contribute to the creation of what has sometimes been described as a "hegemonic" ideology: an ideology of elite standards, submission to authority, and bourgeois aspirations.[6] And yet these institutions were generally quite diverse. They exercised considerable control over their own affairs and consequently provided a context in which a relatively high level of innovation could take place. The institutional autonomy that science had gained in the seventeenth century and the more informal freedoms that writers and philosophers had acquired in the eighteenth century continued. Within the broad framework of action constituted by their own leaders, the state, and the various clienteles they served, scientists and writers were able to initiate and reward a great deal of innovative work. The achievements of Pasteur, Darwin, and Mendel are associated with this period, as are the works of Goethe, Hegel, and Kierkegaard. In literature a prominent new mode of realist writing came into vogue through the contributions of Dickens, Hardy, Balzac, and Flaubert. In the visual arts the period is known for the diversity evident in Constable, Delacroix, Courbet, Manet, Degas, Monet, and Renoir. And intellectual deviations, challenges, and reforms of all kinds were characteristic of the period, as evidenced in the writings of Nietzsche and Saint Simon, the Owenite experiments, and the reforms associated with Lamennais in France and the Oxford Movement in England.

Expansion in the Social Environment

During the course of the nineteenth century, most of the institutions in which cultural production took place were situated in a broader social environment whose overall resources were increasing. Industrial production, international trade, population, and colonial relations between Europe and the rest of the world were all expanding. Along most of these dimensions, growth was already evident early in the nineteenth century as a result of the technological innovations that had been made before the end of the previous century, and in many places this growth was facilitated by the international trade that returned at the conclusion of the American War of Independence. But it was particularly the last third of the nineteenth century and the decade prior to the First World War that witnessed the highest rates of economic growth. For Europe as a whole, the average annual rate of growth in gross national product at constant prices rose from 1.2 percent between 1800 and 1830 to 1.5 percent between 1830 and 1860, edged up to 1.6 percent between 1860 and 1890, and then climbed to 2.5 percent between 1890 and 1913 (after which it fell to 1.6 percent between 1913 and 1939 and 0.9 percent between 1939 and 1950).[7] During this period, indicators of industrial production showed exceptionally rapid growth. For example, steel production in Great Britain increased from 334,000 metric tons in 1870 to 6.776 million metric tons in 1910. Over the same period the figures for France rose from 84,000 to 3.413 million, and for Germany from 126,000 to 13.1 million.[8]

Of course the extent of growth varied from region to region, as did its particular composition, and both kinds of variation influenced the character of the cultural changes that took place. As in both of the earlier historical periods we have examined, though, the economic growth of the nineteenth century was not simply a chance occurrence that happened to take place simultaneously in each individual country; it was a systemic feature of the European economy as a whole. The stimulus to growth among the so-called industrial powers was to an important degree the presence of economic competition among these rivals, while the patterns in less developed areas were often heavily influenced by the opening up of new markets with the more industrialized nations.

This expansion for the most part contributed positively to the growth and vitality of established cultural institutions rather than threatening to undermine or replace them. Many of the ideas, as well as the very style of discourse, that became prominent in the nineteenth century were in fact highly adaptable to the changing social, economic, and political circumstances of the period. The idea of progress, for example, legitimated change, encouraged a positive outlook toward the future, and undergirded new economic and political theories that were thought to be vital adaptations to new conditions in the social environment. Individualism and utilitarianism contributed on a certain level to the legitimation of diversity and the search for more efficient relations between means and ends. The increasingly close ties between scientific research and technological applications also appeared to be well suited to an environment of change. As industrial expansion raised technical questions, scientific practitioners sought to provide answers to these questions.[9] Especially in comparison with the ideologies that had been associated with relatively more stable social environments, such as the medieval church or the political theories of the mercantile period, the dominant perspectives of the nineteenth century, therefore, seemed less likely to become jeopardized by the expansion taking place in the arenas of economic production, the state, the military, and international relations.

The environmental change that was to create the greatest challenge for the established cultural institutions was the emergence of a large industrial working class. By 1880 half of the entire labor force in Great Britain was employed in manufacturing, mining, and construction. By the end of the century at least a third of all laborers in Germany, France, Belgium, the Netherlands, Switzerland, Norway, and Austria were in these industries.[10] Accompanying these statistical shifts in labor force composition was a great deal of geographic and social change as well. Rather than remaining scattered throughout the countryside in small shops, as much of the textile industry had been during the industrial revolution's early phases, the newer kinds of industrial production tended to be concentrated more heavily in urban areas, thereby requiring workers to take up new residences and to sever many of their ties to the land and to the family networks that might otherwise have provided social and economic security during times of hardship. In many of the working-class districts that developed in the medium-sized and large cities, growth was so rapid and resources such as time, money, and leadership so scarce that sizable populations found themselves without the communal support systems on which they had relied in the past.

In addition to the sheer social dislocation that was associated with rapid industrialization, much of the first half of the nineteenth century was a time of political upheaval and instability as well. In France, for example, new constitutions were put into effect in 1789 and 1795 and again in 1815; revisions of the electoral system went into effect in each of these years and in 1802, 1817, 1820, 1831, 1848, 1852, 1871, and 1873; and major regime changes occurred in 1789, 1792, 1795, 1799, 1814, 1815, 1830, 1848, 1852, 1870, and 1871. Less frequently, but often accompanied by violence and domestic upheaval, regime changes occurred in most of the other European countries as well: in the Hungarian and Bohemian sections of the Hapsburg empire, in Sicily and Milan, in Prussia and many of the smaller German states, in Denmark, and in Switzerland. Changes in trade relations and military alliances also added to the political instability of the period. Along with expanding markets and growing military strength came increasing levels of intervention by dominant powers in the affairs of peripheral areas such as Turkey and Poland, and in the affairs of colonies and former colonies, especially in Latin America, the Middle East, and Asia.[11] The major powers, particularly France and Great Britain, alternated between forming mutual alliances and opposing one another. Within all the dominant powers, ruling factions also vacillated between policies of free trade and protectionism, policies of expansion and contraction, and policies of cobelligerence and isolation.

Socialism: Antecedents and Competition

Socialism emerged in this context. Like the tributaries of a great river, its origins can be traced backwards into countless ravines, rivulets, and artesian springs. Groups with occult beginnings such as the Circle of Philadelphians, the Charcoal Burners, and the Brotherly Association are said to have provided the earliest models of organizational commitment and revolutionary zeal which later became the trademarks of the socialist movement.[12] More commonly recognized as antecedents of the Marxist stream of socialist thinking are such early utopian varieties as Owenism, Fourierism, and Saint-Simonianism. From these movements came the words *socialism* and *communism,* first used in publications in the late 1820s and early 1830s, and then deployed more widely in the 1840s, Other, more direct sources of the socialist movement as a political force can be found in the revolutionary episodes that erupted in France in the 1830s and in the Italian states, in the occupied sections of Poland, in Spain, and in the German states during the same period. These uprisings produced exiles with common hopes and grievances who were forced into dependent relations with one another. Living an itinerant existence outside the law, these revolutionary leaders were able to maintain themselves financially and support one another by developing loose social networks. For example, Wilhelm Weitling, who became an associate of Marx and Engels in the 1840s, had been an early exponent of utopian Christian socialism in Germany, a member of the League of the Just in Paris in the 1830s, a founder of communist groups among German workers in Switzerland, and by 1845 a leading member of a small group of German revolutionaries in Brussels. Others who gravitated to Brussels at the same time included Moses Hess, Wilhelm Wolff, and Joseph Weydemeyer, all of whom had been active in previous efforts to organize revolutionary activities among workers.[13] Marx's and Engels's own careers followed this pattern, of course, as did many of those who became their disciples.

The most significant boost to these scattered coteries of socialists came in 1848. In February uprisings in Paris forced the abdication of Louis Philippe, and soon after the same conditions led to eruptions in Germany and Austria. In Bavaria and Württemberg democratic reforms, including a representative parliament and a free press, were instituted; in Hesse-Cassel many concessions were made to save the throne; in Berlin a popular uprising resulted in the convening of a national assembly; and in Vienna an uprising forced Metternich to resign. The socialists generally benefited from these uprisings, but less tangibly than ideologically. In the aftermath of 1848 the League of Communists, which Marx and Engels had supported, actually saw most of its strength disappear as German exiles in the movement in France, England, and Belgium returned to the German states and principalities from which they had emigrated. Nor did the upheavals of 1848 generate widespread enthusiasm among workers for the socialists' revolutionary ideals.[14] To the small numbers of loyal socialist leaders, however, the events of 1848 gave clear indication that history was indeed moving in the direction they had predicted. The triumph of the bourgeoisie over the aristocracy was not a struggle in which they themselves were directly involved, but it proclaimed that the stage was now set and that their turn would be next. Editorials and speeches by socialist leaders offered predictions of which policies would ultimately contribute most to the workers' cause and counseled their followers in proper ways of behaving, but caution was also advised in committing action to revolutionary causes that were as yet too premature to succeed.

The organizational pattern that came increasingly to characterize the socialist movement during the 1850s and 1860s was also a product of these earlier struggles. Founded by political activists who had become disillusioned in France after the 1830 revolution and by German exiles, the early socialist organizations led a semisecret existence among students and artisans. Educational classes and recreational activities provided "above ground" cover for the more subterranean political activities in which the movement was engaged. The most promising workers associated with the public organizations were recruited as members of the underground league. In order to maintain secrecy, oaths were taken and members knew one another by secret names. These early cell groups served explicitly as models for the later activities of the socialist organizations.

The ideologies associated with these early revolutionary and utopian experiments also served as antecedents for the later socialist movement that marched in the footsteps of Marx and Engels. For the most part, however, the earlier experiments provided negative reference points. The very fact that they had failed to attract more than a few adherents made them something of an embarrassment to socialist leaders, who saw their movement as the vanguard of history. Marx and his followers repeatedly distanced themselves from these forerunners, describing them as "utopian" and contrasting them with "scientific" formulations. They also employed the doctrine of historical determination to advantage in separating themselves from these forebears. The earlier experiments were in effect said to have contributed as much as could be expected, given the limits placed on them by historical conditions. They were utopian because they had had to depend on imaginary visions of the future, whereas the present formulations could be scientific because of their grounding in an analysis of the contradictions inherent in capitalism.

These arguments gave the socialist movement some degree of unity in comparison with its varied roots. But like the Enlightenment the unity of the socialist movement owes more to the reconstructive efforts of subsequent leaders, and even of historians, that it does to any single unifying creed or philosophical consensus. Although the leadership and writings of Marx cast a broad shadow across the entire movement, just as Luther does for the Reformation, only a small core of the socialist movement in any country reflected the pure Marxist position, while in every case socialist ideology manifested itself distinctively within the various factions that surrounded different leaders. Indeed historians of socialism have been at pains to identify its common themes at all and have found it necessary to focus their accounts on internal struggles or on conceptual distinctions such as those between cooperative socialism and trade socialism or collectivist socialism and revolutionary socialism. The ideas of collective ownership of the means of production and of revolutionary social transformation through the rise of the proletariat constitute unifying themes in many of these accounts, but even these ideas fail to describe the movement's more practical programs. It is thus to a large degree the organizational structure of the Internationals and the relatively concentrated structure of the movement in historical time as a political force that has allowed it to be treated retrospectively as a single phenomenon.[15]

From the beginning it was virtually an understatement to say that socialist ideology was fraught with strong internal disagreement. Marx and Engels on one side and Bruno Bauer and Max Stirner on the other side fought over the proper formulation of the class struggle. Ludwig Feuerbach and Moses Hess put forth their own criticisms. Attacks and defenses of earlier socialists such as Fourier and Cabet were published, while writers and leaders such as Proudhon, Kriege, and Lassalle put forth their own interpretations.

As was true in the Reformation and the Enlightenment, though, these differences of opinion played a positive role overall in generating a high rate of ideological production. In addition to their competition for intellectual ascendancy, socialist writers were stirred to action by the prospect of their ideas actually playing a role in revolutionary action. Especially in the turbulent period between 1844 and 1848 it appeared that even the slightest nudge might generate the kind of revolutionary uprising that socialist leaders were expecting. Adding to the war of words that resulted was the belief that such an uprising could be successful only if it were united along shared ideological convictions. Consequently, it was of considerable importance to the various socialist writers not only to express their opinion but also to be successful in having their point of view prevail. The likelihood of any single doctrine achieving consensus was remote, though, for the various socialist camps were led by strong willed and able spokespersons; moreover, the very marginal existence they shared with respect to established political and cultural institutions meant that they remained geographically scattered, linked to their own journals and sources of patronage, and in some cases unable to come together collectively to hammer out their differences and forge a common set of doctrines. By virtue of their own energies and collaboration Marx and Engels fared better than most of their rivals in popularizing their particular brand of socialism. Even theirs, however, was far from being the rallying cry around which a single unified movement could develop. It was, therefore, the broader social environment after the movement began to grow into an international phenomenon during the second half of the nineteenth century that played a decisive role in shaping the form and distribution of socialist ideology.

The development of socialism can, from one perspective, be viewed as an opposition movement advanced by leaders, drawn from the working classes themselves, who formulated a radical critique of the established political, economic, and cultural institutions that were regarded as exploiters of this class. The significant extent to which socialist leaders, and especially socialist intellectuals, drew resources from established cultural institutions must also be recognized, however. Engels took courses at the University of Berlin, participated in the city's intellectual subculture, and began his literary career writing for its newspapers and political journals. William Liebknecht was trained in philosophy, theology, philology, and history at the universities of Giessen, Berlin, and Marburg. Jean Jaurès was trained at the prestigious Ecole Normale Supèrieure in Paris, where he was a classmate of Henri Bergson and Emile Durkheim, published his first articles in the great republican newspaper of Toulouse, *La dèpeche de Toulouse,* and began his career in a comfortable teaching post at the lycée of Albi.[16] Even August Bebel, whose humble origins deprived him of most of the cultural benefits available to the rich, was influenced by the speeches to workers' associations given by professors at the University of Leipzig and by the more general intellectual sophistication brought to the city by its publishing industry and newspapers.[17] The socialist movement's ability more generally to draw in intellectual talent for drafting party platforms and organizational rules, and especially for making speeches and producing pamphlets, was of considerable value.

The ideological themes of the movement also reflected its indebtedness to the more established cultural institutions. The virtues of science, an awareness of history and sensitivity to its importance as a legitimating motif, skepticism toward religious dogma, and faith in progress were all rhetorical concepts that the socialists shared with those whose intellectual careers had been shaped by the Enlightenment. Engels himself once acknowledged that "in its theoretical form, modern socialism . . . appears . . . as a more logical extension of the principles laid down by the great French philosophers of the eighteenth century."[18]

Both the Enlightenment and the Reformation, in fact, provided rhetorical antecedents for socialist discourse. They provided historical examples of the role of revolutionaries and reformers in whose lineage socialist leaders could depict themselves. Luther, Calvin, and especially Thomas Müntzer were pictured as great reformers struggling against prevailing economic injustices. Locke, the encyclopedists, and particularly Rousseau provided models of intellectual rebellion against superstition and tradition, rebellion that was said to have contributed directly to the political revolutions in England and France. Because of the prominence given to historical materialism among Marxist socialists, the Reformation and Enlightenment also figured in most attempts to trace the theoretical development of their own movement. The Reformation, according to historical materialism, came in response to the crumbling of feudalism and found its greatest support among the rising bourgeoisie. Although the Lutheran Reformation failed for various reasons to attract the bourgeoisie's full efforts, Calvinism became, in Engels's words, a "doctrine ready cut and dried" for the "boldest of the bourgeoisie."[19] The subsequent religious struggles, especially those involving Puritanism and the English Civil War, constituted a further development in the gradual triumph of the bourgeoisie. The Enlightenment was in Marxist interpretations also a product of this development. In it could be found the legitimating doctrines of liberal individualism but also the groundwork for socialism's own materialistic view of society. It would be inaccurate to say that socialist ideology was modeled in any specific way on either of these previous ideological movements, for socialism was conceived to be an alternative framework that negated, exposed, and superseded all previous ideologies. And yet socialism did in these ways incorporate and reconstruct the history of both the Reformation and the Enlightenment into its own theoretical discourse.

To the extent that socialism was an oppositional movement conveying an ideology that was fundamentally oriented toward the overthrow of established cultural, political, and economic institutions, however, it was important that the more predominant forms of cultural capital in the nineteenth century be debunked. Many of the grassroots socialist organizations kept a wary eye on intellectuals in their midst, and some overtly excluded them from holding office. August Bebel explained, for instance, that he was generally "of the opinion that the workers should choose leaders from their own ranks" and charged that it was evident from experience that "the doctors and professors were of no use to us."[20] Similarly, Paul Lafargue asserted that intellectuals were "mere hirelings"; most of them, he argued, "exhaust their brains to enrich the big capitalist, who need not trouble himself to acquire knowledge, since he finds chemists, engineers and scholars on the market at forty or fifty dollars a month."[21]

Another tactic used in debunking, and in distancing itself from, the cultural capital of the established intellectual elite was to associate this elite with the proletariat itself, thereby stripping it of any privileged status and subjecting it to the more encompassing class analysis of the socialists themselves. According to this perspective, intellectuals had once enjoyed the freedom and prestige to produce valid, autonomous, even critical knowledge, but they were now subordinate to the dynamics of capitalism. Despite noticeable increases in overall educational levels in the population at large, these increases were not a means of personal enhancement or emancipation; they were imposed on the sons and daughters of the petty bourgeoisie as the sole means of obtaining a livelihood, and yet disrupting their adolescence while providing them with only rudimentary technical information. The educated elite was also growing in size, but could not sustain itself apart from the wage system of capitalism. An increasing number were becoming unemployed and were forced to take menial jobs, while the remainder functioned as salaried apologists for the bourgeoisie. In the last analysis the educated were, like nearly everyone else, sinking rapidly into the ranks of the proletariat. As Karl Kautsky observed: "Formerly people spoke of the 'aristocracy of intellect,' today we speak of the 'intellectual' or 'educated' proletariat."[22]

The ideological role of these socialist attacks on their competition was threefold. First, it explicitly debunked the knowledge produced and taught by, or learned from, the established intellectual elite: they had lost the capacity to think clearly; the class struggle shaped their ideas, distorted their vision, and forced them to think only the thoughts that would maintain their class position. If the established cultural elites were in fact salaried employees of the upper bourgeoisie, then clearly their ideas would reflect the bourgeoisie's interests.[23] Second, a kind of leveling process was invoked which in effect elevated socialist intellectuals to a more competitive position relative to the educated elite: not only were the elite's ideas suspect, but their very position in society was crumbling; they might think themselves privileged, but in reality they were rapidly losing influence. Because of the pressures of a glutted intellectual labor market, this elite could no longer enjoy the luxury of pure intellectual pursuits. Whatever prestige they thought they had was merely a delusion. "Most of them," wrote Kautsky, "still imagine they are something better than proletarians." The truth of the matter, he said, was quite different: "Place-hunting takes more and more of their energies. Their first care is, not the development of their intellect, but the sale of it. The prostitution of their individuality has become their chief means of advancement. Like the small producers, they are dazzled by the few brilliant prizes of life. They shut their eyes to the numberless blanks in the wheel and barter away soul and body for the merest chance of drawing such a prize."[24] In contrast to the game of chance in which the bourgeoisie's intellectual lackeys were engaged, socialist intellectuals could find reassurance in the solid fact that historical development was on their side. And third, the vision of an imperiled, self-deluded educational elite could also deter the proletariat (and the petty bourgeoisie) from believing that educational attainment could solve their ills: one should look to the class struggle and the eventual triumph of socialism rather than expecting to move into the bourgeoisie through higher education. Indeed the irony of it all, according to this analysis, was that one's individual efforts to climb the ladder of educational success might prevail, but the whole ladder was sinking irreversibly into the depths of subsistence, unemployment, and exploitation.

Socialism, therefore, was engaged in a struggle to assert its own ideology, its own mode of cultural production as well as economic production, against the established cultural institutions of the nineteenth century. Its constituency was to be the working classes, especially the industrial proletariat whose numbers were being increased daily by the larger processes of economic expansion to which capitalism was contributing. In addition to having to compete with the established cultural institutions, however, socialism was not alone in attempting to draw in the working classes in support of its aims. Other movements were also contending for the loyalties of the laboring masses.

Republicanism remained an attractive option for many segments of the working class throughout the nineteenth century. Organized into the so-called liberal parties because it favored an extension of legislative and representative power in place of monarchic and aristocratic rule, it offered incentives to a wide spectrum of groups in the lower and middle social strata. Shopkeepers, owners of small firms, farmers, artisans, craftsmen, skilled and unskilled laborers all joined, at least periodically, in supporting the republicans' efforts to extend the franchise, to equalize the system of electing deputies to parliament, and to promote the most favorable kinds of economic policies.

Religious loyalties presented another source of competition to socialist organizers. During the domestic social upheavals that spread to most European societies between 1815 and 1848, schisms and reform movements erupted in the established churches, creating religious organizations that were often in closer contact with segments of the lower strata. In France the new wave of religious activity included a number of movements oriented specifically toward working-class constituencies: the Société des Traités Religieux (1821), a Protestant Bible study movement modeled after the Religious Tract Society of London; the Society of Saint Vincent de Paul (1833); a Christian union movement founded in Lyons by evangelical Protestants (1843); and the various Christian socialist organizations, among the most prominent of which were the movements founded by Etienne Cabet, Alphonse Laponneraye, and Philippe Buchez.[25] By the 1870s most of these organizations were defunct, but some of the religious themes they had popularized were assimilated into the republican tradition, giving it a messianic and moralistic fervor that competed powerfully with the Marxian socialists' appeals.[26] In England the extent of new religious activity among the working classes was more prominent. Methodism continued to make inroads in many working-class communities.[27] This growth was facilitated by a number of schisms and mergers that resulted in the creation and consolidation of Methodist denominations more specifically oriented toward working-class constituencies: Primitive Methodists (1811), Bible Christian Methodists (1816), Protestant Methodists (1827), Warrenite Methodists (1831), Associated Methodists (1834), and the Wesleyan Methodist Association (1835). Other denominations and movements in Britain also brought religious organizations into closer contact with the working classes. The Particular Baptists emerged in 1813 as a result of rapid growth among the working classes in both rural and urban areas. In the 1830s various Brethren and Darbyite sects emerged that were to have an increasing attraction among the working classes over the next half century. Mass meetings, revivalism, new sects among Dissenters and Nonconformists in industrial districts, and religiously sponsored service organizations such as the British Temperance Society (1832), the Young Men's Christian Association (1844), Christian Socialists (1848), and the Salvation Army (1878) also promoted religious themes against which the socialist movement would have to compete. In varying degrees much the same was true in Germany, Scandinavia, the Netherlands, and many other parts of Europe. Free, evangelical, and reformed denominations displayed special strength in founding churches in growing industrial cities. So-called friendly societies that provided mutual benefit insurance and other kinds of social protection became popular. Christian charitable associations served similar functions. And by the end of the nineteenth century a number of Christian working-class political movements had been founded.[28]

Trade unions and anarchist groups constituted further competition for the loyalties of the expanding working classes. Trade unions grew naturally from the guilds, confraternities, and mutualist associations that had been in existence long before the nineteenth century. They provided skilled artisans with ways of restricting their numbers, set standards for the relations between masters and journeymen, and played an active role in confrontations with employers. By the eve of the First World War, union membership accounted for as much as 20 percent of the labor force in Belgium and the Netherlands, nearly 40 percent of the British work force, and more than half of all workers in Austria.[29] Anarchism was also particularly suited to making headway in the political and economic environment of the nineteenth century; indeed, some qualitative estimates suggest that prior to the First World War anarchism probably gained a wider following than Marxian socialism.[30] In contrast to the Marxists, anarchists generally placed less emphasis on material progress and the forces of industrialization. They focused on transcendent moral principles, such as justice, equality, and the abolition of authoritarianism. And their tactics, whether violent or nonviolent, were generally related to these higher principles by only the loosest connections. The theoretical framework of the movement was relatively impervious to empirical disconfirmation while its activities could be adapted to a wide variety of situations. Thus it was not uncommon to find strong supporters of the movement in settings as diverse as Catalonia, the rural sections of southern Italy, among grape workers in France, and in the Russian areas of Poland.

If these groups did not provide enough competition for socialist movements, state bureaucracies themselves were also increasingly mindful of ways in which to elicit support from the working classes. Public education provided an incentive for workers in some cases; promises to extend the franchise served a similar function in others. Social welfare reforms also played a growing role, especially toward the end of the nineteenth century. In 1880, for instance, no European country had yet initiated programs of disability, sickness, or old age and survivor insurance, but by 1914, fifteen countries had work injury insurance programs, ten had national insurance programs for illness, and nine had old age and survivor insurance.[31] In some cases these programs were initiated by liberal republican parties. But just as often it was the more conservative aristocratic and monarchic regimes that initiated them as a way of luring working class support away from the liberal parties.

Organizational Means and the Social Environment

For it to triumph over its competitors, socialism needed an institutional vehicle—a vehicle through which its ideology could be given expression. As a student of socialism in England has recently suggested: "To replace a culture requires not only a definite commitment to do so but also the command of the means to do so."[32] And that of course was not a requirement that could be filled easily, for the institutions with which socialism was in competition were in a far stronger position to secure resources.

The vehicle that was identified in much of the discourse produced by socialist leaders was revolution: a violent seizure of power would provide the means by which their movement could triumph. The people would rise up against the state, causing it and ultimately its ideological apparatus, and most important the established bases of economic production, to collapse, much as had been the case in the French Revolution. Indeed, the French Revolution was cited repeatedly as a precedent for what might be accomplished on a grander scale by the socialist movement. No other historical event played as prominent a role in socialist discourse. Neither the Reformation nor the Enlightenment nor any cultural innovation from the advent of Christianity to the birth of romanticism occupied the socialists' attention to any similar degree, for their hope was bent on changing society, not simply bringing about an intellectual revolution. Only the industrial revolution came close to arousing as much interest, but it tended to be conceived of less as a revolution than as an ongoing process, one that had progressed to a high degree in England but had far to go in most other European countries. It was the French Revolution, just far enough below the historical horizon and yet sufficiently still in mind to be a decisive contributor to the shape of all nineteenth-century social relations, that required explanation and that served as a repertoire for lessons in practical strategy.

The French Revolution required explanation because the working class had participated in it but seemingly had not benefited from it. For Marx, the reason for this failure pointed to the inevitable march of economic conditions in determining the outcome of political events. The working class was not ripe in 1789 to seize power; the bourgeoisie was, and did. Through the events associated with the revolution, the bourgeoisie's long struggle with the aristocracy came to an end, feudalism and the traditional monarchy it had sustained came resolutely to termination, and the capitalist classes rose to a position of unrivaled ascendancy.

The revolution of 1789 offered the most usable precedent from which to draw practical lessons about how to organize the socialist movement not only because it was well known, thereby serving as a vehicle for collective discourse, but also because it provided an illustration of the best and worst in relations between the bourgeoisie and the proletariat in times of social upheaval. On the negative side, it provided a narrative with which to illustrate the dangers of co-operating with the bourgeoisie or of expecting help from the bourgeoisie. On the positive side, it symbolized the possibility of society being fundamentally changed through deliberate, organized activity. It showed, for example, that the force of a majority in society, such as the proletariat was soon expected to be, could not be quashed. As Jean Jaurès observed, the French Revolution had been "the work of an overwhelming and perfectly self-conscious majority," so "in the same way" the socialist revolution would be accomplished "by the definite and harmonious will of the immense majority of the citizens."[33]

For all its talk about revolution, though, the socialist movement failed to make it the vehicle by which their ideals were realized. Not a single revolutionary episode broke out under socialist leadership in the decades before the First World War. Revolution served only as an important rhetorical device. In looking backward to the French

Revolution socialists could conceive of radical social transformation as a real possibility, and in looking forward to the revolution of the proletariat they gained hope and inspiration. But the means by which their ideology found expression in the interim were quite different.

The actual vehicle that became the means of embodying and transmitting socialism was the political party. Though their purpose was ostensibly the representation of popular sentiment in the political process, political parties became an important new mode of producing and disseminating cultural products. With the major culture-producing institutions closely aligned with the upper social strata, party mobilization provided the most viable means through which to articulate oppositional views.

Political parties emerged in Europe during the first half of the nineteenth century, although in England they had functioned actively during much of the eighteenth century on a somewhat restricted scale. Their emergence was contingent on a number of factors, not least of which was the growing importance of legislative functions as a check on the activities of monarchs or prime ministers and their executive bureaucracies. In many instances legislative assemblies also performed a coordinating function among the diverse agencies of the expanding central bureaucracy. With the expansion of lower houses in the various legislative assemblies came an increasing need for organization both among deputies in formulating proposals and between deputies and the electorate in mobilizing support during elections. Party organization grew in response to this need, forming coherence around identifiable policy positions, interest groups, and constituencies.[34] As informal bodies without constitutional recognition or official capacities within the established bureaucracy, they relied heavily on patronage and on ideologically defined moral obligations for articulating the social relations of their members. The oppositional role that immediately became part of the relation between parties also contributed to this tendency toward patronage and ideology. Thus parties became one of the chief locations in which ideology was produced, debated, modified, and disseminated.

Indeed, it is significant that the idea of ideology itself developed in close conjunction with the emergence of political parties. Engaged as they were in competition with one another, parties came to represent ideas that were considered expressions not of a "general will" or of an underlying cultural consensus but of a fraction of the public or a special group in pursuit of its own interests. Hence the accusation

of being "ideological" became a frequent charge in the political debates among party members. And in seeking ways to define and
distinguish the character of competing parties, analysts came to consider an ideological position, goal, or set of shared beliefs the essential
component of parties themselves.

Like other carriers of ideology, parties developed a bureaucratic
structure that required resources to maintain and that in turn played
an important role in ideological production. The bureaucratization
of party politics developed, initially, less from the interests of party
leaders themselves than from the close (and yet competitive) relation
that existed between parties and the state. Parties in power typically
drew on the state bureaucracy to supply leadership, to exercise control over party members, and to supply rewards and sanctions for
party service. As a result, opposition parties discovered the importance of organizational machinery for their activities as well.

It was, then, principally the organizational context of the political
party in which socialist ideology developed and spread. Beginning
in 1863 with the formation of the General German Workingmen's
Association, socialist parties spread during the next three decades to
nearly every country in Europe: to Spain in 1879, France in 1882,
Great Britain in 1883, Belgium in 1885, Norway in 1887, Austria
in 1888, Sweden and the Netherlands in 1889, and Italy in 1892.[35]
Usually the formal appearance of socialist parties was preceded by
grass-roots activity at the local level, by some cooperation with international socialist groups or contact with socialist émigrés, and by
efforts to moblize workers for strikes or electoral activities. But the
political party itself became the main mechanism by which socialist
ideals were made known. Parties sponsored newspapers and lectures,
elected deputies to parliamentary assemblies who served as spokespersons for party policies, and more generally utilized their membership rolls and the votes they could obtain in popular elections as
symbols of the strength of the socialist movement.

To say that party organizations were the carriers of socialist
ideology is not to suggest that the rank and file members of these
movements joined for ideological reasons or voted for socialist candidates out of any deep commitment to socialist doctrines. People
joined and voted for a multitude of reasons. What little evidence
there is on the motivations and understandings of socialist workers
during this period indicates that their commitment to orthodox teachings of the movement was often shallow or poorly expressed. Never-

theless, it was precisely their commitment, from attendance at socialist lectures to voting for socialist deputies, that dramatized the reality of socialism. In these collective activities socialism became an ideological force quite different from any mere intellectual orientation or philosophical theory. Its abstract theoretical arguments became embodied in collective discourse and in collective action, thereby rendering it a social reality that had a definite relation with its social environment.

Like other organizational vessels, socialist parties experienced varying degrees of success, depending on the kinds of relations they were able to establish with their environments and the resources these environments supplied. In Germany, for example, the socialist party gained a relatively strong following and was able to make itself the flagship of the international socialist movement by accomplishing sizable victories in German elections. In France and England the socialist parties experienced much more limited success. And in other countries socialist achievements also varied widely.

Why these variations followed the patterns they did has been the question underlying most theories of the social conditions influencing the growth of socialism. In the spirit of socialism itself, most of these theories have emphasized class relations. Taking the proletariat as the main constituency, and therefore the main resource, for the various socialist movements, these theories have attributed variations in socialist accomplishments to such factors as the level, rate, and timing of industrialization; the overall size, growth, and geographic concentration of the industrial working classes; and characteristics of the proletariat—immiseration, exploitation, dislocation—that might render it amenable to socialist appeals.

Some of these theories have found limited support in empirical investigations. But most studies have generated enough anomalous results that the usefulness of examining additional factors is suggested. The chapters that follow will consider not only the broad economic changes that influenced the growth of the industrial working classes but also the ways in which these changes in the social environment interacted with the state to shape the specific institutional context in which socialist party activity was carried out.[36]

The period under scrutiny extends from 1864, the year in which the First International was founded in London, to 1914, the eve of the First World War and the year in which the Second International fell into disarray. Although scattered utopian and socialist movements were in existence well before the last third of the nineteenth century, particularly in England, where Owenites and Chartists had developed socialist experiments, and on the Continent, where socialist collectives had been active during the revolutions of 1848, this was the period in which socialism matured into a mass movement with a well-defined ideology and a vast social infrastructure capable of supporting the production of socialist ideas and of attempting to put these ideas into practice.[37]

At the start of this period most of the intellectual groundwork of Marxian socialism had already been laid: Marx and Engels had formulated the basic principles of dialectical materialism and of working-class revolution in the 1840s, and even Marx's long-overdue first volume of *Capital* was finally published in 1867; pockets of utopian socialist writers had been at work for nearly half a century; and during the struggles of 1848, producers' cooperatives and other forms of collectivism had been experimented with widely. From the 1870s onward, moreover, the socialist movement was increasingly embroiled in its own internecine rivalries to such an extent that later generations of scholars have found it an almost impenetrable morass of personalities, acronyms, and tedious debates over doctrinal subtleties. Indeed, many of the more general surveys of socialist history pass quickly over this period to the more glamorous events of 1917.

Yet it is precisely the period between the 1860s and the First World War that is most telling as far as understanding the institutionalization of European socialist ideology is concerned. Although many of the intellectual antecedents had already been expressed, just as they had in the decades preceding the Reformation and the Enlightenment, these antecedents still remained the scattered thoughts of isolated writers whose work was not yet well known, let alone the basis of any large-scale ideological movement. Neither the social resources necessary for any sustained, organized process of ideological production nor the conditions giving this process its own institutional identity were yet in place. The complex adjustments involved in transforming intellectual utterances into an ideological form distinctly articulated with its social context were also largely in the future. Between 1870 and 1914, amidst the competition among the various socialist factions, the selective interaction between environment and ideas began to mold a distinct form of democratic Marxian socialism. As in the sixteenth and eighteenth centuries, the new ideology prospered to a significantly greater degree under some conditions than it did under others, thereby rendering possible comparisons from which to generate inferences about the social conditions of ideological production, selection, and institutionalization. In the course of its development after the 1860s, the socialist movement also had to contend increasingly with the practical consequences of its own theoretical formulations. The ensuing debate over the relations between theory and practice was in itself to become an important feature of the process of ideological articulation.

12 &

Bismarck's Contribution
to German Socialism

AS AN ORGANIZED movement socialism began in Germany in 1863 with Ferdinand Lassalle's founding of the General German Workers' Association. Six years later a more Marxist-oriented movement came into existence with the formation of the Social Democratic Labor party, and in 1875, as a result of the Gotha conference, the two parties united to form the Socialist Labor party. From 1878 to 1890 the strength of the socialist movement continued to grow, despite Bismarck's antisocialist legislation, and under a reorganization in 1891 the Social Democratic party (SPD) was born. Its successes over the next two decades in enlisting members, publishing socialist newspapers, attracting revenue, sponsoring candidates, and winning elections were nothing short of spectacular. When records began to be kept in 1906, the party's membership stood at 384,327, and by the outbreak of the First World War more than 1 million were on its rolls with another 2.5 million on the rolls of affiliated labor unions.[1]

Much of the SPD's ideology was oriented toward purely practical issues, such as the attainment of universal suffrage, a graduated income tax, the eight hour work day, restrictions on child labor, and social insurance. Yet the party continued to articulate Marx's economic analysis of the contradictions of capitalism and staunchly advanced demands for the social ownership of the means of production. By the end of the period under consideration, the SPD in Germany had thus become one of the principal European locations in which Marxist socialism had become institutionalized.

The SPD's growth occurred during the same period as Germany's rise to industrial prominence, attracting much of its support from the burgeoning industrial proletariat. It thus appeared to represent the fulfillment of its own prophecies: socialism as the ideological consequence of industrial capitalism. Yet neither the proletariat nor socialism was simply the inevitable or predetermined consequence of industrialization alone, as the relative failures of the socialist movements in France and Britain were to demonstrate. German socialism was shaped, just as the German Enlightenment had been, by a complex relation between economic forces and the structure of the German state. That Germany should have become one of the leading bastions of socialism was certainly not the intention of Bismarck or any of his top officials. It was, rather, the unintended consequence of structural arrangements that gave the SPD its unique opportunity to mobilize sufficient resources to become institutionalized.

German Industrialization

Although particular estimates vary, all indications show that the German economy grew rapidly during the nineteenth century, reaching a particularly rapid tempo in the final decades before the First World War. Paul Bairoch, for example, estimates that gross national product at constant prices grew sevenfold between 1830 and 1913, with the largest decadal increases occurring between 1880 and 1913.[2] Knut Borchardt provides a somewhat more conservative estimate for the first half of the nineteenth century, suggesting that net national product remained relatively stable until around 1855, but agrees that the following decades produced a dramatic increase in net national product, totaling approximately 45 million marks in 1913 at constant prices compared with only 10 million marks in 1855—a threefold increase in per capita product.[3]

Increases in agricultural productivity were the source of some of this growth.[4] But the largest share came from rapid expansion in the industrial sector. Alan Milward and S. B. Saul calculate that industrial production rose 3.8 percent annually between 1850 and 1914, while agricultural production grew at a rate of only 1.6 percent annually.[5] B. R. Mitchell's index of industrial production for Germany shows a doubling in volume between 1850 and 1870, another doubling between 1870 and 1890, and a 250 percent increase between 1890 and 1913.[6] Over the same period the contribution of industry to national product increased from 21 percent to 43 percent, while that of commerce grew from 8 percent to 15 percent and agriculture declined from 47 percent to 25 percent. In comparison with other industrialized countries, Germany therefore came to resemble England in sectoral contribution and to a degree exceeded France in industrial proportion.

The growth of German industry was equally reflected in capital stock, the amount of which increased five times between 1850 and 1913, with the most rapid rates of accumulation occurring prior to the crash of 1873 and again after 1896.[7] Railways constituted one of the most significant elements in the growth of capital stock, rising tenfold in mileage between 1850 and 1913, and generating vast growth in related industries such as iron, coal, and lignite production.[8] By 1879 railroads constituted approximately 62 percent of all capital stock in industry and commerce.[9]

The greatest effect of industrialization as far as socialism was concerned was, of course, to add immensely to the size and social prominence of the industrial labor force. As a proportion of the total labor force nonagricultural workers grew from 36 percent in 1871 to 64 percent in 1895.[10] This change dramatically distinguished the period after 1870 from the preceding decades; for example, data from Prussia reveal that nonagricultural workers accounted for 28 percent of the labor force in 1872, almost the same percentage as in 1816 (26.5 percent), but by 1910 this proportion had risen to 60 percent.[11] In absolute terms the number of industrial workers in Germany nearly doubled from 5 million in 1871 to 9.5 million in 1910.[12]

Structurally the composition of the industrial work force also changed in ways generally regarded as conducive to socialist organization. Extremely rapid growth occurred in metals and mining, bringing their total to 33 percent of the industrial labor force in 1913 compared with only 12 percent in 1846, whereas textiles and clothing dropped proportionately, from 47 percent in 1846 to 19 percent in 1913.[13] Thus a growing share of the industrial work force came to be made up of new recruits from rural areas without strong ties to guild forms of organization.[14] By the end of the century only about one eighth of all skilled workers still belonged to guilds, the majority of guild regulations having been abolished in 1871.[15] As the size of industrial establishments expanded, a greater share of the labor force also came to be concentrated in mass settings, both by employment and by residence: between 1882 and 1907 the proportion of industrial workers employed by firms with fifty or more employees grew from 26 percent to 46 percent; and the proportion of the total population living in urban areas rose from 20 percent to 60 percent—an absolute increase from 7 million to 40 million.[16]

The impact of German industrialization was thus to create a vast pool of human resources toward which the socialist movement could direct its appeals and efforts. Migration to the cities, rapid turnover in the composition of neighborhoods, and the dissolution of guilds created a vacuum in community ties that socialist organizations could attempt to fill.[17] In the rapidly industrializing area around Düsseldorf, for example, approximately one resident in every two during the 1890s was a recent immigrant; about one in seven had migrated within the past year; almost as many emigrated each year; and the majority who came were young, male, and single.[18] Socialist groups were, in fact, particularly effective at recruiting such workers, especially the ones who were otherwise unattached and isolated from established neighborhoods and family relationships. Mary Nolan's study of Düsseldorf, for example, shows that from 1897 to 1908, between 80 and 90 percent of all new SPD members were recent immigrants to the district.[19]

The effectiveness of the SPD in attracting the displaced and unattached was in large measure a result of its efforts to reconstruct a moral community for workers of this kind. Although the SPD utilized the printed word to attract members, much of its work focused on building small groups in which the interaction, if not the ideology, would draw workers into its ranks. During the period of antisocialist legislation large numbers of reading societies and athletic clubs were founded, at first to camouflage political activities; but by the 1890s these organizations had become so successful that clubs of virtually every conceivable sort were added. Some were purely recreational; others provided for the material needs of workers. In one writer's words: "The party sponsored extensive social, cultural, and educational endeavors; it owned an impressive network of newspapers and publishing houses; it ran insurance programs, burial societies, and travel clubs; and in conjunction with the closely allied trade unions, it sponsored facilities in which itinerant and indigent workers could find shelter and support."[20] According to a survey of

German workers conducted in 1912, the fears that concerned workers above all were individual calamities owing to accidents and illness.
Any kind of "moral economy" that included insurance and protection
against such disasters was, therefore, likely to prove attractive.[21]

Less formally, there were socialist taverns, cycling and hiking
clubs, choral groups, smoking clubs, brass bands, the People's Stage,
and even a Proletarian Freethinker's League for philosophical discussion.[22] In Nuremberg there were not only formal educational
programs, cooperatives, and housing programs for workers but also
gymnastic, singing, cycling, and discussion groups. A contemporary
estimated that the number of these organizations had grown to more
than fifty by 1905 and that as many as 32,000 workers were involved.[23] In Düsseldorf at least a third of the SPD membership was
involved in some form of organized athletic, musical, or cultural
association.[24] Overall, some 190,000 workers had become members
of socialist athletic groups by 1914, 160,000 had joined cycling organizations, and 100,000 belonged to singing groups.[25] Socialist
ideas, therefore, could be spread by word of mouth in formal gatherings, at local inns and taverns, in workplaces, and through family
networks and kinship relations. Moral obligations were established
which bound individuals to one another perhaps more than to any
formal statement of socialist doctrine. Yet the loyalties established
were also distinctly socialist in identity and were expressed in a richly
connotative socialist jargon. Words like *Vorwärts, Arbeiter, Genosse,*
and *Frei* acquired strong in-group meanings which signaled loyalty
to comrades and set them off from nonsocialists.

In-group loyalty was also cultivated through rituals and festivals
which, like those of the Reformation and Enlightenment, translated
theoretical abstractions into symbolic events that desacralized the
moral basis of established ideologies and dramatized new concepts
of moral obligation. Patriotic festivals that united large segments of
the population in ritual obeisance to the state were singled out for
special ridicule. The socialist press satirized these events, much as
the Protestant reformers had satirized the mass, as superstitious traditions which kept workers in ignorance and bondage.[26] In their place
workers' festivals were established. Imperial banners were replaced
by the red flag; patriotic eulogies found substitutes in memorials for
slain or imprisoned comrades; alternative holidays were designated;
and new songs and rites were made the centerpiece of workers'
festivals.[27]

For workers who became more deeply involved in the movement, the richly symbolic interaction among fellow socialists at the grass-roots level was also supplemented by the pageantry of annual socialist congresses. The SPD developed a highly disciplined form of party organization—so efficient in fact that it served as inspiration for both Max Weber's admiring comments and Robert Michel's more critical treatise on German bureaucratization. The annual congresses played a crucial role in conducting the party's business. Yet they served a ceremonial role much like that of modern political conventions rather than simply performing bureaucratic tasks: "They were also celebrations of the movement's victims, the year's major social event, and a time for . . . spiritual renewal. The pageantry of the congresses . . . was planned by the locals . . . and these organizations often seemed to be competing to hold the grandest festival. Delegates frequently returned home from these gatherings rejuvenated and strengthened by the camaraderie and good will of the three- or four-day gatherings."[28]

In addition to creating a large mass of workers with susceptibilities to such gatherings, industrialization also supplied economic resources that proved to be of immense value to the SPD. Although workers were attracted to socialism because of harsh working conditions and unfair employment practices, economic "immiseration" as such was not a leading factor in the development of the SPD. To the contrary, socialist organizations grew and experienced greater success in achieving their objectives when economic conditions were prosperous than when they were depressed.[29] Workers who lost jobs or who lived near subsistence level could afford neither to pay dues nor to subscribe to socialist newspapers. Thus, during the depression that began in 1873, the movement experienced setbacks rather than gains.

The German economy was not hit as hard by the depression of the 1870s as were the economies of many other countries, however. Despite continued stagnation in the agricultural sector until 1896, the industrial sector actually experienced a relatively quick recovery and grew steadily during the 1880s and 1890s. Indeed, real wages (which had been static since at least 1820) began to rise sometime between 1870 and 1880, and by 1913 had at least doubled in most industries while tripling in some others.[30]

These increases provided the basis from which the socialist movement was able to establish educational societies, pay for lecturers, support party officials, and publish newspapers. One of the features of the SPD that most impressed Robert Michels (writing in 1915), in fact, was its ability: "to pay for all services to the party, from the most trifling notice contributed to a newspaper to the lengthiest public discourse. While this deprives the party to a large extent of the spirit of heroism and of enthusiasm, and of work done by voluntary and spontaneous collaboration, it gives to the organization a remarkable cohesion, and an authority over the personnel which, though doubtless detracting from its elasticity and its spirit of initiative, and, in essence, tending to impair the very socialist mentality, constitutes none the less one of the most important and indispensable bases of the party life."[31] If the ability to pay for party work had negative as well as positive aspects, having the necessary financial resources to engage in political activities was nevertheless a distinct boon to the socialist movement in Germany.

It was a boon, in particular, to the SPD's extensive publishing enterprise, which provided the means for disseminating socialist ideology. In 1890 the movement had sixty newspapers and periodicals with a total circulation of 254,000.[32] By 1913 the number of newspapers and periodicals had risen to eighty and total circulation had mushroomed to 1.5 million.[33] Newspapers served not only as a means of disseminating ideas but also as a revenue-generating mechanism. Individuals who purchased subscriptions to party newspapers generally received membership without paying dues; subscriptions thus became an attractive way of taking in money.

Party revenues rose accordingly, even at a much more rapid pace than membership: from 1.1 million marks in 1891 to 9.5 million marks in 1900 and 82 million marks in 1913, compared with only a tenfold increase in membership over the same period.[34] Much of the income was plowed back into publishing or other educational projects, such as a socialist school founded in Berlin in 1891, a training academy for party officials founded in 1906, and the more than 1,100 workers' libraries which were founded prior to 1914.

But the expense of running candidates in elections as well as paying stipends for those who won required the largest proportion of party funds. In virtually every election prior to 1914 the party was able to run a candidate in nearly every electoral district. Often these candidates had little chance of winning, and in some races the party was forced to run the same candidate in several districts because of a shortage of available leaders. Nevertheless, this strategy successfully established the party's image as a national party and insti-

tutionalized the idea of socialism as a political reality.[35] Candidates
who won, no matter what their party, were forced to pay their own
salaries. Thus the party's finances also made it possible for workers
to sustain the costs of a political career.

The expansion of the German economy, then, contributed in
some direct ways to the socialist movement by creating human and
financial resources which the SPD could mobilize. But the availability
of displaced workers with rising wages and sociability needs was one
thing; the evolution of a massive socialist movement was another.
Rapid industrialization may have contributed to the need for workers'
organizations, but it also made fulfilling this need more difficult.
Workers in large firms, for example, were particularly susceptible to
repression because of fluctuations in the demand and supply of labor
and the ease, especially in unskilled occupations, with which employers could bring in strikebreakers. If studies of cities such as
Düsseldorf and Berlin point to a relation between socialism and rapid
industrialization, other studies cast doubt on this relation; for example, Lawrence Schofer's discussion of worker protest in Upper
Silesia provides a clear example of an area in which socialism had
virtually no appeal despite rapid industrialization and attendant labor
problems.[36] In Leipzig political organizing among workers seems to
have depended more on the persistence of family and neighborhood
ties than on the disruption of these ties.[37] In Bremen rapid industrial
growth appears to have made the bourgeoisie *more* responsive to
workers' needs rather than less, and socialist organizers succeeded
only to the extent that their appeals included broad democratic principles which drew in the petty bourgeoisie as well as the proletariat.[38]
The limitations of industrialization as an explanation for the kind of
socialism that developed in Germany are, however, evident even in
the case of Düsseldorf.

Located on the Rhine between Cologne and the Ruhr, Düsseldorf lay in the heart of German industrialization and underwent all
the dramatic changes associated with this process. Heavy metals,
smelting, railroad equipment, steam engines, machine tools, and instruments were among its principal industries. As demand for these
items grew both nationally and internationally, the city's labor force
expanded dramatically. By the mid-1880s it totaled approximately
67,000, and in the next decade this figure nearly doubled. Over the
same period there was also a growing concentration of workers in
large firms: by the 1890s nearly half the entire labor force was em-

ployed in firms with more than one hundred employees. Yet for all of this, the impact of socialism was quite meager. Despite a labor force of 127,000 in 1907, SPD votes in the district totaled only 25,389, and SPD membership numbered only 2,560.[39] The case of Düsseldorf also raises questions about the effectiveness of the SPD's ideological activities. Attendance at party lectures was sporadic; educational programs were often poorly designed; and workers appear to have been more interested in vivid personalities than in party rhetoric.

Other studies, even those that credit the SPD's grass-roots activities with much significance, raise questions about the degree to which working-class culture was actually penetrated by these activities.[40] Despite the fact that a segment of the working class was available for recruitment into socialist organizations, the German working class was by no means in the throes of disintegration or atomization as a result of industrialization. There were instead numerous organizations competing to provide solidarity and social support for the working class. Evidence from local communities suggests in fact that socialists were forced to organize themselves into such a multiplicity of associations precisely because the working class on the whole was already highly organized.[41] If it was to gain visibility at all amidst the wealth of religious groups, Christian workers' associations, mass political parties, cultural groups, and recreation clubs, the SPD had to develop a similar menu of programs.[42] To the extent that the SPD experienced greater success in organizing the working class than some of its religious and political competitors, then, questions also must be raised concerning the reasons why churches, trade unions, or other political parties failed to make greater headway.

Another difficulty with linking socialism in Germany too directly to industrialization lies in the fact that industrialization was not a spontaneous process developing in isolation from other social conditions, nor was it alone sufficient to produce a homogeneous working class with common interests. Although industrialization came about in Germany, as it did elsewhere, through the stimulus of technological innovation and increased demand, it was also a function of strategic investment, market integration, fiscal planning, and foreign policies, all of which shaped its direction and content.

The consequences of industrialization were also diverse as far as the labor force was concerned. In even the most heavily industrialized areas there were sharp divisions within the working class by sector and by industry so that no more than a quarter might be employed in any one industry while the remainder might be scattered in such diverse employments as carpentry, glassworking, municipal transportation, and metallurgy. Factory size and skill levels also varied, separating workers into groups of no more than five to upwards of a thousand by place and creating differentials in wages and employability by degree of experience and training.

Overall, the total industrial work force still accounted for as little as a quarter of the German laboring population as late as 1907; approximately one-fourth of this number still lived in rural areas, and a sizable minority were women who had yet to receive the franchise.[43] While it was perhaps true that workers were bound to a common destiny by the fact that others controlled the means of production, they nevertheless remained a highly heterogeneous group. In many respects they shaded imperceptibly into the ranks of the skilled artisans, lower middle class, and petty bourgeoisie, rather than forming an identifiable proletariat. As Carl Landauer has remarked, even after the middle of the nineteenth century "the political and ideological separation of the proletariat from the middle classes was still incomplete."[44] Yet, as the socialist movement developed, it was able to create a political agenda which found common cause with a good many workers and forged them into a major political party. It was in fact the political context that shaped both German industrialization and the socialist response.

The Role of the State

The principal roles played by the state in shaping German socialism consisted of, first, encouraging the rapid expansion of German industry; second, maintaining the power of a conservative ruling class which systematically undermined the strength of the liberal parties; third, stamping the socialist movement with a distinct political identity; and fourth, channeling the socialist movement's activities toward parliamentary politics. The state's relation to the churches and educational system also played an indirect role in shaping German socialism.

Germany's rapid rate of industrialization between the 1840s and the First World War was as much a product of state intervention as it was the basis on which a strong national state apparatus was erected.

Other conditions that played an important role in this process included capital accumulation in the agricultural sector, resulting from increasing export demand and an availability of cheap labor, and technical innovations in industries such as textiles, chemicals, and smelting. But profits from agriculture were as likely to be invested in foreign securities or spent on luxury goods as they were to be spent on industrialization unless some other force made the latter a compelling option, and technical innovation alone was scarcely a guarantee of industrialization since competitors in England and France tended to be in the forefront of many of these innovations.[45] The state was thus a key factor in channeling investments and creating favorable markets.

Prior to the 1840s or 1850s the various German states had remained relatively uninvolved in promoting industry. According to Knut Borchardt, "The authorities were inclined rather to tolerate the evolution of industry; they took an interest in fostering the workers' diligence and in safeguarding 'the nourishment of the people,' but their support for the tendency towards concentration was lukewarm."[46] Nevertheless, the bureaucratic apparatus which had developed, especially in Prussia, during the eighteenth century and which had come during the nineteenth century to penetrate the civil society ever more pervasively provided a means for state intervention in the economy. As Reinhart Kosselleck has shown, by the middle of the nineteenth century the Prussian state had established a clear precedent for taking an active part in promoting economic growth.[47]

Other than the Zollverein tariff policies, which created an infrastructure for economic cooperation among the northern German states, the most important activity promoted by the state was the development of the German railway system. For military reasons, and because it was an enterprise of such magnitude that only political supervision could ensure its success, the railway system was largely the creation of the state. During the 1840s and 1850s approximately half of all the investment capital for railways was contributed by the state, and by 1870 approximately half of the German railway system was state owned.[48] The railway system naturally played a major role in stimulating the iron and coal industries as well and provided a valuable facility for the integration of domestic markets.[49]

National unification in 1871 provided a further boon to business investments. Not only did unification create a politically stable environment in which business could grow; it also created an enlarged marketing zone for German products, established uniform legal guarantees for property, made available a large financial pool for industrial loans, and led to the formation of state owned companies. These developments favored private entrepreneurship to the extent that between 1871 and 1873 alone, 726 new joint-stock companies were established, compared with only 276 during the preceding eighty years.[50] In the same two year period 1,500 kilometers of railway were completed, pig iron consumption nearly doubled, and coal output grew by approximately 20 percent.

The financial crash of 1873 temporarily halted these rapid increases, but the reversals within industries closely connected to the state were generally less severe than in other sectors of the economy. Railway construction continued, and by the end of the decade foreign demand for German railway equipment had recovered; protective tariffs saved the textile industry and agricultural markets from foreign competition. The 1880s witnessed another significant expansion in foreign markets through the state's acquisition of colonies in the Kamerun (1884), East and Southwest Africa (1885), and New Guinea (1886). After 1890 the economy again began to expand rapidly, especially in industries such as chemicals and metalworking that were promoted by the state. The fact that German industrialization produced a large industrial labor force from which the socialist movement could arise was, then, in no small measure the product of state intervention.

The formation of a socialist party was, however, shaped in a much more direct, albeit complex, manner by the state insofar as the state also played a decisive role in supporting a conservative element of the ruling class against the more liberal segments of the bourgeoisie. Tracing the contours of this process is by no means a straightforward task, given the complexities of the interests involved, but it requires recognizing the potential for political cooperation across a broad segment of the left, including the working class, and the state's resources for undermining such a coalition, thus leaving the working class to the virtually exclusive appeals of the socialist party.

During the 1850s and 1860s the left became a relatively strong force in German society, developing in such a way as to make it a potential ally of the working class. Economic expansion during this period created some of the same internal factions within the state that had been evident during the Enlightenment. Bureaucratic growth and political centralization raised questions once again about

constitutional bases of opposition and civil liberties. The move toward German unification in particular gave these questions urgency
as the smaller German states vied with Prussia to install a more
loosely integrated federalist system of government rather than being
absorbed into the Prussian oligarchy. An identifiable "liberal" opposition crystallized around the federalist interests of the smaller
German states and gained the support of some segments of the
bourgeoisie, especially the lower middle class of small shopkeepers
and manufacturers, whose interests appeared to be threatened by
greater political centralization. This coalition also included a substantial number of professionals and civil servants within the bureaucracy itself who were ideologically committed to greater
constitutional controls over the state—a position that reflected tensions within the state itself between the more rationalized, semiautonomous segments of the bureaucracy and those more closely
allied with the monarchy.[51] The liberal movement thus represented
a diverse set of interests that stood generally in opposition to the
more conservative interests of the rural aristocracy, army, and monarchy.[52]

Just as in the eighteenth century, the fracture that became evident within the German polity between the 1850s and 1870s generated widespread debate among intellectuals concerning the nature
and legitimate distribution of authority. Among those who contributed to these discussions, Heinrich von Treitschke, David Friedrich
Strauss, Wilhelm Dilthey, Karl Marx, and somewhat later Max Weber
stand as leading examples. But in other respects the political situation
of the mid-nineteenth century was quite different from that of the
eighteenth century, and for this reason the manner in which structural
conflict contributed to the production of ideology was also different.
The development of constitutional representation, which had taken
noticeable strides between 1789 and 1848, now made it possible for
oppositional politics to be channeled through the legislative process.
The gradual extension of the franchise and the rise of the political
press also served to focus political debate on issues of electoral politics. At the time of German unification the liberal opposition had
not yet developed the organizational structure of a modern political
party, but its chief locus of power resided in the imperial Reichstag
and in regional or municipal legislative bodies.

Unification successfully drew some of the upper bourgeoisie
away from this liberal coalition, since a strong central government

promised to open up markets, provide military protection against France and Austria, and guarantee domestic stability. The industrialists whose interests were identified with railway construction and related enterprises such as iron and coal production appear to have fallen into this category.[53] Nevertheless, the liberals' strength in legislative bodies remained a force that any prime minister had to recognize.[54] Indeed, Bismarck seems to have forged his rise to power by carefully exploiting the liberals as ballast against the aristocracy.[55]

The liberal segment of the bourgeoisie was by no means an entirely natural ally of the working class. The two were divided over fundamental economic interests such as wages, work hours, and factory regulations. Like the rural aristocracy, the bourgeoisie was fearful of the potential for social disruption if workers were allowed to participate fully in electoral politics. Sentiment still ran deep that only the propertied elite was capable of exercising power responsibly. It was far easier for the liberals to countenance self-help programs for workers than to give them political power. Yet the liberal bourgeoisie was better situated to make use of an alliance with the working class than any other elite group.

The need for a skilled labor force had been recognized on a sufficiently broad scale that from the 1830s the bourgeoisie had supported both public and private efforts to improve the literacy and educational levels of workers. As in England, these efforts not only focused on the acquisition of technical skills but also included activities aimed at fostering bourgeois tastes and morality among workers. Turnover among employees, often ranging as high as 50 percent in a single year, was a source of much discussion about the need for improved wages and better working conditions. For other members of the bourgeoisie, the line between themselves as owners of small shops or farms and skilled craftsmen tended to be blurred by common neighborhoods, religion, and income levels. But most important, after universal male suffrage was granted in 1871, the working class provided a vast resource for the liberals in their opposition to the conservative aristocracy.

The potential for cooperation between liberals and the working class was in fact realized to a degree in the 1860s, when the leading organizations representing working class interests were the Workmen's Educational Societies. The activities of these organizations, focusing on cultural, literary, self-help, and reform policies, were more wide ranging and more practical than the more radical programs of the early Lassallean socialists and thus attracted a much broader base of support. Bourgeois liberals were particularly prominent in these organizations, especially in central and southern Germany, where anti-Prussian, antimonarchical, and proparliamentary convictions were strong. It was in these organizations that the potential for a broad coalition on the left involving both workers and bourgeoisie could be seen. Indeed it appeared for a brief time that the political arm of this movement, the Volkspartei, might succeed in uniting major segments of the two classes into a powerful political bloc.[56]

Although the socialist leadership seceded from the Volkspartei in 1869, the goals of the two parties remained sufficiently similar to make coalition politics a conceivable option. Anti-Prussian views, republican ideals, suffrage, and parliamentary reforms, as well as numerous secondary issues concerning separation of church and state, municipal administration, and free association provided a strong basis for cooperation. Even the more extreme Marxist assumptions about economic change which began to penetrate the socialist movement in these years were tempered by practical leanings toward educational associations and parliamentary politics as short-term tactics for realizing economic goals.

The failure of the liberals to contain the working class or to draw the socialist movement into a closer alliance has often seemed inevitable with the advantage of hindsight. Yet it is difficult to account for this failure strictly on the basis of assertions about contradictory interests, as comparisons with France and England will illustrate. The socialist movement in Germany grew in direct proportion to the decline of the liberal parties, not because of the rise of the proletariat alone but as a result of the changing relations between the liberal parties and the state.

Although the German state is generally thought to have been impeded in its progress toward consolidating power because of the regional strength of the various principalities, these obstacles were rather quickly overcome after 1871, and an increasingly powerful conservative coalition gave both strength and stability to the new national system of government. The traditional power of the territorial princes was undercut by basing election to the imperial Reichstag on universal suffrage by secret ballot. The idea of a strong state as an essential guarantee of social order against the divisive forces of regional, religious, and economic factions quickly gave the new system legitimacy.[57] But most of all, the dominance of Prussia within the national system and the conservative nature of Prussian politics determined the nature of the state. According to Gordon Craig, "The continued existence within the Reich of an enlarged Prussian state with a virtual monopoly of military power, with a position in the Bundesrat superior to that of the other states, and with a parliamentary system of its own, based on a form of suffrage which was not democratic but favored the propertied classes, was the best possible assurance against any possibility of the federal government succumbing to the forces of liberalism and democracy."[58] Dominating nearly two-thirds of the territory of imperial Germany, Prussia exercised a tremendous influence over the national state. As supreme commander of the army, head of the civil service and diplomatic corps, and supervisor of the administrative apparatus of the Reich ministries, the king of Prussia along with his chancellors and top ministers exercised control over vast social and economic resources and wielded enormous power. Any political parties formed in opposition to this system were bound to be greatly influenced by its character.

The conservative policies of the Prussian and later of the imperial state, including policies opposing the liberal views of many business and professional interests, were in the first instance a result of the continuing influence of the Junker aristocracy. Although the aristocracy's autonomy had been reduced during the eighteenth century and brought under the umbrella of the bureaucracy, these reforms provided a basis for longer term influence through the bureaucracy, particularly as the state came to depend more on the military services of the aristocracy.[59] The economic position of the aristocracy also contributed to its continuing political strength. Land in Prussia was concentrated in large holdings owned by the aristocracy, and much of this land was committed to the production of wheat and rye for export.[60] The share of land owned by the aristocracy actually declined during the nineteenth century, but the interests of smaller operators were sufficiently similar to those of the aristocracy, because both drew income from direct sales rather than rents, that the aristocracy was able to maintain its position as representative of a large rural bloc in Prussian politics.[61] This position tended to be reflected in the composition of the bureaucracy. The German state was not aristocratic simply in the sense of serving aristocratic interests or emulating aristocratic tastes. As Heinrich von Treitschke observed proudly in his treatise on politics in 1916: "In England we find the purely aristocratic ambition, with us it takes monarchic-bureaucratic form."[62]

Arno J. Mayer has suggested that the state bureaucracies everywhere in Europe were characterized by highly conservative orientations right up to the First World War: "The bureaucracies were not politically neutral institutions but instruments of system-maintenance . . . In addition to being conservative by provenance and training, bureaucrats became conservative by function, and their professional mind and interest predisposed them to routine and caution. Moreover, all along and particularly in times of crisis, reflexive conservatism . . . was a prerequisite for promotion, especially to the higher administrative and executive echelons."[63] If this description is generally accurate, it is especially applicable in the case of the German bureaucracy.[64]

During the half century preceding the First World War the aristocracy held a majority of the influential posts and utilized these positions to cast official policy in a conservative direction. In Prussia the aristocracy dominated all levels of government, accounting for 62 percent of the provincial governors, 73 percent of the district superintendents, and 62 percent of the county commissioners in 1888-1891. By 1911 the proportion of provincial governorships held by the nobility had actually increased to 92 percent, while that among the district superintendents had declined only to 62 percent, and the county commissioners to 56 percent.[65] The legislature was less the preserve of the aristocracy than the bureaucracy, but even here the combination of aristocratic and bureaucratic influence was pronounced. Landowners held 17 percent of the seats in the Prussian Landtag in 1849 and 31 percent in 1912; bureaucrats held 37 percent and 21 percent respectively; and despite the growth of trade, the commercial classes held only 4 percent and 10 percent respectively.[66]

At the national level the aristocracy's influence was weaker than in Prussia alone, and the result of universal suffrage was to reduce considerably this influence in the Reichstag as time passed. Thus in 1871 fully 40 percent of the seats were occupied by nobility, whereas by 1912 this proportion had declined to 14 percent. Over the same period the proportion of seats held by landowners declined from 27 percent to 18 percent, and the proportion held by state officials from 26 percent to 9 percent.[67] Nevertheless, even at the latter date there were more nobles in the Reichstag than there were merchants. If state officials are included, since many were members of the aristocracy, the predominance of conservative elements is evident in all the major Reichstag parties; for example, in 1898 85 percent of the Conservative party deputies were landowners or state officials, as were 86 percent of the Free Conservatives and 46 percent of the National Liberal deputies.[68] In the imperial bureaucracy itself aristocratic influence remained much in evidence, especially at high levels. According to one calculation, half the secretaries of state between 1867 and 1890 were nobles, as were half the councilors in the foreign office and 63 percent of the foreign service officers.

In Germany, to a greater extent than in either France or Britain, then, the aristocracy remained a powerful economic elite throughout the period of rising industrialization. Although its wealth and prestige may have declined relative to that of the industrial bourgeoisie, it was able to exercise concerted political power in the defense of its interests. Its economic strength lay chiefly in the expansion of export markets for the grain grown on large estates in the eastern sections of Prussia. Its political strength lay in its role in the army, the size of which grew from 455,000 troops in 1882 to 646,000 in 1907, and in its virtually unlimited access to offices in the bureaucracy.[70]

The bureaucracy's overall effect on German politics increased in approximate proportion to its size. During the first quarter of the nineteenth century the Prussian bureaucracy had employed some 100,000 officials. By 1852 the total number of officials employed in the territory of the empire stood at 352,000. When the empire was unified in 1871 this number was 539,500, and by 1907 it had grown to 2,046,000.[71] By the last date more than 6 percent of the entire adult male population was thus employed by the state. Among the reasons for this dramatic growth was the state's involvement in a number of new services such as gasworks, railroads, expanded postal services, an enlarged customs bureaucracy, factory inspection, education, social welfare administration, and greater centralization of policing and judicial functions.[72] An indication of the bureaucracy's enormously expanded role was the fact that government expenditures multiplied more than twelve times between 1872 and 1914, the same period during which net national product multiplied less than threefold.

The state's expansion was also particularly evident in the cultural sphere. The close relationship that had developed in Prussia during the eighteenth century between the bureaucracy and institutions of cultural production was no less evident during the last half of the nineteenth century. As the bureaucracy expanded, so did the universities and schools. Between 1876 and 1908 the number of university students rose from 16,124 to 46,632; academic staff increased from 1,521 in 1870 to 3,090 in 1909; and university budgets climbed from 4.7 million marks in 1870 to 23 million marks in 1900 and 39.6 million marks in 1914.[73] Nearly three-fourths of the cost of German higher education was borne by the state, making it relatively inexpensive for students with the necessary training to attend. In return, the state absorbed many of those who graduated into various public offices: 95 percent of theology graduates, 70 percent of law graduates, and 66 percent of graduates in teaching.[74] The universities also served as an important ideological prop of the state. As articulated by Fichte and Hegel, among others, the idea of *Kulturstaat* defined spiritual reality as an emanation of the state. Although some tension was evident between scholars and the state, a higher identity was thought to exist between political and cultural ends. German scholars welcomed the state as the protector and supporter of higher education and saw justice in the privileged role which university graduates were given in the bureaucracy.[75]

Beyond the universities, the school system more generally reflected the conservative ideology of the state. By the second half of the century Germany had the most extensive system of elementary schools in the world, and this system was, in Gordon Craig's words, "one of the principal supports of the existing order."[76] Through the Ministry of Education teachers were directed to emphasize discipline, order, and obedience to authority. Education was utilized increasingly as a vehicle for controlling the working class, a practice that was quite deliberate, to judge from William II's remark in 1889 that he had for some time been "preoccupied with the idea of making the school in its various grades useful in combating the spread of socialistic and communistic ideas."[77] In a more fundamental way, the schools also reinforced the elitist orientation of the state. While most children attended public schools for eight years, children of wealthy parents generally transferred to Gymnasium after four years, where they trained for ten years in preparation for university. Direct outlays, opportunity costs, and differences in subcultures and expectations all combined to limit university attendance to the privileged few who then acquired public office in the state, church, universities, or schools.[78]

With firm roots in a coalition comprising the aristocracy, military, bureaucracy, and the educational system, the state represented a powerful force which gradually weakened the liberal opposition by drawing important segments of the bourgeoisie into a position of loyalty and, by some indications, dependence. In the 1860s Bismarck's anti-Hapsburg Austrian policy had given him support from the king, army, and aristocracy in Prussia, but had alienated the liberal bourgeoisie in the Prussian Landtag. The military successes that followed this policy brought a number of the Prussian liberals around to a more supportive role however. In 1871 the majority position in the new imperial Reichstag was liberal, represented chiefly by the National Liberal party, which had been founded in 1867, and the more extreme Progressive party, founded in 1861.[79] Both parties favored economic growth and recognized the potential role that the bureaucracy and unification could play in promoting growth. But they remained opposition parties in that they favored federalization over centralization, stronger constitutional checks on the monarchy, and measures aimed at limiting the power of the Prussian aristocracy. Lower-level professional civil servants, industrialists, merchants, and other members of the wealthy middle class were among the chief advocates of these liberal policies.[80] Yet by the 1880s much of this opposition had dissipated. As Mary Nolan observes: "In the 1860s some resented aristocratic prominence, but by the 1870s and 1880s they abandoned all resistance and emulated aristocratic culture. The feudalization of the upper bourgeoisie had begun."[81]

The state's successes not only in executing military policies but also in promoting economic growth initiated the process by which significant elements of the bourgeoisie were weaned away from the left. Hans Daalder observes that "large sections of the new industrial capitalist classes were drawn into the existing power cluster, [leaving] the fate of German liberalism to the faltering hands of mainly professional and intellectual groups rather than to the strongly unified economic class."[82] In the 1870s those whose economic interests were linked to the state through railway construction and related industries such as smelting and heavy metals shifted their political allegiance decisively in the direction of the conservative aristocratic state.[83] By the end of the decade the combination of depressed economic conditions, foreign competition, and the state's support of protective tariffs had begun to win over the allegiance of a broader segment of the middle class, including some businessmen and small farmers. At first the agitation for protective tariffs came chiefly from the iron

industry, while farmers and merchants continued to favor more liberal trading policies. But with the appearance of cheap American
grain, even the farmers shifted toward protectionism. Remarking
specifically on the protective tariff of 1879, Milward and Saul suggest
that it reconciled the liberal business classes, which had been the
strongest defenders of constitutionalism, with the more conservative
Junker aristocracy.[84]

The 1880s were thus characterized by a relatively strong conservative bloc organized against a relatively weak liberal sector. The
policy of colonial expansion on which Germany embarked at the
time won further support from the bourgeoisie.[85] Expansion into
colonial areas promised an end to the long recession that had been
plaguing Germany by opening up new markets and providing cheap
sources of raw materials. Liberals were also convinced of the need
for colonial expansion as a general policy to maximize Germany's
strength in the international arena. The working class, however was
generally predisposed against imperial expansion because its material
benefits for the working class were not at all obvious. Imperialism
offered greater profits to the railroads and other industries directly
controlled by the state, but for the average worker the threat of
increased military obligations loomed much more clearly than any
possibility of improved working conditions.[86]

Following another temporary resurgence of liberalism in the
early 1890s, the conservative coalition again succeeded in drawing
an increasing number of the bourgeoisie into its ranks. As a result,
two significant changes became evident in the National Liberal party.
First, its own position shifted increasingly toward the right because
of the conservative influence of the officials and industrialists in its
ranks. Second, an even larger number of the upper bourgeoisie defected from its ranks entirely, with the result that the composition
of the party's delegation in the Reichstag shifted from 40 percent
businessmen in 1890 to only 13 percent businessmen in 1912. A
similar change also occurred in the Left-Liberal delegation: from 27
percent to 7 percent. Over the same period the shifting alliances of
the bourgeoisie also became evident in the widening gap between
the two liberal parties. While the National party retained a greater
number of the upper bourgeoisie, the Left-Liberals came to inherit
the more purely liberal doctrines of the past but were able to gain
adherents only from a petty bourgeoisie consisting of small farmers
and shopkeepers.[87] The net effect of this process was not lost on

contemporaries. Robert Michels, for example, summarized the developments well when he wrote in 1915: "In modern Germany, under our very eyes, there has for the last forty years been proceeding an absorption of the young industrial bourgeoisie into the old aristocracy of birth and the process has of late been enormously accelerated."[88] Or, as Ralf Dahrendorf has concluded more recently: "Germany's rapid industrialization . . . did not lead to the social and political hegemony of a new entrepreneurial class. Instead, an older ruling class—largely Prussian, consisting of aristocratic civil servants, officers, diplomats and landowners—strengthened its position."[89]

Government Policy and the SPD

The conservative government's attempts to weaken, if not actually destroy, the liberal opposition included a policy toward the socialists that appeared harsh and reactionary at the time but in retrospect probably played a positive role in the formation of the SPD. In 1864 overtures toward the socialist Universal German Workingmen's Association had been made by Bismarck himself as a means of driving a wedge between the liberal Progressive party and the working class.[90] The passage of universal suffrage which was declared in 1867 and put into effect in 1871, was another overture to the working class which was aimed at limiting the power of the liberals. As Vernon Lidtke has pointed out, universal suffrage "guaranteed in effect that workers would never be obligated to rely on the bourgeois liberals for entrance into politics."[91]

After 1871 Bismarck's willingness to consider socialist demands greatly diminished as a result of fears aroused by the socialists' role in the Paris Commune and because of the fact that his own position was more secure. The antisocialist legislation which began in 1877 and 1878 cannot be understood simply as an attempt to suppress the socialist movement, however. James J. Sheehan, who is one of the leading authorities on German liberalism in this period, interprets the antisocialist legislation as a deliberate policy aimed at weakening Reichstag interference with the power of the bureaucracy.[92] This legislation was actually part of a two-pronged attack against the liberal opposition in the Reichstag: on the one hand, antisocialist measures were intended to drive a wedge between the labor movement and bourgeois elements of the left; on the other hand, protective tariffs and state monopolies were initiated to create an alliance between the bureaucracy and the wealthier members of the Reichstag.[93] The timing of these moves was dictated by Bismarck's desire to expand government revenue without sacrificing power to the liberal Reichstag, and the opportunity was made possible by two assassination attempts on the emperor which aroused antisocialist sentiments. The anticipated result was clearly articulated in Bismarck's remark after the second assassination attempt: "Now I've got them," he is alleged to have said. "The Social Democrats?" he was asked. "No," he replied, "the National Liberals!"[94]

Bismarck's policies were largely successful in weakening the liberals. Conflicting interests surfaced in the liberal parties around both protectionism and antisocialist repression. As a result of these embarrassing divisions the liberal parties lost support at the polls and thus were able to exercise less influence in the Reichstag. Free trade was abandoned against the protests of many municipal officials and merchants, who now found themselves at odds with industrialists and owners of state-protected enterprises. Within the bureaucracy liberals who had been outspoken advocates of democratization and reform were replaced by conservatives, thereby further weakening the left.

For the socialist movement the effect of being outlawed was not disaster but an enforced self-reliance which proved to be especially effective. Socialism gained a distinct cultural identity more quickly from the state's action than from any efforts of its own, and this identity once and for all separated the movement from other parties on the left at the same time that it imposed greater internal uniformity on the movement. As Engels himself acknowledged, looking back on the period in 1892: "Bismarck's hammer blows fell impartially upon Lassalleans and Eisenachers alike with the result that the two groups have been finally forged into a single homogeneous party."[95] More generally, the movement now became a political entity and its development depended heavily on the ways in which its activities were channeled by the state.

The weakening of the liberal parties played an important role in giving the socialist movement untrammeled access to the working class. In countries where liberal parties were capable of achieving their political objectives the working class was often divided in its political loyalties, and even the socialist movement was sometimes torn with dissension over how much to cooperate with other parties. This was the situation that had prevailed in Germany during the

1860s. The Progressive party in particular had worked actively to cultivate the support of the working class: by 1864 it had established approximately 1,000 workers' associations with a combined membership of more than 400,000.[96] One of the critical issues that had kept the two factions of the socialist movement from uniting during this period was the fact that the Social Democratic Workers' party had greater support in the south German states, where liberalism was stronger, and thus favored a more cooperative and reformist program while the Lassalleans were based primarily in Prussia where liberalism was weaker, and thus favored a more militant program.[97] Once Bismarck's policies succeeded in dividing the left and drawing key elements of the bourgeoisie into a more conservative coalition, few of the socialist leaders clung to the idea that cooperation or cooptation into the liberal parties would serve any useful purpose.[98]

The effect of Bismarck's antisocialist legislation was also to create a reluctance on the part of liberal leaders to cooperate with socialist organizations. The legislation did, however, permit socialist candidates to run for election to the Reichstag. As it turned out, this policy was a fortuitous development for the socialist movement because it in effect forced the movement to concentrate nearly all its resources on electoral politics. The existence of a universal franchise together with a relatively emasculated liberal party left the field of electoral politics virtually open to the socialist movement. Thus, despite the antisocialist legislation, socialist votes increased from 493,288 in 1871 to 1,427,298 in 1890, and after the ban was lifted in 1890 to 2,107,076 in 1898 and to 4,250,399 in 1912. Over the same period the number of seats won increased from 12 to 35 and then to 56 in 1898 and 110 in 1912.[99]

The socialist successes owed much to the implementation of disciplined bureaucratic procedures, as both Michels and Weber recognized. But the fact that socialist electoral participation developed during the critical decade and a half when other socialist activities were outlawed by the state also shaped the character and success of the movement. As Vernon Lidtke has pointed out, it was politically inexpedient during this period to form a highly centralized organization that could easily be suppressed. Instead, the party relied heavily on a more decentralized or federated structure which allowed the movement to maintain a lower public profile. This structure offered greater local autonomy to party organizers and to the publishers of local socialist newspapers, thus enabling the movement to develop

a somewhat eclectic ideology and to adapt more effectively to differences in local conditions. At a time when regional differences still
played an important role in orienting attitudes toward German politics and when industrialization had still not progressed far enough
to have created a uniform working culture, this flexibility was of
much value.

A related phenomenon during this period was the development
of a fairly wide-ranging debate over the fundamental principles of
socialist ideology. Lacking the organizational means to exert strict
discipline with respect to formal doctrine, the movement fell prey
to various ideological interpretations of its purpose and direction.
The ensuing debates addressed many of the fundamental tenets of
European socialism: the nature and possibilities of revolution, the
uses of violence and parliamentary measures, the relevance of Marxism to the German situation, and evidence of capitalist crises on
which the movement's triumph would depend. Ironically, the position that prevailed on most of these issues was that of Marx and
Engels; yet in practice the movement became increasingly pragmatic,
oriented toward moderate reforms, and dependent on the state to
implement its demands.[100] As Carl Landauer notes: "Revolutionary
philosophy became more and more a matter of language, greatly
emphasized in propaganda speeches, but without much significance
in practical life."[101] No proposals were ever introduced by socialist
deputies in the Reichstag that would have brought about fundamental
social changes such as the elimination of private property, collectivization, or workers' control over the means of production. The legislative agenda of the SPD always focused on political reforms
concerned with legal equity, worker protection, and worker representation, even to the point of offering proposals which, if passed,
would have strengthened the central power of the state, such as
factory inspection bills and health and housing regulations. The capacity to advance a revolutionary Marxist ideology at the same time
that it focused on practical reforms was, in fact, one of the more
interesting features of German socialism.

The reformist agenda of the movement reflected its relation to
the state and the state's relation to German society. Having been
channeled into parliamentary politics, the movement found its key
resource to be its ability to mobilize voters, and this ability depended
in turn on its capacity to secure legislative successes. The party thus
worked for reforms that were at the time attainable, and in the

absence of a strong central organization independent of parliamentary politics, socialist deputies were able to take the lead in setting the movement's agenda. Much of this agenda focused on the state as a result of the fact that the state's pervasive social role made it the most likely agent of social change.

Although the state was not particularly responsive to socialist demands, it had a long history of intervening in the economy on behalf of workers, and socialist deputies were often placed in a position of having to support these measures despite their opposition to the regime in order to gain workers' support. Among the major initiatives that were passed were a compulsory sickness insurance bill in 1883, workmen's compensation in 1884, and old age and disability insurance in 1890. All were opposed by the liberal parties on the grounds that laissez faire was a more appropriate policy toward economic affairs. But even these measures had been preceded by many similar policies of state intervention, especially in Prussia. These included the Prussian employers' liability law for railway workers (1838), the Prussian system of compulsory insurance for miners (1854), Saxony's comprehensive establishment of compulsory sickness insurance for workers (1868), Bavaria's system of communal aid to factory workers (1869), and unified Germany's plan of employers' liability for workers' accidents in specific industries (1871). Only Belgium had been as active in initiating state-sponsored insurance schemes. Thus the socialist movement was able to unify its objectives around state-sponsored programs rather than having to carve out a distinct agenda amidst competing programs offered by liberal parties, trade unions, and voluntary associations.

The capacity to maintain its commitment to revolutionary rhetoric at the same time that it pursued practical reforms was partly a function of the period of antisocialist legislation. Gary Steenson attributes the radicalization of German socialism directly to persecution during this period: "Official persecution created a heroic spirit that won the SPD ever more followers and preserved a radical tradition well beyond the point it could have been sustained by other objective factors."[102] Whether there is a natural inclination for persecuted movements to grow and become more radical seems debatable. But the antisocialist legislation did have a concrete effect on the production of socialist ideology in that it forced the party's major ideologues and newspaper publishers into exile. When socialist literature was banned in 1878, the main centers of ideological production became physically separated from the centers of parliamentary activity. The *Sozialdemocrat*, which served as the party's official newspaper, for example, was published in Switzerland, where its editorial staff enjoyed safe passage and was able to maintain communication with the international movement. Physically isolated from Berlin, it became the main source in which Marxist ideology was articulated.[103] Marxism thus provided a kind of identity for the movement, even though it did not guide the party's political activities. Its emphasis on class conflict corresponded well with the working class's actual separation from the bourgeoisie both economically and politically. It provided a rationale for the movement's existence, yet it was framed in sufficiently futuristic terms that policies could be formulated largely without reference to specific doctrines. As George Lichtheim has remarked: "Marxism functioned as an integrative ideology, not as a theory of action. It was invoked to explain why the labor movement had to lead a separate existence . . . The paradoxical result was to establish a nominally socialist subculture within the official aristocratic-bourgeois civilization."[104]

Until the mid-1890s the main competitor of the socialist movement for working-class loyalties was the Catholic Center party. Formed in 1870, it remained an opposition party for nearly a quarter of a century, thus providing workers with an alternative means of expressing political grievances.[105] Protestantism was closely identified with the state and, because of the fact that the state supplied it with only meager support, was relatively ineffective in commanding workers' loyalties. In most Protestant areas the number of clergy had declined steadily since the middle of the century, and urban and suburban areas were especially hard hit; for example, Berlin's suburbs had only one pastor for every 25,000 people in 1879.[106] On the average only about 3 percent of the population attended church, of which an estimated three-fourths were women.[107] Some workers retained private religious convictions even though working conditions and social pressure made them unlikely to attend religious services. But even private religiosity appears to have been relatively rare in Protestant districts: according to a survey of workers conducted around the turn of the century, for example, only 13 percent said they believed in God.[108] For all practical purposes, then, Protestantism had ceased to be a serious contender for the ideological allegiance of the German working class both because of its image of conservative support for the state and because the state failed to provide it with sufficient resources to carry out its work.[109]

The Catholic church generally fared better since it was not the official religion and its community level of organization penetrated more deeply into the neighborhood life of the working class. At first it used pulpits and religious meetings to expound its own solutions to workers' problems; later special organizations were set up for associational and political activities; and eventually Christian trade unions and legislative proposals were initiated to reform working conditions.[110] Not only did the church have vast resources in personnel, buildings, and financial reserves; it also advanced an ideology that cut across class lines and offered a corporatist vision of society that enabled it to draw on the support of aristocratic and bourgeois defenders.[111]

In Catholic areas the SPD generally made little headway compared to the Center party in recruiting working class-members and voters. Thus there was a great deal of animosity between the two parties, and SPD ideology came to be filled with antireligious rhetoric. Some of this rhetoric was directed at the Protestant church because of its aristocratic leanings and lack of involvement in working-class causes.[112] But just as much invective was heaped on the Catholic church despite its involvement with the working class, because these efforts were regarded by the socialists as palliative rather than revolutionary. Yet as time passed, even the Center party abandoned the field to the SPD.

During the latter part of the 1890s the state succeeded again in contributing inadvertently to the growth of the SPD by drawing the Center party to the right through a series of overtures on religious issues and economic policies, such as tariff increases, which proved attractive to the party's rural and bourgeois constituents. Perceiving this shift as a sign of weakening commitment to working-class interests, thousands of Catholic workers shifted their votes to the SPD as the only remaining political alternative.[113] By 1903 the SPD was thus in a position to capture 31.7 percent of the popular vote, up from 19.7 percent in 1890.[114]

A Provisional Model

The relative success of the SPD in Germany, then, suggests the importance not only of economic changes associated with industrialization but also of the state as it interacted with the economy, class structure, and cultural institutions. Industrialization contributed significantly to the size of the working class and to the economic resources at the disposal of the working class for supporting party activities. The disruptive effects of industrialization should not be exaggerated, but in many rapidly expanding urban areas the presence of a transient labor force resulted in socially unattached persons who tended to be relatively available to the recruiting efforts of any political party that was capable of providing such a large array of voluntary associations as the SPD. Rapid industrialization was itself a product of forces such as rising external demand and changing technologies, but it also depended on the intervention of a strong state bureaucracy. Initially rooted in a conservative coalition of aristocratic, monarchical, and military interests, the state's intervention in the economy on behalf of trade and industry provided the revenue for rapid growth of the bureaucracy and over time succeeded in drawing an increasing number of the upper bourgeoisie as well as peasants and small farmers into the conservative coalition. The so-called feudalization of the bourgeoisie, along with the state's deliberate efforts to combat the strength of the liberal parties in the Reichstag, effectively eliminated the liberal parties as contenders for working-class loyalties and widened the split between the bourgeoisie and proletariat. The working class was thus left open to the organizing activities of the socialist movement, and this movement was able to concentrate almost exclusively on the working class rather than running the risk of internal division by attempting to form alliances with the liberal parties or devise appeals for the petty bourgeoisie or peasantry.[115] The state also contributed to the unity of the movement by giving it a distinct social identity through the antisocialist legislation and by channeling its resources toward parliamentary politics. The state's dominant position in the economy meant that most of the party's practical programs took a political focus rather than being dissipated among various voluntary associations concerned with trade, direct negotiation with firms, and collective bargaining.

Regional differences between southern Germany (Bavaria, Württemberg, and Baden) and Prussia are particularly indicative of the state's role in shaping the socialist movement. Economic differences between the two regions were partly responsible for the greater successes of socialism in Prussia than in the south, but southern Germany also had a sizable industrial labor force which under the appropriate political circumstances, might have been mobilized by the SPD. The principal difference in political circumstances was that the liberal parties in southern Germany were stronger and more effective in responding to working-class demands. Liberal parties took an early lead in sponsoring workers' associations and often cooperated with workers in pushing for legislation. As in Prussia, one of the principles that consistently united liberals and socialists was opposition to the centralizing tendencies of the imperial government. This concern was even more powerful in southern Germany because it corresponded with regional antagonisms against Prussia, and fewer of the bourgeoisie in southern Germany had economic interests in industries such as mining, heavy metals, or railways that were being promoted by the imperial government. In the south German states the elected representative bodies also had a stronger voice in initiating state policies and were less constrained by the monarchy, army, and bureaucracy. The left in southern Germany was thus in a better position to rule as a broad coalition which transcended class interests. As a result the socialist movement failed to develop as distinct an identity as was forced upon it in the north.[116]

In an ironic sense the socialists' most benevolent ally in Germany, therefore, was the conservative-aristocratic state. The liberal parties thrived by masking class differences and by forming associations and policy initiatives which either cooperated with the socialists or drew the socialists into partisan collaboration with the liberals. The strength of the conservative bureaucracy, however, weakened the liberal parties to the point where the socialist movement was able to carve out a relatively broad niche within the working class. Revolutionary anticapitalist rhetoric served to identify socialism with working-class interests. Yet in an important sense the movement did not so much oppose or attack the state as channel working-class demands into a reformist parliamentary program which ultimately strengthened the state and legitimated an even greater degree of intervention in the economy. While it was ironic on the surface that the state should have been the ally of socialism, then, the even greater irony was that socialism came to function as an ally of the state.[117]

The German case thus serves as a provisional model which identifies several conditions of the broader social fabric as being conducive to the institutionalization of socialist ideology in Europe during the latter part of the nineteenth century: economic expansion leading to the development of an industrial proletariat, a conservative bureaucratic state which actively intervenes in economic and class relations, and an emasculated left incapable of creating coalitions between the working class and the liberal bourgeoisie. France and England provide useful contexts in which to examine the generality of the relations involving the state and the left, since the balance of liberalism and conservatism in both was quite different from that in Germany.

13   🏻

Liberalism in France
and Great Britain

POPULAR IMAGERY of French socialism suggests that it emerged in the producers' cooperatives of the Second Republic, was pushed into exile by Napoleon III's coup d'état, gradually regained strength in the 1860s, fomented the Paris Commune, for which it was again severely repressed, and then quickly recovered under the Third Republic as a result of the liberalism of the regime and the movement's alliance with the petty bourgeoisie, thus growing into a strong national party by 1914. According to this view the socialist movement in France was a huge success, and the reason for this success was mainly the strength of the liberal republican coalition which gave aid to the socialist cause. Yet the conclusion that comes from comparing France with Germany is that this image, along with the understanding of the conditions facilitating socialist development it implies, may need to be reconsidered.

France's contribution to the development of European socialism should not be underestimated, for it was France that inspired some of Marx's most astute observations, and when the Second International was founded in 1889, more than half the delegates assembled were French. Nevertheless, the French movement itself remained organizationally weak for a decade and a half after this notable gathering, and by 1914 few of its original goals had been achieved. If Marxists succeeded in dominating the movement intellectually, they did so only at the cost of opting for an increasingly eclectic approach in practice, and even this compromise failed to win the party the level of popular support that might have been expected and was in fact achieved in Germany.

Socialism in France never succeeded to the same extent that it did in Germany. Despite the fact that much of the early development of socialism during the revolutions of 1830 and 1848 as well as the Paris Commune in 1871 had occurred in France, the fate of French socialism between 1871 and 1914 was generally disappointing in comparison with that of its German counterpart. During much of this period the party was divided into factions with differing views on basic doctrine and practical objectives. From the beginning, the social environment seemed to provide a less clearly identifiable niche for socialism than in Germany, with the result that the French movement failed to realize its early potential. Albert Lindemann has suggested that between 1880 and 1914 the French socialist movement averaged about one-tenth the size of the movement in Germany. Even by 1914 the socialists were able to capture only 17 percent of the popular vote, compared to a proportion nearly twice this size in Germany.[1]

The Character of French Industrialization

Some of the difficulty that the socialist movement experienced in France can be attributed to the pace of French industrialization and hence to the nature of the proletariat. Economic growth was considerable overall, as reflected in a total increase in gross national product from an average of 20 billion francs between 1865 and 1874 to an average of 34.6 billion francs between 1905 and 1913. This growth, however, was neither as dramatic as that in Germany nor for that matter particuarly spectacular in comparison with France's own expansion earlier in the century. Gross national product had doubled, for example, in the forty years between 1815 and 1855, but it took sixty years to double again after 1855.[2]

Industrial production as such began to expand earlier in France than in Germany and developed at a more gradual pace. Whereas industrial production in Germany doubled every twenty years between 1850 and 1910, resulting in a cumulative increase of nearly tenfold, industrial production in France doubled about once every fifty years for a total cumulative increase between 1850 and 1910 of less than threefold. During the critical years from 1870 to 1910, when German industrial production rose more than four times, French industrial production increased only twofold.[3] Like Germany, France experienced more rapid industrialization during the latter half of the nineteenth century than during the former, and throughout most of the nineteenth century its overall level of industrialization was higher than Germany's, but in its rate of growth France underwent considerably less rapid change than Germany.

The differences between France and Germany are especially evident in sectoral distribution of national product between 1870 and 1910. In Germany, as we have seen, industry grew from 28 percent of national product in 1870 to 43 percent in 1910, commerce grew from 10 to 15 percent, and agriculture decreased from 40 percent to 25 percent. In comparison, French industry increased only from 30 percent to 36 percent of national product, commerce remained constant at 7 percent, and agriculture decreased only from 43 percent to 35 percent.[4]

The relatively gradual pace of French industrialization meant that the industrial labor force grew slowly in comparison with Germany's. As a proportion of the total labor force, nonagricultural workers in Germany totaled 36 percent in 1871 and approximately 66 percent in 1910. In contrast, nonagricultural workers in France made up 48 percent of the labor force as early as 1856, but this proportion had risen only to 59 percent by 1911.[5] Thus the 30 percent change in Germany over a forty-year period was matched by only an 11 percent change in France over a period of more than fifty years. This contrast in proportional change was also magnified by the fact that overall population in France grew only about one-fifth as rapidly as in Germany between 1850 and 1911.[6] Accordingly, the nonagricultural population grew by only about 1.7 million in the forty years prior to the First World War, reaching a total of 6.2 million in 1911, whereas the nonagricultural population of Germany grew by 4.5 million over the same period, reaching 9.5 million in 1910.[7] By more rigid definitions, the growth in size of the French industrial population was even smaller during most of this period. Fernand Braudel and Ernest Labrousse, for example, place the number of industrial workers at 2.8 million in 1866, climbing to 3.1 million in 1876, and then rising to only 3.4 million by 1906, after which a sudden spurt in the economy brought the total up to 4.7 million in 1911.[8]

The internal composition of the industrial labor force further accentuates the differences between France and Germany. Heavy industry, which in Germany was advanced by the state through railway construction, and which represented one of the fastest growing sectors of the industrial economy, was in France a less significant sector. On the eve of the war metallurgy and mining in France accounted for approximately 21 percent of the industrial labor force, employing approximately 1.3 million workers, while in Germany 33 percent of the industrial labor force, or 3.1 million workers, were so employed.[9] In contrast, textiles continued to dominate French industry, employing 42 percent of the industrial labor force as late as 1911, while in Germany the proportion employed in textiles dropped from 47 percent in 1846 to 19 percent in 1913.

One of the additional differences associated with these structural characteristics was that French workers tended to remain in the employment of relatively small firms in comparison with German workers. Alfred Cobban estimates that as late as 1900, ten out of every eleven workshops in France had fewer than five employees.[10] Georges Dupeux calculates that of the 3.9 million business concerns in France in 1906, only one-fourth employed anyone other than the proprietor and his wife, while only 4 percent employed more than fifty workers.[11] Braudel and Labrousse's analysis of the same figures, focusing strictly on industrial establishments, shows that 59 percent of these establishments employed fewer than ten workers, 16 percent employed between eleven and one hundred workers, and 25 percent employed more than one hundred workers. By comparison, nearly half of all industrial workers in Germany were employed in firms of fifty workers or more.[12]

The net impact of industrialization on French society during the half century prior to the First World War, therefore, appears to have been considerably less dramatic than that in Germany. Fewer of the French proletariat were concentrated in heavy industry or in large firms, and a larger proportion continued to work in industries that remained geographically decentralized. Thus the rate of urbanization in France was relatively slow, reaching only 41 percent of the total population by the turn of the century, compared with a much more rapid rate and higher overall proportion in Germany.[13] Even in the most rapidly growing industrial districts a relatively large share of the population appears to have come from local stock or from surrounding rural districts and therefore to have maintained fairly close relations with kin and other natural groupings.[14]

The relative stability of communal and associational ties among French workers contrasts sharply with the social disruption seen in German industrial districts. Hard evidence on voluntary associations in France remains sparse, and the available evidence suggests strong regional variations in these activities, but on the whole one gains the impression that informal modes of association remained relatively more important in France than in Germany while the converse was true of formally organized associations with explicit political goals.[15] In most areas informal gatherings in taverns, neighborhoods, homes, and churches seem to have been the settings in which both sociality and political discussion occurred.[16] Cabarets, Freemasonry associations, and clubs devoted to leisure activities also abounded; for example, in St. Etienne one cabaret existed for every 62 residents, and in Lille there were 37 cards-playing clubs, 63 singing clubs, 64 athletic clubs, and approximately 1,300 cabarets.[17] As in the Catholic sections of Germany, the church also provided a continuing source of communal attachments in many areas of France. In Paris and the Nord, for example, Catholic trade unions provided relief benefits and cooperative insurance schemes which proved attractive to many workers in the metal, building, and clothing industries.[18] Secular trade associations also played an important role in some industries in providing educational programs, unemployment and sickness benefits, training for apprentices, and credit cooperatives.[19]

Although some debate exists over the role of trade associations in facilitating or impeding the growth of French socialism, the evidence on informal associations seems to suggest, as in Germany, that these attachments generally worked to the disadvantage of socialist recruiters. This conclusion also tends to be supported by studies showing that workers who retained more intimate ties to the land were less susceptible to socialist organizing.[20] Workers with continuing agrarian links were not only more effectively integrated into family, religious, and community networks, but also enjoyed a kind of economic security which substituted for the political and economic schemes offered by the socialists. Land provided an alternative source of income in the event of recession, lay-off, declining real wages, or old age; it enabled wives and children to contribute to family income; it allowed workers to accept wages below those demanded by the unions since supplemental income and food were available; and in many cases it protected workers from being drawn into company housing, food, insurance, and credit schemes which left their recipients permanently at the mercy of employers. In areas with a long tradition of artisan and rural industry, such as the Lyonnais region, the social dislocation associated with industrialization also appears to have been minimized. Newer industries in these areas tended to absorb workers mainly from declining industries, and these workers for the most part seem to have retained some of the craft unions that protected them in negotiations with employers.[21] To the extent, then, that French industrialization proceeded at a relatively slow, even pace sufficient to maintain these kinds of traditional ties, workers were probably less likely to become available resources for institutionalizing socialist ideology.

Yet the differences between French and German industrialization should not be exaggerated. In a number of respects French industrialization was highly conducive to the development of socialism. If the overall rate of industrialization in France was not as rapid as in Germany, it was nevertheless quite pronounced in several key areas. Private investments in French industry grew from 337 million francs in 1860 to more than 1.8 billion francs in 1900, a sixfold increase in less than half a century, with the result that the capital-to-worker ratio increased dramatically during this period. Over the same period coal consumption more than tripled, while figures for 1830 and 1875 show an increase in the use of steam power of some forty times.[22] Between 1866 and 1911 the total number of salaried employees grew from 0.1 million to 1.9 million, the number of transportation workers increased threefold, and the number of miners more than doubled.[23]

If industrialization in France did not produce as great a degree of social dislocation as in Germany, it still resulted in a great deal of social change. Although the percentage of firms with large numbers of employees was relatively small, these firms carried a disproportionate amount of weight in the overall labor force. According to one estimate, 40 percent of all industrial workers in 1896 were employed in industrial firms that had fifty or more employees, a figure not much below that for Germany.[24] In addition, the period between 1870 and 1914 marked a significant transition away from artisanal labor toward unskilled, mechanized labor, which tended to be less well represented by guild organizations and was less capable than artisan labor of controlling its own labor markets or achieving economic goals through collective bargaining.[25] Although the persistence of artisan labor acted as a barrier against unification of the industrial working class, its decline created strong incentives for workers of all kinds to seek alternative means of protecting themselves against the advances of capitalism.

As in Germany, the relatively steady expansion of some industries toward the end of the century also permitted worker solidarity of the kind that socialism could cultivate to develop over time. Having severed ties with village networks in the countryside, workers in these industries became dependent on other workers for primary and secondary attachments. Where geographic and occupational mobility was low, these attachments could play a vital role in strengthening the socialist movement at the grass roots. Dislocation did not result in permanent isolation; rather, old ties were replaced by new ones that were more specific to the workers' new location in the occupational structure. Co-workers and members of unions stood up for one another at weddings or pledged themselves as godparents for one another's children, and they came out en masse for their fellows' funerals. Especially the latter provided occasions for expressing common grievances and for socialist or protosocialist rhetoric about hardships and exploitation. Stable and complex networks of interaction also engendered trust, bred a common language, and facilitated the tasks of canvasing electoral lists and encouraging bloc voting. Conformity to party standards could, under these conditions, be reinforced with personal favors and mutual respect, or negatively with ostracism.[26]

Industrialization in France, as in Germany, was also accompanied by an overall decline of religious ties as a mode of social organization among workers that often competed with the mobilizing efforts of socialist leaders. Although some evidence of a resurgence in religious interest had existed between 1845 and 1871, this interest appears to have been replaced by a generalized wave of anticlericalism after 1871 among both workers and the bourgeoisie. Having never been as fully subjugated to the state as the church in Germany, the French church constituted a troublesome source of friction at both the national and municipal levels, particularly over matters of school reform, taxes, church buildings, relief programs, and relations with Italy.[27] The presence of anticlericalism among the bourgeoisie made the church no more attractive to the working class, however, with the result that religious resources and religious observance declined seriously between 1870 and 1914. Substantial erosion in religious practice had already occurred between 1829 and 1855 and again between 1855 and 1877.[28] This erosion was now intensified, especially in the cities, where the church's support for royalist causes and its lack of personnel constituted serious obstacles to attracting the working class. Overall, the number of ordinations to the priesthood dropped from 1,753 in 1868 to 704 in 1913.[29]

The effect of religious decline on the rise of French socialism should not be exaggerated, however. Gustav LeBon's 1899 treatise on socialism, for example, argued that socialism was spreading in France *primarily* in response to an underlying need for faith which was no longer being met by the church.[30] The "ebb" of one apparently gave rise to the "flow" of the other, an argument that LeBon and others defended by pointing out the parallels between socialism and religion. Hydraulic arguments of this kind no longer seem compelling, of course, because of the difficulty of establishing either the need for faith in some universal sense or the range of alternatives capable of fulfilling such a need. Nevertheless, the declining strength of French religion does constitute a form of social change similar to that occurring simultaneously in Germany, thereby adding to the complexity of accounting for the relatively greater degree of socialist activity in Germany than in France.

The degree to which slow industrialization and a relative absence of social dislocation may have inhibited the growth of socialism in France must not, therefore, be overemphasized, just as the rapidity of industrialization and the extent of social disruption in Germany should not, as I have suggested, be exaggerated. While the pace of industrialization was slower in France than in Germany, the size of the industrial working class in France was certainly sufficient to have sustained a far larger socialist movement than it did, as evidenced by the fact that the Socialist party never grew beyond approximately 75,000 members in the years prior to the First World War and never gained more than 1.5 million popular votes out of more than 6 million industrial workers.[31]

The difficulty of attaching too much importance to the sheer rate of industrialization is also evidenced by the fact that no simple correlation exists between socialist voting and membership in the industrial sector. Studies of French labor history have focused increasingly on the structure of work and the dynamics of proletarianization within particular industries and locales, but the evidence produced thus far has pointed mostly to the complexity of the relation between occupation and socialist leanings. For example, artisans in

Lyons were as attracted to socialism as were the more heavily industrialized workers in Roanne; coal miners and metalworkers in the Stephanois basin were relatively more attracted to parliamentary reform and class coalition than to socialism; but peasants in the Var were strongly oriented toward socialism despite a virtual absence of industrialization in the region.[32] One survey of this literature concludes: "One must strain mightily ... to see the French socialist movement as uniquely or even chiefly *proletarian* in social origin or inspiration. Craft workers and artisans provided much of the original social base, while the movement's leaders consisted largely of men of petty bourgeois origins. From the start ... the socialist movement was composed of a congeries of social groups, including farmers and small businessmen, farm labourers, artisans, white-collar workers, school teachers, civil servants, professional people, as well as unskilled workers."[33]

The very fact that French socialism attracted such a wide variety of groups contrasts sharply with the much heavier concentration of German socialism among the industrial working class. This diversity appears not only to have accounted for some of the strength that French socialism achieved despite otherwise unfavorable conditions, but also to have created internal tensions within the movement which impeded its ultimate growth. An explanation of both characteristics requires consideration of the interaction between class structure and the state rather than concentrating only on economic processes.

Political Conditions in the Third Republic

In comparison with that of Germany the state bureaucracy in France was relatively weak, thus providing opportunities for a relatively flexible set of bourgeois republican and liberal democratic interests to assume power. Rather than drawing the liberal bourgeoisie into a conservative coalition which would isolate the working class and give it a distinct political identity, the state pursued a policy of coopting working-class demands through concessions for labor unions and cooperation between the working class and liberal parties. The socialist movement, as a result, enjoyed considerable freedom of action but faced severe problems in defining its goals relative to the state, the liberal bourgeoisie, and the unions.

The difference between the French and German states was typified by the outcome of the Franco-Prussian War in 1871: Bismarck won, Louis Bonaparte lost. Through the defeat of the French, Bismarck's alliance with the military and aristocracy was strengthened to the point where members of the bourgeoisie were forced increasingly to rely on this alliance to protect their interests. In defeat the French state lost much of the legitimacy that had previously been attached to monarchist claims, and the Third Republic became the preserve of the liberal bourgeoisie. The strength of this regime derived ultimately from the political past: the revolutions of 1789, 1830, and 1848, and the tenuousness of the regimes that came into existence after each of these crises. Nearly a century of political disorder had proven that any regime not built on a broad base of support within the ruling class was a highly precarious venture. By the mid-1860s the Bonapartist empire had begun to show such signs of precariousness. Drained financially and subject to dissension within the ruling class, it was dependent on the peasantry for support, a fact that once again raised the specter of political disorder from below.

The so-called liberal empire that came into being in 1869 was the work of groups within the state itself and among the broader industrial bourgeoisie, who were oriented toward preserving political stability by expanding the distribution of power. Among the reforms accomplished under the liberal empire were the creation of a more independent legislature and the instituting of constitutional controls over the state budget. With Bonaparte's defeat the opportunity was opened for consolidating these liberal reforms. Not until 1875, however, was the new constitution ratified and monarchical support firmly defeated. By the end of the 1870s a relatively liberal coalition of republicans was finally in control of the government and able to build a power base satisfactory to most of the new industrial bourgeoisie as well as to shopkeepers and "petty producers."[34]

The ruling republican coalition was distinctly oriented toward economic growth and the protection and encouragement of domestic industry, as well as the right of private property, and firmly supported law and order against the threat of upheaval posed by the lower classes. But it was also egalitarian and democratic in principle and deeply suspicious of aristocratic pretensions to control over the state from the right. Its programs were directed toward relatively uniform regional economic growth, the creation of a national market through the development of railway transportation, and the reduction of class antagonism through a system of national education.

The thrust toward universal education was particularly strategic since it provided an opportunity to inculcate national values at the same time that it promised to upgrade the technical skills of the laboring population. As the author of a recent study observes: "To give the shaky Republic a solid foundation, to develop loyalty to it in the thousands of communes of France, republicans turned to primary education as the best means of propaganda at hand. The profound educational transformation that ensued—making elementary school free, secular, and compulsory—made the village schoolmasters those who would henceforth make the republican system work. In one fell swoop the teacher, representing his government, became 'the great influence in the village.' "[35]

In France no less than in Germany the schools thus became the great disseminators of official ideology. They taught children who in most cases had never had contact with the outside world, and whose parents' loyalties were to the local community, to identify with France as a nation and to think of the state as its embodiment. From the earliest grades children learned the importance of obedience and devotion to the state; they heard speeches praising those who had defended their country through military service and learned songs, marches, and drills that instilled a sense of patriotic duty; history and geography lessons extolled patriotism and national unity; provincialism was attacked through the advancement of the national language; arithmetic lessons included instruction in the payment of taxes; and throughout the schooling experience children learned of the state's beneficence in providing them with modern instruction and the skills needed to advance their own destinies.[36]

In a more subtle way the very presence of the teacher served an ideological role for the republic insofar as it symbolized both the state and a higher standard of living potentially available through the benevolence of the state. In villages lacking mass communications (and where many adults could not have read a newspaper if one had been available) teachers had a virtual monopoly over the transmission of certain kinds of knowledge, bringing new ideas, interpreting national events, and serving as notables in the community. Teachers also influenced the associational life of their communities, founding credit societies, occupational interest groups, temperance societies, medical aid groups, and musical clubs.

The French state, to this extent, was clearly in the business of ideology, and any movement advancing an alternative ideology had to contend with the state's control over the educational apparatus as a significant mode of ideological dissemination. Opposition or indifference to the socialist movement stemmed in part from the loyalties, promises, and associational ties transmitted throughout the population by the schools and teachers. Just as in Germany, the educational system also reflected the class composition of the society, particularly at the secondary and university levels to which only the wealthy elite could aspire. French universities were not, as critics sometimes charged, simply the state's pawns: politicians generally showed little interest in them, and those who did were usually frustrated in efforts to involve the universities in overtly political causes.[37] Like the German universities, however, French institutions of higher learning were clearly the exclusive province of the ruling class.

Yet in a broader sense the educational system in France differed from that in Germany in a way that reflected the different structures of the two state systems. Its relation to the state was more subtle than in Germany, thereby making its political content somewhat less obvious to critical observers and, as a result, more difficult for socialists to arm themselves against. The ideological thrust of French education was less overtly personified than the overweening presence of Bismarck made possible in Germany. Rather than teaching explicit obedience to the state itself, the French system attached emphasis mainly to the idea of moral order, as later popularized in the social sciences, particularly in the work of Emile Durkheim. Implicit in the concept of moral order was the notion of loyalty to the state, but explicit mention of the state tended to be minimized relative to concepts of self-discipline, social participation, and solidarity across class lines.

The contrast in state structure between France and Germany was undoubtedly clearest, however, in the relations that existed between the executive bureaucracy and parliamentary institutions. Unlike in Germany, where the bureaucracy served as the focal point of a conservative coalition and all but eliminated liberal opposition in the Reichstag, the bureaucracy in France tended to remain subservient to powerful liberal and republican interests whose strength resided in parliament. As one writer has suggested: "Politics became a kind of game in which a divided parliament prevented the formation of effective political executives."[38] Although many of the characteristics of state centralization that had developed during the seventeenth and eighteenth centuries were retained, the constitutional restrictions that had been implemented after the revolution imposed strict limitations on the bureaucracy and granted sweeping rights to the individual and to the private interests of the ruling classes. "Hence the role of the state," writes Stanley Hoffman, was "a narrow one, meeting the individual's desire not to become a mere instrument of the state, especially in economic affairs, and the desire of the consensus groups for a sharp separation between state and society."[39]

In contrast with Germany, the French state was also limited in the economic sphere to a relatively passive role such as that of fostering protectionism, tax legislation, and tariff policies, rather than being able to promote or participate actively in industry. Another feature that contrasted sharply with Germany was the decentralization of jurisdiction at the local level, thus further weakening the capacity of the central bureaucracy to impose its way.[40] The French state was also characterized in general to a much greater extent by parliamentary supremacy rather than a strong executive. The actual implementation of parliamentary decisions fell to the bureaucracy, but the Council of Ministers which headed the bureaucracy was subordinate to the authority of parliament and was further restrained by a division of responsibility with the Ministry of Justice, which jealously intervened in matters of civil liberties, and by a complex set of relations with departmental and municipal councils whose co-operation was required for governmental action to be effective.[41] The development of a bureaucratic apparatus that could defy liberal principles and become the seat of a repressive regime was, therefore, largely avoided during the Third Republic.

Between 1871 and 1914 the bureaucracy did of course undergo some expansion in personnel and in functions. By 1913 some 470,000 to 550,000 persons were employed as public officials, about twice the number that had been employed in 1870.[42] Much of this increase, however, was accounted for by the rise in numbers of schoolteachers and thus amounted to little in the way of centralized power.[43] Government expenditures also edged upward, from an annual average of 3 billion francs during the 1870s to an annual average of 3.8 billion francs between 1900 and 1910.[44] Most of this growth came about simply as a result of broader economic expansion, however. As a percentage of national product, government expenditures actually *declined* between 1880 and 1912.[45] In contrast with the situation in Germany, state expenditures on railways and public works projects such as bridges, canals, and road construction rose only modestly during this period.

The fundamental division in French politics during the Third Republic was, as Ernest Labrousse observes, a cleavage between those forces in favor of the liberal republic and certain antirepublican forces aligned on the political right: "The major internal issues over which battle raged in this conflict were the consolidation of the Republic itself, civil liberties, secular education, anticlericalism, separation of church and state."[46] After 1871 the supporters of republicanism made strong advances, but their foes on the right were by no means vanquished.[47] Many of the nobility, military officers, higher ecclesiastical officials, and conservative members of the bureaucracy, along with supporters among the peasantry, continued to hope and work for a change in government that would ultimately restore the monarchy or at least give a stronger voice to aristocratic, ecclesiastical, and bureaucratic interests.[48] Between 1876 and 1906 the republicans maintained a strong coalition against the right, never failing to gain at least 60 percent of the seats in the National Assembly.[49] Nevertheless, the continuity of the right was a factor that the liberals could not ignore. This presence was especially apparent in shaping the left's relations with the working class.

Although the Republic was largely under the rule of a relatively wealthy and influential segment of the upper bourgeoisie, it nevertheless remained a product of its own history which, since the revolutions of 1830 and 1848, drew on the support of the middle and lower bourgeoisie, skilled artisans, and some industrial workers. "In principle," Bernard Moss writes, "Republicans were inclined to favor a liberal democracy of small property owners . . . [and] did not see any basic conflict between petty capitalists, the masters of small scale industry, and their workers. Instead of considering capitalist masters as . . . exploiters . . . they would treat them as victims . . . whose interests in association continued with that of their workers."[50]

In the absence of a strong imperial bureaucracy the republicans were able to present themselves as the party most capable of enforcing law and order. Unlike the situation in Germany, where Bismarck held the strongest claim to this role, the French republicans were in a position to call for support from both the middle class and the working class in the name of national defense, civic unity, and economic prosperity. Ronald Aminzade notes in summarizing the period between 1848 and 1871: "Workers . . . did not act collectively as autonomous political forces during the middle decades of the nineteenth century. Their collective political actions were closely linked to the struggle for the creation of a republic, a struggle which was based upon a multi-class alliance centered around a Republican political party that incorporated contradictory class interests."[51] After the government's defeat in 1871 this perspective became increasingly prominent in republican propaganda. Class conflict was pictured even by leaders of the working class as a secondary cleavage that needed to be healed for the sake of the nation, quite unlike concurrent discussions in Germany, which presented class conflict as a necessary form of opposition to Bismarck's plutocracy.[52]

The republican denial of conflicting class interests was a tactical measure that masked actual divisions of interest between the bourgeoisie and proletariat, and these divisions created internal contradictions in republican ideology. Moss observes: "The republican movement contained two souls, socialist and capitalist, struggling in one breast."[53] Nevertheless, at least three characteristics of French social structure softened the class divisions sufficiently to make republicanism a viable reality. One was the relatively gradual rate of industrialization, which secured the existence of a relatively large segment of petty owners and skilled artisans as a buffer between the upper bourgeoisie and the emerging industrial working class. A second was the relatively broad dispersal of capital among private producers, unlike in Germany, which prevented concentration of power in an aristocratic state bureaucracy capable of pressing for rapid industrialization. Finally, the pressure of a conservative aristocratic-monarchical minority provided a continuing threat to the stability of the republican regime, encouraging it to emphasize ties with the working class. The state thus implemented policies aimed at drawing large segments of the working class into the republican majority at the same time that it sought to discourage more radical elements of the working class from developing their own political organizations.

Against the threat of the right, the republican majority sought to broaden its support as well as to create a stable social order by providing mechanisms to ameliorate the condition of the working class. Workers' banks and producers' cooperatives were encouraged and trade unions were legalized in hopes of creating a wage-oriented craft unionism capable of being drawn into the political system.[54] Other measures included republican-financed workers' delegations to international expositions and the establishment of municipally subsidized labor exchanges, the *bourses du travail*. Particularly striking in the French case is the degree to which private entrepreneurs appeared to recognize a potential affinity of interests between capital and labor. Legislation oriented toward the alleviation of inhumane working conditions, proposals for countercyclical measures against the ill effects of recession and unemployment, and tariff laws favorable to the protection of domestic industries were advanced as means of reducing labor strife. Chambers of commerce successfully lobbied for pension benefits and financial incentives that would encourage workers to develop a stake in local enterprises. Even workers' syndicates were established with the favor and financial support of local employers.[55] These measures, along with political freedoms such as the right of assembly, a free press, and universal manhood suffrage, provided the conditions for channeling working class activism into trade union organizations and away from separate political mobilization. What the republicans feared most was the possibility that the right or the bureaucracy might itself enter into a coalition with the working-class.[56]

The Institutionalization of French Socialism

The socialist movement thus developed in a political context in which boundaries between the working class and segments of the bourgeoisie tended to be less than clear. The roots of French socialism blend almost imperceptibly into the history of working class struggles from 1789 to the middle of the nineteenth century, taking the various forms that have been associated with "utopian socialism," "anarchist socialism," and "republican socialism." As early as 1830 Parisian printers had banded together to demand higher wages and to restrict the use of machines. Among their tactics was the formation of a producers' collective to gain ownership of their machines. In the 1840s such activities took on a broader political cast as some spokesmen for the emerging labor movement rejected the idea that a democratic government could do much of value through credit policies and labor legislation and began to envision a socialist state controlled by workers themselves. It was, however, the republican model that prevailed in 1848, and most workers were persuaded to cooperate with the new regime either for concrete gains in labor conditions or in hopes that the state would assist trade unions in collectivizing property.

During the Second Republic over 1,100 trade associations were founded around the country with more than 50,000 members in Paris alone.[57] Many were "socialist" to the extent that they subscribed to the goal of emancipating their own industry from the wage-price system through various collectivization schemes, but they were also closely allied with the republican ideals of the state and saw themselves as part of the republican coalition. By 1871, then, a strong tradition of cooperation between republicans and socialists had already been established which gave sustenance to the socialist movement in the short term but set limits on its growth over the long term.

The fall of the Paris Commune in 1871 and the repression that followed dealt a staggering blow to the socialist movement. The International was outlawed, many of the movement's propagandists and organizers were exiled or imprisoned, and courts meted out harsh punishment to anyone suspected of furthering the socialist cause. The trade associations that had existed before 1871 provided a potential foundation on which socialist organizers could rebuild, but not until 1876 did the political climate relax sufficiently for the movement to demonstrate any signs of new vitality. In 1877 the first socialist newspaper was published; a year later a socialist candidate ran for municipal office in Paris; about the same time groups of socialists began holding public meetings and distributing pamphlets; and in 1879 the French Workers' party, more popularly known as the Guesdists after its leader Jules Guesde, came into being.[58] To the socialism of collective trade associations Guesde added a revolutionary program which envisioned the creation of a socialist state through spontaneous workers' revolt. The distinctive features of the Guesdists' program, all more or less consistent with the writings of Marx and Engels, included demands for the collectivization of property, the doctrine of class conflict, and a political party oriented specifically toward the interests of the proletariat.

Yet the socialist movement was fraught with difficulties from the beginning, and the Guesdist position was relatively slow in attracting adherents. Of the 130 socialist delegates gathered at the Marseilles Congress in 1879, for example, only 17 spoke in favor of revolutionary collectivism while nearly all of the remainder held fast to associationist strategies.[59]

The political development of the Loire, which was one of the more industrialized regions of France in the 1860s and 1870s, illustrates the circumstances that impeded revolutionary socialism. Although an independent workers' party with some affinities for socialist ideas emerged in the Loire, local politics were controlled by the republicans. In the election of 1869 republicans scored their first major electoral victory in this region and consolidated their victory over the next four years into a broadly supported political base. The structure of industry in the Loire tended to inhibit the development of a distinctly working-class movement separate from the republicans. Except for several large metallurgical complexes, most of the region's industry remained scattered among small metalworking and textile firms. The domestic putting out system was sufficiently intact that workers remained closely integrated into the social fabric of village life. Relatively few industrial workers were without some direct ties to the rural sector or to their own employers. The demographic strength of the political movement, therefore, lay primarily in the hands of the petty producers, small farmers, lower middle class, and skilled artisans, all of whom received support from the Republican party.

Much of the workers' political sentiment in the Loire was directed against the Bonapartist regime rather than the republicans because of the fact that working conditions were blamed mainly on the regime's trading policies with England. Socialist organizers thus found their own appeals diluted by working-class attraction to the republican platform, which promised an end to the imperial regime. The republicans were not above using force to suppress outbreaks of unrest among the working class, but their constituency reached down the social hierarchy to include many whose interests overlapped with those of the working class. Universal suffrage, democratic representation, freedom of the press, freedom of assembly, and reforms in the manufacturing establishments all appealed to the working class as well as to the lower bourgeoisie. Lacking the support of a powerful imperial bureaucracy, republicanism depended heavily on its ability to forge a broad coalition of popular support and thus was forced to take seriously many of the specific demands of the working class.[60]

The Loire was not unique in this respect. In the Nord the misfortunes of the textile industry during the 1860s had done much to discredit the imperial regime among the local bourgeoisie. In developing its strength as an opposition party the republican movement had granted concessions to textile workers and co-opted workers' organizations by incorporating them into the party's central committee structure. With the empire's defeat in 1871 the repubicans found themselves virtually unrivaled as masters of the local political machinery. The working class was only poorly differentiated from the lower strata of small producers and independent artisans, who were overwhelmingly loyal to the republican cause. As a result, socialist organizers had only a narrow constituency on which to build.[61]

Had the socialist movement been less concerned with achieving its goals through parliamentary politics it might have been able to ignore the strength of the republicans. But the rules of electoral politics required it to cooperate with the republican party if it was to hope for any degree of success, given the narrowness of its natural constituency. The threat of a conservative monarchical party ready to assert aristocratic privileges at the expense of popular freedoms repeatedly drove the socialists into the arms of the republicans. The particular French system of electioneering, which involved second balloting, also forced greater cooperation between the two parties. The net result, according to Labrousse, was that "a kind of inter-communication between Socialism and the Republic developed at all levels in the country: from municipal councils often elected on a common list of the Left established before the second or even first round, to the parliamentary committees in the Chamber of Deputies or the Bureau of the Chamber itself."[62]

Cooperation with the republicans, together with uncertainty as to how best to achieve working-class demands, and a poorly defined working class itself, all contributed to one of the distinguishing features of French socialism, as contrasted with the German SPD, a feature that is generally credited with further impeding the overall progress of the French movement: the proliferation of rival socialist sects as well as rival parties of other convictions all competing for working-class support. Democratic radicals in the Jacobin tradition functioned as key rivals of Marxist socialists, as did Blanquists, Proudhonists, and Bakuninists. In addition, Independents, Allemanists, and Possibilists, plus remnants of pre-Marxian, anarchist, and utopian socialist movements also competed for working-class adherents.

In 1880, only a year after the founding of the French Workers' party, the noncollectivist trade union elements split off from the Marxist oriented socialists. A year later the Blanquist party was formed as an alternative organization, calling for a revolutionary coup d'état but in practice working chiefly through parliamentary politics. Later in the same year further dissension broke out as a result of the frustrations of an election in which the socialists had received only 60,000 votes out of 7 million and had failed to elect a single candidate. The ensuing conflict pitted revolutionary collectivists against moderate reformists who believed that revolutionary ideology was too radical for the French context. The reformists succeeded in seizing control of the party and in 1882 founded the Federation of Socialist Workers. For the next decade the movement remained deeply divided between its Marxist and reformist factions.[63]

Among the divisions separating the several socialist factions were differences in their locations relative to the state and the bourgeoisie.[64] In contrast to the German socialists, who occupied a relatively uniform political position as a result of the label attached to them by the antisocialist laws, French socialists operated in a more variegated context. Different leaders were thus capable of advancing plausible arguments that differed in their view of both the republican state and the working class. Paul Brousse, for example, advocated gradual reforms achieved through alliances with liberal segments of the bourgeoisie; the disciples of Malon also sought alliances with the liberals and looked to the state as an instrument of reform; Guesde in contrast advocated a more purist revolutionary vision which shunned cooperation with the bourgeoisie.[65]

After 1890 the socialist movement finally began to evidence some noticeable growth. In 1893 nearly 600,000 votes were captured by the various socialist parties, and in 1898 this number climbed to nearly 900,000. Still far from wielding the power of the SPD in Germany, the movement nevertheless had made great strides since the 1880s. Several conditions contributed to this growth, among which were the enlargement of the working class itself, new legislation which gave government employees the right to organize, and a greater degree of unity within each of the main socialist parties concerning reformist goals and the value of focusing on electoral politics rather than dissipating resources on trade unionism and strikes.[66]

In addition, the socialist movement appears to have acquired a somewhat broader political niche in which to operate as a result of a gradual shift toward the right within the dominant parties. Philip Nord's research on the lower bourgeoisie during this period documents a significant shift to the right among shopkeepers' associations after 1890, which placed them in closer alliance with Social Catholicism and nationalist groups than with the working class.[67] By 1902 this trend had become sufficiently pronounced at the local level that even the municipal council in Paris was captured by the right. In the process, shopkeepers also ceased to be as exclusively oriented toward local communities (in which workers' interests were a significant political consideration) and shifted increasingly toward the formation of national syndicates to protect their own interests. The growing cleavage between shopkeepers and industrial workers provided opportunities for socialist organizers to appeal more directly to the working class.

During the decade before the First World War the socialist movement again grew in popularity, rising in the popular vote from about 900,000 in 1902 to nearly 1.5 million in 1910 and increasing in actual membership from 34,688 in 1905 to 72,765 in 1913.[68] Although this growth failed to bring the French movement anywhere near the strength of that in Germany, it set the stage for a continuing socialist presence felt in French politics long after the war. The surprising feature of this growth was that it occurred despite relatively little increase in the overall size of the industrial work force. Part of the explanation, however, must be sought in the fact that between 1900 and 1901, the five competing factions which then characterized French socialism were reduced to two, the French Socialist party and the Socialist party of France, and in 1905 these parties merged to form the Socialist party, giving French socialism its first truly national movement.

Despite efforts by the republicans to maintain support within the working class through various welfare reforms, these measures were largely ineffective in counteracting the ill effects of industrialization, thus giving the socialist movement an opportunity to attract working class support. Wage workers were beset by uneven and sluggish economic forces and by an increasing erosion of community ties in the face of market expansion, compulsory education, conscription, and regional integration. Producer cooperatives and syndical organizations promised economic and cultural remedies to these problems and socialism provided support for these visions. More important, socialism was the only political alternative to a liberal republican tradition which seemed increasingly to have become identified with the privileged classes.[69]

For all its gains during these years, French socialism nevertheless remained subject to many of the problems that had inhibited its early development. Acting through the state as well as through private organizations the bourgeoisie permitted trade unions to expand as

representatives of the working class, thus stripping the socialist movement of its exclusivity in this area and producing factionalism within
the movement.[70] Within the party the state's efforts to accommodate
working class demands also had a decisive effect in reinforcing reformist views and eroding revolutionary Marxist ideology. Minimum
wages were established in many industries, labor unions were given
a greater voice in the formulation of labor legislation, the workday
was reduced to ten hours, an old age pension plan was proposed
(although not adopted), and a Labor Council was established. Mod-
erates within the socialist party were able to press these achievements
to ideological advantage, while radicals and extremists remained divided.[71]

The party thus became less and less an opposition movement,
serving instead as a broad coalition of interests which somewhat
ambivalently supported reform but lacked any particularly distinct
relation to the industrial working class. Aaron Noland suggests, in
fact, that after 1905 the movement became increasingly "a mass party
which sought the support and endeavored to represent the interests
of certain broad non-proletarian segments of the population—the
petite bourgeoisie and the peasantry, including the peasant proprietors—as well as the working class."[72]

There was, finally, yet another way in which the broader political
structure conditioned the development of French socialism. In the
decade between the Congress of Unity in 1905 and the First World
War the party explicitly focused an increasing share of its attention
on ideology. Having conceded the dangers of too close a relation
with the republicans—or as some perceived it the dangers of trying
to accomplish its political objectives too quickly—and yet clinging
to the distinct hope of an eventual crisis that would bring the working
class to power, the party found that the main course of action left
open to it was neither to work in total harmony with the republicans
for concrete reforms nor to sit passively by waiting for revolution,
but to prepare the working class for its role in the postrevolutionary
period.[73] Efforts to disseminate socialist teachings thus proceeded on
all fronts, including speeches and lectures by party leaders, printed
propaganda, and to some extent the symbolic tactics of mass action.
These efforts contributed to the party's successes at the polls, but
the rationale for electoral politics became chiefly that of education.
Thus, the shortcomings of an overzealous commitment to either

reform or revolution led in the end to an emphasis on the production of ideology which created a lasting image for French socialism, but one that far exceeded its actual accomplishments.

Industrial Expansion in Great Britain

Like France, Great Britain also provides an interesting comparison case for examining the social conditions associated with the development of socialism. Here, despite an exceedingly strong record of industrialization, socialism also failed to become institutionalized on any scale comparable to that in Germany. British socialism specialized in electoral politics and in revolutionary ideology, much as its counterpart did in France. The two countries shared some of the more subtle characteristics of economic development that seem to have inhibited socialist movements. But Britain was on the whole considerably more prone to such movements on the basis of its economic characteristics alone than was France. The relative failure of British socialism in spite of these conditions, therefore, points strongly to the importance of other factors such as the role of liberal parties and the state.

By most indications British industrialization in the nineteenth century advanced both steadily and rapidly, not at the rate of Germany, but certainly faster than in France. Over the course of the entire nineteenth century, for example, the index of industrial production calculated by B. R. Mitchell demonstrates that British industrial output doubled approximately every thirty years, compared to a doubling in Germany approximately every twenty years and in France only about every forty years.[74] Overall gross national product at market prices in Britain doubled between 1870 and 1910, compared with an increase of approximately 2.7 in Germany and only 1.6 in France. In absolute terms British GNP exceeded that of Germany by 10 to 20 percent in all years except 1910 and gradually extended its lead over that of France by approximately 35 to 40 percent.[75]

According to sectoral comparisons, Britain was by far the most heavily industrialized of the three countries, even by the middle of the nineteenth century, and retained its lead until the First World War. In 1850 only 21 percent of total national product in Britain came from agriculture, compared with 47 percent in Germany and 45 percent in France. By 1910 this figure had shrunk to 6 percent in Britain, compared with 25 percent in Germany and 35 percent in France.[76] Despite the fact that Germany made tremendous gains on Britain's early position of dominance as a leader in industry, Britain managed to hold on to its lead until the close of the nineteenth century. In these terms Britain and Germany resembled each other as industrial powers to a much greater extent than either resembled France; for example, in 1900 approximately 20 percent of all manufacturing output in the world came from Britain, and Germany contributed nearly as much (17 percent), while France contributed only 7 percent.[77]

As a percentage of the labor force British industry showed relatively little change, rising from only 28 percent in 1871 to 31 percent in 1911. Absolute growth in the industrial labor force was quite pronounced, however, because of the rapid growth in population as a whole. Thus, the already sizable industrial labor force of 6.2 million in 1871 nearly doubled over the next forty years, reaching 11.1 million by 1911. Industries which in other countries were particularly susceptible to socialist organizing grew at an especially rapid pace: manufacturing from 4.4 million to 7.1 million, mining from 0.6 million to 1.2 million, construction from 0.7 million to 1.1 million, and transportation from 0.7 million to 1.6 million. In absolute terms, then, the British industrial proletariat was the largest in western Europe, exceeding that of Germany by more than 1.5 million and France by nearly 5 million. In terms of growth it had also expanded the most in the forty years prior to the First World War, adding some 4.8 million workers, compared with 4.5 million in Germany and approximately 1.7 million in France.[78]

By other indications, the growth of British industry would also appear to have disposed it favorably toward socialist movements to a degree resembling that in Germany and to a much greater degree than in France. The extent of geographic mobility as a measure of potential social disruption was nearly as great in England as in Germany and considerably higher than in France: 28.4 percent of the British population in 1890 recorded residences in counties other than those of their birth, compared with 30.3 percent in Prussia, and 30.9 percent in Saxony but only 18.7 percent in France.[79] Urbanization was even more pronounced: in 1900 53.6 percent of the English population and 42.4 percent of the Scottish population lived in cities of twenty thousand or more residents, compared with only 21.9 percent of the German population and 21.1 percent of the

French population.[80] Between 1850 and 1890 England had also experienced a higher annual rate of increase in urban concentration (.56 percent) than either Prussia (.47 percent) or France (.29 percent).[81] As in Germany, local areas in which industry was heavily concentrated grew at particularly rapid rates; for example, Cardiff in South Wales grew from 33,000 in 1861 to 196,000 in 1911, Edinburgh rose from 168,000 to 298,000 over the same period, and Glasgow and Dundee grew even more rapidly.[82]

As in Germany and France, real wages in Britain rose fairly steadily in the half century or so prior to the First World War. Sidney Pollard's index, anchored at 100 for 1850-1859, shows a rise in real wages from 130 in the 1870s to 146 in the 1880s, 171 in the 1890s, and 196 between 1900 and 1909.[83] Other measures, however, suggest that inequality and immiseration were at least as severe in Britain as in Germany or France. Simon Kuznets's calculations of economic inequality based on distribution of national income, for example, suggest that in 1880 48 percent of British national income went to only 5 percent of the population; by comparison, the top 5 percent of Prussia's population took only 26 percent of its national income.[84] Using death rates per thousand population as an indicator, Theodore Hamerow has suggested that immiseration was higher in England's five largest cities (30.8) than in Paris (26.1), the Nord (25.6), or industrialized sections of Germany such as Düsseldorf (20.3) and Arnsberg (20.6).[85] In absolute terms, Zygmunt Bauman has estimated that about 40 percent of the British labor force lacked the means to provide for their basic needs.[86] Many of these workers were also the victims of periodic unemployment, the rate of which reached highs of 7.5 percent of the labor force in 1893, 6 percent in 1904, and 7.8 percent in 1908.[87]

If socialism were simply the product of rapid industrialization leading to an enlarged industrial working class subject to the miseries of poverty, social dislocation, and urbanization, the British context should have produced a powerful socialist movement of the kind that appeared in Germany. As the comparison of Germany and France has already suggested, however, the institutionalization of socialism was to a very great extent conditioned by the state as well as by industrialization alone. The social construction of an identifiable class-conscious proletariat ready to throw its weight behind a socialist movement was as much a function of political conditions as it was of economic conditions. In Britain, just as in France, the state played a major role in inhibiting the development of a distinct proletariat having these characteristics.

The State as Institutional Context

The rapid rise in economic resources that characterized Britain during the last half of the nineteenth century made possible a dramatic increase in the size of the state bureaucracy. Between 1851 and 1881, for example, the number of public administrators grew from 64,000 to 109,000, and by 1911 this figure had risen to 271,000. Over the same period the size of the armed forces grew from 63,000 to 114,000 to 221,000. Of the total number in public employment, those employed directly by the civil service grew from 50,000 in 1881 to 162,000 in 1911.[88] Much of this growth was made possible by the tremendous increase in government revenue that took place at approximately the same time. Between 1830 and 1870 government revenue had remained virtually constant, rising only 26 percent from £54 million to £68 million. But after 1870 government revenue shot up dramatically, nearly tripling at £204 million in 1910 and rising still further as war became imminent.[89] As a percentage of gross national product, government revenue was high—approximately equivalent to the 7 or 8 percent extracted by the state in Germany. But the growth in absolute revenues came mostly as a result of broader economic expansion rather than an increase in the rate of extraction itself.[90]

In addition to paying for the growth in bureaucratic personnel, the expansion of government revenue permitted an overall increase in a variety of government programs, some of which were directed toward ameliorating the condition of the industrial working class. For example, expenditures on social services of all kinds increased from £27.3 million in 1890 to £100.8 million in 1913, added to which local government expenditures rose from £19.4 million to £64.3 million.[91] As in Germany and France, an important share of these expenditures went to education. Between 1870 and 1910 the number of primary teachers rose from 14,000 to 164,000, while the number of primary pupils rose from 1.2 million to 5.4 million.[92] The state also took an increasingly active role in coercing school attendance (making attendance compulsory at the primary level in 1880) and in securing its own monopoly over the supply of education. By 1880 29.5 percent of all schools were operated by the state, as opposed to religious or charitable institutions, and this proportion rose steadily to 61.5 percent in 1910.[93] Thus, as in Germany and France, the state came increasingly to dominate one of the country's principal means of ideological dissemination.

The expansion of the state, therefore, was of direct relevance to the production of culture. This expansion, nevertheless, was carried out with quite different consequences than in Germany, where the bureaucracy became a major actor in the conservative aristocratic coalition. In Britain the bureaucracy developed in the context of a strong parliamentary system that jealously protected its own power from being subordinated to the bureaucracy. Indeed, decisive steps toward limiting the political strength of the bureaucracy were taken in 1855, when a civil service system based on merit as determined by competitive examination was initiated, and in 1870, when this system became fully operational.[94] The result of this system was to protect the dual party system which had developed in parliamentary politics and to preclude either party or the crown from exploiting patronage or bureaucratic offices to its own advantage, as in Germany. The party system which initiated this policy and which benefited from it was in turn a major factor influencing the development of British socialism.

Power was divided almost evenly between the Conservative and Liberal parties. The Conservatives' stronghold remained the rural aristocracy, while that of the Liberals included the urban industrialists and, after the electoral reforms of 1884, a lower-class constituency among the Celtic fringe, miners, and agricultural laborers. The Liberal party had come into being during the 1860s as a coalition of Whigs, Radicals, and Nonconformists. Although it generally held the upper hand in Parliament, the two parties were sufficiently balanced that the government alternated according to the marginal strength of each party: Liberals held a slight majority from 1868 to 1874, from 1880 to 1885, and from 1906 to 1913, while Conservatives held a small advantage from 1874 to 1880 and from 1886 to 1905.

Political parties as such played a considerably more important role in British politics than in Germany or France, partly as a result of the long history of development of the British party system, and partly because of the uniqueness of the British franchise system. Party organizations were indispensable to political candidates because a high degree of mobility among the population, coupled with residence requirements, meant that armies of volunteers were needed to register voters. After any given election as many as half the voters were likely to be off the lists by the following year.[95] It was chiefly after the Reform Act of 1867 that both parties came to realize the need for greater levels of party organization and discipline in order to attract voters. After being defeated in the 1868 election, the Conservative party set up a Conservative Central Office to co-ordinate registration and campaign efforts. In 1877 the Liberal Central Association, a reorganization of the Liberal Registration Association, was established to perform a similar function for the Liberal party. Following its defeat in 1874, the Liberal party also initiated party organizations at the municipal level based on ward divisions and administered by an oligarchic structure which maintained party control while reaching more effectively to the grass roots in the cities.[96]

The various franchise reforms that were initiated between the 1860s and 1880s also played a role in determining the character of party politics. Although the franchise in Britain was not universal as in Germany or France, it was broadened to a considerable extent during this period, thus for the first time making working-class constituencies relevant to electoral campaigns.[97] Between 1866 and 1885 the population eligible to vote increased from approximately 1 million to 4.4 million, or about 60 percent of all adult males.[98] In the short term the franchise reforms brought immediate gains to the Liberal party, particularly in the years from 1868 to 1874. The more consequential result of an enlarged franchise, however, was to stabilize the strength of the two established parties. As J. A. Hawgood notes: "It helped to restore the clear-cut two party system in the country and in Parliament and ended the dangerous drift toward a system of groups."[99]

The political context that emerged in Britain just prior to the development of a socialist movement, therefore, was characterized by a relatively distinct split between Conservatives and Liberals. Both parties were on their way toward developing a well-disciplined form of party organization which made possible recruiting efforts among the working class. The extension of the franchise made working-class constituents relevant to the vitality of both parties, and the relative equivalence in strength between the two parties provided incentives for each to compete for working-class allegiance. This situation, then, was similar in many respects to that in France, with the exception that the Liberals in Britain were faced by a better organized opposition party on the right and thus had an even greater incentive to seek the loyalty of working-class supporters. Unlike in Germany, where the preponderance of elite strength on the right gave the working class almost exclusively to the socialists, the British working class remained subject to strong efforts by the liberals to capture its allegiance.

British Socialism

The origin of British socialism is generally dated to 1883, the year in which all three of the major socialist organizations with ideological ties to Marxism were founded: the Social Democratic Federation, the Fabian Society, and the Fellowship of the New Life. Although the activities of informal socialist gatherings appear to have waned during the 1870s as a result of depressed economic conditions, the success of the SPD in Germany, which by 1877 had polled nearly half a million votes, was of great inspiration to socialists in Britain. Visions of similar accomplishments in electoral politics encouraged them to organize on a broader scale, and an influx of German exiles helped to create a small cadre of dedicated leaders. As late as 1880, however, socialist ideology remained limited to relatively small pockets of alienated subalterns and clerks rather than having any broader base among the working class.

The Social Democratic Federation came about chiefly as a reaction to power shifts within the Liberal party which were perceived as a move toward the right and away from representing working-class interests. But it was from the start, as the name implied, a federation of diverse groups without any particular fondness for socialist ideology as such. Leaders who held strongly to socialist doctrines were thus forced from the beginning to contend with an organization based on compromise and oriented more toward practical accomplishments than the advancement of a pure ideological program.[100] It was, nevertheless, the most successful of the three socialist organizations in developing a political agenda. The Fabians remained small and were oriented toward abstract intellectual discussion, while the Fellowship of the New Life bore a closer ideological affinity to the Ethical Union than to socialism. All three were largely the creation of middle-class professionals and intellectuals whose meetings, not unlike those at the London coffeehouses of the Enlightenment, blended together various utopian, religious, and

moral ideals.[101] Their ideas combined elements of Scottish human-
ism, the Dissenting tradition, and utilitarianism, but as George
Lichtheim has remarked, "no sizable body of opinion on the British
Left adopted even a watered-down form of Marxism."[102]

The 1890s brought greater success to the socialist movement
than the 1880s. From a combined membership of only 2,056 in 1889,
the various socialist organizations grew to approximately 23,000
members by 1901. Membership in the Social Democratic Federation
grew from 1,000 to 9,000, the Fabian Society increased its membership from 200 to 900, and the Socialist League (which had split
from the Federation in 1885 and then had given birth to the socialist-
oriented Independent Labour party in 1892) had a combined membership of approximately 13,000. Over the same period the various
socialist organizations also succeeded in increasing their vote in electoral politics, gaining 44,000 votes in 1895 and 87,000 in 1899.[103]

British socialism in the 1890s was devoted, as on the Continent,
to an exceptional array of voluntary and leisure activities, including
Saturday night dances, scouting organizations, sing-alongs, labor
picnics, bazaars and junk sales, and charitable activities such as providing hot meals for the poor and care for orphans. In addition to
offering occasions for sociability, often in lieu of religious services,
these activities were designed to capture newspaper attention and
thus to disseminate socialist ideology. Wherever possible, local notables and speakers with national reputations were brought together
to maximize both attendance and press coverage. An eyewitness who
played a personal role in organizing a meeting in London in 1888 at
which the cultural figure William Morris was to speak wrote later:
"Socialist lectures were as a rule designedly ignored by the local
newspapers, but they could not conveniently avoid mentioning the
visit of so great a figure as William Morris, and when the Monday
papers reported that the principal at the University College of the
town had taken the chair at a Socialist meeting, the local philistines
gasped with horror, and became incoherent with rage. Did they
employ a professor of literature to give aid and comfort to a rabble
of confiscating Socialists?[104]

But the purpose of public meetings and voluntary activities was
not simply to propagate socialist rhetoric; it was also to provide a
vivid experience of the unity and uplift that could be gained from
working for the socialist cause. At the grassroots the socialist gatherings that sprang up in Britain during the 1890s were highly emo-

tional and exuded an almost contagious enthusiasm. They contained a vision of hope for the working classes that transcended class conflict and material conditions, often finding expression in the religious language of "brotherhood," "salvation," "mission," and "kingdom." Leaders without any religious affinities in their own backgrounds turned to imagery of the transcendent to capture the sense of liberation and excitement they found in participating in the movement."[105] Many of them looked back later with wistful longing to the time when these visions seemed not only real and compelling but also possible. At the popular level, socialism showed signs of being a spontaneous, visionary, millenarian movement. As George Bernard Shaw wrote in 1897: "Socialism wins its disciples by presenting civilization as a popular melodrama, or as a Pilgrim's Progress through suffering, trial, and combat against the powers of evil to the bar of poetic justice with paradise beyond."[106]

For all its fervor, British socialism was nevertheless severely limited by its social and cultural environment. The lack of clear, unifying objectives which produced factional tendencies in French socialism had the same effect in Britain. In addition to the three major national organizations, there were in the 1890s at least forty-six socialist societies or socialist unions independent of any national grouping. The various socialist sects disagreed on such fundamental questions of policy as their relation to the liberal parties, their relation to the trade union movement, collectivization, imperialism, and welfare reforms. The strength of the Liberal party in working-class districts was particularly problematic for socialist leaders since it encouraged them to adopt much the same set of proposals but at the same time rendered ambiguous the identity of the socialist movement. Although they supported the socialist vision of collectivization, they deemphasized class conflict, sought to involve the middle class in their activities, agreed with the Liberal party on issues such as universal suffrage and land reform, and envisioned welfare reforms coming about chiefly through legislation and the civil service. R. H. Tawney, writing a few years after the First World War, summarized the earlier period by suggesting that "compared with Continental Socialism, British Socialism has been tentative and experimental, saying little about the inevitability of class struggles and much of the possibility of cooperation for communal ends."[107]

In addition to its own problems of identity the socialist movement in Britain was also faced with an extraordinary number of rival organizations. Despite its relatively advanced industrialization, British society was characterized by a large number of voluntary, charitable, religious, and trade organizations which cut across class lines and provided services to the working class.[108] "Friendly societies," with membership numbering upwards of 4 million in 1890 and 14 million in 1909, provided insurance against economic fluctuations as well as old age benefits for large numbers of workers; consumer cooperatives, enlisting at least 500,000 workers, functioned effectively in certain segments of the market; Methodists, Quakers, and Anglicans competed with one another to provide not only religious care but services ranging from poor relief to model housing construction; and trade unions were well organized in many of the more skilled sections of the working class.[109] During the last two decades before the war the trade unions became particularly prominent, growing in membership from approximately 750,000 in 1888 to 4.1 million in 1913.[110] By the latter date nearly one person in ten belonged to a union, compared with only one person in twenty in Germany and one person in forty in France. Moreover, 46 percent of all union expenditures in Britain were paid out in member benefits, compared to only 21 percent in Germany; thus, the British unions were by no means an inconsequential economic factor.[111] Given both legal protection and economic backing by the Liberal party, union leaders tended for the most part to disdain socialism and to support Liberal candidates as well as Liberal positions on issues such as tariffs, education, and temperance.[112]

After 1900 the socialist movement grew more rapidly than it had during the previous two decades, reaching approximately 44,000 members by 1910, of whom 30,000 belonged to the Independent Labour party, 12,000 belonged to the Social Democratic Federation, and 2,000 to the Fabian Society. Much of this growth was again attributable to active associational functions at the local level, such as labor clubs, choirs, and educational societies. These functions were particularly effective in northern counties around Yorkshire, Lancashire, and the Colne Valley, where religious attendance was low and labor unions had failed to become established.[113] Yet in comparison with the Friendly Societies and trade unions, socialist membership was extremely small. By 1914 the various socialist organizations were able to capture only 6 percent of the popular vote, the lowest of any of the industrialized countries in western Europe.[114]

The difficulties that the socialist movement faced in developing a broad working class constituency in Britain were, as in France, to a considerable degree a product of the strength of the Liberal party and its efforts, motivated in large measure by competition from the Conservatives, to win over substantial support from the working class. In Britain these efforts played an important role in laying the groundwork for a strong trade union movement that was virtually free of socialist influences. Between 1867 and 1876 both parties competed to enhance their share of the working-class vote by sponsoring legislation which established a firm legal basis for trade unions. Among the most significant of these acts were the Trade Union Act of 1871, the Conspiracy and Property Protection Act of 1875, and the Trade Union Amendment Act of 1876.[115] According to Stanley Pierson: "The trade unions and the other working class associations helped integrate the workers into the developing capitalistic system and strengthen the spirit of 'labourism' and class collaboration." Pierson also goes on to say: "The narrow range of trade union concerns and their relative effectiveness in protecting the interests of the workers served, in fact, to inoculate broad sections of the British working classes against the appeal of socialism."[116]

The affinity between labor and the Liberal party was, however, deeper than a mutuality of interests built only around the Liberals' support of trade unions. By the 1870s the Liberal party had a well-established reputation as an opposition movement which generally stood for social reform. Born between the 1830s and 1850s, it had attracted widespread support in urban areas, not only among industrialists but among merchants, proprietors of small businesses, and artisans, all of whom were disenchanted with the Tory party's indifference to the towns and its subservience to the rural aristocracy.[117] Liberalism also gained the support of Nonconformists, including Unitarians, Congregationalists, and Independents, who saw in the party a base from which to oppose the ecclesiastical hierarchy and established wealth. In the 1880s much of the working-class support that the party received continued to derive from Nonconformists as well as from ethnic minorities identified with the Celtic fringe. In this respect the strength of British liberalism was based, as in Germany, in minority religions and in regional peripheries. Yet, in contrast with the situation in Germany, the conservative coalition never succeeded in mobilizing the machinery of the state bureaucracy to crush this opposition.

Apart from religious and ethnic factors, there was also wide-spread working-class support for the Liberal party because it constituted a viable means of opposing privilege and achieving social reform. Studies of pre-1914 voting patterns uniformly point toward a strong bias among working-class voters toward the Liberal party.[118] In expressing these preferences, the working class manifested much the same orientation as members of the lower middle class. In a pattern similar to that observed in France, the result of early and somewhat steady industrialization in Britain was an apparent reduction in sharp differences between these two classes. At the upper end, the working class blended almost imperceptibly into the lower middle class of salaried white collar workers such as clerks, bank tellers, and teachers. Most of the latter retained close family ties with the former. They went to the same primary schools, had nearly the same amount of income, and were equally subordinate in the workplace.[119] Bauman writes: "The skilled worker copied the models set up by the lower levels of the middle class in such matters as the furnishings of his home, his style of life and his preferred recreations. He sent his children to the same schools and instilled into his offspring ideals of advancement in life which were borrowed from the lower middle class. Like the main body of that class, he was moderately conservative . . . and valued peace and order above all else as the surest guarantee of his modest but quite important privileges."[120] The chief differences were that lower middle-class families enjoyed slightly greater job security, remained somewhat more active in the churches, and tended to think of themselves as a "cut above" the working class. In political orientations the two were much alike.

An alliance between middle-class Liberals and the working class was also reinforced by the character of the British electoral system. Candidates for political office had to pay their own campaign expenses, officers' fees, and livelihood. It was for this reason unlikely for a working-class candidate to win office without financial backing from one of the established parties. This problem was confounded by the fact that socialist, radical, or labor candidates were reluctant to enter races as opponents of the Liberals for fear of splitting the Liberal vote and thereby contributing to a Conservative victory.[121] The net result of this situation was not to force working-class candidates into the arms of the socialists, as in Germany; instead, the competition between Conservatives and Liberals led to a greater degree of acceptance of working-class candidates within the Liberal party itself. By 1885, eleven candidates from working-class backgrounds had already been elected to Parliament on the Liberal ticket, and this number increased gradually during the following two decades.[122]

In contrast with the situation in Germany, the Conservative coalition in Britain failed to weaken substantially the strength of the Liberals over any extended period prior to the First World War. Some evidence points to the fact that segments of the wealthier industrial bourgeoisie defected to the Conservative party, not unlike in Germany, during the 1890s.[123] This shift was counteracted, however, by an erosion of Conservative strength in rural districts, as estate holders shifted toward foreign investments to escape property taxes, and by a migration to the suburbs among wealthy industrialists, which left urban districts such as London and Manchester firmly in the hands of a liberal bourgeoisie.[124] Thus, contrary to some studies in the 1930s, which suggested that the Liberal party had begun to decline as early as the turn of the century, it appears that both nationally and regionally (with the possible exception of some sections of London) the Liberal party was in no apparent decline until after 1914.

From the 1880s onward, socialist leaders recognized that any success they might hope for would have to come by weaning workers away from their dependence on the Liberal party and the trade unions. This task was in fact most easily accomplished during those times when the Liberal party appeared temporarily to be in decline. The late 1870s and early 1880s, during which the major socialist parties were organized, was one such period. In London Conservative victories continued with significant force until 1890, giving the socialists an even longer period in which to mobilize. The process of mobilization, indeed, spoke strongly to the conditioning effects of the Liberal party. This process was typified by working-class defections from the Liberal party *before* any viable alternative was available, and only then by working-class leaders joining ranks to form socialist organizations. Another period during which socialism made some headway as a result of a temporary lapse in Liberal strength was 1907 and 1908. In these years Conservative gains in working-class districts as a result of rising nationalistic and religious sentiments led some Liberal candidates to step aside voluntarily on the assumption that socialist and labor candidates might be able to make a more effective showing.[125]

But generally the strong presence of the Liberal party not only posed a serious external barrier to the socialist movement but also raised a significant dilemma for socialist leaders. From the very beginning the socialist movement was divided by the issue of whether parliamentary action was a feasible approach or whether the strength of the Liberal party was so incontestable that only extraparliamentary activities could provide a raison d'être for the movement. This issue perhaps more than any other divided the leadership of the Socialist League, leading the parliamentary faction gradually to withdraw and the remainder to veer increasingly toward anarchism. The Social Democratic Federation was split by virtually the same issue. Those who favored building up strength to participate in parliamentary elections saw the desirability of compromising with the Liberals and with the trade unions in order to gain support; others clung to the goal of a separate but purely socialist organization. In the Fabian Society, similarly, a majority favored parliamentary means of achieving reform and saw the most effective method of parliamentary action to be cooperation with the Liberal party, but this strategy kept the Fabians from taking a more aggressive role in courting the working class and in the long run worked against the stability of the Fabian Society.[126]

In a somewhat indirect manner the relatively balanced division of power between the Liberal and Conservative parties also worked to the disadvantage of the socialists by deterring the trade unions from becoming involved in political causes. The official stance of the national Trade Union Congress (T.U.C.), adopted for a variety of reasons among which was the necessity of securing protection early in its existence from both Liberal and Conservative governments, was one of political neutrality. This policy had the effect of focusing labor activity away from direct political organizing and thus dealt a blow to socialist members of the T.U.C. who wished to involve it in such actions. Rather than seeking mass support like the German SPD, the T.U.C. worked mainly for legislative reforms favorable to its membership, thus involving it in compromises and bipartisan programs.

Having permitted the growth of trade unions, the state was also in a position to pass legislation aimed at improving working-class conditions and to co-opt working-class leaders into administrative positions. Had it not been for the establishment of unions in a wide spectrum of industries, it seems doubtful that the state would have been able to administer the social welfare programs it initiated. Union leaders provided information on issues such as industrial safety and workers' compensation. Labor exchanges and national insurance schemes required the same kind of involvement. The success of these programs depended on workers' cooperation, which the unions were able to deliver. Moreover, the cost of distributing benefits would likely have been prohibitive had bureaus and staff been set up from scratch either by the state or by employers. The unions, in contrast, were already organized at the level of the firm, thus providing an effective administrative apparatus which was well articulated with variations across firms, occupations, and industries. This degree of articulation, unlike that of a mass political party, was conducive to the administration of benefit plans which detracted from workers' enthusiasm for socialist political visions.

Welfare programs seem to have inhibited socialism in part by reducing the motivation for more radical economic reforms; at least this was the hope of those who supported the various welfare bills. But socialism was also inhibited much more directly by virtue of the fact that the state incorporated working-class leaders into the administration of these programs. Staffs of administrators distributed unemployment compensation, kept records on strikes and work stoppages, and worked through trade unions to calculate insurance and disability payments. These positions included a sufficient number of socialists and labor activists that a vital element of grass-roots leadership was lost to the socialist movement.[127]

Leaders who remained active in socialist organizations also discovered, often to their chagrin, that on a day-to-day basis the state seemed to function more as a friend than as an enemy. The meritocratic examination system which had been adopted by the civil service made it relatively easy, at least more so than in Germany or France, for members of opposition parties, including socialists, to penetrate the bureaucracy. For example, two of the founding members of the Fabian Society, Sidney Webb and Sydney Oliver, were both employed by the civil service, the latter enjoying a long and distinguished career in the Colonial Office.[128] Others cultivated ties through the Board of Trade and the Bureau of Labor Statistics. The irony of the conservative Charles Booth collecting statistics on the plight of London's poor with the assistance of the protosocialist Beatrice Potter, for example, has not escaped the attention of historians. By the turn of the century the Fabian Society in particular had become a fairly respectable research enterprise and clearinghouse for social reform ideas. Its leaders were able to use personal ties with government officials on more than one occasion to influence policy.[129]

With resources of this kind at its disposal the socialist movement might have been expected to make greater strides than it did. Yet the absorptive quality of the state was a mixed blessing. It provided opportunities for socialists to influence legislative actions, but in so doing it also channeled their attention away from a distinct socialist agenda and toward a program of ameliorative welfare reform. Socialism, therefore, failed to flourish as a distinct ideology or as a separate and identifiable party, but it did serve to strengthen the stability of the established state system and, indeed, legitimated an expansion of the state into a whole realm of welfare activities.[130]

14 ❧

Socialism in the Broader European Context

THE COMPARISONS between Germany on the one hand and England and France on the other suggest the importance of state structures in addition to economic conditions in accounting for the relative success of the socialist movement. Socialist ideology, it appears, became more fully institutionalized in party politics when rapid industrialization was accompanied by the presence of a conservative aristocratic regime that weakened the liberal bourgeoisie's capacity to forge an alliance with the proletariat. Under these conditions, socialist parties had freer rein in mobilizing the working class around their own social-democratic appeals. When a liberal or republican regime was in power, the bourgeoisie was more effective in weaning working-class support away from socialist parties. It thus appears that the broad environmental conditions associated with industrialization influenced the development of socialist ideology through the specific institutional contexts of state bureaucracies, cleavages within the ruling class, political party competition, and the balances among these various forces. There are, however, unique aspects of the German case—especially in the relations between Prussia and the south German states—that make one hesitant to generalize about the effects of these conditions on socialism elsewhere. For this reason, the additional comparisons made possible by the other European countries in which industrialization was taking place on a significant scale—the Scandinavian countries, Belgium and the Netherlands, and Italy and Spain—become particularly important.

Socialism in the Scandinavian Context

The social conditions influencing the development of socialist parties in Scandinavia were for the most part more similar to those in Germany than in France or England. The broader social environment in the Scandinavian countries was characterized generally by rapid industrialization occurring within the specific context of a royalist-aristocratic state. Consequently, liberal bourgeois parties and labor unions were relatively weak. The socialist parties experienced some repression but generally had access to the working class. Their orientations became increasingly political as a result of struggles between the liberal and aristocratic factions over the franchise. They also gained some support from the liberal parties, but these parties were too weak to dominate or thwart the growth of socialism in the ways they did in France and Great Britain. These patterns are most evident in Sweden. To a somewhat lesser degree they also characterize Denmark, while Norway exhibits greater liberal strength and consequently a somewhat weaker and less political socialist movement.

Attempts to account for the development of socialism in Scandinavia have generally focused on economic factors. The so-called Bull-Galenson hypothesis, for example, has emphasized the effects of rapid industrialization in promoting radical socialist orientations among the working class.[1] According to this hypothesis, rapid industrialization in the Scandinavian countries led to a rapid expansion of the industrial labor force, and this expansion was associated with dislocation and atomization, which in turn rendered the working class more susceptible to the appeals of radical socialism. Assuming (from qualitative historical observations) that socialism was more radical in Norway than in Denmark, Edward Bull and Walter Galenson (and their followers) focused on comparing the rates of industrialization and correlative indicators of social dislocation in these two countries.

The Bull-Galenson argument is, of course, similar to ones about the effects of rapid industrialization that we have already considered for Germany, France, and England. In those contexts I presented some counterarguments that cast doubt on the degree to which social dislocation could actually be associated with socialist strength. Nevertheless, on the whole, the fact that Germany did experience more rapid industrialization by many indications than either France or England makes it impossible to dismiss the Bull-Galenson hypothesis entirely. Thus, the comparisons provided by the Scandinavian countries warrant careful consideration.

Some evidence appears to support the Bull-Galenson explanation for the more radical orientation of socialism in Norway than in Denmark. For example, the number of industrial workers in Norway grew from approximately 70,000 in 1897 to approximately 136,000 in 1915, an increase of 94 percent, whereas Denmark's industrial work force grew from only 178,000 to 227,000 over the same period, an increase of only 27 percent.[2] These figures are at least consistent with Galenson's argument that Denmark began to industrialize somewhat earlier in the nineteenth century because of a relatively strong agricultural sector, whereas Norway did not begin to industrialize rapidly until the end of the century, mostly as a result of the introduction of electricity. Consistent with this thesis, as Galenson also demonstrated, urbanization occurred earlier in Denmark than in Norway: by 1870, for instance, 25 percent of the Danish population lived in cities and towns, compared with 17 percent of the Norwegian population. Thus, the potential for social dislocation was greater, Galenson argued, in the country that was less urbanized at the start.

Closer examination of the data, however, yields negative evidence. Studies by Simon Kuznets and William Lafferty, for example, have focused on changes in the relative size of the industrial labor force as a proportion of the total labor force instead of looking at absolute employment figures. Their data confirm that Denmark probably began to industrialize earlier than Norway. For instance, in 1870 24 percent of the Danish labor force was in industry compared with only 16 percent of the Norwegian labor force. These comparisons also suggest that Norway industrialized faster than Denmark between 1870 and 1900, with increases of 62 percent and 17 percent respectively. The negative evidence comes mainly from comparing the two countries between 1890 and 1910, the period in which the differences in socialism supposedly became more apparent. Norway's industrial work force grew only from 22 percent to 25 percent of the labor force, not substantially more than Denmark's, which grew from 26 percent to 28 percent. In other words, neither country showed much change, and even the overall levels of industrialization were much the same. Moreover, both countries' rates of industrialization were low in comparison with Sweden's. Between 1890 and 1910 the proportion of Sweden's labor force engaged in industrial work grew from 19 percent to 29 percent; and over the whole period from 1870 to 1910 Sweden's proportion of the labor force in industry grew 123 percent, compared with 56 percent in Norway and 17 percent in Denmark.[3]

Evidence from studies of social dislocation also cast doubt on the Bull-Galenson hypothesis. At a minimum, crude measures of social dislocation are sufficiently ambiguous to raise questions. For example, in support of the hypothesis Bull showed that the urban population in Norway increased by more than 70 percent between 1870 and 1910, compared with an increase of only 60 percent in Denmark. Yet the actual figures for Norway were 17 percent urban in 1870 and 29 percent urban in 1910, while the actual figures for Denmark were 25 percent and 40 percent respectively. In absolute terms, therefore, Denmark shifted by 15 percentage points, compared to a change of only 12 points for Norway. Furthermore, the greatest single decadal increase occurred in Denmark: a shift from 33 percent to 39 percent urban between 1890 and 1900.[4] More damaging is the evidence produced by Lafferty. Using suicide rates as a measure of social dislocation, Lafferty examined the actual correlations between this measure and socialist voting, taking five-year intervals as units of analysis in Denmark, Sweden, and Norway. In none of the three countries was there a significant positive relation (Norway .007, Sweden −.143, Denmark −.542). If anything, the results suggest that this kind of social dislocation dampened rather than enhanced the likelihood of socialist voting.[5] Lafferty's results also cast doubt on the more general idea of immiseration as a source of socialism. The strongest predictors of socialist voting in all three countries were wage levels: the higher the wages, the greater the socialist voting (Denmark .957, Sweden .840, Norway .786). Income per capita, while a somewhat less direct measure, also showed a strong positive relation.[6]

Such results do not rule out the importance of economic factors. But they do cast into doubt the value of relating differences in the three Scandinavian countries too precisely to differences in economic conditions. Instead, it appears more useful to suggest that changes in economic conditions were important in all three countries but that the strength of their respective socialist movements also depended on other features of the social environment. Discerning the nature of these effects requires taking a closer look at the conditions in each of the three countries.

First of all, the relative degree to which socialism became institutionalized in each of the three countries needs to be established. As elsewhere, the symbolic importance that socialist parties themselves attached to party membership, voting, and newspaper circulation gives these indicators special significance. In both absolute and relative terms, the socialist movement appears to have gained greatest strength in Sweden, followed by Denmark, with Norway showing only slightly weaker representation. By 1900, for example, Socialist party membership in Sweden stood at 44,000, compared with 27,000 in Denmark and only 10,000 in Norway. Not all of these members were industrial workers, but some sense of the relative magnitude of these figures can be obtained by dividing them by the number of industrial workers in each country. Doing so gives figures of 16 percent for Sweden, 14 percent for Denmark, and 12 percent for Norway.[7] Voting results also give similar indications of the relative strength of socialism in the three countries. In Sweden the Socialist party had succeeded in electing only 2 percent of the parliamentary deputies in 1903, but by the eve of the First World War, this proportion had risen to 33 percent. In Denmark socialist representation among parliamentary deputies grew from 7 percent in 1895 to 21 percent in 1906 and then to 28 percent in 1918. And in Norway the comparable figures rose from 3 percent in 1903 to 9 percent in 1909 to 19 percent in the election of 1912.[8] Thus, the Swedish party's strength was among the highest of any country in Europe, rivaling that of Germany, while Denmark's was also relatively high, and Norway's was slightly above that of France and considerably greater than England's.

In Sweden and Norway socialist movements developed relatively late in comparison with Germany, France, and England—a fact that may be associated with the relative lateness of industrialization in Scandinavia but can perhaps also be tied to delays in the extension of the franchise. The Social Democratic party emerged in Sweden in 1889 at a time when only about 6 percent of the population was eligible to vote for the lower house of the Riksdag. Not until 1909, after the franchise had been enlarged, did the party begin to grow rapidly.[9] In Norway the Social Democratic Federation was founded in 1885, but not until 1903 were the first socialist deputies elected.[10] Only in Denmark did the introduction of socialism occur at roughly the same time as in Germany and France: the first socialist organization was founded in 1871 but was quickly repressed; the Danish Socialist party was formed in 1878 and placed its first elected deputies in 1884.[11]

. Characterizations of the ideology of the three socialist parties have been more subjective, but some consensus is evident. Socialism in Sweden has generally been characterized as more radical than its counterpart in Denmark. One reason appears to have been the disappointment that resulted from massive strikes, staged without success, by the trade union movement in 1909. In consequence, reformism within the socialist movement fell out of favor, and several radical splinter groups broke away from the main organization. If Sweden was more radical, Denmark nevertheless advanced a form of socialist ideology that was by all indications orthodox. Although it was moderate, and perhaps oriented more toward reform than revolution, it was neither syndicalist nor ministerialist.[12] Norway's socialism, as I have noted, has enjoyed a reputation of being more radical than that of either Sweden or Denmark. This reputation, however, tends to reflect the interwar years better than it does the period before 1914. During its first two decades, Norwegian socialism was not only moderate and reformist in orientation but also countenanced a nationalistic agenda and favored cooperation with liberal parties.[13] In both party strength and commitment to revolutionary ideology, then, it appears that Sweden ranked first, Denmark second, and Norway third by the end of the period under consideration. These are, however, relatively minor differences in comparison with the larger differences separating all three countries from France and Great Britain.

If precise connections between these characterizations of the three socialist movements and rates of industrialization cannot be drawn, it does need to be emphasized that all three movements developed within a general environment of economic expansion. Between 1897 and the start of the war, the number of industrial workers in Sweden grew by nearly 60 percent, in Norway by nearly 100 percent, and in Denmark by nearly 30 percent.[14] During the four decades between 1870 and 1910, railway expansion alone did much to stimulate the Scandinavian economy. In Denmark this period witnessed an increase in railway lines from only 770 kilometers to 3,445 kilometers, in Norway from 359 kilometers to 2,976 kilometers, and in Sweden from 1,727 kilometers to 13,829 kilometers.[15] Growth was also particularly rapid in metals and machinery, paper, and textiles, while more traditional industries such as quarrying, timber, and mining experienced relative decline. Other more general indicators also attest to the economic growth, as well as to the shifting sectoral distribution of economic activity, during this period. Between 1870 and 1914 gross national product increased by 200 percent in Denmark, by 150 percent in Norway, and by 260 percent in Sweden, thus placing the Scandinavian countries among the most rapidly developing regions of Europe.[16] Over the same period mining, manufacturing, and transportation grew as a proportion of gross domestic product from 52 percent to 70 percent in Denmark, from 28 to 37 percent in Norway, and from 23 to 40 percent in Sweden. And the proportion of the labor force employed in these activities grew from 33 percent to 42 percent in Denmark, from 26 to 41 percent in Norway, and from 20 to 45 percent in Sweden.[17] Apart from short-term fluctuations, these increases were generally associated with rising wages, which (as we have seen) were positively associated with the growth in socialist voting.[18] Nevertheless, income inequality was still widespread; ownership of property was even less equitably distributed; and education levels, though rising, still tended to be low.[19]

If the comparisons of Germany, France, and England have applicability in the Scandinavian context, however, the balance of power within each state must also be considered in accounting for the growth of socialism. Perhaps the most distinguishing feature of the Scandinavian political systems after the middle of the nineteenth century was the peculiar alignment of social sectors with the liberal and conservative parties. Unlike in Britain and France (and even Germany to a lesser degree), where the conservative parties secured strength mainly from rural areas while the liberal parties grew in towns and cities, the situation in the Scandinavian countries was reversed. Liberal parties, particularly in Denmark and Norway, emerged among farmers, while conservative strength resided with the urban industrialists.[20] The reasons for this pattern are not altogether clear but appear to be rooted in the fact that agriculture was to a very large extent composed of small operators rather than aristocracy (more similar to the pattern in Bavaria than Prussia, for example).[21] Progressive land reforms in the early 1800s had reduced the strength of the aristocracy, and public education, state aid, and cooperatives for sharing machinery and technological information

gave the operators of small farms a reasonably strong economic position. Moreover, these operators' income depended on free trade,
exports, and peaceful relations with Britain and France, while the
industrialists were linked closely to the bureaucratic state through
state ownership of mines and public utilities, and they looked to the
state to protect these industries.[22] At any rate, the upshot was that
even where the liberal parties succeeded in capturing sizable segments of the electorate, these segments were separated from the
urban working class both geographically and economically.[23] In short,
the rising industrial sector contributed more to the conservative statist coalition, as in Germany, than to a strong bourgeois liberal coalition of the kind that developed in France and England. Socialists,
therefore, had more latitude to develop their own constituencies
among the urban working classes than might appear to have been
the case on the basis of major party strength alone.

The relations between the state and industry appear, in fact, to
have been as close in the Scandinavian countries as they were in
Bismarck's Germany. A contemporary, for example, observed of
Sweden: "There are few countries where state activity in industry
and production has reached such a high state of development." The
central and municipal authorities, he went on to say, "control almost
entirely the whole railway-, canal-, post-, telegraph-, and telephone-
systems of the country, but frequently also the tramway and the gas
and electricity in the towns."[24] In addition, the state dominated banking and still retained ownership of approximately 20 percent of the
land. Increasingly the state also became a source of employment and
investment.[25]

In part, the state's capacity to govern without making concessions to the liberal opposition was a product of the degree to which
power remained concentrated in the bureaucracy. Hugh Heclo has
observed, for example, that in Sweden the exercise of power throughout the second half of the nineteenth century "resided with the
conservative royalist-bureaucratic oligarchy rather than with parliamentary factions."[26] Until 1905 the king completely controlled the
Council of State and filled its offices with members of the aristocracy.
The upper chamber of the Riksdag also remained closely aligned
with the king, thus reducing pressures on the monarch to grant
broader concessions. Not until 1917 did the crown grant full parliamentary representation. Harry Eckstein has made similar observations in the Norwegian context, arguing that the executive

bureaucracy, which comprised the monarchy, cabinet, and civil service, far outweighed representative structures—and indeed were separated from them by cultural and language differences—until at least 1905.[27]

Another factor that favored the development of socialism in the Scandinavian countries was the relatively late emergence of mass parties of all kinds.[28] To a large degree this failure was also a function of the continuing dominance of the royal-aristocratic bureaucracy. In Sweden a bicameral legislature had been established in 1866, but, as I have noted, the upper house continued to serve mainly as an estate assembly dominated by the aristocracy and tied closely to the crown. In Denmark a bicameral legislature had been introduced in 1849, but a revision of the constitution in 1866 increased the king's power. Norway did not adopt parliamentary principles of government until 1884. Rather than having to struggle to win voters away from other established parties, liberal or conservative, socialist organizers were thus able to mobilize on relatively virgin territory. When the Social Democratic party emerged in Sweden in 1889, for example, it was the first truly national electoral organization.[29] And when the socialists in Norway began to organize for political purposes in 1887, they were only three years behind the efforts of the liberal and conservative parties to develop local organizations.[30]

Just as in other parts of Europe, the conditions promoting mass parties in Scandinavia were, however, related to broader patterns of economic expansion during the second half of the nineteenth century. Weak as it was, the emergence of democratic opposition to the royalist-aristocratic coalition was rooted in the broader changes within the European economy that began to open up new markets and promote trade on a broader scale. One of the reasons why this opposition was as pronounced as it was within the rural sector in the Scandinavian countries was that the repeal of the Corn Laws in England in 1829 had opened new markets for Scandinavian crops. Another was that prices for farm goods had risen considerably between the 1830s and 1860s as a function of increased demand on the international market. Thus, conflicts between those elements represented by the central bureaucracy and those represented by parliamentary structures were set in motion, resulting in heightened demands for an enlarged franchise and new opportunities for the development of mass parties.[31] Gradually the franchise was in fact extended, and as it grew, mass parties became increasingly effective in mobilizing the eligible electorate.[32]

Even after the advent of partisan politics the conservative faction continued to dominate the government, however, just as it did in Germany. It effectively drew the upper bourgeoisie into a royal-aristocratic coalition and prevented the liberal parties from forging an effective coalition between the lower bourgeoisie and the working classes. In Sweden the conservatives enjoyed an absolute majority in both houses until 1905 and held control of the government until 1911, when they were finally forced to form a coalition government. In Denmark the liberal opposition did not succeed in winning concessions from the royalists until 1894, after some thirty years of intensifying rivalry, and not until 1901 did they gain an effective voice in the government. Only in Norway, and there only during the final years before the First World War, did the liberals dominate parliamentary politics to a sufficient extent to force the socialists into a dependent relation and to pursue their own reforms without relying on the socialists' strength among the working classes to restrain the conservatives.[33]

The relations between the state and the various socialist parties in Scandinavia were also fraught with many of the same tensions that prevailed in Germany. On the one hand, state policies actively courted loyalty from the working classes in an effort to preclude alliances from forming between workers and the liberal parties. On the other hand, repressive actions gave the socialists a clear political identity and inadvertently contributed to their ability to mobilize support among the workers. In Sweden the socialist party was never officially banned, as it was in Germany, but the parallels with Bismarck's policies have generally been recognized.[34] From 1876 until the mid-1890s the Swedish socialist movement faced consistent, if somewhat less than effective, opposition from the state. Troops were called out to put down strikes, and socialist meetings were routinely broken up and their leaders occasionally jailed.[35] Much the same was true in Denmark, especially during the formative years of the socialist movement.[36] At the same time, the weakness of the trade union movements and the state's promotion of social welfare policies, as well as its more general role in industrial expansion, made it the obvious focus of attention for socialist aims.[37] In Norway it was the state that initiated factory reform laws in 1892 and accident compensation in 1894. More than becoming a mere economically defined party of the working class, therefore, socialism came to be identified by its political orientations and by its position in the party system.

Belgian and Dutch Socialism

The emergence of socialism in Belgium is usually dated from 1868, but at the time it remained limited primarily to the vicinity of Brussels.[38] Although the movement had ties from the beginning with the International, it was more devoted to the formation of labor unions during the first decade of its existence than to political struggle. This changed in 1877, when the Flemish Socialist party and the Socialist party of Brabant were organized to seek the political emancipation of the proletariat. Two years later the Belgian Socialist party succeeded in uniting these groups into a single national movement. Yet for the next six years the party existed only as a small sect, failing to mold the disparate cooperative, voluntaristic, and anarchistic segments of the working class into a coherent movement. In 1885 the socialists founded the Belgian Labor party, giving them a political role in relation to the working class similar to that of the Social Democrats in Germany and Sweden. From the mid-1880s until the onset of the First World War the strength of socialism, organized in this manner, grew steadily.

The Belgian socialists were probably most successful, perhaps even more so than their German and Scandinavian counterparts, in creating a grass-roots infrastructure that drew workers into the party, as well as giving concrete expression to the movement's ideology and mobilizing commitment to its ideals. Because of restrictive legislation the labor unions and producers' cooperatives had no separate organization at the national level. Consequently they became the local representatives of the Labor party and were subordinate to the socialist leadership. Through its association with these groups the party was able to serve not only as the workers' political voice but also as their agent in negotiating contracts, purchasing food and clothing cheaply, and pressing for unemployment insurance, old age pensions, and better educational opportunities. So extensive were the party's activities that the historian Henri Pirenne was prompted to say: "It makes the observer think of a state and a church in which the class spirit takes the place of the national or the religious spirit."[39] More prosaically, a handbook on Belgium prepared for the British

Foreign Office during the war asserts that "in no country has Socialism, as a political and economic force, been more thoroughly organized or found such widespread support."[40]

Statistically the socialist movement included more than 160 workers' associations representing more than 40,000 workers as early as the mid-1880s. It sponsored two newspapers during these years which achieved a circulation of approximately 27,000 copies.[41] And by 1894 it attracted 237,920 votes, approximately 13 percent of the total, and succeeded in obtaining 15 percent of the seats in parliament. Six years later the number of votes had increased to 461,095, or 23 percent of the total, and its representation accounted for 21 percent of the seats in parliament. By 1914 its share in both the popular vote and in parliamentary seats had risen to 30 percent.[42]

Ideologically the orientation of the Belgian Labor party, while not exclusively devoted to the principles of socialism, took socialism as its guiding philosophy. In many respects its platform resembled the Erfurt program adopted by the German Social Democrats at about the same time. For historical and philosophical inspiration it drew on socialistic assumptions. Yet in practical proposals it took a moderate, reformist stance aimed chiefly at improving the working conditions of the industrial labor force. It also sought to voice appeals capable of attracting the agrarian sector.[43]

Although some attempts have been made to account for the success of the Belgian socialist movement in terms of rapid industrialization and social dislocation, the rate and timing of Belgian industrialization do not support this interpretation. Indeed, the Belgian economy in many respects followed a pattern resembling that in France. It was by no means an instance of late industrialization. As early as 1840 Belgium was already considerably advanced in industrial activity, even more so than France, ranking second only to Great Britain.[44] Starting at this relatively high level, the Belgian economy nevertheless expanded at a modest pace during the remainder of the century. Like France, Belgium was affected by the depression that lasted from around 1873 until 1893, and after this its development was steady but in no way exceptionally rapid. One estimate suggests a growth rate of 2.3 percent annually from 1840 to 1858, 6 percent annually from 1858 to 1873, 0.5 percent annually from 1873 to 1893, and 4 percent annually from 1893 to 1913.[45] Some of these variations reflect changes in agricultural productivity, but the general picture is one of steady growth of a moderate nature for the two decades prior to the First World War.[46] For the whole period from 1860 through 1910, economic growth calculated as gross national product per capita averaged only 2.04 percent annually. This figure was actually lower than the comparable figure for France between 1830 and 1860 and was lower than the growth rates between 1860 and 1910 in Germany, Sweden, and Denmark.[47]

Where the Belgian economy differed from that of France was in industrial concentration. More of Belgium's industrial activity was located in sectors such as coal mines, steel plants, and large cotton factories that employed large numbers of workers. By 1910, for example, half of the industrial labor force worked in joint-stock companies, and the average number of employees in these companies was 175.[48] The increasing concentration of Belgian labor in the newer heavy industries was also reflected in a geographic shift. According to one economic historian: "In 1830 the country's industrial center of gravity was in the Flemish provinces, being based in textile manufacture—at that date still predominantly rural and scattered. Half a century later the center of gravity had clearly passed into the Walloon provinces, to the great string of industrial basins which had grown up from Mons to Liège. No longer was production dependent upon thousands of small, individual enterprises. Rather it was concentrated in great factories, mines, and workshops."[49] But this transition and the growth of heavy industry in Belgium more broadly cannot be understood apart from the actions of the state.

When Belgium gained independence in 1830, the main political divisions that were to shape the subsequent development of the state were between the Catholic landed nobility, who were strong supporters of the monarchy, and the Protestant industrialists, who tended to favor republican policies. The Liberal party became relatively distinct as an orientation, although not yet as an organized movement, in the 1850s. Its advocates consisted mostly of French speaking merchants and professionals in the larger cities who were opposed to protectionist tariffs and the church's dominance over the schools.[50] The Catholic party, however, remained dominant. Effective power lay in the hands of the monarchic bureaucratic elite.

The Constitution of 1830 had formally provided for a progressive parliamentary government in which legislative power was vested in a democratically elected bicameral parliament and individual civil rights were guaranteed. Important restrictions continued, however. All ministers were appointed and dismissed by the king. The electorate was restricted to a mere .075 percent of the population. A large minority of the legislative body were members of the nobility. And the church retained important prerogatives in areas of finance and education. On the whole, the state was structured more as in Germany and the Scandinavian countries than in either England or France. No minister emerged with power comparable to that of Bismarck. Yet the degree of legislative control over important governmental activities remained greatly underdeveloped, leaving the administrative sector largely at the disposal of the royal oligarchy.[51]

During the third quarter of the century, from about 1847 to 1870, this administrative hegemony was tempered somewhat by a succession of liberal ministers who sought to foster economic development through a laissez-faire policy and who jealously guarded themselves against royal dependence by forming party alliances in parliament. In 1884 the end of this period was signaled, however, by the triumph of a conservative Catholic coalition which succeeded in holding power without interruption until 1919. The political structure that prevailed throughout the entire time during which the socialist movement rose from obscurity into a major national party was thus a conservative ministerial oligarchy.

Writing for a British and American audience in 1904, an observer of the Belgian capital drew the following contrast between the strength of the bureaucratic oligarchy and the weakness of the legislative body: "Political personages enjoy no special consideration socially on account of their being members of the legislature: indeed, it is rather the reverse. The majority of them are regarded as persons requiring or seeking emolument; those whose material prosperity is beyond doubt are held in some way to diminish their own importance by becoming deputies . . . It is very different with the permanent officials of the great departments. Employment in the cabinets or secretariats of the chief offices is much sought for, and considerable social influence and position are needed to obtain admission into them."[52] Another observer, the American political scientist Thomas H. Reed, wrote that the king and his bureaucratic chiefs constituted "a great body of functionaries who, in substantial independence of all other authority, dispose of the power of the state."[53] Vested in these offices, Reed pointed out, was the right to appoint all holders of civilian and military posts, the administration of the army and navy, the conclusion of commercial treaties and foreign policy, and the ability to dismiss parliament.

During the first half century of its existence as an independent nation, the Belgian state actively supported industrialization, thereby bringing many of the early supporters of liberal republican views into a more conservative alliance. The international situation that favored an alliance between industry and the state arose from the conditions under which Belgian independence was established between 1830 and 1839, particularly the condition that Britain would guarantee political protection in return for Belgium's remaining a neutral state. Under these terms the commercial classes gained generous trading opportunities but dared not pursue radical republican ideologies of the kind present in France lest the British interpret these pursuits as a hostile gesture. As one writer indicates: "The price the Belgians had to pay for protection was the avoidance of republicanism." And, the same writer goes on to explain, this avoidance helped solidify an elite coalition around the monarchist state: "Paradoxically, this eased resolution of the problem of legitimacy, since otherwise the Belgian political class might have been as sharply divided as was the French between monarchists and republicans."[54]

During the latter half of the nineteenth century, the monarchic oligarchy succeeded in drawing the industrial elite into a stronger position of dependence and support. It initiated the system of national railroads, established the Belgian Congo, founded a government savings bank, and made appointments on the basis of loyalty and patronage. Antwerp, Bruges, Brussels, and Ghent all developed rapidly as port cities with the aid of progressive commercial treaties and state assistance in deepening canals and opening waterways. Mons, Liège, and Namur developed with the help of state-sponsored technical schools and in the coalfields, and the importance of coal was increased by the state's involvement not only in domestic railway construction but also in railway exports.[55] Initially the Walloon provinces had fostered the strongest anti-Catholic sentiment and the greatest support for prorepublican orientations along French lines. But with the state's growing involvement in the economic fortunes of these areas a significant reduction occurred in the strength of these liberal sentiments. Overall, the conservative Catholic party gained strength. And these gains were particularly notable in the major industrial and commercial centers: Antwerp, Bruges, Ostend, Liège, Ghent, and Brussels.[56]

When the socialist movement began to expand and take on national proportions in the 1880s, the strength of the liberal republicans was relatively weak. Their main cause was a more democratic system of education. On economic issues they failed to win over more than a small fraction of the elite. In the election of 1894, for example, they returned only 20 seats to parliament compared to 114 for the Catholic party. And in 1900 the Catholic party still outnumbered liberals in parliament by a margin of nearly three to one.[57]

The socialist-dominated Labor party functioned with legal recognition from the beginning. In other ways, however, political conditions could scarcely be considered conducive to its growth. Workers' demonstrations in the coal basin around Liège, for example, were forcibly suppressed with military troops, involving loss of life and heavy prison sentences. Popular writers associated with the movement, such as Alfred Defuisseux, were imprisoned or exiled. And police spies were used routinely to infiltrate socialist organizations. Just as in Germany, therefore, socialism grew less from explicit encouragement by the state than from the inadvertent effects of an eviscerated liberal republican party incapable of competing effectively with socialism for the loyalties of the working classes.[58]

From the time it emerged as a national entity, the socialist movement was characterized primarily by its political identity. Until 1893 it struggled for universal suffrage as a means of enlarging its political base and this struggle itself oriented the movement clearly toward political organization.[59] Earlier in the century, when liberal republican ideas had been stronger, the state had pioneered a number of welfare programs for the benefit of the working classes: compulsory sickness insurance for seamen (1844), compulsory invalidity and old age insurance for seamen (1844), state subsidies for workers voluntarily insured in mutual benefit societies (1851), and compulsory accident insurance for miners (1868).[60] Consequently the socialists continued to look to the state to pass legislation favorable to the working classes. Soon after the socialist successes in the 1894 election the government did in fact offer concessions in hopes of regaining the loyalty of the industrial labor force. A ministry of labor was established in 1895, factory safety laws were introduced in 1896, compulsory inspection of mines was legislated in 1897, trade unions were legalized in 1898, and a workers' compensation law was passed in 1903.[61] Yet the political situation of the workers remained overwhelmingly conducive to their continuing identification with the socialist movement. A highly disproportionate system of plural voting still denied workers a strong voice in elections.[62] Most of the heavily industrialized sections of the country were Protestant, while the government was firmly in the hands of the Catholic party. Universal education was consistently opposed by the Catholic party. The crown was engaged in military and imperial adventures that threatened to place greater burdens on the working classes in the form of taxes and conscription. And the weakness of the Liberal party gave socialists virtually unrestricted ability to function as the voice of the working classes.

A valuable comparison that brings into sharper relief the circumstances promoting a strong socialist movement in Belgium is provided by the case of the Netherlands. Not only were the two countries similar in size and location, but also the rate of rapid industrialization in the latter would, if anything, suggest that socialism might have found the Netherlands even more fertile than Belgium. Yet the success achieved by the Dutch socialists did not equal that of their Belgian counterparts.

The first socialist association in the Netherlands was organized on a local basis in Amsterdam in 1878. After several years of growth in new locations, including Groningen, Haarlem, and The Hague, the Social Democratic League was founded in 1881, adopting the Gotha Programme as its standard but deemphasizing the goal of collectivism.[63] During its first decade the league failed to gain much support outside of Amsterdam. Its membership was no more than about five thousand during this period—one-tenth as large as in Belgium—and its newspaper sold only about two thousand copies. E. H. Kossmann summarizes the situation as follows: "The number of workers joining socialist organizations was relatively small and the programmes put forward by the socialists, if they took the trouble to put one forward at all, seemed either to consist of wild utopian fantasies or to be dependent on, and indeed subordinated to, the pursuit of universal franchise, which they were not alone in asking for."[64]

Not until 1894 was the Social Democratic Workers party formed, the interim years having seen little growth in actual membership, no initiatives in trade union organization, and a great deal of dissension within the movement's leadership. Although the Dutch delegation was pressed at the meeting of the Second International in Brussels in 1891 to become more active in union organizing, the trade federation that emerged two years later was a separate body and developed independently from the Social Democrats, even though it shared many of their principles. Indeed, the social democratic trade union federation was the more revolutionary wing of the movement in that its activities were geared mainly for preparing the Dutch worker for the revolution that was presumed to be inevitable. In taking this stance it differed both from the political wing, which favored parliamentary action, and the more conventional trade unions, which devoted a greater share of their efforts to strike funds, negotiations, and agitation for workers' compensation. While the political wing represented by the Social Democrats was more reformist in orientation, it was from the beginning divided into several factions differing in the degree to which emphasis should be placed on parliamentary action and on cooperation with other parties. In this it was of course quite similar to its counterparts in Britain and France.[65]

At its inception the Social Democratic party counted only 700 members, and by 1902 it had grown to only 4,500 members. Not until 1910 did it begin to evidence more substantial growth, rising from a total of 9,500 members in that year to 15,500 in 1913 and 25,708 in 1914. The socialist trade unions showed a similar pattern of growth. Numbering 12,700 members in 1896, they rose to approximately 44,000 members in 1910 and reached 87,600 members in 1914. Relative to the labor force and to the size of other unions, however, they remained small even at the end of this period. Fewer than 20 percent of the work force was affiliated with any trade union, and of these, socialist unions accounted for no more than a third of the total membership.[66] The first time seats in parliament were gained by the Social Democrats was in 1897, representing only 3 percent of the total in that year. By 1905 this figure had climbed only to 7 percent, and in 1913 it reached 18 percent, considerably lower than the representation achieved in the same year by the socialists in Belgium.[67]

If the socialist movement experienced relatively modest—and late—advances in the Netherlands, these advances nevertheless appear to have been reinforced by the rapid rate of industrialization and the correlative expansion of the working classes during this period. By some indications the Dutch economy (like the Belgian economy) was already relatively industrialized by the middle of the nineteenth century. For instance, in 1849 24 percent of the Dutch labor force was employed in industry, and nearly half of this number was employed in the textile industry. Over the next forty years the sectoral distribution of the labor force remained relatively constant, with industry rising only to 29 percent by 1889. And even during the period of socialist expansion this figure rose only to 32 percent.[68] It is by no means appropriate, however, to attribute the modest and moderate character of Dutch socialism to early and gradual industrialization. The pattern of Dutch industrialization was actually quite complex, and many indicators point toward a relatively late start with fairly rapid growth occurring during the critical period from about 1890 to 1914 when socialism was experiencing its greatest successes.[69] Capital investment as measured by the size of the domestic securities portfolio was virtually constant during the earlier period, rising only from 1.122 billion guilders in 1854–1857 to 1.22 billion guilders in 1888–1890; but during the next quarter century its value nearly tripled, rising to 3.1 billion guilders in 1913–1915. As a more direct measure of industrialization, the share of the industrial labor force that was employed in medium-sized or large firms rose from 23.5 percent in 1889 to 44.5 percent in 1909; and for large firms alone the shift was from 15.2 percent to 29.2 percent.[70] To the extent that rapid industrialization, the social dislocation caused by the rise of new industries and the sudden growth of urban centers, and the mobilizing potential of labor concentration in large workplaces were all present, therefore, the Dutch socialist movement should have had ample resources on which to draw.[71]

The greatest differences in the institutional contexts affecting Dutch and Belgian socialism were not in the availability of an industrial work force but in the political conditions influencing the strength of the Socialist party. Whereas the Conservative party dominated Belgian politics during much of the latter half of the nineteenth century, its influence steadily declined in Dutch politics. Its representation in parliament, for example, declined from thirty-five seats in 1859 to ten seats in 1879, and then to only one seat in 1888. The two religious parties, the Orthodox Protestants and the Catholics, took up some of the power that the Conservatives lost. But the fact that they were divided along religious lines often prevented them from consolidating an effective bloc on the right.[72] Between 1850 and 1901 the Liberal party always enjoyed a plurality of the seats in parliament.[73] Only after the turn of the century did the new Confessional party become strong enough to form a conservative government.[74]

The conservatives' lack of influence during the latter half of the nineteenth century lay partly in the fact that relations between the state and the industrial elite were relatively weak. During the 1850s and 1860s the main economic policies enacted by the state had the effect of removing it from business and instituting laissez-faire on a large scale. Excise duties on a number of commodities were abrogated, protection of fisheries was abolished, export duties were eliminated, and patent laws were eased.[75] Railroads constituted another area in which the state's role in furthering industrialization was characteristically weak. For a variety of reasons—geographic concentration of industry, high construction costs owing to soil weakness and the number of canal crossings required, division among provincial jurisdictions, and inadequate public finances—the state did not become involved as early or as extensively in railway construction as it did in Belgium. Only the profits from the East Indies trade, which accrued to the state, made it possible for public finances to be allocated to the railway project and not until 1880 was an integrated system of railways and waterways completed. Moreover, since the raw materials for this construction had to be imported, the stimulus to heavy industry which forged an alliance between industrialists and the state in countries such as Belgium and Germany was virtually absent.[76]

Also contributing to the absence of a strong state-industrial alliance was the comparative ineffectiveness of the state bureaucracy itself. Whereas the Belgian bureaucracy was relatively unified, expansive, and capable of dominating parliament, the obverse was true in the Netherlands. In absolute terms the number of government employees rose, as it did elsewhere, but this increase barely kept pace with the broader growth occurring in the civilian labor force.[77] There was also a strong tradition of decentralization in the Dutch government, and among the key policies enacted after the middle of the century were some that militated against greater centralization. A high degree of local community autonomy was preserved, and a clear distinction was drawn between the bureaucracy on the one hand and parliament on the other, which held both constitutional and organizational checks against the bureaucracy.[78] Within the bureaucracy itself, ministers who favored sizable expenditures on public works and substantial loans to industry generally evoked opposition from others who supported a balanced budget. Moreover, the Dutch system included a highly developed judiciary system that placed unwary civil servants in jeopardy of the courts.[79] Accordingly, the bureaucracy seldom functioned as a decisive initiator or promoter of industrial expansion. Throughout the prewar period, one writer notes, "the government left industrial enterprise almost entirely to itself."[80] Even major construction projects, such as the Rotterdam harbor renovation project (which greatly stimulated Dutch trade), were generally financed and directed from private sources. And financial ties between the government and the industrial elite appear to have diminished in importance as well because of an overall reduction in the proportion of national wealth held in the form of government securities.[81] In most observers' judgment, the relations between industrialists and state officials were more often marked by strain than by cooperation.

Between 1870 and 1914 the government passed acts aimed at minimizing the more serious abuses of industrialization: a ban on child labor (1874), regulation of industrial working conditions for women (1889), a factory safety act (1895), accident insurance (1901), mining regulations (1906), and sickness insurance (1913). And it was the liberal government that initiated many of these reforms and took credit for others, not a conservative coalition of the kind that passed similar acts in Belgium and Germany. Moreover, the liberals courted widespread support from the working classes with other kinds of social legislation, with laws aimed at extending schooling to the working classes, and with opposition to conscription laws that would have allowed the wealthy special exemptions. The strongest support for a conservative government came from the rural sector, prompted by promises of protectionist tariffs which were opposed by the industrialists and commercial classes. Much of the bourgeoisie, therefore, remained loyal to the Liberal party.[82]

In the last decade before the war the growth of the Socialist party and of the trade union movement can be traced directly to the triumph of a more conservative regime under the leadership of Abraham Kuyper. Because of internal divisions within the liberal wing over the franchise, a relative lack of grass-roots organization within the Liberal party, and the role of electoral reforms in driving some of the more moderate segments of the Liberal party into the Conservatives' ranks, Kuyper's government was able to win a solid majority in parliament, which gave it the power to risk a policy of determined opposition toward labor unrest. The government's reaction to the railway strikes that developed shortly after the turn of the century was particularly severe and resulted in the strikers' failing to attain their objectives. This defeat left a number of labor leaders convinced that syndicalist or anarchist activity would be futile unless stronger unions and political organizations were created. Thereafter the main thrust of socialist activity lay in these areas, with the result that membership and voting began to increase.[83]

The fact that the trade union movement had developed prior to and to a large extent independently of the socialist movement, as it had in France and England, also played an important role in shaping the trajectory of Dutch socialism.[84] With the legislative support for social reform that was available from the liberal government until the end of the nineteenth century, the unions provided an effective means with which the working classes could cooperate with segments of the middle and upper strata in attaining their objectives. Not until the conservative government effectively weakened this support from the liberals were the socialists able to sustain a convincing argument for the priority of political action.

A comparison of the Netherlands and Belgium, therefore, reveals that local institutional contexts mediated decisively between the broader industrial expansion, on the one hand, that created the demand in a general sense for an ideology oriented toward working-class interests and the specific outcomes of the socialist movement's efforts, on the other hand, to fulfill that demand. Although there were differences in the composition of the two countries' economic expansions, both countries experienced growth in sufficient proportions, late enough and rapidly enough, and with a sufficiently high degree of reorganization of labor into large-scale production to provide the basic circumstances in which a working-class movement might have appeared. In Belgium, however, much of this expansion was encouraged by a monarchic oligarchy in alliance with a strong segment of the industrial elite, whereas in the Netherlands it occurred largely without such encouragement. Their interests being more closely wedded to an aristocratic state bureaucracy, the Belgian industrialists did not support a liberal republican party, thus weakening this party's capacities to build loyalty across a broad range of middle-and working-class constituents. Trade unions also remained relatively weak. Socialist organizers, therefore, had few competitors and were subject to few cross-cutting orientations in defining their objectives. To gain economic, social, or political objectives, the socialists needed to be in a position to make demands from the state. In the Netherlands, in contrast, conservative aristocratic elements within the state diminished in importance during the latter half of the nineteenth century relative to a liberal coalition involving a broad spectrum of the upper and lower bourgeoisie. Faced with the continuing threat of a conservative resurgence, the liberal coalition courted support from the working classes by offering a broad program of welfare legislation. Trade unions flourished, leaving little incentive for revolutionary socialist activity, and even the socialist leadership was divided over the most effective means of attaining its objectives. Not until a conservative government came into power, effectively weakening the Liberal party, and giving the working classes a more distinct sense of their own political identity, did the socialist movement begin to experience significant growth.

Workers' Movements in Italy and Spain

Though vastly different in most other respects, Italy's pattern of economic expansion and the structure of its political parties in many ways resembled those in the Netherlands, certainly to a greater extent than they did the patterns in Belgium. Economic growth followed a course that by itself would have suggested an environment ripe for socialist organizing: it came relatively late and was quite rapid when it did come. A liberal coalition in the government, however, was also fairly strong. As with Dutch socialism, the Italian socialist movement experienced only modest success. Economic conditions favored it, but the political situation weakened the movement, contributed to its internal divisions, and promoted a relatively autonomous trade union movement.

All economic indicators suggest that industrial expansion in Italy was extremely limited, if existent at all, prior to 1896. During much of the latter half of the nineteenth century Italy ranked near the bottom among all European countries in per capita growth in output. Savings and capital accumulation were slow in developing, and even though the state engaged in railroad building and public works spending, these programs did little to stimulate industry since most of the goods had to be purchased abroad. By the mid-1880s some growth was becoming evident. Steel plants were constructed with government assistance; banking reforms began to make loans more readily available for industry; improvements in agriculture gave impetus to national investment; and a rapid increase in foreign trade reversed the country's balance of payments.[85] The main period of growth, however, occurred between 1896 and 1913. Total value added at constant prices grew at a rate of 2.7 percent annually during this period, compared with a rate of only 0.7 percent between 1861 and 1897.[86] National income grew more than three times as rapidly as in the earlier period. Industrial output per capita doubled on the whole and was especially rapid in heavy industry such as iron and steel, chemicals, and engineering.[87] As a percentage of the labor force, industrial workers increased from 20 percent to 24 percent. Industrial contribution to gross national product grew from 21 percent to 26 percent. And gross fixed investment multiplied tenfold.

This growth in the final decade and a half before the First World War meant that the working classes were expanding in overall size and becoming increasingly concentrated in the cities and in large firms. Milan, for example, already had an industrial work force of 134,000 in 1901, including almost 50,000 garment workers, 20,000 machine workers, and 15,000 textile workers. The average number of employees per firm was 49 in the garment industry, 33 in chemicals, and 29 in machinery. Data for the period also reveal the considerable extent of social dislocation among the Milanese working classes: fewer than a third of the male work force were natives of the city.[88]

From 1861 (when the country was unified nationally) until 1922, Italy was governed by a liberal parliamentarian coalition. Although a monarchical system was retained, as in much of Europe, the Italian monarchy was strictly dependent on parliament and could not sustain itself without parliamentary approval. The bureaucracy, modeled after France's rather than Germany's, was centralized but remained subject to parliamentary controls. Because of factionalism it was also generally regarded as less effective than the German bureaucracy. Northern industrialists, men of commerce, lawyers, and other professionals, however, held the upper hand in both the bureaucracy and parliament. Though moderate on matters of social order, they were united by a common interest in economic growth and favored democratic rule by an elite whose social standing, they felt, qualified them to govern. No aristocratic bloc of the Bismarckian kind existed on the right, nor was the left compelled to organize itself as an opposition party.[89]

The first important Italian socialist party was the Partito Operaio Italiano (POI) founded in Milan in 1882. By 1886 its membership had grown to an estimated 40,000, but it was still concentrated almost exclusively among the industrial workers in Milan. It was also subjected to political repression by the government, and many workers gravitated toward the trade union movement, while others in rural areas were more attracted by anarchism. In 1892 the Italian Socialist party was reinitiated, still against resistance by the government. Responding in 1893 to rioting in Sicily the government proclaimed martial law, established military tribunals, and dissolved all workers' organizations. A year later the Socialist party itself was dissolved along with all of its affiliated organizations, and socialist congresses were prohibited. Socialist representation in parliament was permitted, however, and in 1895 the movement elected ten deputies, or approximately 2 percent of the total, while in 1897 its representation increased to fifteen. During this period it also initiated a daily newspaper which attracted a circulation of approximately forty thousand.[90] On a more limited scale, then, the repressive measures in these years led to some of the same unanticipated outcomes in Italy as in Germany.

By the 1890s the government's opposition to the socialists had begun to soften, in large measure because of divisions within the ruling elite itself. These divisions were partially attributable to regional differences between the more agricultural south and the more industrial north. As the economic strength of the north increased, its representatives adamantly opposed the more autocratic, militaristic, and imperialistic policies of leaders from the south. This opposition gave the socialists some room to maneuver but also created divisions within the working classes themselves, as some leaders began to favor the liberal parties and the less politically active unions.

Between 1898 and 1900 the political climate again became more advantageous for socialist organizing. As a result of sporadic labor violence in 1897 and 1898 and an unsuccessful attempt on the life of the king, the government increased its repressive measures. At this point, moreover, the northern industrialists were aligned with the conservatives. Thus the situation, at least for a brief period, resembled that in Germany: an industrial-monarchic alliance on the right and a policy of official repression, with only parliamentary activity left open to the socialists, thus channeling their activities in a political direction. Between 1898 and 1900 the Socialist party increased its representation in parliament from sixteen to thirty-two, partly as a result of alliances with the liberal parties who courted their support in these years.

Over the next decade the rapid rise in industrialization enlarged the population to which the socialist movement could direct its appeals. Party membership increased from approximately 19,000 in 1900 to approximately 60,000 in 1902, and socialist voting increased from approximately 165,000 in 1900 to 326,000 in 1904.[91] Still, the successes experienced in these years were relatively modest in comparison with the growth of the liberal parties and the unions. A liberal coalition succeeded in gaining 52 percent of the seats in parliament in 1900, thereby enabling it to form a liberal government. It advocated tax reforms, universal suffrage, civil rights, and a more tolerant policy toward strikes. In the 1904 election this coalition gained 71 percent of the seats in parliament. The unions also grew rapidly during this period, reaching a membership of nearly 800,000 in 1910, compared with membership in the Socialist party of only a tenth this size.[92] At its peak, the party gained only 11 percent of the popular vote, placing its strength more in the category of the socialist movements in France, Great Britain, and the Netherlands, rather than Germany, Sweden, or Belgium.

Ideologically the movement was most clearly identified as Marxist in orientation. During its formative years its leaders had been in close contact with Engels and drew on the organizational tactics in use among the German Marxists.[93] In the years before the war there was, however, a high degree of internal division within the movement, particularly between those who favored the orthodox Marxist line, those who favored cooperating with the liberal government and working for gradual reform, and the anarcho-syndicalists, who supported violence and political abstention.

If the Italian case provides an example of relatively modest socialist achievements owing to the policies of a liberal regime, despite rapid industrialization, the situation in Spain, finally, provides an illustration of the difficulties that socialists faced when neither the political nor the economic conditions were favorable. Spain's economy grew only marginally during the half century preceding the First World War. Gross national product per capita, for example, increased from only $346 in 1860 to $367 in 1913.[94] Industry on the whole was also relatively stagnant: between 1887 and 1910 the proportion of the economically active population engaged in industry rose only from 14.6 percent to 15.8 percent, and approximately half of these were artisans rather than factory laborers.[95] Textile workers concentrated around Barcelona constituted the largest single category of the industrial labor force. Miners in the Asturias and the more traditional artisans, printers, builders, and transport workers, whose activities were centered in Madrid, made up the balance.[96]

In Barcelona, to a greater extent than in Madrid, the conditions of an impoverished industrial proletariat were most noticeable. By 1900 the rapid growth of immigration from rural areas and villages had combined with a lack of social services and harsh employment conditions to create an exceptionally disadvantaged situation.[97] One writer observes:

> Crammed into the tenement districts . . . near the harbor, in out-lying *barrios* north and south of the city, and on the hills overlooking Barcelona, the newly arrived workers did not have the skills or education to move out of the vast unskilled labor pool that kept wages down and forced them to live in conditions very little better—and often worse—than those in the villages they had left. Public education did not exist; the Church controlled the schools and did not press for a widespread extension of education. There was a government sponsored Institute of Social Reform, but its function was advisory rather than regulatory, and, as a consequence, working conditions and public health were almost always bad. Even public relief was controlled by the Church, whose parsimony made the lack of unemployment compensation and industrial accident insurance even more sorely felt in times of need.[98]

The situation was also severe for most of the working classes who remained in the rural areas and villages. Seigneurial jurisdictions had been abolished only in 1817, and until the end of the century over half the land in southern Spain was concentrated in large estates, many of which had actually increased in size as a result of the state's efforts to break up church lands. Despite a long history of liberal and republican efforts to divide the large estates and to disentail land from the church and from the state, these efforts had largely excluded the average farm worker from obtaining land and had not significantly altered the terms under which most tenants operated the land they leased. In addition, a prolonged flight of capital from agriculture, preventing the introduction of technological improvements, an abandonment of arable land, declining grain prices, and a decrease in rural incomes all contributed to the immiseration of the rural population. But by itself, immiseration in the countryside and among the industrial working classes, as we have seen in other cases, was not enough to bring about a strong socialist movement.

Despite its economic backwardness, Spain progressed toward a republican form of government which had more in common with postrevolutionary France than with any of the autocratic states in central, northern, or eastern Europe. The Constitution of 1812, drawn up by liberal refugees of the French invasion of 1808, gave formal sovereignty to the people and became a model for other democratic reforms. From 1833 to 1868 Isabella II maintained a semblance of monarchical control that was far weaker in practice than in theory. The revolution of 1868, which forced her into exile, and the subsequent abdication of Amadeo of Savoy in 1873 left the country under the de facto rule of a federal republic. The restoration of Alfonso XII in 1875 brought needed unity to the struggling republic, but the state now remained even more firmly in the hands of an oligarchy made up of landed aristocrats, the commercial bourgeoisie, and military leaders.[99]

From the 1870s to the turn of the century, the main elements of the ruling class were the grain growers of Castile and Andalusia, the Catalan cotton manufacturers, and the Basque mine owners. All three depended on protectionist measures to prevent foreign products from invading their markets. But beyond fulfilling this requirement the state had little to offer any of these groups. Certainly none of them wished to see a return to monarchical dominance; all favored the more limited liberal view of constitutional monarchy; and none, including the grain growers whose lands had increased as a result of ecclesiastical land sales, had a strong interest in enlarging the political role of the church.[100]

The state's role in the economy, unlike that in Germany or Belgium, was one of weakness reinforcing weakness. After the loss of Spain's American colonies, the state's financial resources were seriously limited. Rather than being able to stimulate industrial growth through strategic investments, it was forced to borrow wherever it could, thus drawing investment capital away from industry and incurring indebtedness to foreign lenders. Not until 1900 did the state embark on investments in industry. Even the railways constructed during the 1870s represented a lost opportunity to stimulate industry, since they were built largely with foreign capital and by foreign firms using foreign materials.[101]

During the 1880s all the leading elements of the ruling class became increasingly centered on the state, especially since protectionist policies and state finances appeared to be the only ways of maintaining their increasingly precarious position in the international economy. Thus, the potential was there for a conservative statist coalition of the kind that emerged in Germany, especially because the landed aristocracy was still relatively powerful. But instead of a conservative coalition developing, power remained scattered among the various segments of the ruling class. State finances had been extremely limited ever since 1812, thus minimizing the state's effectiveness in drawing the ruling factions into a closer relation of dependence. During the same period in which countries such as England and Prussia were developing the financial capacity to mount large military forces and to support building programs and other infrastructural activities, Spain was suffering from diminishing or static state revenues. Between 1800 and 1830 these revenues had actually declined by approximately a fourth, and by midcentury they had risen by only a third. After this date they rose more rapidly, but only because of makeshift policies such as alienating land from the church and from municipalities. Throughout the nineteenth century a large share of any increase in state revenue was immediately eaten up by interest payments on the national debt, and foreign creditors generally had to be courted on their own terms to keep the state from having to declare bankruptcy.[102]

Rather than the state drawing the various segments of the elite into a strong coalition, these elites increasingly exploited the state for their own ends and sought protection for their particular interests under the guise of liberal republican and democratic traditions. After 1868 the state ceded all mines in perpetuity to private interests in hopes of satisfying some of its desperate need for revenue. During the 1880s and 1890s a growing movement for regional autonomy developed, sparked mainly by the Catalan bourgeoisie—a movement that effected some unity between the republicans and the rural working classes.[103] Members of the bureaucracy used the state for their own gain, drawing resources away from the state and building up vast empires of personal patronage. Indeed the favors, earnings, and gratuities that were channeled into the private coffers of deputies and other officials were estimated at more than twenty times the amount of taxes collected by the state.[104]

The political situation, therefore, was characterized by a divided and financially corrupt state bureaucracy on the one hand and on the other a set of warring liberal factions that were too divided to draw control of the state entirely into their own hands. In combination the two reinforced each other. As Stanley Payne has observed: "The main defect of the democratic monarchy was that it was too democratic in a country riven by elite dissidence and without a developed structure of interest representation." Lacking a strong state bureaucracy or a well-administered parliamentary system that could serve as a moderating agent, he says, "the liberal factions fought each other tooth and nail over issues of access, status, and patronage."[105]

The elements for a conservative aristocratic coalition of the kind that emerged in Germany were all present—except for a strong, financially solvent state bureaucracy. And without a strong state bureaucracy it was harder to mobilize an effective policy of economic expansion of the kind that drew the industrial elites in Germany into an alliance with the bureaucracy. Juan Linz draws this comparison explicitly: "In contrast to Imperial Germany, where the power of the Emperor was securely anchored in the Bismarckian constitutional arrangements, even when the forces of democratization in the Reichstag and the electorate were making gains, in Spain the obstacles did not come from the strength, self-confidence, and legitimacy of the forces of tradition, but from the weaknesses of those who could and should have transformed the system."[106]

The state intervened occasionally on behalf of the working class, as in 1884, when an inquiry into working conditions was commissioned, and again in 1900, when a Worker's Compensation Act was passed. But for the most part the liberal structure of the Spanish state carried over into its relations with the working classes. Amelioration was attempted chiefly through private rather than public means. Thus trade associations were encouraged as mechanisms for negotiating contracts and fostering relief insurance, many of which functioned with religious sponsorship, while an even broader movement aimed at "re-Christianizing" the working class gained widespread support.

It may be argued that the lack of state intervention in areas of social legislation was partly attributable to the fact that in the absence of a large or rapidly growing industrial population private initiatives seemed satisfactory. What argues against this interpretation is the fact that most of the private initiatives actually seem to have had little effect in ameliorating working-class conditions. A more plausible argument is that the lack of state intervention was a function of the way in which the state itself was organized; namely, its lack of financial resources and the extent to which constitutional liberalism permitted the ruling classes to obstruct initiatives from within the bureaucracy. Raymond Carr notes, for example, that "all the legislation was either opposed or sabatoged by the employers as an illegitimate attack on their liberties and an impoverished state lacked the resources to implement any extensive programme of social security, or even pay an efficient factory inspectorate."[107] Spain was like England, insofar as constitutional democracy made private initiatives such as trade unions and voluntary associations more attractive than public initiatives. But Spain was less effective than England in passing social legislation because the state was more divided and severely less capable of raising the necessary funds or finding an effective way of administering them.

From one perspective, these characteristics of the political environment should have given socialist groups ample opportunity to mobilize dissent among the working classes. Particularly the disorganization evident in both the liberal parties and the state bureaucracy, together with their apparent indifference toward the working classes, should have given alternative organizations ample opportunity to mobilize mass support. Yet the relatively underdeveloped size of the industrial working class, the high degree to which the mass population remained in rural areas, the absence of clear political demarcations between the bourgeoisie and the working class, and a state that did not provide a political focus for the aims of working-class organizations all militated against the formation of a strong socialist movement.

Attempts to organize a socialist movement in Spain were actually in progress as early as the 1870s. A socialist party was founded in 1879, and a socialist trade union followed in 1882. From the beginning the socialist movement enjoyed the resources of a strong leader in the person of Pablo Iglesias, as well as a tight communication network and a clear vision of Marxist objectives modeled after the French Guesdists. In theory at least, the movement might also have benefited from the long history of workers' associations, mutual protection societies, work stoppages, and strikes that had characterized Spanish society from the 1840s through the 1870s. Nevertheless, the movement failed to incorporate any sizable proportion of the population. The socialists attracted only .2 percent of the popular vote in 1907 and .6 percent in 1910. By 1913 the party had only 14,729 members.[108] The socialist labor unions were somewhat more successful, achieving their greatest victories among the mining and metalworking industries, but their strength remained quite limited among the textile workers. As late as 1904 their membership accounted for only 2 percent of the industrial labor force, and this figure rose only to 5.7 percent by 1913.

The socialists' difficulties lay in the fact that the republican movement among the petty bourgeoisie was strong enough to lure away many working-class supporters from the more militant policies of the socialists, while others were sufficiently content with the political system to favor directing their activities toward syndicalism and trade associations rather than working to achieve political aims. Some of the political zeal that inspired workers in other countries may also have been preempted by the granting of universal manhood suffrage in 1890.[109]

The workers' movement that captured the greatest loyalty in Spain was anarchism, or perhaps more accurately anarcho-syndicalism, focusing on revolution, the general strike, and scattered acts of violence. Its appeal contrasted sharply with the more disciplined, politicized, gradualist yet revolutionary orientation of the socialists. Between 1870 and 1913 much of the activity of workers' organizations was in fact directed at work stoppages, strikes, mass marches, and violent confrontations with the police rather than being channeled in the directions suggested by orthodox Marxist socialism. Indeed, the history of the Spanish working classes during this period reads like a nearly continuous saga of conflict between workers and their employers. Most of this conflict, however, was quite specifically focused against particular employers and was aimed at gaining practical economic concessions. It may have reinforced a sense of class consciousness, but it seldom acquired political objectives, seldom resulted in revolutionary demands being directed at the state, and seldom solidified into an ongoing national movement.[110]

The growth of anarchism in place of Marxist socialism was, in fact, a lens through which the broader structure of Spanish politics was reflected. Many working-class leaders were able to see the futility of parliamentary activity when, despite universal manhood suffrage, the state was too weak financially to meet their demands. Conventional trade associations, however, tended to be dominated by artisan labor, and their extension into newer industrial sectors was strongly resisted by employers. The key factor distinguishing Spain from England and France in this regard was that the state's resources in Spain were so limited that it made little sense for a parliamentary movement such as the British Labour party to develop, leaving anarcho-syndicalism as the most attractive alternative. This movement also proved relatively successful at attracting the industrial workers in new heavy industries and the poorest segments among the rural working class, both of which were less closely linked to the republicanism of the skilled artisans in trades such as textiles and printing.[111]

Yet even the influence of anarchism should not be overemphasized. Many of its activities were intentionally exaggerated either by movement leaders or by the police for their own purposes. Anarchic violence was strategically planned to have the most visible consequences but was probably quite limited in gaining actual sympathizers. Even at its height in 1914, the main anarcho-syndicalist union had only fourteen thousand members.[112] Indeed, the fact that it appears in retrospect to have been an important movement at all stems primarily from its growth during and after the turbulent years of the First World War rather than its successes before the war.

15

Theory and Practice

THE FOREGOING comparisons bear evidence of both local variations and more general patterns influencing the institutionalization of socialism. The effects of rapid industrialization are especially evident in the decades prior to the First World War. Europe as a whole underwent remarkable industrial expansion during this period, and studies in many areas reveal the social dislocation that resulted. In some instances socialist leaders effectively drew in supporters from the ranks of the dislocated, or at least found their work easier than in areas where workers remained linked to rural, familial, and artisanal networks. Beyond this, however, efforts to identify direct connections between either the rate of industrialization or the size and composition of the industrial proletariat and the success or ideological orientation of the various socialist parties tend to break down.

If industrialization was more rapid in Germany than in England, the two did not differ significantly in geographic dislocation or urban immiseration; and if the pace of industrialization was slower in France than in Germany, approximately the same proportion of workers in both were concentrated in large firms. Yet the socialist movements in England and France remained relatively unsuccessful in comparison with their German counterparts. And if these comparisons can be discounted because of historic differences in the organization of work, trade associations, religion, and so on, other difficulties for the industrialization argument remain: the relative weakness of the socialist movement in industrialized sections of southern Germany, northern France, and London; the fact that socialism was nearly as strong in Denmark as in Sweden despite huge differences in the pace of industrialization; the comparatively weak, reformist socialist movements in Norway and the Netherlands in comparison with those in Sweden and Denmark despite rapid industrialization; Belgium's high level of socialist activity despite a pattern of industrialization that resembled that of France; the negative findings concerning the effects of social dislocation and immiseration on socialist voting in Scandinavia; and the failure of immiseration in Spain to bring about a strong socialist movement.

Greater purchase on the variations in socialist achievements, it appears, comes from examining the political contexts of this activity. It was, after all, the political arena toward which socialist parties were primarily oriented. Changes in the broad economic environment were accompanied by struggles for resources in the political arena. Socialist parties may have regarded the proletariat as their natural constituency, but they had to compete with republicans, liberals, state bureaucrats, and even aristocratic regimes to gain this constituency's support.

Where parliamentary parties oriented toward liberal or republican ideals were strong, the bourgeoisie was able to penetrate into the working classes and draw support away from the socialist movement. England, France, the Netherlands, and to some extent Norway, Italy, and Spain all manifested these tendencies. Faced with continuing competition from conservative aristocratic or monarchic interests, liberal parliamentary interests catered to working class demands and encouraged trade unions. Socialist organizers themselves were thus more likely to seek alliances across class lines, to be divided over reformist or revolutionary tactics, to experience conflicts between economic and political agendas, and in general to achieve only modest success at the polls. Germany, Belgium, Sweden, and Denmark provided political contexts that proved more amenable to socialist movements. Strong monarchic state bureaucracies not only gained the support of rural elites but also managed to draw the upper bourgeoisie into a conservative coalition, leaving a seriously weakened and often divided faction on the left. With liberal parties thus eviscerated, socialist parties were often in the strongest position to represent working class interests. Moreover, the ruling coalitions' efforts to prevent alliances from forming on the left by outlawing or repressing socialist activities generally appears to have backfired: socialists gained a distinct identity, were less likely to be drawn toward cross-class activities, did not devote their energies toward purely economic organizations, and were more likely to focus on winning parliamentary victories. Party activities took on symbolic importance as indications of movement legitimacy and served as the vehicle for producing and disseminating socialist ideology.

In this respect, then, the institutionalization of socialism bears some of the marks that were evident in the Reformation and the Enlightenment. The half century preceding the First World War was a time of economic expansion, like the periods of the Reformation and the Enlightenment. But the effects of this expansion were mediated by specific institutional contexts. In particular, the state played an important mediating role. In all three periods economic expansion was associated with alterations in the relations among dominant factions of the ruling elite. Where these alterations opened new opportunities, the ideological movements in question were more likely to gain a solid footing. Like the divisions that created a public sphere in which the Enlightenment could take hold, the effects of industrialization on monarchic bureaucratic regimes created a political space on the left in which socialism could gain the resources it needed to become institutionalized.

Articulation in Socialist Discourse: Theory and Practice

There was, however, at least one significant way in which the social circumstances under which socialist ideology emerged differed from those of the Enlightenment. Whereas the Enlightenment had developed within the highly fluid atmosphere of intellectual speculation, socialism was by its own dictates concerned with matters of practical social reform. Its legitimacy rested less on taste or force of argument than on its effectiveness in empowering and improving the social conditions of the working class. In this respect the mode of articulation between ideology and its social context was for socialism more similar to that of the Reformation than the Enlightenment. Socialism, like Protestantism, required its own fulfillment in the practice of its followers. The task of fulfillment in the Reformation, however, was facilitated by the relatively less complex political institutions of the sixteenth century and by the more personalistic orientation of Protestant ideology itself. Protestantism succeeded or failed at the political level primarily on the basis of whether or not the highest authorities gave it their approval. Where it received approval, outward manifestations of religious practice conformed at least in principle to the patterns specified by the reformers. Inward conformity, however, could vary considerably, but this variation was anticipated and dealt with by the reformers' emphasis on faith, conviction, and the inner disciplining of the will. Socialism, in contrast, emerged in a highly complex political context and required a mode of practice that made it more vulnerable to pragmatic considerations. The political context was conditioned by the rise of representative legislative politics and by the fact that socialists were nowhere in western Europe in a position to dictate policy apart from the legislative process. Theirs was a world of deputies, elections, bills, and compromise. The reformist orientations of socialist ideology also required it to be more than a matter of personal conviction. Redistribution of wealth, changes in labor conditions, insurance and welfare benefits all demanded effective implementation of ideology in social practice.

In the development of the various social-democratic movements there is, then, a distinctive and fundamental preoccupation with questions of practice, with the relations between theory and practice, and ultimately with moral principles and compromise. Socialist leaders and their opponents struggled persistently with these questions, and the very legitimacy of socialist ideology seems to have depended on finding some satisfactory resolution to the relation between theory and practice.

Two methods of relating theory and practice appear with increasing regularity in the socialist discourse of this period. On the one hand, socialist ideology veers toward utopian formulations that cannot be expected to have practical ramifications. On the other hand, it is reduced to reformist programs that can be more readily implemented but which have little relation to abstract socialist ideals. Examples of both these tendencies have been seen in the previous chapters and have, of course, been the subject of much critical discussion in socialist literature itself. Either tendency in effect reduced the pressure for having to advance theoretical formulations that articulated closely with the socialists' own practical attempts to alter their social situation. But neither was considered entirely legitimate by strategists and theoreticians within the movement. Theory and practice remained inextricably intertwined. Thus, it became necessary within the field of discourse itself to distinguish the two and assign them to their appropriate roles.

On the theoretical side, genre itself played an important role in separating theory from practice, thereby permitting theoretical reflection to proceed without constant reference to actual behavior. In comparison with all that literary criticism has suggested about the relation between innovation in literary genres in the eighteenth century and their attractiveness to literate audiences, nothing in the genres of nineteenth-century socialist literature would give any reason to see a potentially large or interested audience for this literature. There were, to be sure, elements of this literature that could be expected on stylistic grounds alone to have evoked a receptive audience: socialist fiction graphically depicted the miseries of working-class life; newspaper editorials commented on public affairs; manifestos called for devotion to the movement. The fact that socialist newspapers were produced by writers and editors in touch with working-class life was also a positive factor, as was the prominent role played by the spoken word, especially in reaching semiliterate audiences. Much of the work that became regarded as the theoretical basis for the movement, however, was scarcely crafted in a way that made it approachable to any sizable audience. *The German Ideology,* for example, was (and is) no easy book to read, both because of its length (over five hundred pages in the unabridged text) and because of the fact that it was never finished. Even the parts that were completed deviated considerably from their authors' original design for the book. "No wonder," writes one historian, "that the publishers to whom the manuscript was submitted rejected it. They recognized that very few readers could be expected to have the stamina required to read the whole of this lengthy philosophical diatribe from beginning to end."[1] Much the same could be said about Marx's *Capital.* Although it was immediately hailed by many of Marx's disciples as a profound study of the scientific laws of capitalist economics, there is little evidence of its being widely read. Even socialists like August Bebel and Jean Jaurès who read it carefully seem not to have been noticeably influenced by it.[2]

If the theoretical works of socialism were not written in a form that actually reinforced their influence, their form was nevertheless conducive to reinforcing the distinction between theory and practice. Written in an obscure, unapproachable style, they served mainly as abstract debates to which leaders of the movement could refer ceremonially. Their very obscurity symbolized "theory" and differentiated them from the activities and programmatic statements that were regarded as "practice."[3]

In contrast, "practical ideology" tended to be put forth in a way that permitted it to relate more directly to its social context. Its claims were often presented in the genre of abbreviated lists, or party platform "planks," that reflected the outcome of much behind-the-scenes negotiating as well as public deliberation among delegates at labor congresses. The typical list of demands was presented as self-evidently desirable to the working class, if not to large segments of the peasantry and petty bourgeoisie as well. No extended theoretical justification or explanation of the origins of each demand was offered, nor was the list related internally as far as the various demands were concerned, except through a numbered sequence. No effort was made to demonstrate that each demand reinforced the others or that the package as a whole amounted to a sum greater than its parts.[4] This format was highly conducive to the politics of compromise from which it resulted. Single items could be, and typically were, included that fell outside certain theoretical orthodoxies common within the movement. For example, a list of demands such as that forming the Gotha program included proposals for socialistic productive establishments, Sunday closing laws, and regulation of mining safety as well as appeals that more closely reflected the ideas of Marxian analysis. Thus, Marx could criticize the program for its lack of theoretical rigor. And yet the various items included in it could be subscribed to or rejected in practice with little effect on the other demands. Lists of this kind could be assembled, disassembled, added to, deleted from, and rearranged according to the interests of particular constituents. Their very format gave the movement flexibility in adapting its practice to diverse environments.

The strong emphasis on practice in socialist discourse did predispose it, of course, to address particular events as they arose. Like their Lutheran predecessors, socialist leaders articulated their ideology with its social milieu by bringing their rhetoric to bear on the outcome of concrete decisions of public importance. Agitation is the word that has often seemed most appropriate: editorials in socialist newspapers, impassioned speeches before legislative assemblies, pleas to gatherings of workers stirred men and women to take actions which in measurable ways transformed the social milieu into the image projected on it ideologically. To suggest that ideology worked mainly as an instrument of agitation, however, casts the process of articulation in overly narrow terms. Ideological articulation also occurred, perhaps even more profoundly, through interpretation.[5]

An event from the celebrated labor history of Carmaux illustrates the significant role played by interpretation. Although unrest had broken out among the miners of Carmaux intermittently since 1869, it was in 1892 that a decisive work stoppage took place in response to the mining authorities' firing of a socialist worker who had recently been elected mayor. Socialist leaders became active in the cause, giving it national publicity, exhorting workers to take militant action, and using political leverage against the company. At the local level, workers' solidarity was both strengthened by the event and played a large role in bringing pressure to bear on the city's elite. Socialist slogans, red flags, and other regalia signifying the collective spirit of the workers were much in evidence.[6] Whether the eventual settlement was in any positive way attributable to the broader intervention of socialist spokespersons from the outside remains unclear. Addressing themselves to the event, nevertheless, gave socialists a legitimate occasion to interpret the event's significance. The actual settlement represented a clear compromise between the two sides: the mayor was reinstated, the company retained charge of the mine, most strikers were rehired, and some of the socialist leaders permanently lost their jobs. In the socialist press, however, the event was hailed as a victory for universal suffrage, a manifestation of the potential power of worker solidarity, and a great blow struck for workers' freedom.[7] In a clear sense, then, the movement's discourse interacted with its own activities and with its broader theoretical agenda: ideology was neither a static reflection of the social world nor an intellectual framework imposed on reality; it was the revisable ingredient, and outcome, of the movement's action sequences.

Insofar as the leaders of ideological movements are typically unable to control any but a few of the circumstances that actually affect their movements, it can also be argued that the secret to a program of successful articulation is to anticipate correctly what other decision makers are likely to do. In predicting what courses of action others will take, it then becomes possible to shape the movement's strategies and ideas accordingly. There is, in fact, much evidence in the socialist case that movement leaders spent considerable time in strategy sessions aimed at devising the most effective plans of action based on predictions concerning the outcomes of electoral contests, insurrections, power struggles, and the like, and some leaders in particular have been credited with a canny sense of being able to anticipate moods and circumstances well enough to achieve exceptional records of success. In addition to their own initiatives, these leaders' success also appears to have been contingent on two conditions that characterized the socialist movement more generally during this period. One was the movement's access to centers of power and information. Although it was often in a relatively precarious position, it generally had elected representatives in central governing bodies who understood and had personal contact with those in power, and it had sufficiently intimate contact with local workers' organizations that reasonable predictions could be made concerning workers' interests, grievances, political inclinations, and propensities for violence. The other condition was that many aspects of European society were, as has been previously suggested, relatively stable or moving in predictable directions. In comparison with the half century preceding it and the half century succeeding it, the period from 1870 to 1914 was remarkably free of international war and major civil upheavals. Ironically, the very stability of the regimes that revolutionary socialists opposed gave a degree of continuity to their environments that was conducive to the familiarization of popular pleas. In addition, the growth of industrial capitalism, the expansion of the working class, the periodicity of business cycles, the constancy of economic hardship, and the rising importance of electoral politics were all features of the environment that could be anticipated with reasonable certainty.

When the socialists' record at making the right guesses about specific events is taken as a whole, however, the results do not suggest that ideological survival depended on achieving a high rate of accuracy. Despite the fact that a mark of correct theory was often taken to be its capacity to generate effective action, socialist leaders repeatedly made the wrong guesses, as did the leaders of other political factions. Sometimes the accuracy or inaccuracy of their predictions resulted in serious gains or setbacks for specific leaders. The movement as a whole, however, was sufficiently differentiated—even fragmented—that one leader's failure was often another's success. Indeed, this internal differentiation was a key to the movement's ability to articulate its ideology with varied and uncertain social conditions.[8]

Despite their efforts, Marx and Engels together (and Engels alone after Marx's death) were unable to impose doctrinal uniformity on the movement. Their attacks on leaders who espoused deviant views were often extremely sharp, but these leaders were generally in closer contact with the workers' organizations themselves than was the "high command" in London. And Marx's own writings were sufficiently complex that leaders could pick and choose from among the various themes they wished to emphasize. In consequence, a rather diverse set of socialist ideologies came to be enunciated, as we have seen. Common to all of these were certain core concerns about the role of capitalism in exploiting workers and the desire to reform social conditions for the workers' benefit. Beyond this, different versions of socialism stressed a variety of specific proposals, ranging from demands for universal suffrage to stronger alliances with the liberal bourgeoisie to agrarian reforms to trade unionism and the general strike. To those who saw the importance of a single, strong, unified, international movement for gaining political objectives, this disarray represented a major weakness in socialist ideology. In more practical terms, however, internal disagreement was not an entirely ineffective means of adapting socialism to its heterogeneous social environment. In Prussia the nationalistic sentiments of Lassalle made socialism at least temporarily tolerable to the Prussian authorities. In Saxony the anti-Lassallean, reformist orientations of socialist leaders such as August Bebel helped to gain support from, and reflected, the interests of the Leipzig workers' organizations, which included large numbers of anti-Prussian shopkeepers and artisans. In France, Jaurès's syncretic moral idealism and materialism bent orthodox Marxism in a direction that was more attractive to former republicans and representatives of the petty bourgeoisie. From one vantage point, each of these variants constituted a dangerous compromise of pure Marxian socialism. From a different view, however, each variant was a crucible in which some of the basic propositions of socialist ideology could be disseminated to diverse environments. Having drawn at least a partial distinction between theory and practice at the operative level, socialist leaders were able to adopt different strategies in different settings. And, as in the Reformation and the Enlightenment, this diversity often resulted in particular ideological themes being selectively reinforced by the unique constellation of social factors in the settings in which they emerged.

The practical emphasis in socialist ideology, nevertheless, led many of the movement's branches increasingly to elevate the pursuit of political power to a position of preeminence. This emphasis was hotly debated within the movement itself, and yet from the standpoint of understanding how the movement's ideology articulated with its social environment, it represented a compromise that was not clearly understood at the time. The problem of articulation came to be resolved, as it were, by an expected fusion of ideology and power. Rather than the movement's legitimacy being measured primarily in, say, spiritual terms or according to aesthetic standards, it became identified with the political struggle. To a considerable degree the movement thereby sacrificed control over its own credentialing capacity to forces largely beyond itself. The Protestant reformers, in making scriptural truth the highest criteria of their arguments' success, had in effect reserved for themselves the right to serve as competent judges of their own work. Similarly the Enlightenment writers, in championing aesthetic and scientific standards, especially in favor of technical utility, also maintained a standard of judgment over which they themselves exercised almost exclusive control. The socialist leaders, in contrast, increasingly assumed that the essential components of their own ideology had already been worked out, and devoted their attention to anticipating the day when socialism would capture control of the state and thereby transform society into its own image. In so doing, they necessarily evoked criteria of assessment over which representatives of the state, rather than leaders of the movement itself, had a high degree of influence.

Had this sacrifice of jurisdiction over the certification of their own claims been complete, the socialists' principles would clearly have been judged a failure, for no branch of the socialist movement actually captured the state prior to the First World War. However, the movement did manage in other ways to control its own process of legitimation to a large extent, chiefly by finding ways of associating concrete activities with its professed aim of seizing power. On the one hand, the seizure of power became an objective that was explicitly pushed well into the future, defined in relatively utopian terms, and linked to deterministic historical processes, thereby making it less readily susceptible to disconfirmation or subject to alternative definitions. On the other hand, virtually any activity in which the movement became involved, and indeed most of the negative circumstances that happened to befall it, were interpreted as steps toward the eventual attainment of power. Whether the specific action at issue was the passage of workmen's insurance, the debate over military expenditures, or the national consolidation of Bismarck's power in Germany, socialist leaders saw in them signs of their own inevitable political triumph.

The socialist leaders had just enough resources at their disposal to run a few candidates for political office, to launch party newspapers, and to become involved in local strikes and other controversies involving working men and women. Being on the scene, as it were, provided them opportunities to comment with some authority on what had happened. And they were able to do so increasingly with reference to their own internally coherent set of doctrines and goals. Rather than having to submit their claims entirely to a process of external validation, therefore, they were able to provide their own interpretations of events.

It was, then, as much through ideological interpretation as through any sacrifice of ideology for action that practice came to be of vital concern to socialist thought. At the same time that practice, insofar as it was effective, provided workers with tangible reasons to vote for socialist delegates, it also gave socialist leaders opportunities to point out that ideology led not to idle theoretical reflection but toward concrete historical steps along the road to the eventual attainment of power.[9] Much of the internal controversy that characterized the movement consisted, in fact, of claims and counterclaims about the significance of particular actions for the longer-range goal of political ascendancy. And in this sense the debates were no more subject to external validation than were the theological controversies of the Protestant reformers or the aesthetic judgments of the Enlightenment writers.

The Construction of a Discursive Field

A major issue that merits attention within this context is the manner in which the concept of the proletariat came to forge a closer degree of articulation between socialist ideology and this particular segment of its social environment—that is, the working class. Much evidence has been presented in the foregoing chapters to demonstrate that the proletariat in which socialism gained a foothold was as much a product of political circumstances as it was of industrial development. And this fact was by no means invisible to the movement's leaders themselves, especially in view of the frequency with which they were forced to struggle with the question of how much or how little cooperation to encourage between their own movement and the political parties representing the liberal bourgeoisie. In these debates the proletariat itself became a product of ideological definition. Just as the concept of the bourgeois became a kind of figural actor, defined by the discursive field that the Enlightenment writers created, so the concept of a proletariat developed as a symbolically laden category that stood somewhere between, as it were, the institutional experience of actual working men and women and the potentiality attributed to them by socialist visions of the transformed society.

In constructing this discursive field it was crucial, in the first place, to invent a clear designation of what the proletariat was *not*. Prevailing institutional circumstances were identified as products of social forces beyond the proletariat's control. Not only were these forces different from the proletariat, but their designation itself implied the proletariat's negation. Capitalism, the bourgeoisie, and the middle class more loosely all implied this negation of the working class by virtue of the terminology that was used. Thus, for example, Engels in describing the German working class's relation to the predominantly aristocratic, landowning Prussian ruling class always insisted on treating this elite as a single manifestation of capitalist society: "Although Germany is ruled by a semi-feudal monarchy its policy is ultimately determined by the economic interests of the middle classes."[10] More generally, bourgeois society took on negative connotations by being contrasted with scenarios of more primitive, or at least traditional, harmony and goodness. In *The Communist Manifesto,* for example, Marx and Engels develop a sequence of such contrasts, the impact of which is heightened by their parallel form: the bourgeoisie's actions have turned social ties into egotistical, self-interested, exploitative relations; prestigious occupations into wage labor; family sentiments into mere money relations; vigor into slothful indolence. Not only is the contrast clear in terms of movement from the desirable to the undesirable, but this motion itself is dramatized by verbs of violence and disruption: torn asunder, left naked, drowned, stripped, torn away.[11] Having taken these actions, the bourgeoisie becomes personified as an agent that can be not only blamed but also combated. It provides a tangible symbol against which the movement's struggle can be defined. In addition, the "bourgeois," as adjective, provides a summary designation that both subsumes and explains the essential, common features of the present institutional order: bourgeois society, bourgeois ideology, bourgeois morality, bourgeois family relations, bourgeois property, bourgeois rule.

At the more ideal end of the axis around which this discursive field operated, the vision of a classless society in which social democratic principles would be ascendant suggests an image of the proletariat that is identifiably more working class than not, and yet clearly different from the vale of woes common to actual working-class men and women. Within the horizon of working-class life itself, the proletariat is depicted as exploited, demoralized, degraded, and destitute, even stunted spiritually and physically. But in the classless society to come, the proletariat will consist of free comrades, a fraternal association of strong, free, and equal persons. The proletariat, in the dual sense conveyed by these joint images, stands between the two poles of present reality and future ideal, providing a character to whom the virtues necessary for moving from the present to the future can be ascribed.

The two poles of the socialists' discursive field, similar to those of the Reformation and the Enlightenment, were constructed by attaching graphic symbols to realities and potentials readily apparent in the movement's own social context. On the negative end, graphic imagery helped to define the negative pole as one of scorn and ridicule. Just as the Protestant reformers desacralized many of the church's cherished teachings and the Enlightenment writers parodied the traditional customs of elite society, so the socialist leaders profaned the accepted virtues of bourgeois society. Religion, dogma, and superstition naturally came under attack. So did the more apparently "progressive" ideals of liberal democracy. For example, Marx characterized the German liberals' attempt to champion religious liberty during the *Kulturkampf* as a trivial matter being exploited for political purposes. "Everyone must be able to relieve his religious needs," he wrote sarcastically, "like his bodily needs, without the police sticking their noses in."[12] More generally, concepts of "rights" were excoriated as props of bourgeois class domination. Rather than regarding them, as in Hegel and Kant, as universal principles, Marx and his followers showed them to be relativistic conceptions having their roots in the material conditions of life. Property rights were especially onerous, but so were principles of liberty and justice. Marx vilified them as "dogma," "nonsense," and "myth," much in the same way that Luther had denounced the superstitious beliefs of the medieval church.[13] Similar words and phrases were added to the list of charges against other bourgeois institutions: education was "bourgeois clap-trap"; family virtues were belied by the fact that the bourgeois "take the greatest pleasure in seducing each other's wives"; eternal laws of reason were merely "selfish misconceptions"; and ideals such as freedom and independence were nothing more than "brave words."[14] And, of course, many of the economic principles of bourgeois capitalism came in for particularly vigorous attack. Not only were they subjected to dispassionate theoretical critique; they were also objectified, personified (by association with their proponents), and satirized to the point of providing a tangible reference point for the negative end of the socialists' discursive framework. "Our boasted civilization," wrote Paul Lafargue, "will pass down into history as the age of trash." Economic conditions are "the great criminals"; the modern factory "robs the baby of its mother and the father of his wife"; its products are "all imitations, all adulterated"; it engenders "intrigue, trickery, lying, avarice, egoism."[15]

These epithets, moreover, were not limited to formal speeches or to the movement's polemical tracts; differentiation of the working class from the bourgeoisie was also accomplished through collective rituals, gatherings, and other activities. One of the reasons for initiating workers' gymnastic, singing, and cycling associations was to give workers an identity separate from that of the bourgeoisie. Participation in these associations accentuated the physical and cultural distances between workers and the bourgeoisie. Workers interacted with other workers, gave their associations distinctive names (like Verein Vorwärts and Solidarität), and engaged in electioneering for their own candidates. They also sang songs that mocked the religious music of the bourgeoisie, held counterfestivals and counterparades, and heard speakers who derided the bourgeoisie.[16]

The contamination of sacred ideals with images of pollution served two purposes. First, it relativized these concepts, thereby allowing them to be called into question. Rather than their being legitimate by virtue of merely being taken for granted as features of the natural order, they could be questioned as somehow "out of place" in the same way that images of pollution symbolized disorder and the need for cleansing. Second, they provided by negative example clarification of what the proletariat and its representatives in the socialist movement were not. Beyond their association with images of pollution, the concepts attached to the negative discursive pole were characteristically labeled bourgeois. Other than in the more complex theoretical treatises of party leaders, the bourgeoisie was not precisely defined, however, especially not in terms of who specifically fell within its circumference. By default the bourgeoisie was, as more recent neo-Marxist theories have increasingly emphasized, a relational concept. It designated, primarily by the actions ascribed to it, a negative valence in relation to which the movement stood in opposition. As much as being an actual social class, the bourgeoisie was a symbolic construction. In anchoring the negative end of discourse, it provided a space in which the proletariat could be conceived.

At the opposite end of the ideological field, the concept of a classless society was particularly important. It represented the negation and transformation of present social conditions. Yet it was also a product of these conditions. It was not, as Marxists themselves recognized clearly, simply an ideal or a dream but a particular vision of the future that depended on an understanding of the social situation. Like Luther's concept of God and the Enlightenment's concept of nature or freedom, the socialists' classless society grew out of a conjuncture of specific social and cultural resources. It depended on the growing sense of linear historical movement that had emerged during the Enlightenment. It drew on long-standing images of cooperation and equality. The French Revolution, as we have seen, provided both a positive image, in the sense of total social change being possible, and a negative image, in the sense of bourgeois revolution not having gone far enough. And above all, the effects of industrialization, which were widely seen as promoting the growth and inevitable numerical triumph of the working class, made conceivable the idea of progressing toward a classless society. All these were conditions in the socialists' social milieu that provided them with the raw materials from which an ideological agenda could be defined—an agenda that, in turn, was recognizably articulated with its social context.

Though much of the socialists' literature is rooted in complex philosophical understandings that do not themselves translate easily into such simple formulas, many of the specific concepts that became active ingredients in socialist ideology can be viewed as attributes associated with one end or the other of this basic polarity. Illusory and real, illusion and awareness, ideal and material, ideological and scientific, past and future, competitive and cooperative, bondage and emancipation—all take their form within this framework. As abstractions they provide sharp and seemingly timeless contrasts. And yet they were also defined in terms that made them recognizable to contemporaries, terms that drew from the immediate social context the necessary valences to provide evaluative connotations. Metaphors from family life and from work were particularly amenable to such uses, but images of time, of historical movement, and of progress also came into play. Progress, a commitment to reason, and science especially served in this manner. As one pamphlet explained, socialist theory was "the science of the *irrational* regulation of [society] at present." The same author held forth the image of a "*reasonable* order" to be brought into being by the socialist movement.[17]

The discursive polarity that socialist ideology established between the negative aspects of bourgeois society and the positively valued classless society provided a space in which many of the important debates generated by the movement were located.[18] For instance, the historical trejectory that ran along the major axis of this polarity constitued the context in which the state was discussed. Although socialist strategists could not ignore the state in practice, their most systematic theoretical treatments of the state emerged not in the context of empirical observation but in the framework of dialectical history. As the development of capitalism was depicted within this framework, the state entered the picture primarily as an abstract entity that responds to the growing crises of capitalist production by socializing certain sectors of the economy. The emphasis on this activity at the neglect of all other state functions clearly depended on the thematized conception of historical development characterizing the socialist framework. In addition, the more intractable questions of how the state itself changes and how these changes must be responded to by the proletariat were largely wished away by treating the state itself as a figural actor. As Engels observes, the state "shows itself" the way to accomplish socialist revolution.[19] That is to say, the state's socialization of property becomes important chiefly as an exemplar, a vehicle of education, that suggests to the proletariat how it must proceed. Thus, the proletariat, seeing the state taking the lead in this direction, "seizes political power and turns the means of production into state property."[20] How this is to be done does not figure as an important question within this immediate framework because the very direction of history, as symbolized in the state's action, assumes that the proletariat will succeed. Furthermore, the question of what the proletariat is to do with this state property is also immediately resolved by the declaration that once private property has been seized, both the proletariat and the state, along with all class divisions and class antagonisms, will have been abolished.

In practical discourse questions of the proletariat's role as dictator over the state and of the state's role in transforming society into a classless entity of course surfaced prominently in the decade prior to the First World War, especially after the 1905 uprising in Russia, and again with even greater force after 1917. Marxist theory, however, was not dependent on finding successful or compelling answers to these questions. Theoretical discourse concerning the state did not, in terms of the present discussion, have to articulate closely with actual political conditions. As a thematized entity, the state came on the scene only as a signal of the final death throes of capitalism, and then dropped out of consideration as a theoretical issue once the socialization of property had been achieved. To assume that this treatment of the state was either arbitrary or untrue to social conditions, however, is to miss its essential consistency with the broader framework in which it was developed. Both the action and the disappearance of the state referred back to the historical dialectic, thereby reinforcing the conceptual core of the Marxist framework.

There is, nevertheless, a certain degree of ambiguity in the discursive field underlying socialist ideology. Especially at the positive end of this field ambiguity is evident that helps explain some of the diversity that came to characterize the various branches of the movement. In insisting that theirs was a materialist philosophy with no room for idealism, Marx and Engels rejected characterizing the positive end of their discursive axis as an ideal to be striven toward in contrast with the real or known world of capitalist society. A purely classless society is to be understood not as an ideal but as a future reality. Its existence as scientific fact is assured through the materialist movement of history itself. Yet, in contrasting its positive benefits with the negative features of capitalist society, they relied on terminology that sounds both idealistic and utopian. Steven Lukes observes, for example, that "in Marx and Engels, these two positions co-exist in constant tension with one another. In the subsequent marxist tradition they have separated out. The over-all drift of the mainline marxism of the Second and Third Internationals (and of

Trotskyism and many social democratic variants) has been scientific–anti-utopian; but utopian counter-currents have always existed."[21] Lukes treats this ambiguity as if it were distinctly attributable to inconsistencies in the writings of Marx and Engels. And to some extent their desire to be "scientific" and yet to motivate political action may be seen as an underlying problem. In view of the fact that certain utopian and antiutopian controversies are also evident in the Reformation and the Enlightnment, however, it can legitimately be asked whether or not this problem may be a more endemic characteristic of the kinds of discursive frameworks I have been describing.

The Protestant reformers' image of God and the bourgeois ideal of the eighteenth century, like the vision of a classless society, were clearly utopian categories that had no discernible referent in observable reality. In all three cases, however, that very fact resulted in the formulation of more proximate goals that could be more readily attained. These were not merely means to an ultimate end but more qualified statements of the ends toward which action could realistically be devoted. They bore recognition of the fact that the positive always reflected in it the negative as well, and that action had to take place within the framework defined by both: between sin and divine perfection, custom and enlightenment, capitalist struggle and the classless society. In all three cases room in the middle was specified for individual discretion, responsibility, and the inevitable variation that resulted. And these formulations tended to prove most adaptable to the large, heterogeneous environments in which each movement developed.

There were in each case, however, utopian variants as well. In these formulations a sharper sense of the ideal was maintained, less of a distinction was made between the pure and the good, and less room was provided for individual discretion and variation. In consequence, these variants generally remained smaller in terms of participants but also engaged the dominant movement in continuous counterdiscourse, one result of which was to maintain an image of the purest ideals.

In turn, the very presence of these utopian variants provided a rhetorical occasion for the dominant ideological movement to distinguish between hope and action, between theory and practice, for it was the contention of its leaders that the utopians were deluded mainly by the unreality of the steps by which they saw utopia being realized. To be utopian was, as Lenin cautioned, "to indulge in idle guesswork about what cannot be known."[22]

In arguing against utopian variants of the vision of a classless society, socialists brought this ideal into a closer relation with practice and with actual social conditions. A temporal connection, welded solidly into the assumption of historical determinism, brought tangible programs into a definite relation with the more utopian goal of liberating humanity.[23] To the extent that the vision of a classless society was legitimated in terms of the inevitable movement of history, however, leverage was also put into effect for disarticulating ideology from its social context. In the socialist case this meant refusing to resolve all uncertainties with definite prescriptions and, instead, specifying the field of relevant concepts in relation to which such decisions should be made on a case-by-case basis. An answer is provided, rather than simply allowing for the possibility that anyone's answer might be correct, but the answer takes the form of specifying a method of arriving at an answer instead of giving a substantive response. And the method suggested operates within a conceptual framework instead of pertaining directly to empirical reality. Jaurès, for example, insists on the impossibility of determining ahead of time "the innumerable combinations by means of which Socialism will be instituted." And yet he also argues with certainty "that the direction of economic evolution will itself determine the infinitely complex relations according to which the new society will be organized." The most specific advice he can offer, then, is "to observe constantly the trend of affairs, to grasp the points at which the society of to-day touches the new idea." This is a method, a strategy for making decisions rather than a prescription for those decisions. It depends specifically on having in mind the broader theoretical framework in which economic evolution is emphasized.[24] Karl Kautsky's discussion of the minimal size for a successful "commonwealth" of socialist production demonstrates the use of a similar method. In response to the question of what size such a commonwealth must be, he refuses either to give a specific figure or to leave the matter entirely open: "As the socialist republic is not an arbitrary creation of the brain, but a necessary product of economic development, the size of such a commonwealth cannot be determined. It must conform to the stage of social development out of which it grows."[25] Thus, the question of size can be answered in specific situations but only by understanding the Marxist theory of economic development. The relevance of the general framework is at once affirmed, while its detachment from any specific social situation is made possible.[26]

The Ideological Formation of the Proletariat

As the major figural actor in socialist ideology, the proletariat must be understood ultimately as a construction made possible by the distinctive discursive space which opened up along a historical axis between the present contradictions of bourgeois society and the anticipated future of a classless society. And yet the very possibility for conceiving of the proletariat in this way depended on the social context in which this discourse emerged. Although there was no one-to-one relation between the size of the industrial working class and the strength of socialism or the clarity with which the proletariat was conceptualized, there was a relation between the complexity of the working class and the socialist movement's tendency to define the proletariat in less than purely empirical terms. An understanding of this relation requires recognition, first, of the diversity of ways in which the proletariat was defined substantively, and second, of the ways in which functional and relational concepts of the proletariat substituted for these substantive definitions.

The diversity of substantive conceptions has already been alluded to in previous chapters with reference to the factionalization that occurred within the movement over relatively more or less inclusive political strategies vis-à-vis the petty bourgeoisie, and in certain cases the rural sector. These differences also became evident in the various formal statements of movement ideology itself.[27] Toward the end of the prewar period, writing primarily from the basis of the German experience, Kautsky, for example, was relatively confident about including the petty bourgeoisie and farmers, given their seemingly inevitable decline along with the industrial laboring sector. In his conception the proletariat included all "workers who are divorced from their instruments of production so that they can produce nothing of their own efforts," but also "the majority of the farmers, small producers and traders."[28] Lafargue vacillated amidst a number of competing conceptions of the proletariat, focusing at times on all "producers," at others on "wage workers," in other instances on the more limited set of workers who live "in the presence of the colossal machinery which employs them," and in still other instances reverting to the more inclusive category of "manual and intellectual workers alike."[29] These conceptual difficulties were, of course, not entirely without basis in social reality. For, as the previous chapters have shown, the working class—and even that segment of the working class most attracted to socialism—was quite diverse. Political conditions sometimes tended to overcome these internal distinctions, giving the socialist movement room in which to define its objectives more clearly. And yet even in these situations the economic conditions of the working class provided no easy way of distinguishing it from other classes.[30]

Although the proletariat was conceivable in purely substantive (that is, occupational) terms, the differences of opinion over its exact composition resulted in its being defined operationally instead, in relational and functional language. The program adopted at the Fifth Congress of German Workers' Societies at Nuremberg in 1867, for example, referred simply to the "working classes" and to "workers" without supplying any specific indication of their composition. Their unity was defined relationally as one of "dependence," "misery," and "degradation."[31] To take another example, Kautsky spoke of the proletariat as an amorphous entity defined mainly by (1) its subjection to economic exploitation; (2) its growth, which had already made it the most sizable segment of the population; and (3) its declining economic power, freedom, and means of self-determination. Jaurès cautioned specifically against trying to resolve the substantive diversity of the proletariat, pointing out, for example, that Proudhon had quickly discovered that the proletariat was actually "a mixture of factory-workers, still weak in numbers and power, of a lower middle-class composed of petty manufacturers and small tradespeople, and of an artisan class which the absorbing power of capital was eyeing greedily but had not yet done away with." To focus on this diversity was, in Jaurès's view, to make oneself vulnerable to "all that is hazy and contradictory." Instead, he argued, the proletariat should be conceived of in terms of its *relation* to the movement of history. Rather than focusing on "all the reservations and restrictions which result from the study of the complicated and many-sided reality," one should emphasize only that the proletariat is on the ascendancy. Like Kautsky, Jaurès stressed the proletariat's increasing numbers in both absolute and relative terms and the changes in modes of production that would ensure its continued growth. Above all, the proletariat could be treated as a unitary whole, Jaurès insisted, because of its relation (which he likened to a kind of tax) of dependence on the class that owned the means of production.[32]

It is perhaps noteworthy, given what we have seen in previous chapters about the political determination of the proletariat, that socialist ideology largely did not identify the proletariat in political terms. For example, the proletariat was scarcely ever identified as politically disenfranchised, despite the fact that demands for universal enfranchisement were frequently part of the socialists' platform. Nor was the proletariat associated with those who might be members of the Socialist party or supporters of its candidates, or who might be presumed to be in sympathy with its objectives. To have adopted the former strategy would have not only introduced complications because of national differences in the franchise but also failed in distinguishing socialist demands clearly from the demands of republican and liberal democratic parties. To have adopted the latter definition would greatly have restricted the size of the constituency to which the socialist movement's appeals were directed.

Rather than being identified with any concrete economic or political group, therefore, the proletariat came to be an ideological construct whose outlines depended at least partly on the broader categories in which socialists conceived of society and history. In Marx's own writings the internal diversity of the proletariat is explicitly acknowledged in passages about the contrasts between industrial workers, the reserve army of unemployed labor, and the lumpenproletariat. These empirical differences are resolved with arguments about the primacy of the means of production in determining class relations. But such arguments themselves require making abstractions from the empirical conditions of the working class itself—abstractions that depend on broader theoretical assumptions. The proletariat was not unified in all respects within the horizon of institutional contexts itself but was a *unitary concept* within the discursive framework of Marxist theory. To oversimplify only slightly: the proletariat became a symbolic representation that stood for many of the negative features of industrial society and at the same time pointed toward a redemptive escape from these negative conditions. Relationally the proletariat stood for exploitation, alienation, and deprivation. Functionally it symbolized action, the forward movement of history, a means to overcoming present woes and moving toward a more humane society.

One need not follow those who have seen in this conception of the proletariat a mere imitation in Marx of Hegel or in socialism of Christian eschatology.[33] Yet there was some of the power in this conception that has been observed in systems of myth and symbolism more generally. Rather than its appeal resting strictly on an empirical analysis of occupational or political conditions, it was a conceptual system that extracted elements from the lives of working men and women and generalized these elements into an objectified symbol. Moreover, the proletariat was more than simply an isolated word or slogan; its very meaning depended on the discursive framework created by the movement's ideology. As Marx had recognized as early as midcentury in debating his opponents, the proletariat could not be called on to take immediate, heroic action without consideration of the economic forces to which it was subject. The proletariat's composition and its vision of revolutionary action depended entirely on a broader framework of interpretation.

The relation between the proletariat as an ideological construct and the social environment in which it was articulated resembles the relation that was seen earlier between the ideological formation of the bourgeoisie and its social environment. The concept of the bourgeosie did not grow directly from a previously distinct bourgeois class in the social environment but developed indirectly, as it were, from the diversity of the public sphere, which in turn evoked a problematic relation between private selves and public roles. The bourgeoisie came to be defined as a symbolic construct in which both the worst and best elements of this relation could be put together and thereby envisioned as a model for concrete action. In much the same way the proletariat as an ideological construct grew only loosely from its counterpart in the occupational structure. Rather than the working class being an empirically distinct societal unit that provided a model for conceptions of the proletariat, it was both internally diverse and differentiated in its relations with the ruling elites and the state.[34] This very ambiguity created a problematic relation between the working class as it then existed and the socialist movement's conception of historical tendencies and revolutionary action. Within the framework of this problematic relation, the proletariat emerged as a symbolic construct in which elements of both the present situation and the anticipated direction of history came together. As was the case with the ideological creation of the bourgeoisie, that of the proletariat depended on the construction of a distinct discursive field.

It was, moreover, not merely the empirical complexity of the economy—and therefore of economic groups—but also the ambiguities of the state that led to functional and relational rather than substantive conceptions of the proletariat. Because the leaders of the socialist movement regarded the seizure of state power as an important means of bringing about the socialization of property relations, they could scarcely ignore the realities of political conditions. The eventual triumph of the proletariat was contingent not only on projected growth in the size of the industrial sector but also on its potential for mobilizing these numbers for political purposes either in the form of direct action or through parliamentary processes. Questions of actual and potential alliances among different segments of the working class, as a result, were always important as political considerations as much as they were matters for abstract reflection based on assumptions about the economic determination of class relations. Much of the conflict between the Lassalleans and the Eisenachers in Germany, for example, reflected differing assessments of the importance of coalitions among industrial workers, peasants, and the petty bourgeoisie for electoral purposes. Indeed, Marx came as close in this controversy as he did anywhere to allowing political expediency to determine his views of class relations.

The key problem in dealing with the state's role in defining the proletariat, however, was that no solid theoretical basis was available in Marxism for systematically analyzing this relation. With the possible exception of Marx's distinction between *Klass an sich* and *Klass für sich,* which was seldom invoked in the context of discussing political contingencies, the central empirical referent for the proletariat remained that of the economy. The state's role was limited in theory to that of reaffirming class relations. Empirical issues that arose from practical considerations such as the question of how much or how little to cooperate with Bismarck were dealt with largely on an ad hoc basis which at most recognized variations in national histories and in the strength of political parties as added factors influencing class relations. Only gradually, especially toward the end of the prewar period, with the increasing growth of the socialist movement as a political actor itself, did more systematic attention turn to the development of a theory of the state. And even these treatments paid greater attention to the state's role in regulating giant trusts and in contributing directly to the socialization of production than to the state's indirect role in creating a political space in which socialist parties could grow.

Thus, the broader political influences on the proletariat that have been examined in the foregoing chapters were only partially reflected in the self-analysis of the socialist movement itself. These influences could scarcely be ignored entirely because they determined in practice much of the movement's success or failure in capturing votes and achieving electoral successes. But the movement's theoretical framework did not provide a means of giving these influences full or systematic treatment. In the absense of any such framework the movement's ideology developed in a way, therefore, that systematically removed itself from having to correspond exactly with actual social conditions.

Figural Action: The Proletariat and Moral Behavior

In defining the activities of the proletariat, socialist ideology was faced with a quandary imposed by the categories of which it itself consisted. All action should promote the eventual rise to power of the proletariat. Yet in different circumstances, various means to that end might be most effective. A simple differentiation of means and ends was sufficient to justify defending different courses of action in different situations. Nevertheless, the very courses of action that had to be defended—namely, cooperating with the bourgeoisie, taking immediate violent actions, working gradually through parliamentary processes—were the ones that orthodox socialists felt compelled to brand as heresy in order to maintain their own control of the movement. To suggest a particular course of action as a short-term strategy, therefore, was tantamount to suggesting that bad must be tolerated in order to bring about good. These actions were in effect treated not simply as means but as immoral behavior, as violations of principle. In a revealing letter written in the 1840s, for example, Marx and Engels had exhorted their German followers: "Forget your German honour, candour and respectability! Support middle class petitions for freedom of the press, a constitution, and so on. When these middle class demands have been achieved the ground will be prepared for communist propaganda. Then we shall have a better chance of getting our way since the rivalry between the middle classes and the proletariat will have been accentuated. To aid the communist party you should support any policy which will be to our advantage in the long run. And do not be deterred by any stuffy moral scruples."[35] This kind of argument was to reappear repeatedly over the next half century as socialist leaders debated practical policies. It was nevertheless problematic because it suggested that the proletariat should at least in the short run be willing to abandon "moral scruples" in order to attain socialist goals. Was the proletariat in fact to behave immorally? Or could the proletariat be conceived in such a way as to be upheld as an exemplar of moral virtue?[36]

One resolution to this dilemma would have been to adopt the purely pragmatic form of rationality expressed by Weber in his discussion of *Zweckrationalität*. As long as means were organized efficiently and consistently, questions of abstract moral principles could be excluded within this form of reasoning. To a considerable extent the socialist movement did in fact conform to this style of rationality, at least in practice, as both Weber and Michels recognized. However, the strong commitment of socialist theory, especially in its Marxian version, to the principle of attaining a classless society as an absolute value prevented ideological formulations from departing entirely from a form of *Wertrationalität*.

The distinction between theory and practice, of course, alleviated some of the tension between behavioral compromise and moral ideals. Insofar as cooperation with the bourgeoisie could be discussed strictly within the horizon of practical policy, questions of principle did not need to be addressed. This tactic was in fact somewhat more manageable than it might otherwise have been by virtue of the physical separation, and indeed role differentiation, that isolated socialist deputies from Marx, Engels, and other theoreticians of the movement. As we have seen, the exile of some of the leading German theoreticians during the period of Bismarck's antisocialist legislation seems to have reinforced this tendency in Germany in the 1870s.[37] Nevertheless, compartmentalizing theory and practice could not be an entirely effective resolution to the problem of morality, especially as long as critics within the movement were eager to point out inconsistencies in official policy.

The answer at a discursive level lay in attributing to the proletariat an enlightened mode of consciousness. Not simply any worker but the socialist worker, by virtue of his participation in the revolutionary struggle, became aware, it was argued, of higher principles, needs, and opportunities to which the bourgeoisie was blinded. What seemed immoral from one perspective, therefore, acquired different meaning within this expanded horizon. Moreover, this awareness necessarily required an understanding of the theoretical principles

on which socialism was based. Two workers could be engaged in the
same revolutionary movement, but only the one who understood
the underlying principles of the movement was capable of acting
morally. Only this worker, as Marx and Engels put it, had "the advantage of clearly understanding the line of march, the conditions,
and the ultimate general results of the proletarian movement."[38]
Thus, the movement always had to be concerned with defining and
propagating its ideology as well as merely encouraging mass action.

The possibility of heightened consciousness among the proletariat also provided a way of bridging the gap between theory and
practice. If, in theory, the problem of moral action was to be resolved
by each worker taking greater responsibility to reconcile his own
needs with the collective good, then practice was the means by which
the worker came to develop these sensitivities. Once socialism was
achieved, people would—again in theory—be more in possession of
their own lives, better able to assess their own needs, and capable
of interacting on a basis of mutual concern. The way to attain these
ideals, while requiring instruction in the theoretical principles of
socialism, not only lay in the contemplation of abstract ideals but
depended on a commitment to practice. By engaging in the self-
sacrificial acts associated with party work, the individual was able to
anticipate some of the benefits of socialism in the here and now.
Indeed, it is not uncommon in the accounts written by participants
in the movement to find that a sense of elevation, moral uplift, and
intimate identification with the collectivity was actually present.

Practice bridged the gap between the real world of competitive
self-interest and the theoretical world of moral action much in the
way that Durkheim was to suggest only a few years later in considering the role of ritual in social life.[39] Participation in the rituals of
socialist party work disciplined the individual and magnified the person's sense of identification with the collectivity no less visibly than
did the primitive religious rites with which Durkheim was concerned.
The collective effervescence that came on a small scale from this
participation provided a tangible, experiential glimpse of what life
could possibly be like under the eventual conditions of a socialist
society. For the worker actually caught up in the full round of party
behavior, socialism stood for something more than either an abstract
ideology or a mere hope of improvement in material conditions. The
image of the worker-participant, as would become even more pronounced after the Russian revolution, was that of a valorized hero—

one who had escaped the limitations of ordinary human existence, had communed with the gods, gained in personal efficacy, and, by example, showed that others could follow the same path. Socialism, in Max Adler's words: "brings about a self-transcendence in every worker who is genuinely inspired by it. From that moment he no longer feels himself to be merely a worker. His mind becomes filled with hopes which direct his attention to a better future, and all those other interests in a brighter more joyous existence and a richer content to life are awakened, far beyond what a merely working-class interest could provide."[40]

Put differently, as Louis Althusser does in his analysis of *Capital,* the proletariat consists of persons with vision.[41] The worker sees instinctively what all the classical bourgeois economists have missed—namely, that capital accumulation comes about only from the appropriation of the laborer's surplus value. The role of the revolutionary ideologue, consequently, is to make explicit what the worker already knows. The proletariat's vision does not depend on faith in a model of the future set forth in doctrine alone. It consists of seeing the present as it really is, of having the blinders of false consciousness stripped away, and then of realizing the practical steps that must be taken to correct the artificiality of the conditions prevailing under capitalism. Like the bourgeoisie in Enlightenment discourse, the proletariat suffers from inauthenticity, from a gap between the real and the actual, but also bears the potential for bridging this gap.

Significantly, the proletariat's potential to bridge the gap between present conditions and a fuller realization of itself is contingent on the very discursive field in which the proletariat is defined. Only by grasping the horizon of discourse do present conditions and future possibilities become visible. This is the secret of why bourgeois economists could be wrong. What they say is based on an improper horizon that fails to suggest the appropriate questions and therefore fails to provide correct answers. Within the new horizon of socialist analysis, the terrain can be viewed differently. Indeed, once the gaps in classical economic understanding become evident, a natural place for socialist concepts opens up. What would be regarded as interpolation now becomes a matter of substitution, of replacing the false with reality. The socialist has merely to fill in blank spaces in a jigsaw puzzle, rather than constructing an entirely new picture of the world.[42]

Although a certain degree of freedom and will on the part of the proletariat is thereby implied, it is nevertheless not up to the heroic virtue of the individual worker alone to bring about the necessary social transformation. Merely by placing himself or herself within the horizon of socialist discourse, the worker gains vision. And the vision gained is not so much a property of the individual but a feature of the discursive terrain itself. For purposes of legitimation, this particular formulation is of great importance: it reduces the potentially arbitrary, willful act of the worker to an inevitable characteristic of the conceptual landscape. Moreover, it supplies the worker with an unexpected resource: insight is not entirely to be won at the expense of great personal effort and sacrifice; it is an abundant gift, a manifestation of grace, a realization that cannot be escaped within the terrain of the theoretical formulation itself.

The tangible rewards associated with socialist practice reinforced the connection between ideological production and the social means of ideological production in the same manner that had been the case in the Reformation and the Enlightenment. In the earlier instances, part of the ideological message suggested that a true understanding and appreciation of the ideological principles required putting them into practice, whether in the Calvinist struggle to exemplify faith in one's behavior or in the Enlightenment's commitment to advanced knowledge as a prerequisite for appreciating the higher aesthetic qualities of Enlightenment literature. Now, commitment to the propagation of socialism and its political realization became an act on which the higher morality of socialist ideology itself was contingent. In short, ideology provided the reward for its own preservation. Thus, to return to the question of articulation, socialist theory engendered practice of the kind that not only contributed to the furtherance of theory in general but also created the ideal conditions on a restricted scale within the movement itself that were conducive to the kinds of experience the ideology prescribed.

For western socialists following in the Marxist tradition, the idea that participation in the movement was in a sense its own reward provided a powerful argument that became a recurring element of the movement's discourse. And yet it also presented the movement with sufficient practical problems that it became a subject of counterdiscourse as well. In the face of long years of effort, sometimes at considerable personal sacrifice, which nevertheless yielded no revolution and no seizure of power through legislative means, the claim that "the movement is everything" could provide an incentive or at least a rationale for continued participation. Unlike the more purely reformist ideologies advanced by some of its leading competitors, Marxian socialism offered those in the vanguard of the movement a rhetoric that depended neither on continuous success in ameliorating the economic conditions of the working class nor on an entirely altruistic motivation in the interim before the revolution. Motivation could be based on experience that was itself rewarding, and yet this experience could be regarded as a legitimate source of satisfaction because it promoted a heightened consciousness of the very kind that would be needed when the revolution came.

The basis for counterdiscourse lay inevitably in the tendency for strategic action of a reformist kind to be replaced by these internal sources of reward and motivation. As long as the movement remained committed both to the revolutionary ideal and to the concrete program of economic and political reforms, it was inescapably subject to this kind of discourse and counterdiscourse. Perhaps as much as anything else, the Marxist version was advanced at the level of ideological formulation by the contradictions within its own rhetorical and motivational structure—contradictions that themselves encouraged an ongoing debate.

The degree to which these subtleties of interpretation were actually incorporated into the discourse of rank and file members of the movement should not, of course, be exaggerated. Rather, the struggles to provide adequate answers to issues of this complexity took the form primarily of debates between the leading theoreticians of the movement and became resolved symbolically by becoming affixed to the various personalities involved. Conflicts between Marx and Lassalle, Bakunin and Proudhon, Kautsky and Bernstein, and others, came to stand as shorthand designations for much more subtle ambiguities and differences of interpretation within the broader socialist canon. One could indeed say that different interpretations became personified. Ideological debates hinged to a certain extent, therefore, on ad hominem claims and on caricatures of arguments that in fact displayed greater sophistication. To the extent that these personalities also tended to be engaged actively as leaders of particular parties and factions within the movement, the success or failure of interpretations identified with them depended on collective processes that went beyond the mere force of intellectual assertion. As in the debates between Luther and his contemporaries, or between

Voltaire and his rivals, the personification of ideological variations within the larger movement, therefore, brought the movement into a closer relation with its own actions and with the environment in which these actions took place.

These considerations suggest an additional feature of socialist thought that also helps to account for its success under relatively heterogeneous and, certainly over the entire course of its history, changing conditions. There are in socialism neither any absolute values against which particular courses of action can be evaluated in all cases nor any specific prescriptions for action that can be defended under all circumstances. To say this may seem at odds with the idea that achieving socialism or seizing power sometimes functions as an absolute value. Yet the idea of moving toward a socialist society is always couched, certainly by Marx and Engels, in assertions about the empirical direction of historical development, rather than being defended on the basis of any consistent set of higher-order values (freedom, equality, justice, productivity), and no particular means of attaining this goal is ever consistently advanced. A relatively ad hoc set of higher-order values is specified, as are the situationally contingent means of action that are discussed.[43] By standards of philosophical rigor, the lack of greater consistency and coherence may be regarded as a distinct weakness of socialism. This very weakness, however, can be regarded as a strength for any ideology faced with adapting to diverse and changing social conditions. Rather than providing for a strictly logical defense of any course of action on the basis of ideology alone, socialism requires a relatively high level of choice and interpretation on the part of its followers.

Much like the Lutheran concept of faith as a mechanism that tempers scriptural fixity, so the ambiguity built into the socialist view of revolutionary action mitigates tendencies toward dogmatic inflexibility. The revolutionary member of the proletariat is defined as a product of his own ideology and circumstances. Thus, it is always necessary for this actor to decide on an appropriate course of action. Some actions are clearly excluded by the collective interests of the movement, but different actions, although subject to constant scrutiny and deliberation, can seldom be proven decisively to be unacceptable on grounds of doctrine alone. As William Liebknecht observes: "We set up no especial principles according to which the movement shall model itself. Our theoretical propositions rest in no way upon 'ideas' or 'principles' that this or that reformer has 'discovered.' They are only . . . expressions of actual relations of an existing class struggle—of an historical movement going on before our eyes."[44]

Indeed, socialism does not merely leave a great deal of discretion to the individual by default but explicitly calls on the individual to exercise discretion knowledgeably and responsibly. Like the figural Protestant and the enlightened bourgeois, the proletarian is required by the vision within socialist ideology to make choices. Various standards for making the right choices are discussed, but even this repertoire is incomplete. Only by taking initial steps to participate in the revolutionary struggle, and then by determining where these steps lead, can the socialist decide. This, of course, is no more tantamount to saying that the good socialist must at heart be an individualist than it is to say that the Protestant could defy the authority of Scripture and the counsel of fellow believers. The socialist, however, must have "character," which is to say, must not only have internalized the movement's values but also have a sense of personal freedom and responsibility. If socialist writings fail to provide a precisely codified statement of the criteria of strong character, they are nevertheless replete with adulations of the "heroic deeds" of persons who contributed to the struggle and filled with vilifications of those not to be imitated.

The distinctive contribution of socialism to arguments about character, however, is its explicit insistence on the individual's weakness apart from the collectivity. As Marx and Engels assert in *The German Ideology:* "Only in community with others has each individual the means of cultivating his gifts in all directions; only in the community, therefore, is personal freedom possible."[45] Or as Kautsky insists: "It is only the class war and not the single-handed efforts of individuals acting on their own behalf which has the necessary strength to advance social development, and to bring needs into conformity with the higher level of development of the productive forces."[46] Motivation to undertake the risks required for revolutionary action depends on strong identification with one's fellows in similar circumstances. Moreover, it depends on certain initial changes in these circumstances being made so that the individual can feel a sense of support and visualize the possibility of change.

The prevalence of competitiveness in capitalist society provides an explanation for the general reluctance of workers to side with the movement. Thus any initial step toward cooperative action should result in some reduction of this reluctance. In much of the revisionist socialism that characterized western Europe between 1870 and 1914, it was also assumed that incremental improvements in living conditions would inspire greater commitment to the party. The weakness of generating collective action on the basis of utilitarian self-interest, however, showed itself in the relative lack of commitment to the party other than at the polls. As in the case of socialism's predecessors in the sixteenth and eighteenth centuries, the movement's reliance on a strong sense of individual discretion contributed, as it were, to a relatively modest level of commitment. Only with the more disciplined collective orientations of the Bolshevik revolutionary vanguard, much like the Calvinist "elect," was a greater degree of control imposed on the individual.

Socialist Action, Theory, and Practice

The moral action of the proletariat added an element of discretion, and thereby, significantly, of responsibility, to the otherwise deterministic conception of historical materialism in socialist theory. The individual proletarian was not free, however, simply to choose any course of action based on abstract moral principles or considerations of self-interest. The proletarian's moral action was always framed by, and therefore constrained within, the rhetorical structure from which its very being emanated. Within Marxist orthodoxy, this meant that the proletarian's moral behavior depended on having a clear understanding of present class conditions on the one hand and a vision of revolutionary socialist action on the other. Kautsky, for example, put the matter clearly in his debate with Otto Bauer over the nature of Kantian ethics when he asserted that morality is socially beneficial "only for as long as it remains dependent on society, and as long as it continues to fulfill those social needs which produce it."[47] In other words, morality should not be thought of as an independent force but in relation to a proper (that is, materialist) conception of society. Within that framework, and only there, can morality sharpen one's ethical vision, promote solidarity, and motivate progressive behavior.[48]

Kautsky's view of morality again demonstrates the specific dependence of figural action on a broader set of discursive relations. In its orientation toward the class distinctions of capitalist society, the proletariat becomes aware, as it were, of "powerful interests," "repression," and the "force of habit," all of which serve as obstacles to the performance of proper moral action. Yet as the proletariat is defined in an anticipatory relation with the classless society to come, it receives a kind of transcendent power that suggests a lack of compulsion, a reconciliation between "public opinion" and morality, and a happy blending of freedom and restraint. Here, paradoxically, the individual's conscience is utterly free of restraint but continues to function for the public good even "when there is no one watching us." The vision of a classless society, therefore, serves not only as a broad goal toward which to orient moral action but also as a resolution of the problems inherent in defining moral action. Significantly, it is here, at the figural juncture between class society and a vision of classless society, that the seeming disjuncture between theory and practice is also resolved.

Although the distinction between theory and practice is fundamental to the underlying structure of Marxist discourse, any explicit acknowledgment of this distinction as a possible discrepancy or contradiction appears, as I have noted, to be inadmissable as such. The negative pole provided by the image of class society in Marxist rhetoric, however, presents a context in which to acknowledge, and thereby to disarm, this possibility. The "contradiction between theory and practice," Kautsky says, actually manifests itself in two ways, both of which can be understood as a function of capitalist class relations: "Classes and individuals which believe themselves to be in a position of strength openly disregard the traditional morality while doubtless considering it to be necessary for others. Classes and individuals which feel themselves to be weak, on the other hand, disregard the moral code secretly while preaching it openly."[49] Within this context, Kautsky claims, the distinction between theory and practice must be understood as one of "cynicism" or "hypocrisy."

At the opposite extreme, no contradiction between theory and practice is said to be possible within a purely classless society, for in that setting theory will already have been realized in practice, and practice will have no constraints compelling it to deviate from theory. Thus, the potentially contradictory gap between theory and practice does not come to rest finally on the shoulders of the proletariat but is located, with the appropriate valences, at both ends of the discursive spectrum within which the proletariat stands.

The appropriate response called for by this construction is for the proletariat to reject the inevitable cynicism and hypocrisy that must arise from class-based conceptions of theory and practice and to strive toward the reconciliation envisioned in conjunction with a classless society. The proletariat adopts a "new morality" which serves not so much as a dialectic resolution of the old contradictions but as a higher vantage point from which to understand the tensions between theory and practice. This vantage point is attained as part of the broader materialist conception of history and of the class struggle.[50] Insofar as practice may be forced to deviate from theory, it is because of the transitional phase in which the class struggle remains and, therefore, need not be associated with cynicism or hypocrisy. Moreover, the very definition of appropriate practice depends on a theoretical conception of this struggle.

There is, then, no simple or final resolution to the relation between theory and practice. Neither is modeled directly on actual social experience. Nor does one or the other reflect reality while the other stands over against reality as an ideal. The proletarian as a figural embodiment of moral action always arises in the midst of any treatments of theory and practice. It is through the discretionary moral behavior of the proletariat that theory and practice both come into being and come together. But the proletariat is itself a construction that depends on a mixture of actual social experience and a conceptual reworking of that experience. Its action can resolve only those contradictions that are identified within this conceptual reworking. And the very notion of moral action implies both an active negation of the negative valence of class society and a negation in the breach of the positive valence of classless society. As much as the proletariat is a reflection of the historical working class itself, therefore, it also presents an image of timeless becoming that escapes the bonds of its own social creation.

PART IV

Sociology and Cultural Change

16 ⁓

The Legacy of Classical Theory

HE WAYS IN WHICH changes in social structure have brought about changes in culture have, of course, been of interest in sociology since the discipline's inception. All the founding theorists wrote about it: Durkheim in discussing the effects of increasing levels of complexity in the social division of labor, Weber in describing the processes of rationalization, and of course Marx in formulating a materialist theory of history. They placed the question of cultural change permanently on the discipline's agenda.

My examination of the social conditions under which the Reformation, the Enlightenment, and socialism arose falls directly in the lineage of the classical theorists' interest in cultural change. I have paid close attention to the specific circumstances that varied from country to country and from period to period, but questions about the general processes underlying cultural change have also been raised. How the patterns that have emerged compare—both in substance and in the formal method of analysis they imply—with the received wisdom concerning cultural change is the question to which I now turn.

For this purpose, it will be helpful to draw a distinction between two general strands of thinking that have been prominent in the social science literature on cultural change. There is, on the one hand, a tradition of thought that emphasizes the ways in which culture adapts to increasing levels of societal complexity. For brevity's sake, this tradition might be referred to as a theory of cultural adaptation. On the other hand, a mode of thinking about cultural change that emphasizes the roles of social classes and their requirements for legitimation can also be identified. This tradition might be referred to as a theory of class legitimation. Both of these perspectives are rooted in assumptions about society that ultimately derive from classical political theory: they presuppose social interdependence, the necessity of cooperation, the threat of social conflict, and the basic goal-oriented character of human action. Cultural adaptation tends to focus more on the problems of arriving at collectively desired goals under conditions of cooperation, although these conditions are also characterized by certain unresolved problems or strains, while class legitimation assumes conditions essentially fraught with conflict. Both perspectives have appeared at various points in the preceding chapters. Historians' efforts to account for specific instances of cultural change have been as likely to draw on these traditions as sociologists' attempts to delineate the general contours of change. Some of the foregoing has provided support for the general utility of these perspectives; much of it has suggested a need for critical reformulations. To see most clearly how the foregoing may contribute to a different theoretical understanding of the general role of social factors in cultural change, let us briefly reconsider the assumptions that have guided each strand of the classical heritage and then identify the limitations and weaknesses inherent in these assumptions.

Cultural Adaptation

In discussions reflecting this tradition, cultural change is generally depicted as an evolutionary or developmental process that occurs in analytically distinguishable stages as a response to changing societal conditions. The changes in societal conditions that evoke changes in culture are variously described as institutional differentiation, increases in societal complexity, or, at a somewhat lower level of abstraction, as master tendencies inherent in urbanization and industrialization. Episodes of major cultural transformation, such as the Reformation, the Enlightenment, and socialism, are thus attributed to broad changes in social organization. Such changes in the way that societies are organized are said to generate problems that lead to new patterns of culture becoming prominent as modes of resolving these problems. The process of cultural change, in this respect, is not simply neutral but plays a positive role in the society's capacity to survive. Only as certain cultural changes come about does it become possible for a society to adapt to the burdens of increasing complexity. Consequently, the cultural changes that prove to be theoretically interesting are those that contribute to the "adaptive upgrading" or "adaptive modification" of a society.[1] A movement such as the Reformation, therefore, arises from problematic features of society in the course of its evolution but also contributes to the resolution of these problems.

An early formulation of the theory of cultural adaptation is found in Emile Durkheim's *Division of Labor in Society*.[2] Durkheim linked cultural change specifically to the increasing institutional differentiation that comes about as societies grow larger and become more complex. In a relatively small, localized, undifferentiated society, Durkheim argued, everyone tends to be related to things "in the same way"; cultural expressions can thus remain tied to the concrete ("this animal," "this tree," "this plant"). But in a larger, geographically diverse, differentiated society, experiences will inevitably be more varied. Consequently, cultural expressions can no longer be limited to concrete, specific references; they must also include higher levels of abstraction that can subsume the specific and order local variations into more general categories (not "such an animal" but "such a species"). Durkheim summarized this argument in the following formula: culture "changes its nature as societies become more voluminous." And more specifically: "Because these societies are spread over a vaster surface, the common conscience is itself obliged to rise above all local diversities, to dominate more space, and consequently become more abstract."[3]

Directly or indirectly, the Durkheimian perspective on cultural change has found its way into the work of a variety of more recent social theorists. Talcott Parsons, for example, described cultural change as a process of "value generalization" induced by the growing complexity of social patterns. He wrote: "When the network of socially structured situations becomes more complex, the value pattern itself must be couched at a higher level of generality in order to ensure social stability."[4] As examples he cited changes in religious conceptions, the development of empirical and theoretical knowledge, and changes in legal codes. Together, in Parson's view, these constitute the critical form of cultural change: "The generalization of value systems, so that they can effectively regulate social action without relying upon particularistic prohibitions, has been a central factor in the modernization process."[5]

Much the same argument has been outlined by other social theorists in treatises on cultural change. In a succinct statement the German theorist Niklas Luhmann explains, for instance: "The reason for . . . the rise of ideologies lies in . . . an increase in the range of possible actions among which choices can be made, and thus in a heightening of the complexity of society—a heightening that, in turn, is attainable only when more effective mechanisms for the reduction of complexity can be institutionalized."[6] Others who have taken a similar view of cultural change include Robert Bellah, whose stage theory of religious evolution represents a major effort to depict broad patterns of cultural change from the standpoint of increasing levels of societal differentiation, and Jürgen Habermas, who has borrowed directly from Parsons and Bellah in developing his own stage theory of cultural evolution.[7] Both Bellah and Habermas depict cultural evolution primarily as a response to increasing societal complexity.

An emphasis on cultural adaptation can also be found among leading students of culture whose orientations can in no way be as easily linked to the Durkheimian or Parsonian traditions. In discussing the development of modern art and literature, for example, Pierre Bourdieu writes of the effects of increasing societal differentiation. These effects, he asserts, become manifest in several important ways: as a growing economic division of labor that generates greater economic independence on the part of cultural producers, as a heightened degree of complexity among authorities the result of which is to provide culture producers with greater intellectual freedom, and as a more highly differentiated mass public that becomes the basis for producing a broader range of marketable symbolic products.[8] In focusing on culture producers, products, and markets, Bourdieu's discussion differs from the more implicit concepts of culture that dominate much of the literature on cultural adaptation. He nevertheless demonstrates the continuing impact of this tradition on contemporary thinking about the sources of cultural change. Indeed, his work draws specifically on the cultural adaptation legacy to provide an interpretation of the effects of markets and cities on the production of new literary genres in the eighteenth century.

The notion of societal complexity usually remains at an abstract level in these formulations, but two specific kinds of social change are often emphasized as concrete sources of cultural adaptation. One is urbanization. Durkheim, for instance, singled out rapid urbanization as a particularly likely impetus to heightened levels of cultural abstraction, rationality, and individuality. In rapidly growing cities, he observed, the population will inevitably include large numbers of immigrants from the countryside or from other cities. The experience of these immigrants will be colored by two overriding features: they will have to adjust to a new set of social circumstances other than the ones in which they were reared, and the composition of the city itself will become highly varied because of the migrants' diverse backgrounds. Both, he suggested, will encourage new outlooks and habits of thought. The other specific source of cultural adaptation is economic expansion. Especially when economic growth occurs rapidly, dramatic effects on culture can be expected. The exact causal sequence envisioned differs from one theory to the next, but in general the breakdown of established social relations during times of rapid economic growth is identified as a significant factor. Durkheim, for example, emphasized the extent to which rapid economic growth leads to an uprooting of local communities and a potential for disorientation. During such times of transition, he suggested, people will be especially vulnerable to new ideas.

Theories of cultural adaptation have generally emphasized gradual, continuous, long-term change. But specific historical episodes such as the ones that have been considered here have also been identified as the major examples of such change. Durkheim's own discussion alludes specifically to three such episodes. The first began in the fifteenth century, he suggested, and consisted chiefly of a breakdown in the communal bonds uniting masters and workers as a result of growing specialization in artisan labor. "Beginning with the fifteenth century, things began to change," he observed. Prior to this time, "the worker everywhere lived at the side of his master." Workers shared a common experience and a common, concrete culture. But after the fifteenth century, "a sharp line is drawn between masters and workers." The two became "an order apart" and were forced to develop a more differentiated set of cultural abstractions.[9] The second period is the industrial revolution in the late seventeenth and eighteenth centuries. During this period the separation of workers from employers became more pronounced, specialization became greater, and symptoms of social stress, such as worker unhappiness and revolts, became more frequent. Not only were new ideas about social arrangements initiated in these years, Durkheim observed, but science also became more specialized, and scientific theories were forced to become more abstract.[10] The third period was Durkheim's own: the end of the nineteenth century. In a lengthy discussion of the rapid growth of cities during the 1870s and 1880s, for instance, he pointed both to the social disruption involved and to the potential for cultural innovation. He wrote: "Since common beliefs and practices, in large part, extract their strength from the strength of tradition, it is evident that they are less and less able to prevent the free expansion of individual variations."[11] Durkheim's references to each of these historical periods were necessarily brief, meant as they were to illustrate more general evolutionary tendencies. Nevertheless, it is significant that these references indicate, at least in passing, the applicability of Durkheim's broader theoretical emphases to the three specific periods that have been the subject of the foregoing chapters.

In other formulations these same periods have also been identified as particularly salient moments in the evolution of modern culture. For example, Parsons identified the breakup of the feudal mode of social integration during the late medieval period as the social change that culminated in the Renaissance and the Reformation. Particularly the Reformation served in Parsons's evolutionary framework as a key example of cultural adaptation. It was, he suggested, "a movement to upgrade secular society to the highest religious level."[12] In a brief passage he also focused on the eighteenth century, and particularly prerevolutionary France, as a time of rapid growth in societal complexity. Central to this growth were the state's efforts to extend the political system to encompass the entire nation. This growth in complexity, he suggested, set up the conditions that necessitated increased emphasis on empirical knowledge and mass education—two specific features of the Enlightenment. In this sense the Enlightenment provided an instance of cultural adaptation to the increasing societal complexity of the period. Similarly, the rapid industrial expansion of the late nineteenth century seemed, in Parson's view, to exemplify the relations between increased societal complexity and cultural upgrading. He suggested specifically that the emergence of socialist ideology in this period was a response to the fact that capitalist ideology had not fully extended the conception of rights and equality to all social strata. Socialism was at once facilitated by an erosion of ascriptive ties and in turn assisted in the process of mobilizing "government power to institute fundamental equality."[13]

In the preceding chapters I have noted variants of the cultural adaptation perspective in a number of instances. Though seldom framed in the more sweeping terms of Durkheimian or Parsonian propositions, arguments have been put forth by historians that in essence suggest that new cultural forms came into being because they helped the adherents of these ideas adapt more effectively to their social surroundings. I have cited studies of the Reformation that held the religious reforms in general to be the response to new horizons and expectations resulting from rapid urbanization, population change, and expanding trade. Other studies saw in the reformers' views better ways of dealing with the social complexity of the cities, depicted religious zeal arising from the disruptions of relations between landlords and peasants, and recognized advantages in Protestant theology for looser, more specialized, and more individualistic commercial relationships. For the Enlightenment, arguments of this nature are generally less in evidence, but a similar logic is occasionally apparent in the studies considered here. For example, the general effects of expanding horizons, achieved through industry and trade, on writers' outlooks and expectations have often been emphasized, as have the effects of urban life in promoting anonymity and individualism. And studies of the rise of socialism have generally placed considerable emphasis on the socially disruptive tendencies inherent in urbanization and industrialization as well. Thus, it seems evident on the surface at least that the accounts of these three historical episodes developed in the preceding chapters bear directly on the empirical assessment of this theoretical tradition.

Class Legitimation

The alternative theoretical tradition has held that cultural change of the kind we have been considering comes about as a result of the shifting position of social classes in relation to one another. As a new social class becomes more powerful, generally speaking, it apparently needs to legitimate itself both in relation to segments of the older ruling class and in the eyes of subordinate elements of the population. New ideologies therefore come into being at such moments in history in order to fulfill these requirements for legitimation. Cultural change is considered adaptive as far as the rising ruling class is concerned, but in contrast with the cultural adaptation perspective, this change is said to come about more abruptly and in the service of a specific set of social interests. The leading source of this theory of cultural change has, of course, been Marx, but similar arguments can also be found in Weber's discussion of the role of status groups in bringing about cultural change. Because vestiges of these arguments have arisen repeatedly in the foregoing, they too warrant closer attention.

In Marxist theory the need for ideological legitimation is said to arise primarily from the fact that an emerging social class is inevitably faced with opposition from existing elites. It becomes necessary, if this class is to succeed, for it to develop a broader coalition of support. As Marx and Engels wrote in *The German Ideology:* "Each new class which puts itself in the place of one ruling before it, is compelled, merely in order to carry through its aim, to represent its interest as the common interest of all the members of society."[14] This is the impetus that leads to the formulation of a new ideology, a set of ideas framed in universalistic terms and disseminated broadly throughout a society. The universalistic notions of science, history, and human rights that emerged in the eighteenth century in conjunction with the rising strength of the bourgeoisie is generally cited as an example.

The specific content of a new ideology is shaped, in the Marxist view, by two conditions: first, by the fact that new ideas reflect the particular historical experience of the rising ruling class, and second, by the fact that the new ruling class controls the means of ideological production. In explaining the rise of new political doctrines during the Enlightenment, for example, Marx and Engels argued that the idea of a separation of powers reflects the bourgeoisie's actual experience of contending with the aristocracy and monarchy for power. They also likened the production of ideas to the production of goods, thereby making control over the means of cultural production a decisive factor. As they say, the class that has "the means of material production at its disposal, has control at the same time over the means of mental production, so that, thereby, generally speaking, the ideas of those who lack the means of mental production are subject to it."[15]

Elements of the class legitimation argument can also be found, as noted previously, in Weber. In *Economy and Society,* for example, he argued that the Reformation was "codetermined," at least indirectly, by economic factors; namely, the rise of the bourgeoisie as a class characterized by a more rationalized ethic, a preoccupation with self-justification, and less exposure to "organic natural events" than in rural areas. It was, he wrote, "the peculiar piety of the intensely religious bourgeois strata that made them side with the reformist preachers against the traditional ecclesiastic apparatus." Moreover, it was the relative power of the bourgeoisie that determined which of the different branches of the Reformation were to prevail in different areas. Wherever the bourgeoisie gained the upper hand, the "ascetic varieties of Protestantism" prevailed, while the retention of power by princes and the nobility was more conducive to the rise of Anglicanism or Lutheranism.[16]

Much the same line of reasoning is evident in Weber's scattered remarks about the Enlightenment. Here his concern was, again, more with addressing the consequences of Enlightenment teachings for subsequent economic development than with giving a full account of their origins. Accordingly, he suggested in passing that charisma played a role in initiating the Enlightenment. Nevertheless, he also suggested that the growing importance of ethical rationality among the bourgeoisie contributed to the principal doctrine of the Enlightenment—the basic rights of the individual—and that the Enlightenment was reinforced over time by its affinities with the advance of capitalism. Specifically, he suggested that the eighteenth century was characterized by a heightened sense of individual rights in the economic sphere, including "the right to pursue one's own economic interests," "the inviolability of individual property," "freedom of contract," and "vocational choice." These ethical norms, he argued, "find their ultimate justification in the belief of the Enlightenment in the workings of individual reason which, if unimpeded, would result in the at least relatively best of all worlds."[17] Weber, in fact, likened the Enlightenment doctrine of the rights of man to that of ascetic Protestantism, suggesting that it had a corrosive effect on traditional patrimonial norms, that it "facilitated the expansion of capitalism," and "made it possible for the capitalist to use things and men freely."[18]

In discussing the rise of socialist ideology, Weber again stressed the role of status groups and economic interests. Here, however, it was no longer the laissez-faire bourgeoisie but the "bureaucratic literati" whose interests were advanced by the new ideology. He wrote: "It is this sober fact of universal bureaucratization that is behind the so-called 'German ideas of 1914,' behind what the literati euphemistically call the 'socialism of the future,' behind the slogans of 'organized society,' 'cooperative economy,' and all similar contemporary phrases. Even if they aim at the opposite, they always promote the rise of bureaucracy."[19] The unintended consequence of socialist ideology, in his view, was to legitimate an extended rationalization of society, an enlarged conception of rights and responsibilities (for public welfare, full employment, old age insurance, and so on), which would require a growing cadre of bureaucrats to administer. It was in the interest of this cadre, therefore, to advance some version of socialist ideology.

Like the cultural adaptation perspective, class legitimation theories have been much in evidence in the explanations surveyed in the preceding chapters. Students of the Reformation and of the Enlightenment have, as those chapters have shown, referred often to the rising bourgeoisie and to its apparent need for legitimation in attempting to account for the birth of these new ideologies, and studies of socialism have emphasized the proletariat's rise and its requirements for a legitimating ideology. In the sociological literature more generally, theories of class legitimation have also received much elaboration beyond their initial formulations in classical theory. Rather than simply tracing the development of these literatures, however, it will be more useful to discuss these various contributions in the context of raising critical issues related to both perspectives. These frameworks have provided a general structure within which to think about cultural change, but they also contain problematic elements that limit their effectiveness. In the present context, the following merit particular consideration: the concept of culture implicit in each approach; the clarity of the explanatory variables in each; variations in the rate and timing of cultural change; the mechanisms of cultural change; and the relation between theory and history.

Problematic Elements

Concepts of culture. The definition of culture in these theories—and hence the status of what is being explained—has been, to say the least, highly ambiguous. The possibilities range from Durkheim's metaphoric idea of a collective conscience (or consciousness) to Marx's specific discussion of ideology, to Weber's analytic abstractions (rationality, asceticism, theodicy, soteriology), to Parson's notions about values and value orientations, all of which are rooted in more complex philosophical and epistemological frameworks. Whether the cultural change at issue is a broad tendency that can only be extracted from the general orienting principles of an entire society (individualism) or is composed of specific arguments, creeds, and doctrines (freedom of contract) has often been unclear. Equally unclear is whether culture stands apart from the social processes that induce cultural change (urbanization, industrialization) or whether culture is primarily to be inferred from these processes.

There is, nevertheless, an epistemological tendency within the classical theoretical tradition that has influenced the manner in which more recent theoretical treatments of cultural change have often been framed. The concept of culture that implicitly informs both the cultural adaptation and class legitimation models of cultural change has tended to place emphasis on the subjective features of culture. This emphasis is evident in the very terms used to identify culture: "collective conscience" (Durkheim), "orientations that guide action" (Parsons), "class consciousness" (Marx), "beliefs and conceptions" (Weber), "mental structures" (Mannheim). Although there are other, more objective aspects of ideology in these conceptions as well, the basic orientation has derived from a variant of subject-object dualism in which ideas are associated with the subjective while behavior and social structure are conceived of as objective realities. In Marx, for instance, the superstructure in which ideology and class consciousness are located is composed of "feelings, illusions, habits of thought and conceptions of life," while the base or infrastructure that determines the content of the superstructure consists of the accessible, material conditions of human life. The former are located essentially "in the brains of the participants," in contrast with the real historical struggles of which the latter are composed.[20] When taken to an extreme, this tendency has resulted in culture's being located primarily in the subjective beliefs and attitudes of individuals, while social structure has tended to be associated with the more obdurate facts of their collective experience. In less extreme interpretations, culture has been associated more with collectivities than with individuals; yet the observer is still hard-pressed to say exactly where culture resides: it becomes a free-floating Zeitgeist without clear empirical referents, or it consists of norms and expectations that ultimately have to be inferred by observing regularities in the very social conditions that are invoked as the sources of these norms and expectations. Conceiving of culture in this manner contrasts sharply, of course, with the historical manifestations of culture that have proven important to consider throughout the foregoing analysis: with an emphasis on concrete expressions of public discourse, the rhetorical patterns of specific ideological performances, and the sermons, tracts, books and newspapers, party platforms, and ideological statements that constitute the tangible products of cultural institutions.

One of the difficulties with the concept of culture inherited from the classical theorists is that culture ceases to have readily available empirical referents. Instead of consisting primarily of observable artifacts, it remains a matter of beliefs and outlooks, of moods and motivations which are in the best of cases difficult to pin down. Efforts to identify these subjective meanings and motivations even in contemporary situations have shown the difficulty of eliciting what is ultimately thought to lie deep within the individual's consciousness. But in historical circumstances such meanings and motivations have been nearly impossible to reconstruct. The analyst is thus likely to engage either in an act of simplification or in an act of reduction: simplification by abstracting tangible cultural artifacts into more pervasive values and orientations, reduction by emphasizing the observable features of social behavior while minimizing the importance of the less tractable mentalities of the times. What results is either a general discussion of vague axiological principles which has only the barest connection with the observable externalities of cultural production, or a materialist version of society in which culture plays no role at all.

In addition to these difficulties, much of the emphasis in these theoretical traditions has been on the psychological functions of ideology for the individual—a bias that was closely associated, of course, with conceiving of culture in subjective terms in the first place. Weber, for example, grounded his discussion of cultural change in psychological arguments. In discussing the relation between social stratification and religious belief, he stated that the disprivileged classes' hunger for worthiness was a "psychological condition."[21] He also suggested that the legitimating beliefs of privileged classes were "rooted in certain basic psychological patterns." And he went on to say that "everyday experience proves that there exists just such a need for psychic comfort."[22]

It is important, of course, to note that extensions of the cultural adaptation and class legitimation approaches have often gone beyond purely subjective conceptions of culture and have specified more complex relations between social structure and cultural change. Nevertheless, it is fair to say that these traditions gave rise to a subjective bias that has by no means been overthrown. Despite emphasis in some discussions on the material artifacts of culture, the apparatuses by which ideology is produced and reproduced, and the more practical or enacted aspects of culture, a major focus of cultural studies continues to be the internalized, taken-for-granted world views and assumptions of individuals and of collectivities of individuals. Indeed this emphasis appears, if anything, to have been heightened, especially in the class legitimation literature, by the prominence of discussions in which notions of cultural hegemony, totalization, and one-dimensionality have surfaced as answers to questions about the continuing legitimacy of advanced capitalism.[23] As one critical examination of the literature in which notions of legitimacy and class consciousness have guided empirical investigations has concluded: "They all have a subjectivist conception of history, according to which political processes are decided by unitary conscious subjects, legitimate or illegitimate governments, consenting or dissenting peoples, consciously revolutionary or unconscious classes. They leave no room for de-centred constraints and fissures, contradictions and reinforcements, such as are inscribed in the economic and political structure and process. Nor do they allow for the complexities of social heterogeneity and compartmentalization."[24]

Clarity of explanatory variables. In the cultural adaptation literature the most general source of cultural change is identified as increasing societal complexity. But complexity has a host of diverse empirical indicators: population size, population density, occupational diversity, urbanization, cultural heterogeneity, institutional differentiation, technological specialization, to name several. In class legitimation theories the concept of class is equally vague. It ranges from distinct conceptions of social position in capitalist societies to vague notions of economic process to highly general ideas about power, authority, prestige, and status. In attempting to account for specific episodes of cultural change, therefore, concepts often appear to be invoked, as we have seen, more on the basis of convenience than in any rigorous fashion. In the extreme, virtually any event since the sixteenth century becomes subject to explanation as a product of increasing social complexity or the dynamics of bourgeois class formation.[25]

An illustration of this problem is evident in Marx's discussion of the English and French Enlightenment. Several particular aspects of eighteenth-century social experience in the two countries are singled out and related to the content of a few writers of the Enlightenment, but Marx's discussion fails to develop a more systematic or comprehensive view of the relations between the bourgeoisie and the Enlightenment. He seems more intent on illustrating certain biases in utilitarian theory than in articulating a theory of the effects of bourgeois class position on enlightened culture. What he provides, therefore, is only a general sense of these effects. At most, it becomes possible to infer that the rise of the bourgeoisie in England and France was associated with certain economic problems' being given special intellectual attention in the work of scholars such as Locke and d'Holbach. What is lacking is any sense of whether the bourgeoisie as such is essential to this argument or whether it is sufficient to suggest only that commercialization had a general influence on eighteenth-century thought.

The picture that has emerged from the historical evidence we have been considering is that the effects of general processes, such as urbanization, industrialization, and class formation, vary considerably from one specific context to another. It is evident from the theoretical literature as well, though, that explanatory variables cannot be treated as neatly or as simply as the more general formulations would suggest. This is a point I made in the previous section in discussing the writings of Marx and Engels on the relations between the proletariat and socialism. It is equally evident in the Marxist literature on other episodes of cultural change. For instance, Engels sought in some instances to portray the Reformation as a simple example of feualism being opposed by the rising bourgeoisie; yet his analysis also suggests that class conflict was overridden by the tensions between Rome and local seats of power in central Europe.[26] The problematic aspect of the theoretical literature, therefore, lies not in the fact that explanatory complications have gone unrecognized but that these complications, once recognized, have not resulted in efforts to develop a more systematic treatment of the factors involved.

Variations in the rate and timing of cultural change. The thrust of my discussion of the Reformation, the Enlightenment, and the rise of socialism has been to suggest that the trajectory of modern culture needs to be understood in terms of relatively abrupt periods of cultural upheaval, not as the gradual accumulation of minor incremental changes. Careful reading of the specific statements on cultural change of Marx, Durkheim, and Weber or more recent theorists such as Parsons or Mannheim reveals a persistent ambiguity on this score as well: although some attention is devoted to specific episodes of notable change in cultural systems, such as the Enlightenment or the rise of socialism, theoretical statements also tend to give the impression that cultural change must be conceived of as gradual, linear, and for the most part continuous. The latter emphasis, in fact, works against offering satisfactory theoretical explanations for specific variations in the rate and timing of cultural change, for if cultural change is simply incremental, then only the broadest sources of its general direction can be of interest.

In some measure this issue has arisen from ambiguities concerning the appropriate level of generality at which to examine cultural change. If culture is conceived of not as specific symbolic expressions but as the most general patterns or orientations underlying social behavior, then attention is inevitably drawn to prevailing forms rather than particular episodes of cultural change. Weber, for example, has often been interpreted as having identified rationalization as the most general tendency underlying the development of modern culture. In examining the process of rationalization, Weber was thus led to discover it everywhere insofar as the Occident was concerned: in law, music, economic relations, science, bureaucracies, museums, the state, religion, military organization. Given this prevalence, it becomes bootless in a sense to inquire into the sources of any of its particular manifestations. One instance of rationalization simply reinforces another.

At this high level of generality, each manifestation of cultural change ceases to be important in its own right. Instead it becomes significant only as an indication that some deeper process is at work. Understanding the origins of a particular cultural episode becomes less interesting than interpreting its meaning in relation to some larger pattern. Habermas, in discussing Weber's contribution to the sociology of music, for example, suggests that it is less important to know how rational musical structures originated or became institutionalized than to recognize that this development was a symptom of the increasing differentiation of autonomous cultural spheres, of the increasing differentiation of aesthetic and technical realms, and of the increasing differentiation of theoretical and practical reason.[27] This type of argument is conducive, of course, to an interpretive style of social science that is concerned with discovering the meanings of events rather than explaining their sources. Such an approach, however, depends mainly on having an a priori conception of the master tendencies in modern culture (for example, differentiation, class conflict). With such a conception in mind, the investigator merely has to find instances of cultural change that seem to fit the overall pattern. But the processes by which cultural change actually becomes institutionalized remain unilluminated. This tendency is also related, as I shall show, to an increasing bifurcation in the study of cultural change between purely theoretical and more historical or empirical approaches. For the moment it will suffice to say that efforts to relate these general perspectives to specific historical cases, while numerous, have proven less than satisfactory. Two examples will illustrate the point.

Although (as we have already seen) the Enlightenment has been regarded in the theoretical literature as a key instance of cultural change coming about in response to changing needs for class legitimation, many of the most recent and extensive historical studies from which I have drawn evidence in the foregoing chapters straightforwardly reject the notion that cultural change in this period was in any way connected with a rising bourgeoisie or its need for class legitimation. "A new vision of the future certainly emerged," the author of one such study concludes, "but its apostles were to be found among both nobles and bourgeois—of the famous *Philosophes* of the Enlightenment most were either born or bought themselves into the nobility—and the first people who tried to translate the enlightened ideas into practice were members of the government, all of whom, apart from Necker, were nobles."[28] This author goes on to assert that commercial and industrial wealth did not constitute more than a small share of the eighteenth-century economy, that nobles and the bourgeoisie were largely indistinguishable in terms of the sources of their wealth, and that the nobility did not suffer any relative or absolute decline.

The rise of socialism also provides an example. Of all modern cultural changes, this development, perhaps ironically, seems to have created the most difficult explanatory problems, especially for the class legitimation model. These problems may be partially attributable to the fact that some of the theoretical formulations in this tradition have themselves been associated with the rise of socialism. But other problems also seem to be evident. At the simplest level, class legitimation models attribute the rise of socialism to the emergence of the proletariat as a new class in need of legitimation—and the empirical problems in defending this argument have been demonstrated clearly in the preceding chapters. More sophisticated versions, however, have not been content with this explanation. Wanting to maintain the significance of socialist ideology as a *precursor* of the proletarian struggle, these arguments have taken a different view. Lukács, for example, writes that "nothing has changed in the objective situation" of the proletariat and that only the "vantage point . from which it is judged" has altered.[29] This kind of argument, of course, undermines the basic thrust of the class legitimation model, for if nothing changes in objective social relations, how then is the change in "vantage point" to be explained?

Mechanisms of cultural change. Since many of the more general theoretical formulations are concerned primarily with broad evolutionary tendencies, they specify a general relation between increasing societal complexity or increasing economic capacity but do not provide an explanation of the intervening processes by which these changes influence culture. In this respect, these approaches have served best as models of macro-level comparisons rather than models of actual processes of change. With these macro-level approaches it has been possible to make hypotheses based on static, cross-sectional comparisons of societies at different levels of complexity or development or on comparisons of a single society at two or more widely separated periods. But the manner in which change in complexity or development actually leads to cultural change has for the most part remained unspecified.

Symptomatic of the lack of specificity about intervening social mechanisms is the tendency in these approaches to resort to explanations rooted in assumptions about individual psychology (as I have already noted). It may well be that some kinds of cultural change come about primarily through the conversions of individuals, or in other instances, that the unsettled periods in which ideologies are born create anxiety for the individuals living in these periods. From the evidence that has been adduced for the Reformation, the Enlightenment, and socialism, little indication of the importance of such processes has appeared. Even if psychological processes were involved, however, these processes could not substitute for a more explicit consideration of the conditions under which they operated.

Marxist theory, in particular, emphasizes the fact that individuation, and therefore individual psychology, is itself contingent on the nature of the productive process. If ideology is conceded to change primarily because of changes in individual experience, this experience must then be understood as a product of particular social conditions. In the first place, it occurs under conditions in which market relations and "the principle of rational mechanization and calculability" have permeated society to such an extent that the "atomized individual" has come into existence; and second, it tends to be limited to those aspects of ideology that concern an individual's self-perception as an externally governed commodity.[30] Within this formulation of the class legitimation model itself, therefore, individual experience can provide only a partial explanation of cultural change.

The main alternative to identifying psychological states as the intervening mechanisms connecting societal changes and cultural changes has been to assert a simple mechanistic connection. Especially in the more macroscopic levels of analysis that have focused on broad patterns of social evolution it has simply been asserted that one kind of change leads to another, rather than raising the question of how these changes are effected. Some of the functionalist imagery already cited has served this purpose. Deterministic imagery has also been evident in some formulations.[31] The development of science and art, Durkheim suggested, came about because of "a necessity which is imposed." The advance of modern culture, therefore, should not be attributed to the values or desires of individuals; nor should it be understood in terms of its attractiveness or as something toward which people strive. Culture is, rather, moved along by the increasing size, density, and diversity of society: "It develops because it cannot fail to develop."[32]

More recent studies of cultural change have naturally taken issue with this extreme form of sociological determinism, arguing for the value of seeing a dialectical relation between social and cultural change. In the work of Bourdieu that was mentioned previously, for example, the problem of identifying a plausible mechanism of ideological change is to a certain extent resolved, or at least circumvented, by suggesting that cultural production becomes increasingly autonomous from its social surroundings.[33] A dialectical process is envisioned in which social conditions influence cultural production, but then the latter, having once gained relative autonomy, exercises a reciprocal force on the former. The heightened levels of societal complexity to which Bourdieu points as sources of ideological change bring about this transformation neither deterministically nor by mysteriously altering the perceptions of individuals but by emancipating the producers of art and literature. In the process, artists and writers gain the capacity to act according to their own norms rather than responding to broader societal pressures.[34] Bourdieu's interest, however, is not to provide a detailed account of these historical developments. He therefore takes largely as a given the relative autonomy of the culture-producing community rather than specifying the particular circumstances under which this autonomy may have been attained.

A somewhat more satisfactory line of argument has been presented by Göran Therborn, who suggests that studies of cultural change would benefit by an approach that not only takes a more dialectical view but also gives greater attention to *process* and *competition*.[35] In emphasizing process, he attaches importance to the fact that ideologies develop in interaction with social conditions over a period of time. In emphasizing competition (among different ideologies), he also wishes to stress the fact that the outcomes of these interactions are to a degree indeterminate. Rather than envisioning a straightforward ideological outcome associated either with rising social complexity or with changing class relations, he wants to consider the specific situations that provide room for new ideologies to develop, how they influence one another, and what the eventual outcome of a particular sequence of action may be. Therborn's approach, therefore, leads to greater consideration of the actual processes and the more immediate conditions that link broad societal changes with specific episodes of cultural innovation.

Therborn's emphasis on processes and competition points, of course, in the same direction as that of the foregoing empirical chapters. Rather than envisioning the Reformation, the Enlightenment, and socialism as instances of long-term, unilineal, or deterministic tendencies associated with the general growth of modernization or capitalism, I have made an effort to suggest specific historical conjunctures that made cultural innovation possible. If, on the basis of the evidence considered, it seems reasonable to treat episodes of cultural innovation in this manner, it should nevertheless be recognized that this approach runs against the grain of the dominant ways in which cultural change has been conceived in the theoretical literature.[36]

Disjuncture between theory and history. Finally, both the cultural adaptation and class legitimation theories have shown a tendency to separate theoretical specification on the one hand from historical analysis on the other. Indeed, much of the interest in cultural change among sociological theorists appears to have moved in the direction of abstract, normative, or reconstructive models, which in some discussions are specifically regarded as having no connection with historical analysis. From the cultural adaptation tradition has emerged a variety of reconstructive formulations of cultural evolution, while the class legitimation literature has produced an increasing number of philosophical and epistemological specifications, especially in the Marxist and neo-Marxist traditions. Studies of concrete historical episodes of cultural change have not abandoned the assumptions of these more general traditions entirely, as we have seen, but they have increasingly expressed dissatisfaction with these traditions and have been developed from what might be called a more ad hoc or inductive perspective.

Both tendencies—toward the raising of theoretical questions and toward more inductive historical approaches—probably reflect the growing awareness in epistemological thought of the hermeneutic circle in which the social analyst is caught. In this the two tendencies undoubtedly continue to influence each other. Nevertheless, there has also been a tendency for the two variants of scholarship to grow farther apart. Indeed, a virtual impasse has been reached in some of the more philosophical discussions.[37]

17

Social Structure and Ideology

*T*RACING THE SOCIAL circumstances in which the ideologies of the Reformation, the Enlightenment, and socialism came to be institutionalized has necessitated paying attention to a more complex set of conditions and processes than is suggested by the established theoretical traditions. It has proven necessary to consider, in addition to the effects of economic expansion, urbanization, and class formation, such conditions as regional variations in patterns of trade and taxation, state officials' relations with landed elites, the size of state bureaucracies, factional cleavages within ruling elites, the development of political parties, and alliances across classes, as well as a variety of more localized secondary factors. Rather than conceiving of these social conditions as having a purely unidirectional impact on the rise of new ideologies, it has also proven necessary to posit an interactive relation—a process—in which the internal patterns of elements within ideologies play an important role in determining the eventual fit between ideologies and their environments.

Reconstructing the relations between ideology and social structure in each of the three historical periods and providing an account of how ideological innovation came about has not been strictly a matter of induction, however. At the outset of this book a conceptual scaffold was set in place to facilitate the task. I suggested the value of identifying features of the general social environment, of relating changes in these features that affected the specific institutional contexts in which ideology was produced, and of depicting the action sequences involved in ideological production within these contexts. I further suggested distinguishing processes of ideological production, of selection among competing ideologies, and of institutionalization. Relating the social horizons of the experienced world to the discursive fields evident within ideological constructions themselves, and relating both to the figural actions identified in particular ideologies, were discussed as well. Together these conceptual platforms were shown to offer a standpoint from which to assemble an account of the ways in which ideology and social structure come into articulation with each other. Now that these frameworks have been employed, it remains to summarize what has been learned and to suggest some of the theoretical connections between what has been learned and current theoretical developments in the literature on cultural analysis. Tracing these connections will demonstrate the extent to which the approach to cultural change that has been developed in the foregoing chapters reflects a broader redirection of current thought about the nature of culture and the conditions under which it changes.

Theoretical Developments in Cultural Analysis

Considerable rethinking of the concept of culture itself has been taking place. Although the subjective perspective in which culture is conceived of as taken-for-granted beliefs and values remains in evidence, current definitions focus increasingly on the observable features of culture, namely, discourse and other symbolic-expressive acts or practices. Anthropological conceptions of culture, for example, have shifted increasingly away from thinking of symbols primarily as vehicles for meanings toward thinking of symbols themselves as a focus of study. Rather than consisting of internalized habits of mind or generalized value orientations, culture has come increasingly to be understood as being embodied in public, observable symbols. Moreover, these symbols are not static, dehumanized accretions but are constituted in action. Practice is the key word. Culture is produced: it comes about through a series of actions, is expressed in action, and through action shapes the relations of individuals and societies.[1] Other disciplines have reflected similar shifts in thinking about culture. Increasing emphasis has been placed on utterances, speech acts, enunciative fields, symbolic codes, cultural production, culture in action, and the institutionalization of cultural products.[2]

Once culture is understood in this fashion, it becomes apparent that the study of culture must pay attention to speakers and audiences, discursive texts, the rituals in which discourse is embedded, and the social contexts in which it is produced. As something not simply affirmed subjectively or internalized unconsciously but produced collectively, culture depends on social resources, and the availability and distribution of these resources is likely to play a major role in influencing the direction of cultural change. Conceived in this manner, cultural change necessitates, even more so than before, an approach that focuses on the institutional contexts in which it is produced, enacted, and disseminated.

The fact that cultural change comes about not so much from the experiences of masses of individuals but as the result of culture-producing organizations has been deemphasized in the classical theoretical literature, but it has not been overlooked entirely. It is possible, for instance, to find suggestive passages in Marx that point toward a less subjective conception of culture. Writing in *The Communist Manifesto* about the creation of a cosmopolitan world market for economic goods, for example, Marx and Engels add: "As in material, so also in intellectual production. The intellectual creations of individual nations become common property. National one-sidedness and narrow-mindedness become more and more impossible, and from the numerous national and local literatures, there arises a world literature."[3] Again, they liken cultural production to material production in discussing the problem of oversupply in advanced capitalism, asserting that there is an overabundance of intellectual products just as there is an excess of industrial production. They also speak directly of cultural change in these terms, asking rhetorically: "What else does the history of ideas prove, than that intellectual production changes in character in proportion as material production is changed?"[4]

Similarly, it is possible to read Weber and Durkheim in a way that gives greater tangibility to cultural products. Weber examined sermons and the writings of Puritan divines in *The Protestant Ethic and the Spirit of Capitalism,* paid attention to the codification of religious texts and the discourse of charismatic leaders in his work on patterns of authority, wrote extensively about formalized theodicies and soteriologies, and discussed legal and musical codes. Durkheim wrote not only of the interiorized conceptions of collective consciousness but also of the concrete rituals and symbols—the totems, dances, flags, and anthems—that represented these conceptions.

In more recent work the complex circumstances under which innovations in these symbolic expressions come about have received increasing attention. Richard Ashcraft's study of the social conditions under which Locke's *Two Treatises of Government* were written, for instance, was mentioned in the section on the Enlightenment.[5] Ashcraft does not portray Locke's ideas as a reflection of expanding economic horizons or of bourgeois aspirations in general but situates them in the concrete political struggles of the period. He argues that a political theory such as Locke's should be regarded as "a set of structured meanings that are understandable only in reference to a specified context, wherein the concepts, terminology, and even the internal structure of the theory itself are viewed in relation to a comprehensive ordering of the elements of social life."[6] Ideology is not simply a taken-for-granted way of viewing the world but a tangible expression, in this case observable "not only through the highly formalized medium of books, but also through newspapers, pamphlets, sermons, broadsides, and various literary forms."[7]

To understand how an ideology is shaped by its social environment, one must therefore examine the specific circumstances under which these expressions come into being, the audience to whom they are enunciated, the slogans and other materials that are available at the time for incorporation into discursive acts, the roles of speakers and audiences relative to one another and in relation to positions of power, and even the financial resources that make publishing activities possible. Examining these contexts of ideological production enables one to establish with greater clarity why a particular constellation of ideas comes to be institutionalized successfully in a particular setting. Ashcraft's advice is applicable to studies of ideological innovation of all kinds: "Attention needs to be paid to the usage of a social language that has a particular salience for identifiable social groups, the appeal to respected cultural authorities and important historical events, and the manner in which presuppositions drawn from other . . . areas of social life are deployed."[8]

A similar strategy has been employed in a study of ideological innovation among seventeenth-century Puritans. Focusing on the origins of covenant theology, the author argues for placing the question of change within the context of concrete organizational pressures facing Puritan clergy and their audiences. These pressures were shaped, he suggests, by various preconditions in the larger society: the penetration of market forces into the countryside, the growth of artisan industry, the availability of printing technology for the dissemination of ideas, the existence of a largely literate population, and a strong tradition of rational, skeptical forms of argumentation. Within these broader circumstances, attention is then drawn to the structure of the Puritan hierarchy, its relations with the state and aristocratic patrons, the roles of local clergy in relation to their ecclesiastical superiors, and the geographic and occupational composition of the Puritan laity and their relations with the clergy. The study also examines specific pamphlets and sermon texts to determine their use of analogies with secular contracts, references to biblical and ecclesiastical authorities, and attention to ameliorating demands from the laity.[9]

These examples are in-depth studies of two quite specific instances of ideological innovation. They differ only from similar studies in the historical literature in that they have also sought to illustrate the utility of bringing specific social contexts into the study of ideological innovation more generally and have been concerned with correcting theoretical impressions in the sociological and political science literature. Other studies have examined broader ideological patterns and thus have had to pitch the analysis of social circumstances at a more macroscopic level, but they too have demonstrated the value of transcending monocausal treatments of the influences of institutional differentiation and social class.[10]

The thrust of these and similar historical studies has been to underscore the value of taking into careful consideration the actual circumstances in which ideological products were produced and disseminated rather than merely identifying general affinities between ideological patterns and broad features of the social environment, such as its degree of institutional differentiation or the evolution of social classes in need of legitimacy. These studies have linked ideological change to specific historical movements rather than portraying it as the long-term result of imperceptible incremental modifications in values and beliefs. At the same time, the role of predisposing intellectual currents is retained in the analysis by emphasizing the incorporation of these precedents into the specific products of discourse itself. In addition, the fact that ideological products are at issue means the activities of culture producers cannot be neglected: their relations with other producers, authorities, and specifically targeted audiences must be taken into consideration. Broader features of the social milieu, such as economic resources, technologies, and political conditions, also come into play.

In the theoretical literature some important efforts have also been made to integrate these kinds of considerations into formal statements concerning the effects of social factors on ideology. One particularly valuable outline of these factors, for instance, has been provided by the Marxist literary critic Terry Eagleton.[11] His discussion emphasizes the shaping of concrete cultural products such as books, manuscripts, and other texts. These result, Eagleton argues, from distinct literary modes of production—writers, scribes, printers, booksellers—and these literary modes bear a determinate relation with the more general (economic) mode of production on the one hand and with the form and content of specific texts on the other: "The literary text bears the impress of its historical mode of production as surely as any product secretes in its form and materials the fashion of its making."[12] Thus, one can expect a certain genre of literature to emerge under the market conditions of advanced capitalism that differs markedly from the literature produced under the patronage relations of early capitalism, and both genres will be distinct from the texts associated with peripatetic bards or ecclesiastical scribes in earlier settings.

Eagleton's discussion goes beyond most other Marxist approaches to the production of ideology in specifying the importance of literary producers, patrons, authorities, channels of dissemination, and consumers as institutional links connecting base and superstructure. He also gives credit to the relatively autonomous influences of literary genre and authorial ideology in shaping the actual content of literary products. Rather than following more limited unicausal perspectives, he asserts that a text is a "multiply articulated structure" and that it is shaped "only in the last instance" by a particular phase of economic development.[13] In concentrating ultimately on the effects of class relations, however, Eagleton allows his own text to be framed at a level of generality that is insufficient for examining the actual historical conjunctures associated with cultural innovation. His outline, moreover, provides only an introduction to the relevant considerations rather than a systematic model for the analysis of these factors.

Suggestive indications of the range of social influences needing to be considered can also be found in the writings of Raymond Williams, Göran Therborn, and Frederic Jameson.[14] In each of these instances, though, the primary effects of class relations have been posited as a starting point rather than a more abstract model capable of subsuming class relations and other social factors being formulated. If the historical evidence that has been considered in previous chapters is any indication, the concrete combination of social conditions influencing the production of ideology is likely to vary from one period or society to another. It seems most useful, therefore, to specify the range of relevant considerations at a relatively abstract level of generality, and then with the benefit of empirical examples to suggest at a more concrete level the particular manifestations of these abstractions that are most likely to become operative.

Environments, Institutions, Actions

In classic theories of cultural change, as well as in most contemporary approaches to the study of social structure and ideology, broad features of the general social milieu serve as a starting point. Levels of economic development, urbanization, literacy, degrees of unrest, and political climates receive attention. In deterministic approaches some effect on the form or content of ideology is generally posited, while in less deterministic approaches (such as standard guides to the literature of a period) some reference to these conditions is considered useful as a way of situating the discussion. In my examination of the Reformation, the Enlightenment, and socialism, these general economic, political, and religious circumstances have been given a prominent place.

Attempting to identify relevant features of the broader social environment in which cultural change occurs clearly reflects sociology's emphasis on social conditions. It does not preclude alternative epistemological approaches in which greater emphasis is placed on intellectual history, serendipitous innovations, or the seminal work of great thinkers. It does, however, necessitate an assumption that ideas exist primarily in the world of human society and, for this reason, are likely to be influenced in some way by social circumstances. Typically the logic of sociological inquiry also suggests that if change in culture is at issue, then change in the broader social environment is also likely to be a relevant consideration.

The sociological tradition, as I have suggested, has generally emphasized the so-called material conditions of the social environment as possible sources of cultural change. In this tradition economic activities, modes of production, demographic patterns, urbanization, class relations, income levels, and the like have been given special attention. The emphasis on these material conditions rests, in addition to whatever theoretical framework may be invoked, on at least three practical considerations: that material conditions are sufficiently distinguishable from cultural phenomena that one is unlikely to become involved in purely tautological arguments by attempting to establish the influence of one on the other; that societies and individuals are relatively dependent on their capacity to extract resources from the material environment and are, therefore, likely to be affected in significant ways by their relations to this environment; and that material conditions, by their very materiality, are likely to have left traces of themselves, thereby facilitating the task of empirical reconstruction. In arguing for both a broader conception of environmental conditions, especially one that includes intellectual precedents and implicit features of the cultural tradition, and a more empirical or behavioral concept of culture itself, some of these practical advantages may be diminished. Nevertheless, the general value of paying attention to the broad environmental conditions under which ideological change comes about would appear to remain beyond dispute.

Environmental conditions, as the term has been used in this study, consist of economic, political, and cultural resources, characterized in terms of overall levels, distributions, and rates of change that determine the nature of broad societal patterns. Unlike more specific concepts, such as bourgeoisie or urbanization, that are intended to denote actual historical formations, the idea of environmental conditions is a purely sensitizing device free of historical content. It therefore requires operationalization in more concrete terms in specific historical settings. As a general category of social factors, however, it points toward the probable importance of economic resources that affect capacities to engage in culture production; political resources such as guarantees of intellectual freedom, legal guarantees underlying relevant contracts and property relations, and the prestige or legitimacy that political entities may be capable of bestowing on cultural products; communication technologies such as river transportation, postal services, printing, bookshops, or electronic media that influence genres of cultural production and their capacity to reach particular audiences; and cultural resources such as shared languages, literacy, religious and ethnic traditions, and orientations toward particular values. In the case of the Reformation, for instance, the specific manifestations of these general conditions that proved relevant to the analysis include the cultural uniformity that spanned most of Europe as a result of the historic influences of Christianity, the existence of printing and of rising levels of literacy, the prevalence of agrarian modes of economic production, the continent's division into numerous political entities that were often in conflict with one another, a gradual rise in population, expansion in trade, and correlative increases in prices and the circulation of money.

In the cases considered, several points about these environmental conditions appear worth emphasizing. Of particular importance, insofar as ideology is conceived of as the result of a process of production, is the extent to which broad social environments function as pools of resources. Changes in population, trading networks, wages and price levels have all been considered in this manner, as have such relevant conditions as literacy rates, military obligations, levels of national political integration, and tensions within the religious sphere. Treating these conditions as resources has placed emphasis on their potential for altering or maintaining the specific contexts in which ideological production takes place. Changes in the profitability of particular commodities thus become important, for instance, insofar as these changes permit some actors involved in the production of ideology greater latitude in making decisions. This view is, of course, quite different from a perspective that understands ideology to be merely a constitutive element of the broad social environment. It also differs from a purely structural approach that emphasizes certain tacit homologies between environmental conditions and their associated ideologies. In these cases ideology is shaped directly and determinatively by the social environment. Conceiving of environments as resources adds an element of indeterminacy. Resources affect the range of ideologies that are likely to be produced, but these resources are also channeled by the more proximate contexts in which ideological production occurs.

Another point is that the abstract notion of environmental resources takes on meaning only in specific historical settings. What constitutes a relevant resource in one setting clearly may not be an important factor in another setting. The economic changes that permitted towns to fortify themselves against surrounding nobility clearly had greater relevance in the sixteenth century than in the eighteenth or nineteenth centuries. It also bears noting, however, that this very lack of conceptual specificity has advantages in pointing toward a wide variety of relevant resources. Not only can the role of economic conditions and class relations be considered, but also the influences of intellectual antecedents, prevailing literary genres, precedents for voicing dissent, and so on. The concept of environmental conditions thus subsumes the more generalized, implicit, embedded features of culture that have been emphasized in other perspectives.

Broad changes in dominant ideologies such as those associated with the Reformation, the Enlightenment, and socialism appear to have been facilitated by overall increases in the level of resources available in the social environment. Demographic, commercial, and political expansion opened the way for new elites to gain power and for new mechanisms of ideological production to emerge without fundamentally undermining established institutions (until later in the process). The effects of resource expansion were, however, mediated. They did not facilitate new ideologies simply by altering the outlooks of disaggregated individuals. Nor did their effects occur uniformly. Changes in resources were decisively channeled by pre-existing patterns of social relations, by the particular kinds of resources available, and by prevailing modes of appropriating and distributing resources.

The critical mediating connection between shifts in environmental conditions and changes in ideology appears in all three of the episodes examined to have been the specific institutional contexts in which ideologies were produced, disseminated, and authorized. None of these ideologies sprang into bloom on a thousand hilltops as if scattered there by the wind. They grew under the careful cultivation of particular movements that arose in specific places and that bore specific relations to their surroundings. The Reformation grew in urban pulpits, within certain ranks of the clergy, and in the offices of some ecclesiastical and secular hierarchies; the Enlightenment in salons, academies, bureaus, and universities; the socialist movement in party offices, legislative halls, and clandestine associations. Broadly speaking, institutional contexts are the organizational positions and relations that form the matrix in which ideas are produced and disseminated, including the relations between these organizations and other institutions in the broader environment.

The study of the institutional contexts of ideological production must focus first on the producers themselves: their numbers, conditions of work, sources of patronage, and channels of communication. Second, it must focus on the immediate audiences toward which ideological production is directed: their size and social composition, the channels connecting them with producers, the resources they can place at the disposal of producers, and the limitations they can impose. Finally, it must focus on the broader web of institutional linkages in which these specific activities are embedded: relations with established culture producing institutions, relations with agencies of the state, informal relations with ruling elites, integration into market relations and patronage networks, vulnerability to institutional schisms. These, much more so than the general spirit of the times or even the specific conditions under which culture producers' personalities are shaped, constitute the immediate contexts in which ideology is produced. It is in these contexts that particular forms of patronage can facilitate one kind of ideology more than another, or that audiences with particular grievances can gain the attention of writers capable of articulating these grievances, or that literary markets sizable enough to sustain an interactive and competitive community of literary producers can be created.

Within these institutional contexts ideology is generated and shaped, not all at once but through a series of action sequences. These are the work of historical agents. Their activities occur within the structural constraints of the institutional arrangements to which they are exposed. But within these constraints discretion is exercised, and variability in the cultural products that emerge is the inevitable result. The producers of ideology and those in a position to channel it in one direction or another respond to specific pressures, to crises, to demands that must be met if further crises are to be avoided. These responses occur in time; they follow one another and depend on the precedents and limitations set by their own predecessors.

The ideologies that result from these processes are likely, over time, to bend in the direction of the resources and situational constraints that went into their formation. They may not, however, reflect the interests of their creators. The decisions from which they emanate are more likely to be made with partial knowledge of the immediate situation, with an even more limited knowledge of the future, and with the intention of resolving short-term crises more than perpetuating long-term interests.

The idea of action sequences also points toward a reciprocal influence (a kind of feedback mechanism) of ideas on the social environment. If, as I have suggested, the social environment consists of resources, then ideology may be recognized as one of the ways in which actors attempt to gain control over these resources. Ideologies are seldom neutral with respect to the distribution of resources. Rather than merely describing the environment, ideologies specify how social resources should be distributed. Claims are made on authorities; scripts are provided that become operative in situations of decision making; standards are set forth for evaluating the propriety of behavior. If an ideology succeeds in becoming institutionalized, therefore, it may play a decisive role in acting back on its environment. This, of course, becomes the point at which to consider the processes involved in articulating a distinct relation between an ideology and its environment.

Production, Selection, Institutionalization

It has been suggested that cultural change comes about as a result of relatively abrupt, episodic ideological innovations, such as those associated with the Reformation, the Enlightenment, and socialism, in addition to the more gradual, incremental migration of outlooks that has often been described in the literature. In these episodes of marked ideological innovation, the conjuncture of changing resources and shifting institutional contexts can be seen clearly. The resulting ideological change does not, however, consist of a simple replacement of an old ideology by a new one. The process, as I have suggested, can be divided into three phases or subprocesses.

The production phase is characterized by an increase in the overall range of variation in ideological forms. Older, well-established forms continue but are faced with deviant alternatives, some of which will eventually fail while others will eventually triumph. The heightened degree of diversity may be evident along a number of dimensions: substantive or thematic emphases, modes of ideological production, genres, distinct charismatic leaders and devotees of a particular ideological orientation, ritual practices. In the Reformation this diversity was evident in an expanded array of biblical interpretations, views of the sacraments, styles of worship, and charismatic figures whose names came to symbolize clusters of alternative beliefs and practices. In the Enlightenment a heightened variety of ideological forms became evident in the use of alternative genres, in an enlarged number of literary and scientific topics, in the increasing range of media and sources of patronage, and again in the proliferation of charismatic figures with distinct ideological positions. The socialist movement demonstrated a similar proliferation of charismatic figures, a variety of programmatic emphases, experimentation with new genres of discourse, and the adoption of a wide range of discursive vehicles. The accepted ideas of the past were confronted not so much by a single innovative revelation as by many ideological contenders. Permutations compounded, and their advocates often found themselves at odds with one another as much as with the more traditional ideological practices.

All three periods were characterized by a combination of circumstances that expanded the opportunities available for this kind of diversity to be produced. Economic expansion alone contributed to an increasing availability of patronage, opportunities for a larger number of talented writers or speakers to pursue careers in theology or literature or politics, and an enlarged segment of the population with requisite literacy levels or excess income to devote to books, newspapers, and the support of literary associations. In addition, changing configurations of power among fractions of the ruling elite created stalemates that prevented established cultural authorities from repressing the new alternatives, or expanded the variety of patrons from whom support could be obtained or of officials from whom protection could be sought. Changing configurations of power also created structural ambiguities that appear to have encouraged efforts to redefine prevailing ideologies. In the Reformation these ambiguities were evident in uprisings within the lower strata of the towns and cities, in the relations between state officials and the landowning elite, and in the relations among the leading regimes. In the Enlightenment a critical source of ambiguity lay in the altered balance of power between central bureaucracies and representative bodies and in the heterarchic structure of patronage networks and state agencies. The socialist movement grew in response to ambiguities created by competition between liberal republican parties and monarchic aristocratic parties and by the numeric increases evident in the working class itself. Combined with the resources and de facto opportunities to respond to these ambiguities, circumstances of these kinds became rife with competing communities of discourse.

As the historical evidence has indicated, heightened levels of ideological diversity in these periods, once produced, also became subject to processes of social selection. Certain variants gradually proved more successful at securing resources under particular circumstances, while other contenders gradually fell by the wayside or became relegated to relatively small, marginalized niches. These processes were evident in the trajectories of Lutheranism, Calvinism, Catholicism, and the various Anabaptist sects during the Reformation. Local circumstances reinforced different religious tendencies in different parts of Europe. In the Enlightenment local conditions favored more philosophic orientations in some areas and technical orientations in others. Socialist leaders found some contexts more conducive to revolutionary rhetoric, others to reformist coalitions.

In each instance the very possibility of selective processes coming into being was contingent on two decisive characteristics of the broader society. It was contingent on preexisting ideological diversity, for without heightened variation in ideological forms, fewer options for selection would have been present. It was also contingent on the relation I have emphasized between resources and ideological production. Were ideologies simply the private ruminations of individuals, any number of conceivable permutations could coexist in happy mutual accommodation. But to be produced, ideologies require resources and, in turn, specify how resources ought to be used. Thus, the various purveyors of ideologies in each of these periods were indeed one another's competitors. Ideologies that secured the necessary resources flourished; others declined.

The competition on which selective processes rested also depended on several broad features of the social environment in which these ideological movements developed. One was the relative ease with which communication occurred. Without it, the Reformation or the Enlightenment or socialism would not have been a single movement with internal competition but a congeries of separate movements. In a general sense, communication in each instance was facilitated by the fact that Europe, even by the sixteenth century, had achieved a remarkable degree of economic integration, was crisscrossed with an increasing amount of trade and travel, and enjoyed a single religious heritage that, despite language differences, provided common values and interests. At the same time, is was also crucial that Europe consisted of a heterogeneous array of local and regional niches. It was possible in all three periods for leaders of ideological movements to gain control over needed resources by adapting to certain of these niches. This adaptation furthered the overall ideological diversity of each period and yet facilitated the survival quotient of the movement as a whole by linking it to a broader array of conditions. None of the three movements depended only on the success or failure of a particular regime.

In addition to the selective processes that connected specific ideological variants with specific geographic locations, more general selective processes are also evident in the three movements. Dependent as they were on the state for patronage of all kinds, the leaders of each movement found themselves constrained by the interests of state officials. This did not mean that state officials encouraged only those ideologies that aggrandized their regimes or adopted ideologies that legitimated the broader class interests on which their power was based. But it did mean, in nearly all instances, that officials were more likely to bestow resources on ideological movements that posed no immediate challenge to their authority and that enhanced their own capacity in the short term to make decisions. Henry VIII's Reformation placed the ecclesiastical hierarchy under the crown's control but militated against Lollardy and other heresies that demanded greater lay control over the church. Town magistrates in central Europe for the most part followed courses of action that they hoped would quiet popular dissent and avoid intervention by outside regimes. The Enlightenment writers produced works of virtually every conceivable kind, but the works that gained them prominence, patronage, and appointments to prestigious academies were more likely to emphasize moral and utilitarian themes, appeal to high-brow aesthetic tastes, and disguise more critical themes in satire and historical treatises than to cater openly to the masses or encourage blatant dissent. Even the socialists, whose revolutionary rhetoric posed direct challenges to the established order, produced an ideology prior to the First World War that largely favored parliamentary debate, moderate reform, and cooperation with the state in achieving legislation favorable to the working classes. At a more general level, we have also seen examples of the degree to which rational procedures for the conduct of scholarly business, rational forms of discourse, utilitarian criteria of evaluation, and universalistic appeals were reinforced by the movements' association with the state.

The fact that selective processes occurred in the context of relatively high levels of ideological diversity and structural ambiguity also resulted in some tendencies for genres of discourse capable of expressing this diversity and ambiguity to be reinforced. For instance,

Reformation discourse tended to favor the homily, the tract, and verse-by-verse commentary, all of which were suited to discrete observations about contemporary events, to a greater extent than the more systematically integrated theological tome. Enlightenment literature gradually turned away from the more constricted forms of epic poetry and classical drama and experimented with epistolary fiction, travelogues, and the novel. Socialist writers found advantages in formulating programs around seriatim lists of demands, disaggregated theses, and short polemical tracts and newspaper commentaries. In each instance, a symbolic differentiation also occurred between these more practical modes of discourse and the theoretical treatises that defined the movement's ideology in more abstract terms.

As these examples indicate, selective processes involve the active efforts of ideological producers as well as the effects of impersonal social mechanisms. But in both ways, selective processes draw ideological manifestations into closer articulation with their social contexts and demonstrate the shaping influences of these contexts. Processes of institutionalization, in contrast, point more toward ideologies gaining the capacity to shape their own destinies, as it were, and even to have an effect on the social contexts in which they occur. Institutionalization is characterized by an increasing level of differentiation between other arenas of social activity and those in which ideology is produced. In this process the producers of ideology gain a greater degree of autonomy in setting their own standards of evaluation. This autonomy, together with a more highly developed system of internal communication and greater routinization of the means by which resources are channeled toward ideological production, generally implies a stronger sense of stability for the resulting ideologies.

Institutionalization implies that ideas become embedded in concrete communities of discourse rather than floating freely in the creative minds of their inventors. Despite the loftiness of its ideals, the Enlightenment was grounded firmly in the concrete activities of writers and patrons, publishers and booksellers, the gatherings in salons and academies, classrooms, libraries, and laboratories. So were the ideals of the Protestant reformers and revolutionary Marxists. Indeed, a distinguishing feature of each of the periods examined was that new ideas ceased to be the sporadic contributions of a few inventive minds and became the regular products of social organizations devoted to their cultivation and dissemination. Reading clubs, academies, salons, university chairs, book fairs, subscription lists, and periodicals, in this sense, gauge the success of the Enlightenment as much as do the more ethereal virtues of rationality, skepticism, empiricism, and freedom.

Yet institutionalization also implies the emancipation of ideas from the social contexts in which they are embedded. Clergy made Scripture the measure of their authority, writers their own standards of aesthetic virtue, and revolutionaries the deterministic movement of material conditions that only they and their disciples could claim to understand. Discourse contemporizes itself by addressing concrete issues of collective importance, but it also refers reflexively to its own central themes. The competition separating different wings of the movement is not resolved by fiat but is allowed to continue, thereby necessitating further discourse and ensuring the perpetuation of its own production. Discretion in the interpretation of dogma is enjoined, giving it flexibility in adapting to unforeseen situations. At the same time, responsibility, deliberation, ritual enactments, festivals, and gatherings are prescribed, increasing the likelihood that fellow producers and their audiences will sustain contact with one another and acquire a tangible identity that reinforces the more abstract levels of their discourse.

Institutionalization, therefore, overlaps with the processes of production and selection but also plays a distinct role in ideological innovation. Like production and selection, it results from the actions of culture producers and involves not only responses to social conditions but also adaptations of the internal structure of discourse itself. It strengthens an ideology's capacity to withstand subsequent changes in its social environment. But it also depends on an appropriate combination of social circumstances. In each of the cases examined, broader expansion in the resource environment made possible an increase in the range of ideologies produced and a more dependable assortment of patronage networks, publishing arrangements, recruitment mechanisms, and offices for culture producers. The relative abundance of resources also made possible an extended period of internal competition which encouraged higher overall levels of ideological productivity. More important perhaps, the particular distribution of these resources among fractions of the ruling elite opened up zones of activity that were relatively free of control by established cultural institutions: urban pulpits, state-initiated academies, working-class political parties. Divisions within religious institutions and other established cultural organizations and in the ruling elite more generally also created conditions that culture producers could exploit to gain greater control over their own affairs. In each case these favorable conjunctures were relatively short-lived, lasting no more than a few generations, but new ideas became sufficiently institutionalized that they could not be ignored in the more turbulent times that followed.

Discursive Fields and Figural Action

The content of ideology in each of these instances was thus shaped in a variety of ways by the social circumstances in which it appeared. To pin down these relations more specifically, I have drawn attention to the connections among social horizons, discursive fields, and figural action. Examining these connections necessitates shifting the primary focus of attention to the discursive texts in which an ideology is expressed. All the foregoing is required in order to grasp the conditions of which the experienced social horizons of culture producers are composed, but the clues for linking these horizons to the internal composition of texts themselves come largely from a different source. They come from structuralist and formalist methods of literary analysis: from Bakhtin, Todorov, Althusser, Jameson, and others.[15]

Linking the internal structure of discourse with the social contexts of its production must also be understood in relation to the problem of articulation that was raised at the outset. Efforts to identify direct homologies between belief systems and the experienced world, such as those prevailing in standard approaches to the sociology of knowledge, have generally proven theoretically sterile and empirically futile. That ideologies should bear the decisive imprint of class relations, authority structures, or some other feature of the social environment has proven impossible to defend in the face of the vast creative variety that characterizes culture production. At the same time, a distinctly inferior theoretical position is taken if one asserts that culture production is free of all social influences or related to social contexts only in idiosyncratic ways. If ideologies are produced, rather than merely happening by some subjective process, then they are produced in time and space, and these coordinates limit the horizons from which resources can be obtained. Some degree of articulation with these horizons seems inevitable. And yet some degree of disarticulation seems equally inevitable, particularly if the ideologies under consideration have any continuing appeal. This delicate balance between articulation and disarticulation is, of course, partly achieved by the process of institutionalization, insofar as this process places culture producers within a tangible social setting and yet emancipates them from some of the constraints of the surrounding social environment. It is, however, a balance that depends on the more dynamic interaction between experience and discourse as well.

The ideologies purveyed by the Reformation, the Enlightenment, and socialism constitute a distinct mode of discourse: not only are they ideologies that attempt to persuade (for example, in contrast with discourse aimed merely at description, factual communication, or entertainment), but they are also the work of oppositional movements. Through the processes of production, selection, and institutionalization, they generated an enlarged range of ideas and significantly challenged those of established cultural institutions. To a degree more pronounced than in other forms of discourse, therefore, questions of authority, of sacralization and desacralization, and of opposing views play a prominent role in these ideologies.

Beyond the usual binary categories evident in all discourse, the ideologies of the Reformation, the Enlightenment, and Marxism, it has been argued, display a distinct oppositional structure characterized by such polarities as ecclesiastical tradition versus scriptural authority, inherited knowledge versus nature, and capitalist society versus the vision of a classless community. These are not single polarities but an oppositional form to which symbols of a wide variety become attached. Nor are they simple oppositions that only negate each other; they anchor widely separated ends of a continuum, thereby defining a space or field in which discourse can be framed.

The origins of these discursive fields, it appears, can be traced to various intellectual precedents rather than being attributable entirely to the creative work of leading figures of the Reformation, the Enlightenment, or socialism. Nevertheless, these figures appear to have sharpened the rhetorical use to which such oppositions were put, and in so doing effected a greater degree of articulation between them and contemporary social circumstances. In part, the creation of a distinct discursive field appears to have constructed an alternative source of authority with which to challenge the authority of prevailing ideas. But elements of the experienced social context can also be found at each end of the discursive continuum. The social setting in which ideologies were produced was sufficiently heterogeneous that both negative and positive models could be found. Luther attached the church and the nobility to the negative end of his discursive fields but found positive examples in the actions of some rulers and his fellow reformers. Rousseau criticized the pretensions of courtly society and modeled republican ideals after his native city of Geneva. Marx and Engels castigated the hypocrisy of bourgeois society and extrapolated from economic trends to predict the numerical superiority of the working classes.

In each instance the raw materials of social experience were lifted directly, as it were, and placed into the symbolic frameworks that made up the new ideologies. Movement leaders themselves evoked responses from other actors in their social milieu, and these responses provided grist for the mills that ground out ideological statements. This was one of the ways in which the movements' own action sequences fed back into the formulation and reformulation of movement discourse. Social experience became incorporated as elements of movement ideology, thus forging a higher degree of articulation between ideology and social conditions. As it was incorporated, though, it was also transformed by the other symbolic materials to which it was related. Marxist characterizations of the bourgeois family were not simply factual descriptions; they took on meaning as negative anchors in Marxist discourse, were associated with more trenchant criticisms of bourgeois society, and provided examples of exploitation and oppression. The same was true of Voltaire's satire and Calvin's polemics.

The central concepts that grew from each ideological movement were not modeled directly after the activities of some concrete status group or rising social class but were figural actions that depended on the discursive fields in which they were framed. Luther's and Calvin's admonitions concerning faith, worship, the calling, individual moral responsibility, and even the righteous conduct of rulers were seldom defenses of behavior they witnessed directly in their social environment. These admonitions focused on figural or representative characters and behavior. The legitimation of the reformers' own behavior or that of their secular patrons was sometimes in question, to be sure. But just as frequently this behavior provided instances for making points about the validity of the theological tenets at issue rather than the other way around.

The main role filled by formulations of figural action was to resolve the tensions built into the discursive fields of the ideological system itself. Rather than simply holding up a positive ideal against the negative circumstances of the experienced world, movement leaders provided more subtle and complex examples of behavior that remained in the experienced world and yet aspired to higher ideals. The very problems that inspired discussions of the righteous individual, the enlightened person of liberty, or the valorized revolutionary proletarian were set by the discursive fields in which these discussions were framed.

The moral constructs that specified models for behavior, therefore, were at least one significant step removed from the immediate social experience from which movement leaders produced their ideas. They grew out of this experience but were mediated by the symbolic frameworks in which they were placed. They were as much, or more, dependent on an ideological structure as they were on their social contexts. They consisted of representative actions and characters, and their generality was contingent on the symbolic space that removed them from concrete events. They provided models that could be emulated long after the specific events had changed— models of the righteous individual, the conscientious bourgeois, the heroic worker. These models were loosely recognizable within their immediate contexts of origin because of the tangible examples that were used in formulating the relevant discursive fields. But they were also disarticulated from these contexts. And this degree of disarticulation permitted them to function as some of the more abiding elements of modern culture.

The most general lesson to be learned from these considerations, it appears, is to situate the study of cultural change within a multifactoral perspective that emphasizes both the tangible social contexts in which culture is produced and the internal structures of the resulting cultural products. Shifts in broad environmental conditions influence the supply and distribution of social resources on which the production of ideology depends. Of special importance are the institutional arrangements that channel these resources and set the constraints that limit the activities of culture producers, their audiences, and patrons. The conditions that shape the various subprocesses involved in cultural change must also be distinguished, especially those augmenting the range of variability in ideological production, those selectively furthering particular ideological orientations in some contexts and impeding the survival of others, and those affecting the institutionalization of ideological forms. These influences, moreover, appear to function not as mechanical processes but as part of a dynamic sequence of action in which culture producers and other relevant agents respond to their circumstances. Part of this response involves modifications to the structure of ideology itself, which at the same time draw on features of the experienced social context and remove ideology from the immediate limitations of this context. The shaping of ideology is thus historically contingent. Certain relevant factors can be identified for bringing these contingencies into sharper relief, but no single overarching framework can be imposed apart from the specific historical conditions of cultural change themselves. It remains, therefore, to indicate at a more substantively specific level what the foregoing implies about the social conditioning of modern culture.

18

Capitalism and the Shaping of Culture

T HE THREE PERIODS I have examined cover a relatively small fraction of the capitalist epoch. These periods nevertheless provide insight into the ways in which capitalist development has contributed to the shaping of modern culture. The three hundred years separating the beginning of the Reformation from the culmination of nineteenth-century socialism also span the centuries in which capitalism rose from a relatively localized artisanal trading system to a vast industrial enterprise that reached into nearly every corner of the globe. In this long trajectory the Reformation, the Enlightenment, and the rise of socialism emerge as turning points, as transitional periods or episodes of exceptional cultural fervor in which the dynamic relations between social conditions and shifting ideas become especially prominent. What then can be said, in concluding, about the imprint of capitalism at these critical junctures in the development of modern culture?

Markets and Cultural Production

An interpretation that has gained expression particularly in studies of the development of literature emphasizes the role of markets as the leading influence of capitalism on culture. Modes of cultural production, and in turn cultural content itself, were shaped, this interpretation suggests, by the gradual penetration of market relations into all areas of society and thus by the increasing commoditization of cultural products. This interpretation attaches clear significance to the broad influences of the capitalist system. It also differs in emphasis from the empirical relations that have been stressed in the foregoing, although much of the foregoing also implicitly suggests the importance of commercial expansion and other forms of market penetration. It therefore makes sense to bring some of these arguments about the market into more explicit focus.

It is in discussions of the Enlightenment period that arguments about the effects of market relations have been expressed most clearly and compellingly. Studies of English literature during the eighteenth century have been particularly likely to emphasize these relations. In the half century or so separating Alexander Pope and Samuel Johnson, a notable shift is seen in the degree to which the life of letters was shaped by market relations. An oral tradition governed by private patronage and courtly manners gradually yielded, it has been argued, to a style of writing dominated by a commercial market, the technologies of printing, and an anonymous audience. Addison and Steele were among the first to recognize the significance of these changes, and their work contributed to the emergence of a new style of literature that was especially suited to the new situation. In addition to the periodical literature that resulted, writers such as Richardson, Fielding, and Smollett were able to exploit the new conditions to their advantage as pioneers of the modern novel, and with Samuel Johnson it becomes possible to see the emergence of a fully institutionalized literary community oriented to the exigencies of market relations.

Set in a somewhat broader context, several features of this argument make it an attractive interpretation, even within the theoretical framework that was discussed in the previous chapter. For one thing, it is an argument that can be readily extended in both directions to encompass the broader period of capitalist development. Studies of printing technology have emphasized the gradual penetration of this technology into the cultural sphere since the middle of the fifteenth century. These studies often attach greatest significance to technology itself as the motivating force, but they also recognize the dynamics of market expansion. The Reformation is thus portrayed as the first major episode of cultural innovation influenced by the availability of printing technologies. In the century and a half following the Reformation, printing is said to have been incorporated only gradually into the commercial market, remaining limited largely to the production of Bibles and other religious materials. The eighteenth century proved most conducive to the commoditization of cultural products, so that a large share of the production that has occurred in the past two centuries has been subject to market influences. Socialism itself depended on such precedents as the commercially produced newspaper and political pamphlet, but also needed to distance itself from the bourgeois institutions of cultural production in order to advance a truly revolutionary ideology.

Another feature of this argument is its potential to incorporate the processes of cultural production, selection, and institutionalization. As a mechanism of cultural dissemination, the market provides an interpretation of the manner in which all three of these processes may function. Production—especially the production of an expanded array of cultural materials—can be understood in terms of the expanded audiences and opportunities for culture producers that are likely to be associated with an expanding market. Market relations in the cultural sphere, as in the sphere of goods and services more generally, provide a mechanism for reaching a more diverse audience. These relations also enhance the likelihood that profitability incentives will draw a larger variety of culture producers into the literary market. Selection in favor of or against particular cultural forms is thus accomplished by the invisible hand of the market itself. Producers whose work appeals to a large or affluent segment of the market are rewarded, and their work gradually prevails; others are driven out of the field by their inability to attract a sufficient market. This process also ensures some degree of institutionalization. As profits accumulate, some publishing houses and individual authors gain the resources to dominate markets and squeeze out their less resourceful competitors.

The market also suggests a potentially acceptable argument about the ways in which broader social conditions and ideological orientations come to articulate with one another. It is, after all, the bourgeoisie that gradually dominates market relations, both as the producers of cultural materials and as those with sufficient surplus income to become the consumers of these materials. Bourgeois tastes thus come increasingly to set the standard for cultural production because the market favors the selection of ideologies that appeal to these tastes. In contrast to simpler theories of cultural adaptation and class legitimation, arguments that emphasize the market provide a more tangible account of the ways in which broad experiences come to effect cultural change. Experience does not eventuate in cultural change by a direct psychological process in which each individual more or less invents a new world view in isolation from others or even through the informal processes of socialization and interaction. It results in cultural change instead through a process mediated by the market in which individual consumers register their orientations by purchasing certain kinds of cultural products, and the profits generated thereby encourage producers to cater to these interests.

Beyond these general themes, an emphasis on the market has also permitted arguments to be made about some of the specific changes in form and content that have been observed in studies of modern literature. Profits from the commercial marketing of cultural products apparently played an important role in gradually emancipating cultural producers from church and court, thereby permitting cultural production to become more fully secularized, oriented toward aesthetic criteria, and professionalized. As markets increased, printing costs decreased, and cultural production therefore became democratized and indeed may have gradually incorporated the democratic ideals that have often been attributed to the literary community since the Enlightenment. At the same time, markets induced new pressures on writers to appeal to mass audiences, thereby lowering the quality of cultural products, or at least resulting in a greater degree of differentiation between popular culture and elite culture. Other influences that have sometimes been attributed to the market include greater emphasis on individual tastes, the self, and individualism generally; a greater fixity and systematization of style; greater specialization of the various functions involved in producing cultural materials; and a heightened sense of competition among culture producers.

Some of the evidence considered in the preceding chapters attests to the potential importance of market relations as one of the ways in which the growth of capitalism in general may have influenced the development of modern culture. Market relations were already drawing Europe together into a more closely integrated economy in the sixteenth century, and although these relations were still largely removed from the world of cultural production itself, they did provide channels of communication. The Reformation was disseminated along these channels, embodied as it was both in printed materials and in the discourse of merchants and traders. Commercial printing remained a relatively small industry, but in some towns it grew rapidly, and its growth appears to have augmented the number of Protestant adherents in these towns. The eighteenth century was characterized, as we have seen, by rapid growth in the number of books and by the introduction of newspapers and other printed media. This expansion depended to some degree on the revenues that market relations brought to publishers and authors. Audiences for these materials were also enlarged in the major cities in which Enlightenment literature flourished by the more general commercial resources created in conjunction with expanding markets. As the eighteenth century progressed, a wider audience for literature and public commentary did seem to be reached through commercial publishing. Socialism in the nineteenth century was preceded by the creation of national publics, at least partly as a result of newspapers and other commercialized media, and probably could not have emerged as an international movement had it not been for these publics. Leaders of the movement, most notably Marx himself, earned their livelihood by writing for commercial newspapers, served as salaried editors, and secured royalties from their books and pamphlets. In these ways it is difficult to imagine any of the three periods of cultural innovation having been the same without the contextualizing influences of the capitalist market.

It should also be evident from the foregoing, however, that interpretations in which exclusive or even primary emphasis is given to market relations must be viewed with caution. Studies in which printing has received prominence generally place greater emphasis on technology itself than on the integration of this technology into the capitalist market. And printing technology does in fact need to be sharply distinguished from market relations. In the sixteenth century printing depended almost entirely on church and state for support; in the eighteenth century the state still continued to supply the lion's share of printers' business, or at least played an active role in regulating the commercial market; and the printing activities in which socialists engaged in the nineteenth century merely imitated market relations rather than fitting squarely into any model of supply, demand, and profitability. Moreover, a relatively large share of cultural production and dissemination in all three periods remained independent of either the printed word or the publishing market. Sermons were the key mode of cultural dissemination in the Reformation, and oral disputations and private correspondence played a critical role in linking the reformers to one another. The Enlightenment was characterized as much by the verbal exchanges in salons and coffeehouses, by the noncommercial publications of scientific societies and universities, by classroom instruction, and by the resources of patrons and subscription lists as it was by the commercial market. And socialism depended as much on public lectures and legislative discourse as it did on newspapers and pamphlets.

Even the particular features of the Enlightenment that were presumably most influenced by the growth of market relations in the publishing industry suggest that one apply caution in attributing too much to these relations. Studies that skip from Pope to Johnson pass too easily over some of the most critical decades of the Enlightenment itself. If anything, the Enlightenment was more a product of the oral tradition in which Pope worked, or at least of the public sphere created by the academies and salons, as it was of the narrower printed media with which Johnson was associated. And if this is the case in England, it is even more so in France. The great outpouring of ideas in the first half of the eighteenth century that became known as the Enlightenment probably contributed more to the subsequent rise of commercial publishing than commercial publishing did to the rise of the Enlightenment. Indeed, some of the studies I have mentioned point to the dampening effects of commercial publishing on the vitality of the Enlightenment during the closing decades of the eighteenth century.

The same can be said of many other alleged effects of the market on cultural production. Market relations may have heightened competition among authors, thereby contributing to the overall growth of cultural production. But the evidence points clearly to other forms of competition that preceded market relations in the sixteenth and eighteenth centuries, or that circumvented them in the nineteenth century. These bases of competition were rooted in broader institutional relations, depended on the internal dynamics of social movements, and yet contributed immensely to the overall growth of cultural production. Intellectual competition in any of these periods scarcely depended on the market: it was a product of different views of the Eucharist, different geographic contingencies in the Reformation cities, strong personalities and struggles for personal fame in the Enlightenment, state-sponsored essay contests, the scarcity of patronage, political cleavages, contending socialist factions, and differences in the relations between socialist movements and liberal republican parties. Authors in the Enlightenment may have gained autonomy by making profits from commercial publications. But the eighteenth-century comparisons indicate other sources of autonomy that did not depend on commercial production, particularly the fluidity of political cleavages and writers' ability to play poorly institutionalized positions in the emerging state bureaucracies to their own advantage. And if commercial markets freed some authors from the whims of individual patrons, they also generated limitations on autonomy of their own kind, such as the limitations of having to adhere to strict publication schedules and writing for marketable tastes. Other factors, as I have suggested, played as much of a role in creating the separation between private selves and public roles that characterized Enlightenment literature as did the market; indeed, the temporal and geographic comparisons presented here suggest that market relations in general provide a less adequate explanation of these developments than do arguments about writers' location in relation to the public sphere and the distinctive institutional characteristics of the public sphere.

The most general point to be recognized about arguments focusing on market effects is that markets themselves are embedded in social relations. Rather than commercial publishing and printing technology being depicted as an inevitable tendency in modern culture, leading perhaps to more egalitarian and professionalized tastes, these developments must be understood as human creations and as the products of specific historical circumstances. If copyright laws were enacted because of pressures from commercial publishing, it was still in the hands of the state to pass these laws, and some states proceeded more quickly in that direction than others. If market expansion in general brought larger audiences for authors, this expansion was itself a function of military campaigns, diplomacy, protective tariffs, monopoly companies, and deliberate regulation. Culture producers generally remained in communication with one another and reacted to the criticisms of their colleagues not because of market relations but because of formal and informal networks of interaction and correspondence. Even the proverbial anonymity of the literary market in the eighteenth century has been much overemphasized, for publishers depended heavily on subscription lists, and writers remained in personal contact with many of their readers and wrote for patrons or for themselves as much as they did for the anonymous reader. Market relations have, of course, generated their own symbols, their own defenses and legitimations, and these have become a prominent feature of capitalist culture. But the effects of market relations on such episodes of cultural innovation as the Reformation, the Enlightenment, and socialism appear primarily to be partial and indirect. The market certainly did not spark cultural innovation in these periods as if driven by some inevitable logic of the market itself; instead, market tendencies were themselves the product of social arrangements.

Class Formation

An emphasis on class as the key influence of capitalism on modern culture has been seen to be problematic on both conceptual and empirical grounds. Arguments about rising classes' requirements for a legitimating ideology too often succumb to faulty teleological reasoning or fail to specify the mechanisms by which new ideologies are produced and disseminated; historical studies of the connections between membership in particular social classes and support for the Reformation, Enlightenment, or socialism increasingly yield results that confound the wisdom of simple class-based arguments. Like markets, however, class influences cannot be ruled out entirely. Broadly conceived, classes and class fractions appear to have been important features of the social contexts in which each episode of cultural change took place. Established cultural institutions were embedded in dominant hierarchies of class control. The church on the eve of the Reformation was an integral feature of the moral economy that bound peasants and landlords together in vertically stratified relations of dominance and dependence; the universities, seminaries, scientific academies, and patronage for writers and musicians at the end of the seventeenth century remained tied to aristocratic and courtly wealth; schools, colleges, newspapers, literary markets, libraries, and most state churches in the nineteenth century provided opportunities for the bourgeoisie that remained closed to the proletariat. It took a special conjuncture of circumstances among shifting factions of the ruling elite in each instance to create the space in which new ideologies could gain support.

The role of the bourgeoisie in furthering cultural change is most evident, perhaps ironically, in the Reformation. Its significance is ironic because recent Marxist historiography of the Reformation has tended to concentrate on Luther's support of the princes and Müntzer's role in the peasant uprisings rather than emphasizing the bourgeoisie. There are features of the Reformation, however, that come closer to a more theoretically informed version of Marxist interpretation. If the bourgeoisie is conceived of broadly as a set of social relations determined by trade and industry, its role in advancing the Reformation is readily apparent. Urban dwellers with direct or indirect ties to the commercial expansion of the period became the reformers' staunchest allies. Support came not only from the narrow class of merchants and traders themselves but also from artisans in trades such as textiles and metalwares that depended on the commercial revolution and even from displaced members of the lower strata whose lives were shaped by the shifting demands for an urban labor force. Moreover, the bourgeoisie, such as it was, confronted opposition from the landed elite on a number of issues, including policies toward the Reformation. Indeed, religious policies were among the most sharply contested issues because they held far-reaching implications for the traditional moral economy of rural life.

The Enlightenment, in contrast, was much less clearly a product of the rising bourgeoisie despite widespread arguments emphasizing this relation. Study after study has now challenged the idea that men of commerce and industry played a special role in promoting the Enlightenment, and broader comparisons reveal major anomalies in any general relation between the bourgeoisie and Enlightenment scholarship. Only if the concept of the bourgeoisie is broadened to include men and women of inherited wealth, nobility, members of the royal family, magistrates, bureaucrats, lawyers, physicians, and other professionals—virtually the entire elite—can a connection be drawn with the Enlightenment. An emphasis on class relations also fails to illuminate the changing content of cultural production during the Enlightenment. Understanding the dynamics of patronage networks, the overlapping cleavages of political life, the expanding resource base of state bureaucracies, the collective orientations of the public sphere, and the separation of private selves from public roles, it has been argued, provides a greater awareness of the actual circumstances in which the content of the Enlightenment was shaped than does a preoccupation with the bourgeoisie's alleged needs for legitimation.

The rise of socialism also bore a problematic relationship with the class relations emphasized in its own theories. The growth of an impoverished industrial working class appears to have contributed to the possibilities for socialist ideology to become institutionalized, but only in very general ways and in conjunction with other conditions. Neither the overall size of the industrial working class nor the rapidity of its growth was an accurate predictor of the socialist movement's strength from country to country. Large segments of the industrial working class opted for liberal and republican ideologies in some contexts, while in other settings socialist organizers were able to gain as much support from peasants, skilled artisans, and the petty bourgeoisie as from the industrial proletariat itself.

If arguments about the effects of class formation were to prove useful in understanding the shaping of modern culture, they should have proven useful in these specific episodes of cultural change. These episodes have been cited frequently in the literature from which such arguments are derived. The evidence on economic expansion also provides support for the idea that each period was in fact a time of opportunity for rising classes—for the commercial bourgeoisie (or protobourgeoisie) in the sixteenth century, a mercantilist bourgeoisie in the eighteenth century, and an industrial proletariat in the nineteenth century. The relations between class formation and cultural production, however, turn out to be neither as central nor as uniform as much of the theoretical literature would suggest. In none of the three periods do arguments about class relations clarify the essential dynamics between social horizons and the structure of discourse. No simple equation can be drawn between the polarities of discourse and polarities conceived to have been present between social classes: Luther and Calvin had nearly as much to say against merchants and artisans as they did against landlords and peasants; the reformers' discourse focused on the legitimacy of holy writ rather than the legitimacy of the bourgeoisie, and their concept of righteousness scarcely reflected the life style of any actual social class. Similarly, Voltaire and Rousseau pitted the virtues of nature against the pretenses of civilization, not in a way that directly championed the bourgeoisie but in a more complex pattern that reflected the internal logic of their discourse and only later provided a model for subsequent generations of the bourgeoisie to imitate. Marx and Engels, in turn, castigated bourgeois society but created an image of the proletariat that again served more as a figural abstraction from theoretical oppositions than as a reflection of the working class itself. In all three cases the relations among various segments of the elite, or between the elite and lower strata, are sufficiently important to continue to provoke discussion about class formation. But in each instance any specific effects of class formation turn out to be understandable only with reference to a variety of other social conditions. The Reformation was institutionalized not directly at the bidding of the bourgeoisie but by political authorities who maximized their own short-term interests; merchant oligarchies often temporized in the face of religious unrest, and many cities with a sizable bourgeoisie failed to institute religious reforms. The differences depended more on broad political relations than they did on the strength of the bourgeoisie alone. In the Enlightenment, commercial expansion interacted most closely with the state instead of creating an across-the-board division between the aristocracy and the bourgeoisie; as a result, the immediate context of Enlightenment production consisted of state bureaus and political patrons. Socialism, too, depended on an appropriate mixture of political relations to give it space in which to emerge; the proletariat that socialism was able to attract was a product of political cleavages as much as it was of industrialization.

It is also worth noting in this context that a variant of class theory focusing on the social dislocations associated with shifting class relations gains little support as an explanation for cultural change either. According to this line of reasoning, the effects of changing economic conditions on ideology occur less directly among the rising elites themselves than among those whose lives are becoming marginalized by these changes. In the sixteenth century it would thus have been the weakening moral bonds between peasants and feudal lords that should have resulted in ideology-ridden social movements. In the eighteenth century it should again have been the peasantry whose localistic ties were most disrupted by the corporatistic tendencies of mercantilist capitalism, while in the nineteenth century the social dislocations of the industrial working classes ought to have been most conducive to movements carrying new ideologies. In short, crisis and strain should predict ideology.

The evidence, however, has mostly cast doubt on this thesis. Despite the rather serious erosion of feudal relations at the start of the sixteenth century, most peasants' moral economies appear to have adapted effectively to changing conditions, and even those faced with extreme dislocation did not for the most part take this as an occasion to adopt the new religious ideologies of the reformers. The eighteenth century witnessed its share of peasant uprisings, and centralizing tendencies aroused periodic dissent from local, ethnic, and regional factions. But the success of the Enlightenment depended more on its isolation from these mass movements than it did on its gaining support from them. The nineteenth century provides the strongest confirmation for arguments relating ideology to social dislocation, but even for this period the evidence is mixed. Socialism attracted support in some instances because workers were geographically dislocated and economically immiserated; in other instances support depended on strong informal networks of association and on rising levels of economic resources.

The other point about class formation that has been emphasized is the extent to which notions of class were an outcome of cultural change itself, perhaps even more than they were a source of this change. Luther and Calvin, Voltaire and Rousseau, Marx and Engels, and their compatriots forged conceptions of appropriate behavior that were to become increasingly influential in subsequent decades. These conceptions were not, except possibly in Marx's case, full-blown arguments about social classes. They were, as we have seen, conceptions of representative behavior, discussions of figural action that provided models of virtue for individuals as representative social actors. These figurative characters grew out of concrete situations and were narratively contextualized in situations that could be recognized by those who read or heard about them. They were at the same time products of the discursive frameworks that defined the problems and range of possible actions that could be conceived. The behaviors, roles, and self-conceptions that emerged were thus both relevant to present circumstances and sufficiently disarticulated from these circumstances to have longer-term appeal. These models for action, coupled as they were with institutionalized resources of cultural dissemination, were to provide the symbolic materials around which subsequent conceptions of class could crystallize. The virtues defined by the reformers of the sixteenth century were thus to become models of ethical action of the kind that Weber identified with entrepreneurial capitalists of the seventeenth century. The reflective, socially responsible character of the eighteenth-century novel provided a prototype for later conceptions of the bourgeoisie. Similarly, Marx's discussions of the socialist worker and the worker's place in historical evolution generated a concept of the proletariat that has played a powerful role in defining all subsequent discussions of class relations. In each instance, therefore, class formation must be seen as a feature of ideological construction itself rather than a prior characteristic of the social environment that ideology merely came to reflect.

Capitalism and State Structures

The broad effects of expansion in the capitalist economy, I have suggested, were mediated most directly by the state. Economic growth did not occur simply because of competitive markets, technological innovation, or rising demand. It was encouraged by state officials who were in turn motivated by military competition with other rulers, by fears of popular uprisings, and by a need for revenue sufficient to purchase their autonomy from rival factions of the ruling elite. Officials' effectiveness in achieving these aims was, in turn, contingent on past levels of economic development, natural resources, geography, alliances, and administrative patterns. No simple relation between capitalism and political development can be specified. Preexisting social arrangements, the relative position of class fractions, and an interplay of environmental resources and economic specialization channeled overall rates of economic growth into different political outcomes. Thus, it was a particular type of economic growth that made the regime of Henry VIII in England a more conducive factor in the Reformation than the regime of Charles V in Spain, and the geography of the German states compared with that of France played an important role in differentiating these regions in the growing economic division of labor of the period; it was the combination of state policy and mercantilist expansion that differentiated England and France from the Dutch Republic in the Enlightenment, and the infusion of English trade and Silesian industry, among other things, that distinguished Scotland and Prussia from Austria or Sweden; and in the nineteenth century, strong aristocratic regimes pressing for rapid industrialization in Germany and Belgium did more for the socialist cause than did the more balanced industrialization of France and England.

Generally speaking, greater centralization of state structures tended to be associated with higher rates of economic growth and more progressive forms of capital accumulation, although there were some notable exceptions. These types of growth tended to be more readily appropriated by central state agencies through tax and loan schemes on the one hand, and required greater amounts of capital investment, which could be supplied and orchestrated by the state, on the other hand. Capital accumulation was thus both the result of strategic action by state officials and the means by which these officials enhanced their capacity to govern. Centralization, in this sense, was not so much the presence of a huge bureaucracy as a concentration of power that did not depend on the allegiances of elites with interests in strictly local or regional social arrangements. It depended on foreign trade, national markets, international competition, and innovations in commerce and industrial production. Examples of this type of relation between central regimes and the promotion of economic growth from which taxable revenues could be derived were evident in the comparisons between Reformation England and France, in the activities of the Danish and Swedish sovereigns during the Reformation, and in the dynamic sectors of the English, French, Scottish, and Prussian economies in the eighteenth century. In contrast, the relative decentralization of Austria, Sweden, and the Dutch Republic during this period seems to have inhibited economic growth. And in the nineteenth century, the weaknesses of countries such as Spain and Italy, both politically and economically, of course stand in sharp contrast to the political and economic strength of countries like England, France, and Germany. There were, however, centralized regimes that failed to create conditions conducive to sustained economic growth (often because of military reversals or inadequate natural resources), and there were instances of marked economic growth that did not result in political centralization. As we have seen, the particular opportunities that officials had at their disposal for promoting certain kinds of economic growth, and for reaping the rewards of this growth, need to be emphasized, rather than painting generalizations about the relations between economic growth and global concepts such as "strong" or "weak" states.

The political conditions most conducive to cultural innovation in each period, however, consisted less of simple centralization than of a division within the ruling elite—a division that was itself associated with the simultaneous occurrence of a particular type of economic expansion. In the Reformation it was the division between monarchic or magisterial governing bodies and the landowning elite that created opportunities for innovative religious policies to be institutionalized. In the eighteenth century it was the heterarchic division of power between central administrative bureaucracies and parliamentary bodies, together with cross-cutting cleavages within both, that opened up a public sphere in which resources and incentives for the production of Enlightenment ideas became available. In the socialist period, conservative oligarchic regimes that drew important fractions of the upper industrial bourgeoisie into an alliance with the monarchic-aristocratic elite proved most susceptible to socialist movements insofar as these regimes undermined the strength of liberal or republican parties that sought to unite segments of the bourgeoisie and the working classes. Commercial, mercantilist, and industrial expansion, respectively, altered the balance of power among the various fractions of the ruling elite and, depending on the ways in which these arrangements were worked out, an institutional space became available in which ideological movements could grow.

In broad terms, the decisive effect of relatively rapid capitalist expansion in each period was to heighten the divisions between fractions of the ruling elite, and these divisions, in turn, supplied opportunities, resources, and motivation to the producers and disseminators of new ideologies. Growth in the capitalist system during these episodes of cultural innovation was characterized not so much by the rise of one distinct social class relative to another as by a transitional period in which the boundaries between ruling-class fractions became blurred, alliances became more fluid, temporary opportunities to promote new ideas opened up, and exploitable resources not tied to any single established fraction became available. These were distinct periods of transition, characterized by relatively unusual relations among class fractions and state officials and set off from preceding and succeeding periods, rather than mere phases in long-term, gradual evolutionary processes. By virtue of the overall expansion of material resources and opportunities, new actors were incorporated into the ruling elite. The cultural innovations that resulted, however, remained the work of relatively small minorities, even in the socialist case, rather than representing massive inputs from the general population. The dynamism of each period depended as much on the balance, uncertainty, and relative autonomy of the various elite fractions as it did on any sheer increment of new interests with fresh insights.

It was, then, a conjuncture of economic and political conditions that proved conducive to ideological change in each of these periods.

Economic expansion of a particular kind contributed resources that facilitated the growth of state agencies, and these agencies became sufficiently differentiated from more established segments of the ruling elite to provide at least tacit encouragement to the leaders of ideological movements. Economic growth enhanced the likelihood of resources being made available to culture producers, enlarged the size of potential audiences, facilitated communication between the two, and raised new issues to be addressed. State structures channeled the results of economic expansion in ways that diversified the policy options that could be pursued, deflected resources away from established cultural elites, organized the conflict between segments of the ruling elite, and brought culture producers into this context of political conflict.

The three periods differed from one another in ways that also bear evidence of the importance of long-term economic and political development. In the sixteenth century the states that furthered the Reformation remained little more than small deliberative bodies carrying out the business of monarchs, territorial princes, or town patricians. By the middle of the eighteenth century the major European states consisted of functionally differentiated bureaus, legislative bodies, centralized judiciaries, and professional staffs often numbering in the thousands. A century later these agencies had expanded even further and were supplemented by national electoral systems and formally organized political parties. As the states' administrative structures grew, so did the realms over which centralized control was exercised. Single states administered larger and more diverse territories in the nineteenth century than in the sixteenth century. They also supervised a larger and more diverse assortment of functional activities. Taxatory and military powers gradually expanded, and to these were added an increasing array of financial responsibilities, diplomatic activities, laws aimed at promoting and regulating industry, supervision of a much-enlarged system of transportation and communication, and an increasing role in education.

Cultural production depended on the state in many ways as much in the sixteenth century as in the eighteenth or nineteenth centuries. Its relations to the state nevertheless changed with the course of political development. The Protestant reformers depended on state officials for military protection and looked to them to supervise doctrinal disputes, but the disputes at issue focused chiefly on questions of faith rather than political matters, and the movement's aims were directed ultimately toward the hearts and minds of masses of believers. The Enlightenment writers depended, at least as much as the Protestant reformers had, on the state to create organizations to train disciples and to support and protect the activities of their literary academies and scientific societies. Much of their writing dealt with intellectual issues that went well beyond the immediate concerns of the state. But their audience to a great extent was composed of persons with direct connections to the state, and a significant share of their work focused on political theory and practical matters of political policy. For them the state more nearly set the bounds of the public sphere in which scholarly discourse could take place. By the end of the nineteenth century, the state not only set the context of ideological debate but also provided both the mechanisms and the objectives around which socialist discourse was organized. Socialists focused on the state either as an ally from which reforms could be extracted or as a foe to be overthrown, and the activities and organizations that carried their appeals were in large measure those of political parties. Legislative victories became a central symbol of their success.

In this sense it might be argued that the power of ideology gradually came to be more closely integrated with the power of political agencies. In the sixteenth century religious reformers could still make claims on believers' consciences quite apart from political considerations, and despite the territorial settlements that attempted to impose religious identities on the basis of political boundaries, the religious wars of the next century and a half, resulting in declarations of religious diversity and freedom of conscience, demonstrated the extent to which ideology could still hold sway over the powers of temporal rulers. The Enlightenment also demonstrated the capacity of culture producers to create abstract philosophy, fiction, and works for leisure consumption independently of political concerns. Insofar as the Enlightenment developed within the public sphere, however, it was from the beginning closely associated with political power, and its institutionalization over the following century came about primarily through the state's promotion of science and higher education, the extension of mandatory public schooling, and the constitutional definition of rights and responsibilities. Socialism was not only conditioned by the political context in which it arose but also formed itself as a political party, gained strength through legislative victories, and set its aim as the seizure of state power. In each period smaller movements and countermovements of course developed with more diverse relations to the state. But overall, the tendency of each succeeding movement to define itself more closely to political power than the last had a cumulative effect. Thus, the relation of religious movements to the state is now generally weakest, and that of religious conviction to individual conscience generally strongest, while socialism is imposed by central regimes or the rights and duties it champions are protected and carried out by welfare state bureaucracies. The main themes of the Enlightenment occupy a middle ground, on the one hand being defined as individual rights and freedoms and institutionalized in organizations with relatively high autonomy, such as universities, but on the other hand being defended constitutionally and legislatively and perpetuated through public systems of education.

More than a strict increase in the politicization of ideology, however, the three periods demonstrate a shift in the strategies required to effect ideological change in the face of expanding state structures. In the sixteenth century religious reformers were able to gain the ear of individual rulers and then look to these rulers to supply personal protection and to declare formally (if often ineffectively) the truth of the reformers' views. Where rulers held heavy concentrations of power in their own hands, the reforms accomplished were often rapid and severe. Whole religious institutions and traditional practices were swept away and new modes of worship were implemented. Folk traditions may have survived, but official practices were brought under the monopoly of new leaders with new ideas. By the eighteenth century the mechanisms of ideological innovation were already becoming more subtle and complex. The Enlightenment writers did not supplant entire religious institutions with the stroke of an executive pen. New organizations were founded that largely added to, rather than replaced, established modes of cultural production. Literary academies coexisted with community churches, and chairs in natural philosophy complemented chairs in theology. As states became more highly bureaucratized, culture producers also found it necessary to imitate this form of organization. Many held offices in state bureaucracies; many held positions in universities; others organized societies and academies along parliamentary lines. Some writers enjoyed access to individual rulers, but increasingly the lines of access became formalized and depended on participating in formal organizations. To an even greater degree, the socialist movement reflected the state's capacity to determine the available means of public discourse. Socialist leaders organized political associations, ran candidates in local elections, and looked to parliamentary debates as a means of expressing their views. Their hopes lay ultimately in seizing control of the state or overthrowing it.

In each case the new ideology that became institutionalized was but one of a number of competing alternatives. It was the one that succeeded in gaining support from the state. Anabaptists challenged the authority of secular rulers and found themselves relegated to a tiny, oppressed margin of European society. Mesmerists, radical Freemasons, utopian socialists, and anarchists suffered similar fates in subsequent periods. The mainstream of the Reformation, the Enlightenment, and socialism did not capitulate entirely to the demands of the state, but these movements did for the most part (if sometimes inadvertently) strengthen the authority of central regimes and encourage them to expand into new functional areas. Whatever the direct relations may have been between capitalism and ideology, the ideologies that prevailed were primarily those in which the state structures that fostered capitalism were encouraged.

Cultural Themes

The present study also bears on questions about the effects of capitalism in particular, or of modernity in general, on substantive cultural themes such as individualism, rationalization, pluralism, discretion, virtue, and so on. These questions have generally been framed in terms of origins and legitimation; for example, did individualism originate with capitalism, and was capitalist development legitimated by individualism? General affinities have been sought and historical evidence has generally raised doubts about how much emphasis should be attributed to capitalist influences. Within the present framework these questions can be recast: given the multifactoral or conjunctural conditions under which specific episodes of cultural innovation appear to have arisen, is there nevertheless any evidence that these episodes reinforced particular substantive themes, and given the nexus of social horizons and discursive fields in which particular substantive themes arose, did these themes gain articulation in a way that made them relevant both to their specific contexts and to the capitalist epoch more generally?

Modern individualism indeed appears to have been reinforced by each of these episodes of cultural change, although antecedents can be found well before the advent of capitalism itself. In none of the three episodes were freedoms, rights, or duties of the individual championed to the exclusion of ideas about community attachments and collective responsibilities. Nevertheless, the discursive frameworks that were enunciated focused on sufficiently complex normative issues that an expression of individual autonomy provided the only viable means of resolving these issues. At the same time, the manner in which these notions of individual autonomy were formulated reflected the specific historical situations in which they emerged. In the process, new individuals came into being, as it were, through the creative joining together of situational experiences and symbolic constructs. Desires for individual autonomy did not, as far as can be discovered from the historical evidence, arise simply in the hearts of scattered individuals who then put these feelings into words and joined movements that privileged these meanings. Discourse about individual autonomy was instead an active creation of culture producers who not only reflected on their own experiences but borrowed ideas from the intellectual genres of their day.

Ideological expressions of individual autonomy did not, as some theoretical reconstructions have suggested, pit the individual against the constraints of established social obligations in a strict oppositional relation. In none of the periods examined did individualism emerge simply as a negation of social ties. It emerged within discursive frameworks that pitted higher-order ideals against established social conventions. Concepts of the individual served as a means of resolving the tensions between these poles. Individualized moral action became the way of reconciling life in the experienced world with a vision of a more perfect realm. Elements of both became attached to the figural individual, and the tensions pulling at the individual from both directions created the boundaries against which individual action was to be defined.

The Protestant Reformation, in this respect, added to the possibilities for individual action on which subsequent levels of capitalist development seemed to depend. The Protestant, as a representative type or model of moral behavior, was constrained to live, as it were, not only in the present world, as opposed to taking an otherworldly orientation, but suspended between the real and the ideal. The tension of living in this condition could not be escaped, and particularly in the Calvinist tradition it became imperative to identify even an appropriate mixture of the earthly and the divine. Enlightenment constructions of the individual secularized the discursive context in which moral action was to be determined, removing it from the polarity of ecclesiastical tradition and biblical virtue and placing it in the nexus of social convention and the rights and truths of nature. The individual was not so much freed as redefined. Individual autonomy, responsibility, and discretion all became updated by being placed in the context of considerations most likely to bear on moral action in the eighteenth century. Socialism extended these conceptions and updated them again, at the same time that it stressed the collective features of social reality, by creating for the masses of workers both a sense of the mutability of social conditions and a heightened conception of their own responsibilities as moral agents.

Over against the situational flexibility provided by conceptions of individual discretion, guidelines were also articulated that reintroduced levels of predictability and social conformity. Beyond the purely idiosyncratic origins of these guidelines in local subcultures, a special degree of emphasis was placed on conceptions of rationality. These conceptions were in part contingent on the fact that figural characters were indeed representative actors whose behavior was set forth as a standard to emulate and was framed by the tensions between experienced realities and hypothetical worlds. Actions were, in this sense, goal directed, or were at least matters of choice that were to be carried out within a given normative context. To the extent that action was associated with concrete symbolic characters, rationality in the sense of behavioral consistency was also a given.

As with the construction of ideological themes more generally, rationality was to an important degree an ideological form that depended on the joining together of models from the social environment itself and features of ideological structure. From the social environment models of rationality tended to be incorporated, as has been seen, by virtue of culture producers' close relations with the state. In resolving disputes and advancing claims to truth, culture producers sometimes permitted these claims to be resolved within the rational-legal mechanisms provided by the state itself, and more often borrowed the language of these mechanisms in their own deliberations. From the structure of their own genres they also derived a semblance of consistency of style and argumentation that provided norms of rationality with which to conform. Competition and imitation reinforced conformity to canons of style and argumentation that cast discourse into recognizable genres. Within these genres substantive variations allowed for closer degrees of articulation with specific social situations, but the common features of discursive structure itself permitted communication across relatively heterogeneous settings.

The heterogeneity of these ideological contributions can be understood both in terms of the internal flexibility of discourse itself and in terms of the selective processes that adapted different ideologies to different social situations. Although certain substantive and structural emphases, such as individualism and rationality, appear to have been reinforced, the overarching pattern that becomes evident between the beginning of the sixteenth century and the end of the nineteenth century is one of accumulating cultural heterogeneity. The Reformation, the Enlightenment, and socialism all achieved partial successes. At the close of each period, Europe remained divided between sections that had participated more actively in the ideological innovations of the time and those that had resisted these innovations or remained indifferent to them. In addition, each set of innovations was itself internally divided around competing movements, alternative formulations, rival leaders, and so on. Subsequent revolutions, wars, and efforts to mobilize mass support contributed to the reduction of some of this diversity. But over the longer term, each subsequent episode of ideological innovation added further diversity. Whereas the cultural landscape of Europe on the eve of the capitalist epoch was a patchwork of local and regional customs, therefore, the cultural patterns that grew with the development of capitalism displayed their own special varieties of tradition and innovation.

It can be argued that the heterogeneity of modern culture has contributed to its own adaptive potential in that a nearly infinite variety of permutations and situational variations is conceivable. And yet the very fact of this heterogeneity should point toward a greater awareness of the indeterminateness of theories about the sources of cultural change, including theories emphasizing inevitable advances in adaptive potential. It is possible to reconstruct some of the social

conditions that contributed to the production, selection, and institutionalization of cultural change in the past and even to identify
common patterns among these conditions. Such efforts necessitate
paying greater attention to the conceptual tools on which thinking
about the past inevitably depends. It also demonstrates, however,
that the pieces from which the past is reconstructed have come together in a multitude of patterns.

Conjuncture and Cultural Innovation

The fact that the Reformation, the Enlightenment, and the development of European socialism all grew out of a conjuncture of complex historical circumstances should give one pause in advancing the
kinds of arguments about cultural innovation that have often arisen
in the literature. These episodes that contributed so much to the
shaping of modern culture cannot be understood, as some theories
have suggested, simply as a response to the growing social complexity
of the modern era. They cannot be accounted for by pointing to the
disruptive effects of urbanization and industrialization. They did not
result from rising status groups who happened to be in a position to
develop new ideas and then use these ideas to legitimate their claims
to wealth and power. Above all, we cannot understand these periods
of innovation as the inevitable consequence of capitalism, either
decrying them as part of the breakdown of traditional values supposedly accompanying capitalism or praising them as the great side
benefits of civilization which capitalism has brought our way. Nothing
was inevitable about these movements, nor was the development of
capitalism itself inevitable.

It is always dangerous to extrapolate from the past to the future,
but these conclusions should also give us pause in making predictions
about the nature, likelihood, and timing of future periods of cultural
innovation on a grand scale. Some theories of capitalism point to a
future of ever-increasing intellectual creativity, a sharpening of our
sense of individuality and freedom, and an inevitable capacity to
reformulate our values and think of new ones as the situation may
arise. They complacently associate the future of capitalism with all
these possibilities. Other theories predict more turbulence and discontinuity but also closely link changes in culture to the trajectory
of capitalism. There is, some have argued, a new social class whose
rise to power is rooted in a new mode of production—the production

of knowledge—just as the bourgeoisie was rooted in industrial production and the aristocracy in agrarian production: this new class, they say, will bring about a fundamentally new ideology. Taking cues from arguments about markets and technology, others claim that the next major episode of cultural innovation is now emerging through the effects of television, computers, and mass communication, just as the Reformation was born of the printing press and the Enlightenment from the commercial market for published material. We should be skeptical of all these predictions.

The Reformation, Enlightenment, and socialist movements were, of course, not the only sources of cultural innovation in the past. The mystics and Anabaptists who stood near the edge of the Reformation's mainstream, the alchemists and Freemasons, the great discoveries of Copernicus and Kepler, and the work of Napoleon, Jefferson, and Freud all contributed as well. The Enlightenment has come to stand as a symbol of cultural achievement, and the Reformation and socialism are depicted as watersheds in the rise of modern thought. But we should take caution from knowing what they consisted of, from recognizing their internal diversity, their continuity with the past, and the degree to which economic and political forces shaped them into the institutional realities they became.

For us it should be a matter of learning from the past rather than simply extrapolating from it to the future. We learn from these episodes that history is not determined by the invisible dynamics of capitalist development; it is made by actors who exercise choice on the basis of partial information; but it is also shaped within the constraints defined by tradition, special interests, economic conditions, and political circumstances. We do not have to wait until the conjunctures that facilitated cultural movements in the past repeat themselves: in abstract terms, the conditions that facilitated each episode of cultural innovation were much the same; but in concrete terms, each period was unique. The ideological themes advanced in each period, moreover, bore only a loose connection to these conditions. They were inventive and powerful themes. They achieved a lasting effect through the form and content of their own discourse.

In each historical episode the leading contributors to the new cultural motifs recognized the extent to which the institutional conditions of their day were flawed, constraining, oppressive, arbitrary. Their criticism of these conditions was often extreme and unrelenting. It was sharpened by an alternative vision, a vision constructed discursively, a vision that was pitted authoritatively against the established order, not as its replacement but as a conceptual space in which new modes of behavior could be considered. The strength of their discourse lay in going beyond negative criticism and beyond idealism to identify working models of individual and social action for the future.

Notes

Introduction

1. Martin Luther, *Werke: Kritische Gesamtausgabe* (Weimar: H. Böhlau, 1883), vol. 10, no. 4, p. 10.

2. Quoted in Heinrich Bornkamm, *Luther in Mid-Career, 1521-1530* (Philadelphia: Fortress Press, 1983), pp. 74–75. Bornkamm concludes: "These March weeks proved decisive for the future course of the Reformation" (p. 77). Roland H. Bainton, *Here I Stand: A Life of Martin Luther* (New York: New American Library, 1950), p. 166, describes the return to Wittenberg as a turning point for Luther as well, a turn from negative polemics toward positive engagement with the practical implications of theological reform: "The leader of the opposition was called to be the head of the government. . . . The demolisher was summoned to build. . . . The change was vast between the role of railing against 'the execrable bull of Antichrist' and that of providing a new pattern of Church, state, and society, a new constitution for the Church, a new liturgy, and a new Scripture in the vernacular." In short, theory was from this point on wedded to practice.

3. Luther, *Werke,* vol. 10, no. 42, p. 9. The essence of the contrast Luther sought to make was between discourse that leaves action voluntary and action that accomplishes its ends through legislative or political means: "We must promote and practice and preach the Word, and then afterwards leave the result and execution of it entirely to the Word, giving everyone his freedom in this matter. . . . We have the *jus verbi* [right to speak], but not the *executio* [power to accomplish]." For a discussion of this distinction in relation to Luther's views of civil order, see Marjorie O'Rourke Boyle,

Rhetoric and Reform: Erasmus' Civil Dispute with Luther (Cambridge, Mass.: Harvard University Press, 1983), esp. pp. 99–131. For a description of the events surrounding the Wittenberg sermons, see Walther von Loewenich, *Martin Luther: The Man and His Work* (Minneapolis: Augsburg, 1986), pp. 214–230; Bernhard Lohse, *Martin Luther: An Introduction to His Life and Work* (Philadelphia: Fortress Press, 1986), pp. 50–52; and Bainton, *Here I Stand,* pp. 152–166.

4. Lewis W. Spitz, *The Protestant Reformation, 1517–1559* (New York: Harper and Row, 1985), pp. 90–91.

5. Harold Jantz, "German Renaissance Literature," *Modern Language Notes* 81 (1966), 418; Maria Grossman, "Wittenberg Printing, Early Sixteenth Century," *Sixteenth Century Essays and Studies* 1 (1970), 54–74; Elizabeth L. Eisenstein, "The Advent of Printing and the Protestant Revolt: A New Approach to the Disruption of Western Christendom," *Annales, E.S.C.* 26 (1971), 1355–1382; Elizabeth L. Eisenstein, "Some Conjectures about the Impact of Printing on Western Society and Thought: A Preliminary Report," *Journal of Modern History* 47 (1968), 1–56; Richard G. Cole, "The Dynamics of Printing in the Sixteenth Century," in *The Social History of the Reformation,* ed. by Lawrence P. Buck and Jonathan W. Zophy (Columbus: Ohio State University Press, 1972), 93–105; Richard G. Cole, "Propaganda as a Source of Reformation History," *Lutheran Quarterly* 22 (1970), 166–171.

6. Luther, *Werke,* vol. 10, no. 2, p. 72.

7. Martin Luther, *Luther's Works,* vol. 48, ed. Jaroslav Pelikan, Hilton C. Oswald, and Helmut T. Lehmann (Philadelphia: Fortress Press, 1957), p. 197.

8. For example, the contrast between externalities and matters of the heart is much in evidence in Luther's denunciations of Carlstadt in the months following his return to Wittenberg; see James S. Preus, *Carlstadt's "Ordinaciones" and Luther's Liberty: A Study of the Wittenberg Movement, 1521–22* (Cambridge, Mass.: Harvard Theological Studies, 1974), no. 27.

9. Luther, *Werke,* vol. 10, no. 2, p. 25.

10. For a useful discussion of the metonymic functions of figures, see Michael Shapiro and Marianne Shapiro, *Figuration in Verbal Art* (Princeton: Princeton University Press, 1988), pp. 23–45.

11. On the relation between metonymy and the problem of articulation and disarticulation, as presented here, see especially Roman Jakobson, "Quest for the Essence of Language," *Diogenes* 51 (1965), 21–37.

12. I have discussed definitions of culture and approaches to the study of culture more extensively in my book *Meaning and Moral Order: Explorations in Cultural Analysis* (Berkeley: University of California Press, 1987).

13. For an attempt at a more general periodization and comparison of these movements with other ideological movements, see Ibid., Chap. 7.

1. Contexts and Perspectives

1. E. Harris Harbison, *The Age of Reformation* (Ithaca: Cornell University Press, 1955), p. 7; Roger Mols, "Population in Europe, 1500–1700," in *The Fontana Economic History of Europe: The Sixteenth and Seventeenth Centuries,* ed. Carlo M. Cipolla (Glasgow: William Collins Sons, 1974), p. 39.

2. Fernand Braudel, *The Mediterranean and the Mediterranean World in the Age of Philip II* (New York: Harper and Row, 1973), p. 705.

3. Perez Zagorin, *Rebels and Rulers, 1500–1660* (Cambridge: Cambridge University Press, 1982), p. 95.

4. See Francis Oakley, *The Western Church in the Later Middle Ages* (Ithaca: Cornell University Press, 1979), p. 82; H. S. Bennett, *Life on the English Manor: A Study of Peasant Conditions, 1150–1400* (Cambridge: Cambridge University Press, 1960), p. 29.

5. Some examples are discussed in Martin Ingram, "Religion, Communities, and Moral Discipline in Late Sixteenth- and Early Seventeenth-Century England: Case Studies," in *Religion and Society in Early Modern Europe, 1500–1800,* ed. Kaspar von Greyerz (London: George Allen and Unwin, 1984), p. 177.

6. For an excellent survey, see André Burguière, "Le rituel du mariage en France: Pratiques ecclésiastiques et pratiques populaires (XVIᵉ–XVIIIᵉ siècles)," *Annales, E.S.C.* 33 (1978), 637–649. Another historian suggests that because of the church's prohibition against familial marriages to the fourth degree villagers were keenly aware of extended family relations; see Robert Muchembled, *Culture populaire et culture des élites dans la France moderne (XVᵉ–XVIIIᵉ siècles)* (Paris: Presses universitaires de France, 1978), chap. 1.

7. See, for example, the discussion in John Bossy, "Blood and Baptism: Kinship, Community, and Christianity in Western Europe from the Fourteenth to the Seventeenth Centuries," in *Sanctity and Secularity: The Church and the World,* ed. Derek Baker (Oxford: Basil Blackwell, 1973), p. 131.

8. Examples are given in A. N. Galpern, "Late Medieval Piety in Sixteenth-Century Champagne," in *The Pursuit of Holiness in Late Medieval and Renaissance Religion,* ed. Charles Trinkaus (Leiden: E. J. Brill, 1974), pp. 141–176; A. C. F. Koch, "The Reformation at Deventer in 1579–1580: Size and Social Structure of the Catholic Section of the Population during the Religious Peace," *Acta Historiae Neerlandicae* 6 (1973), 51; Emmanuel LeRoy Ladurie, *Montaillou: The Promised Land of Error* (New York: Vintage Books, 1979), pp. 310–311. The classic analysis of godparentage relations is Sidney W. Mintz and Eric R. Wolf, "An Analysis of Ritual Co-Parenthood (Compadrazgo)," *Southwestern Journal of Anthropology* 6 (1950), 341–368.

9. This function is discussed in R. W. Southern, *Western Society and the Church in the Middle Ages* (London: Penguin Books, 1970), p. 8.

10. These restrictions are mentioned by John Bossy. "The Counter-Reformation and the People of Catholic Europe," *Past and Present* 47 (1970), 57.

11. A number of insightful examples are discussed in William A. Christian, Jr., *Local Religion in Sixteenth-Century Spain* (Princeton: Princeton University Press, 1981).

12. A. N. Galpern, *The Religions of the People in Sixteenth-Century Champagne* (Cambridge, Mass.: Harvard University Press, 1976), p. 43.

13. Janusz Tazbir, "The Cult of St. Isidore the Farmer in Europe," in *Poland at the 14th International Congress of Historical Sciences in San Francisco* (Warsaw: Polish Academy of Sciences, Institute of History, 1975), p. 107.

14. These points are stressed in Carlos M. N. Eire, *War against the Idols: The Reformation of Worship from Erasmus to Calvin* (Cambridge: Cambridge University Press, 1986), pp. 11–13; and Charles Garside, Jr., *Zwingli and the Arts* (New Haven: Yale University Press, 1966), p. 90.

15. Mervyn James, "Ritual, Drama, and the Social Body in the Late Medieval English Town," *Past and Present* 98 (1983), 3–29; John Bossy, "Essai de sociographie de la masse, 1200–1700," *Annales, E.S.C.* 36 (1981), 44–70; John Bossy, "The Social History of Confession in the Age of the Reformation," *Transactions of the Royal Historical Society* 25 (1975), 21–38; cf. Clifford Geertz, *The Interpretation of Cultures* (New York: Basic Books, 1973), pp. 142–169, for a discussion of the tension-resolving functions of ritual in another context.

16. Robin Briggs, *Early Modern France, 1560–1715* (Oxford: Oxford University Press, 1977), p. 181; Sidney Oldall Addy, *Church and Manor: A Study of English Economic History* (New York: Augustus M. Kelley, 1970), pp. 415–450; C. S. L. Davies, *Peace, Print, and Protestantism, 1450–1558* (London: Paladin, 1977), p. 32; J. C. Dickinson, *The Later Middle Ages: From the Norman Conquest to the Eve of the Reformation* (London: Adam and Charles Black, 1979), p. 360; Cezaria Baudouin de Courtenay Jedrzejewicz, "Polish Peasant Rituals and Seasonal Customs," in *Polish Civilization: Essays and Studies,* ed. Mieczyslaw Giergielewicz (New York: New York University Press, 1979), pp. 1–24; see also the more general information on social status and burial customs in Philippe Ariès, *The Hour of Our Death* (New York: Knopf, 1981).

17. For a useful general survey of attitudes toward the poor, see Michel Mollat, *The Poor in the Middle Ages: An Essay in Social History* (New Haven: Yale University Press, 1986), esp. pp. 251–293.

18. Quoted in Alexander Murray, *Reason and Society in the Middle Ages* (Oxford: Clarendon Press, 1985), p. 361.

19. Lucien Febvre, *Life in Renaissance France* (Cambridge, Mass.: Harvard University Press, 1977), p. 74.

20. Some local studies of wages and prices have suggested increases in peasants' standard of living during this period, but these conclusions are generally contested by evidence of increasing tax burdens and tighter restrictions on the usage of common lands for grazing, hunting, and timber; specific studies are discussed in the following chapters.

21. For some examples, see W. P. Blockmans and W. Prevenier, "Poverty in Flanders and Brabant from the Fourteenth to the Mid-Sixteenth Century: Sources and Problems," *Acta Historiae Neerlandicae* 10 (1978), 20–57; Roland Mousnier, *The Institutions of France under the Absolute Monarchy, 1598–1789,* vol. 1, *Society and the State* (Chicago: University of Chicago Press, 1979), pp. 557–558.

22. This role is discussed in Jean-Pierre Gutton, *La sociabilité villageoise dans l'ancienne France* (Paris: Presses universitaires de France, 1979), chap. 5. Where differences in income were substantial, however, conflicts between priests and parishioners were more likely.

23. Dickinson, *The Later Middle Ages,* p. 360; Miriam Usher Chrisman, *Strasbourg and the Reform: A Study in the Process of Change* (New Haven: Yale University Press, 1967), p. 277.

24. William Monter, *Ritual, Myth, and Magic in Early Modern Europe* (Athens, Ohio: Ohio University Press, 1983), p. 15.

25. In another context, Jeffrey M. Paige, *Agrarian Revolution: Social Movements and Export Agriculture in the Underdeveloped World* (New York: Free Press, 1975), emphasizes the importance of competition for scarce resources in peasant economies.

26. Jerome Blum, "The European Village as Community: Origins and Functions," *Agricultural History* 45 (1971), 157–178, is a particularly useful discussion of these aspects of village life.

27. Marceli Kosman, "Programme of the Reformation in the Grand Duchy of Lithuania and How It Was Carried Through," *Acta Poloniae Historica* 35 (1977), 21–50. Kosman presents some wide-ranging material on the size of parishes in different sections of Europe.

28. Christian, *Local Religion in Sixteenth-Century Spain,* is again one of the more useful sources. Conformity to these obligations was also enforced in many instances by ecclesiastical courts; see Ralph Houlbrooke, *Church Courts and the People during the English Reformation, 1520–1570* (Oxford: Oxford University Press, 1979), esp. p. 7.

29. For a sense of the continuing importance of church bells in rural life, see Dorothy L. Sayers, *The Nine Tailors* (New York: Harcourt Brace Jovanovich, 1934); and for a vivid description of the centrality of the church building itself in village life, see Thomas Merton, *The Seven Storey Mountain* (New York: Harcourt Brace Jovanovich, 1948), pp. 36–37.

30. The quotation and examples are from Robert W. Scribner, "Cosmic Order and Daily Life: Sacred and Secular in Pre-Industrial German Society," in Greyerz, *Religion and Society in Early Modern Europe,* p. 17.

31. Ibid., pp. 18–21.

32. I am indebted to Robert W. Scribner, "Ritual and Popular Religion in Catholic Germany at the Time of the Reformation," *Journal of Ecclesiastical History* 35 (1984), 47–77, for the examples given here.

33. Some recent studies of the peasants' uprisings in 1525 have suggested that anticlericalism was a significant part of these revolts. Indeed, instances of anticlerical unrest among peasants had occurred periodically for more than a century before the Reformation. The bulk of opinion, however, seems to suggest that: (a) economic and legal grievances outweighed religious issues; (b) rural anticlericalism was limited geographically; (c) this anticlericalism generally did not translate into demands for wholesale reforms of the church; and (d) peasants more often resisted religious reforms in neighboring towns than joined forces with it. This evidence is discussed in greater detail in later chapters. For a brief discussion, see Tom Scott, *Freiburg and the Briesgau: Town-Country Relations in the Age of Reformation and Peasants' War* (Oxford: Clarendon Press, 1986), pp. 229–235.

34. Special bequests went to priests and friars who could be counted on to pray regularly for the departed; for example, in England, even as late as the 1530s, two-thirds of all wills included such bequests, and many of the remainder seem to have taken them for granted. See J. J. Scarisbrick, *The Reformation and the English People* (London: Basil Blackwell, 1984), p. 5. On these patterns in Europe more generally, see Carlo M. Cipolla, *Before the Industrial Revolution: European Society and Economy, 1000–1700* (New York: W. W. Norton, 1976), pp. 54–58.

35. Thomas Aquinas, *Summa Theologica*, II, 2, q. 100, a. 3.

36. Murray, *Reason and Society in the Middle Ages*, pp. 317–325.

37. Aloys Schulte, *Der Adel und die deutsche Kirche im Mittelalter: Studien zur Social-, Rechts-, und Kirchengeschichte* (Darmstadt, 1909), pp. 261–293.

38. Murray, *Reason and Society in the Middle Ages*, p. 346.

39. Mary Douglas and Baron Isherwood, *The World of Goods* (New York: Basic Books, 1979), p. 32.

40. J. H. Elliott, *Imperial Spain, 1469–1716* (London: Edward Arnold, 1963), p. 88.

41. Penry Williams, *The Tudor Regime* (Oxford: Clarendon Press, 1979), p. 63.

42. See, for example, the discussion of France in J. H. Shennan, *Government and Society in France, 1461–1661* (London: George Allen and Unwin, 1969), esp. p. 23. Often the church served as an instrument of *direct* transfer from peasants to landlords as well, reinforcing a system of tithes in which a share of the proceeds was paid to the landlord himself; see Jerome Blum, *The End of the Old Order in Rural Europe* (Princeton: Princeton University Press, 1978), p. 63.

43. Franz Lau and Ernst Bizer, *A History of the Reformation in Germany to 1555* (London: Adam and Charles Black, 1969), pp. 11–12.

44. Gerhard Benecke, *Society and Politics in Germany, 1500–1750* (London: Routledge and Kegan Paul, 1974), p. 11; see also Lawrence G. Duggan, *Bishop and Chapter: The Governance of the Bishopric of Speyer to 1552* (New Brunswick, N.J.: Rutgers University Press, 1978), pp. 163–166.

45. Kosman, "Programme of the Reformation," p. 37.

46. Evidence from some areas, which will be considered later, suggests conflict between monastic and secular landowners as a result of changing views toward farming and land use; other research, however, suggests that monastic landholders were as progressive as secular landholders and that the two cooperated in making improvements; see J. N. Hare, "The Monks as Landlords: The Leasing of the Monastic Demesnes in Southern England," in *The Church in Pre-Reformation Society: Essays in Honour of F. R. H. Du Boulay,* ed. Caroline M. Barron and Christopher Harper-Bill (Suffolk: Boydell Press, 1985), pp. 82–94. Christopher Haigh, "Anticlericalism and the English Reformation," in *The English Reformation Revised,* ed. Christopher Haigh (Cambridge: Cambridge University Press, 1987), p. 59, observes: "Bishops and abbots shared property interests and a common social life with the country nobles and gentry who were their stewards, bailiffs, lessees and neighbours."

47. Examples of the importance of these arrangements are given in R. Po-chia Hsia, *Society and Religion in Munster, 1535–1618* (New Haven: Yale University Press, 1984); see esp. pp. 44–45.

48. For a discussion of these relations in the rural Lyonnaise area, see Philip T. Hoffman, *Church and Community in the Diocese of Lyon, 1500–1789* (New Haven: Yale University Press, 1984), esp. pp. 58–60. After the Reformation, especially during the seventeenth century, greater integration of local community government into the central state bureaucracy on the one hand and greater efforts by the church to provide central administration over the local parish on the other began to widen the divisions between community and parish; see, for example, Gutton, *La sociabilité villageoise dans l'ancienne France,* chap. 5.

49. These variations have been discussed in conjunction with two contributions by Robert Brenner, "Agrarian Class Structure and Economic Development in Pre-Industrial Europe," *Past and Present* 70 (1976), 30–75, and "The Agrarian Roots of European Capitalism," *Past and Present* 97 (1982), 16–113.

50. These relations are alluded to in passing by Michael Hechter and William Brustein, "Regional Modes of Production and Patterns of State Formation in Western Europe," *American Journal of Sociology* 85 (1980), 1061–1094.

51. Studies of these patterns include John B. Freed, "The Mendicant Orders in German Society" (Ph.D. diss., Princeton University, 1969); Christian, *Local Religion in Sixteenth-Century Spain;* David Knowles and R. Neville Hadcock, *Medieval Religious Houses: England and Wales* (London: Longman, 1971); Richard W. Emery, *The Friars in Medieval France* (New York: Columbia University Press, 1962); Felicity Heal, *Of Prelates and Princes: A Study of the Economic and Social Position of the Tudor Episcopate* (Cambridge: Cambridge University Press, 1980), pp. 21–23.

52. Benecke, *Society and Politics in Germany,* p. 6; Jan DeVries, *The Dutch Rural Economy in the Golden Age, 1500–1700* (New Haven: Yale University Press, 1974), pp. 42–43; Jonathan Dewald, *The Formation of a Provincial Nobility: The Magistrates of the Parlement of Rouen, 1499–1610* (Princeton: Princeton University Press, 1980), p. 174; G. R. Elton, "The Reformation in England," in *The New Cambridge Modern History,* vol. 2, *The Reformation, 1520–1559,* ed. G. R. Elton (Cambridge: Cambridge University Press, 1958), p. 226; Eli F. Hecksher, *An Economic History of Sweden* (Cambridge, Mass.: Harvard University Press, 1954), p. 67; Jaime Vicens Vives, *An Economic History of Spain* (Princeton: Princeton University Press, 1969), p. 340; J. P. Cooper, "The Social Distribution of Land and Men in England, 1436–1700," in *Essays in Quantitative Economic History,* ed. Roderick Floud (Oxford: Clarendon Press, 1974), p. 109.

53. Kosman, "Programme of the Reformation," p. 24.

54. Some examples are given in Christian, *Local Religion in Sixteenth-Century Spain;* David G. Hey, *An English Rural Community: Myddle under the Tudors and Stuarts* (Leicester: Leicester University Press, 1974); Michael Roberts, *The Early Vasas: A History of Sweden, 1523–1611* (Cambridge: Cambridge University Press, 1968), esp. p. 59.

55. Some statistics are presented in Robert Weinstein and David Bell, *Saints and Society* (Berkeley: University of California Press, 1982), pp. 188–189.

56. Braudel, *The Mediterranean,* pp. 770–777; more generally, see Keith V. Thomas, *Religion and the Decline of Magic* (London: Weidenfeld and Nicholson, 1971).

57. Scholars emphasizing the deep integration of late medieval religion in rural social life have suggested that the very intensity of this integration may have been oppressive and therefore conducive to the Reformation. The principal contributions to this literature include Bernd Moeller, "Religious Life in Germany on the Eve of the Reformation," in *Pre-Reformation Germany,* ed. Gerald Strauss (New York: Macmillan, 1972), pp. 13–42; Steven E. Ozment, *The Reformation in the Cities* (New Haven: Yale University Press, 1975); W. D. J. Cargill Thompson, "Seeing the Reformation in Medieval Perspective," *Journal of Ecclesiastical History* 25 (1974), 297–308; Thomas Tentler, *Sin and Confession on the Eve of the Reformation* (Prince-

ton: Princeton University Press, 1977). This argument potentially undermines the conclusion that seems to arise from this evidence: that the rural
social order depended on established religious patterns to such an extent
that it was likely to be a force *against* the Reformation. It must be recognized, however, that, with the exception of some ambiguity in Moeller's
essay, most of the debate has centered on the nature of urban religion; few
questions seem to have been raised about the depth, persistence, or tra-
ditionality of rural religious practices. Moreover, recent contributions concerning the extent of oppressiveness—some of which have drawn examples
from rural areas—have focused mainly on the balance between external
control by the church and voluntary compliance to the church. None has
questioned the overall intensity of rural religious practices or the extent of
their embeddedness in the moral economy of rural life.

58. Particularly valuable general sources on trade in the sixteenth century include Kristof Glamann, "European Trade, 1500–1750," in Cipolla,
*The Fontana Economic History of Europe: The Sixteenth and Seventeenth Cen-
turies,* pp. 427–526; Kristof Glamann, "The Changing Patterns of Trade,"
in *The Cambridge Economic History of Europe,* vol. 5, *The Economic Organi-
zation of Early Modern Europe,* ed. E. E. Rich and C. H. Wilson (Cambridge:
Cambridge University Press, 1977), pp. 185–289; M. M. Postan, *Medieval
Trade and Finance* (Cambridge: Cambridge University Press, 1973); M. M.
Postan, "The Trade of Medieval Europe: The North," in *The Cambridge
Economic History of Europe,* vol. 2, *Trade and Industry in the Middle Ages,* ed.
M. Postan and E. E. Rich (Cambridge: Cambridge University Press, 1952),
pp. 119–256; Robert S. Lopez, "The Trade of Medieval Europe: The
South," in *The Cambridge Economic History of Europe,* vol. 2, pp. 257–354;
J. H. Parry, "Transport and Trade Routes," in *The Cambridge Economic
History of Europe,* vol. 4, *The Economy of Expanding Europe in the Sixteenth
and Seventeenth Centuries,* ed. E. E. Rich and C. H. Wilson (Cambridge:
Cambridge University Press, 1967), pp. 155–222.

59. Recent discussions also point out the importance of changes in
agriculture that created surplus profits for investment in commerce, supplied
excess food for urban populations, and drove surplus labor into the towns
or into rural artisanal production; see the review in John Langton and Göran
Hoppe, *Town and Country in the Development of Early Modern Western Europe*
(Norwich: Historical Geography Research Series, 1983), no. 11; and on
the role of rural industry, see Peter Kriedte, Hans Medick, and Jürgen
Schlumbohm, *Industrialization before Industrialization: Rural Industry in the
Genesis of Capitalism* (Cambridge: Cambridge University Press, 1981).

60. Figures on grain prices are from Wilhelm Abel, *Agricultural Fluc-
tuations in Europe: From the Thirteenth to the Twentieth Centuries* (London:
Methuen, 1980); other price series referred to are from F. P. Braudel and
F. Spooner, "Prices in Europe from 1450 to 1750," in *The Cambridge Eco-*

nomic History of Europe, vol. 4, pp. 378–486. The effects of American bullion are discussed in Earl J. Hamilton, *American Treasure and the Price Revolution in Spain, 1501–1650* (Cambridge, Mass.: Harvard University Press, 1934). Glamann, "The Changing Patterns of Trade," p. 188, points out the relevance of unit costs for long-distance trading. Real wages and profit margins are discussed in Abel, *Agricultural Fluctuations in Europe;* and Walter Minchinton, "Patterns and Structure of Demand, 1500–1750," in Cipolla, *The Fontana Economic History of Europe,* pp. 83–176.

61. Walther von Loewenich, *Martin Luther: The Man and His Work* (Minneapolis: Augsburg, 1982), p. 21.

62. Lacey Baldwin Smith, *Treason in Tudor England: Politics and Paranoia* (Princeton: Princeton University Press, 1986), p. 180.

63. Ibid., p. 182. She goes on to say: "Anxiety bred of spiritual agitation and a sense of terror that the beast was at the gate took on institutional form when . . . dynastic politics and economic self-interest allied themselves with ideology to create the conditions of fear and instability in which paranoia for the next five generations could thrive" (p. 182).

64. Other historians have been mindful of this problem. For example, Chaunu has suggested that economic expansion was associated with a diffusion of the written word and with the development of schools, both of which contributed to the Reformation. More generally, he stresses that the choice of Protestantism was rarely an individual decision; it was essentially collective, involving the church, state, city, and seigneury. This argument represents a step toward specifying the institutional changes facilitating the Reformation, but remains too broadly concerned with the social environment to illuminate the complexities of these changes. See Pierre Chaunu, "Niveaux de culture et Réforme," *Bulletin de la Société de l'Histoire du Protestantisme français* 118 (1972), 305–325.

65. Lewis W. Spitz, *The Protestant Reformation, 1517–1559* (New York: Harper and Row, 1985), p. 24, insists that the Reformation period as a whole was "a time of profound discontent"; yet he correctly observes that "one cannot superimpose a map of Protestant Europe upon a sketch of the inflationary pattern, for some Protestant areas were the last to be affected, while some that remained Catholic suffered economically most grievously."

66. Studies that have characterized the commercial revolution primarily as a dissolution of the feudal system have generally overemphasized the extent to which peasant-landlord relations were disrupted, at least for the early sixteenth century; it is for this reason that the foregoing discussion of rural religion is cast in terms of concrete social relations rather than abstract ideas about the nature of feudalism.

67. Hoffman, *Church and Community in the Diocese of Lyon,* p. 54.

68. "People were afraid not so much of the beggar's indigence as of

his idleness, his rootlessness, and his anonymity. They no longer knew with whom they were dealing." Mollat, *The Poor in the Middle Ages,* p. 251. Mollat also observes that wills increasingly referred to the poor as an abstract category. The role of insecurity in the city, fed by fear of vagabonds, as a source of aggressiveness toward outsiders has also been stressed by Muchembled, *Culture populaire et culture des élites,* esp. chap. 3.

69. Mollat, *The Poor in the Middle Ages,* p. 265.

70. For example, of the thirty-six almshouses still in existence in York, Norfolk, and Birmingham, fourteen were in dire economic straits and six were close to ruin. In London the situation was even worse: only eight of twenty-two almshouses were still in operation by the end of the fifteenth century. Ibid., p. 270. A study of Lille examines in some detail the pressures that migration and increases in food prices placed on the urban poor and shows how these pressures led the town magistrates to assume a greater role in administering public charity; see Robert Saint-Cyr Duplessis, "Charité municipale et autorité publique au XVIᵉ siècle: L'example de Lille," *Revue du Nord* 59 (1977), 193–219.

71. Mollat argues that the religious charities in general tended to be less effective than secular charities, both royal and municipal, because of certain customs that had developed over a long period which permitted bishops to reap a substantial share of the bequests given; *The Poor in the Middle Ages,* pp. 265–268.

72. For a similar point, see Charles Tilly, "Reflections on the History of European State-Making," in *The Formation of National States in Western Europe,* ed. Charles Tilly (Princeton: Princeton University Press, 1975), p. 41.

73. Some of this literature is reviewed in David Gold et al., "Some Recent Developments in Marxist Theories of the State," *Monthly Review* 27 (1975), 36–51.

74. Versions of these arguments are discussed in Nicos Poulantzas, *Classes in Contemporary Capitalism* (Atlantic Highlands, N.J.: Humanities Press, 1975), pp. 89–174; Erik Olin Wright, *Class, Crisis, and the State* (London: Verso, 1978), pp. 230ff.; Colin Barker, "The State as Capital," *International Socialism* 2 (1978), 16–42; Christopher Chase-Dunn, "Interstate System and Capitalist World-Economy: One Logic or Two?" *International Studies Quarterly* 25 (1982), 19–42; Fred Block, "Beyond Relative Autonomy: State Managers as Historical Subjects," *Socialist Register* 2 (1980), 227–242.

75. For example, the role of strong and weak states in economic development is discussed extensively in Immanuel Wallerstein, *The Modern World-System: Capitalist Agriculture and the Origins of the European World-Economy in the Sixteenth Century* (New York: Academic Press, 1974). Criticisms of this formulation of the role of the state appear in Theda Skocpol,

"Wallerstein's World Capitalist System: A Theoretical and Historical Critique," *American Journal of Sociology* 82 (1977), 1075–1090; Peter Gourevitch, "The International System and Regime Formation: A Critical Review of Anderson and Wallerstein," *Comparative Politics* 10 (1978), 419–438; Aristide R. Zolberg, "Origins of the Modern World System: A Missing Link," *World Politics* 23 (1981), 253–281.

76. On clergy recruitment in England, see Josiah Russell, "The Clerical Population of Medieval England," *Traditio* 2 (1944), 177–212; Margaret Bowker, *The Secular Clergy in the Diocese of Lincoln, 1495–1520* (Cambridge: Cambridge University Press, 1968); Jo Ann Hoeppner Moran, "Clerical Recruitment in the Diocese of York, 1340–1530: Data and Commentary," *Journal of Ecclesiastical History* 34 (1983), 19–54; A. H. Thompson, *The English Clergy and Their Organization in the Later Middle Ages* (Oxford: Oxford University Press, 1947).

2. State Autonomy and the Reformation

1. Elizabeth L. Eisenstein, *The Printing Press as an Agent of Change*, 2 vols. (Cambridge: Cambridge University Press, 1979), and Miriam Usher Chrisman, *Lay Culture, Learned Culture: Books and Social Change in Strasbourg, 1480–1599* (New Haven: Yale University Press, 1982), are particularly valuable sources on the role of literacy, books, and learning in central Europe during the Reformation. See also Natalie Zemon Davis, *Society and Culture in Early Modern France* (Stanford: Stanford University Press, 1975), pp. 189–226, for a discussion of the effects of printing. Robert W. Scribner, *For the Sake of Simple Folk: Popular Propaganda for the German Reformation* (Cambridge: Cambridge University Press, 1981), gives greater weight to the use of visual media for the dissemination of reformed ideas. Chrisman's book (esp. pp. 151–155) presents evidence that challenges the idea that literacy alone accounts for the Reformation's appeal. Marshall McLuhan, *The Gutenberg Galaxy* (Toronto: University of Toronto Press, 1962), has given a popular but greatly exaggerated account of the effects of printing.

2. H. Soly, "The 'Betrayal' of the Sixteenth-Century Bourgeoisie: A Myth? Some Considerations of the Behaviour Patterns of the Merchants of Antwerp in the Sixteenth Century," *Acta Historiae Neerlandicae* 8 (1975), 47; Gerald Strauss, *Nuremberg in the Sixteenth Century* (New York: Wiley, 1966); Robert W. Scribner, "The Reformation as a Social Movement," in *Stadtbürgertum und Adel in der Reformation: Studien zur Sozialgeschichte der Reformation in England und Deutschland,* ed. Wolfgang J. Mommsen (Stuttgart: Klett-Cotta, 1979), pp. 49–79; E. William Monter, *Calvin's Geneva* (New York: Wiley, 1967), p. 44. Robert W. Scribner, "Practice and Principle in the German Towns: Preachers and People," in *Reformation Principle and Practice: Essays in Honour of Arthur Geoffrey Dickens,* ed. Peter Newman Brooks (London: Scolar Press, 1980), shows that a disproportionate share

of Protestant clergy were sons of town magistrates, merchants, and artisans; only one in nine was of rural origin. Other local studies of the Reformation in specific towns are rapidly adding to the nuanced description of the institutional forces shaping the adoption of religious reforms. I will emphasize only the main themes of these studies. Among several useful surveys of the literature cited elsewhere in the text, see Gerhard Müller, *Reformation und Stadt: Zur Rezeption der evangelischen Verkündigung* (Wiesbaden: Franz Steiner Verlag, 1981), esp. pp. 3–19.

3. Alastair Duke, "The Face of Popular Religious Dissent in the Low Countries, 1520–1530," *Journal of Ecclesiastical History* 26 (1975), 44–45; Miriam Usher Chrisman, *Strasbourg and the Reform: A Study in the Process of Change* (New Haven: Yale University Press, 1967), pp. 93–97.

4. Kaspar von Greyerz, *The Late City Reformation in Germany: The Case of Colmar, 1522–1628* (Wiesbaden: Franz Steiner Verlag, 1980), p. 46; for more general sources, see George Hunston Williams, *The Radical Reformation* (Philadelphia: Westminster Press, 1962), and Claus-Peter Clasen, *Anabaptism: A Social History* (Ithaca: Cornell University Press, 1972), and *The Anabaptists in South and Central Germany, Switzerland, and Austria* (Ann Arbor: University Microfilms International, 1978).

5. Examples are given in Robert W. Scribner, "Civic Unity and the Reformation in Erfurt," *Past and Present* 66 (1975), 29–60; and Strauss, *Nuremberg in the Sixteenth Century,* pp. 176–177.

6. Thomas A. Brady, Jr., *Turning Swiss: Cities and Empire, 1450–1550* (Cambridge: Cambridge University Press, 1985), p. 158.

7. Harold Grimm, "Luther's Contribution to Sixteenth-Century Organization of Poor Relief," *Archiv für Reformationsgeschichte* 61 (1970), 222–223. Laicization of welfare programs was not unique to Protestant areas, but appears to have been initiated more widely in these areas and accomplished with less resistance; see Robert M. Kingdon, "Social Welfare in Calvin's Geneva," *American Historical Review* 76 (1971), 50–69; Natalie Zemon Davis, "Poor Relief, Humanism, and Heresy: The Case of Lyon," *Studies in Medieval and Renaissance History* 5 (1968), 217–275; and Robert Jütte, "Poor Relief and Social Discipline in Sixteenth-Century Europe," *European Studies Review* 11 (1981), 25–52.

8. C. Verlinden, J. Craeybeck, and E. Scholliers, "Price and Wage Movements in Belgium in the Sixteenth Century," in *Economy and Society in Early Modern Europe,* ed. Peter Burke (New York: Harper and Row, 1972), pp. 59–68; Scribner, "The Reformation as a Social Movement"; and E. Maschke, "Verfassung und soziale Drafte in der deutschen Stadt des spaten Mittelalters, vornehmlich in Oberdeutschland," *Vierteljahrschrift für Sozial und Wirtschaftsgeschichte* 46 (1959), 289–349, 433–476, and "Deutsche Stadte am Ausgang des Mittelalters," in *Die Stadt am Ausgang des Mittelalters,* ed. Welhelm Rausch (Linz: Donau, 1974), pp. 40ff.

9. Hermann Aubin, "Medieval Agrarian Society in Its Prime: The Lands East of the Elbe and German Colonization Eastward," in *The Cambridge Economic History of Europe,* vol. 1, *The Agrarian Life of the Middle Ages,* ed. M. M. Postan (Cambridge: Cambridge University Press, 1966), pp. 464–486; Robert Brenner, "Agrarian Class Structure and Economic Development in Pre-Industrial Europe," *Past and Present* 70 (1976), 56–59.

10. Useful sources on the German Peasant War are Robert W. Scribner and Gerhard Benecke, eds., *The German Peasant War of 1525—New Viewpoints* (London: George Allen and Unwin, 1979), and Robert W. Scribner, "The German Peasants' War," in *Reformation Europe: A Guide to Research,* ed. Steven Ozment (St. Louis: Center for Reformation Research, 1982), pp. 107–134.

11. Estimates are given in Clasen, *Anabaptism;* other evidence is discussed in James M. Stayer, "The Anabaptists," in Ozment, *Reformation Europe,* pp. 135–160.

12. Heinrich Bornkamm, *Luther in Mid-Career, 1521–1530* (Philadelphia: Fortress Press, 1983), p. 177.

13. Kenneth J. Dillon, *King and Estates in the Bohemian Lands, 1526–1564* (Brussels: Les Editions de la Libraire Encyclopedique, 1976), pp. 21–72. In Saxony and Hesse the nobility objected strongly to the dissolution of the monasteries but were too weak to muster effective resistance; see F. L. Carsten, *Princes and Parliaments in Germany* (Oxford: Clarendon Press, 1959), p. 207.

14. Quoted in Brady, *Turning Swiss,* p. 19.

15. The political circumstances of central Europe are described in Hajo Holborn, *A History of Modern Germany: The Reformation* (New York: Knopf, 1959); Carsten, *Princes and Parliaments;* and Gerhard Benecke, *Society and Politics in Germany, 1500–1750* (London: Routledge and Kegan Paul, 1974). Some useful information is also presented in M. L. Bush, *Renaissance, Reformation, and the Outer World, 1450–1660* (London: Blandford Press, 1967); and in Hermann Heimpel, "Characteristics of the Late Middle Ages in Germany," in *Pre-Reformation Germany,* ed. Gerald Strauss (New York: Macmillan, 1972), pp. 43–72.

16. Evidence of these activities is presented in Wolfgang Von Stromer, "Commercial Policy and Economic Conjuncture in Nuremberg at the Close of the Middle Ages: A Model of Economic Policy," *Journal of European Economic History* 10 (1981), 119–130; Monter, *Calvin's Geneva,* p. 49; Philip Broadhead, "Politics and Expediency in the Augsburg Reformation," in Brooks, *Reformation Principle and Practice,* p. 81; and Alice C. Carter, "Survey of Recent Historical Works on Belgium and the Netherlands Published in Dutch," *Acta Historicae Neerlandica* 8 (1975), 159–200. Throughout most of central Europe the cities were well-represented in parliamentary bodies; Carsten, *Princes and Parliaments.* This was especially true in the Low Coun-

tries. Here the States General had grown out of representative assemblies called for the purpose of regulating trade and were made up almost totally of representatives from the towns; see H. G. Koenigsberger, "Crown and Estates in the Low Countries," in *The "New Monarchies" and Representative Assemblies: Medieval Constitutionalism or Modern Absolutism?* ed. Arthur L. Slavin (Boston: D. C. Heath, 1964), pp. 37–42.

17. Useful background on the political and economic circumstances of the Reformation in Württemberg is given in David Warren Sabean, *Power in the Blood: Popular Culture and Village Discourse in Early Modern Germany* (Cambridge: Cambridge University Press, 1984), esp. pp. 4–7; see also James Martin Estes, *Christian Magistrate and State Church: The Reforming Career of Johannes Brenz* (Toronto: University of Toronto Press, 1982), esp. pp. 10–13, 60–61.

18. Income and activities of the territorial princes are discussed in John U. Nef, "Mining and Metallurgy in Medieval Civilisation," in *The Cambridge Economic History of Europe,* vol. 2, *Trade and Industry in the Middle Ages,* ed. M. M. Postan and E. E. Rich (Cambridge: Cambridge University Press, 1952), pp. 430–493; Henry J. Cohn, *The Government of the Rhine Palatinate in the Fifteenth Century* (Oxford: Oxford University Press, 1965); Benjamin R. Barber, *The Death of Communal Liberty: A History of Freedom in a Swiss Mountain Canton* (Princeton: Princeton University Press, 1974); and Brenner, "Agrarian Class Structure and Economic Development," 30–75. Revenue from mining was particularly important in Saxony. Silver production from the Marienberg and Saigerhutten mines doubled in volume during the first half of the sixteenth century; see John U. Nef, "Silver Production in Central Europe, 1450–1618," *Journal of Political Economy* 49 (1941), 575–591; and E. Westermann, *Das Eislebener Garkupfer und seine Bedeutung für den europaischen Kupfermarkt, 1460–1560* (Cologne: Greven-Verlag, 1971), p. 287. With these revenues the dukes of Saxony significantly expanded their land-holdings; see Carsten, *Princes and Parliaments,* pp. 191–196. About two-thirds of their entire income came from mining.

19. Helen P. Liebel, "The Bourgeoisie in Southwestern Germany, 1500–1789: A Rising Class?" *International Review for Social History* 10 (1965), 283–307.

20. Hermann Kellenbenz, "Rural Industries in the West from the End of the Middle Ages to the Eighteenth Century," in *Essays in European Economic History, 1500–1800,* ed. Peter Earle (Oxford: Clarendon Press, 1974), p. 58. Some question exists, however, concerning the effectiveness of these restrictions; see Jerome Blum, "The European Village as Community: Origins and Functions," *Agricultural History* 45 (1971), 175.

21. See Holborn, *A History of Modern Germany,* p. 59; and Eberhard Weis, "Ergebnisse eines Vergleichs de grundherrschaftlichen Strukturen Deutschlands und Frankreiches vom 13. bis zum Ausgang des 18. Jahr-

hundrets," *Vierteljahrschrift für Sozial- und Wirtschaftsgeschichte* 57 (1970), 1–14. Weis indicates that free tenancy also expanded to a much larger extent by the end of the sixteenth century. Relations between nobles and peasants were particularly weak in Saxony and in several of the Swiss cantons; see Jerome Blum, *The End of the Old Order in Rural Europe* (Princeton: Princeton University Press, 1978), pp. 29–39. The princes were partly responsible for protecting the peasants' rights against the nobles; see Carsten, *Princes and Parliaments,* p. 195.

22. Soly, "The 'Betrayal' of the Sixteenth-Century Bourgeoisie"; also H. Van Werveke, "The Rise of the Towns," in *The Cambridge Economic History of Europe,* vol. 3, *Economic Organization and Policies in the Middle Ages,* ed. E. E. Rich and Edward Miller (Cambridge: Cambridge University Press, 1963), pp. 3–41. Carsten, *Princes and Parliaments,* p. 195, suggests that the merchants drove up the price of land and squeezed many of the lesser nobility out of the land market.

23. Thomas A Brady, Jr., *Ruling Class, Regime, and Reformation at Strasbourg, 1520–1555* (Leiden: E. J. Brill, 1978), p. 44; also see Francis Rapp, "Die soziale und wirtschaftliche Vorgeschichte des Bauernkrieges im Unterclass," in *Bauernkriegs-Studien,* no. 189, Bernd Moeller (Gutersloh: Schriften des Vereins fur Reformationsgeschichte, 1975), pp. 29–45.

24. Evidence on the decline of the lower nobility is given in Hermann Van der Wee, "Prices and Wages as Development Variables: A Comparison between England and the Southern Netherlands, 1400–1700," *Acta Historiae Neerlandicae* 10 (1978), 58–78; Jan DeVries, *The Dutch Rural Economy in the Golden Age, 1500–1700* (New Haven: Yale University Press, 1974), p. 38; Geoffrey Barraclough, *The Origins of Modern Germany,* 2d ed. (Oxford: Basil Blackwell, 1947), pp. 336–337; and Aubin, "Medieval Agrarian Society in Its Prime."

25. A particularly valuable source on the tensions between towns and the nobility is Brady, *Turning Swiss,* esp. pp. 8–15, 127–133.

26. Bernd Moeller, "Religious Life in Germany on the Eve of the Reformation," in Straus, *Pre-Reformation Germany,* p. 41. Cologne was one of the imperial cities that did not adopt the Reformation, apparently in part because of an absence of political autonomy: "For all its claims to freedom, Cologne was by no means autonomous"; Robert W. Scribner, "Why Was There No Reformation in Cologne?" *Bulletin of the Institute of Historical Research* 49 (1976), 221.

27. Manfred Hannemann, *The Diffusion of the Reformation in Southwestern Germany, 1518–1534* (Chicago: Chicago University Press, 1975), p. 70.

28. Van Werveke, "The Rise of the Towns," pp. 30–31.

29. Hannemann, *The Diffusion of the Reformation,* pp. 37–41. Part of this relation was, of course, attributable to the larger cities' closer integration into trading and communication networks.

30. Williams, *The Radical Reformation,* pp. 342–360; Aldo de Maddalena, "Rural Europe, 1500–1750," in *The Fontana Economic History of Europe: The Sixteenth and Seventeenth Centuries,* ed. Carlo M. Cipolla (Glasgow: William Collins Sons, 1974), p. 296; L. G. Rogier, "De Protestantisering van het Noorden," in *Algemeene Geschiedenis der Nederlanden,* vol. 5, ed. J. A. Van Houtte et al. (Utrecht: Gent en Leuven, 1952), p. 328; Jan Juliaan Woltjer, "Stadt und Reformation in den Niederlanden," in *Kirche und gesellschaftlicher Wandel in deutschen und niederländischen Städten der werdenden Neuzeut,* ed. Franz Petri (Cologne: Böhlau Verlag, 1980), pp. 155–167.

31. DeVries, *The Dutch Rural Economy,* pp. 25–41; C. A. J. Armstrong, "Had the Burgundian Government a Policy for the Nobility?" in *Britain and the Netherlands,* vol. 2, *Papers Delivered to the Anglo-Dutch Historical Conference, Utrecht and Amsterdam, 1962,* ed. J. S. Bromley and E. H. Kossmann (Groningen: J. B. Wolters, 1964), pp. 9–10.

32. Norman Birnbaum, "The Zwinglian Reformation in Zurich," *Past and Present* 15 (1959), 27–47; Barber, *The Death of Communal Liberty.*

33. One of the most useful sources on the Reformation in Basel is Hans R. Guggisberg, *Basel in the Sixteenth Century: Aspects of the City Republic before, during, and after the Reformation* (St. Louis: Center for Reformation Research, 1982).

34. William Martin, *Switzerland from Roman Times to the Present* (New York: Praeger, 1971), pp. 81–84.

35. Gerald Strauss, "Protestant Dogma and City Government: The Case of Nuremberg," *Past and Present* 36 (1967), 38–58; Gottfried Seebass, "The Reformation in Nürnberg," in *The Social History of the Reformation,* ed. Lawrence P. Buck and Jonathan W. Zophy (Columbus: Ohio State University Press, 1972), pp. 17–40; Jackson Spielvogel, "Patricians in Dissension: A Case Study from Sixteenth-Century Nürnberg," in Buck and Zophy, *The Social History of the Reformation,* pp. 73–92.

36. Strauss, *Nuremberg in the Sixteenth Century,* pp. 172–173; Thomas F. Sea, "Imperial Cities and the Peasants' War in Germany," *Central European History* 12 (1979), 3–37, makes a similar point concerning other cities.

37. Chrisman, *Strasbourg and the Reform,* pp. 93–97; Brady, *Ruling Class, Regime, and Reformation.*

38. Lorna Jane Abray, *The People's Reformation: Magistrates, Clergy, and Commons in Strasbourg, 1500–1598* (Ithaca: Cornell University Press, 1985).

39. Monter, *Calvin's Geneva,* p. 44.

40. Soly, "The 'Betrayal' of the Sixteenth-Century Bourgeoisie," pp. 46–49.

41. A. C. F. Koch, "The Reformation at Deventer in 1579–1580: Size and Social Structure of the Catholic Section of the Population during the Religious Peace," *Acta Historiae Neerlandicae* 6 (1973), 50.

42. A. G. Dickens, *The German Nation and Martin Luther* (London: Edward Arnold, 1974), pp. 169–174; Scribner, "Civic Unity and the Reformation in Erfurt," pp. 29–60; Williams, *The Radical Reformation,* p. 87.

43. Franz Lau, "Der Bauernkrieg und das angebliche Ende der lutherischen Reformation als spontaner Volksbewegung," *Luther Jahrbuch* 26 (1959), 109–134; Suzanne Ritter, *Die kirchenkritische Tendenz in den deutschsprachigen Flugschriften der fruhen Reformationszeit* (Tübingen: Weidlich, 1970).

44. Steven E. Ozment, *The Reformation in the Cities: The Appeal of Protestantism to Sixteenth-Century Germany and Switzerland* (New Haven: Yale University Press, 1975), p. 131. Often the protection given was passive, however; reformers were tolerated but not actively supported for fear of evoking external intervention in the cities' affairs. For an example, see Hans-Christoph Rublack, "Nördlingen zwischen Kaiser und Reformation," *Archiv für Reformationsgeschichte* 71 (1980), 113–133. In the Nördlingen case the main threat to the city's autonomy was the emperor; in other cases, especially where unrest among the peasantry was likely, it was associated directly with the nobility. For example, see Hans-Christian Rublack, "Die Stadt Würzburg im Bauernkrieg," *Archiv für Reformationsgeschichte* 67 (1976), 76–100; Müller, *Reformation und Stadt,* pp. 19–35.

45. At the Nuremberg Diet in 1522, for example, the rate assessed against the nobility was 1 percent of income, while that against towns was 1 percent of total assets; see Brady, *Turning Swiss,* p. 130.

46. R. Po-chia Hsia, *Society and Religion in Münster, 1535–1618* (New Haven: Yale University Press, 1984), p. 44.

47. Tom Scott, *Freiburg and the Briesgau: Town-Country Relations in the Age of Reformation and Peasants' War* (Oxford: Clarendon Pres, 1986), p. 62.

48. Ibid., p. 196.

49. Ibid., pp. 198–199.

50. G. R. Elton, *Reformation Europe, 1517–1559* (New York: Harper and Row, 1963), p. 61.

51. Fritz Hartung, "Imperial Reform, 1485–1495: Its Course and Its Character," in Strauss, *Pre-Reformation Germany,* pp. 73–135; Steven Rowan, "Imperial Taxes and German Politics in the Fifteenth Century," *Central European History* 13 (1980), 203–217.

52. For a discussion of the Council of Regency, see Bornkamm, *Luther in Mid-Career,* pp. 295–309.

53. Heimpel, "Characteristics of the Late Middle Ages in Germany," p. 52.

54. Hans-Stephan Brather, "Administrative Reforms in Electoral Saxony at the End of the Fifteenth Century," in Strauss, *Pre-Reformation Germany,* pp. 225–262. Carsten, *Princes and Parliaments,* p. 201, observes that

the power of the nobility in relation to the dukes of Saxony had deteriorated substantially by the end of the fifteenth century.

55. Alton O. Hancock, "Philipp of Hesse's View of the Relationship of Prince and Church," *Church History* 35 (1966), 168; J. C. Stalnaker, "Anabaptism, Martin Bucer, and the Shaping of the Hessian Protestant Church," *Journal of Modern History* 48 (1976), 601–643; Hastings Eells, *The Attitude of Martin Bucer toward the Bigamy of Philipp of Hesse* (New Haven: Yale University Press, 1924), pp. 44–57. Hans J. Hillerbrand, *Landgrave Philipp of Hesse, 1504–1567: Religion and Politics in the Reformation* (St. Louis: Foundation for Reformation Research, 1967), p. 1, suggests that "without Philipp Luther's cause may well have tumbled like a house of cards." Carsten, *Princes and Parliaments,* pp. 150–172, concludes that the central regime in Hesse was able to exert autonomous influence over the nobility, relying on its own military strength, administrative and financial support from the towns, and weaknesses within the nobility from factionalism. By the time Landgrave Philipp introduced the Reformation in 1527, the power of the nobility had been effectively curbed.

56. Estes, *Christian Magistrate and State Church,* pp. 10–11, emphasizes the role of Hesse in advancing the Reformation in Württemburg.

57. Useful material on the social conditions surrounding the Reformation in the Electoral Palatinate is presented in Volker Press, "Stadt und territoriale Konfessionsbildung," in Petri, *Kirche und gesellschaftlicher Wandel in deutschen und niederländischen Städten der werdenden Neuzeut,* esp. pp. 250–265.

58. Peter Blickle, *The Revolution of 1525* (Baltimore: Johns Hopkins University Press, 1981), esp. pp. 78–81, has emphasized the conflicts present in general between territorial princes and local nobility because the two competed within fairly narrow limits for tax revenues from peasants. His analysis also indicates that rising tax demands constituted one of the principal reasons for peasant uprisings. To the extent that this analysis is correct, it suggests yet another advantage that princes with relatively autonomous incomes may have enjoyed in supporting the Reformation: they could do so, even to the point of supplying military aid, without fear of precipitating peasant unrest. Blickle observes: "Any growth in the chancery or cameral revenues of the prince also served peasant interests [for it] was an indispensable prerequisite to lowering the territorial tax burden" (p. 80).

59. In considering the role of the territorial princes one should note, however, that princely politics remained sufficiently subject to the influences of personal background and patronage networks that territorial size and economic interests alone did not dictate religious leanings. Duke George of Albertine Saxony, for example, proved to be one of the Reformation's staunchest opponents and engaged Luther personally in an ongoing battle of theological wits despite landownings and economic resources

similar in size and composition to those of his cousin, John of Saxony. An explanation of Duke George's religious inclinations can be found only by looking more deeply at the political rivalries that had developed between him and his cousin, at the legacy of family obligations to the emperor that he had inherited from his father, and the intensity of his own religious training. These kinds of factors meant that the Reformation in central Europe gained only partial territorial support, and as a result became increasingly embroiled in the political struggles that dominated the region during the following century.

60. It is illustrative of the salience of the emperor to contemporary minds that when in April 1525 Philipp of Hesse wrote of his conversion to his mother, she responded with concern about how the emperor might react to the news; see Hancock, "Philipp of Hesse's View," p. 162. Hesse's own power vis-à-vis the emperor, however, was sufficiently strong that he went farther even than Luther in maintaining his right to resist the emperor, given the emperor's dependence on him and the other German princes for his election and for financial support; on these relations, I am indebted to George W. Grubb, "Landgrave Philipp of Hesse: Politics, Religion, and Moral Order" (Department of Sociology, Princeton University, 1980).

61. For a discussion of the relations between Charles V and the German princes, see Steven Ozment, *The Age of Reform, 1250–1550: An Intellectual and Religious History of Late Medieval and Reformation Europe* (New Haven: Yale University Press, 1980), pp. 245–260.

62. Valuable information on northern Europe during this period is found in N. K. Andersen, "The Reformation in Scandinavia and the Baltic," in *The New Cambridge Modern History*, vol. 2, *The Reformation, 1520–1559*, ed. G. R. Elton (Cambridge: Cambridge University Press, 1958), pp. 134–160; Carl Ingvar Andersson, *History of Sweden* (London: Geroge Allen and Unwin, 1956), pp. 120–131; Carl Ingvar Andersson, "Sweden and the Baltic," in *The New Cambridge Modern History*, vol. 3, *The Counter-Reformation and Price Revolution, 1559–1610*, ed. R. B. Wernham (Cambridge: Cambridge University Press, 1968), pp. 404–426; Thomas Riis, "Towns and Central Government in Northern Europe from the Fifteenth Century to the Industrial Revolution," *Scandinavian Economic History Review* 29 (1981), 33–52; and Michael Roberts, *The Early Vasas: A History of Sweden, 1523–1611* (Cambridge: Cambridge University Press, 1968).

63. These figures are reported in Antoni Maczak, "The Structure of Power in the Commonwealth of the Sixteenth and Seventeenth Centuries," in *A Republic of Nobles: Studies in Polish History to 1864*, ed. J. K. Federowicz, Maria Bogucka, and Henryk Samsonowicz (Cambridge: Cambridge University Press, 1982), pp. 109–134.

64. In addition to the aforementioned, useful sources on the Scandinavian Reformation include E. H. Dunkley, *The Reformation in Denmark*

(London: S.P.C.K., 1948), and Conrad Bergendoff, *Olavus Petri and the Ecclesiastical Transformation in Sweden, 1521–1552: A Study in the Swedish Reformation* (Philadelphia: Fortress Press, 1965).

65. Dickens, *The German Nation*, pp. 163–165; Wilson King, *German Free Cities: Hamburg, Bremen, Lübeck* (New York: E. P. Dutton, 1914).

66. Martin S. Lausten, "König Christian III von Dänemark und die deutschen Reformatoren: 32 ungedruckte Briefe," *Archiv für Reformationsgeschichte* 66 (1975), 151–182; Martin S. Lausten, "Johann Bugenhagen und die Treptower Vitte in Dragor: Ein ungedruckte Brief Bugenhagens," *Hansische Geschichtsblätter* 86 (1968), 80–84; see also Dunkley, *The Reformation in Denmark*, pp. 13–98; Guy E. Swanson, *Religion and Regime: A Sociological Account of the Reformation* (Ann Arbor: University of Michigan Press, 1967), pp. 122–129.

67. Andersen, "The Reformation in Scandinavia and the Baltic," p. 140; Kenneth Scott Latourette, *A History of Christianity*, vol. 2, *Reformation to the Present*, rev. ed. (New York: Harper and Row, 1975), p. 735.

68. Oskar Garstein, "The Reformation in Norway," *The Month* 21 (1959), 95–103; H. Rieber-Mohn, "Catholicism in Norway since the Reformation," *The Month* 21 (1959), 104–113.

69. H. G. Koenigsberger and George L. Mosse, *Europe in the Sixteenth Century* (London: Longman, 1968), pp. 219–220; Bergendoff, *Olavus Petri*, pp. 1–61.

70. Owen Chadwick, *The Reformation* (Baltimore: Penguin Books, 1972), p. 384.

71. Roberts, *The Early Vasas*, pp. 171–173.

72. Roland H. Bainton, *The Age of the Reformation* (Princeton: D. Van Nostrand, 1956), p. 158; Bergendoff, *Olavus Petri*, p. 225.

73. Roberts, *The Early Vasas*, p. 172; see also John Wordsworth, *The National Church of Sweden* (London: Longmans, 1911); Eric Yelverton, *An Archbishop of the Reformation* (London: Longmans, 1958).

74. G. R. Elton, "The Reformation in England," in *The New Cambridge Modern History*, vol. 2, p. 226.

75. T. M. Parker, *The English Reformation to 1558*, 2d ed. (Oxford: Oxford University Press, 1966), p. 47.

76. Claire Cross, *Church and People, 1450–1660: The Triumph of the Laity in the English Church* (Atlantic Highlands, N.J.: Humanities Press, 1976), p. 53; also see Arthur Joseph Slavin, *The Precarious Balance: English Government and Society* (New York: Knopf, 1973), pp. 117–152; and A. G. Dickens, *The English Reformation* (New York: Schocken, 1964). Viewing the Reformation from below, another writer concludes that "English men and women did not want the Reformation and most of them were slow to accept it when it came." In this writer's opinion, the English Reformation "was in only a limited sense popular and 'below.' " See J. J. Scarisbrick, *The

Reformation and the English People (London: Basil Blackwell, 1984), p. 1.

77. J. Cornwall, "The English Population in the Early Sixteenth Century," *Economic History Review* 23 (1970), 32–44, gives estimates of 2.3 million in 1525 and 3.8 million in 1603; also see David Grigg, *Population Growth and Agrarian Change: An Historical Perspective* (Cambridge: Cambridge University Press, 1980), p. 55.

78. M. M. Postan, *Medieval Trade and Finance* (Cambridge: Cambridge University Press, 1973), p. 162.

79. Peter Bowden, *The Wool Trade in Tudor and Stuart England* (London: Macmillan, 1962); J. H. Parry, "Transport and Trade Routes," in *The Cambridge Economic History of Europe*, vol. 4, *The Economy of Expanding Europe in the Sixteenth and Seventeenth Centuries*, ed. E. E. Rich and C. H. Wilson (Cambridge: Cambridge University Press, 1967), pp. 155–222; F. J. Fisher, "Commercial Trends and Policy in Sixteenth-Century England," in *Essays in Economic History*, vol. 1, ed. E. M. Carus-Wilson (London: Edward Arnold, 1954), p. 153. A. R. Bridbury, *Economic Growth: England in the Later Middle Ages* (London: George Allen and Unwin, 1962), p. 32, documents sizable growth during the last quarter of the fifteenth century as well. Also significant is the fact that about nine-tenths of these exports consisted of manufactured cloth, unlike the situation in Spain, whose involvement in the cloth trade consisted mainly of raw wool exports; see Peter Ramsey, *Tudor Economic Problems* (London: Gollancz, 1965), p. 48.

80. Frederick C. Dietz, *English Government Finance, 1485–1558* (London: Frank Cass, 1964); Postan, *Medieval Trade and Finance*, pp. 214–218.

81. F. V. Emery, "England circa 1600," in *A New Historical Geography of England*, ed. H. C. Darby (Cambridge: Cambridge University Press, 1973), pp. 293–301. About 88 percent of the cloth trade passed through London; see Ramsey, *Tudor Economic Problems*, p. 53.

82. A. R. Myers, *England in the Late Middle Ages*, 8th ed. (Baltimore: Penguin, 1971), p. 206; Ramsey, *Tudor Economic Problems*, p. 55, remarks that "Tudor despotism consisted in London's dominance over the rest of the country." Perez Zagorin, *Rebels and Rulers, 1500–1660*, 2 vols. (Cambridge: Cambridge University Press, 1982), p. 72, notes that London's magistracy was far more independent of the nobility than were the urban magistracies in Spain and France.

83. Penry Williams, *The Tudor Regime* (Oxford: Clarendon Press, 1979), p. 450. During the fifteenth century these merchants had also begun to loan substantial sums to the crown; see Caroline M. Barron, "London and the Crown, 1451–61," in *The Crown and Local Communities in England and France in the Fifteenth Century*, ed. J. R. L. Highfield and Robin Jefts (Gloucester: Alan Sutton, 1981), pp. 88–109.

84. Gordon Batho, "Landlords in England: The Crown," in *The Agrarian History of England and Wales*, vol. 4, *1500–1640*, ed. Joan Thirsk (Cam-

bridge: Cambridge University Press, 1967), p. 257; B. P. Wolffe, "Henry VII's Landed Revenues," *Economic History Review* 79 (1964), 253–264; B. P. Wolffe, *The Crown Lands, 1461–1536* (London: George Allen and Unwin, 1970).

85. Williams, *The Tudor Regime,* p. 58; Slavin, *The Precarious Balance,* pp. 98–103; J. D. Alsop, "The Theory and Practice of Tudor Taxation," *English Historical Review* 97 (1982), 1–30.

86. G. R. Elton, *The Tudor Revolution in Government: Administrative Changes in the Reign of Henry VIII* (Cambridge: Cambridge University Press, 1953), pp. 33–34.

87. H. Miller, "London and Parliament in the Reign of Henry VIII," in *Historical Studies of the English Parliament,* vol. 2, *1399–1603,* ed. E. B. Fryde and Edward Miller (Cambridge: Cambridge University Press, 1970), pp. 125–146.

88. Stanford E. Lehmberg, *The Reformation Parliament, 1529–1536* (Cambridge: Cambridge University Press, 1970).

89. Lehmberg's conclusions regarding the relative weight of landowners and burgesses in the Reformation Parliament must be qualified to some extent, of course, because some of the towns returned members of the landed gentry to Parliament. J. E. Neale, *The Elizabethan House of Commons* (Cambridge: Cambridge University Press, 1949), p. 155, for instance, cites some examples of the problems small boroughs faced in maintaining burgesses at Parliament unless a member of the gentry was sent who could pay his own expenses. A detailed examination of the burgesses returned from Suffolk county, however, reveals that a substantial majority were either "true burgesses" (i.e. principal residents of the towns) or men elected because of close ties to London, whereas only a minority were local gentry whose power depended primarily on networks of influence in the countryside; moreover, the proportion of true burgesses was considerably higher during the first half of the sixteenth century than it was by the end of the century; see Diarmaid MacCulloch, *Suffolk and the Tudors: Politics and Religion in an English County, 1500–1600* (Oxford: Clarendon Press, 1986), pp. 46–47, 422–423.

90. M. E. James, "Obedience and Dissent in Henrician England: The Lincolnshire Rebellion, 1536," *Past and Present* 48 (1970), 70. The view that the English monarchy was in fact subordinate to Parliament has been defended by William Huse Dunham, Jr., and Charles T. Wood, "The Right to Rule in England: Depositions and the Kingdom's Authority, 1327–1485," *American Historical Review* 81 (1976), 738–761; but this view has been shown to have little merit by J. W. McKenna, "The Myth of Parliamentary Sovereignty in Late-Medieval England," *English Historical Review* 94 (1979), 481–506.

91. Williams, *The Tudor Regime,* pp. 407–420.

92. Peter Clark, *English Provincial Society from the Reformation to the Revolution: Religion, Politics, and Society in Kent, 1500–1640* (Sussex: Harvester Press, 1977), pp. 19–20; Williams, *The Tudor Regime*, pp. 462–463.

93. MacCulloch, *Suffolk and the Tudors*, pp. 68–76, cites a number of instances in which members of the nobility were moved "like chess pieces" and local patrimonies were dismantled.

94. Clark, *English Provincial Society*, p. 17; Williams, *The Tudor Regime*, pp. 381–382.

95. G. R. Elton, *Policy and Police: The Enforcement of the Reformation in the Age of Thomas Cromwell* (Cambridge: Cambridge University Press, 1972).

96. I have benefited from a useful survey of the relevant literature by Richard Lachmann, "Local Elite Structure and State Formation in Sixteenth- and Seventeenth-Century England and France" (Department of Sociology, University of Wisconsin, Madison, 1984); for a thorough study of the relations between landowners and the crown in one locality, see MacCulloch, *Suffolk and the Tudors*, pp. 53–82.

97. Elton, "The Reformation in England," p. 229. Other useful sources include Felicity Heal, *Of Prelates and Princes: A Study of the Economic and Social Position of the Tudor Episcopate* (Cambridge: Cambridge University Press, 1980), and Lacey Baldwin Smith, *Tudor Prelates and Politics, 1536–1558* (Princeton: Princeton University Press, 1953).

98. David Birch, *Early Reformation English Polemics* (Salzburg: Institute für Anglistik und Amerikanistik, 1983), pp. 37–58. Although the role of the state in implementing the English Reformation has been debated by a long line of historians, this work has until recently focused on the personal efforts of Henry VIII and his leading ministers rather than considering the state as an institution embedded in a larger matrix of social constraints. A recent review of this literature suggests that even its most notable contributors adhere to "the view that the course of events was determined by the will of people in high places," and the author of this review bluntly asserts that these contributors display "little or no understanding of the interaction of socio-economic and religious factors with the world of politics." Rosemary O'Day, *The Debate on the English Reformation* (London: Methuen, 1986), p. 131.

99. John N. King, *English Reformation Literature: The Tudor Origins of the Protestant Tradition* (Princeton: Princeton University Press, 1982), pp. 76–121.

100. The exception, beginning with the reign of Henry VII, was that several prominent writers of chivalric prose in the Burgundian style had been attached to the royal household; see Gordon Kipling, "Henry VII and the Origins of Tudor Patronage," in *Patronage in the Renaissance*, ed. Guy Fitch Lytle and Stephen Orgel (Princeton: Princeton University Press, 1981), pp. 117–164.

101. Ibid., pp. 48–49.

102. A. G. Dickens, "Heresy and the Origins of English Protestant-ism," in Bromley and Kossmann, *Britain and the Netherlands,* vol. 2, p. 64.

103. Lehmberg, *The Reformation Parliament.*

104. Miller, "London and Parliament in the Reign of Henry VIII," points out that the cities did not succeed in getting their way in Parliament on all the issues they introduced, but they had by this time developed an effective means of advancing legislative proposals at the local level and bringing them before Parliament.

105. Lehmberg, *The Reformation Parliament,* pp. 81–82; Christopher Haigh, "Anticlericalism and the English Reformation," in *The English Reformation Revised* (Cambridge: Cambridge University Press, 1987), p. 60, notes conflict between the London Mercers' Company and the church over "war taxation, trading privileges and the . . . disruption of the cloth trade."

106. D. M. Palliser, *Tudor York* (Oxford: Oxford University Press, 1979), pp. 233–234, suggests that York was relatively less affected by the Reformation than towns to the south, but notes that "orthodox citizens had a viewpoint which in certain respects can only be called Erastian or anti-clerical, and . . . must have smoothed the path of at least some of the Reformation changes."

107. Clark, *English Provincial Society,* p. 40.

108. Claire Cross, "Priests into Ministers: The Establishment of Protestant Practice in the City of York, 1530–1630," in Brooks, *Reformation Principle and Practice,* p. 210.

109. Roger B. Manning, *Religion and Society in Elizabethan Sussex: A Study of the Enforcement of the Religious Settlement, 1558–1603* (Leicester: Leicester University Press, 1969), p. 243; also see Parker, *The English Reformation,* p. 19.

110. Susan Brigden, "Tithe Controversy in Reformation London," *Journal of Ecclesiastical History* 32 (1981), 285–301.

111. James, "Obedience and Dissent," p. 70.

112. MacCulloch, *Suffolk and the Tudors,* p. 129.

113. Cross, *Church and People,* p. 83; M. H. Dodds and R. Dodds, *The Pilgrimage of Grace and the Exeter Conspiracy* (Cambridge: Cambridge University Press, 1915); A. G. Dickens, "Religious and Secular Motivation in the Pilgrimage of Grace," *Studies in Church History* 4 (1968), 39–54; C. S. L. Davies, "The Pilgrimage of Grace Reconsidered," *Past and Present* 41 (1968), 54–76; James, "Obedience and Dissent,"; Dickens, *The English Reformation,* pp. 122–128.

114. The conflict between central government and local forces is sum-marized by Haigh, "Anticlericalism and the English Reformation," p. 72, who writes: "From the point of view of the parishes, the Reformation was an external, autonomous event, which they had in no sense chosen, caused or contributed towards."

115. Margaret Bowker, *The Henrician Reformation: The Diocese of Lincoln under John Longland, 1521–1547* (Cambridge: Cambridge University Press, 1982), p. 147; Clark, *English Provincial Society*; David G. Hey, *An English Rural Community: Myddle under the Tudors and Stuarts* (Leicester: Leicester University Press, 1974); James E. Oxley, *The Reformation in Essex to the Death of Mary* (Manchester: Manchester University Press, 1965); Christopher Haigh, *Reformation and Resistance in Tudor Lancashire* (Cambridge: Cambridge University Press, 1975), esp. pp. 98–117; Ronald Hutton, "The Local Impact of the Tudor Reformations," in *The English Reformation Revised,* ed. Christopher Haigh (Cambridge: Cambridge University Press, 1987), pp. 114–138.

116. James, "Obedience and Dissent," pp. 51–52. Elton, *Policy and Police,* pp. 384–425, also credits the crown's use of treason proceedings and its police power with a strong role in enforcing the Reformation.

3. The Failure of Reformation

1. Maria Bogucka, "Towns in Poland and the Reformation: Analogies and Differences with Other Countries," *Acta Poloniae Historica* 40 (1979), 55–74.

2. Aleksander Gieysztor et al., *History of Poland* (Warsaw: Polish Scientific Publishers, 1968), p. 186.

3. Marceli Kosman, "Programme of the Reformation in the Grand Duchy of Lithuania and How It Was Carried Through," *Acta Poloniae Historica* 35 (1977), 21–50.

4. Aleksander Bruckner, "The Polish Reformation in the Sixteenth Century," in *Polish Civilization: Essays and Studies,* ed. Mieczyslaw Giergielewicz (New York: New York University Press, 1979), pp. 68–87.

5. For a general discussion of the history of this migration, see Geoffrey Barraclough, *The Origins of Modern Germany,* 2d ed. (Oxford: Basil Blackwell, 1947).

6. Walther Hubatsch, "Albert of Brandenburg-Ansbach, Grand Master of the Order of Teutonic Knights and Duke in Prussia, 1490–1568," in *Government in Reformation Europe, 1520–1560,* ed. Henry J. Cohn (New York: Macmillan, 1971), pp. 169–202. In Ducal Prussia Albert of Brandenburg retained virtual autonomy over matters of trade, taxation, and jurisdiction. The influence of Catholicism, which had been strong under the Order of Teutonic Knights in the fifteenth century, had waned as that order declined; folk religious customs indigenous to the peasants themselves, over which the landlords had little control, such as the sacrificial feasts observed in reverence to the "goat divinity," had become widespread; and some of the landlords, including Duke Albert, saw Protestantism as a means of recovering control over the religious life of the area, particularly in view of the fact that popular unrest appears to have included demands

for religious reform. Karol Gorski, "The Royal Prussian Estates in the Second half of the XVth Century and Their Relation to the Crown of Poland," *Acta Poloniae Historica* 10 (1964), 64, concludes: "Great discontent of the masses . . . disquieted life in Prussia for a quarter of the century (1493–1517). The new generation was to link this discontent with the Reformation movement." In short, Ducal Prussia resembled Saxony and Hesse to the west to a somewhat greater extent in both political and religious affairs than it did the rest of eastern Europe.

7. Janusz Tazbir, "The Fate of Polish Protestantism in the Seventeenth Century," in *A Republic of Nobles: Studies in Polish History to 1864,* ed. J. K. Fedorowicz, Maria Bogucka, and Henryk Samsonowicz (Cambridge: Cambridge University Press, 1982), pp. 198–217; Stanislaw Grzybowski, "The Gentry and the Beginnings of Colonization," in *Poland at the 14th International Congress of Historical Sciences in San Francisco* (Warsaw: Polish Academy of Sciences, Institute of History, 1975), pp. 24–43.

8. Kosman, "Programme of the Reformation," and Bruckner, "The Polish Reformation," mention the existence of 208 Protestant chapels in Lithuania in the 1550s, mostly Calvinistic in orientation. Catholicism's difficulties here were exacerbated by resistance from some of the landlords who refused to build churches in their private towns for fear of losing control over local affairs; see Tazbir, "The Fate of Polish Protestantism," p. 204.

9. Gieysztor et al., *History of Poland,* pp. 171–174.

10. Bruckner, "The Polish Reformation," pp. 73–74.

11. Gieysztor et al., *History of Poland,* p. 186.

12. Jerzy Topolski, "The Manorial-Serf Economy in Central and Eastern Europe in the 16th and 17th Centuries," *Agricultural History* 48 (1974), 341–352, emphasizes these factors in his account of the economic development of eastern Europe.

13. These estimates are given in Marian Malowist, "The Economic and Social Development of the Baltic Countries from the Fifteenth to the Seventeenth Centuries," *Economic History Review* 12 (1959), 177–189; see also Malowist, "Poland, Russia, and Western Trade in the 15th and 16th Centuries," *Past and Present* 13 (1958), 28. Jerzy Topolski, "Continuity and Discontinuity in the Development of the Feudal System in Eastern Europe (Xth to XVIIth Centuries)," *Journal of European Economic History* 10 (1981), 391, estimates that only about 2.5 percent of all Polish grain produced during the second half of the sixteenth century was exported; nevertheless, he suggests that the profits from these exports were of great marginal value to the economic well-being of the nobility.

14. These flows are discussed in Kristof Glamann, "The Changing Patterns of Trade," in *The Cambridge Economic History of Europe,* vol. 5, *The Economic Organization of Early Modern Europe,* ed. E. E. Rich and C. H.

Wilson (Cambridge: Cambridge University Press, 1977), esp. pp. 262–264. Discussions of the Polish nobility's positive trade balance are also found in Malowist, "Poland, Russia, and Western Trade," and Malowist, "The Economic and Social Development of the Baltic Countries."

15. See Topolski, "The Manorial-Serf Economy," p. 348. Malowist, "The Economic and Social Development of the Baltic Countries," p. 184, estimates that nearly 80 percent of the rye imported by sea to Amsterdam came from Gdansk.

16. Population estimates for Poland are reported in Roger Mols, "Population in Europe," in *The Fontana Economic History of Europe: The Sixteenth and Seventeenth Centuries,* ed. Carlo M. Cipolla (Glasgow: William Collins Sons, 1974), p. 38; Topolski, "Continuity and Discontinuity," p. 384, and Irena Gieysztorowa, "Research into the Demographic History of Poland: A Provisional Summing-Up," *Acta Poloniae Historica* 18 (1968), 5–17.

17. R. R. Betts, "Constitutional Development and Political Thought in Eastern Europe," in *The New Cambridge Modern History,* vol. 2, *The Reformation, 1520–1559,* ed. G. R. Elton (Cambridge: Cambridge University Press, 1958), p. 465, writes: "What gives to this part of sixteenth-century Europe its homogeneity is the great economic supremacy that was enjoyed and exploited there by the landowners, who, however large or small their estates, were nobles."

18. See especially Antoni Maczak, "Export of Grain and the Problem of Distribution of National Income in the Years 1550–1650," *Acta Poloniae Historica* 18 (1968), 75–98; and Antoni Maczak, "The Social Distribution of Landed Property in Poland from the Sixteenth to the Eighteenth Centuries," *Third International Conference of Economic History* 1 (1968), 455–469.

19. This figure is reported in Z. P. Pach, "The Development of Feudal Rent in Hungary in the Fifteenth Century," *Economic History Review* 19 (1966), 1; see also Z. P. Pach, "Sixteenth-Century Hungary: Commercial Activity and Market Production by the Nobles," in *Economy and Society in Early Modern Europe,* ed. Peter Earle (New York: Harper and Row, 1972), pp. 113–133; and Denis Sinor, *History of Hungary* (New York: Praeger, 1959). While the course of economic development in Hungary was different from that in Poland, the landed elite in Hungary was able to retain supremacy for much the same reasons that it did in Poland: "(i) accumulation by the feudal class of considerable stocks of farm crops in the form of feudal rent; (ii) relative weakness of towns; (iii) political and social supremacy of the feudal lords and their trading privileges which made it possible to use extra-economic pressure both when purchasing peasant farm produce and in creating a sales market in their own estates"; see Leonid Zytkowicz, "Directions of Agrarian Development in South-Eastern Europe in 16th–18th Centuries," *Acta Poloniae Historica* 43 (1981), 34.

20. The relation between rising grain prices and expansion of the demesne system is emphasized in most discussions of this period in eastern European economic development; for example, see Stanislaw Hoszowski, "The Polish Baltic Trade in the 15th–18th Centuries," in *Poland at the XIth International Congress of Historical Sciences in Stockholm* (Warsaw: Polish Academy of Sciences, Institute of History, 1960); Witold Kula, *An Economic Theory of the Feudal System* (London: NLB, 1976); and B. H. Slicher van Bath, "Agriculture in the Vital Revolution," in *The Cambridge Economic History of Europe,* vol. 5, esp. p. 119.

21. For a brief account of the "second serfdom," see Slicher van Bath, "Agriculture in the Vital Revolution," pp. 114–116; also see Zytkowski, "Directions of Agrarian Development," and Pach, "The Development of Feudal Rent."

22. Jerzy Topolski, "Sixteenth-Century Poland and the Turning Point in European Economic Development," in Fedorowicz et al., *A Republic of Nobles,* p. 77.

23. Kula, *An Economic Theory of the Feudal System,* p. 65; cf. Andrzej Wyrobisz, "Small Towns in 16th- and 17th-Century Poland," *Acta Poloniae Historica* 34 (1976), 153–164.

24. Henryk Sansonowicz, "Polish Politics and Society under the Jagiellonian Monarchy," in Fedorowicz et al., *A Republic of Nobles,* p. 58; cf. Andrzej Wyczanski, "The Problem of Authority in Sixteenth-Century Poland: An Essay in Reinterpretation," ibid., pp. 91–108.

25. Betts, "Constitutional Development and Political Thought," p. 465.

26. Maczak, "The Structure of Power in the Commonwealth."

27. Wyczanski, "The Problem of Authority in Sixteenth-Century Poland."

28. Edward Opalinski, "Great Poland's Power Elite under Sigismund III, 1587–1632," *Acta Poloniae Historica* 42 (1980), 41–66.

29. Maczak, "The Structure of Power in the Commonwealth," p. 121.

30. Frederich Lütge, "Economic Change: Agriculture," in *The New Cambridge Modern History,* vol. 2, p. 36.

31. Jan Ptasnik, "Towns in Medieval Poland," in Giergielewicz, *Polish Civilization,* pp. 25–50.

32. Gieysztor et al., *History of Poland,* p. 175; Maczak, "The Structure of Power in the Commonwealth," p. 115.

33. Topolski, "Continuity and Discontinuity in the Development of the Feudal System," p. 378; Slicher van Bath, "Agriculture in the Vital Revolution," p. 123; Maczak, "Export of Grain," p. 76.

34. Malowist, "Poland, Russia, and Western Trade," p. 32; Topolski, "Sixteenth-Century Poland," p. 71; Kula, *An Economic Theory of the Feudal System,* p. 68.

35. Maria Bogucka, "Polish Towns between the Sixteenth and Eighteenth Centuries," in Fedorowicz et al., *A Republic of Nobles,* p. 146.

36. Bogucka, "Towns in Poland and the Reformation," p. 57. Although Bogucka cites instances of Reformation activity in a number of towns, she concludes: "As a rule the Polish urban population remained faithful to Catholicism" (p. 58).

37. Bogucka writes: "It was obvious that the Reformation opened up for the gentry an additional path for intervention into urban questions; in this situation the burghers received not so much advantages from a change of religion, it rather brought further limitation of their rights . . . In Polish towns one sees a lack of the most important factor which elsewhere was the basis for the victory of the Reformation; i.e. the support of numerous groups of people who were not so much engaged because of the ideological values of the new faith but because of their definite economic or social interests." Ibid., p. 67.

38. Tazbir, "The Fate of Polish Protestantism in the Seventeenth Century," cites figures of 260 Protestant congregations in Great Poland and Little Poland in 1600 and 191 in Lithuania; Bruckner, "The Polish Reformation in the Sixteenth Century," p. 71, indicates that by 1650 the numbers remaining were 28 in Great Poland, 69 in Little Poland, and 140 in Lithuania.

39. F. C. Spooner, "The Reformation in Difficulties: France, 1519–59," in *The New Cambridge Modern History,* vol. 2, p. 210.

40. Cf. Immanuel Wallerstein, *The Modern World-System: Capitalist Agriculture and the Origins of the European World-Economy in the Sixteenth Century* (New York: Academic Press, 1974), p. 297.

41. France's population is discussed briefly in Philip Benedict, *Rouen during the Wars of Religion* (Cambridge: Cambridge University Press, 1981), p. 3; and in J. H. M. Salmon, *Society in Crisis: France in the Sixteenth Century* (New York: St. Martin's, 1975), pp. 27–37. Paris, with approximately 200,000 residents, was by far the largest city in Europe at the time.

42. This point is elaborated by Lütge, "Economic Change: Agriculture," pp. 45–46. Data on woolen manufactures at Amiens indicate that the volume of this trade must have doubled between 1525 and 1550, but these increases were highly localized; see P. Deyon, "Variations de la production textile aux 16ᵉ et 17ᵉ siècles," *Annales, E.S.C.,* 18 (1963), 948–959.

43. Fourquin's study of land-holding in the vicinity of Paris suggests that tenure arrangements were sufficiently closed that few urban merchants were able to acquire land. This study also reveals little intermarriage between the rural and urban elites; see Guy Fourquin, *Les campagnes de la région parisienne à la fin du Moyen Age du milieu du XIIIᵉ siècle au debut du XVIᵉ siècle* (Paris: Presses universitaires de France, 1964), pp. 523–524. A

study of Bayeux in Normandy shows only 11 percent of the nobility married to women of Third Estate background, again suggesting the relative separation of the rural and urban elite; see James B. Wood, *The Nobility of the Election of Bayeux, 1463–1666: Continuity through Change* (Princeton: Princeton University Press, 1980), p. 106. As other evidence suggests, this separation did not mean that the nobility lacked influence in the towns, but their interests and social relations appear to have remained more distinctly rural than was the case in the sections of central Europe in which the towns supported Protestantism.

44. Marc Bloch, *French Rural History: An Essay on its Basic Characteristics* (Berkeley: University of California Press, 1966), p. 125.

45. Elizabeth S. Teall, "The Seigneur of Renaissance France," *Journal of Modern History* 37 (1965), 131–150, argues that a "sense of loyalty and mutual obligation" between seigneurs and peasants persisted in France well into the seventeenth century. A study of the Champagne area, which, with open fields, large estates, and close-knit villages, was relatively typical of rural France, notes: "The seigneurs . . . commonly provided for a distribution of bread or money to all the village poor. Seigneurs were responding to a moral obligation to relieve . . . the needy among their peasants, who expected the distribution as a matter of custom. It formed one link in a complex network of exchanges—asymmetrical exchanges, to be sure—between the two." See A. N. Galpern, *The Religions and the People in Sixteenth-Century Champagne* (Cambridge, Mass.: Harvard University Press, 1976), pp. 33–34. Another study emphasizes the seigneurs' hold over the peasantry in judicial matters, as their protectors against the state, and as creditors; see Jean-Pierre Gutton, *La sociabilité villageoisie dans l'ancienne France* (Paris: Presses universitaires de France, 1979), esp. chap. 5.

46. Among the many sociological studies that have taken the sixteenth-century French state as an example of centralized absolutism, two that bear closely on the issues under consideration here are Guy E. Swanson, *Religion and Regime: A Sociological Account of the Reformation* (Ann Arbor: University of Michigan Press, 1967), and Perry Anderson, *Lineages of the Absolutist State* (London: NLB, 1974).

47. R. J. Knecht, *Francis I* (Cambridge: Cambridge University Press, 1982), emphasizes the accomplishments of Francis I in bringing a more centralized structure to the French state, but his account largely ignores the French state's continuing indebtedness to the landed elite. Martin Wolfe, *The Fiscal System of Renaissance France* (New Haven: Yale University Press, 1972), in contrast, is more sensitive to fiscal issues and concludes that "absolutism comes only with the Old Regime in the seventeenth century" (p. 98).

48. These quotations are taken from J. Russell Major, "The French Renaissance Monarchy as Seen through the Estates General," in Cohn,

Government in Reformation Europe, 1520–1560, p. 44. This point is sometimes obscured by comparisons of the "early modern" state in France and
England, which turn out to be based more on the seventeenth century than
the first half of the sixteenth. A more accurate appraisal of the comparison
is given in Lewis W. Spitz, *The Protestant Reformation, 1517–1559* (New
York: Harper and Row, 1985), pp. 39–40, who writes: "On the surface it
seemed that the kings of France had most nearly arrived at autocracy,
whereas those of England had to deal with a powerful Parliament . . . yet
the power of the king [in France] was still hemmed in by the customary
rights and ancient liberties of the nobility and other segments of society
[while] England developed a modernized consolidated monarchy." Even
this kind of broad assessment, though, is (as I have tried to suggest) less
useful for understanding the Reformation than is a more specific analysis
of the relations between central governing agencies and the landowning
sector.

49. Useful sources on these relations include P. S. Lewis, *Later Medieval France: The Polity* (New York: St. Martin's, 1968), and J. H. Shennan,
Government and Society in France, 1461–1661 (London: George Allen and
Unwin, 1969). For a brief analysis, see Joseph Strayer, *Medieval Statecraft
and the Perspectives of History* (Princeton: Princeton University Press, 1971),
pp. 346–347. In comparing the nobility in England and France, Lewis writes
that "the judicial and fiscal rights of French magnates were much greater"
(p. 195).

50. James Westfall Thompson, "The Domination of Political Motives,"
in *The French Wars of Religion*, ed. J. H. M. Salmon (Boston: D. C. Heath,
1967), p. 2; cf. Marilyn Manera Edelstein, "The Social Origins of the Episcopacy in the Reign of Francis I," *French Historical Studies* 8 (1974), 377–
392.

51. Alain Guéry, "Les finances de la monarchie français sous l'Ancien
Régime," *Annales, E.S.C.* 33 (1978), 216–239. Another source reveals that
revenues continued to fall during the middle decades of the century. See
Claude Michaud, "Finances et guerres de religion en France," *Bulletin de
la Société d'Histoire Moderne* 78 (1979), 3–10. This writer also suggests that
the Wars of Religion arose as a reaction to the crown's attempts to salvage
its deteriorating financial condition and should be seen in this light rather
than as a cause of this condition. At the same time, the crown became
increasingly dependent on the church during this period by virtue of its
decision to tax the clergy. Among the specific reasons generally cited for
the crown's financial difficulties are its loss of Milan in 1521, military reversals and ransom payments between 1522 and 1526, declining returns
from the *taille*, and the effects of inflation in precious metals.

52. Salmon, *Society in Crisis*, p. 92. J. Russell Major, "The Crown and
the Aristocracy in Renaissance France," *American Historical Review* 69

(1964), 631–645, attributes the nobility's continued political influence to two factors: rising incomes from land-holdings, and the development of a "new feudalism" involving stronger patron-client networks between the upper and lower nobility.

53. J. Russell Major, *The Deputies to the Estates General in Renaissance France* (Madison: University of Wisconsin Press, 1960), p. 115; see also J. Russell Major, *The Age of the Renaissance and Reformation* (Philadelphia: J. B. Lippincott, 1970), pp. 146–157.

54. Robert R. Harding, *Anatomy of a Power Elite: The Provincial Governors of Early Modern France* (New Haven: Yale University Press, 1978).

55. Shennan, *Government and Society in France,* p. 50; Wolfe, *The Fiscal Sysem of Renaissance France,* p. 11.

56. Richard Bonney, *The King's Debts: Finance and Politics in France, 1589–1661* (Oxford: Clarendon Press, 1981), pp. 1–21.

57. Salmon, *Society in Crisis,* pp. 76–77. Wolfe, *The Fiscal System of Renaissance France,* p. 93, shows that the crown did not borrow on a large scale from merchants and urban financiers. And unlike in England, where relations between London and the crowd were complementary, relations between Francis I and Paris were often strained because of the king's military adventures and taxation policies, which were perceived as inimical to trade; see R. J. Knecht, "Francis I and Paris," *History* 66 (1981), 24–33.

58. Thompson, "The Domination of Political Motives," p. 2; cf. Gordon Griffiths, "The State: Absolute or Limited?" in *Transition and Revolution: Problems and Issues of European Renaissance and Reformation History,* ed. Robert M. Kingdon (Minneapolis: Burgess, 1974), p. 29; and Major, "The Crown and the Aristocracy," p. 643.

59. Wood, *The Nobility of the Election of Bayeux,* p. 170. Another writer concludes: "The crown, it is now felt, did not skirt the obstructionist interests of a decaying nobility, but rather, willingly relied on leading noblemen as agents of administration and control in a still fragmented kingdom"; see Kristen B. Neuschel, "The Picard Nobility in the Sixteenth Century: Autonomy and Power," *Proceedings of the Annual Meeting of the Western Society for French History* 10 (1982), 42.

60. Brief accounts of this phase of the Reformation are included in G. R. Elton, *Reformation Europe, 1517–1559* (New York: Harper and Row, 1963), pp. 118–119; R. J. Knecht, "The Early Reformation in England and France: A Comparison," *History,* 57 (1972), 9–10; and David S. Hempsall, "Martin Luther and the Sorbonne, 1519–21," *Bulletin of the Institute of Historical Research* 46 (1973), 28–40.

61. The most extensive study of the Faculty of Theology, from which the present discussion draws, is James K. Farge, *Orthodoxy and Reform in Early Reformation France: The Faculty of Theology of Paris, 1500–1543* (Leiden: E. J. Brill, 1985).

62. David Nicholls, "Social Change and Early Protestantism in France: Normandy, 1520–62," *European Studies Review* 10 (1980), 42–49; David Nicholls, "The Nature of Popular Heresy in France, 1520–1542," *Historical Journal* 26 (1983), 261–275. Benedict, *Rouen during the Wars of Religion,* p. 53, also based on extensive research of the area, cites a somewhat lower figure of 15 to 20 percent.

63. Henry Heller, "Reform and Reformers of Meaux" (Ph.D. diss., Cornell University, 1969); James Jordan, "Jacques Lefèvre d'Etaples: Principles and Practice of Reform at Meaux," in *Contemporary Reflections on the Medieval Christian Tradition: Essays in Honor of Ray C. Petry* (Durham, N.C.: Duke University Press, 1974), pp. 94–115.

64. Denis Richet, "Aspects socio-culturels des conflits religieux à Paris dans la seconde moitié du XVIᵉ siècle," *Annales, E.S.C.* 32 (1977), 764–789; Yves-Marié Bercé, *Révoltes et révolutions dans l'Europe moderne* (Paris: Presses universitaires de France, 1980). Richet suggests that Protestants and Catholics alike believed the success or failure of the Reformation in Paris would depend on the nobility.

65. Galpern, *The Religions of the People in Sixteenth-Century Champagne.*

66. Natalie Zemon Davis, "The Sacred and the Body Social in Sixteenth-Century Lyon," *Past and Present* 90 (1981), 40–70.

67. Gabriel Loireth, "Catholiques et protestants en Languedoc à la veille des guerres civiles (1560)," *Revue d'histoire de l'église de France* 23 (1937), 503–525. Loireth attributes some of the strength of Protestantism in this region during the 1550s to the conversion of lesser nobles whose socioeconomic position had declined relative to that of the upper nobility.

68. David Rosenberg, "Social Experience and Religious Choice: A Case Study, the Protestant Weavers and Woolcombers of Amiens in the Sixteenth Century" (Ph.D. diss., Yale University, 1978).

69. Emmanuel LeRoy Ladurie, *The Peasants of Languedoc* (Urbana: University of Illinois Press, 1974), pp. 158–164.

70. Although variations in literacy rates can be adduced from a variety of sources, local studies of book ownership are generally cited as the strongest evidence; see for example, A. Labarre, *Le livre dans la vie amiénoise du seizième siècle: L'enseignement des inventaires après décès, 1503–1576* (Paris: Presses universitaires de France, 1971). Literate book-owning merchants and artisans constituted a sizable number in Amiens because merchants and artisans in general made up a large share of the population. In percentage terms, a larger proportion of the nobility actually owned books than of merchants and artisans; see Roger Chartier, *The Cultural Uses of Print in Early Modern France* (Princeton: Princeton University Press, 1987), p. 147.

71. For printers, it is easy to assume that literacy came first and provided a basis for becoming attracted to Protestantism; more generally, though, it appears that the causal order may have been reversed, since

Protestant services became "one of the places in which training in group reading took place, as they brought together men and women, the literate and the illiterate, and the faithful of different professions and of different parts of the city"; see Chartier, *The Cultural Uses of Print*, p. 153.

72. Benedict, *Rouen during the Wars of Religion*, p. 49. Major, "The Crown and the Aristocracy," p. 632, also suggests that merchants who bought land generally became part of the nobility in outlook and life style.

73. Jonathan Dewald, *The Formation of a Provincial Nobility: The Magistrates of the Parlement of Rouen, 1499–1610* (Princeton: Princeton University Press, 1980), draws these conclusions from an extensive study of the social origins, wealth, land-holdings, and commercial transactions of the magistrates of Rouen between 1499 and 1610. His evidence points overwhelmingly to the importance of rural interests in the economy of the area and to the economic partnership between peasants and landlords: "It was this partnership that really 'tied and untied' them" (p. 181). The role of these magistrates in deterring the growth of Protestantism in Rouen has been documented by Benedict, *Rouen during the Wars of Religion,* and Nicholls, "Social Change and Early Protestantism in France."

74. Galpern, *The Religions of the People in Sixteenth-Century Champagne,* pp. 123–140.

75. Claire Dolan, "L'image du protestant et le counseil municipal d'Aix au XVIᵉ siècle," *Renaissance and Reformation* 4 (1980), 152–164.

76. M. Greengrass, "The Anatomy of a Religious Riot in Toulouse in May 1562," *Journal of Ecclesiastical History* 34 (1983), 367–391.

77. Philip T. Hoffman, *Church and Community in the Diocese of Lyon, 1500–1789* (New Haven: Yale University Press, 1984), pp. 11–15.

78. Ibid., pp. 16–17.

79. Shennan, *Government and Society in France,* p. 61; Major, "The Crown and the Aristocracy," p. 631.

80. Harding, *Anatomy of a Power Elite,* pp. 36–37.

81. Examples are given in Galpern, *The Religions of the People in Sixteenth-Century Champagne,* pp. 139–140; and in Robert M. Kingdon, *Geneva and the Coming of the Wars of Religion in France, 1555–1563* (Geneva: Librairie E. Droz, 1956), esp. p. 55.

82. Cf. Harding, *Anatomy of a Power Elite,* pp. 40–43. A somewhat different argument is suggested by Chaunu, who argues that the greater success of Protestantism in the south than in the north was partly attributable to the fact that the southern nobility were in a *stronger* social position. See Pierre Chaunu, "L'état," in *Histoire économique et sociale de la France,* vol. 1, pt. 2, ed. Emmanuel LeRoy Ladurie and Michel Morineau (Paris: Presses universitaires de France, 1977), pp. 9–224. The two arguments can perhaps be reconciled by observing that Chaunu also suggests that the southern nobility's strength lay in the fact that the seigneury had greater control over

the means of justice and the police than did the parish community. Thus, although the nobility may have been able to exert their will in social matters, their power may have been less fully integrated with the local patterns of village life, including the church. In this sense, the nobility, like the towns in other parts of Europe, and like their counterparts in forested areas or in the newly settled areas of Lithuania, were freer to experiment religiously because they were less dependent on the religiously ceremonialized patron-client relations of the rural village.

83. Salmon, *Society in Crisis,* pp. 79–89.

84. N. M. Sutherland, *The Huguenot Struggle for Recognition* (New Haven: Yale University Press, 1980), p. 20.

85. Edelstein, "The Social Origins of the Episcopacy," pp. 383–384. It has also been observed that the Concordat benefited the pope more than the king; see R. J. Knecht, "The Concordat of 1516: A Reassessment," in Cohn, *Government in Reformation Europe,* pp. 91–112.

86. Major, *Deputies to the Estates General,* p. 136.

87. These conclusions, concerned as they are with the first half of the sixteenth century, are not inconsistent with those of more traditional studies that have emphasized the role of Protestant nobles in the religious wars; see, for example, the assertions in Spitz, *The Protestant Reformation,* p. 193. That role, as has been suggested, emerged only during the second half of the century and was rooted in the radically altered political and religious dynamics of this later period, particularly the coalescence of rival noble factions around religiously contested claimants to the throne.

88. See H. G. Koenigsberger, "The Empire of Charles V in Europe," in *The New Cambridge Modern History,* vol. 2, pp. 301–333, for useful background information on the fate of humanism and Lutheranism in Spain. Bartolomé Bennassar, *The Spanish Character: Attitudes and Mentalities from the Sixteenth to the Nineteenth Century* (Berkeley: University of California Press, 1979), suggests that popular religious ferment was widespread in sixteenth-century Spain.

89. The remarks of Fernand Braudel, *The Mediterranean and the Mediterranean World in the Age of Philip II* (New York: Harper and Row, 1973), p. 767, on this subject are of interest.

90. John Lynch, *Spain under the Habsburgs,* vol. 1, *Empire and Absolutism, 1516–1598* (Oxford: Oxford University Press, 1964), p. 61.

91. This view is stated by Christopher Hill, *Reformation to the Industrial Revolution, 1530–1780* (London: Penguin Books, 1967), p. 34.

92. M. L. Bush, *Renaissance, Reformation, and the Outer World, 1450–1660* (London: Blandford Press, 1967), pp. 58–61; J. H. Parry, *The Spanish Theory of Empire in the Sixteenth Century* (Cambridge: Cambridge University Press, 1940), p. 3.

93. Wallerstein, *The Modern World-System,* emphasizes this conception

of Spain. The importance of religion to the legitimacy of empires is stressed in S. N. Eisenstadt, *The Political System of Empires* (New York: Free Press, 1969), esp. pp. 141–142; and more specifically in discussions of Spanish political theory in the sixteenth century such as those of Bernice Hamilton, *Political Thought in Sixteenth-Century Spain: A Study of the Political Ideas of Vitoria, DeSoto, Suarez, and Molina* (Oxford: Clarendon Press, 1963), and J. A. Fernandez-Santamaria, *The State, War, and Peace: Spanish Political Thought in the Renaissance, 1515–1559* (Cambridge: Cambridge University Press, 1977).

94. Wallerstein, *The Modern World-System,* for example, acknowledges Spain's dependence on Castile for revenue, but exaggerates the role of finance from Antwerp and Augsburg and generally focuses on Spain's efforts to construct an empire rather than on its domestic social structure.

95. It has been argued that Charles V might have succeeded in capturing all of Europe had he embraced the Lutheran cause; see A. J. P. Taylor, *The Course of German History* (London: Hamilton, 1945), p. 163.

96. John E. Longhurst, *Luther's Ghost in Spain, 1517–1546* (Lawrence, Kans.: Coronado Press, 1969), p. 14.

97. These figures are cited in Antonio Dominguez Ortiz, *The Golden Age of Spain, 1516–1659* (New York: Basic Books, 1971).

98. Pierre Chaunu, *Seville et l'Atlantic (1504–1650),* vol. 8, *La conjuncture* (Paris: S.E.V.P.E.N., 1959).

99. Glamman, "The Changing Patterns of Trade," p. 499.

100. Ruth Pike, "The Genoese in Seville and the Opening of the New World," *Journal of Economic History* 22 (1962), 348–378; see also Jaime Vicens Vives, *Approaches to the History of Spain,* 2d ed. (Berkeley: University of California Press, 1970), pp. 97–98.

101. Hermann Van der Wee, "Monetary, Credit, and Banking Systems," in *The Cambridge Economic History of Europe,* vol. 5, p. 371.

102. Stanley G. Payne, *A History of Spain and Portugal,* vol. 1 (Madison: University of Wisconsin Press, 1973), p. 178.

103. Earl J. Hamilton, *American Treasure and the Price Revolution in Spain, 1501–1650* (Cambridge, Mass.: Harvard University Press, 1934), p. 34; see also Parry, "Transport and Trade Routes," p. 210.

104. Pierre Vilar, *Spain: A Brief History* (New York: Pergamon Press, 1967), p. 28.

105. Henry Kamen, "The Decline of Spain: A Historical Myth?" *Past and Present* 81 (1978), p. 47.

106. Wallerstein, *The Modern World-System,* p. 176.

107. J. P. Cooper, "Patterns of Inheritance and Settlement by Great Landowners from the Fifteenth to the Eighteenth Centuries," in *Family and Inheritance: Rural Society in Western Europe, 1200–1800,* ed. Jack Goody et al. (Cambridge: Cambridge University Press, 1976), p. 235.

108. Vicens Vives, *Approaches to the History of Spain,* p. 94.

109. Stephen Haliczer, *The Comuneros of Castile: The Foraging of a Revolution, 1475–1521* (Madison: University of Wisconsin Press, 1981), p. 207.

110. The costs associated with the military had already risen substantially under the reign of Isabella—by some estimates, as much as four times between 1482 and 1504 alone—and had forced the crown to depend more heavily on loans from the nobility, as well as legitimating its expenditures on the basis of religious appeals. For example, see Miguel Angel Ladero Quesada, "Les finances royales de Castlle à la veille des temps modernes," *Annales, E.S.C.* 25 (1970), 775–788.

111. Payne, *History of Spain and Portugal,* p. 283.

112. Lynch, *Spain under the Habsburgs,* p. 55.

113. J. H. Elliott, *Imperial Spain, 1469–1716* (London: Edward Arnold, 1963), pp. 193–195. Also see I. A. A. Thompson, "The Purchase of Nobility in Castile, 1552–1700," *Journal of European Economic History* 8 (1979), 319–331; and Carla Rahn Phillips, *Cuidad Réal, 1500–1750: Growth, Crisis, and Readjustment in the Spanish Economy* (Cambridge, Mass.: Harvard University Press, 1979).

114. Lynch, *Spain under the Habsburgs,* p. 53.

115. R. Ruiz-Martin, *Letters marchandes échangées entre Florence et Medina del Campo* (Paris: S.E.V.P.E.N., 1965), p. 14; Frederic Mauro, "Spain," in *An Introduction to the Sources of European Economic History, 1500–1800,* ed. Charles Wilson and Geoffrey Parker (Ithaca: Cornell University Press, 1977), p. 49.

116. Elliott, *Imperial Spain,* p. 175.

117. J. R. L. Highfield, "The Catholic Kings and the Titled Nobility of Castile," in *Europe in the Late Middle Ages,* ed. J. R. L. Highfield and B. Smalley (Evanston, Ill.: Northwestern University Press, 1965), p. 377.

118. The basic source on the Mesta remains Julius Klein, *The Mesta: A Study in Spanish Economic History, 1273–1836* (Cambridge, Mass.: Harvard University Press, 1919).

119. Elliott, *Imperial Spain,* p. 72.

120. Aldo de Maddalena, "Rural Europe," in Cipolla, *The Fontana Economic History of Europe: The Sixteenth and Seventeenth Centuries,* p. 299.

121. Braudel, *The Mediterranean,* pp. 709–710.

122. Elliott, *Imperial Spain,* p. 75; Richard L. Kagan, *Lawsuits and Litigants in Castile, 1500–1700* (Chapel Hill: University of North Carolina Press, 1981), p. 14.

123. H. G. Koenigsberger and George L. Mosse, *Europe in the Sixteenth Century* (London: Longman, 1968), p. 229.

124. Ortiz, *The Golden Age of Spain,* p. 119.

125. Henry Kamen, *Inquisition and Society in Spain in the Sixteenth*

and Seventeenth Centuries (Bloomington: Indiana University Press, 1985), p. 142.

126. Ibid., p. 145.
127. Ibid.

4. Social Conditions and Reformation Discourse

1. Some of these activities of the state are discussed in Gerald Strauss, "Lutheranism and Literacy: A Reassessment," in *Religion and Society in Early Modern Europe,* ed. Kaspar von Greyerz (London: Allen and Unwin, 1984), pp. 109–123.

2. Lacey Baldwin Smith, *This Realm of England: 1399–1688* (Lexington, Mass.: D. C. Heath, 1976), p. 114. See also Felicity Heal, *Of Prelates and Princes: A Study of the Economic and Social Position of the Tudor Episcopate* (Cambridge: Cambridge University Press, 1980), p. 3, who points out that the ecclesiastical hierarchy retained much of its wealth and power.

3. These practices are discussed in William Monter, *Ritual, Myth, and Magic in Early Modern Europe* (Athens, Ohio: Ohio University Press, 1983), pp. 26–27.

4. On these defensive alliances, see Fritz Hartung, "Imperial Reform, 1485–1495: Its Course and Its Character," in *Pre-Reformation Germany,* ed. Gerald Strauss (New York: Macmillan, 1972), pp. 73–135; Geoffrey Barraclough, *The Origins of Modern Germany* (Oxford: Basil Blackwell, 1947), p. 374; Gerald Strauss, *Nuremberg in the Sixteenth Century* (New York: Wiley, 1966), pp. 148–149.

5. On this point, see Joseph Lortz, *The Reformation in Germany* (New York: Herder and Herder, 1968), p. 40; Lewis Spitz, *The Renaissance and Reformation Movements* (Chicago: University of Chicago Press, 1971), p. 121.

6. Claus-Peter Clasen, *The Anabaptists in South and Central Germany, Switzerland, and Austria* (Ann Arbor: University Microfilms International, 1978), pp. 5–38; George Hunston Williams, *The Radical Reformation* (Philadelphia: Westminster Press, 1962), pp. 398–404; James M. Stayer, "The Anabaptists," in *Reformation Europe: A Guide to Research,* ed. Steven Ozment (St. Louis: Center for Reformation Research, 1982), p. 143.

7. Among the sources that agree on this conclusion are G. R. Elton, *Reformation Europe, 1517–1559* (New York: Harper and Row, 1963), pp. 309–310; Gerhard Zschäbitz, *Zur mitteldeutschen Wiedertäuferbewegung nach dem grossen Bauernkrieg* (Berlin: Rütten and Loening, 1958), pp. 155–156; Walther Kirchner, "State and Anabaptists in the Sixteenth Century: An Economic Approach," *Journal of Modern History* 46 (1974), 1–25; Kaspar von Greyerz, *The Late City Reformation in Germany: The Case of Colmar, 1522–1628* (Wiesbaden: Franz Steiner Verlag, 1980), p. 70.

8. Claus-Peter Clasen, *Anabaptism: A Social History* (Ithaca: Cornell University Press, 1972).

9. On the functions of these communities, see Williams, *The Radical Reformation*, p. 165; Henry Heller, "Famine, Revolt, and Hersey at Meaux, 1521–1525," *Archiv für Reformationsgeschichte* 68 (1977), 133–157; Peter James Klassen, *The Economics of Anabaptism, 1525–1560* (The Hague: Mouton: 1964).

10. In subsequent decades, the composition and interests of the town council continued to influence the direction of the Reformation in Basel. Its internal divisions, as well as the broader circumstances that forced it to emphasize peace and prosperity, inhibited it from implementing a uniform set of theological doctrines. Instead, a great deal of doctrinal diversity was retained, including pockets of humanism, Anabaptists, and even Catholics. These conclusions follow those of Hans R. Guggisberg, *Basel in the Sixteenth Century: Aspects of the City Republic before, during, and after the Reformation* (St. Louis: Center for Reformation Research, 1982).

11. A thorough discussion of the social processes favoring certain teachings in place of others during the Reformation in Strasbourg is presented in Lorna Jane Abray, *The People's Reformation: Magistrates, Clergy, and Commons in Strasbourg, 1500–1598* (Ithaca: Cornell University Press, 1985).

12. For a discussion of these restrictions, see John F. Davis, *Heresy and Reformation in the South-East of England, 1520–1559* (London: Royal Historical Society, 1983), esp. p. 17.

13. John N. King, *English Reformation Literature: The Tudor Origins of the Protestant Tradition* (Princeton: Princeton University Press, 1982), pp. 134–140.

14. Of the many studies of the development of Calvin's thought, one that pays particular attention to the Genevan context in which his ideas were formulated is Harro Höpfl, *The Christian Polity of John Calvin* (Cambridge: Cambridge University Press, 1982); see esp. pp. 56–76.

15. Peter Blickle, "Social Protest and Reformation Theology," in *Religion, Politics, and Social Protest: Three Studies on Early Modern Germany*, ed. Kaspar von Greyerz (London: Allen and Unwin, 1984), pp. 1–23.

16. On the role of urban oaths as theological models, see Hans-Christoph Rublack, "Political and Social Norms in Urban Communities in the Holy Roman Empire," in von Greyerz, *Religion, Politics, and Social Protest*, pp. 24–60.

17. Ibid., pp. 38–39.

18. Roland H. Baiton, *Here I Stand: A Life of Martin Luther* (New York: New American Library, 1950), p. 173, provides a succinct summary of the manner in which Luther's emphasis on the Word combined both tangible and intangible imagery: "[The Word] is not to be equated with Scripture nor with the sacraments, yet it operates through them and not apart from them. The *Word* is not the Bible as a written book because 'the gospel is really not that which is contained in books and composed in letters,

but rather an oral preaching and a living word, a voice which resounds throughout the whole world and is publickly proclaimed.' This Word must be heard." The reformers' self-legitimation of discourse is, of course, evident in this statement as well.

19. Martin Luther, *Werke: Kritische Gesamtausgabe* (Weimar: H. Böhlau, 1883), vol. 8, no. 143, pp. 33, 35.

20. Quoted in Marjorie O'Rourke Boyle, *Rhetoric and Reform: Erasmus' Civil Dispute with Luther* (Cambridge, Mass.: Harvard University Press, 1983), p. 47. Boyle argues that Luther's method of debate was neither the modern dialectic nor its precursor, which Erasmus exemplified, that of skeptical comparison and harmonization: "The divine method, he [Luther] argues, is not to collect the world into a harmony but to set it in opposition to itself: Not *collatio* but *collisio*" (p. 46). Or, in deconstructionist terminology, Luther's discourse is characterized by alterity: the poles stay apart.

21. Luther, *Werke*, vol. 12, no. 391, pp. 25–26.

22. Among the numerous studies of iconoclasm, see especially Jean Wirth, "Against the Acculturation Thesis," in *Religion and Society in Early Modern Europe*, ed. Kaspar von Greyerz (London: Allen and Unwin, 1984), pp. 66–78; and Carlos M. N. Eire, *War against the Idols* (Cambridge: Cambridge University Press, 1986).

23. Guggisberg, *Basel in the Sixteenth Century*, pp. 23–25.

24. Philip T. Hoffman, *Church and Community in the Diocese of Lyon, 1500–1789* (New Haven: Yale University Press, 1984), p. 20.

25. Clifford Geertz, *The Interpretation of Cultures* (New York: Harper and Row, 1973), chap. 4.

26. For a particularly impressive example of these relations, see Dieter Demandt and Hans-Christoph Rublack, *Stadt und Kirche in Kitzingen: Darstellung und Quellen zu Spätmittelalter und Reformation* (Stuttgart: Ernst Klett, 1978), esp. pp. 36–46. Having examined a number of conflicts between the townspeople of Kitzingen in southwest Germany and the church prior to the Reformation, the authors show how a debate over the priest's salary in 1522 was quickly transformed into a more general negative characterization of the church by the town council, and that the council relied on reform rhetoric about the Scriptures to sharpen this characterization. In this case the application of reform discourse was also effective in that the priest responded not in terms of the more specific question at issue but by attacking reform teachings more generally. Inadvertently his own response, therefore, dramatized the opposition between institutional practice and idealized scriptural spirituality.

27. For an excellent discussion of the varieties and functions of redundancy in ideological discourse, see Susan R. Suleiman, *Authoritarian Fictions: The Ideological Novel as a Literary Genre* (New York: Columbia University Press, 1983).

28. Luther, *Werke*, vol. 7, nos. 580–590, pp. 18–25.

29. An examination of the vocabulary, syntax, and imagery in the writings of John Calvin over a twenty-year period also suggests that consistency was reinforced by a remarkably stable usage of clear sentence structure, a limited lexical pool, and words with unambiguous meanings; see Francis M. Higman, *The Style of John Calvin in His French Polemical Treatise* (Oxford: Oxford University Press, 1967).

30. The rhetorical style of the commentary, written specifically to persuade, also carried over into the more prosaic works of the Reformation, often giving them a popular appeal that might otherwise have been lacking. Luther's translation of the New Testament, for example, accomplished in a remarkable period of only eleven weeks in 1522, was notable not only because it brought Scripture to German readers in their own tongue but also because it incorporated the cadence and style of Luther's most persuasive previous writings, rendering the New Testament in an eminently appealing form. From dry historical texts, the passages took on contemporary practical importance in the same way that Luther's ideology more generally did. The gospel was for Luther a hallowed story, and he freely translated it in a style that made it come alive. As one historian remarks: "He conveys its tone so that the reader grasps it as a living, spoken word. Through sentence structure and punctuation he turns the Bible into a book to be heard and not simply read." Heinrich Bornkamm, *Luther in Mid-Career, 1521–1530* (Philadelphia: Fortress Press, 1983), p. 47.

31. Readers of these accounts cannot help being impressed with the richness of detail with which they allow the history of the Reformation to be reconstructed. One has, for example, a detailed account of an obscure meeting between Luther and Carlstadt on August 22, 1524, that provides a blow-by-blow account of what each participant said to the other, reported almost verbatim, together with remarks about facial expressions, moods, gestures, and the physical surroundings. Two days later, a confrontation between Luther and the town council of Orlamünde is preserved in equally graphic detail. Indeed, it has been possible for historians to chart Luther's activities on a nearly day-by-day basis. And this level of detail has not been reserved only for the leading figures of the Reformation but has also been recorded for many of its minor figures.

32. Reflexive narratives of this kind also contributed to the unification of public and private lives that was characteristic of the leading reformers. Bringing abstract thought to bear on specific encounters, disputations, and public deliberations not only reinforced the connections between reformers' own private and public lives but provided occasion for commentators to forge accounts in which these connections were interpreted and emphasized. Significantly, it is not primarily on the autobiographical writings of the reformers themselves that one has to depend in order to gain insight into their character; the secondary discourse generated by their contemporaries is rich with accounts that, however apocryphal, purport to shed light on the

reformers' thoughts and feelings, and in so doing create a public image of these thoughts and feelings that can generally withstand scrutiny in relation to the public episodes themselves.

33. That the disputation was not merely a social event involving debate but a well-understood rhetorical convention, rooted in the leading reformers' classical education, is argued compellingly in Boyle, *Rhetoric and Reform,* esp. pp. 5–42.

34. As one indication of the role of internal competition within the Reformation as a stimulus to literary production, the proportion of printings in Wittenberg of Luther's works that were directed against evangelical competitors rose from only 22 percent for the period 1521–1525 to 60 percent for the period 1531–1540; see Mark U. Edwards, *Luther's Last Battles: Politics and Polemics, 1531–46* (Ithaca: Cornell University Press, 1983), p. 11. The reformers themselves were not unmindful that disputations played a positive role in furthering their work beyond merely resolving theological issues; for example, Boyle, *Rhetoric and Reform,* p. 36, reports that on one occasion Erasmus wrote to Luther: "Perhaps Erasmus writing against you will profit the gospel more than certain coarse men writing for you." She also observes that Luther "welcomed hostility: it summoned in him the courage to retort vehemently, and the opportunity to color the justice of his case with heightened hues" (p. 42).

35. The reformers themselves were, of course, keenly aware of the epistemological relations between constructs and things, schooled as they were in medieval theological discussions of these relations and practically concerned with them in such central questions as debates concerning the nature of Christ's presence in the Eucharist; as background, see Richard Waswo, *Language and Meaning in the Renaissance* (Princeton: Princeton University Press, 1987), esp. pp. 250–283.

36. Bainton, *Here I Stand,* p. 187, also stresses the structural similarity between Luther's discussion of church and state and the more general categories of his discourse: "The demarcation of the spheres of Church and state corresponds in a rough way to dualisms running through the nature of God and man. God is wrath and mercy. The state is the instrument of his wrath, the church of his mercy. Man is divided into outward and inward. Crime is outward and belongs to the state. Sin is inward and belongs to the church."

37. For a systematic enumeration of the dualistic concepts that frequented Calvin's writing, see Nicole Malet, *Dieu selon Calvin: Des mots à la doctrine* (Lausanne: L'Age d'Homme, 1977). Eire writes that "Calvin systematically juxtaposed the divine and the human, contrasted the spiritual and the material, and placed the transcendent and omnipotent *solus* of God above the contingent multiple of man and the created world." See Eire, *War against the Idols,* p. 197.

38. Higman, *Style of John Calvin,* p. 154, concludes from a close analy-

sis of Calvin's polemical writings that descriptions of the spiritual realms
generally rely on "biblical or devotional expressions and imagery" and use
classical rhetoric that "provides harmonious rhythms and oratorical mod-
ulations of tone, elegant without ever becoming flamboyant, which present
an image of dignity, sobriety, and simplicity"; in contrast, the fleshly, evil,
and false is depicted in "markedly popular langauge" that draws from "the
indigenous stock of the common people, not the learned sources of scholarship," uses "bizarre neologisms" to caricature them, employs a "conver-
sational, or broken and discordant" syntax, and uses "figurative colloquial
expressions and vulgar images" to degrade them. Another writer observes
that in formal structure, the use of parallelism, and even alliteration, "Calvin's writing is a binding of opposites, the emphatic quality of its binding
nature serving to underline the distance (and it is a distance of polarities)
between the things that it binds"; Suzanne Selinger, *Calvin against Himself:
An Inquiry in Intellectual History* (Hamden, Conn.: Archon, 1984), p. 176.

39. See Mary Douglas, *Purity and Danger* (London: Penguin, 1967),
for a discussion of pollution as symbolic boundary.

40. Higman, *Style of John Calvin,* pp. 146–149, catalogs examples of
Calvin's uses of the following imagery: sewage, defecation and latrines, the
drunkard and his vomit, robbers and prostitutes, and animals.

41. The importance of the fact that Calvin's were a second generation
of reforms is generally stressed in discussions of the Reformation; see esp.
Joachim Rogge, "Kritik Calvins an Luthers Zwei-Reich-Lehre?" in *Theologie
in Geschichte und Kunst: Walter Elliger zum 65. Geburtstag* (Witten: Luther-
Verlag, 1968), pp. 152–168.

42. John Calvin, *De necessitate reformandae Ecclesiae* (1543), quoted in
Eire, *War against the Idols,* p. 199.

43. Richet, on the basis of accounts in Paris, suggests that Protestant
converts actually did think of themselves as models of religious virtue and
imitated traditional rituals of purification in distancing themselves from the
ignorant Catholic mobs. This interpretation, incidentally, suggests that the
reformers' discursive field, which placed moral action "above" traditional
religious practices, resonated with artisans' and merchants' status aspirations
relative to the lower classes. It is difficult, however, to determine how strong
this resonance may have been. See Denis Richet, "Aspects socio-culturels
des conflits religieux à Paris dans la seconde moitiè du XVIᵉ siècle," *Annales,
E.S.C.* 32 (1977), 764–789. Data from Catholic sources in Aix also suggests
that Catholic discourse depicted Protestants as opponents not of individuals
but of institutions. Protestants thereby became symbols of danger threatening the community's established way of life. See Claire Dolan, "L'image
du protestant et le counseil municipal d'Aix au XVIᵉ siècle," *Renaissance
and Reformation* 4 (1980), 152–164. This evidence suggests that the reformers' discursive field, in which the life of virtue was pitted against es-

tablished institutions, articulated sufficiently with the way in which actual social relations were experienced to be reinforced in Catholic discourse.

44. E. William Monter, *Calvin's Geneva* (New York: Wiley, 1967), p. 158.

45. Robert M. Kingdon, *Geneva and the Coming of the Wars of Religion in France, 1555–1563* (Geneva: Librairie E. Droz, 1956).

46. Robert W. Scribner, "Civic Unity and the Reformation in Erfurt," *Past and Present* 66 (1975), 29–60.

47. Miriam Usher Crisman, *Strasbourg and the Reform: A Study in the Process of Change* (New Haven: Yale University Press, 1967); Strauss, *Nuremberg in the Sixteenth Century;* Harold Grimm, "Luther's Contribution to Sixteenth-Century Organization of Poor Relief," *Archiv für Reformationsgeschichte* 61 (1970), 222–233; I. Schoffer, "Protestantism in Flux during the Revolt of the Netherlands," in *Britain and the Netherlands,* vol. 2, *Papers Delivered to the Anglo-Dutch Historical Conference, Utrecht and Amsterdam,* ed. J. S. Bromley and E. H. Kossmann (Groningen: J. B. Wolters, 1962), p. 76.

48. Karl E. Demandt, *Geschichte des Landes Hessen,* 2d ed. (Kassel: Barenreiter-Verlag, 1972), pp. 226–227; H. C. Erik Midelfort, "Protestant Monastery? A Reformation Hospital in Hesse," in *Reformation Principle and Practice: Essays in Honour of Arthur Geoffrey Dickens,* ed. Peter Newman Brooks (London: Scolar Press, 1980), pp. 71–94; F. L. Carsten, *Princes and Parliaments in Germany* (Oxford: Clarendon Press, 1959), pp. 150–172.

49. Lawrence G. Duggan, *Bishop and Chapter: The Governance of the Bishopric of Speyer to 1552* (New Brunswick, N.J.: Rutgers University Press, 1978), p. 154. Similar gains accrued to Duke Ulrich in Württemberg; see Carsten, *Princes and Parliaments,* p. 20.

50. T. K. Derry, *A History of Scandinavia: Norway, Sweden, Denmark, Finland, and Iceland* (Minneapolis: University of Minnesota Press, 1979), p. 87; Franklin D. Scott, *Sweden: The Nation's History* (Minneapolis: University of Minnesota Press, 1977), pp. 118–161; Owen Chadwick, *The Reformation* (Baltimore: Penguin Books, 1972), p. 384; actual ownership of land by the crown grew from 5 percent in 1500 to 28 percent in 1560; see Carlo M. Cipolla, *Before the Industrial Revolution: European Society and Economy, 1000–1700* (New York: W. W. Norton, 1976), p. 56.

51. N. K. Andersen, "The Reformation in Scandinavia and the Baltic," in *The New Cambridge Modern History,* vol. 2, *The Reformation, 1520–1559,* ed. G. R. Elton (Cambridge: Cambridge University Press, 1958), p. 140.

52. Smith, *This Realm of England,* pp. 214–215; Penry Williams, *The Tudor Regime* (Oxford: Clarendon Press, 1979), p. 63; Heal, *Of Prelates and Princes,* pp. 180–201.

53. David Knowles and R. Neville Hadcock, *Medieval Religious Houses: England and Wales* (London: Longman, 1971); Joyce Youings, "The Terms

of Disposal of the Devon Monastic Lands, 1536–58," *English Historical Review* 59 (1954), 18–38; H. J. Habakkuk, "The Market for Monastic Property, 1539–1603," *Economic History Review* 10 (1958), 362–380; H. R. Trevor-Roper, "The Gentry, 1540–1640," *Economic History Review* 7 (1955), Supplement 1; John U. Nef, *The Conquest of the Material World* (Chicago: University of Chicago Press, 1964), pp. 215–239.

54. R. B. Smith, *Land and Politics in the England of Henry VIII: The West Riding of Yorkshire, 1530–46* (Oxford: Clarendon Press, 1970), pp. 214–215; Peter Clark, *English Provincial Society from the Reformation to the Revolution: Religion, Politics, and Society in Kent, 1500–1640* (Sussex: Harvester Press, 1977), p. 52.

55. Aldo de Maddalena, "Rural Europe, 1500–1750," in *The Fontana Economic History of Europe: The Sixteenth and Seventeenth Centuries,* ed. Carlo M. Cipolla (Glasgow: William Collins Sons, 1974), p. 296; Pieter Geyl, *The Revolt of the Netherlands, 1555–1609* (London: Williams and Norgate, 1932), pp. 139–140.

56. Stephen A. Fischer-Galati, *Ottoman Imperialism and German Protestantism, 1521–1555* (Cambridge, Mass.: Harvard University Press, 1959), pp. 46–47; I. Andersson, "Sweden and the Baltic," in *The New Cambridge Modern History,* vol. 3, *The Counter-Reformation and Price Revolution, 1559–1610,* ed. R. B. Wernham (Cambridge: Cambridge University Press, 1968), p. 408; Robert M. Kingdon, "Was the Protestant Reformation a Revolution? The Case of Geneva," in *Transition and Revolution: Problems and Issues of European Renaissance and Reformation History,* ed. Robert M. Kingdon (Minneapolis: Burgess, 1974), p. 65.

57. Monter, *Calvin's Geneva,* pp. 233–234.

58. Michel Baelde, "Financial Policy and the Evolution of the Demesne in the Netherlands under Charles V and Philip II (1530–1560)," in *Government in Reformation Europe, 1520–1560),* ed. Henry J. Cohn (New York: Macmillan, 1971), pp. 203–224.

59. Immanuel Wallerstein, *The Modern World-System* (New York: Academic Press, 1974).

60. Gerhard Ritter, "Why the Reformation Occurred in Germany," *Church History* 27 (1958), 99–106; Miriam Usher Chrisman, *Lay Culture, Learned Culture: Books and Social Change in Strasbourg, 1480–1559* (New Haven: Yale University Press, 1982), p. 156. In examining Reformation publications, Chrisman shows that anti-Catholic polemic was the most frequent theme, outnumbering theological tracts by two to one.

61. Donald R. Kelley, *The Beginnings of Ideology: Consciousness and Society in the French Reformation* (Cambridge: Cambridge University Press, 1981), p. 32.

62. Phyllis Mack Crew, *Calvinist Preaching and Iconoclasm in the Netherlands, 1544–1569* (Cambridge: Cambridge University Press, 1978); Rob-

ert W. Scribner, "Reformation, Carnival, and the World Turned Upside-Down," *Social History* 3 (1978), 303–329.

63. Robert W. Scribner, "The Reformation as a Social Movement," in *Stadtbürgertum und Adel in der Reformation: Studien zur Socialgeschichte der Reformation in England und Deutschland,* ed. Wolfgang J. Mommsen (Stuttgart: Klett-Cotta, 1979), pp. 49–79.

64. A. G. Dickens, *The German Nation and Martin Luther* (London: Edward Arnold, 1974), pp. 67–68.

65. Natalie Zemon Davis, "The Sacred and the Body Social in Six-teenth-Century Lyon," *Past and Present* 90 (1981), 40–70.

66. Pierre Joseph Proudhon, *La révolution sociale démontrée par le coup d'état du deux décembre* (Paris: Garnier, 1852), p. 47; quoted in Lucien Febvre, *Life in Renaissance France* (Cambridge, Mass.: Harvard University Press, 1977), p. 89.

67. H. G. Koenigsberger and George L. Mosse, *Europe in the Sixteenth Century* (London: Longman, 1968), p. 130; Quentin Skinner, *The Foundations of Modern Political Thought,* vol. 2, *The Age of Reformation* (Cambridge: Cambridge University Press, 1968), pp. 12–20.

68. Chrisman, *Strasbourg and the Reform,* p. 122.

69. G. R. Elton, "The Reformation in England," in *The New Cambridge Modern History,* vol. 2, p. 236.

70. For example, by the 1550s Württemberg had institutionalized a system of discipline in religious matters that closely paralleled the relatively centralized character of its state apparatus. In contrast to the imperial cities, where church discipline was generally vested in the local community, a more centralized system was adopted that used district superintendents and a central church council to follow up on the warnings of local pastors. The state worked closely with this system, taking responsibility for the actual punishment of persons convicted of moral or religious infractions. For a discussion of these practices, see David Warren Sabean, *Power in the Blood: Popular Culture and Village Discourse in Early Modern Germany* (Cambridge: Cambridge University Press, 1984), esp. p. 39.

5. Mercantilism and the House of Learning

1. Robert Darnton, "In Search of the Enlightenment: Recent Attempts to Create a Social History of Ideas," *Journal of Modern History* 43 (1971), 123, observes that the Enlightenment "never penetrated far below the elite in any area of eighteenth-century Europe." Similarly, Rolf Reichardt, "Zu einer Sozialgeschichte der französischen Aufklärung: Ein Essay," *Francia* 5 (1977), 240, notes that it "is by no means as clear as many have assumed" that the philosophes succeeded in changing the way people thought.

2. Between 1600 and 1700, overall population in the German terri-tories declined from 20 million to 15.5 million; in the Low Countries from

3 million to 2.7 million; in Spain from 8 million to 7.3 million; and in the Italian states from 13 million to 11.3 million. These figures are reported in F. C. Spooner, "The European Economy, 1609–50," in *The New Cambridge Modern History,* vol. 4, *The Decline of Spain and the Thirty Years War, 1609–48/59,* ed. J. P. Cooper (Cambridge: Cambridge University Press, 1970), pp. 70–71.

3. Stanley G. Payne, *A History of Spain and Portugal,* vol. 1 (Madison: University of Wisconsin Press, 1973), p. 283.

4. Ibid., p. 69. Immanuel Wallerstein, *The Modern World-System,* vol. 2, *Mercantilism and the Consolidation of the Euroepan World-Economy, 1600–1750* (New York: Academic Press, 1980), p. 21, cites authorities suggesting that "depression began in Spain around 1600, in Italy and part of central Europe in 1619, in France and part of Germany in 1630, in England and the United Provinces in 1650." Wallerstein provides a critical review of the major theories of crisis and contraction during the seventeenth century; see esp. pp. 13–34.

5. Of the closer supervision provided by the state, one writer suggests: "What was new is the greater degree of control and supervision exercised over the activities of these officials and institutions by the prince's councils and central offices. The officials became increasingly mere executors of the instructions and orders emanating from the center, which provided rational and comprehensive direction." Marc Raeff, "The Well-Ordered Police State and the Development of Modernity in Seventeenth- and Eighteenth-Century Europe: An Attempt at a Comparative Approach," *American Historical Review* 80 (1975), 1227.

6. Quincy Wright, *A Study of War,* 2d ed. (Chicago: University of Chicago Press, 1965), p. 660, estimates total English casualties for the seventy-year period from 1640 to 1709 at 128,400, compared with casualties of 102,995 for the century between 1710 and 1809. The largest decadal figures occurred between 1650 and 1659, and between 1700 and 1709.

7. See C. H. Wilson, *Profit and Power: A Study of England and the Dutch Wars* (London: Longman, 1957), esp. pp. 1–10, for a discussion of the extent to which war became institutionalized as a feature of international relations.

8. One writer says of Colbert, for example, that he "believed that he was working in a relatively static European economy, in which there was just so much bullion, so much shipping, and so much consumption and production of industrial goods. He was out to make sure that France got the most of everything and that other countries, especially Holland, got less." Harold T. Parker, *The Bureau of Commerce in 1781 and Its Policies with Respect to French Industry* (Durham, N.C.: Carolina Academic Press, 1979), p. 16.

9. Klaus Knorr, *British Colonial Theories, 1570–1850* (Toronto: University of Toronto Press, 1944), p. 5.

10. Barry E. Supple, *Commercial Crisis and Change in England, 1600–1642: A Study in the Instability of a Mercantile Economy* (Cambridge: Cambridge University Press, 1959), p. 230.

11. "The essence of the system lies not in some doctrine of money, or of the balance of trade; not in tariff barriers, protective duties, or navigation laws; but in something far greater: namely, in the total transformation of society and its organization, as well as of the state and its institutions, in the replacing of a local and territorial economic policy by that of the national state." Gustav Schmoller, *The Mercantile System and Its Historical Signifance* (New York: Macmillan, 1896), p. 51. Schmoler's thesis has been challenged and reworked in a number of studies, among the most important of which are Eli F. Hecksher, *Mercantilism,* 2 vols. (New York: Macmillan, 1955); Charles Wilson, *Mercantilism* (London: Routledge and Kegan Paul, 1958); and D. C. Coleman, "Mercantilism Revisited," *Historical Journal* 23 (1980), 773–791.

12. Some evidence of these developments in England and France is available in Chantal Rondet, "Fidélités et clientèles dans l'Angleterre d'Elizabeth et des Stuarts," *Revue du Nord* 59 (1977), 317–342, and F. Secret, "La première académie française de musique, selon les témoignages de Genebrard et de Jean Bodin," *Bibliothèque d'humanisme et Renaissance* 40 (1978), 119–121.

13. The importance of this geographical centralization is emphasized in P. J. Yarrow, *A Literary History of France,* vol. 2, *The Seventeenth Century, 1600–1715* (London: Ernest Benn, 1967), pp. 74–80.

14. R. J. W. Evans, "Learned Societies in Germany in the Seventeenth Century," *European Studies Review* 7 (1977), 129–152.

15. The role of international competition is evident in a statement by Dryden, who was one of the promoters of this venture: "I am sorry," he wrote, "that (speaking so noble a language as we do) we have not a more certain measure of it, as they have in France, where they have an Academy erected for that purpose, and endowed with large privileges by the present king." Quoted in Michael Foss, *The Age of Patronage: The Arts in Society, 1660–1750* (London: Hamish Hamilton, 1971), p. 103.

16. Reinhard Bendix, "Province and Metropolis: The Case of Eighteenth-Century Germany," in *Culture and Its Creators: Essays in Honor of Edward Shils,* ed. Joseph Ben-David and Terry Nichols Clark (Chicago: University of Chicago Press, 1976), p. 131, offers this revealing observation about the German states: "At the German courts, imitation of French fashion, use of French as the language of high society, demonstrations of homage to the French monarch—these seemed a small price to pay for an unofficial but unchallengeable verification of sovereign status." A similar point has

been made about the relations between Russia's imitation of French culture and its diplomatic aspirations; see Marc Raeff, "The Enlightenment in Russia and Russian Thought in the Enlightenment," in *The Eighteenth Century in Russia*, ed. J. G. Garrard (Oxford: Clarendon Press, 1973), esp. p. 42.

17. An extensive literature has dealt, for example, with the conflict between Newton and Leibniz, some of which points to the role of political factors in these debates; see esp. A Rupert Hall, *Philosophers at War: The Quarrel between Newton and Leibniz* (Cambridge: Cambridge University Press, 1980), and Steven Shapin, "Of Gods and Kings: Natural Philosophy and Politics in the Leibniz-Clarke Disputes," *Isis* 72 (1981), 187–215.

18. German scholars, including Theodore Haak and Samuel Hartlib, escaped the disruptions of the wars and religious conflicts that ravaged their homelands by emigrating to England or France. French Huguenots migrated to England, the Low Countries, and the German states.

19. The diffusion of Newton's ideas to Holland as a result of 'sGravesande, who came to England as secretary to the Dutch ambassador, is a familiar example; see Trevor H. Levere, "Relations and Rivalry: Interactions between Britain and the Netherlands in Eighteenth-Century Science and Technology," *History of Science* 9 (1970), 42–53. It has also been suggested, for another example, that the role of merchants and foreign diplomats was particularly instrumental in transmitting scientific ideas to Russia during the latter half of the seventeenth century; see Alexander Vucinich, *Science in Russian Culture: A History to 1860* (Stanford: Stanford University Press, 1963), esp. pp. 16–17. In France and England publishing and regular mail service were, of course, becoming increasingly important means of international communication; yet the role of trade was still extremely important. J. H. Plumb records, for example, that as late as the end of the seventeenth century Samuel Pepys felt obliged to make routine visits to the Royal Exchange in order to pick up foreign news by talking with merchants; see J. H. Plumb, *The Commercialization of Leisure in Eighteenth-Century England* (Reading: University of Reading Press, 1973), p. 5. I have written about the role of the mercantilist system in nurturing the legitimacy, patronage, autonomy, and communication networks in seventeenth-century science in greater detail in another context; see Robert Wuthnow, *Meaning and Moral Order: Explorations in Cultural Analysis* (Berkeley: University of California Press, 1987), chap. 8.

20. Racine provides another example of a prominent writer who enjoyed close relations with the court, in his case for nearly thirty-five years.

21. Yarrow, *A Literary History of France*, pp. 339–340.

22. See Theodore Besterman, *Voltaire* (London: Longmans, 1969), p. 35, who describes the Jesuit catechism that Voltaire, Diderot, Helvétius, and other Enlightenment writers learned as "essentially a practical guide

for the man of the world." In his view, it glossed over the subtleties of doctrine, dismissed concepts of evil and divine justice, and secularized the meaning of the eucharist.

23. See, for instance, Alexander Koyré, *Newtonian Studies* (Chicago: University of Chicago Press, 1965), esp. p. 22. In support of this argument it has been shown that Newton's immediate followers consciously put forth arguments relating economic self-interest to natural philosophy; see Margaret C. Jacob, "Newtonianism and the Origins of the Enlightenment," *Eighteenth-Century Studies* 11 (1977), 1–25.

24. For one example of an attempt to spell out this kind of connection between science and Enlightenment, see Michael Hunter, *Science and Society in Restoration England* (Cambridge: Cambridge University Press, 1981), esp. pp. 27–31.

25. Maurice Crosland, "The Development of a Professional Career in Science in France," *Minerva* 13 (1975), 40, observes that "the man of science had hardly been distinguished from the man of letters." The terms *savant* and *philosophe,* he notes, could be applied to both. The same point is underscored by Roger Hahn, "Scientific Research as an Occupation in Eighteenth-Century Paris," *Minerva* 13 (1975), esp. 503, in suggesting that scientists were not clearly distinguished from historians and antiquarians even in eighteenth-century France.

26. Foss, *The Age of Patronage,* p. 63, for example, suggests that in Restoration England a strong connection between reason and the state had been established which spilled over into other areas: "The arts—literature in particular, as the most articulate—were driven towards rationalism, not just by contemporary fashions in thought, but also by politics."

27. A detailed account of the relations between Locke and Shaftesbury is presented in Richard Ashcraft, *Revolutionary Politics and Locke's Two Treatises of Government* (Princeton: Princeton University Press, 1986); see esp. pp. 17–127.

28. Ibid., pp. 406–466.

29. Ibid., pp. 354, 365–370.

30. L. W. Sharp, "Charles Mackie: The First Professor of History at Edinburgh University," *Scottish Historical Review* 41 (1962), 23–45. In addition to Mackie, the networks that connected Locke and Shaftesbury to the Scottish Enlightenment included Thomas Reid, William Wishart, and Francis Hutcheson, all of whom had received patronage from Robert, Viscount Molesworth, a leading parliamentarian and one-time teacher of Shaftesbury. From Molesworth they had been exposed to the writings of both Locke and Shaftesbury. See Peter Jones, "The Scottish Professoriate and the Polite Academy, 1720–46," in *Wealth and Virtue: The Shaping of Political Economy in the Scottish Enlightenment,* ed. Istvan Hont and Michael

Ignatieff (Cambridge: Cambridge University Press, 1983), esp. pp. 93–99.

31. A. Owen Aldridge, *Voltaire and the Century of Light* (Princeton: Princeton University Press, 1975), pp. 42–45.

32. This connection is discussed in Ira O. Wade, *The Intellectual Development of Voltaire* (Princeton: Princeton University Press, 1969), pp. 44–81.

33. Historians have not been unmindful of the importance of this growth for the Enlightenment, and some have specifically compared the period with that of the Reformation. For example, see Georges Duby and Robert Mandrou, *A History of French Civilization* (New York: Random House, 1964), p. 351, who write: "Let us recognize that the period of the *philosophes* was one of great prosperity, flooding all of French life with riches; it was a period comparable to the long sixteenth century's revival, even to its appetites for luxury items."

34. Roger Mols, "Population in Europe, 1500–1700," in *The Fontana Economic History of Europe,* vol. 2, *The Sixteenth and Seventeenth Centuries,* ed. Carlo M. Cipolla (Glasgow: William Collins Sons, 1974), pp. 38–39.

35. E. N. Williams, *The Ancien Régime in Europe: Government and Society in the Major States, 1648–1789* (New York: Harper and Row, 1970), p. 194.

36. André Armengaud, "Population in Europe, 1700–1914," in *The Fontana Economic History of Europe,* vol. 3, *The Industrial Revolution,* ed. Carlo M. Cipolla (Glasgow: William Collins Sons, 1973), p. 61.

37. Wilson, *Profit and Power,* p. 28.

38. The role of the bourgeoisie, printing, and an expanding literary market in eighteenth-century literature has been much emphasized; see, for example, Georg Lukács, *The Historical Novel* (Lincoln: University of Nebraska Press, 1962), esp. pp. 19–30; Arthur Humphreys, "The Social Setting," in *The New Pelican Guide to English Literature,* vol. 4, *From Dryden to Johnson,* ed. Boris Ford (Hammondsworth: Penguin, 1982), pp. 15–52; Terry Eagleton, *Criticism and Ideology* (London: NLB, 1976),pp. 45–53; Raymond Williams, *The Sociology of Culture* (New York: Schocken, 1981), pp.163–171; Pierre Bourdieu,"The Market of Symbolic Goods," *Poetics* 14 (1985), 13–44; and Alvin Kernan, *Printing Technology, Letters, and Samuel Johnson* (Princeton: Princeton University Press, 1987), esp. pp. 3–70.

39. The role of the bourgeoisie in intellectual developments in specific societies will be examined in subsequent chapters. As a general supposition, the connection between the bourgeoisie and the Enlightenment has been emphasized repeatedly in the literature. Some writers go as far as to build this connection into the very definition of the Enlightenment. See, for example, Hiroshi Mizuta, "Towards a Definition of the Scottish Enlightenment," *Studies on Voltaire and the Eighteenth Century* 154 (1976), 1459, who asserts: "The Enlightenment can be defined as a system of ideas whose

function was to legitimise a bourgeois civilisation at an early stage of its growth." Other writers, as we shall see, have been more skeptical of this connection or have noted difficulties in arriving at precise estimates of the composition and influence of the bourgeoisie. To cite one example, M. S. Anderson, *Historians and Eighteenth-Century Europe, 1715–1789* (Oxford: Clarendon Press, 1979), p. 105, observes emphatically that "any explanation of the Enlightenment in terms of classes and their economic interests seems implausible."

6. Cultural Production in France and England

1. Olwen H. Hufton, *Bayeux in the Late Eighteenth Century: A Social Study* (Oxford: Clarendon Press, 1967), p. 5.

2. Olwen Hufton, "The French Church," in *Church and Society in Catholic Europe of the Eighteenth Century,* ed. William J. Callahan and David Higgs (Cambridge: Cambridge University Press, 1979), pp. 13–33.

3. Cyril B. O'Keefe, *Contemporary Reactions to the Enlightenment* (Geneva: Librairie Slatkine, 1974), p. 58, observes a direct connection between the religious controversies and the Enlightenment: "The domestic troubles helped to provide a screen to hide the radicalism of the writings of the philosophers, Voltaire, Diderot, d'Alembert, and Rousseau. The censorship authorities were too preoccupied with the deluge of literature occasioned by the ecclesiastical controversies to pay close attention to the new works of the *philosophes*." Official government policy also aggravated these controversies by vacillating between the Jesuit and Jansenist perspectives. The philosophes mainly took the occasion as an opportunity to argue for reason in place of religious dogma.

4. Frederick B. Artz, *The Development of Technical Education in France, 1500–1850* (Cambridge, Mass.: MIT Press, 1966), pp. 33–34; Roger Chartier, "Student Populations in the Eighteenth Century," *British Journal for Eighteenth-Century Studies* 2 (1979), 150–162.

5. Thomas L. Hankins, *Jean d'Alembert: Science and the Enlightenment* (Cambridge: Cambridge University Press, 1970), p. 19; this is not to suggest, however, that the universities were insignificant or in a state of decay. Although they did not serve as the primary institutional bases of the Enlightenment, they remained important as centers for training in legal, clerical, and medical professions; see Jean de Viguerie, "Quelques remarques sur les universités françaises aux dix-huitième siècle," *Revue histoire* 262 (1979), 29–49.

6. Colm Kiernan, *The Enlightenment and Science in Eighteenth-Century France,* 2d ed. (Banbury: The Voltaire Foundation, 1973), p. 161.

7. Georges Duby and Robert Mandrou, *A History of French Civilization* (New York: Random House, 1964), pp. 401–402: "The *colleges* are the period's greatest triumph: they spring up everywhere, even in the smallest

towns of some thousand inhabitants, gathering together twenty or a hundred and fifty pupils." Estimates indicate that by 1750, 90 percent of the towns with inhabitants of 10,000 or more had at least one college and that these institutions enrolled a total of between 150,000 and 200,000 pupils; see Roger Chartier et al., *L'education en France du XVIe au XVIIIe siècles* (Paris: Société d'èdition d'enseignement supérieur, 1976), pp. 179–196; Willem Frijhoff and Dominique Julia, *Ecole et société dans la France d'Ancien Régime* (Paris: A Colin, 1975), pp. 35–40.

8. Charles R. Bailey, "Attempts to Institute a 'System' of Secular Secondary Education in France, 1762–1789," in *Facets of Education in the Eighteenth Century,* by James A. Leith (Oxford: Voltaire Foundation at the Taylor Institution, 1977), pp. 105–124.

9. Joseph Klaits, "Men of Letters and Political Reform in France at the End of the Reign of Louis XIV: The Founding of the Académie Politique," *Journal of Modern History* 43 (1971), 577–597.

10. Kiernan, *The Enlightenment and Science,* pp. 149–154; John A. Armstrong, "Old-Regime Administrative Elites: Prelude to Modernization in France, Prussia, and Russia," *International Review of Administrative Sciences* 38 (1972), 35; Roland Mousnier, *The Institutions of France under the Absolute Monarchy, 1598–1789,* vol. 1, *Society and the State* (Chicago: University of Chicago Press, 1979), pp. 455–457.

11. Alan Charles Kors, *D'Holbach's Coterie: An Enlightenment in Paris* (Princeton: Princeton University Press, 1976), pp. 216–217.

12. Daniel Roche, "Milieux académiques provinciaux et société des lumières," *Livre et société dans la France du XVIIIe siècle* 9 (1965), 96.

13. The most extensive study of the provincial academies is Daniel Roche, *Le siècle des lumières en province: Académies et académiciens provinciaux, 1680–1789,* 2 vols. (Paris: Mouton, 1978).

14. Charles C. Gillispie, *Science and Polity in France at the End of the Old Regime* (Princeton: Princeton University Press, 1980), pp. 81–99; James E. McClellan III, "The International Organization of Science and Learned Societies in the Eighteenth Century" (Ph.D. diss., Princeton University, 1975); Roger Hahn, "Scientific Research as an Occupation in Eighteenth-Century Paris," *Minerva* 13 (1975), 501–513.

15. Hankins, *Jean d'Alembert,* pp. 36–39.

16. Often the salons' hostesses had more than passing connections with the state. For example, the salon that set the patterns for many of the gatherings that developed later in the century was organized around 1700 by the duchesse du Maine. She was married to the legitimized son of Louis XIV, became involved in the Cellamare conspiracy of 1718, and spent two years in the Bastille as a result. Another influential salon early in the century was that of Mme. de Tencin, who was a sister of the powerful bishop of Grenoble, later made archbishop of Lyons and then cardinal. She was also

known for her affairs with leading officials, including the English diplomat Matthew Prior and the police lieutenant d'Argenson. She too spent a brief period in the Bastille. Yet another influential salon was that of Mme. Geoffrin, who was married to a rich manufacturer who was lieutenant-colonel of the National Gaurd. Still another salon was hosted by Mme. du Deffand, whose credits included that of mistress of the regent. For an overview of these salons, see Robert Niklaus, *A Literary History of France: The Eighteenth Century, 1715–1789* (London: Ernest Benn, 1970), pp. 40–55. According to Daniel Mornet, the principal salons in Paris during the first half of the eighteenth century were those of the duchesse du Maine, the marquise de Lambert, Mme. de Tencin, and Mme. du Deffand, while the most prominent centers of the following period were those of Mlle. de Lespinasse, Mme. Helvétius, Mme. d'Holbach, Mme. d'Epinay, and Mme. Necker. Daniel Mornet, *French Thought in the Eighteenth Century* (New York: Prentice-Hall, 1929), p. 21. For the earlier period, Wade mentions the salons sponsored by the duchess of Bouillon, the duke of Nevers, and the duke of Vendôme. The last of these, also known as the Temple, provided the literary environment in which Voltaire developed his talents between 1706 and 1723. See Ira O. Wade, *The Intellectual Development of Voltaire* (Princeton: Princeton University Press, 1969), pp. 18–19.

17. Daniel Roche, "Négoce et culture dans la France du XVIIIᵉ siècle," *Revue d'histoire moderne et contemporaine* 25 (1978), 375–395.

18. Robert Shackleton, "The Enlightenment," in *The Eighteenth Century: Europe in the Age of the Enlightenment,* ed. Alfred Cobban (New York: McGraw-Hill, 1969), p. 271.

19. Priscilla P. Clark and Terry Nichols Clark, "Patrons, Publishers, and Prizes: The Writer's Estate in France," in *Culture and Its Creators: Essays in Honor of Edward Shils,* ed. Joseph Ben-David and Terry Nichols Clark (Chicago: University of Chicago Press, 1977), pp. 197–225. They note that the four leading writers of seventeenth-century France—Corneille, Racine, Molière, and Boileau—all received patronage from the court. Robert Darnton, "In Search of the Enlightenment: Recent Attempts to Create a Social History of Ideas," *Journal of Modern History* 43 (1971), 123, suggests that state subsidies for writers were probably greater under Louis XVI than under Louis XIV. James A. Leith, "Nationalism and the Fine Arts in France, 1750–1789," *Studies on Voltaire and the Eighteenth Century* 89 (1972), 919–937, observes that with some 1,800 to 2,000 paintings the crown was also a substantial patron of the visual arts. Kiernan, *The Enlightenment and Science,* p. 153, writes: "A most important reason for a developing interest in the life sciences and in technology was royal patronage, which rendered fashionable what was already an established interest."

20. Before rising to prominence, writers were sometimes especially dependent on securing patronage or odd jobs associated with government

activities. Diderot, during his critical first decade in Paris, for instance, took odd jobs such as tutoring in mathematics, ghost writing, and translating, and submitted occasional articles to the many gazettes and journals that the capital supported. See Otis Fellows, *Diderot* (Boston: Twayne, 1977), p. 30.

21. Kors, *D'Holbach's Coterie,* pp. 200–201. Darnton observes that men of letters such as Suard managed to live largely from patronage rather than having to rely on income from the literary market for a living. Robert Darnton, *The Literary Underground of the Old Regime* (Cambridge, Mass.: Harvard University Press, 1982), pp. 3–7.

22. Joseph Ben-David, *The Scientist's Role in Society: A Comparative Study* (Englewood Cliffs, N.J.: Prentice-Hall, 1971), p. 98.

23. McClellan, *The International Organization of Science,* p. 564, emphasis added.

24. Kors, *D'Holbach's Coterie,* pp. 200–208. Having substantial incomes of their own, some of the Enlightenment's leading figures were of course less dependent on government patronage, and thereby gained some financial autonomy from the state. Montesquieu provides a vivid example. At the age of seven he inherited from his mother a valuable wine-producing estate in Bordeaux. At age twenty-six he married a wealthy Protestant who brought him a dowry of 100,000 livres. And a year later he inherited the estates of a wealthy uncle. Five years before the publication of his first major work, therefore, he was in a position to devote all his attention to literary pursuits. His wealth, however, did not separate him from the broader influences of the state. Indeed the same wealth that freed him to pursue intellectual interests placed him in contact with members of the government and exposed him to the major political debates of the day. From his uncle he inherited not only estates but also the socially prominent position of deputy president in the parlement of Bordeaux. Through the contacts this position provided, and particularly the assistance of the duke of Berwick (military governor of Bordeaux), Montesquieu was introduced to Parisian social life and soon after began to appear as a regular member of the salon of Mme. de Lambert and the Club of the Entresol, which included among its members d'Argenson and the exiled Bolingbroke.

25. Remy Saisselin, *The Literary Enterprise in Eighteenth-Century France* (Detroit: Wayne State University Press, 1979), p. 76.

26. Of general interest on this topic is François Furet, "La 'libraire' du royaume de France au XVIIIᵉ siècle," *Livre et société dans la France du XVIIIᵉ siècle* 1 (1970).

27. Otis Fellows, "Buffon's Place in the Enlightenment," *Studies on Voltaire and the Eighteenth Century* 25 (1963), 603–629.

28. Ralph H. Bowen, "The *Encyclopédie* as a Business Venture," in *From the Ancien Régime to the Popular Front,* ed. Charles K. Warner (New

York: Columbia University Press, 1969), pp. 1–22. The importance of capital and organizational skills is especially apparent in the case of the *Encyclopédie:* it involved the contributions of 150 authors, the labor of 1,000 artisans, the support of 4,000 subscribers, and a total turnover of some 7.6 million livres, which, it has been pointed out, exceeded the value of France's entire trade with the East and West Indies. See Niklaus, *A Literary History of France,* p. 374.

29. Lawrence Stone, "Literacy and Education in England, 1640–1900," *Past and Present* 42 (1969), 120. Another estimate suggests that adult literacy on the whole increased from 21 percent in 1686 to 37 percent in 1786. François Furet and William Sachs, "La croissance de l'alphabetisation en France, XVIIIᵉ–XIXᵉ siècles," *Annales, E.S.C.* 29 (1974), 714–737.

30. J. Queniart, *Culture et société urbaines dans la France de l'ouest au XVIᵉ–IIᵉ siècles,* 2 vols. (Lille: Nord, 1977), pp. 552–565. In all, some three thousand works of fiction are estimated to have been written in France between 1715 and 1789; Niklaus, *A Literary History of France,* p. 372.

31. Daniel Roche, "Urban Reading Habits during the French Enlightenment," *British Journal for Eighteenth-Century Studies* 2 (1979), 220.

32. O'Keefe, *Contemporary Reactions to the Enlightenment,* p. 44; Stephen Botein et al., "The Periodical Press in Eighteenth-Century English and French Society: A Cross-Cultural Approach," *Comparative Studies in Society and History* 23 (1981), 470.

33. Robert Darnton, *The Business of Enlightenment: A Publishing History of the Encyclopédie, 1775–1800* (Cambridge, Mass.: Belknap Press, 1979), pp. 282–286.

34. Roche, "Urban Reading Habits," p. 148. Other historians of the period have generally argued that writers could not support themselves strictly from sales and, therefore, were dependent on patronage. For example, Niklaus asserts: "With no protection . . . , a small public, and poor returns, the writer was hard put to make ends meet, without financial aid"; *A Literary History of France,* p. 42.

35. Cf. Frédéric Barbier, "L'imprimerie Strasbourgeoise au siècle des lumières (1681–1789)," *Revue d'histoire moderne et contemporaine* 24 (1977), 161–188; Daniel Droixhe, ed., *Livres et lumières au pays de Liège, 1730–1830* (Liège: Desoer Editions, 1980).

36. Edmond Soreau, "Quelques remarques sur les papeteries, imprimeries, librairies au XVIIIᵉ siècle," *Annales d'histoire de la Révolution française* 34 (1962), 306–335.

37. Furet observes that the Parlement of Paris and the monarchy were frequently divided on cases of censorship and that this division worked against an effective system of repression; during the course of the eighteenth century an increasing number of books that were considered objectionable nevertheless received authorization under the system of *permission tacite,* a

practice that appears to have been used primarily in the case of historical, scientific, and literary works rather than religious books; see Furet, "La 'libraire' du royaume."

38. D. W. Smith, *Helvétius: A Study in Persecution* (Oxford: Clarendon Press, 1965), p. 2.

39. Voltaire, for example, was arrested in 1717 and imprisoned in the Bastille for thirteen months; in 1726 he was arrested again and this time was forced to exile himself to England in order to escape imprisonment.

40. Jacques LeBrun, "Censure preventive et literature religieuse en France au début du XVIIIᵉ siècle," *Revue d'histoire de l'Eglise de France* 61 (1975), 201–226.

41. Mornet, *French Thought in the Eighteenth Century,* pp. 174–175; Kors, *D'Holbach's Coterie,* p. 297; Theodore Besterman, *Voltaire* (London: Longmans, 1969), pp. 297–298. Rousseau is often considered the exception because of his psychological and emotional distance from the French capital; yet even he was significantly influenced by his contacts with the state. His stint as secretary to the French ambassador in Venice (1743–1744) gave rise to the reflections about political democracy that were later incorporated into *The Social Contract.* From writing daily dispatches on affairs in the city, Rousseau learned that Venice was not the great republican example eulogized in history books but a dissolute aristocracy. The disillusionment he felt, he wrote later in the *Confessions,* awakened within him a continuing interest in political institutions (bk. 7, pt. 1); for a discussion of this experience, see James Miller, *Rousseau: Dreamer of Democracy* (New Haven: Yale University Press, 1984), pp. 59–60.

42. Alexis de Tocqueville, *The Old Régime and the French Revolution* (New York: Doubleday, 1955), p. 139.

43. These earlier views include those of Henri Hauser, "The Characteristic Features of French Economic History from the Middle of the Sixteenth to the Middle of the Eighteenth Century," *Economic History Review* 4 (1933), 257–272, and Benjamin T. Hoselitz, "Entrepreneurship and Capital Formation in France and Britain since 1700," in *Capital Formation and Economic Growth,* ed. Moses Abramovitz (Princeton: Princeton University Press, 1955), pp. 142–175. Among those who have directly challenged these views, see Don R. Leet and John A. Shaw, "French Economic Stagnation, 1700–1760: Old Economic History Revisited," *Journal of Interdisciplinary History* 8 (1978), 531–544.

44. Denis Richet, "Economic Growth and Its Setbacks in France from the Fifteenth to the Eighteenth Century," in *Social Historians in Contemporary France,* ed. Marc Ferro (New York: Harper and Row, 1972), pp. 209–210; Earl J. Hamilton, "The Political Economy of France at the Time of John Law," *History of Political Economy* 1 (1969), 135; Peter Mathias and Patrick O'Brien, "Taxation in Britain and France, 1715–1810: A Compar-

ison of the Social and Economic Incidence of Taxes Collected for the Central Governments," *Journal of European Economic History* 5 (1976), 601–650.

45. Jan Marczewski, "Some Aspects of the Economic Growth of France, 1660–1958," *Economic Development and Cultural Change* 9 (1961), 369–386; Roger Price, *The Economic Modernization of France, 1730–1800* (New York: Wiley, 1975), p. 171.

46. François Crouzet, "England and France in the Eighteenth Century," in Ferro, *Social Historians in Contemporary France*, p. 69; J. C. Toutain, *Le produit de l'agriculture française de 1700 à 1958*, vol. 2, *La croissance* (Paris: Mason, 1961), pp. 128–129.

47. Duby and Mandrou, *A History of French Civilization*, p. 51.

48. Thomas M. Doerflinger, "The Antilles Trade of the Old Regime: A Statistical Overview," *Journal of Interdisciplinary History* 6 (1976), 397–415; Arthur McCandless Wilson, *French Foreign Policy during the Administration of Cardinal Fleury, 1726–1743: A Study in Diplomacy and Commercial Development* (Cambridge, Mass.: Harvard University Press, 1936), pp. 290–317; Ruggiero Romano, "Documenti e prime considerazioni interno alla 'balance du commerce' della Francia dal 1716 al 1780," *Studi in onore di Armando Sapori* 2 (1957), 1265–1300.

49. Crouzet, "England and France in the Eighteenth Century," pp. 63–69; Charles P. Kindleberger, "Commercial Expansion and the Industrial Revolution," *Journal of European Economic History* 4 (1975), 632–635.

50. Marczewski, "Some Aspects of the Economic Growth of France," p. 372.

51. Charles Tilly, *The Contentious French* (Cambridge, Mass.: Belknap, 1986), pp. 209–211, stresses the importance of the fact that, despite the overall increase in tax revenues, the economy grew even faster; thus "in real cost per capita, direct taxes actually declined slightly over the century," a decline that Tilly associates with the state's more general capacity in these years to maintain domestic order.

52. Van der Wee, "Monetary, Credit, and Banking Systems," in *The Cambridge Economic History of Europe*, vol. 5, *The Economic Organization of Early Modern Europe*, ed. E. E. Rich and C. H. Wilson (Cambridge: Cambridge University Press, 1977), pp. 376–377.

53. G. P. Gooch, *Louis XV: The Monarchy in Decline* (Westport, Conn.: Greenwood Press, 1976), pp. 5–8.

54. Vivian R. Gruder, *The Royal Provincial Intendants: A Governing Elite in Eighteenth-Century France* (Ithaca: Cornell University Press, 1968), pp. 59–72; J. F. Bosher, *The Single Duty Project: A Study of the Movement for A French Customs Union in the Eighteenth Century* (London: Athlone Press, 1964), pp. 2–14.

55. For example, Leonard R. Berlanstein, *The Barristers of Toulouse in the Eighteenth Century, 1740–1793* (Baltimore: Johns Hopkins University

Press, 1975), suggests that in Toulouse, the provincial capital of Languedoc, there were over 1,000 functionaries attached to the court, including the 100 magistrates of the parlement. This study also gives evidence that the growth in the state bureaucracy in Paris was reproduced in the provinces; for example, the number of barristers at the parlement in Toulouse grew from 87 in 1740 to 215 in 1789. See also Alfred Cobban, "The *Parlements* of France in the Eighteenth Century," *History* 35 (1950), 64–80. Tilly, *The Contentious French*, p. 208, summarizes: "A fortified, bureaucratized fiscal structure became the framework of the whole state."

56. Artz, *The Development of Technical Education*, p. 56.

57. Gillispie, *Science and Polity in France*, provides an extensive treatment of the relations between science and the state during Turgot's ministry.

48. General overviews of these developments are presented in Mousnier, *The Institutions of France under the Absolute Monarchy*, and Price, *The Economic Modernization of France*, pp. 1–25.

59. Cf. Harold T. Parker, *The Bureau of Commerce in 1781 and Its Policies with Respect to French Industry* (Durham, N.C.: Carolina Academic Press, 1979), pp. 17–28.

60. Betty Behrens, "Government and Society," in *The Cambridge Economic History of Europe*, vol. 5, p. 555; Michael Howard, *War in European History* (Oxford: Oxford University Press, 1976), pp. 63–66.

61. Lionel Rothkrug, *Opposition to Louis XIV: The Political and Social Origins of the French Enlightenment* (Princeton: Princeton University Press, 1965), pp. 414–415.

62. Parker, *The Bureau of Commerce*, p. 23.

63. E. Lavaquery, *Necker: Fourrier de la Révolution, 1732–1804* (Paris: Libraire Plon, 1933), pp. 17–118; Douglas Dakin, *Turgot and the Ancien Régime in France* (London: Methuen, 1939), pp. 288–289.

64. Roland Mousnier, "La fonction publique en France du début du seizième siècle à la fin du dix-huitième siècle," *Revue histoire* 261 (1979), 321–335.

65. Hankins, *Jean d'Alembert*, p. 13.

66. Shackleton, "The Englightenment."

67. Hahn, "Scientific Research as an Occupation," 505.

68. The close relation between writers and the state, nevertheless, gave this competition a political tone and sometimes aggravated it. Voltaire's struggles with the censorship officials, for example, which are usually understood in terms of his relations with the church, can also be interpreted in this light. From 1733 to 1762, the office of royal censor was held by Prosper Jolyot de Crébillon, with whom Voltaire was perpetually at odds. Crébillon, however, was not principally a representative of the church. He was instead a member of the Académie Française, the leading writer of French tragedy, and Voltaire's chief rival for preeminence on the French stage. That Cré-

billon was also held in high regard by the crown, received a pension from the king, and served as royal censor merely intensified the intellectual rivalry that divided the two writers. For a discussion of this relationship, see Niklaus, *A Literary History of France,* pp. 293–295.

69. Duby and Mandrou, *A History of French Civilization,* p. 380; William Doyle, "The Parlements of France and the Breakdown of the Old Regime, 1771–1788," *French Historical Studies* 6 (1970), p. 426.

70. Olwen Hufton, *Europe: Privilege and Protest, 1730–1789* (Glasgow: William Collins Sons, 1980), p. 299.

71. Norman Hampson, "The Enlightenment in France," in *The Enlightenment in National Context,* ed. Roy Porter and Mikulas Teich (Cambridge: Cambridge University Press, 1981), p. 53.

72. Gruder, *The Royal Provincial Intendants,* pp. 83–84.

73. Doyle, "The Parlements of France," p. 454.

74. Behrens, "Government and Society," p. 553.

75. Bailey Stone, *The Parlement of Paris, 1774–1789* (Chapel Hill: University of North Carolina Press, 1981), pp. 15–16; J. H. Shennan, *The Parlement of Paris* (London: Eyre and Spottiswoode, 1968), pp. 285–325.

76. Gruder, *The Royal Provincial Intendants,* p. 206.

77. Keith Michael Baker, "French Political Thought at the Accession of Louis XVI," *Journal of Modern History* 50 (1978), 279–303.

78. Parker, *The Bureau of Commerce,* pp. 3–15; Paul Walde Bamford, "French Shipping in Northern European Trade, 1660–1789," *Journal of Modern History* 26 (1954), 207–219.

79. Mark Hulliung, *Montesquieu and the Old Regime* (Berkeley: University of California Press, 1976), p. 20.

80. Doyle, "The Parlements of France."

81. Crouzet, "England and France in the Eighteenth Century," p. 73; see also Franklin L. Ford, *Robe and Sword: The Regrouping of the French Aristocracy after Louis XIV* (Cambridge, Mass.: Harvard University Press, 1953).

82. Betty Behrens, "Nobles, Privileges, and Taxes in France at the End of the Ancien Régime," *Economic History Review* 15 (1963), 455.

83. See also Marie-Thérèse Allemand, "Les grandes remontrances de la cour des aides et la réforme de l'état," *Bulletin d'histoire economic et sociale de la Révolution française* (1976), 37–103; Guy Chaussinand-Noggaret, *La noblesse au XVIIIᵉ siècle: De la Féodalité aux lumières* (Paris: Hachette, 1976); Price, *The Economic Modernization of France,* pp. 32–33.

84. John A. Armstrong, "Old-Regime Governors: Bureaucratic and Patrimonial Attributes," *Comparative Studies in Society and History* 14 (1972), 19; Tom Kemp, *Economic Forces in French History* (London: Dennis Dobson, 1971), p. 56.

85. John A. Lynn, "A Pattern of French Military Reform, 1750–1790:

Speculations Concerning the Officer Corps," *Proceedings of the Consortium on Revolutionary Europe, 1750–1850* (1974), 113–128.

86. Gruder, *The Royal Provincial Intendants,* pp. 161–163, 205–207; Lynn A. Hunt, "Local Elites at the End of the Old Regime: Troyes and Reims, 1750–1789," *French Historical Studies* 9 (1976), 379–399.

87. Hulliung, *Montesquieu and the Old Regime,* p. 16.

88. Rothkrug, *Opposition to Louis XIV,* pp. 372–392.

89. Cf. Alfred Cobban, "The Pattern of Government," in Cobban, *The Eighteenth Century,* pp. 11–40. Tilly, *The Contentious French,* p. 212, asserts that statemaking generally imposed standardization, while economic expansion reinforced regional distinctions.

90. Doyle, "The Parlements of France," p. 447.

91. Cf. Bailey Stone, "Robe against Sword: The Parlement of Paris and the French Aristocracy, 1774–1789," *French Historical Studies* 9 (1975), 278–303.

92. Peter Gay, *Voltaire's Politics* (Princeton: Princeton University Press, 1959), p. 126.

93. Gruder, *The Royal Provincial Intendants,* p. 37; Stone, "Robe against Sword."

94. For specific discussions of these problems, see especially the following: C. B. A. Behrens, *The Ancien Régime* (New York: Harcourt Brace, 1967), p. 140; J. F. Bosher, "The French Crisis of 1770," *History* 57 (1972), 17–30; P. G. M. Dickson, *The Financial Revolution in England: A Study in the Development of Public Credit, 1688–1756* (London: Macmillan, 1967), p. 11; Price, *The Economic Modernization of France,* p. 162.

95. Behrens, "Nobles, Privileges, and Taxes in France"; Kemp, *Economic Forces in French History,* pp. 59–62; Shennan, *The Parlement of Paris,* pp. 297–298; Thomas F. Sheppard, *Loumarin in the Eighteenth Century: A Study of a French Village* (Baltimore: Johns Hopkins University Press, 1971), pp. 49–81.

96. Doyle, "The Parlements of France," p. 429.

97. Hufton, *Europe,* p. 326. Some evidence also suggests that the salons in which writers and government officials participated were becoming more factionalized and competitive during this period. For example, several of the salons had become preserves of the high nobility; another consisted of members faithful to Choiseul; and still another was frequented by devotees of Turgot. Choiseul, Turgot, and Necker also hosted their own dinner gatherings. Still another salon became the center of the encyclopedists; others were organized by coteries of philosophes whose loyalties tended toward Helvétius or Grimm or Diderot. Although the salons kept the leading figures of the Enlightenment in touch with one another, therefore, they also promoted some internal differentiation.

98. Anthony Strugnell, *Diderot's Politics: A Study of the Evolution of*

Diderot's Political Thought after the Encyclopedia (The Hague: Martinus Nijhoff, 1973), p. 96.

99. Roche, "Milieux académiques provinciaux," pp. 100–133.

100. Rolf Reichardt, "Zu einer Sozialgeschichte der französischen Aufklärung: Ein Essay," *Francia* 5 (1977), 232–240.

101. Keith Michael Baker, "French Political Thought at the Accession of Louis XVI."

102. Kors, *D'Holbach's Coterie,* p. 233. This point is also emphasized in Roche's discussion of Kors's study; Daniel Roche, "Lumières et engagement politique: La coterie d'Holbach dévoilée," *Annales, E.S.C.* 33 (1978), 720–728. There were of course exceptions to the link suggested here between the public sphere located in Paris and the development of the French Enlightenment, for other contexts also played significant roles: Geneva in Rousseau's case, for example. Still, the effect of Geneva on Rousseau should not be exaggerated: his experience there was actually quite limited, for he had fled the city at the age of sixteen; he was not directly exposed there to the constitutional struggles that some historians have associated with his work; and the Geneva he mused about explicitly clearly differed from the actual Geneva.

103. Gay, *Voltaire's Politics,* p. 137.

104. Michael Sturmer, "An Economy of Delight: Court Artisans of the Eighteenth Century," *Business History Review* 53 (1979), 496–528.

105. Jean-Marie Goulemot, "Démons, merveilles, et philosophie à l'âge classique," *Annales, E.S.C.* 35 (1980), 1223–1250.

106. Darnton, *The Business of Enlightenment,* pp. 14–15.

107. Ibid., pp. 525–526.

108. Roche, *Le siècle des lumières en province.*

109. Roche, "Négoce et culture dans la France." Approximately 10 percent of the letters to Rousseau came from the bourgeoisie; the figures for Diderot were 7 of 135 correspondents; for Montesquieu 4 of 202; Séguier 11 of 338; and Voltaire 64 of 1,385 (p. 385). Roche also suggests that the outlook of the broader segment of the bourgeoisie (merchants, physicians, lawyers) who were members of the academies was scarcely forward-looking but was that of a social formation that "appealed to an antiquated model of association, which used privileges and patronages in order to protect its ownership"; see Roche, "Die 'Sociétés de pensée' und die aufgeklärten Eliten des 18. Jahrhunderts in Frankreich," in *Sozialgeschichte der Aufklärung in Frankreich: 12 Originalbeiträge,* ed. Hans Ulrich Gumbrecht, Rolf Reichardt, and Thomas Schleich (Munich: R. Oldenbourg Verlag, 1981), p. 95. See also Roger Chartier, *The Cultural Uses of Print in Early Modern France* (Princeton: Princeton University Press, 1987), esp. pp. 186–187, 192–197.

110. Gruder, *The Royal Provincial Intendants,* pp. 107–110.

111. These conclusions draw especially from the work of Guy Chaussinand-Nogaret, *La noblesse au XVIIIᵉ siècle: De la féodalité aux lumières* (Paris: La Haye, 1976); Jean Bastier, *La féodalité au siècle des lumières dans la région de Toulouse* (Paris: LaHaye, 1976); M. Cubells, "La politique d'annoblissement de la monarchie en Provence de 1715 à 1789," *Annales du Midi* 94 (1982), 173–196; and Philippe Goujard, " 'Féodalité' et lumières au XVIIIᵉ siècle: L'example de la noblesse," *Annales histoire de la Révolution française* 49 (1977), 103–118.

112. Roy Porter, "The Enlightenment in England," in Porter and Teich, *The Enlightenment in National Context,* p. 1; cf. J. G. A. Pocock, "Post-Puritan England and the Problem of the Enlightenment," in *Culture and Politics from Puritanism to the Enlightenment,* ed. Perez Zagorin (Berkeley: University of California Press, 1980), pp. 91–111. Pocock echoes Porter's sentiment, noting that England did contribute significantly to the Enlightenment, but when one attempts to speak of an English Enlightenment as such, "an ox sits upon the tongue."

113. Pocock, "Post-Puritan England," attributes this lack of anticlericalism to a longer tradition of anticlerical sentiment within the church itself, dating to the English Reformation and advanced most strongly by the Puritans.

114. E. P. Thompson, *The Poverty of Theory* (London: Merlin Press, 1978), p. 58. Thompson also notes that the Enlightenment in England seemed less vigorous than in France because it lacked anticlericalism.

115. Cited in Geoffrey S. Holmes, "Gregory King and the Social Structure of Pre-Industrial England," *Transactions of the Royal Historical Society* 27 (1977), 58–65.

116. Michael Foss, *The Age of Patronage: The Arts in Society, 1660–1750* (London: Hamish Hamilton, 1971), p. 163; cf. Pat Rogers, "Introduction: The Writer and Society," in *The Eighteenth Century,* ed. Pat Rogers (London: Methuen, 1978), p. 41, who suggests that in 1720 there were about a hundred booksellers in London who regularly published books as well.

117. Botein et al., "The Periodical Press in Eighteenth Century English and French Society," p. 470. These authors emphasize the differences rather than similarities between English and French periodicals, which they see as reflections of differences in social structure: "The French press continued to arrange society in traditionally aristocratic terms, whereas increasingly the English press affirmed the worth and dignity of the industrious order" (p. 484). But like their French counterparts, English periodicals carried news of major political decisions, economic analyses, and items about members of the elite.

118. R. M. Wiles, "Provincial Culture in Early Georgian England," in *The Triumph of Culture: 18th-Century Perspectives,* ed. Paul Fritz and David

Williams (Toronto: Hakkert, 1972), pp. 49–68. Wiles provides a useful summary of newspapers, libraries, and theater performances in the provinces.

119. Rogers, "Introduction: The Writer and Society," p. 42.

120. Louis D. Mitchell, "Command Performances during the Reign of George I," *Eighteenth-Century Studies* 7 (1974), 343–349.

121. J. H. Plumb, *The Commercialization of Leisure in Eighteenth-Century England* (Reading: University of Reading Press, 1973), p. 12. The first half of the eighteenth century was still a relatively difficult time for drama, however. Approximately one-quarter of the plays performed were Shakespearean; leaving these aside, fewer than a dozen seem to have enjoyed any degree of success. It has been estimated that the average play earned only about £20 for its author. For discussions of these difficulties, see C. B. Hogan, *Shakespeare in the Theatre, 1701–1800* (Oxford: Oxford University Press, 1952), esp. pp. 460–461; A. H. Scouten, *The London Stage, 1660–1800* (Carbondale, Ill.: University of Southern Illinois Press, 1968); and Rogers, "Introduction: The Writer and Society," p. 53.

122. George Rudé, *Hanoverian London, 1714–1808* (Berkeley: University of California Press, 1971), p. 68.

123. C. W. Chalkin, "Capital Expenditure on Building for Cultural Purposes in Provincial England, 1730–1830," *Business History* 22 (1980), 51–70, attributes this growth of intellectual and aesthetic interest solely to the rising affluence of the leisure class, citing the extent to which private funding was used to construct concert halls, theaters, museums, and libraries. Most of this private investment came relatively late in the Enlightenment, however, dating mainly from the last quarter of the eighteenth century.

124. Michael Hunter, *Science and Society in Restoration England* (Cambridge: Cambridge University Press, 1981), pp. 32–58, stresses the relative modesty of the Royal Society's contributions to science prior to the eighteenth century.

125. Michael Hunter, "The Debate over Science," in *The Restored Monarchy, 1660–1688*, ed. J. R. Jones (Totowa, N.J.: Rowman and Littlefield, 1979), pp. 176–177.

126. Valuable background on the overlap between science and literature in England is given in Barbara Shapiro, "History and Natural History in Sixteenth- and Seventeenth-Century England: An Essay on the Relationship between Humanism and Science," in *English Scientific Virtuosi in the 16th and 17th Centuries,* ed. Barbara Shapiro and Robert G. Frank, Jr. (Berkeley: University of California Press, 1980), pp. 1–55. The limits of this overlap are discussed in J. H. Plumb, "La diffusione della modernità," *Quaderni storici* 14 (1979), 887–911. The relation between the Enlightenment and medicine in England is discussed in Roy Porter, "Was There

a Medical Enlightenment in Eighteenth-Century England?" *British Journal for Eighteenth-Century Studies* 5 (1982), 49–64.

127. Richard S. Westfall, "Isaac Newton in Cambridge: The Restoration University and Its Scientific Creativity," in Zagorin, *Culture and Politics from Puritanism to the Enlightenment,* pp. 135–164; on enrollments, see Roger Chartier, "Student Populations in the Eighteenth Century," *British Journal for Eighteenth-Century Studies* 2 (1979), 152–153.

128. Roy Porter, *English Society in the Eighteenth Century* (London: Allen Lane, 1982), pp. 177–178.

129. Rogers, "Introduction: The Writer and Society," pp. 17–18.

130. Rudé, *Hanoverian London,* p. 77.

131. Trevor Fawcett, "Eighteenth-Century Debating Societies," *British Journal for Eighteenth-Century Studies* 3 (1980), 217–229.

132. McClellan, *The International Organization of Science and Learned Societies in the Eighteenth Century,* passim; D. G. C. Allan, "The Society of Arts and Government, 1754–1800: Public Encouragement of Arts, Manufactures, and Commerce in Eighteenth-Century England," *Eighteenth-Century Studies* 7 (1974), 434–452.

133. C. H. George, "The Making of the English Bourgeoisie," *Science and Society* 35 (1971), 411.

134. Marvin Rosen, "The Dictatorship of the Bourgeoisie: England, 1688–1721," *Science and Society* 45 (1981), 25.

135. Ibid., p. 51.

136. Christopher Hill, "A Bourgeois Revolution?" in *Three British Revolutions: 1641, 1688, 1776,* ed. J. G. A. Pocock (Princeton: Princeton University Press, 1980), p. 135; Isaac Kramnick, "Children's Literature and Bourgeois Ideology: Observations on Culture and Industrial Capitalism in the Later Eighteenth Century," in Zagorin, *Culture and Politics from Puritanism to the Enlightenment,* p. 205. Kramnick goes on to say: "Science was seen by all as the source of endless improvement and it was a bourgeois science that flourished, science as a practical ameliorative enterprise, science as useful. Science was applied physics, mechanics, electricity, and chemistry, all with useful and material applications . . . a science that would serve industry and manufacture well" (p. 207). See also Christopher Hill, *Reformation to Industrial Revolution* (Hammondsworth: Penguin, 1978), esp. p. 247; and J. H. Plumb, *England in the Eighteenth Century* (Hammondsworth: Penguin, 1951), esp. p. 167.

137. Rudé, *Hanoverian London,* estimates that there were as many as 4,500 aristocratic families in London compared with about 1,000 families in high finance and large-scale trade. These estimates are largely supported by tax return data; see L. D. Schwarz, "Income Distribution and Social Structure in London in the Late Eighteenth Century," *Economic History Review* 32 (1979), 250–259.

138. A study of London aldermen illustrates the difficulty of establishing an empirical definition of the bourgeoisie. Although a majority of the aldermen were directly involved in trade or banking, many had landholdings; intermarrige with the landed gentry was also common, and the manner in which they educated their sons was largely indistinguishable from that of the aristocracy. See Nicholas Rogers, "Money, Land, and Lineage: The Big Bourgeoisie of Hanoverian London," *Social History* 4 (1979), 437–454. And in the country, the aristocracy was heavily involved in capitalist agriculture and had interests that coincided with those of the commercial bourgeoisie; see Hill, "A Bourgeois Revolution?"

139. J. H. Plumb, "The Public, Literature, and the Arts in the 18th Century," in Fritz and Williams, *The Triumph of Culture: 18th-Century Perspectives,* emphasizes the importance of rising affluence in creating an expanded market for books, periodicals, music, and paintings. His discussion also points out, however, that this demand was largely filled at the local level without any common standards of taste or style being evident. It was, he suggests, the relationship between "culture" and the "central elite" within the state that gave unity to the production of culture.

140. Rogers, "Introduction: The Writer and Society," p. 16.

141. For general economic trends, see Anthony J. Little, *Deceleration in the Eighteenth-Century British Economy* (London: Croom Helm, 1976).

142. N. C. R. Crafts, "The Eighteenth Century: A Survey," in *The Economic History of Britain since 1700,* vol. 1, *1700–1860,* ed. Roderick Floud and Donald McCloskey (Cambridge: Cambridge University Press, 1981), esp. pp. 1–3.

143. E. J. Hobsbawn, *Industry and Empire* (Hammondsworth: Penguin, 1969), p. 48; see also Phyllis Deane and W. A. Cole, *British Economic Growth, 1688–1959: Trends and Structure* (Cambridge: Cambridge University Press, 1962), pp. 41–98, who show that foreign trade rose by about 300 percent between 1700 and the end of the Seven Years' War.

144. Hobsbawn, *Industry and Empire,* p. 50; Porter, *English Society in the Eighteenth Century,* p. 205.

145. P. G. M. Dickson, *The Financial Revolution in England: A Study in the Development of Public Credit, 1688–1756* (London: Macmillan, 1967), p. 10.

146. Peter Mathias, *The Transformation of England: Essays in the Economic and Social History of England in the Eighteenth Century* (London: Methuen, 1979), p. 118.

147. Porter, *English Society in the Eighteenth Century,* pp. 131–132.

148. Dickson, *The Financial Revolution in England,* p. 10.

149. Rosen, "The Dictatorship of the Bourgeoisie," pp. 34–36.

150. Dickson, *The Financial Revolution in England,* p. 11.

151. Ibid., pp. 284–298.

152. Mathias, *The Transformation of England*, pp. 171–190; Geoffrey S. Holmes, *Augustan England: Professions, State, Society, 1680–1730* (London: George Allen and Unwin, 1982), p. 255; Henry Roseveare, *The Treasury: The Evolution of a British Institution* (London: Allen Lane, 1969), p. 84.

153. Roger L. Emerson, "The Enlightenment and Social Structures," in *City and Society in the Eighteenth Century,* ed. Paul Fritz and David Williams (Toronto: Hakkert, 1973), p. 107; J. H. Plumb, *The Growth of Political Stability in England, 1675–1725* (London: Macmillan, 1967), p. 108; Geoffrey S. Holmes, "Gregory King and the Social Structure of Pre-Industrial England," *Transactions of the Royal Historical Society* 27 (1977), 58–65.

154. Howard Tomlinson, "Financial and Administrative Developments in England, 1660–88," in Jones, *The Restored Monarchy, 1660–1688,* pp. 100–101.

155. Plumb, *The Growth of Political Stability in England,* p. 112.

156. Porter, *English Society in the Eighteenth Century,* p. 122.

157. Norma Baker, "Changing Attitudes toward Government in Eighteenth-Century Britain," in *Statesmen, Scholars, and Merchants,* ed. Anne Whiteman et al. (Oxford: Clarendon Press, 1973), p. 204.

158. Patrick Crowhurst, *The Defence of British Trade, 1689–1815* (Kent: Dawson, 1977), pp. 45–80; W. A. Speck, "Politics," in Rogers, *The Eighteenth Century,* pp. 81–92. See also Dickson, *The Financial Revolution in England,* p. 11, who writes that "the wars of 1739–63 were crucial, not so much for national prestige, however much this was boosted, as for the decisive increases in export demand resulting from the preservation and extension of the North American and West Indian markets." Plumb, *The Growth of Political Stability in England,* p. 3, also links this commercial expansion with changes in the state: "The more complex trade is, the more involved its financial structure, the greater is the necessity for political stability."

159. Holmes, *Augustan England,* p. 241.

160. Rudé, *Hanoverian London,* p. 76, writes, for example, that London was "quite different from Paris and other Continental cities, whose cultural and social life was dominated by the Court and the landed classes."

161. Leslie Stephen, *Selected Writings in British Intellectual History* (Chicago: University of Chicago Press, 1979), p. 120.

162. Pat Rogers, *The Augustan Vision* (London: Weidenfeld and Nicholson, 1974), p. 70; cf. Bertrand G. Goldgar, *Walpole and the Wits: The Relation of Politics to Literature, 1722–1742* (Lincoln: University of Nebraska Press, 1976), p. 220.

163. Rudé, *Hanoverian London,* pp. 60–61.

164. Quoted in Foss, *The Age of Patronage,* p. 153.

165. Porter, *English Society in the Eighteenth Century,* p. 127.

166. Foss, *The Age of Patronage,* p. 143.

167. Ibid., p. 179.

168. Rogers, "Introduction: The Writer and Society," pp. 52–56.

169. Holmes, *Augustan England,* pp. 32, 252; much the same point is made about medical developments in N. D. Jewson, "Medical Knowledge and the Patronage System in Eighteenth-Century England," *Sociology* 8 (1974), 369–385.

170. Rogers, "Introduction: The Writer and Society," pp. 37–39.

171. For a discussion of this level of literary life, see Pat Rogers, *Grub Street: Studies in a Subculture* (London: Methuen, 1972). This study also stresses the degree to which London writers were absorbed with political issues; see esp. pp. 3–4.

172. Stephen, *Selected Writings in British Intellectual History,* p. 122.

173. Paul J. Korshin, "Types of Eighteenth-Century Literary Patronage," *Eighteenth-Century Studies* 7 (1974), p. 473.

174. Foss, *The Age of Patronage,* p. 50: "The king became less and less able to pay for the arts from a Privy Purse which was always lean and very often completely empty; and as the king's policies brought violence and the threat of civil war, the needs and expectations of poor artists ranked very low in the royal list of priorities."

175. Stephen, *Selected Writings in British Intellectual History,* p. 123.

176. John Brewer, *Party Ideology and Popular Politics at the Accession of George III* (Cambridge: Cambridge University Press, 1976), p. 6; cf. Linda Colley, *In Defiance of Oligarchy: The Tory Party, 1714–1760* (Cambridge: Cambridge University Press, 1982), p. 19.

177. J. C. D. Clark, *The Dynamics of Change: The Crisis of the 1750s and English Party Systems* (Cambridge: Cambridge University Press, 1982), pp. 10–13; Westminster and St. James were, in Clark's words, "hermetically sealed."

178. W. R. Brock, "England," in *The New Cambridge Modern History,* vol. 7, *The Old Regime, 1713–1763,* ed. J. O. Lindsay (Cambridge: Cambridge University Press, 1957), p. 242; Rogers, "Money, Land, and Lineage."

179. Dickson, *The Financial Revolution in England,* p. 47; Mathias, *The Transformation of England,* pp. 125–128; Ralph Davis, *English Overseas Trade, 1500–1700* (London: Macmillan, 1973), pp. 37, 56; Michael W. McCahill, "Peerage Creations and the Changing Character of the British Nobility, 1750–1830," *English Historical Review* 96 (1981), 259–284; H. J. Habukkuk, "England's Nobility," in *Aristocratic Government and Society in Eighteenth-Century England,* ed. Daniel Baugh (New York: New Viewpoints, 1975), pp. 96–114. Land and improvements still made up two-thirds of the country's capital stock. Thus, the interests of landowners could hardly be ignored: impediments to enclosures had been removed; subsidies were

granted to protect cattle producers, and until 1750 bounties were routinely provided to encourage exports of grain; credit institutions made loans available for capital improvements; and public projects for the construction of roads and waterways facilitated the transportation of agricultural produce to markets. E. L. Jones, "Agriculture," in *The Economic History of Britain since 1700,* vol. 1, pp. 66–86; Thompson, *The Poverty of Theory,* p. 42, writes: "The beneficiaries of the settlement were exactly those who were represented in Parliament: that is, the men of substantial property, and especially landed property. Title to the enjoyment of their property was secured by the constitutional impedimenta with which the crown was surrounded, and by the rule of a law which was both dispassionate in its adjudication of substantial property-rights and passionately vengeful against those who transgressed against them."

180. Cf. J. H. Plumb, "Robert Walpole's World: The Structure of Government," in Baugh, *Aristocratic Government and Society in Eighteenth-Century England,* pp. 116–154.

181. Roseveare, *The Treasury,* p. 95, writes: "Everywhere, considerations of electoral influence compromised unhappily with considerations of administrative efficiency." These problems are also discussed in Tomlinson, "Financial and Administrative Developments."

182. J. B. Owen, "Political Patronage in 18th-Century England," in Fritz and Williams, *The Triumph of Culture: 18th-Century Perspectives,* p. 372. As a system of influencing parliamentary elections, patronage appears to have increased over the eighteenth century. Between 1690 and 1761, for example, the number of borough seats influenced by individual patrons grew from 153 to 255. These findings are from a computer analysis of electoral voting; see John A. Phillips, *Electoral Behavior in Unreformed England: Plumpers, Splitters, and Straights* (Princeton: Princeton University Press, 1982), pp. 46–64. Plumb, *The Growth of Political Stability in England,* p. 188, draws a similar conclusion: "Patronage has been, and is, an essential feature of the British structure of power, no matter how varied the costume it may wear. In the eighteenth century it scarcely bothered to wear a figleaf. It was naked and quite unashamed." Studies of local electoral politics also reveal the high degree to which party politics were structured by the patronage system; e.g. for Kent, see Norma Landau, "Independence, Deference, and Voter Participation: The Behaviour of the Electorate in Early-Eighteenth-Century Kent," *Historical Journal* 22 (1979), 561–583.

183. Some examples are given in Norma Baker, "Changing Attitudes towards Government in Eighteenth-Century Britain," in Whiteman et al., *Statesmen, Scholars, and Merchants;* see esp. p. 209.

184. Porter, *English Society in the Eighteenth Century,* p. 121; see also Lawrence Stone, "The Results of the English Revolutions of the Seventeenth Century," in Pocock, *Three British Revolutions: 1641, 1688, 1776,*

p. 75: "England from 1689 to 1721, and more especially from 1701 to 1716, was a deeply fissured society, perhaps more passionately divided in the reign of Anne than at any other time in English history—except of course the Interregnum."

185. Phillips, *Electoral Behavior in Unreformed England,* pp. 253–305.

186. For a useful overview of this background, see J. C. D. Clark, "A General Theory of Party, Opposition, and Government, 1688–1832," *Historical Journal* 23 (1980), 295–326; also Clark, *English Society, 1688–1832* (Cambridge: Cambridge University Press, 1985), pp. 42–118.

187. Speck, "Politics," pp. 81–92.

188. J. B. Owen, *The Pattern of Politics in Eighteenth-Century England* (London: Macmillan, 1962).

189. J. C. D. Clark, "The Decline of Party, 1740–1760," *English Historical Review* 93 (1978), 499–527. According to Clark, there was a direct trade-off between "principle" and party "structure": "Principle mattered to a party in the 1740s and 1750s not because parties existed directly to promote programmes but because, in the absence of a 'structure,' 'principle' was the only mark of identity which could establish the integrity of personal conduct" (p. 509). Clark quotes a number of contemporary sources in support of this conclusion.

190. I. F. Burton et al., "Political Parties in the Reigns of William III and Anne: The Evidence of Division Lists," *Bulletin of the Institute of Historical Research,* Supplement no. 7 (1968), 34–37; Geoffrey S. Holmes, "The Commons' Division on 'No Peace without Spain,' 7 December 1711," *Bulletin of the Institute of Historical Research* 33 (1960), 223–234; Geoffrey S. Holmes, "The Attack on 'The Influence of the Crown,' 1702–16," *Bulletin of the Institute of Historical Research* 39 (1966), 47–68; H. Horwitz, "The Structure of Parliamentary Politics," in *Britain after the Glorious Revolution,* ed. Geoffrey S. Holmes (London: Macmillan, 1969), pp. 23–49; H. L. Snyder, "Party Configurations in the Early Eighteenth-Century House of Commons," *Bulletin of the Institute of Historical Research* 45 (1972), 38–72; W. A. Speck, "The Choice of a Speaker in 1705," *Bulletin of the Institute of Historical Research* 37 (1964), 20–46; W. A. Speck and W. A. Gray, "Computer Analysis of Poll Books: An Initial Report," *Bulletin of the Institute of Historical Research* 43 (1970), 105–112; W. A. Speck et al., "Computer Analysis of Poll Books: A Further Report," *Bulletin of the Institute of Historical Research* 48 (1975), 64–90; J. G. Sperling, "The Division of 25 May 1711, on an Amendment to the South Sea Bill: A Note on the Reality of Parties in the Age of Anne," *Historical Journal* 4 (1961), 191–202. According to these studies upwards of 80 to 85 percent of Parliament voting appears to have followed party lines during the first two decades of the eighteenth century.

191. Stone, "The Results of the English Revolutions," p. 78.

192. Dame Lucy Sutherland, "The City of London in Eighteenth-Century Politics," in Baugh, *Aristocratic Government and Society in Eighteenth-Century England,* p. 162, writes that the commercial classes were "exceedingly bellicose."

193. H. T. Dickinson, *Liberty and Property: Political Ideology in Eighteenth-Century Britain* (London: Weidenfeld and Nicolson, 1977), pp. 91–117. Dickinson suggests that a "symbiotic relationship" developed between the ideologies associated with these two factions, such that members of each felt it necessary to produce constant barrages of resistance toward the other, even though neither side expected to attain a major or lasting victory over the other.

194. Betty Kemp, *King and Commons, 1660–1832* (London: Macmillan, 1957), pp. 90–102. Kemp characterizes the years from 1716 to 1783 as the "period of balance" between the king and the House of Commons.

195. The reasons why conflicts were contained in this manner are discussed in Geoffrey S. Holmes, "The Achievement of Stability: The Social Context of Politics from the 1680s to the Age of Walpole," in *The Whig Ascendancy,* ed. John Cannon (London: Edward Arnold, 1981), pp. 1–22.

196. Shackleton, "The Enlightenment," p. 270, makes a similar point: "Its [the English Enlightenment's] exponents differed in outlook and emphasis as much as they differed in education and in class."

197. These writers' role in English politics is discussed in Isaac Kramnick, *Bolingbroke and His Circle: The Politics of Nostalgia in the Age of Walpole* (Cambridge, Mass.: Harvard University Press, 1968).

198. Mathias, *The Transformation of England,* pp. 295–317.

199. Jewson, "Medical Knowledge and the Patronage System," p. 370.

200. Stone, "The Results of the English Revolutions," p. 75: "The antagonism between the two parties gave rise to not only some of the most brilliant but also some of the most savage political pamphleteering in the English language."

201. Foss, *The Age of Patronage,* pp. 146–152; Stephen, *Selected Writings in British Intellectual History,* pp. 120–123.

202. Plumb, *The Growth of Political Stability in England,* p. 43.

203. Foss, *The Age of Patronage,* p. 161.

204. Hunter, "The Debate over Science."

205. Foss, *The Age of Patronage,* p. 138, observes that political factionalism was associated with a sense of political responsibility among the period's leading writers: "What weighed most with them was a sense of their own importance as rational and articulate men—the epithet *articulate* being in this context exactly right—which drove them to speak out: rhetoric in the service of reason to establish right government."

206. Dickinson, *Politics and Literature in the Eighteenth Century,* pp. ix–xxii.

207. A study of the London theater also emphasizes the extent to which politics penetrated art, particularly because of the interest of contemporaries in finding and maintaining a political balance or equilibrium: "From this search for the precise point of equilibrium . . . grew something of an obsession with government, an obsession revealed in the recurrence of symbols involving affairs of state." Leo Hughes, *The Drama's Patrons: A Study of the Eighteenth-Century London Audience* (Austin: University of Texas Press, 1971), p. 3.

7. Enlightenment Developments in Prussia and Scotland

1. The relatively late efflorescence of the German Enlightenment has been attributed to the absence of a strong empiricist tradition in the seventeenth century, although there were social reasons as well, including the severe devastation of the Thirty Years' War and the political decentralization of the region; see Wilhelm Schmidt-Biggemann, "Emanzipation durch Unterwanderung: Institutionen und Personen der deutschen Früaufklärung," in *Aufklärung in Deutschland,* ed. Paul Raabe and Wilhelm Schmidt-Biggemann (Bonn: Hohwacht Verlag, 1979), esp. pp. 45–48.

2. Joachim Whaley, "The Protestant Enlightenment in Germany," in *The Enlightenment in National Context,* ed. Roy Porter and Mikulas Teich (Cambridge: Cambridge University Press, 1981), pp. 106–117; and G. P. Gooch, *Studies in German History* (London: Longmans, 1948), pp. 55–74, provide general overviews of the Enlightenment in Prussia.

3. Henri Brunschwig, *Enlightenment and Romanticism in Eighteenth-Century Prussia* (Chicago: University of Chicago Press, 1974), p. 5.

4. John A. Armstrong, *The European Administrative Elite* (Princeton: Princeton University Press, 1973), p. 133.

5. Reinhard Bendix, "Province and Metropolis: The Case of Eighteenth-Century Germany," in *Culture and Its Creators: Essays in Honor of Edward Shils,* ed. Joseph Ben-David and Terry Nichols Clark (Chicago: University of Chicago Press, 1976), p. 127. If anything, these estimates are low; another writer estimates that the actual figure in 1790, for instance, was probably closer to five thousand; see Paul Raabe, "Aufklärung durch Bücher: Der Anteil des Buchhandels an der kulturellen Entwicklung in Deutschland, 1764–1790," in Raabe and Schmidt-Biggemann, *Aufklärung in Deutschland,* p. 90.

6. W. H. Bruford, *Germany in the Eighteenth Century: The Social Background of the Literary Revival* (Cambridge: Cambridge University Press, 1935), p. 289; Bendix, "Province and Metropolis," pp. 127–129.

7. Raabe, "Aufklärung durch Bücher," pp. 92–93.

8. Cf. Brunschwig, *Enlightenment and Romanticism,* pp. 34–36.

9. Weeklies and news sheets printed at irregular intervals had already become common by the end of the seventeenth century, reaching perhaps

as many as 250,000 readers altogether; see Martin Welke, "Gemeinsame Lektüre und frühe formen von Gruppenbildungen im 17. und 18. Jahrhundert: Zeitungslesen in Deutschland," in *Lesegesellschaften und bürgerliche Emanzipation: Ein europäischer Vergleich,* ed. Otto Dann (Munich: C. H. Beck'sche Verlagsbuchhandlung, 1981), pp. 29–30.

10. Walther Hubatsch, *Frederick the Great: Absolutism and Administration* (London: Thames and Hudson, 1975), p. 40.

11. James van Horn Melton, "From Enlightenment to Revolution: Hertzberg, Schlözer, and the Problem of Despotism in the Late Aufklärung," *Central European History* 12 (1979), p. 11.

12. Bendix, "Province and Metropolis," pp. 127–129.

13. Welke, "Gemeinsame Lektüre," pp. 30–31.

14. The institutionalization of research in the Prussian universities is usefully examined in R. Steven Turner, "The Prussian Universities and the Research Imperative, 1806–1848" (Ph.D. diss., Princeton University, 1973).

15. Ronald Calinger, "Kant and Newtonian Science: The Pre-Critical Period," *Isis* 70 (1979), 349–362.

16. Karl Hufbauer, "Social Support for Chemistry in Germany During the Eighteenth Century," *Historical Studies in the Physical Sciences* 3 (1971), 207.

17. Ulrich Hermann, "Lesegesellschaften an der Wende des 18 Jahrhunderts," *Archiv für Kulturgeschichte* 57 (1975), 475–484.

18. Brunschwig, *Enlightenment and Romanticism,* pp. 38–40.

19. Marlies Stützel-Prüsener, "Die deutschen Lesegesellschaften im Zeitalter der Aufklärung," in Dann, *Lesegesellschaften und bürgerliche Emanzipation,* p. 74.

20. Hans-Heinrich Muller, "Wirtschaftshistorische und agrarökonimische Preisaufgaben der deutschen Akademien der Wissenschaften im 18 Jahrhundert," *Jahrbuch für Wirtschaftsgeschichte* 1 (1972), 183–214.

21. Turner, "The Prussian Universities," pp. 37–38; cf. R. Stephen Turner, "University Reformers and Professional Scholarship in Germany, 1760–1806," in *The University in Society,* vol. 2, *Europe, Scotland, and the United States from the 16th to the 20th Century,* ed. Lawrence Stone (Princeton: Princeton University Press, 1974), pp. 501–502.

22. R. J. W. Evans, "German Universities after the Thirty Years' War," *History of Universities* 1 (1981), 169–190.

23. Schmidt-Biggemann, "Emanzipation durch Unterwanderung," pp. 59–61.

24. Rolf Lieberwirth, *Der Staat als Gegenstand des Hochschulunterrichts in Deutschland vom 16. bis zum 18. Jahrhundert* (Berlin: Akademie-Verlag, 1978), pp. 20–26.

25. Turner, "The Prussian Universities," pp. 20–86.

26. Charles E. McClelland, "German Universities in the Eighteenth Century, Crisis and Renewal," in *Facets of Education in the Eighteenth Century,* ed. James A. Leith (Oxford: Voltaire Foundation at the Taylor Institution, 1977), pp. 169–190.

27. Roger Chartier, "Student Populations in the Eighteenth Century," *British Journal for Eighteenth-Century Studies* 2 (1979), 153; complete time-series figures for this period are given in R. Steven Turner, "The *Bildungsbürgertum* and the Learned Professions in Prussia, 1770–1830: The Origins of a Class," *Social History* 13 (1980), esp. 112.

28. Bruford, *Germany in the Eighteenth Century,* p. 1.

29. Klaus Epstein, *The Genesis of German Conservatism* (Princeton: Princeton University Press, 1966), pp. 238–244.

30. For example, the court at Württemberg had a musical staff of 41, at Saxony a musical staff of 146.

31. Bruford, *Germany in the Eighteenth Century,* pp. 81–92; R. J. W. Evans, "Learned Societies in Germany in the Seventeenth Century," *European Studies Review* 7 (1977), 129–152.

32. McClelland, "German Universities in the Eighteenth Century."

33. Charles E. McClelland, *State, Society, and University in Germany, 1700–1914* (Cambridge: Cambridge University Press, 1980), p. 37.

34. T. C. W. Blanning, "The Englightenment in Catholic Germany," in Porter and Teich, *The Enlightenment in National Context,* p. 122.

35. McClelland, *State, Society, and University,* p. 41.

36. Turner, "The Prussian Universities," p. 509.

37. McClelland, "German Universities in the Eighteenth Century"; Norman Hampson, *The First European Revolution, 1776–1815* (New York: Harcourt Brace, 1969), p. 63.

38. Quoted in Bruford, *Germany in the Eighteenth Century,* p. 303.

39. Otto Hintze, "The Hohenzollern and the Nobility," in *The Historical Essays of Otto Hintze,* ed. Felix Gilbert (Oxford: Oxford University Press, 1975), pp. 44–58; Hans Rosenberg, *Bureaucracy, Aristocracy, and Autocracy: The Prussian Experience, 1660–1815* (Boston: Beacon, 1958), pp. 33–34.

40. Bruford, *Germany in the Eighteenth Century,* p. 25.

41. Reinhold A. Dorwart, *The Administrative Reforms of Frederick William of Prussia* (Cambridge, Mass.: Harvard University Press, 1953), pp. 5–29.

42. Cf. Walter L. Dorn, "The Prussian Bureaucracy in the Eighteenth Century, I," *Political Science Quarterly* 46 (1931), 403–423; Walter L. Dorn, "The Prussian Bureaucracy in the Eighteenth Century, II," *Political Science Quarterly* 47 (1932), 75–94; Walter L. Dorn, "The Prussian Bureaucracy in the Eighteenth Century, III," *Political Science Quarterly* 47 (1932), 259–273.

43. Otto Busch, *Militarsystem und Sozialleben im alten Preussen, 1713–1807* (Berlin: DeGruyter, 1962), p. 95; Michael Howard, *War in European History* (Oxford: Oxford University Press, 1976), pp. 66–72.

44. Bruford, *Germany in the Eighteenth Century*, p. 98; Hubert C. Johnson, *Frederick the Great and His Officials* (New Haven: Yale University Press, 1975), pp. 16–17; Hubatsch, *Frederick the Great*, p. 37; Rosenberg, *Bureaucracy, Aristocracy, and Autocracy*, p. 175; T. C. W. Blanning, *Reform and Revolution in Mainz, 1743–1803* (Cambridge: Cambridge University Press, 1974), p. 11.

45. Brunschwig, *Enlightenment and Romanticism*, pp. 41–50.

46. H. W. Koch, *A History of Prussia* (London: Longman, 1978), pp. 86–95.

47. Bruford, *Germany in the Eighteenth Century*, pp. 293–294.

48. W. O. Henderson, *Studies in the Economic Policy of Frederick the Great* (London: F. Cass, 1963), p. 126.

49. W. O. Henderson, *The State and the Industrial Revolution in Prussia, 1740–1870* (Liverpool: Liverpool University Press, 1958), pp. 1–11.

50. Leonard Krieger, *The German Idea of Freedom: History of a Political Tradition* (Boston: Beacon Press, 1957), p. 29; Hubatsch, *Frederick the Great*, p. 99.

51. Rosenberg, *Bureaucracy, Aristocracy, and Autocracy*, p. 175; Bruford, *Germany in the Eighteenth Century*, p. 48.

52. Brunschwig, *Enlightenment and Romanticism*, pp. 119–121.

53. Blanning, *Reform and Revolution*, pp. 9–10. Prussian economic thought during the eighteenth century appears to have reflected this situation insofar as it tended to emphasize state-centered mercantilism and manifested little evidence of bourgeois attitudes favoring free trade or the interests of rising industrial classes. See Peter Thal, "Bürgerliche Elemente im Denken deutscher Okonomen des 17. und 18. Jahrhunderts: Voraussetzungen, Grenzen, Resultate (Grundlinien des okonomischen Denkens in Deutschland)," *Jahrbuch für Wirtschaftsgeschichte* 22 (1979), 165–184. Another factor that militated against the growth of bourgeois power was the practice of garrisoning troops in major cities, often in numbers up to 20 percent of the total population, thus presenting a serious obstacle to the development of any kind of self-government by the bourgeoisie that might have run counter to royal policy. See Johnson, *Frederick the Great and His Officials*, p. 13.

54. Johnson, *Frederick the Great and His Officials*, p. 289; Rosenberg, *Bureaucracy, Aristocracy, and Autocracy*, p. 60; Armstrong, *The European Administrative Elite*, p. 77.

55. Krieger, *The German Idea of Freedom*, p. 20.

56. Ibid., p. 13. Because of the agrarian export economy that characterized much of Prussia, its towns and communities remained relatively

small and geographically isolated, apparently with the result that the state
was better able to pursue centralizing policies than in areas with traditions
of strong solidarity at the local community level. Even in the nineteenth
century the average distance between towns in Prussia was more than three
times greater than in most other parts of Germany; see Mack Walker,
German Home Towns: Community, State, and General Estate, 1648–1871
(Ithaca: Cornell University Press, 1971), pp. 22–24.

57. Alfred Cobban, "The Pattern of Government," in *The Eighteenth
Century: Europe in the Age of Enlightenment*, ed. Alfred Cobban (New York:
McGraw-Hill, 1969), p. 37.

58. Bruford, *Germany in the Eighteenth Century*, pp. 237–247.

59. McClelland, *State, Society, and University in Germany*, pp. 41–52.

60. Turner, "The *Bildungsbürgertum* and the Learned Professions";
Robert M. Bigler, *The Politics of German Protestantism: The Rise of the Protestant Church Elite in Prussia, 1815–1848* (Berkeley: University of California Press, 1972), pp. 1–35; Hans-Heinz Eulner, *Die Entwicklung der
medizinischen Specialfächer an den Universitäten des deutschen Sprachgebietes*
(Stuttgart: Ferdinant Enke, 1970).

61. Dorwart, *The Administrative Reforms of Frederick William*, pp. 96–
108.

62. Johnson, *Frederick the Great and His Officials*, pp. 124–131.

63. Hartwig Notbohm, *Das evangelische Kirchen- und Schulwesen in
Ostpreussen* (Heidelberg: Quelle und Meyer, 1959), pp. 86–87.

64. Johnson, *Frederick the Great and His Officials*, p. 130. Another
writer states: "The *Aufklärung* grew primarily out of the universities, the
bureaucracies of the various territorial states, and out of the Protestant
clergy, each of which was closely tied to, if not actually an organ of, the
monarchical state"; see Melton, "From Enlightenment to Revolution," p.
103.

65. In a different sphere—music—the significance of state patronage
is well illustrated by the fact that no operas were produced at the court
between 1756 and 1763 because of the crown's shortage of revenues during
the Seven Years' War.

66. Hermann, "Lesegellschaften an der Wende des 18 Jahrhunderts";
Bendix, "Province and Metropolis," p. 135.

67. Stützel-Prüsener, "Die deutschen Lesegesellschaften," pp. 76–79.

68. Karl A. Schleunes, "Enlightenment, Reform, Reaction: The
Schooling Revolution in Prussia," *Central European History* 12 (1979), 315–
342; Whaley, "The Protestant Enlightenment in Germany."

69. "Academicians and civil servants considered the merchant's education deficient, his interests too mundane. They responded to his presence
in society with no great warmth, when not with outright, even printed
ridicule"; John W. Van Cleve, *The Merchant in German Literature of the*

Enlightenment (Chapel Hill: University of North Carolina Press, 1986), p. 39. Even merchants engaged in long-distance trade were seldom trained in the arts of philosophy and had little understanding of law or political theory. The standard level of training attained by young merchants can be seen in the royal decree promulgated in 1755 as an attempt to *improve* the education of the commercial community. At the age of fifteen, boys were permitted to become full-time apprentices in merchants' households. All that was required for entry was an examination by a local pastor in three subjects: writing, arithmetic, and Christian dogma. In short, even after these improvements went into effect, merchants were not likely to have the educational background to prompt an appreciation of literature and the arts.

70. Ibid. Officials and professionals were also in the best financial position to support the arts and literature. One estimate, for example, shows that the average income of the professional community was twice that of the petty bourgeoisie (small shopkeepers) in 1700 and rose to two and a half times by 1750. These figures are for Frankfurt but are likely to have been roughly comparable in Berlin and Leipzig. See Helmuth Kiesel and Paul Münch. *Gesellschaft und Literatur im 18. Jahrhundert: Voraussetzungen und Entstehung des literarischen Markts in Deutschland* (Munich: Beck, 1977), p. 57.

71. Bruford, *Germany in the Eighteenth Century,* p. 275.

72. This practice may have developed as a means of conforming to mercantilist policies that discouraged the transfer of currency across state boundaries; see Reinhard Wittman, "Soziale und okonomische Voraussetzungen des Buch- und Verlagwesens in der zweiten Hälfte des 18. Jahrhunderts," in *Buch- und Verlagswesen im 18. und 19. Jahrhundert: Beiträge zur Geschichte der Kommunikation in Mittel- und Osteuropa,* ed. Herbert G. Göpfert, Gerard Kozielek, and Reinhard Wittman (Berlin: Verlag Ulrich Camen, 1977), p. 6.

73. Raabe, "Aufklärung durch Bücher," pp. 87–90, 92–93.

74. Peter Lundgreen, "Gegensatz und Verschmelzung von 'alter' und 'neuer' Bürokratie im Ancien Régime: Ein Vergleich von Frankreich und Preussen," in *Sozialgeschichte Heute: Festschrift für Hans Rosenberg,* ed. Hans-Ulrich Wehler (Göttingen: Vandenhoeck und Ruprecht, 1974), pp. 104–118.

75. Raabe, "Aufklürung durch Bücher," p. 99.

76. Blanning, *Reform and Revolution,* pp. 13–14.

77. D. M. Knight, "German Science in the Romantic Period," in *The Emergence of Science in Western Europe,* ed. Maurice Crosland (New York: Science History Publications, 1976), pp. 161–178.

78. Krieger, *The German Idea of Freedom;* Blanning, *Reform and Revolution,* pp. 15–38; Marc Auchet, "Aspects particuliers des lumières en Prusse: Remarques concernant le livre de H. Möller sur F. Nicolai," *Francia* 5 (1977), 769–76.

79. Koch, *A History of Prussia,* pp. 80–82.

80. Rosenberg, *Bureaucracy, Aristocracy, and Autocracy,* pp. 90–94.

81. Krieger, *The German Idea of Freedom,* pp. 26–34.

82. Richard van Dülman, "Die Aufklärungsgesellschaften in Deutschland als Forschungsproblem," *Francis* 5 (1977), 251–275; Charles E. McClelland, "Aristocracy and University Reform in 18th-Century Germany," in *Schooling and Society,* ed. Lawrence Stone (Baltimore: Johns Hopkins University Press, 1976), pp. 146–173.

83. Brunschwig, *Enlightenment and Romanticism,* pp. 67–86.

84. It has been observed that the academies and reading societies, although typically referred to in historical studies as "bourgeois" institutions, represented an intermediate phase between feudal cooperation and bourgeois association; not until the rise of the "reform monarchies" after the Napoleonic Wars did these associations begin to manifest definable class interests and become emancipated from the state; see van Dülmen, "Die Aufklärungsgesellschaften in Deutschland als Forschungsproblem," 254–255.

85. Peter-Michael Hahn, " 'Absolutistische' Polizeigesetzgebung und ländliche Sozialverfassung," *Jahrbuch für die Geschichte Mittel- und Ostdeutschlands* 29 (1980), 13–29.

86. Johnson, *Frederick the Great and His Officials,* p. 282; cf. Hubatsch, *Frederick the Great,* pp. 7–9; Otto Hintze, *Die Hohenzollern und ihr Werk* (Berlin: P. Parey, 1916).

87. Brunschwig, *Enlightenment and Romanticism,* p. 17; cf. Dorwart, *The Administrative Reforms of Frederick William,* p. 187.

88. Rosenberg, *Bureaucracy, Aristocracy, annd Autocracy,* p. 43.

89. Herman Weill, *Frederick the Great and Samuel von Cocceji* (Madison: University of Wisconsin Press, 1961).

90. Johnson, *Frederick the Great and His Officials,* p. 274. Cf. Bernd Wunder, "Zum Problem der Kontrolle der Dienerschaft im 18. Jahrhundert," *Francia* 9 (1980), 182–187. As in France and England, the Prussian bureaucracy was also deeply affected by changes in foreign circumstances. For instance, Prussia's rivalries with Austria during the 1730s and 1740s had promoted closer ties with France. But after 1748 France became aligned with Austria and Britain with Prussia (in what has been known as the "Diplomatic Revolution"). This reversal of alliances gave pro-British interests in the Prussian government a considerably stronger hand and greatly curtailed the French influences at court. Reverberations of these changes were also felt within the literary community. Johann Christoph Gottsched, whose work had borrowed heavily on French standards of reason and good taste, and whose French sympathies were widely shared, came under growing attack by a younger generation of pro-German writers based mainly in Berlin who had also become favorable toward the work of British writers. A dispute betwee these two factions broke out into the open in 1752 with

Nicolai's defense of Milton against Gottsched and became part of the basis for an enduring friendship among Nicolai, Mendelssohn, and Lessing, all of whom held English literature in high esteem. The three, moreover, gained increasing popularity with German audiences by attacking French influences on poetry and drama and calling for a national drama.

91. Wilhelm Treue, "Das Verhältnis der Universitäten und technischen Hochschulen zueinander und ihr Bedeutung für die Wirtschaft," in *Die wirtschaftliche Situation in Deutschland und Osterreich um die Wende vom 18. zum 19. Jahrhundert,* ed. Friedrich Lütge (Stuttgart: Werner Verlag, 1964), pp. 233–238.

92. As in France and England, the presence of multiple centers of power within the Prussian state sometimes contributed quite directly to the relative autonomy of the literary elite as well. One of the most notable examples occurred in conjunction with the new all-inclusive censorship law promulgated by the king in 1737 in response to a wave of antipietist drama. The decree would have given the censor absolute control over every published word. Despite the king's support, the law was never put into effect, however, principally because of opposition from influential segments of the bureaucracy who thought it both impractical and undesirable. For the context of this episode, see William E. Petig, *Literary Antipietism in Germany during the First Half of the Eighteenth Century* (New York: Peter Lang, 1984), pp. 41–75.

93. Rosenberg, *Bureaucracy, Aristocracy, and Autocracy,* p. 75; cf. Carl Hinrichs, "Hille und Reinhardt: Zwei Wirtschafts-und-Sozialpolitiker des preussichen Absolutismus," in *Preussen als historisches Problem,* ed. Gerhard Oestreich (Berlin: DeGruyter, 1964), pp. 161–171.

94. Rudolfine Freiin von Oder, "Estates and Diets in Ecclesiastical Principalities of the Holy Roman Empire," in *Liber Memorialis Georges de Lagrande* (Louvain: Editions Neuwelaerts, 1968), pp. 259–281.

95. Blanning, "The Enlightenment in Catholic Germany, p. 125; Rudolf Vierhaus, "Aufklärung und Freimaurerei in Deutschland," in *Das Vergangene und die Geschichte: Festschrift fur Reinhard Wittram zum 70. Geburtstag,* ed. Rudolf von Thadden et al. (Göttingen: Vandenhoeck und Ruprecht, 1973 , p. 28.

96. Blanning, *Reform and Revolution,* p. 121.

97. F. L. Carsten, *Princes and Parliaments in Germany: From the Fifteenth to the Eighteenth Century* (Oxford: Clarendon Press, 1959), pp. 123–148; F. L. Carsten, "The German Estates in the 18th Century," *Recueils de la Société Jean Bodin* 25 (1965), 227–238; on the religious dimensions of these political conflicts, see Mary Fulbrook, *Piety and Politics: Religion and the Rise of Absolutism in England, Württemberg, and Prussia* (Cambridge: Cambridge University Press, 1983), pp. 130–152.

98. Gooch, *Studies in German History,* pp. 46–47; on the relations

between the Enlightenment and constitutionalism in the duchy, see Heinz Liebing, *Zwischen Orthodoxie und Aufklärung: Das philosophische und theologische Denken Georg Bernhard Bilfingers* (Tübingen: J. C. B. Mohr, 1961).

99. Walker, *German Home Towns,* pp. 25–26; Eric G. Forbes, "The Foundation of the First Göttingen Observatory: A Study in Politics and Personalities," *Journal for the History of Astronomy* 5 (1974), 22–29; McClelland, "Aristocracy and University Reform"; McClelland, *State, Society, and University,* pp. 50–51; Bruford, *Germany in the Eighteenth Century,* pp. 237–247; Gerhard Benecke, "Review of *Aufklärung und Katholisches Reich,*" *Social History* 13 (1980), 498.

100. Johnson, *Frederick the Great and His Officials,* p. 24.

101. Carsten, *Princes and the Parliaments,* pp. 415–422; Bruford, *Germany in the Eighteenth Century,* pp. 20–24; Isser Woloch, *Eighteenth-Century Europe: Tradition and Progress, 1715–1789* (New York: Norton, 1982), pp. 266–267. The inability of a strong bourgeoisie alone to provide the conditions necessary for institutionalizing Enlightenment scholarship is well illustrated by Bremen. Despite its prominence in trade, it failed to provide a sufficient readership to support a literary supplement to the local weekly newspaper. See Pamela Currie, "Moral Weeklies and the Reading Public in Germany, 1711–1750," *Oxford German Studies* 3 (1968), 69–86. Other evidence indicates that the education received by the typical Bremen merchant was scarcely conducive to an appreciation of literary activities: only the bare rudiments of Latin were obtained; reading skills were quite limited; and the kinds of training in ciphering and accounts that the merchant received was not calculated to imbue a burning desire to widen his horizons. See, for example, Rolf Engelsing, *Der Bürger als Leser: Lesergeschichte in Deutschland, 1500–1800* (Stuttgart: Metzler, 1974), pp. 138–141. A similar conclusion has been drawn for the merchant community in Hamburg. See Johann Michael Hudtwalcker, "Elternhaus und Jugendjahre eines Hamburger Kaufmanns in der Mitte des 18. Jahrhunderts," in *Kaufleute zu Haus und über See: Hamburgische Zeugnisse des 17., 18., und 19. Jahrhunderts,* ed. Percy Ernst Schramm (Hamburg: Hoffmann und Campe, 1949), pp. 185–209.

102. The connection between the origins of social science and the Scottish Enlightenment has been stressed in a number of studies, including Gladys Bryson, *Man and Society: The Scottish Inquiry of the Eighteenth Century* (Princeton: Princeton University Press, 1945); Charles Camic, *Experience and Enlightenment: Socialization for Cultural Change in Eighteenth-Century Scotland* (Chicago: University of Chicago Press, 1983); Louis Schneider, "Introduction," in *The Scottish Moralists,* ed. Louis Schneider (Chicago: University of Chicago Press, 1967), pp. xi-lxxvi; Susan Schott, "Society, Self, and Mind in Moral Philosophy: The Scottish Moralists as Precursors of Symbolic Interactionism," *Journal of the History of the Behavioral Sciences*

12 (1972), 39–46; and Alan William Swingewood, "Origins of Sociology: The Case of the Scottish Enlightenment," *British Journal of Sociology* 21 (1970), 164–180. The role of the Scottish Enlightenment in the origins of Marxist thought is examined in Ronald L. Meek, "The Scottish Contributions to Marxist Sociology," in *Economics and Ideology and Other Essays,* ed. Ronald L. Meek (London: Chapman and Hall, 1967), pp. 34–50; and Andrew S. Skinner, "Economics and History—The Scottish Enlightenment," *Scottish Journal of Political Economy* 12 (1965), 1–22.

103. Vern L. Bullough, "Intellectual Achievement in Eighteenth-Century Scotland: A Computer Study of the Importance of Education," *Comparative Education Review* 14 (1970), 90–102; Bonnie Bullough and Vern Bullough, "Intellectual Achievers: A Study of Eighteenth-Century Scotland," *American Journal of Sociology* 76 (1971), 1048–1063; Vern Bullough and Bonnie Bullough, "Historical Sociology: Intellectual Achievement in Eighteenth-Century Scotland," *British Journal of Sociology* 24 (1973), 418–430.

104. Quoted in J. B. Morrell, "The University of Edinburgh in the Late Eighteenth Century, *Isis* 62 (1971), 159.

105. Quoted in D. A. Horn, *A Short History of the University of Edinburgh* (Edinburgh: Edinburgh University Press, 1967), p. 64.

106. For example, one writer states: "It has long been accepted that among the countries which participated in the Enlightenment of the eighteenth century Scotland held a position of remarkable distinction"; see Ronald G. Cant, "The Scottish Universities and Scottish Society in the Eighteenth Century," *Studies on Voltaire and the Eighteenth Century* 58 (1967), 1953. The importance of Scottish philosophy for the development of British physics has been examined in R. V. Jones, "Physical Science in the Eighteenth Century," *British Journal for Eighteenth-Century Studies* 1 (1978), 73–88, and in Richard Olson, *Scottish Philosophy and British Physics, 1750–1800* (Princeton: Princeton University Press, 1975). See also John R. R. Christie, "The Rise and Fall of Scottish Science, in Crosland, *The Emergence of Science in Western Europe,* pp. 111–126. This author suggests that intellectuals and intellectual activity "attained an abnormally high social status in eighteenth-century Scotland." The importance of Scotland in the Enlightenment can also be evinced from the sheer number of writers and intellectuals who gained international stature. A recent study by an author who has gone to some pains to "define" the Scottish Enlightenment lists twenty-eight such figures; see Richard B. Sher, *Church and University in the Scottish Enlightenment: The Moderate Literati of Edinburgh* (Princeton: Princeton University Press, 1985), pp. 8–9. For a general overview, see Nicholas T. Phillipson, "The Scottish Enlightenment," in Porter and Teich, *The Enlightenment in National Context,* pp. 19–40.

107. Ronald G. Cant, "Origins of the Enlightenment in Scotland: The

Universities," in *The Origins and Nature of the Scottish Enlightenment,* ed. R. H. Campbell and Andrew S. Skinner (Edinburgh: Donald, 1982), pp. 42–64; Donald J. Withrington, "Education and Society in the Eighteenth Century," in *Scotland in the Age of Improvement,* ed. N. T. Phillipson and Rosalind Mitchison (Edinburgh: Edinburgh University Press, 1970), pp. 169–199; Morrell, "The University of Edinburgh in the Late Eighteenth Century."

108. Roger L. Emerson, "Scottish Universities in the Eighteenth Century, 1690–1800," in Leith, *Facets of Education in the Eighteenth Century,* pp. 453–474.

109. Anand C. Chitnis, *The Scottish Enlightenment: A Social History* (London: Croom Helm, 1976), p. 134; Emerson, "Scottish Universities in the Eighteenth Century."

110. Significant advances were made in medicine, law, and moral philosophy; see Cant, "The Scottish Universities and Scottish Society." Writing of the Scottish universities generally, Ogg states that they were "among the foremost in Europe"; see David Ogg, "The Emergence of Great Britain as a World Power," in *The New Cambridge Modern History,* vol. 6, *The Rise of Great Britain and Russia, 1688–1715/25,* ed. J. S. Bromley (Cambridge: Cambridge University Press, 1970), p. 279. Glasgow University served as a base for important intellectual activity as well, but it was Edinburgh that became most significant to the Scottish Enlightenment; as Phillipson observes: "the history of the Scottish enlightenment *is* the history of Edinburgh"; see Phillipson, "The Scottish Enlightenment," p. 125. See also Walter Karp, "The Golden Age of Edinburgh," *Horizon* 17 (1975), 10–23.

111. Nicholas Hans, *New Trends in Education in the Eighteenth Century* (London: Routledge and Kegan Paul, 1951), p. 32.

112. The Rankenian Club, founded in 1717 and named after the tavern in which it met, included a number of prominent faculty members from the University of Edinburgh and was to play an important role in bringing reformed thinking to the university. Many of its members became founding members of the Select Society in 1754. For more details on its activities, see Peter Jones, "The Scottish Professoriate and the Polite Academy, 1720–46," in *Wealth and Virtue: The Shaping of Political Economy in the Scottish Enlightenment,* ed. Istvan Hont and Michael Ignatieff (Cambridge: Cambridge University Press, 1983), pp. 89–118.

113. David Daiches, *Edinburgh* (London: Hamish Hamilton, 1978), pp. 105–121; Davis Dunbar McElroy, *Scotland's Age of Improvement: A Survey of Eighteenth-Century Literary Clubs and Societies* (Pullman: Washington State University Press, 1969); Phillipson, "The Scottish Enlightenment," p. 133.

114. Roger L. Emerson, "The Social Composition of Enlightened Scotland: The Select Society of Edinburgh, 1754–1764," *Studies on Voltaire and the Eighteenth Century* 114 (1973), 291–329.

115. Warren McDougall, "Gavin Hamilton, Bookseller in Edinburgh," *British Journal for Eighteenth-Century Studies* 1 (1978), 1–19.

116. Chitnis, *The Scottish Enlightenment,* p. 16.

117. Lawrence Stone, "Literacy and Education in England, 1640–1900," *Past and Present* 42 (1969), 120; Jane Rendall, *The Origins of Scottish Enlightenment* (New York: St. Martin's, 1978), p. 44. The role of literacy alone should not be overemphasized, however. Clive notes as one of the crucial differences between England and Scotland the fact that in Scotland there were no "professional men of letters"; instead, writers were generally supported by patronage or government office, a fact that Clive attributes to the absence of a reading public sufficiently large to support authors on the sale of books alone; see John Clive, "The Social Background of the Scottish Renaissance," in Phillipson and Mitchison, *Scotland in the Age of Improvement,* pp. 227–228.

118. R. H. Campbell, *Scotland since 1707: The Rise of an Industrial Society* (New York: Barnes and Noble, 1965), pp. 1–75.

119. T. C. Smout, "Scotland in the 17th and 18th Centuries: A Satellite Economy?" in *The Satellite State in the 17th and 18th Centuries,* ed. Stale Dryvik et al. (Bergen: Universitetsforlaget, 1980), pp. 9–35; T. C. Smout, "Scotland and England: Is Dependency a Symptom or a Cause of Underdevelopment?" *Review* 3 (1980), 601–630.

120. Ogg, "The Emergence of Great Britain as a World Power," p. 278. Cf. S. G. E. Lythe and J. Butt, *An Economic History of Scotland, 1100–1939* (Glasgow: Blackie, 1975), pp. 70–84.

121. Henry Hamilton, "Economic Growth in Scotland, 1720–1770," *Scottish Journal of Political Economy* 6 (1959), 85–98; Alastair J. Durie, "The Scottish Linen Industry in the Eighteenth Century: Some Aspects of Expansion," in *Comparative Aspects of Scottish and Irish Economic and Social History, 1600–1900,* ed. L. M. Cullen and T. C. Smout (Edinburgh: Donald, 1977), pp. 88–99. One of the most useful overviews of Scottish economic development during this period is Bruce Lenman, *An Economic History of Modern Scotland, 1660–1976* (Hamden, Conn.: Archon Books, 1977), esp. pp. 44–100.

122. R. H. Campbell, "An Economic History of Scotland in the Eighteenth Century," *Scottish Journal of Political Economy* 11 (1964), 17–24.

123. R. H. Campbell, "The Union and Economic Growth," in *The Union of 1707: Its Impact on Scotland,* ed. T. I. Rae (Glasgow: Blackie, 1974), pp. 58–74; cf. Nicholas T. Phillipson, "Culture and Society in the Eighteenth-Century Province: The Case of Edinburgh and the Scottish Enlightenment," in Stone, *The University in Society,* vol. 2, pp. 407–448.

124. T. M. Devine, "Colonial Commerce and the Scottish Economy," c. 1730–1815," in Cullen and Smout, *Comparative Aspects of Scottish and Irish Economic and Social History,* pp. 177–190; T. M. Devine, "The Scottish Merchant Community, 1680–1740," in Campbell and Skinner, *The Origins*

and Nature of the Scottish Enlightenment, pp. 26–41; David Daiches, *The Paradox of Scottish Culture: The Eighteenth-Century Experience* (Oxford: Oxford University Press, 1964), esp. p. 3; Basil Williams, *The Whig Supremacy, 1714–1760* (Oxford: Clarendon Press, 1962), pp. 175–179.

125. P. W. J. Riley, "The Structure of Scottish Politics and the Union of 1707," in Rae, *The Union of 1707,* pp. 1–29; Phillipson, "Culture and Society in the Eighteenth-Century Province," p. 411.

126. Alexander Murdoch, *"The People Above": Politics and Administration in Mid-Eighteenth-Century Scotland* (Edinburgh: Donald, 1980), pp. 1–12.

127. David Kettler, *The Social and Political Thought of Adam Ferguson* (Columbus: Ohio State University Press, 1965), p. 20. Ferguson himself was a product of these "favors": at the age of thirty-four he succeeded Hume as keeper of the Advocates Library in Edinburgh and two years later received an appointment in natural philosophy (and later in moral philosophy) at the University of Edinburgh. Hume had benefited considerably from the ample time his appointment provided as well as from having access to the thirty thousand volumes housed in the Advocates Library.

128. Rendall, *The Origins of the Scottish Enlightenment,* p. 2.

129. Bruce Lenman, *Integration, Enlightenment, and Industrialization: Scotland, 1746–1832* (London: Edward Arnold, 1981), p. 14.

130. R. H. Campbell, "The Scottish Improvers and the Course of Agrarian Change in the Eighteenth Century," in Cullen and Smout, *Comparative Aspects of Scottish and Irish Economic and Social History,* pp. 204–215; Douglas Young, "Scotland and Edinburgh in the Eighteenth Century," *Studies on Voltaire and the Eighteenth Century* 58 (1967), 1967–1990; George S. Pryde, *Central and Local Government in Scotland since 1707* (London: Routledge and Kegan Paul, 1960), pp. 3–12.

131. Riley, "The Structure of Scottish Politics," p. 11.

132. Lenman, *Integration, Enlightenment, and Industrialization,* pp. 18–22.

133. Murdoch, *"The People Above,"* pp. 11–12; Chitnis, *The Scottish Enlightenment,* p. 22. Another writer describes Edinburgh as "a city where a considerable amount of political power resided and where, to a very large extent, knowledge meant power"; see Steven Shapin, "Property, Patronage, and the Politics of Science," *British Journal for the History of Science* 7 (1974), 4.

134. P. W. J. Riley, *The English Ministers and Scotland, 1707–1727* (London: Athlone Press, 1964), pp. 50–60; Rosalind Mitchison, *A History of Scotland,* 2d ed. (London: Methuen, 1982), pp. 325–326; Hugh Ousten, "York in Edinburgh: James VII and the Patronage of Learning in Scotland, 1679–1688," in *New Perspectives on the Politics and Culture of Early Modern Scotland,* ed. John Dwyer et al. (Edinburgh: Donald, 1982), p. 137.

135. Kettler, *The Social and Political Thought of Adam Ferguson,* p. 29.

136. Charles Camic, "The Enlightenment and Its Environment: A Cautionary Tale," in *Knowledge and Society: Studies in the Sociology of Culture Past and Present*, vol. 4, ed. Robert Alun Jones and Henrika Kuklick (Greenwich, Conn.: JAI Press, 1983), p. 155.

137. Hamilton, "Economic Growth in Scotland"; Hugh Trevor-Roper, "The Scottish Enlightenment," *Studies on Voltaire and the Eighteenth Century* 58 (1967), 1635–1658.

138. Ousten, "York in Edinburgh," p. 133.

139. Lenman, *Integration, Enlightenment, and Industrialization*, p. 28; Athol L. Murray, "Administration and Law," in Rae, *The Union of 1707*, pp. 30–57. Murray presents the interesting case of Sir John Clerk, who served as baron of the Exchequer in Scotland for more than forty years. Clerk was an active patron of the arts, held an interest in antiquities, and valued higher education as a means of preparing men for responsible civic office. As a mine owner he was also interested in science and technology. Clerk was clearly a member of the centralizing party in Scottish politics and was a supporter of the union. His own post had been created by the administration in London, and he was charged with carrying out London's orders in matters of taxation and revenue.

140. Ian Ross and Stephen Scobie, "Patriotic Publishing as a Response to the Union," in Rae, *The Union of 1707*, pp. 94–119.

141. Rosalind Mitchison, "Scottish Landowners and Communal Responsibility in the Eighteenth Century," *British Journal for Eighteenth-Century Studies* 1 (1978), 41–45.

142. Steven Shapin, "The Audience for Science in Eighteenth-Century Edinburgh," *History of Science* 12 (1974), 95–121. Another writer states: "As allies and patrons the professors looked to the landed proprietors, whom the Commonwealthmen taught them to admire as the backbone of any true republic, and whom they flattered by association in their clubs and societies, dedicated to the patriotic tasks of improvement and refinement"; Jones, "The Scottish Professoriate," p. 90.

143. Roger L. Emerson, "The Philosophical Society of Edinburgh, 1737–1747," *British Journal for the History of Science* 12 (1979), 173.

144. Emerson, "The Enlightenment and Social Structures," p. 107.

145. Emerson, "The Social Composition of Enlightened Scotland.".

146. Emerson, "The Philosophical Society of Edinburgh," pp. 133–176. Shapin suggests that the society required at least one-third of its members to be nonscientists and nonacademics in order to bring intellectuals together with patrons and, thereby, "to make the patrons of science sensitive to the range of social, cultural and economic benefits which might be seen to flow from science in its various forms"; Shapin, "The Audience for Science in Eighteenth-Century Edinburgh," p. 8.

147. Emerson, "Scottish Universities in the Eighteenth Century"; Phillipson, "Culture and Society in the Eighteenth-Century Province."

148. W. M. Mather, "The Origins and Occupations of Glasgow Students, 1740–1839," *Past and Present* 33 (1966), 74–94.

149. James Scotland, *The History of Scottish Education*, vol. 1, *From the Beginning to 1872* (London: University of London Press, 1969), pp. 134–173; McDougall, "Gavin Hamilton, Bookseller in Edinburgh.".

150. Largely under the influence of the earl of Bute, who wielded considerable power in London after the accession of George III in 1760, the leading circle of Enlightenment writers managed to secure nearly all the top positions at the University of Edinburgh and increased their personal revenue by as much as six or seven times in only a few years. And these incomes permitted a further consolidation of their power: "Henceforth they moved easily in polite society as men of distinction in their own right. They visited London more frequently and more stylishly . . . and associated with members of the nobility, gentry, and the liberal professions at social gatherings and in clubs." Sher, *Church and University in the Scottish Enlightenment*, pp. 120–121. Having close contacts with one another and with the broader elite, they were also able to control the major policy-making body of the church, the general assembly, thereby ensuring that major appointments and votes on theological issues would go their way. By the 1770s, these resources had effectively won them dominance over the major ecclesiastical and academic institutions of Scotland, a fact of no small significance in explaining why their ideas came to be so widely disseminated.

151. Emerson, "Scottish Universities in the Eighteenth Century," p. 457.

152. Lenman, *Integration, Enlightenment, and Industrialization*, p. 28.

153. Simpson stresses the extent to which fissures in the Scottish patronage networks were dependent on the fortunes of various factions in the British state more broadly: "Eighteenth-century politics was a politics of balance—between king and ministry, between minister and minister, between ministry and parliament—and . . . Scotland was run from Westminster, with the Scottish balance a product of the other balances." John M. Simpson, "Who Steered the Gravy Train, 1707–1766?" in Phillipson and Mitchison, *Scotland in the Age of Improvement*, p. 5.

154. J. H. Burns, "Scotland and England: Culture and Nationality, 1500–1800," in *Britain and the Netherlands*, vol. 4, *Metropolis, Dominion, and Province*, ed. J. S. Bromely and E. H. Kossmann (The Hague: Martinus Nijhoff, 1971), pp. 17–41; Neil MacCormick, "Law and Enlightenment," in Campbell and Skinner, *The Origins and Nature of the Scottish Enlightenment*, pp. 150–166; Mitchison, *A History of Scotland*, p. 324.

155. Phillipson, "The Scottish Enlightenment," p. 28; Riley, "The Structure of Scottish Politics," p. 3. In addition to their more general effects on the intellectual climate of the period, the rivalries in Scottish politics appear to have directly augmented literary autonomy. The so-called moderate literati, of whom Hugh Blair, Alexander Carlyle, Adam Ferguson,

John Home, and William Robertson were the most prominent, appear to have benefited specifically from such rivalries in the 1750s, for example. The members of this group who held clergy positions were indebted to the duke of Argyll because of the traditional patronage system by which clergy appointments were made. By midcentury, however, the Argyll faction was at odds with the Pitt-Bute-Leicester House party in London. And the moderate literati also had contact with this faction. The latter contacts played an important role in shielding the literati from the Argyll network's politics during the crucial period before they themselves came to dominate Edinburgh's churches and universities. This argument follows that of Sher, *Church and University in the Scottish Enlightenment,* pp. 74–92. On the Argyll-Bute rivalry, see Murdoch, *"The People Above."*

156. See Daiches, *The Paradox of Scottish Culture,* pp. 14–28, for a useful discussion of the cross-cutting sentiments that continued to pervade Scottish political life during the half century following the union.

157. Nicholas T. Phillipson, "Toward a Definition of the Scottish Enlightenment," in *City and society in the Eighteenth Century,* ed. Paul Fritz and David Williams (Toronto: Hakkert, 1973), pp. 125–147.

158. George E. Davie, *The Scottish Enlightenment* (London: The Historical Association, 1981).

159. Phillipson, "The Scottish Enlightenment," p. 26.

160. George E. Davie, "Hume, Reid, and the Passion for Ideas," in *Edinburgh in the Age of Reason,* ed. Douglas Young (Edinburgh: Edinburgh University Press, 1967), pp. 23–39; Shapin, "Property, Patronage, and the Politics of Science."

8. The Enlightenment in Decentralized Societies

1. Simon Schama, "The Enlightenment in the Netherlands," in *The Enlightenment in National Context* ed. Roy Porter and Mikulas Teich (Cambridge: Cambridge University Press, 1981), p. 56.

2. E. H. Kossmann, "Some Meditations on Dutch Eighteenth-Century Decline," in *Failed Transitions to Modern Industrial Society: Renaissance Italy and Seventeenth-Century Holland,* ed. Frederick Krantz and Paul M. Hohenberg (Montreal: Interuniversity Centre for European Studies, 1975), p. 54.

3. J. L. Price, *Culture and Society in the Dutch Republic during the 17th Century* (London: B. T. Batsford, 1974), p. 211.

4. Charles Wilson, *The Dutch Republic and the Civilisation of the Seventeenth Century* (New York: McGraw-Hill, 1968), pp. 242–243.

5. Schama, "The Enlightenment in the Netherlands."

6. I. L. Leeb, *The Ideological Origins of the Batavian Revolution: History and Politics in the Dutch Republic, 1747–1800* (The Hague: Martinus Nijhoff, 1973), p. 98; cf. E. H. Kossmann, "The Dutch Case: A National

or a Regional Culture?" *Transactions of the Royal Historical Society* 29 (1979), 155–168. Some studies also suggest that Enlightenment literature may have penetrated more quickly and widely into the French-speaking sections of Belgium than into the Dutch sections of the Low Countries because of language differences; see, for example, Daniel Droixhe, "Note relative à l'histoire de la lecture wallonne au XVIIIe siècle," *Le livre et l'estampe* 30 (1984), 7–16; Guy Biart, "Lesegesellschaften im Dienste der Gegenaufklärung: Ein belgisches Beispiel," in *Lesegesellschaften und bürgerliche Emanzipation: Ein europäischer Vergleich,* ed. Otto Dann (Munich: C. H. Beck'sche Verlagsbuchhandlung, 1981), pp. 197–211.

7. G. C. Gibbs, "Some Intellectual and Political Influences of the Huguenot Emigrés in the United Provinces, c. 1680–1730," *Bijdragen en Mededelingen betreffende de geschiedenis der Nederlanden* 90 (1975), 264–265; Roger Chartier, "Student Populations in the Eighteenth Century," *British Journal for Eighteenth-Century Studies* 2 (1979), 152–153.

8. W. D. Hackmann, "The Growth of Science in the Netherlands in the Seventeenth and Early Eighteenth Century Centuries," in *The Emergence of Science in Western Europe,* ed. Maurice Crosland (New York: Science History Publications, 1976), p. 93.

9. J. J. Woltjer, "Introduction," in *Leiden University in the Seventeenth Century: An Exchange of Learning,* ed. T. H. Lunsingh Scheurleer and G. H. M. Posthumus Meyjes (Leiden: E. J. Brill, 1975), p. 7; J. MacLean, "Science and Technology at Groningen University (1698–1702)," *Annals of Science* 29 (1972), 187–202; J. W. Van Spronsen, "The Beginning of Chemistry," in Scheurleer and Meyjes, *Leiden University in the Seventeenth Century,* pp. 329–344.

10. G. A. Lindeboorn, *Herman Boerhaave: The Man and His Work* (London: Methuen, 1968), esp. pp. 29, 51. The fact that Boerhaave stayed till his death in 1738 has even been regarded as an anomaly, attributable to his dislike of court life, which caused him to turn down several offers.

11. Hackmann, "The Growth of Science in the Netherlands."

12. H. A. M. Snelders, "Physics and Chemistry in the Netherlands in the Period 1750–1850," *Janus* 65 (1978), 1–20; P. P. Bockstaele, "Mathematics in the Netherlands from 1750 to 1830," *Janus* 65 (1978), 67–95.

13. Schama, "The Enlightenment in the Netherlands," p. 68.

14. Hemmo Vander Laan, "Influences on Education and Instruction in the Netherlands, Especially 1750 to 1815," in *Facets of Education in the Eighteenth Century,* ed. James A. Leith (Oxford: Voltaire Foundation at the Taylor Institution, 1977), p. 289.

15. Margaret C. Jacob, "Newtonianism and the Origins of the Enlightenment," *Eighteenth-Century Studies* 11 (1977), 1–25.

16. One estimate, drawn from sources in the 1780s, enumerates at least sixty-eight reading societies in existence at that point, but a large

number of these were likely to have been religious groups or political clubs; see P. J. Buijnsters, "Lesegesellschaften in den Niederlande," in Dann, *Lesegesellschaften und bürgerliche Emanzipation,* pp. 143–158. This study also suggests that members of the aristocracy and government officials did not join these circles because their wealth was sufficient to purchase books privately. The period of most rapid growth in reading societies was during the French Revolution. During this period Dutch republicans founded illegal political societies and used reading clubs as a cover for them.

17. Robert Wuthnow, "The World-Economy and the Institutionalization of Science in Seventeenth-Century Europe," in *Studies of the Modern World-System,* ed. Albert Bergesen (New York: Academic Press, 1980), pp. 46–50.

18. Trevor H. Levere, "Relations and Rivalry: Interactions between Britain and the Netherlands in Eighteenth-Century Science and Technology," *History of Science* 9 (1970), 42–53.

19. Hackmann, "The Growth of Science in the Netherlands," p. 101; J. A. Van Houtte, *An Economic History of the Low Countries, 1500–1800* (London: Weidenfeld and Nicolson, 1977), p. 288.

20. P. Smit, "International Influences on the Development of Natural History in the Netherlands and Its East Indian Colonies between 1750 and 1850," *Janus* 65 (1978), 45–65; Levere, "Relations and Rivalry."

21. Price, *Culture and Society in the Dutch Republic,* p. 213.

22. Van Houtte, *An Economic History of the Low Countries,* pp. 227–229, 271–286; J. G. Van Dillen, "Economic Fluctuations in the Netherlands, 1650–1750," in *Essays in European Economic History, 1500–1800,* ed. Peter Earle (Oxford: Clarendon Press, 1974), pp. 199–211.

23. E. N. Williams, *The Ancien Régime in Europe: Government and Society in the Major States, 1648–1789* (New York: Harper and Row, 1970), pp. 51–55; David Ormrod, "Dutch Commercial and Industrial Decline and British Growth in the Late Seventeenth and Early Eighteenth Centuries," in Krantz and Hohenberg, *Failed Transitions to Modern Industrial Society,* pp. 36–43.

24. Max Barkhausen, "Government Control and Free Enterprise in Western Germany and the Low Countries in the Eighteenth Century," in Earle, *Essays in European Economic History,* pp. 212–273.

25. Ibid., p. 245.

26. Williams, *The Ancien Régime in Europe,* pp. 51–55.

27. Barkhausen, "Government Control and Free Enterprise," p. 246.

28. Williams, *The Ancien Régime in Europe,* p. 52.

29. Van Houtte, *An Economic History of the Low Countries,* pp. 287–310; another writer, who attributes the Dutch Republic's economic decline largely to its form of government, suggests that the Dutch state was "more effective in obstructing unpopular measures than in initiating constructive policies"; K. W. Swart, "Holland's Bourgeoisie and the Retarded Indus-

trialization of the Netherlands," in Krantz and Hohenberg, *Failed Transitions to Modern Industrial Society*, p. 44.

30. Olwen H. Hufton, *Europe: Privilege and Protest, 1730–1789* (Glasgow: William Collins Sons, 1980), p. 290.

31. Alice Clare Carter, *The Dutch Republic in Europe in the Seven Years' War* (London: Macmillan, 1971), pp. 19–20.

32. Williams, *The Ancien Régime in Europe*, p. 23; cf. E. H. Kossmann, "The Crisis of the Dutch State, 1780–1813: Nationalism, Federalism, Unitarism," in *Britain and the Netherlands*, vol. 4, ed. J. S. Bromley and E. H. Kossmann (The Hague: Martinus Nijhoff, 1971), pp. 156–175.

33. Swart, "Holland's Bourgeoisie and the Retarded Industrialization of the Netherlands," p. 45.

34. Leeb, *The Ideological Origins of the Batavian Revolution*, p. 16.

35. R. J. Roorda, "The Ruling Class in Holland in the Seventeenth Century," in *Britain and the Netherlands*, vol. 2, ed. J. S. Bromley and E. H. Kossmann (Groningen: J. P. Wolters, 1964), pp. 109–132.

36. H. Wansink, "Holland and Six Allies: The Republic of the Seven United Provinces," in Bromley and Kossmann, *Britain and the Netherlands*, vol. 4, p. 137.

37. J. G. Van Dillen, "Amsterdam's Role in Seventeenth-Century Dutch Politics and Its Economic Background," in Bromley and Kossmann, *Britain and the Netherlands*, vol. 2, pp. 133–147; cf. H. Van Dijk and D. J. Roorda, "Social Mobility under the Regents of the Republic," *Acta Historiae Neerlandicae* 9 (1976), 76–102.

38. E. H. Kossmann, *The Low Countries, 1780–1940* (Oxford: Clarendon Press, 1978, p. 40.

39. Carter, *The Dutch Republic in Europe in the Seven Years' War*, p. 30.

40. Leeb, *The Ideological Origins of the Batavian Revolution*.

41. Price, *Culture and Society in the Dutch Republic*, pp. 195–226.

42. Kossmann, "The Crisis of the Dutch State."

43. Wansink, "Holland and Six Allies," p. 150.

44. Vander Laan, "Influences on Education and Instruction."

45. Hackmann, "The Growth of Science in the Netherlands," p. 90.

46. Voltaire, for example, pronounced Sweden "the freest country in the world," and Rousseau called the Swedish system of government "an example of perfection." Quoted in Michael Roberts, *The Age of Liberty: Sweden, 1719–1772* (Cambridge: Cambridge University Press, 1986), p. 59.

47. Roger L. Emerson, "The Enlightenment and Social Structures," in *City and Society in the Eighteenth Century*, ed. Paul Fritz and David Williams (Toronto: Hakkert, 1973), p. 104.

48. Tore Frangsmyr, "The Enlightenment in Sweden," in Porter and Teich, *The Enlightenment in National Context*, p. 164.

49. James E. McClellan III, "The International Organization of Science

and Learned Societies in the Eighteenth Century" (Ph.D. diss., Princeton University, 1975), p. 111–121.

50. Tore Frangsmyr, "Swedish Science in the Eighteenth Century," *History of Science* 12 (1974), 29–42. Some advances in science were also made in Denmark, but generally Danish science lagged far behind that of Sweden. Mathematics in Denmark was limited to the work of several figures whose reputations remained local; experimental physics attracted little interest, and virtually no work was done in chemistry. Medicine and biology fared somewhat better, a college of anatomy being founded in 1736; but these achievements mostly reflected German influences from the University of Halle. B. J. Hovde, *The Scandinavian Countries, 1720–1865: The Rise of the Middle Classes* (Boston: Chapman and Grimes, 1943), pp. 119–128.

51. Frangsmyr, "The Enlightenment in Sweden"; H. Arnold Barton, "Gustav III of Sweden and the Enlightenment," *Eighteenth-Century Studies* 6 (1972), 1–34. Intellectual activity in Denmark experienced a temporary surge of interest during the reign of Frederick V, who invited foreign scholars and teachers to Copenhagen, but an indigenous community of enlightened scholars failed to develop. Hovde, *The Scandinavian Countries,* pp. 119–128.

52. Franklin D. Scott, *Sweden: The Nation's History* (Minneapolis: University of Minnesota Press, 1977), pp. 240–242; R. M. Hatton, "Scandinavia and the Baltic," in *The New Cambridge Modern History,* vol. 7, *The Old Regime, 1713–63,* ed. J. O. Lindsay (Cambridge: Cambridge University Press, 1957), pp. 341–342.

53. Hatton, "Scandinavia and the Baltic," pp. 339–340.

54. Hovde, *The Scandinavian Countries,* pp. 15–58.

55. Robert V. Eagly, "Monetary Policy and Politics in Mid-Eighteenth-Century Sweden," *Journal of Economic History* 29 (1969), 739–757.

56. Eli F. Hecksher, *An Economic History of Sweden* (Cambridge, Mass.: Harvard University Press, 1954), pp. 173–197.

57. Sven Lundkvist, "The Experience of Empire: Sweden as a Great Power," in *Sweden's Age of Greatness, 1632–1718,* ed. Michael Roberts (London: Macmillan, 1973), pp. 22–26.

58. Carl Lennart Lundquist, *Council, King, and Estates in Sweden, 1713–1714* (Stockholm: Almquist and Wiksell International, 1975), pp. 11–23.

59. J. O. Lindsay, "The Western Mediterranean and Italy," in *The New Cambridge Modern History,* vol. 7, pp. 144–145.

60. Sven-Erik Astrom, "The Swedish Economy and Sweden's Role as a Great Power, 1632–1697," in Roberts, *Sweden's Age of Greatness,* pp. 74–75.

61. Michael Roberts, *The Swedish Imperial Experience, 1560–1718* (Cambridge: Cambridge University Press, 1979), pp. 140–143.

62. Michael F. Metcalf, *Russia, England, and Swedish Party Politics,*

1762–1766 (Stockholm: Almquist and Wiksell International, 1977), p. 3–4; Sven Ulrich Palme, "The Bureaucratic Type of Parliament: The Swedish Estates during the Age of Liberty, 1719–1772," in *Liber Memorialis Georges de Lagrande* (Louvain: Editions Neuwelaerts, 1970), pp. 237–257; Scott, *Sweden: The Nation's History,* p. 241.

63. Sten Carlsson, "The Dissolution of the Swedish Estates, 1700–1865," *Journal of European Economic History* 1 (1972), 574–624; Hecksher, *An Economic History of Sweden,* p. 141.

64. Stein Rokkan, "Dimensions of State Formation and Nation-Building: A Possible Paradigm for Research on Variations within Europe," in *The Formation of National States in Western Europe,* ed. Charles Tilly (Princeton: Princeton University Press, 1975), p. 588.

65. Eagly, "Monetary Policy and Politics."

66. Scott, *Sweden: The Nation's History,* p. 237.

67. Hatton, "Scandinavia and the Baltic," pp. 355–364.

68. This discussion is based on the valuable essay by Michael Roberts that compares Swedish government with English government during the same period; see Michael Roberts, *The Age of Liberty,* pp. 59–110.

69. Quoted ibid., p. 105.

70. The political situation in Denmark also failed to prove conducive to Enlightenment cultural activity, although for reasons that paralleled those of Russia and Spain (discussed in Chapter 9) more than Sweden or the Dutch Republic. Evidence is relatively sparse, but the general contours appear to include the following: royal absolutism had been firmly imposed by 1660, stripping the aristocracy of independent legislative representation and drawing the bourgeoisie into close dependence on royal policy. See Rokkan, "Dimensions of State Formation and Nation-Building," p. 588. In contrast with that of Sweden, this system prevailed until the end of the eighteenth century. As in Sweden, though, the state in Denmark was by the start of the century already on the verge of bankruptcy; its economy remained on insecure footing, and its very survival depended mostly on aid from Sweden's enemies. Immanuel Wallerstein, *The Modern World-System,* vol. 2, *Mercantilism and the Consolidation of the European World-Economy, 1600–1750* (New York: Academic Press, 1980), p. 224. Wallerstein writes that the Danish state was "largely a facade and bolstered by outside interests." The bureaucracy did expand to some extent as the state sought to initiate economic growth through mercantilist policies. But this growth remained limited, and most governmental functions continued to be arrogated under the personal rule of the monarch. Rather than state functions becoming subject to debate by a broad clientele of elite representatives or civil servants, they remained the closely guarded prerogative of the king and his top advisers. See Hovde, *The Scandinavian Countries,* pp. 202–207.

71. J. W. Stoye, "The Austrian Habsburgs," in *The New Cambridge*

Modern History, vol. 6, *The Rise of Great Britain and Russia, 1688–1715/ 25,* ed. J. S. Bromley (Cambridge: Cambridge University Press, 1970), pp. 572–589.

72. William E. Wright, *Serf, Seigneur, and Sovereign: Agrarian Reform in Eighteenth-Century Bohemia* (Minneapolis: University of Minnesota Press, 1966), p. 26.

73. Ernst Wangermann, *The Austrian Achievement, 1700–1800* (London: Thames and Hudson, 1973), pp. 41–42.

74. Victor-L. Tapie, *The Rise and Fall of the Habsburg Monarchy* (New York: Praeger, 1971), p. 142.

75. Stoye, "The Austrian Habsburgs," pp. 572–575; Tapie, *The Rise and Fall of the Habsburg Monarchy,* pp. 176–177. Tapie asserts: "The barrier which the aristocracy formed between the sovereign and the subjects of his different states continued to hinder the administration of the monarchy and made it impossible to bring each country's resources into harmony with general policy." Another writer argues that diverse legal traditions in the various Austrian domains was an important factor that impeded political centralization; see Robert A. Kann, *The Hapsburg Empire: A Study in Integration and Disintegration* (New York: Praeger, 1957), esp. pp. 72–77; see also Robert A. Kann, *A Study in Austrian Intellectual History* (New York: Praeger, 1960), pp. 19–23. The lack of an effective centralized bureaucracy is also stressed in R. J. W. Evans, *The Making of the Habsburg Monarchy, 1550–1700: An Interpretation* (Oxford: Clarendon Press, 1979), pp. 146–154.

76. W. O. Henderson, *Studies in the Economic Policy of Frederick the Great* (London: F. Cass, 1963), pp. 104–114; Wangermann, *The Austrian Achievement,* pp. 24–27; Arnost Klima, "Mercantilism in the Habsburg Monarchy—With Special Reference to the Bohemian Lands," *Historica* 11 (1965), 95–119.

77. N. T. Gross, "The Habsburg Monarchy, 1750–1914," in *The Fontana Economic History of Europe: The Emergence of Industrial Societies,* vol. 4, pt. 1, ed. Carlo M. Cipolla (Glasgow: William Collins Sons, 1973), pp. 237–247.

78. Wangermann, *The Austrian Achievement,* p. 45.

79. General surveys of cultural production in Austria during the Enlightenment include R. Muhlher, "Die Literatur zur Zeit der Aufklärung in Osterreich," *Osterreich in Geschichte und Literatur* 8 (1964), 144–166; Eduard Winter, *Fruhaufklärung* (Berlin: Akademie-Verlag, 1966); Heinz Ischreyt, "Zur Aufklärung in Mittel- und Osteuropa: Probleme und Tendenzen," in *Aufklärung in Deutschland,* ed. Paul Raabe and Wilhelm Schmidt-Biggemann (Bonn: Hohwacht Verlag, 1979), 185–199; and T. C. W. Blanning, *Joseph II and Enlightened Despotism* (London: Longman, 1970).

80. C. A. Macartney, "The Habsburg Dominions," in *The New Cambridge Modern History,* vol. 7, p. 398.

81. Wangermann, *The Austrian Achievement,* p. 29.

82. Tapie, *The Rise and Fall of the Habsburg Monarchy,* pp. 166–167.

83. H. Demelius, "Beitrage zur Haushaltsgeschichte der Universität Wien," *Studien zur Geschichte der Universität Wien* 1 (1965), 208–218.

84. Tapie, *The Rise and Fall of the Habsburg Monarchy,* pp. 196–197.

85. Paul B. Bernard, *Jesuits and Jacobins: Enlightenment and Enlightened Despotism in Austria* (Urbana: University of Illinois Press, 1971), p. 4.

86. Wangermann, *The Austrian Achievement,* pp. 60–89; Ernst Wangermann, "Reform Catholicism and Political Radicalism in the Austrian Enlightenment," in Porter and Teich, *The Enlightenment in National Context,* p. 134; Alfred Cobban, "The Pattern of Government," in *The Eighteenth Century: Europe in the Age of Enlightenment,* ed. Alfred Cobban (New York: McGraw-Hill, 1969), p. 36.

87. Hufton, *Europe: Privilege and Protest,* p. 159.

88. Macartney, "The Habsburg Dominions," pp. 410–415.

89. Hufton, *Europe: Privilege and Protest,* p. 155; general sources on this period include Paul B. Bernard, *Joseph II* (New York: Twayne, 1968), and Saul K. Padover, *The Revolutionary Emperor: Joseph II of Austria* (New York: Archon Books, 1967). On the tensions between members of the central bureaucracy and the nobility, see especially Ernst Wangermann, *From Joseph II to the Jacobin Trials: Government Policy and Public Opinion in the Hapsburg Dominions in the Period of the French Revolution* (Oxford: Oxford University Press, 1959); and, for a parallel discussion of the Rumanian Principalities, Vlad Georgescu, *Political Ideas and the Enlightenment in the Rumanian Principalities (1750–1831)* (New York: Columbia University Press, 1971).

90. Wangermann, *The Austrian Achievement,* pp. 117–118.

91. Richard Plaschka, "Austrian Policy toward the Balkans in the Second Half of the Eighteenth Century: Maria Theresa and Joseph II," *East European Quarterly* 9 (1975), 471–478; Wangermann, "Reform Catholicism and Political Radicalism," p. 128.

92. Bernard, *Jesuits and Jacobins,* is the most useful source on these writers.

93. Wangermann, *The Austrian Achievement,* p. 131.

94. Kann, *A Study in Austrian Intellectual History,* gives greater emphasis to the achievements of the Austrian Enlightenment between 1740 and 1780 but focuses more on political reforms deemed compatible with the Enlightenment than on the existence of an enlightened intellectual movement itself.

95. Wangermann, *From Joseph II to the Jacobin Trials.*

96. The problems associated with the fact that patronage during this period remained largely a function of personal whim are captured well in the following statement: "Even under the ostensibly liberal Joseph, the Emperor's own whims and the alacrity with which officials anticipated them

made nonsense of any literary programme. *Romeo and Juliet* was banned because Joseph disliked scenes in funeral vaults, *Macbeth* was withdrawn lest Joseph take offence at regicide, Klinger's *Zwillinge* was taken off because it shocked Joseph by calling in question the Fourth Commandment; and the young writers of the Sturm und Drang generation were surely discouraged." T. James Reed, "Theatre, Enlightenment, and Nation: A German Problem," in *The Theatre of the French and German Enlightenment,* ed. S. S. B. Taylor (New York: Barnes and Noble, 1978), p. 53.

97. Ibid., p. 26; see also Wangermann, *The Austrian Achievement,* p. 142; and B. Becker-Cantarino, "Joseph von Sonnenfels and the Development of Secular Education in Eighteenth-Century Austria," in Leith, *Facets of Education in the Eighteenth Century,* pp. 32–33.

98. Isser Woloch, *Eighteenth-Century Europe: Tradition and Progress, 1715–1789* (New York: Norton, 1982), p. 268.

99. Quoted in Hufton, *Europe: Privilege and Protest,* p. 185.

9. Autocracy and the Limits of Enlightenment

1. Robert D. Givens, "Eighteenth-Century Nobiliary Career Patterns and Provincial Government," in *Russian Officialdom: The Bureaucratization of Russian Society from the Seventeenth to the Twentieth Century,* ed. Walter McKenzie Pintner and Don Karl Rowney (Chapel Hill: University of North Carolina Press, 1980), pp. 106–129.

2. Antony Lentin, *Russia in the Eighteenth Century from Peter the Great to Catherine the Great* (London: Heinemann, 1973), pp. 14–17.

3. The extent to which the tsars succeeded in this aim is discussed in four works by Robert O. Crummey: "The Reconstitution of the Boiar Aristocracy, 1613–45," *Forschungen zur osteuropaischen Geschichte* 18 (1973), 187–220; "Peter and the Boiar Aristocracy, 1689–1700," *Canadian-American Slavic Studies* 8 (1974), 274–287; "The Origins of the Noble Official: The Boyar Elite, 1613–1689," in Pintner and Rowney, *Russian Officialdom,* pp. 46–75; and *Aristocrats and Servitors* (Princeton: Princeton University Press, 1983). See also Werner Philipp, "Russia: The Beginning of Westernization," *Forschungen zur osteuropaischen Geschichte* 33 (1983), 63–80.

4. Richard Wortman, "Peter the Great and Court Procedure," *Canadian-American Slavic Studies* 8 (1974), 311–318, and *The Development of a Russian Legal Consciousness* (Chicago: University of Chicago Press, 1976); another general source on these developments is George L. Yaney, *The Systematization of Russian Government: Social Evolution in the Domestic Administration of Imperial Russia, 1711–1905* (Urbana: University of Illinois Press, 1973); and for a brief overview, see M. S. Anderson, "Russia under Peter the Great and the Changed Relations of East and West," in *The New Cambridge Modern History,* vol. 6, *The Rise of Great Britain and Russia, 1688–*

1715/25, ed. J. S. Bromley (Cambridge: Cambridge University Press, 1970), pp. 716–740.

5. Brenda Meehan-Waters, *Autocracy and Aristocracy: The Russian Service Elite of 1730* (New Brunswick, N.J.: Rutgers University Press, 1982), pp. 29–70; also useful on the role of nobility are three other works by Brenda Meehan-Waters: "The Muscovite Noble Origins of the Russians in the Generalitat of 1730," *Cahiers du monde russe et sovietique* 12 (1970), 28–75; "The Russian Aristocracy and the Reforms of Peter the Great," *Canadian-American Slavic Studies* 8 (1974), 288–302; and "Social and Career Characteristics of the Administrative Elite, 1689–1761," in Pintner and Rowney, *Russian Officialdom*, pp. 76–105.

6. Lentin, *Russia in the Eighteenth Century*, pp. 29–32.

7. Phillip, "Russia," p. 69; cf. Hans J. Torke, "Continuity and Change in the Relations between Bureaucracy and Society in Russia, 1613–1861," *Canadian Slavic Studies* 5 (1971), 462. Richard Pipes, in describing the service elite, notes that "they were not a nobility in the western sense because they lacked the corporate privileges which in the west distinguished nobles from ordinary mortals. Even the most eminent Muscovite servitor could be deprived of life and property at his sovereign's whim"; Richard Pipes, *Russia under the Old Regime* (London: Weidenfeld and Nicolson, 1974), p. 86. And Jerome Blum observes: "In no other European land was the sovereign able to make all non-clerical landholding conditional upon the performance of service for him"; Jerome Blum, *Lord and Peasant in Russia from the Ninth to the Nineteenth Century* (Princeton: Princeton University Press, 1961), p. 169.

8. Meehan-Waters, *Autocracy and Aristocracy*, pp. 29–30; Anderson, "Russia under Peter the Great," p. 723.

9. Marc Raeff, *The Origins of the Russian Intelligentsia: The Eighteenth-Century Nobility* (New York: Harcourt, Brace, 1966), pp. 22–30.

10. Meehan-Waters, *Autocracy and Aristocracy*, p. 70.

11. Lentin, *Russia in the Eighteenth Century*, pp. 36–37; Alexander Vucinich, *Science in Russian Culture: A History to 1860* (Stanford: Stanford University Press, 1963), p. 52.

12. John T. Alexander, "Medical Developments in Petrine Russia," *Canadian-American Slavic Studies* 8 (1974), 198–221.

13. Gary Marker, *Publishing, Printing, and the Origins of Intellectual Life in Russia, 1700–1800* (Princeton: Princeton University Press, 1985), p. 17.

14. Cf. Michael Confino, "On Intellectuals and Intellectual Traditions in Eighteenth- and Nineteenth-Century Russia," in *Intellectuals and Tradition*, ed. S. N. Eisenstadt and S. R. Graubard (New York: Humanities Press, 1973), p. 122; Lothar A. Maier, "Wissenschaft und Staatsinteresse zur Zeit Peters des Grossen: Die erschliessung Sibiriens und des Nord-

pazifik durch wissenschaftliche Expeditionen," *Osterreichische Osthefte* 20 (1978), 435–449.

15. Vucinich, *Science in Russian Culture,* pp. 65–122; James E. McClellan, "The International Organization of Science and Learned Societies in the Eighteenth Century" (Ph.D. diss., Princeton University, 1975), pp. 99–111.

16. Confino, "On Intellectuals and Intellectual Traditions"; cf. A. A. Kartashev, "Church Reform," in *Peter the Great: Reformer or Revolutionary?* ed. Marc Raeff (Boston: D. C. Heath, 1963), pp. 45–49; and Nicholas Zernov, "The Establishment of the Russian Church," in Raeff, *Peter the Great,* pp. 50–56.

17. Raeff, *The Origins of the Russian Intelligentsia,* pp. 137–147; J. Scott Carver, "A Reconsideration of Eighteenth-Century Russia's Contributions to European Science," *Canadian-American Slavic Studies* 14 (1980), 389–405.

18. Marker, *Publishing,* p. 25.

19. Sumner Benson, "The Role of Western Thought in Petrine Russia," *Canadian-American Slavic Studies* 8 (1974), 265.

20. Lothar A. Maier, "Die Krise der St. Petersburger Akademie der Wissenschaften nach der thronbesteigung Elisabeth Petrovnas und die 'affare Gmelin,'" *Jahrbucher für Geschichte Osteuropas* 27 (1979), 353–373.

21. J. Laurence Black, "Citizenship Training and Moral Regeneration as the Mainstay of Russian Schools," in *Facets of Education in the Eighteenth Century,* ed. James A. Leith (Oxford: Voltaire Foundation at the Taylor Institution, 1977), p. 432.

22. Carver, "Eighteenth-Century Russia's Contributions to European Science."

23. Stuart Ramsey Tompkins, *The Russian Mind: From Peter the Great through the Enlightenment* (Norman: University of Oklahoma Press, 1953), pp. 43–46; Walter M. Pintner, "The Evolution of Civil Officialdom, 1755–1855," in Pintner and Rowney, *Russian Officialdom,* p. 215.

24. Cf. Kerry R. Morrison, "Catherine II's Legislative Commission: An Administrative Interpretation," *Canadian Slavic Studies* 4 (1970), 464–484; James A. Duran, Jr., "The Reform of Financial Administration in Russia during the Reign of Catherine II," *Canadian Slavic Studies* 4 (1970), 485–496.

25. Lentin, *Russia in the Eighteenth Century,* pp. 14–17.

26. Marc Raeff, *Imperial Russia, 1682–1825: The Coming of Age of Modern Russia* (New York: Knopf, 1971), p. 91; Yaney, *The Systematization of Russian Government,* p. 53.

27. Duran, "The Reform of Financial Administration in Russia."

28. Marker, *Publishing,* p. 41.

29. Ibid., pp. 25, 59.

30. Cf. Lentin, *Russia in the Eighteenth Century*, pp. 68–71; Meehan-Waters, *Autocracy and Aristocracy*, pp. 23–48; more generally, see Dan Altbauer, "The Diplomats of Peter the Great, 1689–1725" (Ph.D. diss., Harvard University, 1976), and Robert E. Jones, *The Emancipation of the Russian Nobility, 1762–1785* (Princeton: Princeton University Press, 1973). Although it was once widely regarded that this period was strictly one of rising noble influence, this interpretation has been challenged by a somewhat more balanced view of the relations between the nobility and the bureaucracy. Jones writes, for example: "Whether they are looked at in . . . a historical perspective or are treated as individual acts, modifications in the nobility's service obligations from 1725 to 1762 can be explained more easily and more sensibly if they are seen as the results of the state's efforts to bring the supply of manpower into balance with the demand rather than as the results of political 'deals' between the various sovereigns and the *dvorianstvo*" (p. 180).

31. Blum, *Lord and Peasant in Russia*, p. 287; Herbert H. Kaplan, "Russia's Impact on the Industrial Revolution in Great Britain during the Second Half of the Eighteenth Century: The Significance of International Commerce," *Forschungen zur osteuropaischen Geschichte* 29 (1981), 7–60; David S. Macmillan, "The Scottish-Russian Trade: Its Development, Fluctuations, and Difficulties 1750–1796," *Canadian Slavic Studies* 4 (1970), 426–442; Arcadius Kahan, "The Costs of 'Westernization' in Russia: The Gentry and the Economy in the Eighteenth Century," *Slavic Review* 25 (1966), 40–66, and "Observations on Petrine Foreign Trade," *Canadian-American Slavic Studies* 8 (1974), 222–236.

32. Blum, *Lord and Peasant in Russia*, p. 278; Raeff, *Imperial Russia*, p. 89.

33. Lentin, *Russia in the Eighteenth Century*, pp. 82–92.

34. Pipes, *Russia under the Old Regime*, pp. 112–138.

35. Jones, *The Emancipation of the Russian Nobility*, pp. 180–187.

36. Victor Kamendrowsky and David M. Griffiths, "The Fate of the Trading Nobility Controversy in Russia: A Chapter in the Relationship between Catherine II and the Russian Nobility," *Jahrbucher für Geschichte Osteuropas* 2 (1978), 198–221.

37. Wilson Augustine notes in his discussion of the Great Commission of 1767–1768 that "fear of criticizing the central government, together with the natural interest of the franchised group in local problems concerning ownership of land, resulted in the [nobility] centering their attention on parochial issues"; Wilson Augustine, "Notes toward a Portrait of the Eighteenth-Century Russian Nobility," *Canadian Slavic Studies* 4 (1970), pp. 373–425.

38. Raeff, *The Origins of the Russian Intelligentsia*, p. 107.

39. Jones, *The Emancipation of the Russian Nobility*, p. 154.

40. Torke, "Continuity and Change in the Relations between Bureaucracy and Society in Russia," p. 458; cf. J. Michael Hittle, *The Service City: State and Townsmen, 1600–1800* (Cambridge, Mass.: Harvard University Press, 1979), pp. 190–236.

41. David Ransel, "Nikita Panin's Imperial Council Project and the Struggle of Hierarchy Groups at the Court of Catherine II," *Canadian Slavic Studies* 4 (1970), 443–463; Alfred J. Rieber, "Bureaucratic Politics in Imperial Russia," *Social Science History* 2 (1978), 399–413; and more generally, David Ransel, *The Politics of Catherinian Russia: The Panin Party* (New Haven: Yale University Press, 1975).

42. Jones, *The Emancipation of the Russian Nobility,* pp. 97–100.

43. Pipes, *Russia under the Old Regime,* pp. 130–138.

44. On the nature of this debate, see Andrzej Walicki, *A History of Russian Thought from the Enlightenment to Marxism* (Stanford: Stanford University Press, 1979).

45. Carver, "Eighteenth-Century Russia's Contributions to European Science," p. 389.

46. Max J. Okenfuss, "Popular Educational Tracts in Enlightenment Russia: A Preliminary Survey," *Canadian-American Slavic Studies* 14 (1980), 307–326; Max J. Okenfuss, "Education and Empire: School Reform in Enlightened Russia," *Jahrbucher für Geschichte Osteuropas* 27 (1979), 41–68.

47. Marker, *Publishing,* pp. 72–76.

48. Lentin, *Russia in the Eighteenth Century,* p. 116.

49. Marker, *Publishing,* pp. 76–77.

50. Gary Marker, "Merchandising Culture: The Market for Books in Late Eighteenth-Century Russia," *Eighteenth-Century Life* 8 (1982), 46–71; Tompkins, *The Russian Mind,* pp. 98–119.

51. Cf. Ransel, *The Politics of Catherinian Russia,* pp. 216–221.

52. Pipes, *Russia under the Old Regime,* p. 254.

53. Raeff, *The Origins of the Russian Intelligentsia,* p. 11.

54. Isabel DeMadariaga, *Russia in the Age of Catherine the Great* (New Haven: Yale University Press, 1981), p. 328. This is a brief but useful discussion of the aesthetic aspects of court life under Catherine the Great.

55. Walter J. Gleason, *Moral Idealists, Bureaucracy, and Catherine the Great* (New Brunswick, N.J.: Rutgers University Press, 1981).

56. For example, Jones, *The Emancipation of the Russian Nobility,* pp. 210–243; Walicki, *A History of Russian Thought,* pp. 26–34; Raeff, *Imperial Russia,* pp. 131–158; also see Hans Roggers, *National Consciousness in Eighteenth-Century Russia* (Cambridge, Mass.: Harvard University Press, 1960).

57. See Okenfuss, "Popular Educational Tracts"; David Ransel, "Ivan Betskoi and the Institutionalization of the Enlightenment in Russia," *Canadian-American Slavic Studies* 14 (1980), 327–338; R. P. Bartlett, "Culture

and Enlightenment: Julius von Caritz and the Kazan' Gimnazii in the Eighteenth Century," *Canadian-American Slavic Studies* 14 (1980), 339–360; Gilbert H. McArthur, "Freemasonry and Enlightenment in Russia: The Views of N. I. Novikov," *Canadian-American Slavic Studies* 14 (1980), 361–375; and George Vernadsky, "Rise of Science in Russia, 1700–1917," *Russian Review* 28 (1969), 37–52.

58. Olwen H. Hufton, *Europe: Privilege and Protest, 1730–1789* (Glasgow: William Collins Sons, 1980), pp. 256–257.

59. Vicente Palacio Atard, "Der Aufgeklärte Absolutismus in Spanien," in *Der Aufgeklärte Absolutismus,* ed. Karl Otmar von Aretin (Cologne: Neue Wissenschaftliche Bibliotek, 1974), pp. 293–300.

60. W. N. Hargreaves-Mawdsley, *Eighteenth-Century Spain, 1700–1788: A Political, Diplomatic, and Institutional History* (Totowa, N.J.: Rowman and Littlefield, 1979), pp. 2–3.

61. Richard Herr, *The Eighteenth-Century Revolution in Spain* (Princeton: Princeton University Press, 1958), p. 12.

62. Jaime Vicens Vives, *An Economic History of Spain* (Princeton: Princeton University Press, 1969), pp. 590–595.

63. William J. Callahan, "The Spanish Church," in *Church and Society in Catholic Europe of the Eighteenth Century,* ed. William J. Callahan and David Higgs (Cambridge: Cambridge University Press, 1979), pp. 34–50.

64. Herr, *The Eighteenth-Century Revolution in Spain,* p. 12; the process by which the upper nobility, the grandees, were stripped of power between 1703 and 1717 is detailed in Henry Kamen, *The War of Succession in Spain, 1700–15* (London: Weidenfeld and Nicolson, 1969), pp. 83–117.

65. Herr, *The Eighteenth-Century Revolution in Spain,* pp. 120–128.

66. Ibid., pp. 134–142.

67. Vicens Vives, *An Economic History of Spain,* pp. 540–551.

68. On these changes, see Earl J. Hamilton, *War and Prices in Spain, 1651–1800* (Cambridge, Mass.: Harvard University Press, 1947).

69. J. O. Lindsay, "The Western Mediterranean and Italy," in *The New Cambridge Modern History,* vol. 7, *The Old Regime, 1713–63,* ed. J. O. Lindsay (Cambridge: Cambridge University Press, 1957), p. 275.

70. It has been estimated that the number of nobility fell by half between 1750 and 1800; see Pierre Vilar, "Structures de la société espagnole vers 1750," *Mélanges à la mémoire de Jean Sarrailh* 2 (1966), 425–447.

71. Vicens Vives, *An Economic History of Spain,* pp. 483–539.

72. Other than textiles and long-distance trade, there was virtually no infrastructure to support a commercial or industrial bourgeoisie; see Vilar, "Structures de la société espagnole vers 1750."

73. Ibid., p. 473.

74. Herr, *The Eighteenth-Century Revolution in Spain,* pp. 57–66.

75. Vicens Vives, *An Economic History of Spain,* pp. 479–481.

76. Robert Jones Shafer, *The Economic Societies in the Spanish World* (*1763–1821*) (Syracuse: Syracuse University Press, 1958).

77. Vicens Vives, *An Economic History of Spain*, pp. 479–481.

78. Herr, *The Eighteenth-Century Revolution in Spain*, pp. 154–157; Nigel Glendinning, *A Literary History of Spain: The Eighteenth Century* (London: Ernest Benn, 1972), p. 8.

79. Herr, *The Eighteenth-Century Revolution in Spain*, pp. 131–136.

80. James Clayburn LaForce, Jr., *The Development of the Spanish Textile Industry, 1750–1800* (Berkeley: University of California Press, 1965), p. 152.

81. George M. Addy, "The First Generation of Academic Reform in Spanish Universities, 1760–1789," in Leith, *Facets of Education in the Eighteenth Century*, pp. 475–490; Richard L. Kagan, *Students and Society in Early Modern Spain* (Baltimore: Johns Hopkins University Press, 1974), pp. 227–229; and more generally, George M. Addy, *The Enlightenment in the University of Salamanca* (Durham, N.C.: Duke University Press, 1966).

82. Roger Chartier, "Student Populations in the Eighteenth Century," *British Journal for Eighteenth-Century Studies* 2 (1979), 152–153.

83. Anthony H. Hull, *Charles III and the Revival of Spain* (Washington, D.C.: University Press of America, 1980), pp. 153–155.

84. E. N. Williams, *The Ancien Régime in Europe: Government and Society in the Major States, 1648–1789* (New York: Harper and Row, 1970), pp. 101–103.

85. C. C. Noel, "The Clerical Confrontation with the Enlightenment in Spain," *European Studies Review* 5 (1975), 103–122.

86. Herr, *The Eighteenth-Century Revolution in Spain*, p. 199.

87. There appears to have been, one observer concludes, "an obsession with the most pressing needs of the day" but "superficial answers to deeper questions." See Atard, "Der Aufgeklärte Absolutismus in Spanien," p. 285.

10. Text and Context

1. Owen A. Aldridge, *Voltaire and the Century of Light* (Princeton: Princeton University Press, 1975), p. 16.

2. Ibid.

3. Patricia McKee, *Heroic Commitment in Richardson, Eliot, and James* (Princeton: Princeton University Press, 1986), p. 52, says the self in *Pamela* is "neither self-possessed nor determined by others but is always part of a relation." See also Roy Roussel, "Reflections and the Letter: The Reconciliation of Distance and Presence in *Pamela*," *English Literary History* 41 (1974), 389–398, who suggests that the novel's construction by letters renders the self an "act of correspondence."

4. Heinrich Bornkamm, *Luther in Mid-Career* (Philadelphia: Fortress Press, 1983), p. 343.

5. For the details of Müntzer's capture and confession, see G. Franz, ed., *Akten zur Geschichte des Bauernkrieges zur Mittledeutschland* (Leipzig, 1934), vol. 1, nos. 184–190.

6. James Miller, *Rousseau: Dreamer of Democracy* (New Haven: Yale University Press, 1984), pp. 18–25, has shown the ways in which Rousseau's image of Geneva was an idealization quite different from the actual Geneva and has argued that Rousseau went to some trouble to maintain this fiction, for example, often by creating a euphemistic reference for the city rather than calling it by name. Miller concludes: "What he praised as an ideal republic . . . bore scant resemblance to the real one" (p. 25).

7. After 1726, Voltaire's experience in England provided him with another socially concretized axis around which to organize his reflections. France still provided the negative pole of this axis, but increasingly England came to serve as the positive symbol. All the institutions and customs he examined in England—religion, the state, science, letters—exemplified for him a spirit of liberty. And, unlike that of the freethinkers of the Temple, the English case could be associated with widely shared virtues of the period, namely, economic progress and intellectual achievement.

8. For discussions of Haller, see Christoph Siegrist, *Albrecht von Haller* (Stuttgart: Metzler, 1967); Werner Kohlschmidt, *Dichter, Tradition, und Zeitgeist: Gesammelte Studien zur Literaturgeschichte* (Bern: Francke, 1965); and Karl S. Guthke, *Hallers Literaturkritik* (Tübingen: Niemeyer, 1970).

9. On Rousseau's uses of history in both his political and autobiographical writings, see expecially Lionel Gossman, "Time and History in Rousseau," *Studies on Voltaire and the Eighteenth Century* 30 (1964), 311–349.

10. Robert Niklaus, *A Literary History of France: The Eighteenth Century, 1715–1789* (London: Ernest Benn, 1970), p. 389, emphasis added.

11. Ibid., pp. 389–390.

12. On the relatively neglected theme of Scottish poetry, see John MacQueen, *The Enlightenment and Scottish Literature*, vol. 1, *Progress and Poetry* (Edinburgh: Scottish Academic Press, 1982); among other discussions of the continuation of moral themes in German literature, see Marvin Bragg, *From Gottsched to Goethe: Changes in the Social Function of the Poet and Poetry* (New York: Peter Lang, 1984), esp. pp. 41–64.

13. Ira Konigsberg, *Narrative Technique in the English Novel: Defoe to Austen* (Hamden, Conn.: Archon Books, 1985), p. 10.

14. Theodore Besterman, *Voltaire* (London: Longmans, 1969), p. 77, writing of Voltaire, notes: "The combination of a fixed structure, rigid unities of time and place, and a mechanical metre effectively stifled Voltaire's inspiration." As early as the 1720s there was a tendency among younger writers in Paris to discount poetry as mere tradition-laden fluff in comparison with philosophy. Much the same trend away from poetry in

favor of other genres was evident in German literature. For a discussion that emphasizes the moral motivations for poetry in these changes, see Bragg, *Fzom Gottsched to Goethe.*

15. Besterman, *Voltaire,* pp. 12–13.

16. Hugh Blair, *Lectures on Rhetoric and Belles Lettres,* quoted ibid., p. 2.

17. Quoted ibid.

18. For a general discussion of these explanations, see especially Wayne C. Booth, *The Rhetoric of Fiction* (Chicago: University of Chicago Press, 1961).

19. For example, see W. J. Harvey, *Character and the Novel* (London: Chatto and Windus, 1965); see also John Preston, *The Created Self: The Reader's Role in Eighteenth-Century Fiction* (London: Heinemann, 1970).

20. On William Robertson's historical style, see Jeffrey Smitten, "Robertson's *History of Scotland*: Narrative Structure and the Sense of Reality," *Clio* 11 (1981), 29–47. Smitten also emphasizes the importance of what he terms "binary oppositions" in Robertson's work.

21. See William Harlin McBurney, *A Check List of English Prose Fiction* (Cambridge, Mass.: Harvard University Press, 1960, pp. ii–ix.

11. *Institutional and Intellectual Antecedents*

1. Napoleon's revisions of the French university system went into effect in 1808. Two years later the University of Berlin was founded, increasingly setting the standard for all European universities. Other advances in higher education included the founding of new universities in Zurich in 1833, in Belgium in 1834, in Basle in 1835, in London in 1836, and in Manchester in 1851; the passage of the Education Law in Italy in 1859, which brought universities under secular control; and the opening of the Ecole Pratique des Hautes Etudes in France in 1868.

2. A study of writers in France, for example, shows that the number of persons employed as authors increased from 1,700 in 1820 to 2,500 in 1841. This study also shows that an increasing percentage of these authors were employed full-time as writers and that the proportion earning moderate to high incomes rose as well; see James Smith Allen, *Popular French Romanticism: Authors, Readers, and Books in the Nineteenth Century* (Syracuse: Syracuse University Press, 1981), esp. pp. 92–93. On the expansion of journalism more geneally, see César Graña, "The New Literary Market," in *Modernity and Its Discontents: French Society and the French Man of Letters in the Nineteenth Century,* ed. César Graña (New York: Harper and Row, 1967), pp. 29–36.

3. The Gothic revival that became popular in mid-nineteenth-century England, for example, owed much to the decisions that surrounded the construction of the new Houses of Parliament.

4. Data for five categories of university enrollment in France between 1848 and 1879, for instance, show that the proportions of students from petty bourgeois, artisan, skilled worker, and agricultural worker backgrounds varied from 1 percent to 19 percent, despite the fact that these social strata still constituted the majority of the French population. These data, from various sources, are summarized in George Weisz, *The Emergence of Modern Universities in France, 1863–1914* (Princeton: Princeton University Press, 1983), p. 24.

5. John Roach, "Education and the Press," in *The New Cambridge Modern History,* vol. 10, *The Zenith of European Power, 1830–1870,* ed. J. P. T. Bury (Cambridge: Cambridge University Press, 1964), p. 120. Data on the locations of lending libraries in Paris and evidence from wills and auctions also reveal how limited the penetration of literature was to the working classes and even to large segments of the middle classes; see Allen, *Popular French Romanticism,* pp. 136–146.

6. This term is of course from Antonio Gramsci, *Selections from the Prison Notebooks* (New York: International Publishers, 1971), esp. pp. 12, 52, 175–182. Numerous extensions and criticisms of the idea also have appeared. Two of the most useful are Perry Anderson, "The Antinomies of Antonio Gramsci," *New Left Review* 100 (1977), 5–78, and Raymond Williams, *Marxism and Literature* (Oxford: Oxford University Press, 1977), pp. 108–114.

7. Calculated from figures in Paul Bairoch, "Europe's Gross National Product: 1800–1975," *Journal of European Economic History* 5 (1976), 273–340.

8. Daniel Chirot, *Social Change in the Modern Era* (New York: Harcourt Brace Jovanovich, 1986), p. 91.

9. Between 1800 and 1850 the number of prominent scientists living in England, France, and Germany, and the number of technological discoveries in each of these countries, doubled; see Robert Wuthnow, *Meaning and Moral Order: Explorations in Cultural Analysis* (Berkeley: University of California Press, 1987), chap. 8.

10. Colin Clark, *The Conditions of Economic Progress,* 3d ed. (London: Macmillan, 1960), pp. 510–520.

11. It has been estimated that in 1830, 67 percent of the world's export trade originated in Europe, with Great Britain, France, and the German states ranking first, second, and third, respectively, as the leading exporters; see Paul Bairoch, "European Foreign Trade in the XIX Century: The Development of the Value and Volume of Exports (Preliminary Results)," *Journal of European Economic History* 2 (1973), 5–36. The extent of the European powers' dependence on trade outside of Europe can be seen by the fact that in 1830, 28 percent of all European exports were shipped outside of Europe, a figure that remained virtually constant until 1880; see

Paul Bairoch, "Geographical Structure and Trade Balance of European Foreign Trade from 1800 to 1970," *Journal of European Economic History* 3 (1974), 557–608. The number of formal colonial ties, however, grew steadily; one source lists a low of 81 in 1825, rising to 100 in 1848 and 123 in 1885, reaching a high of 162 in 1912 (these figures are slightly inflated for Europe, though, because of a failure to separate out the United States' colonies); see Albert Bergesen and Ronald Schoenberg, "Long Waves of Colonial Expansion and Contraction, 1415–1969," in *Studies of the Modern World-System,* ed. Albert Bergesen (New York: Academic Press, 1980), p. 275.

12. One of the most useful treatments of these groups is found in James H. Billington, *Fire in the Minds of Men: Origins of the Revolutionary Faith* (New York: Basic Books, 1980), pp. 86–145.

13. W. O. Henderson, *The Life of Friedrich Engels,* vol. 1 (London: Frank Cass, 1976), pp. 77–83.

14. A recent study that casts doubt on Marx's own estimates of the extent of working-class participation in the June days in Paris is Mark Traugott, *Armies of the Poor: Determinants of Working-Class Participation in the Parisian Insurrection of June 1848* (Princeton: Princeton University Press, 1985).

15. A substantive definition that will prove adequate for present purposes describes socialism as "the doctrine which advocates the collective ownership by the masses of the means of production and distribution, introduced either through parliamentary methods or through the dictatorship of the proletariat inaugurated after a violent revolution"; Samuel Bernstein, *The Beginnings of Marxian Socialism in France,* rev. ed. (New York: Russell and Russell, 1965), p. 186.

16. Harvey Goldberg, *The Life of Jean Jaurès* (Madison: University of Wisconsin Press, 1962), pp. 8–32.

17. William Harvey Maehl, *August Bebel: Shadow Emperor of the German Workers* (Philadelphia: American Philosophical Society, 1980), pp. 20–24.

18. Karl Marx and Friedrich Engels, *Selected Works* (New York: International Publishers, 1968), p. 399.

19. Ibid., p. 388.

20. August Bebel, *My Life* (London: T. Fisher Unwin, 1912), p. 110.

21. Paul Lafargue, *Economic Evolution* (Chicago: Charles H. Kerr, 1892), p. 19.

22. Karl Kautsky, *The Class Struggle* (Chicago: Charles H. Kerr, 1910), p. 40.

23. Or as Max Adler declared, the misery of the intellectual "is even greater than that of the purely manual occupations, because it involves at the same time an atrophy, if not a prostitution, of the spiritual ego." Max

Adler, *Der Sozialismus und die Intellektuellen* (Vienna: Wiener Volksbuch-handlung Ignaz Brand, 1910), p. 56.

24. Kautsky, *The Class Struggle,* pp. 40–41.

25. For an overview of these organizations' activities, see Edward Berenson, *Populist Religion and Left-Wing Politics in France, 1830–1852* (Princeton: Princeton University Press, 1984), pp. 36–73.

26. Ibid., pp. 225–238. Berenson writes that French workers in the 1870s "showed little interest in the doctrines and principles of an explicitly revolutionary ideology." Instead, their commitment, he asserts, was "highly religious in quality" and was oriented toward "a moralistic and messianic socialist republicanism that formed part of the legacy of 1848" (p. 237).

27. The classic examination of Methodism's role among the British working class is, of course, E. P. Thompson, *The Making of the English Working Class* (New York: Random House, 1963), esp. pp. 350–400. Thompson cites membership figures of 60,000 in 1789 and 90,000 in 1795, rising to 237,000 in 1827 (p. 389). Two other particularly useful sources are Alan D. Gilbert, *Religion and Society in Industrial England: Church, Chapel, and Social Change, 1740–1914* (London: Longman, 1976), and Robert Currie, Alan D. Gilbert, and L. H. Horsley, *Churches and Churchgoers: Patterns of Church Growth in the British Isles since 1700* (Oxford: Clarendon Press, 1978).

28. A great deal of useful historical and statistical material on these movements is contained in Michael P. Fogarty, *Christian Democracy in Western Europe, 1820–1953* (London: Routledge and Kegan Paul, 1957), esp. pp. 149–231.

29. Some evidence on union membership and growth for various countries is reported in E. H. Kossmann, *The Low Countries, 1780–1940* (Oxford: Clarendon Press, 1978), p. 479; E. H. Hunt, *British Labour History, 1815–1914* (Atlantic Highlands, N.J.: Humanities Press, 1981), pp. 295–296; and Vincent J. Knapp, *Austrian Social Democracy, 1889–1914* (Washington, D.C.: University Press of America, 1980), p. 51.

30. For example, see Albert S. Lindemann, *A History of European Socialism* (New Haven: Yale University Press, 1983), p. 159.

31. Hugh Heclo, *Modern Social Politics in Britain and Sweden* (New Haven: Yale University Press, 1974), p. 10.

32. David Clark, *Colne Valley: Radicalism to Socialism, the Portrait of a Northern Constituency in the Formative Years of the Labour Party, 1890–1910* (London: Longman, 1981), p. 181.

33. Jean Jaurès, *Studies in Socialism* (New York: G. P. Putnam's Sons, 1906), pp. 58–59.

34. For a general discussion of the origins of political parties, see Eugene N. Anderson and Pauline R. Anderson, *Political Institutions and*

Social Change in Continental Europe in the Nineteenth Century (Berkeley: University of California Press, 1968), pp. 345–376.

35. This chronology follows that given in Theodore S. Hamerow, *The Birth of a New Europe: State and Society in the Nineteenth Century* (Chapel Hill: University of North Carolina Press, 1983), p. 223.

36. The call for this kind of approach has been made in an excellent ethnographic study of the origins of socialism in Düsseldorf, Mary Nolan, *Social Democracy and Society: Working-Class Radicalism in Düsseldorf, 1890–1920* (Cambridge: Cambridge University Press, 1981), p. 4: "What is needed is a social history of politics on the one hand and a structural analysis of the society in which the working class and its organizations developed on the other."

37. The same point is made in George Lichtheim, *The Origins of Socialism* (New York: Praeger, 1969), pp. 157–236, which also associates this period with the maturation of European socialism.

12. *Bismarck's Contribution to German Socialism*

1. Wolfgang Abendroth, "The Absolutism of the Hohenzollern State and the Rise of the Social Democratic Party," in *Upheaval and Continuity: A Century of German History,* ed. E. J. Feuchtwanger (London: Oswald Wolff, 1973), pp. 47–66; Gary P. Steenson, *"Not One Man! Not One Penny!"*: *German Social Democracy, 1863–1914* (Pittsburgh: University of Pittsburgh Press, 1981), p. 94. The development of socialism in Austria paralleled that in Germany and occurred under sufficiently similar conditions that it will be most efficient simply to note the similarities and differences in the course of the present discussion of Germany. Just prior to the First World War, Austrian socialism had reached a level comparable to that in Germany, given the fact that Austria's industrial work force was approximately one-fourth the size of Germany's in absolute numbers. Voting for socialist candidates exceeded a million votes, party membership was estimated at approximately 150,000, and more than 425,000 workers were members of trade unions affiliated with the socialists. See C. A. Macartney, *The Habsburg Empire, 1790–1918* (New York: Columbia University Press, 1968), p. 797, and Melanie A. Sully, *Continuity and Change in Austrian Socialism: The Eternal Quest for the Third Way* (New York: Columbia University Press, 1982), pp. 11–32.

2. Paul Bairoch, "Europe's Gross National Product: 1800–1975," *Journal of European Economic History* 5 (1976), 281. For the period 1860–1910, Bairoch reports an annual growth rate in GNP per capita for Germany of 1.39 percent; Austria's rate of growth was 0.98 percent, a figure more comparable to that of England (0.97 percent).

3. Knut Borchardt, "Germany, 1700–1914," in *The Fontana Economic History of Europe,* vol. 4, *The Emergence of Industrial Societies,* pt. 1, ed. Carlo

M. Cipolla (Glasgow: Collins, 1973), pp. 76–80; cf. Hajo Holborn, *A History of Modern Germany, 1840–1945* (New York: Knopf, 1969), p. 4.

4. J. A. Perkins, "The Agricultural Revolution in Germany, 1850–1914," *Journal of European Economic History* 10 (1981), 71–118.

5. Alan Milward and S. B. Saul, *The Development of the Economics of Continental Europe, 1850–1914* (Cambridge, Mass.: Harvard University Press, 1977), p. 19. Their figure for Austria is 3.3 percent.

6. B. R. Mitchell, "Statistical Appendix," in *The Fontana Economic History of Europe*, vol. 4, *The Emergence of Industrial Societies*, pt. 2, ed. Carlo M. Cipolla (Glasgow: Collins, 1973), pp. 738–820.

7. Borchardt, "Germany, 1700–1914," pp. 117–118.

8. Holborn, *Modern Germany*, p. 375; R. H. Tilly, "Capital Formation in Germany in the Nineteenth Century," in *The Cambridge Economic History of Europe*, vol. 7, *The Industrial Economies: Capital, Labour, and Enterprise*, pt. 1, *Britain, France, Germany, and Scandinavia*, ed. Peter Mathias and M. M. Postan (Cambridge: Cambridge University Press, 1978), p. 385.

9. Rainer Fremdling, "Railroads and German Economic Growth: A Leading Sector Analysis with a Comparison to the United States and Great Britain," *Journal of Economic History* 37 (1977), 583–601. The tremendous importance of the railways in Germany can also be seen by the fact that railroad construction during the 1860s accounted for 28 percent of all pig iron production in Germany, compared with only 6 percent in Great Britain.

10. Vernon L. Lidtke, *The Outlawed Party: Social Democracy in Germany, 1878–1890* (Princeton: Princeton University Press, 1966), p. 11.

11. Borchardt, "Germany, 1700–1914," pp. 111, 121. Austria had a higher percentage of nonagricultural workers in 1870 (33 percent) than Germany but a lower percentage in 1910 (47 percent), meaning that the rate of industrial growth was less pronounced in Austria than in Germany. See N. T. Gross, "The Habsburg Monarchy, 1750–1914," in Cipolla, *The Fontana Economic History of Europe*, vol. 4, pt. 1, p. 248, and Hans Rosenberg, *Grosse Depression und Bismarckzeit* (Berlin: Walter de Gruyter, 1967), pp. 227–228. Evidence from financial data also suggests that Austria did not experience a rapid "take-off" period as far as industrialization or capital accumulation was concerned; David F. Good, "Stagnation and 'Take-Off' in Austria, 1873–1913," *Economic History Review* 27 (1974), 72–87, and David F. Good, "Financial Integration in Late Nineteenth-Century Austria," *Journal of Economic History* 37 (1977), 890–910.

12. John L. Snell, *The Democratic Movement in Germany, 1789–1914* (Chapel Hill: University of North Carolina Press, 1976), p. 186.

13. J. J. Lee, "Labour in German Industrialization," in *The Cambridge Economic History of Europe*, vol. 7, pt. 1, p. 446.

14. Richard Biernacki has suggested to me in a personal communication, however, that his research on factory organization in the German

woolens industry during this period suggests a continuing impact of the guild legacy, particularly in the tendency to organize and reward work on the basis of labor power instead of placing emphasis on the output of labor expended; this tendency, of course, may have reinforced the socialists' demands.

15. Lee, "Labour in German Industrialization," p. 456.

16. The standard definition of an "urban" area as a town of more than 2,000 people is of course misleading in this context. A more accurate indication of the role of industrialization in producing growth in *large* cities is the fact that in 1871 only 4.8 percent of the German population lived in cities of 100,000 or more, whereas by 1910 this proportion had risen to 21.3 percent. Arnold Klönne, *Die deutsche Arbeiterbewegung: Geschichte— Ziele—Wirkungen* (Düsseldorf: Eugen Diederichs Verlag, 1980), p. 95.

17. Lidtke, *The Outlawed Party,* p. 12.

18. Mary Nolan, *Social Democracy and Society: Working-Class Radicalism in Düsseldorf, 1890–1920* (Cambridge: Cambridge University Press, 1981), p. 17.

19. Ibid., p. 114; cf. James J. Sheehan, *German Liberalism in the Nineteenth Century* (Chicago: University of Chicago Press, 1978), p. 215.

20. Steenson, *"Not One Man!"* p. xii.

21. Barrington Moore, Jr., *Injustice: The Social Bases of Obedience and Revolt* (White Plains, N.Y.: M. E. Sharpe, 1978), pp. 197–201.

22. Lidtke, *The Outlawed Party,* pp. 89–105.

23. Georg Gärtner, *Die Nürnberger Arbeiterbewegung, 1868–1908* (1908; reprint, Berlin: Dietz, 1977), pp. 212–215.

24. Nolan, *Social Democracy and Society,* p. 135.

25. Klönne, *Die deutsche Arbeiterbewegung,* pp. 113–114. Hartmann Wunderer, *Arbeitervereine und Arbeiterparteien: Kultur- und Massenorganisationen in der Arbeiterbewegung, 1890–1933* (Frankfurt: Campus Verlag, 1980), gives a figure of 270,000 for the singing organizations (pp. 43–44). He also reports that the athletic organizations sponsored a newspaper with 107,000 subscribers in 1911, and that the singers' league published a newspaper with a press run of 65,000 in 1908. Many of these organizations continued to show strong growth after the First World War.

26. Alex Hall, *Scandal, Sensation, and Social Democracy: The SPD Press and Wilhelmine Germany, 1890–1914* (Cambridge: Cambridge University Press, 1977), pp. 29–30.

27. Werner K. Blessing, "The Cult of Monarchy: Political Loyalty and the Workers' Movement in Imperial Germany," *Journal of Contemporary History* 13 (1978), 357–376; Klaus Tenfelde, "Mining Festivals in the Nineteenth Century," *Journal of Contemporary History* 13 (1978), 377–412. May Day festivals sponsored by the socialists in Frankfurt drew crowds of 10,000 in 1891, 15,000 in 1892, and 20,000 in 1893. Other popular events included

Christmas parties, summer festivals, and forest festivals. For a discussion, see Eichler Volker, *Sozialistische Arbeiterbewegung in Frankfurt am Main, 1878–1895* (Frankfurt am Main: Verlag Waldemar Kramer, 1983), pp. 242ff.

28. Tenfelde, "Mining Festivals," p. 410.

29. Cf. Richard Tilly, "Popular Disorders in Nineteenth-Century Germany: A Preliminary Survey," *Journal of Social History* 4 (1970), 1–40. Unemployment among industrial workers, for example, exceeded 6 percent only twice between 1887 and 1914; during the decade before the First World War, when socialist membership increased most rapidly, it varied from a low of 1.2 percent to a high of 2.9 percent. Over the same period the government's social insurance program also covered an increasing number of workers. Accident insurance, for example, covered 25.8 million workers in 1913 compared with 13.7 million in 1890, and health insurance covered 14.6 million compared with 6.6 million. Klönne, *Die deutsche Arbeiterbewegung,* pp. 98–106. Klönne, pp. 13–35, argues that the German socialist movement did not begin until 1860 primarily because it was not until this period that economic conditions were sufficiently prosperous to give workers a chance to focus on issues other than mere survival. His comparisons of real wages, unemployment, and socialist membership figures between 1870 and 1913 also indicate that socialism prospered most when workers prospered most.

30. Borchardt, "Germany, 1700–1914," p. 112; Lee, "Labour in German Industrialization," p. 472; Moore, *Injustice,* p. 185. Overall, real wages in Germany (indexed at 100 in 1900) rose from 77 in 1870 to 79 in 1880, 92 in 1890, 100 in 1900, 120 in 1910, and 130 in 1913. Klönne, *Die deutsche Arbeiterbewegung,* p. 99.

31. Robert Michels, *Political Parties: A Sociological Study of the Oligarchical Tendencies of Modern Democracy* (1915; reprint, New York: Free Press, 1962), p. 137.

32. Bertrand Russell counted thirty-nine daily newspapers, twenty newspapers published three times a week, eight published twice a week, and nine published weekly. *Vorwärts* claimed a circulation of 48,000 and earned a profit of 55,000 marks annually. See Bertrand Russell, *German Social Democracy* (1896; reprint, New York: Simon and Schuster, 1965).

33. Steenson, *"Not One Man!"* p. 132; Hall, *Scandal, Sensation, and Social Democracy,* p. 37.

34. Carl Landauer, *European Socialism: A History of Ideas and Movements from the Industrial Revolution to Hitler's Seizure of Power* (Berkeley: University of California Press, 1959), p. 313.

35. Cf. Steenson, *"Not One Man!"* p. 45.

36. Lawrence Schofer, "Patterns of Worker Protest: Upper Silesia, 1865–1914," *Journal of Social History* 5 (1972), 447–463.

37. Hartmut Zwahr, *Zur Konstituierung des Proletariats als Klasse: Strukturuntersuchung über das Leipziger Proletariat während der industriellen Revolution* (Berlin: Akademie-Verlag, 1978).

38. C. Paulmann, *1864–1964: Die Sozialdemokratie in Bremen* (Bremen: Sozialdemokratische Partei Deutschlands, 1964); see esp. pp. 81–115.

39. Nolan, *Social Democracy and Society,* passim.

40. Cf. Gerhard A. Ritter, "Workers' Culture in Imperial Germany," *Journal of Contemporary History* 13 (1978), 165–190; although Ritter attaches special significance to the cultural activities of the socialist movement, he rightly points out that relatively little is known about the extent of penetration of these activities into working-class culture more broadly.

41. M. Rainer Lepsius, "Parteiensystem und Sozialstruktur: Zum Problem der Demokratisierung der deutschen Gesellschaft," in *Die deutschen Parteien vor 1918,* ed. Gerhard A. Ritter (Cologne: Kiepenheuer und Witsch, 1973), pp. 56–80.

42. The role of imitation and competition is especially emphasized in Wunderer, *Arbeitervereine und Arbeiterparteien,* pp. 11–37.

43. Moore, *Injustice,* pp. 175–184.

44. Landauer, *European Socialism,* p. 223.

45. Tilly, "Capital Formation in Germany," pp. 384–385.

46. Borchardt, "Germany, 1700–1914," p. 102.

47. Reinhart Kosselleck, *Preussen zwischen Reform und Revolution* (Stuttgart: Heiner Verlag, 1967).

48. Borchardt, "Germany, 1700–1914," p. 107; Holborn, *Modern Germany,* p. 12.

49. Milward and Saul, *Economies of Continental Europe,* p. 21; Tilly, "Capital Formation in Germany," writes: "It seems clear that the decisive breakthrough came . . . when government-subsidized railway-building exploded, so to speak, supplying the coal-, iron-, and machinery-producing sectors with an expanding market and transportation-using sectors with rapidly improving facilities" (p. 385).

50. Gordon A. Craig, *Germany, 1866–1945* (Oxford: Oxford University Press, 1978), p. 81.

51. John R. Gillis, "Aristocracy and Bureaucracy in Nineteenth-Century Prussia," *Past and Present* 41 (1968), 117–120.

52. John C. G. Röhl, *Germany without Bismarck: The Crisis of Government in the Second Reich, 1890–1900* (Berkeley: University of California Press, 1967); John C. G. Röhl, "Staatsstreichplan oder Staatsstreichbereitschaft? Bismarck's Politik in der Entlassungskrise," *Historische Zeitschrift* 203 (1966), 610–624; Michael Stürmer, "Staatsstreichgedanken im Bismarckreich," *Historische Zeitschrift* 209 (1969), 566–615.

53. After the 1860s the state in Austria also became increasingly in-

volved in the regulation of trade, industry, and working conditions, with the result that capitalists were drawn into a closer alliance with the state; see Francis H. E. Palmer, *Austro-Hungarian Life in Town and Country* (New York: G. P. Putnam's Sons, 1903), pp. 240–263. Friedrich Funder, *From Empire to Republic: An Austrian Editor Reviews Momentous Years* (New York: Albert Unger, 1963), pp. 95–96, also argues that the state maintained a remarkable degree of centralized control in Austria, despite ethnic and national schisms.

54. Holborn, *Modern Germany*, p. 132.

55. Ibid., pp. 194–197; Holborn argues that the period between 1865 and 1871 was characterized by relative peace between Bismarck and the liberals since Bismarck needed their support in order to put pressure on the territorial princes to enter into the plans for national unification.

56. Lidtke, *The Outlawed Party*, pp. 27–30.

57. Ralf Dahrendorf, *Society and Democracy in Germany* (New York: Norton, 1967), pp. 199–202.

58. Craig, *Germany, 1866–1945*, p. 43; cf. Heinrich von Treitschke, *Politics* (1916; reprint, New York: Harcourt Brace, 1963), p. 235.

59. Daniel J. Hughes, "Occupational Origins of Prussia's Generals, 1871–1914," *Central European History* 13 (1980), 3–33.

60. Steenson, *"Not One Man!"* p. 163.

61. James J. Sheehan, "Conflict and Cohesion among German Elites in the Nineteenth Century," in *Modern European Social History*, ed. Robert Bezucha (Lexington, Mass.: D. C. Heath, 1972), pp. 3–27.

62. Treitschke, *Politics*, p. 138.

63. Arno J. Mayer, *The Persistence of the Old Regime: Europe to the Great War* (New York: Pantheon, 1981), p. 178.

64. Cf. Gillis, "Aristocracy and Bureaucracy."

6т. Theodore S. Hamerow, *The Birth of a New Europe: State and Society in the Nineteenth Century* (Chapel Hill: University of North Carolina Press, 1983), p. 327.

66. Louis Rosenbaum, *Beruf und Herkunft der Abgeordeneten zu den deutschen und preussischen Parlamenten 1847 bis 1919* (Frankfurt am Main: Frankfurter Societäts-Druckerei, 1923); Eugene N. Anderson and Pauline R. Anderson, *Political Institutions and Social Change in Continental Europe in the Nineteenth Century* (Berkeley: University of California Press, 1968), pp. 195–196.

67. Rosenbaum, *Beruf und Herkunft*.

68. Woodruff Smith and Sharon A. Turner, "Legislative Behavior in the German Reichstag, 1898–1906," *Central European History* 14 (1981), 9.

69. Anderson and Anderson, *Political Institutions*, pp. 195–196.

70. Cf. Hall, *Scandal, Sensation, and Social Democracy*, pp. 1–11.

71. Walther G. Hoffman, *Das Wachstum der deutschen Wirtschaft* (Berlin: Springer-Verlag, 1965).

72. Anderson and Anderson, *Political Institutions,* p. 167.

73. Joseph Ben-David, *The Scientist's Role in Society: A Comparative Study* (Englewood Cliffs, N.J.: Prentice-Hall, 1971), p. 129; Konrad H. Jarausch, *Students, Society, and Politics in Imperial Germany: The Rise of Academic Illiberalism* (Princeton: Princeton University Press, 1982), p. 44.

74. Ibid., p. 74.

75. Cf. Edward Shils, *Max Weber: On Universities* (Chicago: University of Chicago Press, 1973).

76. Craig, *Germany, 1866–1945,* p. 188.

77. Quoted ibid., p. 189.

78. Fritz Ringer, "Higher Education in Germany in the Nineteenth Century," *Journal of Contemporary History* 2 (1967), 123–128; cf. A. Zloczower, *Career Opportunities and the Growth of Scientific Discovery in 19th-Century Germany* (Jerusalem: Hebrew University Press, 1966).

79. Hans Jürgen Puhle, "Parlament, Parteien, und Interessenverbände, 1890–1914," in *Das kaiserliche Deutschland: Politik und Gesellschaft, 1870–1918,* ed. Michael Stürmer (Düsseldorf: Droste Verlag, 1970), pp. 340–377; Manfred Rauh, *Die Parlamentarisierung des deutschen Reiches* (Düsseldorf: Droste Verlag, 1977); Peter Molt, *Der Reichstag vor der improvisierten Revolution* (Cologne: Westdeutscher Verlag, 1963).

80. Craig, *Germany, 1866–1945,* pp. 62–69.

81. Nolan, *Social Democracy and Society,* p. 19; Gillis, "Aristocracy and Bureaucracy," p. 108, makes a similar point: "By the time of national unification much that had once divided the aristocracy and bureaucracy had disappeared; both were now part of one relatively homogeneous upper class which also included the officer corps and the upper bourgeoisie." The relation between the economically liberal bourgeoisie and the state in Austria was as conservative and centrist as it was in Germany, but the path by which this unity came about was quite different. In Austria the mutuality of interests between the bourgeoisie and the state developed earlier and more gradually. Throughout much of the nineteenth century the Austrian state lacked the resources necessary to enable it to intervene aggressively in matters of civil society. It did, however, represent the main bastion against the centrifugal tendencies of ethnic nationalism to which the bourgeoisie (located mainly in Austria proper) was opposed. German liberalism had for a time favored provincial against centrist interests; Austrian liberalism favored centrism against provincial interests; see John W. Boyer, *Political Radicalism in Late Imperial Vienna: Origins of the Christian Social Movement, 1848–1897* (Chicago: University of Chicago Press, 1981), pp. 4–39. Carl E. Schorske, *Fin-de-Siècle Vienna: Politics and Culture* (New York: Vintage Books, 1981), pp. 5–7, writes that the liberal bourgeoisie from the first

"had to share their power with the aristocracy and the imperial bureaucracy" and suggests that even in the 1880s "it remained both dependent upon and deeply loyal to the emperor" and sought "integration with the aristocracy." A similar point is made in Andrew Gladding Whiteside, *Austrian National Socialism before 1918* (The Hague: Martinus Nijhoff, 1962), pp. 1–20.

82. Hans Daalder, "Parties, Elites, and Political Developments in Western Europe," in *Political Parties and Political Development,* ed. Joseph LaPalombara and Myron Weiner (Princeton: Princeton University Press, 1966), p. 49.

83. Sando Segre, "The State and Society in Imperial Germany, 1870–1914," *Cahiers internationale d'histoire économie et sociale* 12 (1980), 323–343.

84. Milward and Saul, *The Economies of Continental Europe,* p. 55, write: "The agitation for protective tariffs came first from the iron industry which was suffering from the lower production costs of its foreign competitors. There was no support from farmers because Germany was still a grain exporter to the London market. With the appearance of cheap American grains at the end of the decade, however, agitation for protective tariffs from German grain producers began. The major wheat and rye producers in Germany were not peasant farmers but the large estate farmers of the north-east whose political influence was still very strong. The protective tariff of 1879 reconciled the two political interests which had divided the country: the Junker landlords who had controlled the political destiny of Prussia and the more liberal business and entrepreneurial classes who had been their main opponents in the hard-fought constitutional struggles after 1848."

85. Holborn, *Modern Germany,* p. 244, writes: "The motives of Bismarck's sudden entry into the colonial race lay almost exclusively in domestic politics, the wish to please the merchants."

86. Sheehan, *German Liberalism,* pp. 189–203.

87. Ibid., pp. 240–259; cf. Craig, *Germany, 1866–1945,* pp. 85–97.

88. Michels, *Political Parties,* p. 54.

89. Dahrendorf, *Society and Democracy in Germany,* p. 50.

90. Landauer, *European Socialism,* p. 242.

91. Lidtke, *The Outlawed Party,* p. 32.

92. Sheehan, *German Liberalism,* pp. 181–188.

93. Gerhard Schulze, "Schwerindustrie und Arbeiterbewegung am Vorabend des Sozialistengesetzes: Zur Rolle des Grosskapitals bei der Durchsetzung der Politik der Ausnahmegesetzgebung," *Jahrbuch für Geschichte* 22 (1981), 51–110.

94. Quoted in Sheehan, *German Liberalism,* p. 183. This interpretation is also shared by Klönne, *Die deutsche Arbeiterbewegung,* pp. 45–125, who argues that Bismarck feared that the liberal bourgeoisie would exploit the

socialists, and the working class more generally, as allies in their quest for democratic reforms. Klönne suggests that Bismarck used fear of the red specter to break the back of the liberal opposition, who finally opted for what they saw as greater state security at the expense of their earlier political principles. Bismarck's statement appears also to have expressed the way in which the socialist leadership interpreted the antisocialist legislation. For example, *Vorwärts* (June 14, 1878) observed: "He [Bismarck] does not yet fear the social democrats, for him they're just an excellent bow-wow. The 'pig' that he actually wants to get is liberalism, in the political, industrial, and religious realm." Quoted in Detlef Lehnert, *Sozialdemokratie zwischen Protestbewegung und Regierungspartei, 1848–1983* (Frankfurt am Main: Suhrkamp, 1983), p. 68.

95. Friedrich Engels, "Socialism in Germany, 1891–1892," in *The Life of Friedrich Engels,* ed. W. O. Henderson (London: Frank Cass, 1976), p. 798.

96. Steenson, *"Not One Man!"* pp. 6–7.

97. Roger Morgan, *The German Social Democrats and the First International, 1864–1872* (Cambridge: Cambridge University Press, 1965), pp. 1–33.

98. As early as 1862, Ferdinand Lassalle had advocated that the German working class sever ties with the liberal bourgeoisie and forge its own political identity. Lassalle was suspicious, rightly so as it turned out, that the bourgeois leadership would be drawn into an alliance with the conservative Prussian aristocracy. In pursuing his aims, however, Lasalle himself came increasingly to be regarded by other socialists as an agent of the Junkers. See Harvey Maehl, *August Bebel: Shadow Emperor of the German Workers* (Philadelphia: American Philosophical Society, 1980), pp. 25–35.

99. Dieter Fricke, *Die deutsche Arbeiterbewegung, 1869–1914: Ein Handbuch über ihr Organisation und Tätigkeit im Klassenkampf* (Berlin: Verlag das europaisch Buch, 1976), pp. 509–526.

100. Peter Nettl, "The German Social Democratic Party, 1890–1914, as a Political Model," *Past and Present* 30 (1965), 75, draws a useful contrast in this regard between the SPD and Lenin's Bolsheviks: "The SPD was always in search of correct policies, its nature and size gave it the right or even the duty to take issue on nearly all the major questions of the day. Lenin on the other hand could only influence Russian society sporadically. His universe was one of small competing conspiratorial groups, and internal problems of organization could easily appear pre-eminent in that world. Without a correct power structure there could be no control, and hence no party."

101. Landauer, *European Socialism,* p. 360.

102. Steenson, *"Not One Man!"* p. xiv.

103. Lidtke, *The Outlawed Party,* pp. 130–135; Marianne Schmidt,

"Die Arbeiterorganisationen in Dresden 1878 bis 1890: Zur Organisationsstruktur der Arbeiterbewegung im Kampf gegen das Sozialistengesetz," *Jahrbuch für Geschichte* 22 (1981), 175–226.

104. George Lichtheim, *A Short History of Socialism* (New York: Praeger, 1970), p. 234; cf. Kenneth R. Calkins, "The Uses of Utopianism: The Millenarian Dream in Central European Social Democracy before 1914," *Central European History* 15 (1982), 124–148.

105. Holborn, *Modern Germany,* p. 259; Hall, *Scandal, Sensation, and Social Democracy,* p. 30.

106. John E. Groh, *Nineteenth-Century German Protestantism: The Church as Social Model* (Washington, D.C.: University Press of America, 1982), p. 475.

107. Hugh McLeod, "Protestantism and the Working Class in Imperial Germany," *European Studies Review* 12 (1982), 328.

108. Richard J. Evans, "Religion and Society in Modern Germany," *European Studies Review* 12 (1982), 281.

109. Cf. Groh, *Nineteenth-Century German Protestantism.*

110. Michael Schneider, "Religion and Labour Organization: The Christian Trade Unions in the Wilhelmine Empire," *European Studies Review* 12 (1982), 345–368.

111. Nolan, *Social Democracy and Society,* pp. 42–47.

112. Lee, "Labour in German Industrialization," pp. 456–458.

113. Evans, "Religion and Society in Modern Germany"; Smith and Turner, "Legislative Behavior in the German Reichstag"; Smith and Turner's analysis of the social composition and voting among Reichstag deputies between 1898 and 1906 confirms impressions that the Center party had moved substantially to the right by this time.

114. In Austria socialist candidates captured 23 percent of the popular vote in the 1907 election and 29 percent in the 1911 election. Brief descriptions of the socialists' activities and their relations to the state in these years are presented in Kurt L. Shell, *The Transformation of Austrian Socialism* (New York: State University of New York Press, 1962), pp. 1–11, and Anson Rabinbach, *The Crisis of Austrian Socialism: From Red Vienna to Civil War, 1927–1934* (Chicago: University of Chicago Press, 1983), pp. 7–24. The weakness of the trade union movement as a competitor to the Socialist party is given special emphasis in Vincent J. Knapp, *Austrian Social Democracy, 1889–1914* (Washington, D.C.: University Press of America, 1980). Knapp also credits antisocialist legislation between 1884 and 1891 in Austria with shaping the party toward reformist, parliamentary strategies similar to those employed in Germany.

115. Cf. Landauer, *European Socialism,* p. 302; Nolan, *Social Democracy and Society,* pp. 100–102; Ralf Lutzenkirchen, *Der socialdemokratische Verein für den Wahldreis Dortmund-Horde* (Dortmund: Verlag des Historischen

Vereins Dortmund, 1970), pp. 122–123. Although it has always been assumed that SPD membership was largely working class, statistical studies by Nolan annd Lutzenkirchen confirm this impression and reveal the overwhelming prepondernace of working-class membership: for example 98 percent in Düsseldorf, 92 percent in Leipzig, 85 percent in Dortmund, and 77 percent in Munich. The Munich figure is also consistent with impressions that class cleavages were weaker in Bavaria than in northern Germany.

116. Cf. Steenson, *"Not One Man!"* pp. 178–188. The greatest successes in the south were achieved in Bavaria, where by 1894 more than 20 percent of the labor force was already employed in shops with more than fifty employees. By 1912 socialist candidates had attracted 27 percent of the electorate, but this figure was still below the average for the Reich as a whole. Cooperation with the bourgeoisie was traditionally more prominent in this region, causing the Social Democrats to portray themselves as a party of the people rather than a narrow party of the industrial working class. For an excellent study of Bavarian socialism, see Heinrich Hirschfelder, *Die bayerische Sozialdemokratie, 1864–1914,* 2 vols. (Erlangen: Verlag Palm und Enke, 1979), esp. pp. 355–688.

117. Part of the irony is that socialist leaders at the beginning of the period had been suspicious that Bismarck was consciously trying to use them to weaken the liberal opposition and had, as a result, tried to avoid any actions that would make him seem to be their ally. For example, Wilhelm Liebknecht offered the following observations to a gathering in London in 1865: "Mr. Bismarck did everything in his power to get the working-class movement thoroughly and directly into his hands. He promised them through his go-betweens universal suffrage, the repeal of the Anti-Combination Laws and other concessions; asking in return that the working classes should support his annexation policy, and help him to destroy radically the 'liberal' middle-class movement. The temptation was great." Liebknecht, "Report on the Working-Class Movement in Germany," in *The General Council of the First International, 1864–1866: Minutes* (1865; reprint, Moscow: Foreign Languages Publishing House, 1963), pp. 257–258.

13. *Liberalism in France and Great Britain*

1. Albert S. Lindemann, *A History of European Socialism* (New Haven: Yale University Press, 1983), pp. 139–140.

2. Maurice Lévy-Leboyer, "Capital Investment and Economic Growth in France, 1820–1930," in *The Cambridge Economic History of Europe,* vol. 7, *The Industrial Economies: Capital, Labour, and Enterprise,* pt. 1, *Britain, France, Germany, and Scandinavia,* ed. Peter Mathias and M. M. Postan (Cambridge: Cambridge University Press, 1978), p. 287.

3. B. R. Mitchell, *European Historical Statistics, 1750–1970* (New York: Columbia University Press, 1975), pp. 355–356.

4. Ibid., pp. 799ff.

5. Ives Lequin, "Labour in the French Economy since the Revolution," in *The Cambridge Economic History of Europe,* vol. 7, pp. 304–309.

6. Ibid., p. 296; J. J. Lee, "Labour in German Industrialization," in *The Cambridge Economic History of Europe,* vol. 7, p. 443.

7. Lequin, "Labour in the French Economy," pp. 304–309; John L. Snell, *The Democratic Movement in Germany, 1789–1914* (Chapel Hill: University of North Carolina Press, 1976), p. 186.

8. Fernand Braudel and Ernest Labrousse, *Histoire économique et sociale de la France,* vol. 4 (Paris: Presses universitaires de France, 1979), p. 457; cf. Adam Przeworski, Barnett R. Rubin, and Ernest Underhill, "The Evolution of the Class Structure of France, 1901–1968," *Economic Development and Cultural Change* 28 (1980), 725–752.

9. Lequin, "Labour in the French Economy," p. 308; Lee, "Labour in German Industrialization," p. 446.

10. Alfred Cobban, *A History of Modern France,* vol. 3, *France of the Republics, 1871–1962* (New York: Penguin, 1965), p. 71.

11. Georges Depeux, *French Society, 1789–1970* (London: Methuen, 1976), p. 160.

12. Braudel and Labrousse, *Histoire économique et sociale de la France,* p. 465.

13. Claude Fohlen, "France, 1700–1914," in *The Fontana Economic History of Europe,* vol. 4, *The Emergence of Industrial Societies,* pt. 1, ed. Carlo M. Cipolla (Glasgow: William Collins Sons, 1973), pp. 25–26.

14. In Saint-Etienne, which grew fivefold between 1801 and 1881, for example, 54 percent of the population at the latter date were still living in the commune of their birth, another 22 percent had been born in the department of the Loire, and most of the remainder came from a neighboring department; see Michael P. Hanagan, *The Logic of Solidarity: Artisans and Industrial Workers in Three French Towns, 1871–1914* (Urbana: University of Illinois Press, 1980), p. 35; see also Roland Trempé, *Les mineurs de Carmaux, 1848–1914,* 2 vols. (Paris: Les editions ouvrièrs, 1971); and Elinor Accampo, "Entre la classe sociale et la cité: Identité et integration chez les ouvrièrs de Saint Chamond, 1815–1880," *Mouvement social* 118 (1982), 39–59.

15. Political organizations had become fairly common even before 1870 in regions such as Languedoc, Gascony, and Provence as a result of competition between republicans and monarchists for citizen support; at the other extreme, only 287 political clubs, none with more than a handful of members, could be found as late as 1901 in the Vosges, with a population of over 400,000. Eugen Weber, *Peasants into Frenchmen: The Modernization of Rural France, 1870–1914* (Stanford: Stanford University Press, 1976), p. 269.

16. Stanley Hoffman, "Paradoxes of the French Political Community," in *In Search of France*, ed. Stanley Hoffman (Cambridge, Mass.: Harvard University Press, 1963), pp. 11–12. The relative weakness of intermediate organizations was not, however, contrary to Hoffman's suggestion, tantamount to "individualism."

17. Theodore Zeldin, *France, 1848–1945: Ambition and Love* (Oxford: Oxford University Press, 1979), p. 270; Cobban, *A History of Modern France*, p. 59.

18. Zeldin, *France, 1848–1945*, pp. 253–260; John McManners, *Church and State in France, 1870–1914* (London: SPCK, 1972), pp. 89–90.

19. Samuel Bernstein, *The Beginnings of Marxian Socialism in France*, rev. ed. (New York: Russell and Russell, 1965), p. 6.

20. For example, see Alain Touraine and Orietta Ragazzi, *Ouvrièrs d'origine agricole* (Paris: Laboratoire de Sociologie Industrielle, 1961).

21. Ives Lequin, *Les ouvrièrs de la région lyonnaise, 1848–1914*, 2 vols. (Lyon: Presses universitaires de Lyon, 1977).

22. Claude Fohlen, "Entrepreneurship and Management in France in the Nineteenth Century," in *The Cambridge Economic History of Europe*, vol. 7, pp. 48–51.

23. Ibid., p. 359; Lequin, "Labour in the French Economy," p. 308; Dupeux, *French Society, 1789–1970*, p. 154.

24. Fohlen, "Entrepreneurship and Management in France," p. 359.

25. Hanagan, *The Logic of Solidarity*, pp. 1–27.

26. Examples are given in Joan Wallach Scott, *The Glassworkers of Carmaux: French Craftsmen and Political Action in a Nineteenth-Century City* (Cambridge, Mass.: Harvard University Press, 1974), pp. 116–124.

27. The growing tensions between mayors and priests after 1870 is discussed in Barnett Singer, *Village Notables in Nineteenth-Century France: Priests, Mayors, Schoolmasters* (Albany: State University of New York Press, 1983).

28. Roger Magraw, "The Conflict in the Villages: Popular Anticlericalism in the Isère (1852–70)," in *Conflicts in French Society: Anticlericalism, Education, and Morals in the Nineteenth Century*, ed. Theodore Zeldin (London: George Allen and Unwin, 1970), pp. 173–174.

29. Weber, *Peasants into Frenchmen*, p. 371.

30. See Donald Baker, "Seven Perspectives on the Socialist Movement of the Third Republic," *Historical Reflections* 1 (1974), 175–176, for a more detailed summary of LeBon's argument.

31. Aaron Noland, *The Founding of the French Socialist Party, 1893–1905* (Cambridge, Mass.: Harvard University Press, 1956), pp. 187–204; Peter Campbell, *French Electoral Systems and Elections, 1789–1957* (London: Faber and Faber, 1958), pp. 69–85.

32. Lequin, *Les ouvrièrs de la région lyonnaise*; Maurice Agulhon, *La*

République au village: Les populations du Var de la révolution à la Second République (Paris: Seuil, 1979); Simone Derruau-Boniol, "Le socialisme dans l'Allier, 1848–1914," *Cahiers d'histoire* 2 (1957), 115–161; Tony Judt, *Socialism in Provence, 1871–1914: A Study in the Origins of the Modern French Left* (Cambridge: Cambridge University Press, 1979).

33. Baker, "Seven Perspectives on the Socialist Movement," p. 183; cf. Annie Kriegel, "Mouvement ouvrièr et socialisme: Identification ou différençiation?" in *Le pain et les roses: Jalons pour une histoire des socialismes,* ed. Annie Kriegel (Paris: Presses universitaires de France, 1968), pp. 1–30.

34. Sanford Elwitt, *The Making of the Third Republic: Class and Politics in France, 1868–1884* (Baton Rouge: Louisiana State University Press, 1975), pp. 1–18.

35. Singer, *Village Notables in Nineteenth-Century France,* p. 108; see also Jacques Chastenet, *La France de M. Fallières* (Paris: Fayard, 1949), p. 148; Lequin, "Labouur in the French Economy," pp. 309–318; Elwitt, *The Making of the Third Republic,* pp. 170–229.

36. Weber, *Peasants into Frenchmen,* pp. 332–338.

37. George Weisz, *The Emergence of Modern Universities in France, 1863–1914* (Princeton: Princeton University Press, 1983), pp. 272–273.

38. Bernard Brown, "The French Experience of Modernization," *World Politics* 21 (1969), 374.

39. Hoffman, "Paradoxes of the French Political Community," p. 12.

40. A. Fryar Calhoun, "The Politics of Internal Order: French Government and Revolutionary Labor, 1898–1914" (Ph.D. diss., Princeton University, 1973), p. 23; Brian Chapman, *The Prefects and Provisional France* (London: George Allen and Unwin, 1955), pp. 32–54.

41. Labrousse makes a similar observation: "The Chamber controlled the Government, which was indeed a sort of Executive born of the Assembly. The senate—'conserver' of the Republic *par excellence*—checked swings either to the Right or Left. Both the Chamber and the Senate took care not to elect too strong a personality to Presidency." Ernest Labrousse, "Observations on a New History of Modern France," *New Left Review* 86 (1974), 98.

42. Dupeux, *French Society, 1789–1970,* pp. 158–159.

43. Pierre Sorlin, *Waldeck-Rousseau* (Paris: Colin, 1966), p. 451.

44. Mitchell, *European Historical Statistics,* pp. 707–710.

45. Lévy-Leboyer, "Capital Investment and Economic Growth in France," p. 252.

46. Labrousse, "Observations on a New History of Modern France," p. 94.

47. Theodore Zeldin, *The Political System of Napoleon III* (London: Macmillan, 1958), p. 3.

48. Cobban, *A History of Modern France,* pp. 15–21; René Rémond,

The Right Wing in France: From 1815 to de Gaulle (Philadelphia: University of Pennsylvania Press, 1969), pp. 166–253; Michael Stephen Smith, *Tariff Reform in France, 1860–1900: The Politics of Economic Interest* (Ithaca: Cornell University Press, 1980), p. 23. According to Smith: "The upper bourgeoisie, along with its middle-class clients . . . ran the show with the tacit support of . . . the peasantry, which had also rallied to the Republic after 1871 in order to preserve the Revolutionary land settlement against the supposed threat of 'feudal reaction' posed by the monarchists. As thus defined, the emergent Third Republic was democratic, but also conservative and bourgeois."

49. Campbell, *French Electoral Systems,* pp. 69–85.

50. Bernard H. Moss, "Parisian Producers Associaton (1830–51): The Socialism of Skilled Workers," in *Revolution and Reaction: 1848 and the Second Republic,* ed. Roger Price (London: Croom Helm, 1975), p. 76.

51. Ronald Aminzade, *Class, Politics, and Early Industrial Capitalism: A Study of Mid-Nineteenth-Century Toulouse, France* (Albany: State University of New York Press, 1981), p. xiv.

52. Elwitt, *The Making of the Third Republic,* pp. 54–59.

53. Bernard H. Moss, *The Origins of the French Labour Movement, 1830–1914: The Socialism of Skilled Workers* (Berkeley: University of California Press, 1976), p. 102.

54. Jeanne Gaillard, "Les associations de production et la pensée politique en France, 1852–1870," *Mouvement social* 52 (1965), 59–85.

55. Borghese's data on Mulhouse shows the considerable extent of solidarity between the industrial working class and the petty bourgeoisie as well as the relatively liberal orientation of factory owners toward welfare reforms. Arthur Borghese, "Industrial Paternalism and Lower-Class Agitation: The Case of Mulhouse, 1848–1851," *Social History* 13 (1980), 55–84. Nor was the concession of freedom to form independent workers' associations in any way antithetical to bourgeois interests; as Elwitt notes: "Class collaboration under the fiction of an equality restrained within limits not only maintained the fact of bourgeois rule, but established the mechanics to settle industrial disputes, making strikes unnecessary"; Elwitt, *The Making of the Third Republic,* p. 259.

56. Landauer attributes the quick recovery of French socialism after the repression of the Commune to the potential strength of the right, which forced the repulicans to cultivate an alliance with the extreme left; Carl Landauer, "The Origin of Socialist Reformism in France," *International Review of Social History* 12 (1967), 85; see also Bernstein, *The Beginnings of Marxian Socialism in France,* p. 75. The ambivalent character of the liberal republic as far as the fortunes of socialism were concerned has been a source of continuing debate among French socialists themselves; for example, see

Jolyon Howorth, "From the Bourgeois Republic to the Social Republic," in *Socialism in France: From Jaurès to Mitterand,* ed. Stuart Williams (London: Frances Pinter, 1983), pp. 1–14.

57. Carl Landauer, *European Socialism: A History of Ideas and Movements from Industrial Revolution to Hitler's Seizure of Power,* 2 vols. (Berkeley: University of California Press, 1959), pp. 209–221.

58. Noland, *The Founding of the French Socialist Party,* pp. 1–5.

59. Bernard H. Moss, "Producers' Associations and the Origins of French Socialism: Ideology from Below," *Journal of Modern History* 48 (1976), 80–89.

60. See, for example, J. Merley, "Les elections de 1869 dans la Loire," *Cahiers d'histoire* 6 (1961), 59–83; Elwitt, *The Making of the Third Republic,* pp. 81–96.

61. Claude Fohlen, "Crises textiles et troubles sociaux: Le Nord à la fin du Second Empire," *Revue du Nord* 35 (1953), 107–123; Robert Vandenbussche, "Aspects de l'histoire politique du radicalisme dans le département du Nord, 1870–1905," *Revue du Nord* 47 (1965), 223–268.

62. Labrousse, "Observations on a New History of Modern France," *European Socialism,"* p. 99.

63. Noland, *The Founding of the French Socialist Party,* pp. 9–12; Moss, *The Origins of the French Labor Movement,* pp. 71–73.

64. Lindemann, *A History of European Socialism,* pp. 141–143.

65. The debilitating effects of intramural divisions on the socialist movement are generally emphasized at the parliamentary level; for some observations on their role in diverting socialist leaders' attention from important needs at the grass-roots level, and thereby reducing grass-roots support, see Patricia Hilden, *Working Women and Socialist Politics in France, 1880–1914: A Regional Study* (Oxford: Clarendon Press, 1986), pp. 231–266.

66. Robert Wohl, *French Communism in the Making, 1914–1924* (Stanford: Stanford University Press, 1966), p. 4; Thomas Moodie, "The Reorientation of French Socialism, 1888–90," *International Review of Social History* 20 (1975), 347–369; Noland, *The Founding of the French Socialist Party,* pp. 48–60.

67. Philip Nord, "Le mouvement des petits commerçants et la politique en France de 1888 à 1914," *Mouvement social* 114 (1981), 35–55.

68. Wohl, *French Communism in the Making,* pp. 16–18.

69. Scott, *The Glassworkers of Carmaux,* pp. 108–109, provides illustrations of the socialists' rhetorical efforts to depict the republicans as "reactionary"; her examples, however, also show the considerable extent to which socialist and republican rhetoric drew from the same pool of slogans and imagery.

70. Peter Schöttler, "Politique sociale ou lutte des classes: Notes sur

le syndicalisme 'apolitique' des bourses du travail," *Mouvement social* 116 (1981), 3–20.

71. Landauer, *European Socialism,* pp. 318–339.

72. Noland, *The Founding of the French Socialist Party,* p. 206; cf. Hanagan, *The Logic of Solidarity,* pp. 141–142.

73. Madeleine Rebérioux, "Party Practice and the Jaurèsian Vision: The SFIO (1905–1914)," in Williams, *Socialism in France,* pp. 15–26.

74. Mitchell, *European Historical Statistics,* pp. 355–356.

75. Paul Bairoch, "Europe's Gross National Product: 1800–1975," *Journal of European Economic History* 5 (1976), 273–340.

76. Mitchell, *European Historical Statistics,* pp. 799ff.

77. Theodore S. Hamerow, *The Birth of a New Europe: State and Society in the Nineteenth Century* (Chapel Hill: University of North Carolina Press, 1983), p. 12.

78. Mitchell, *European Historical Statistics,* p. 163.

79. Hamerow, *The Birth of a New Europe,* p. 91.

80. Ibid., p. 93.

81. According to another source, the percentage of the British population living in rural areas declined from 39 percent in 1841 to 19 percent in 1911; A. K. Cairncross, *Home and Foreign Investment, 1870–1913* (Cambridge: Cambridge University Press, 1953), pp. 64, 83.

82. P. Massey, *Industrial South Wales* (London: Gollanz, 1940), p. 26; Robert Q. Gray, *The Labour Aristocracy in Victorian Edinburgh* (Oxford: Clarendon Press, 1976), pp. 9–10.

83. Sidney Pollard, "Labour in Great Britain," in *The Cambridge Economic History of Europe,* vol. 7, p. 171.

84. Simon Kuznets, *Modern Economic Growth: Rate, Structure, and Spread* (New Haven: Yale University Press, 1966), pp. 208–209.

85. Hamerow, *The Birth of a New Europe,* pp. 113–115.

86. Zygmunt Bauman, *Between Class and Elite: The Evolution of the British Labour Movement, A Sociological Study* (Manchester: Manchester University Press, 1972), p. 139.

87. Mitchell, *European Historical Statistics,* pp. 799ff.; E. H. Hunt, *British Labour History, 1815–1914* (Atlantic Highlands, N.J.: Humanities Press, 1981), p. 319.

88. Ibid., pp. 7, 29.

89. Mitchell, *European Historical Statistics,* p. 708.

90. Ibid., pp. 781–785.

91. Alan T. Peacock and Jack Wiseman, *The Growth of Public Expenditure in the United Kingdom* (Princeton: Princeton University Press, 1967), pp. 164–208.

92. Mitchell, *European Historical Statistics,* pp. 799ff.

93. Kenneth D. Wald, *Crosses on the Ballot: Patterns of British Voter*

Alignment since 1885 (Princeton: Princeton University Press, 1983), p. 232; Gillian Sutherland, *Elementary Education in the Nineteenth Century* (London: The Historical Association, 1971), p. 18.

94. Ivor Bulmer-Thomas, *The Growth of the British Party System,* vol. 1, *1640–1923* (London: John Baker, 1965), pp. 106–107.

95. Paul Thompson, *Socialists, Liberals, and Labour: The Struggle for London, 1885–1914* (Toronto: University of Toronto Press, 1967), p. 71; P. F. Clarke, "Electoral Sociology of Modern Britain," *History* 57 (1972), 33.

96. Bulmer-Thomas, *The Growth of the British Party System,* pp. 108–125.

97. A different view on the effectiveness of these reforms is given in J. Roy Hay, *The Origins of the Liberal Welfare Reforms, 1906–1914* (London: Macmillan, 1975), p. 26.

98. Neal Blewett, "The Franchise in the United Kingdom, 1885–1918," *Past and Present* 32 (1965), 27–56; Thompson, *Socialists, Liberals, and Labour,* pp. 69–70.

99. J. A. Hawgood, "The Evolution of Parties and the Party system in the Nineteenth Century," in *The British Party System,* ed. S. D. Bailey (London: Hansard Society, 1953), p. 32.

100. Henry Pelling, *The Origins of the Labour Party, 1880–1900* (Oxford: Clarendon Press, 1965), pp. 1–18.

101. A. M. McBriar, *Fabian Socialism and English Politics, 1884–1918* (Cambridge: Cambridge University Press, 1962), pp. 1–28.

102. George Lichtheim, *The Origins of Socialism* (New York: Praeger, 1970), p. 202.

103. Pelling, *The Origins of the Labour Party,* p. 229.

104. H. H. Snell, *Men, Movements, and Myself* (London: J. M. Dent and Sons, 1936), p. 57.

105. Stephen Yeo, "A New Life: The Religion of Socialism in Britain, 1883–1896," *History Workshop* 4 (1977), 5–56.

106. G. B. Shaw, "The Illusions of Socialism," in *Forecasts of the Coming Century,* ed. E. Carpenter (London: Mackenzie, 1897), p. 31.

107. R. H. Tawney, *The British Labor Movement* (New Haven: Yale University Press, 1925), p. 158.

108. According to a contemporary survey taken in one district in London, the workers who were considered "poor" were served by four benevolent societies, six Anglican churches, three or four Nonconformist churches, two Roman Catholic churches (all with their own relief programs), three hospitals, two dispensaries, a visiting nurse program, "immense numbers of charitable ladies," a workhouse, a state-run infirmary, and a network of orphanages and primary schools; Bernard Bosanquet, "The Principles and Chief Dangers of the Administration of Charity," in *Philanthropy and*

Social Progress, ed. Henry C. Adams (New York: Thomas Y. Crowell, 1892), pp. 251–253.

109. Gray, *The Labour Aristocracy*; J. F. Wilkinson, *The Friendly Society Movement* (London: Longmans, 1891); Stanley Pierson, *The British Socialists: The Journey from Fantasy to Politics* (Cambridge, Mass.: Harvard University Press, 1979), pp. 140–143.

110. Hunt, *British Labour History,* pp. 295–296.

111. Landauer, *European Socialism,* p. 314.

112. Henry Pelling, *Popular Politics and Society in Late Victorian Britain* (London: Macmillan, 1979), p. 15.

113. Deian Hopkin, "The Membership of the Independent Labour Party, 1904–10: A Spatial and Occupational Analysis," *International Review of Social History* 20 (1975), 175–197; David Clark, *Colne Valley: Radicalism to Socialism, the Portrait of a Northern Constituency in the Formative Years of the Labour Party, 1890–1910* (London: Longman, 1981), p. 182.

114. Hamerow, *The Birth of a New Europe,* pp. 224–225.

115. Ross M. Martin, *T.U.C.: The Growth of a Pressure Group, 1868–1976* (Oxford: Oxford University Press, 1980), pp. 18–19.

116. Pierson, *British Socialists,* p. 19.

117. I. G. Jones, "The Politics of a Rural Economy," *Journal of the Merioneth Historical and Record Society* 5 (1968), 285–313.

118. Michael Kinnear, *The British Voter* (London: B. T. Betsford, 1968); T. J. Nossiter, "Recent Work on English Elections, 1832–1935," *Political Studies* 18 (1970), 525–528; Wald, *Crosses on the Ballot*; David E. Butler and Donald Stokes, *Political Change in Britain* (New York: St. Martin's, 1969).

119. Hugh McLeod, "White Collar Values and the Role of Religion," in *The Lower Middle Class in Britain, 1870–1914,* ed. Geoffrey Crossick (London: Croom Helm, 1977), pp. 61–88.

120. Bauman, *Between Class and Elite,* p. 135.

121. Martin Petter, "The Progressive Alliance," *History* 58 (1973), 45–59.

122. A. W. Purdue, "The Liberal and Labour Parties in North-East Politics, 1900–14: The Struggle for Supremacy," *International Review of Social History* 26 (1981), 1–24.

123. Clarke, "Electoral Sociology of Modern Britain," pp. 48–49.

124. Avner Offer, "Empire and Social Reform: British Overseas Investment and Domestic Politics, 1908–1914," *Historical Journal* 26 (1983), 123; Clarke, "Electoral Sociology of Modern Britain," pp. 47–48.

125. Pierson, *British Socialists,* pp. 153–154.

126. Pelling, *The Origins of the Labour Party,* pp. 54–55.

127. Yeo, "A New Life," pp. 41–49.

128. McBriar, *Fabian Socialism and English Politics,* p. 4.

129. Hugh Heclo, *Modern Social Politics in Britain and Sweden* (New Haven: Yale University Press, 1974), pp. 81–85.

130. H. V. Emy, "The Impact of Financial Policy on English Party Politics before 1914," *Historical Journal* 15 (1972), 129; Kenneth D. Brown, "Conflict in Early British Welfare Policy: The Case of the Unemployed Workmen's Bill of 1905," *Journal of Modern History* 43 (1971), 615–629; Pelling, *Popular Politics and Society*, pp. 2–13; Hay, *The Origins of the Liberal Welfare Reforms*, p. 27.

14. Socialism in the Broader European Context

1. This argument was originally presented in Edward Bull, "Die Entwicklung der Arbeiterbewegung in der drei skandinavischen Ländern," *Archiv für die Geschichte des Sozialismus und der Arbeiterbewegung* 10 (1920), 329–361, and was expanded in Walter Galenson, "Scandinavia," in *Comparative Labor Movements*, ed. Walter Galenson (New York: Prentice-Hall, 1952), pp. 25–55, and Walter Galenson, *The Danish System of Labor Relations* (Cambridge, Mass.: Harvard University Press, 1952).

2. William M. Lafferty, *Economic Development and the Response of Labor in Scandinavia: A Multi-Level Analysis* (Oslo: Universitetsforlaget, 1971), p. 38.

3. Simon Kuznets, "Quantitative Aspects of the Economic Growth of Nations," *Economic Development and Cultural Change* 5 (1957), supplement; and Lafferty, *Economic Development*, p. 43.

4. Bull, "Die Entwicklung der Arbeiterbewegung."

5. Lafferty, *Economic Development*, p. 94.

6. Unfortunately, Lafferty's correlations are based on only seven cases (five-year intervals) for each country, and these cases, spanning the period from 1900 to 1935, are only partly relevant to the prewar period, with which the present discussion is concerned.

7. Lafferty, *Economic Development*, p. 206.

8. Ibid., pp. 123, 153. See also Hugh Heclo, *Modern Social Politics in Britain and Sweden* (New Haven: Yale University Press, 1974), p. 38. In 1906 Swedish socialists accounted for 6 percent of the deputies to the second chamber of parliament, and in 1911 28 percent. The high point of their popularity was reached in 1914, when they captured 36 percent of the popular vote. The popular vote in Denmark grew from 11 percent socialist in 1895 to 25 percent in 1906 to 29 percent in 1918. For an overview of Danish socialism before the First World War, see John Logue, *Socialism and Abundance: Radical Socialism in the Danish Welfare State* (Minneapolis: University of Minnesota Press, 1982), esp. pp. 56–57. Logue estimates that the Danish socialists had 25,000 members in 1900 and 50,000 members by 1910. He states: "When the Danish party hosted the congress of the International in Copenhagen in 1910, it was among the strongest of

the members" (p. 57). A useful source on socialist newspapers during this period is B. G. de Montgomery, *British and Continental Labour Policy: The Political Labour Movement and Labour Legislation in Great Britain, France, and the Scandinavian Countries, 1900–1922* (London: Kegan Paul, Trench, Trubner, 1922). Montgomery says there were eighteen socialist newspapers in Sweden by 1914. In Denmark the first socialist newspaper was founded in 1871, and by 1906 there were twenty-five socialist dailies with a combined circulation of 97,000 copies (pp. 125–140). In Norway the first socialist newspaper, the *Social-Democraten,* was founded in 1886, transformed into the official organ of the Norwegian party in 1892, and supported by the party until 1904, when it became financially self-sustaining. Its circulation grew from about 4,000 in 1898 to around 38,000 at the start of the First World War. In all, twenty-nine socialist newspapers were established in Norway before 1914 with a combined circulation of 103,785. This figure equaled 20 percent of all newspaper circulation in Norway; see Svennik Höyer, "The Political Economy of the Norwegian Press," *Scandinavian Political Studies* 3 (1968), 85–143.

9. For a discussion of Swedish politics during this period, see Douglas Verney, *Parliamentary Reform in Sweden, 1866–1921* (Oxford: Clarendon Press, 1957).

10. Montgomery, *British and Continental Labour Policy,* pp. 110–124.

11. Ibid., pp. 125–140.

12. Logue, *Socialism and Abundance,* p. 57.

13. A shift away from an ideology of class conflict toward a greater emphasis on becoming a "people's party" and cooperating with the state rather than overthrowing the state has been traced between 1891 and 1911. See especially the useful discussion of these developments in John Eric Nordskog, *Social Reform in Norway: A Study of Nationalism and Social Democracy* (Westport, Conn.: Greenwood Press, 1973), pp. 40–66.

14. Lafferty, *Economic Development,* p. 38. See also K. G. Hildebrand, "Labour and Capital in the Scandinavian Countries in the Nineteenth and Twentieth Centuries," in *The Cambridge Economic History of Europe,* vol. 7, *The Industrial Economies: Capital, Labour, and Enterprise,* pt. 1, *Britain, France, Germany, and Scandinavia,* ed. Peter Mathias and M. M. Postan (Cambridge: Cambridge University Press, 1978), p. 600, for estimates of the size of the total labor force. As a brief overview of Swedish economic development, Eli R. Hecksher, *An Economic History of Sweden* (Cambridge, Mass.: Harvard University Press, 1954), esp. pp. 209–266, remains useful. Overviews of industrial development in Norway are given in Fritz Hodne, *An Economic History of Norway, 1815–1970* (Trondheim: Tapir, 1975), and Sima Lieberman, *The Industrialization of Norway, 1800–1920* (Oslo: Universitetsforlaget, 1970).

15. Figures listed in B. R. Mitchell, "Statistical Appendix," in *The*

Fontana Economic History of Europe, vol. 4, *The Emergence of Industrial Societies,* pt. 2, ed. Carlo M. Cipolla (Glasgow: William Collins Sons, 1973), pp. 738–820.

16. Lennart Jörberg, "The Nordic Countries, 1850–1914," in Cipolla, *The Fontana Economic History of Europe,* vol. 4, pt. 2, esp. pp. 377–379. Jörberg observes that Norway's exports of manufactured goods increased 600 percent between 1897 and 1915.

17. Ibid., p. 392.

18. One estimate shows that real wages in Sweden grew by 150 percent between 1880 and 1910 for general laborers; see Montgomery, *British and Continental Labour Policy,* p. 68. Another estimate reports an index figure of 33 for real wages in 1860, rising to 90 for 1914; see E. H. Phelps Brown and P. E. Hart, "The Share of Wages in National Income," *Economic Journal* 62 (1952), 253–277. In Norway real wages rose 190 percent between 1897 and 1911.

19. Stein Kuhnle, "The Beginnings of the Nordic Welfare States: Similarities and Differences," *Acta Sociologica* 21 (1978), 18, cites figures showing that 36.1 percent of the income received in Denmark in 1870 went to the top decile of income earners; in Norway 41.8 percent went to the top decile (reported for 1891); and in Sweden 44.5 percent did (reported for 1908). The percentage of all property that was owned by the top decile of property owners was 53 percent in Denmark (1904), 55.5 percent in Norway (1911), and 66.6 percent in Sweden (1921). Montgomery, *British and Continental Labour Policy,* p. 66, says that 14,000 people owned half the total wealth in Sweden in 1913 and that 110,000 owned two-thirds of the nation's wealth. Kuhnle's estimates of changes in education are based on the proportions of fifteen- to nineteen-year-olds who were enrolled in secondary schools. These proportions rose from 3.4 percent in 1880 to 10.2 percent in 1910 in Denmark; from 8.5 percent to 9.7 percent over the same period in Norway; and from 3.1 percent to 4.2 percent in Sweden. See Stein Kuhnle, *Patterns of Social and Political Mobilization: A Historical Analysis of the Nordic Countries* (Beverly Hills: Sage, 1975), p. 46.

20. Ibid., pp. 24–27.

21. According to Montgomery, *British and Continental Labour Policy,* p. 66, 85 percent of the farms in Sweden in 1913 were farmed by their owners.

22. Another reason why the small farm producers favored the Liberal party was their resentment of public expenditures, which meant higher taxes, coupled with a relative lack of representation in political and religious affairs. Since the 1820s rights of free association had been present; consequently, by the 1870s all kinds of voluntary movements (savings clubs, occupational groups, unions) were in existence, giving a stronger basis at the grass roots for the liberal parties. But these organizations generally did

not link the middle classes with members of the urban working class. See Sverre Steen, "The Democratic Spirit in Norway," in Lauwerys, *Scandinavian Democracy,* pp. 139–149.

23. Writing of Denmark, W. Glyn Jones, *Denmark* (New York: Praeger, 1970), p. 76, observes that the left "was in essence the voice of the farmers large and small." He also argues that the left did not represent the urban working population: "Indeed, although the demands for equality of some factions within the Left would have favoured the workers, they were not really interested in them." For Norway, election results tabulated by Eckstein show that the left's strength in rural districts was greater than the right's in every election between 1882 and 1924; indeed, not until 1953 was this pattern effectively reversed; see Harry Eckstein, *Division and Cohesion in Democracy: A Study of Norway* (Princeton: Princeton University Press, 1966), pp. 208–209. Structurally, the weakness of a coalition between liberal elements among the petty bourgeoisie and the working classes can also be attributed to the fact that the bulk of the petty bourgeoisie was not located in the cities. Epsing-Anderson provides statistics for 1900 showing that less than a third of the petty bourgeoisie in Denmark and Norway resided in urban areas, and less than a quarter of the petty bourgeoisie did in Sweden; see Gosta Epsing-Anderson, *Politics against Markets: The Social Democratic Road to Power* (Princeton: Princeton University Press, 1985), p. 53.

24. Montgomery, *British and Continental Labour Policy,* p. 67.

25. Hildebrand, "Labor and Capital in the Scandinavian Countries," p. 604, reports that in Sweden "public services" (that is, government-sponsored projects) grew as a proportion of gross investment in fixed assets from 8 percent in the period 1881–1885 to 15 percent in the period 1911–1915. Similar growth apparently occurred in Denmark as well, and the state, through financial inducements and restrictive legislation, played an active role in promoting the rise to prominence of several large firms.

26. Heclo, *Modern Social Politics in Britain and Sweden,* p. 39.

27. Eckstein, *Division and Cohesion in Democracy,* p. 39. See also J. Andenaes, "The Development of Political Democracy in Scandinavia," in Lauwerys, *Scandinavian Democracy,* pp. 93–107, for evidence on the degree to which the bureaucracy dominated legislative politics between 1814 and 1884. After 1884 liberal representation was much stronger, but internal divisions between farmers and industrialists, and a shift toward more conservative economic policies among the latter, made a concerted stand against the Conservative party impossible.

28. Gunnar Hecksher, "The Role of the Voluntary Organization in Swedish Democracy," in Lauwerys, *Scandinavian Democracy,* esp. p. 127, emphasizes this point.

29. Heclo, *Modern Social Politics in Britain and Sweden,* p. 39.

30. Ulf Torgerson, "The Formation of Parties in Norway: The Problem of Right-Left Differences," *Scandinavian Political Studies* 2 (1967), 43–68.

31. For a useful discussion of these relations in the Danish case, see Jones, *Denmark,* esp. pp. 47–48.

32. In Norway, for instance, 9 percent of the total population was eligible to vote in 1885; by 1900 this figure had risen to 20 percent; moreover, actual voter turnout in urban areas grew from 31 percent of the electorate in 1880 to 78 percent in 1898. These figures are reported in Stein Rokkan and Henry Valen, "The Mobilization of the Periphery: Data on Turnout, Party Membership, and Candidate Recruitment in Norway," in *Approaches to the Study of Political Participation,* ed. Stein Rokkan (Bergen: The Christian Michelsen Institute, 1962), pp. 25–52.

33. Lafferty, *Economic Development,* p. 123, reports that liberals in the Norwegian parliament were overshadowed by conservatives by a margin of fifty to sixty-nine in 1903 and by a margin of forty-eight to sixty-four in 1909; in 1912 liberals finally achieved a decisive advantage of seventy-six to twenty-four over the conservatives.

34. Heclo, *Modern Social Politics in Britain and Sweden,* p. 15, writes that "Sweden is often seen as closely related to Bismarckian influences, with social policy serving as an antisocialist tool."

35. This history is discussed briefly in Lafferty, *Economic Development,* pp. 129–131.

36. Ibid., pp. 146–147.

37. In Sweden the first labor union emerged in 1884, and as late as 1908 only 4 percent of the labor force were union members; Heclo, *Modern Social Politics in Britain and Sweden,* p. 68. See also Walter Korpi, "Social Democracy in Welfare Capitalism—Structural Erosion, Welfare Backlash, and Incorporation?" *Acta Sociologica* 21 (1978), 97–112. In Denmark and Norway the labor unions were preoccupied during their early years with achieving political aims, namely, an extension of the franchise.

38. Prior to this time Marx and Engels had of course lived in Brussels in the 1840s, and the latter had served briefly as an officer in the revolutionary Democratic Association.

39. Henri Pirenne, *Histoire de Belgique,* vol. 7 (Brussels: H. Lamertin, 1935), p. 343.

40. G. W. Prothero, *Belgium* (London: Historical Section of the Foreign Office, 1920), p. 199.

41. E. H. Kossmann, *The Low Countries, 1780–1940* (Oxford: Clarendon Press, 1978), p. 343.

42. M. Moyne, *Resultats des elections belges entre 1847 et 1914* (Brussels: Institut Belge de Science Politique, 1970).

43. On the early development of Belgian socialism, see Maxime

Sztejnberg, "La fondation du parti ouvrier belge et le ralliement de la classe ouvrière à l'action politique, 1882–1886," *International Review of Social History* 8 (1963), 198–215.

44. Paul Bairoch, "Niveaux de développement économique de 1810 à 1910," *Annales, E.S.C.* 20 (1965), 1091–1117.

45. The high rate of growth during the 1860s appears to have come after 1863, when major treaties were concluded with France, Britain, Prussia, the Zollverein, Spain, Italy, and the Netherlands; see Vernon Mallinson, *Belgium* (New York: Praeger, 1970), p. 73.

46. See also Angus Maddison, *Economic Growth in the West: Comparative Experience in Europe and North America* (New York: Twentieth Century Fund, 1964), p. 28.

47. Paul Bairoch, "Europe's Gross National Product: 1800–1975," *Journal of European Economic History* 5 (1976), 273–340.

48. Alan Milward and S. B. Saul, *The Development of the Economies of Continental Europe, 1850–1914* (Cambridge, Mass.: Harvard University Press, 1977), p. 178. See also M. Gadisseur, "La production industrielle au XIXe siècle en Belgique: Construction de l'indice," in *Histoire économique de la Belgique: Traitement des sources et état des questions,* ed. H. Coppejans-Desmedt (Brussels: Archives et Bibliothèques de Belgique, 1973), pp. 79–96.

49. Allan H. Kittell, "The Revolutionary Period of the Industrial Revolution: Industrial Innovation and Population Displacement in Belgium, 1830–1880," *Journal of Social History* 1 (1967), 132. As industrial production increased, the relative role of agriculture decreased. These decreases, therefore, can also be used as measures of the steady shifts undergone by the Belgian economy. As a percentage of gross domestic product, agriculture declined steadily from 70 percent in 1846 to 50 percent in 1875 to 32 percent in 1913; J. De Belder, "Changes in the Socio-Economic Status of the Belgian Nobility in the Nineteenth Century," *Acta Historiae Neerlandicae* 15 (1982), 1–20. As a proportion of the working population, agricultural workers decreased from 32 percent in 1846 and 1866 to 24 percent in 1890 and 17 percent in 1910; Benoit Verhaegen, *Contribution à l'histoire économique des Flandres,* vol. 1 (Louvain: Editions Nauwelaerts, 1961), p. 330. Correlatively, the urban population grew dramatically—in Brussels, for example, from 251,000 in 1850 to 421,000 in 1880 and 720,000 in 1910; Mitchell, "Statistical Appendix," p. 750.

50. Barbara Emerson, *Leopold II of the Belgians: King of Colonialism* (London: Weidenfeld and Nicolson, 1979), p. 122.

51. This discussion draws primarily from John Fitzmaurice, *The Politics of Belgium: Crisis and Compromise in a Plural Society* (London: C. Hurst and Company, 1983), pp. 25–34.

52. Demetrius C. Boulger, *Belgian Life in Town and Country* (New York: G. P. Putnam's Sons, 1904), pp. 54–55.

53. Thomas H. Reed, *Government and Politics of Belgium* (New York: World Book Company, 1924), p. 85.

54. Aristide A. Zolberg, "Belgium," in *Crises of Political Development in Europe and the United States,* ed. Raymond Grew (Princeton: Princeton University Press, 1978), p. 111

55. Between 1843 and 1870 railways expanded from 593 kilometers to 3,350 kilometers, stimulating growth in the steel and machine industries as well as providing a necessary infrastructure for the transport of manufactured goods; coal production quadrupled between 1850 and 1895 to become larger in terms of employment than the textile, metalworking, and machinery industries combined; textiles in contrast became increasingly depressed; see Fitzmaurice, *The Politics of Belgium,* pp. 59–60.

56. Moyne, *Resultats des elections belges.* Between 1848 and 1892 the liberal vote declined 24 percentage points for the country as a whole but 31 points for the eight largest industrial and commercial centers.

57. Mallinson, *Belgium,* p. 82.

58. The socialist movement was also in a relatively advantageous position because the trade union movement had not succeeded in establishing itself as an independent representative of the working classes. As late as 1904, the weakness of unions and other competing organizations was evident. Writing of the mining districts, for example, Boulger observed: "No steps whatever are taken to improve the lot of the miners, to elevate their ideas or even to improve them with amusement or recreations. There are no clubs, except the *cercles* of the Socialists." Boulger, *Belgian Life in Town and Country,* pp. 100–101. The socialist movement was thus able to incorporate the more practical economic programs of the trade unions into their own political agenda.

59. Kossmann, *The Low Countries,* p. 276.

60. Kuhnle, *Patterns of Social and Political Mobilization,* p. 13.

61. Mallinson, *Belgium,* pp. 81–82.

62. According to the franchise law of 1893, 850,000 workers were given one vote apiece, while 290,000 members of the upper strata received two votes apiece and 220,000 received three votes apiece. In an ironic twist of political history, the same franchise act that created the electoral base on which the socialist movement built its strength also sutained the Belgian monarchy for the next half century by granting it the right of dynastic succession and the authority to pursue a colonial policy in the Congo. See Emerson, *Leopold II of the Belgians,* pp. 136–141.

63. On the development of socialism in Groningen, see G. Bruintjes, *Socialisme in Groningen, 1881–1894* (Amsterdam: Van Gennep, 1981).

64. Kossmann, *The Low Countries,* p. 341.

65. One of the best introductions to Dutch socialism is Erik Hansen, "The Origins and Consolidation of Dutch Social Democracy, 1894–1914," *Canadian Journal of History* 12 (1977), 145–172.

66. Kossmann, *The Low Countries,* p. 479, indicates that the 1913 total Dutch union membership stood at 266,000, of which 84,000 members belonged to socialist unions, 29,000 to Catholic unions, 11,000 to Protestant unions, and 142,000 to nonfederated unions. Kossmann's study provides the main comparative treatment of Dutch and Belgian socialism. He maintains throughout his discussion that socialism was significantly less influential in the Netherlands than in Belgium.

67. Johan Gerard Westra, *Confessional Political Parties in the Netherlands, 1913–1946* (Ann Arbor: University Microfilms, 1972). In the closing years before the First World War, the SDAP's fragile unity was also broken by the defection of a group of Marxist dissidents to form the rival Social Democratic party (which became the Communist party of Holland in 1918). The sources and effects of this defection are examined in Erik Hansen, "Crisis in the Party: *De Tribune* Faction and the Origins of the Dutch Communist Party, 1907–9," *Journal of Contemporary History* 11 (1976), 43–64.

68. Sectoral composition and other economic indicators are reported in R. W. J. M. Bos, "Industrialization and Economic Growth in the Netherlands during the Nineteenth Century: An Integration of Recent Studies," *Acta Historiae Neerlandica* 15 (1982), 21–58.

69. As evidence of the lateness of Dutch industrialization, one author notes that in 1860 the Dutch provinces had only 335 kilometers of railways compared with 1,713 kilometers in Belgium; in the same year 794 steam engines were in use in the Netherlands compard with 4,410 in Belgium; see P. E. Kraemer, *The Societal State: The Modern Osmosis of State and Society as Presenting Itself in the Netherlands in Particular* (Meppel: J. A. Boom en Zoon, 1966). Milward and Saul, *The Development of the Economies of Continental Europe,* p. 201, observe: "More recent historians see the maturing of Dutch industry coming in the last two decades before 1914, with a slow but distinct growth of capacity during the previous quarter of a century." Emphasis is also placed on the lateness of Dutch industrialization by Joel Mokyr, *Industrialization in the Low Countries, 1795–1850* (New Haven: Yale University Press, 1976).

70. Mokyr, *Industrialization in the Low Countries,* pp. 47–48. Also indicative of the changes taking place was the fact that textile production declined as a percentage of the industrial labor force while employment in chemicals, utilities, and metalworking increased. Bos, "Industrialization and Economic Growth," dates the period of rapid industrialization from the 1890s, citing technological breakthroughs such as the gas engine and the electric motor as significant contributing factors. On the changing size of firms, see J. A. DeJonge, "Industrial Growth in the Netherlands (1850–1914)," *Acta Historiae Neerlandica* 5 (1971), 159–212. For the years 1909–12, 1,445 firms with 50 or more employees employed a total of 222,813

employees, or approximately 28 percent of the industrial labor force; reported in C. J. P. Zaalberg, "The Manufacturing Industry," in *The Netherlands and the World War: Studies in the War History of a Neutral,* vol. 2, ed. H. B. Greven (New Haven: Yale University Press, 1928), pp. 3–114.

71. Some of these relations are examined in R. Jurriens, "The Miners' General Strike in the Dutch Province of Limburg (21 June–2 July 1917)," *Acta Historiae Neerlandica* 14 (1981), 124–153, and Erik Hansen, "Workers and Socialists: Relations Between the Dutch Trade-Union Movement and Social Democracy, 1894–1914," *European Studies Review* 7 (1977), 199–226.

72. Catholics owed a special debt to the liberal government for their emancipation in relation to the established Reformed Church and for this reason served as a lever against the consolidation of a conservative bloc.

73. Kraemer, *The Societal State,* 179

74. Kossmann, *The Low Countries,* p. 478, lists the percentage of seats held by the Confessional party as fifty-eight in 1901, forty-eight in 1905, sixty in 1909, and forty-five in 1913.

75. Kraemer, *The Societal State,* p. 38.

76. Griffiths, *Industrial Retardation in the Netherlands, 1830–1850* (The Hague: Martinus Nijhoff, 1979), pp. 71–74.

77. Kraemer, *The Societal State,* p. 80.

78. Willem Verkade, *Democratic Parties in the Low Countries and Germany: Origins and Historical Developments* (Leiden: Universitaire Pers Leiden, 1965), pp. 38–41.

79. Some interesting examples are given in F. L. Van Holthoon, "Beggary and Social Control: Government Policy and Beggary, Particularly in the Province of Groningen between 1823 and 1870," *Economisch- en sociaalhistorisch Jaarboek* 43 (1980), 154–193.

80. Eric Schiff, *Industrialization without National Patents* (Princeton: Princeton University Press, 1971), p. 27.

81. According to DeJonge, "Industrial Growth in the Netherlands," p. 195, this proportion declined from 20 percent in 1860 to 10 percent in 1913.

82. Westra, *Confessional Political Parties,* pp. 189–211.

83. This discussion follows that of Verkade, *Democratic Parties in the Low Countries and Germany,* pp. 47–50.

84. Unlike Belgium, where restrictive legislation prevented the formation of a national federation of trade unions, federations came into being in the Netherlands as early as 1866, and in 1871 the first successful national federation of workers' associations representing different trades was formed.

85. J. S. Cohen, "Economic Growth," in *Modern Italy: A Topical History*

since 1861, ed. Edward R. Tannenbaum and Emiliana P. Noether (New York: New York University Press, 1974), pp. 171–196.

86. Milward and Saul, *The Development of the Economies of Continental Europe,* p. 254.

87. Alexander Gerschenkron, "Notes on the Rate of Industrial Growth in Italy, 1881–1913," *Journal of Economic History* 24 (1955), 25–44.

88. Louise A. Tilly, "I Fatti di Maggio: The Working Class of Milan and the Rebellion of 1898," in *Modern European Social History,* ed. Robert J. Bezucha (Lexington, Mass.: D. C. Heath, 1972), pp. 124–160.

89. Useful surveys of Italian politics during this period are provided in Salvatore Saladino, "Parliamentary Politics in the Liberal Era: 1861–1914," in Tannenbaum and Noether, *Modern Italy,* pp. 27–51, and Raymond Grew, "Italy," in Grew, *Crises of Political Development,* pp. 271–312. The factionalism that prevented crystallization of a more effective central bureaucracy is described in John Thayer, *Italy and the Great War: Politics and Culture, 1870–1915* (Madison: University of Wisconsin, 1964), and Serge Hughes, *The Fall and Rise of Modern Italy* (New York: Minerva Press, 1967).

90. One of the most useful general surveys of Italian socialism is Spencer Discala, *Dilemmas of Italian Socialism: The Politics of Filippo Turati* (Amherst: University of Massachusetts Press, 1980). For a brief overview, see Franco Andreucci, "Problèmes d'histoire du parti socialiste italien à l'époque de la Deuxième Internationale," *Mouvement social* 111 (1980), 155–164. The formative years are discussed in Richard Hostetter, *The Italian Socialist Movement* (Princeton: Van Nostrand, 1958).

91. Discala, *Dilemmas of Italian Socialism,* p. 67. Some of the developments between 1900 and 1914, but with little evidence on the party's relations to the state, are described in Daniel Horowitz, *The Italian Labor Movement* (Cambridge, Mass.: Harvard University Press, 1963).

92. William A. Salomone, *Italy in the Giolittian Era: Italian Democracy in the Making, 1900–1914* (Philadelphia: University of Pennsylvania Press, 1960), p. 54.

93. Norman Kogan, "Socialism and Communism in Italian Political Life," in Tannenbaum and Noether, *Modern Italy,* pp. 102–122.

94. Bairoch, "Statistical Appendix."

95. Raymond Carr, *Modern Spain, 1875–1980* (Oxford: Oxford University Press, 1980), p. 34.

96. Barcelona and Madrid each had populations exceeding 500,000 by 1900; overall fewer than 10 percent of the Spanish population lived in cities of 100,000 or more, however; see Jaime Vicens Vives, *An Economic History of Spain* (Princeton: Princeton University Press, 1969), p. 621. Although the textile industry was still concentrated in small firms, it was

one area in which the Spanish economy showed expansion; for instance, per capita consumption of raw cotton rose from approximately 2 kilograms in 1870 to 4.3 kilograms in 1909; see Milward and Saul, *The Development of the Economies of Continental Europe,* pp. 238–247; and for a more general discussion, see Jordi Nadal, "The Failure of the Industrial Revolution in Spain, 1830–1914," in *The Emergence of Industrial Societies,* ed. Carlo M. Cipolla (Glasgow: William Collins Sons, 1973), pp. 532–626.

97. Between 1857 and 1900 the population of Barcelona had increased 200 percent, compared with an increase of 92 percent in Madrid.

98. Robert W. Kern, *Liberals, Reformers, and Caciques in Restoration Spain* (Albuquerque: University of New Mexico Press, 1974), p. 14.

99. For a discussion of this period, see Carr, *Modern Spain, 1875–1980,* pp. 1–15.

100. Vicens Vives, *An Economic History of Spain,* pp. 614–616, 702–712.

101. This point is elaborated in G. Tortella Casares, "An Interpretation of Economic Stagnation in Nineteenth-Century Spain," *Historia Ibérica* 1 (1973), 121–132.

102. Nadal, "The Failure of the Industrial Revolution in Spain, 1830–1914," p. 567.

103. Murray Bookchin, *The Spanish Anarchists: The Heroic Years, 1868–1936* (New York: New York University Press, 1977), p. 37. Beck's assessment of the reign of Alfonso XII, while devoted mainly to narrative history, also supports the view that the state exercised little influence over the economically powerful elites in agriculture and commmerce.

104. Kern, *Liberals, Reformers, and Caciques,* p. 26.

105. Stanley G. Payne, "Spain and Portugal," in Grew, *Crises of Political Development,* pp. 203–204.

106. Juan J. Linz, "The Party System of Spain: Past and Future," in *Party Systems and Voter Alignments: Cross-National Perspectives,* ed. Seymour M. Lipset and Stein Rokkan (New York: Free Press, 1967), p. 202.

107. Carr, *Modern Spain, 1875–1980,* p. 38.

108. Linz, "The Party System of Spain," pp. 223–225.

109. Carr, *Modern Spain, 1875–1980,* pp. 53–56. Linz, "The Party System of Spain," p. 223, also shares this view, writing: "It is probable that the importance of petty bourgeois republicanism, particularly in Catalonia but also in Madrid and Levante, must have prevented many workers from turning to the party."

110. With the general strike that was called in 1909 in conjunction with protests against the Moroccan campaign, evidence finally begins to point toward a political dimension in Spanish working-class violence, a dimension that became more pronounced during the First World War.

111. On the contrasts between Spanish anarchism and socialism, see

Temma Kaplan, *Anarchists of Andalusia, 1868–1903* (Princeton: Princeton University Press, 1977).

112. For this history, see especially Robert W. Kern, *Red Years/Black Years: A Political History of Spanish Anarchism, 1911–1937* (Philadelphia: Institute for the Study of Human Issues, 1978).

15. Theory and Practice

1. W. O. Henderson, *The Life of Friedrich Engels,* vol. 1 (London: Frank Cass, 1976), p. 85.

2. The obscurity of *Capital* has received much comment. Kautsky, for example, wrote that "complaints are made about the unintelligibleness of Marx, and most people have read more about 'Capital' than they have of 'Capital' itself"; Karl Kautsky, *Frederick Engels: His Life, His Work, and His Writings* (Chicago: Charles H. Kerr, 1899), p. 17. Bertrand Russell once said of the book that it is developed with "a patience often exceeding that of the reader"; Bertrand Russell, *German Social Democracy* (1896; reprint, New York: Simon and Schuster, 1965), p. 15.

3. One indication of the effect of this obscurity is that the readership of theoretical journals appears to have been quite restricted. For example, it has been estimated that the theoretical journal *Die neue Zeit* had only 10,000 subscribers in 1913, while at least one socialist magazine containing more popular content had a subscription of 370,000. See Arnold Klönne, *Die deutsche Arbeiterbewegung: Geschichte—Ziele—Wirkungen* (Düsseldorf: Eugen Diederichs Verlag, 1980), p. 124.

4. William Liebknecht, *Socialism: What It Is and What It Seeks to Accomplish* (Chicago: Charles H. Kerr, 1897), pp. 34–35, wrote: "One. is inclined to say more in a platform than belongs there. We must not confuse a platform with a manifesto." This pamphlet illustrates in a number of ways the distinctions that were drawn between theory and practice. For example, Liebknecht states explicitly that "theory and practice are . . . two very different things," associates theory specifically with Marx's writings, and asserts that practice should take precedence over theory.

5. In other words, practice was not simply dependent on empirical or pragmatic verification; the very definition of practice, of action, and of its consequences was a product of the movement's discourse itself. Althusser makes a similar point: "The proof of the pudding is in the eating! So what! We are interested in the *mechanism* that ensures that it really is a pudding we are eating and not a poached baby elephant, though we *think* we are eating our daily pudding!" Louis Althusser, *Reading Capital* (London: NLB, 1970), p. 57.

6. Joan Wallach Scott, *The Glassworkers of Carmaux: French Craftsmen and Political Action in a Nineteenth-Century City* (Cambridge, Mass.: Harvard University Press, 1974); see esp. pp. 130–138.

7. For another account of this event, see Harvey Goldberg, *The Life of Jean Jaurès* (Madison: University of Wisconsin Press, 1962), pp. 100–107.

8. Furthermore, the differentiation of theory from practice meant that practical failures did not necessarily arouse doubts about theoretical statements. Writing in the 1930s, at a time when the proletariat in both Italy and Germany had been crushed, for example, Max Adler could still assert confidently that what critics described as "the crisis, or even the collapse of Marxism does not affect Marxism as a theory but only as a movement." Max Adler, "Wandlung der arbeiter Klasse?" *Der Kampf* 26 (1933), 367.

9. For instance, August Bebel's biographer has suggested that Bebel, "being himself a man of toil and practical expedients . . . knew that he could not refuse his loyal followers whatever could legally be done to expand the area of civil liberties, social justice, protective legislation, direct taxes, and parliamentary control over the armed forces. In the measure, too, that the masses advanced towards these intermediate goals, the political power of the party would grow and the day of social democracy would approach." See William Harvey Maehl, *August Bebel: Shadow Emperor of the Germany Workers* (Philadelphia: American Philosophical Society, 1980), p. 115.

10. Karl Marx and Frederick Engels, *Selected Works* (New York: International Publishers, 1968), p. 801.

11. Karl Marx and Friedrich Engels, *The Communist Manifesto* (1848; Baltimore: Penguin, 1967), pp. 82–83.

12. Karl Marx, *Selected Works,* vol. 2 (Moscow: Foreign Languages Publishing House, 1951), p. 33. In the initial version, before Engels altered the sentence in the 1891 publication of Marx's *Critique of the Gotha Program,* Marx had more explicitly likened religious needs to excretory functions.

13. For example, *Capital* (1867; reprint, Moscow: Foreign Languages Publishing House, 1959), pp. 84–85, and *Critique of the Gotha Programme* (1875; reprint, Moscow: Foreign Languages Publishing House, 1962), p. 25.

14. Marx and Engels, *The Communist Manifesto,* pp. 98–101.

15. Paul Lafargue, *Economic Evolution* (Chicago: Charles H. Kerr, 1892), pp. 12–27. Lafargue and others also found in the interpolation of religious images and descriptions of the economy an especially powerful means of desacralizing the institutional context. For instance, Lafargue wrote in response to the catechistic question "How does thy God [capital] reward thee?" "Our God allows us to help still our hunger, by looking through the large pier glass windows of stylish restaurants . . . Out of His kindness we are also allowed to warm our limbs, numb with cold, by affording us occasional opportunities to admire the soft fur and thick-spun woolen clothes exhibited in large stores and intended for the comfort of the chosen ones and their high priests only. He also grants us the exquisite joy of regaling

our eyes on the streets and public resorts, with the sight of the sacred crowds of Capitalists and Landlords, to admire their sleekness and roundness, together with their gorgeously decked lackeys and footmen as they drive by in brilliant equipages." Paul Lafargue, *The Religion of Capital* (New York: New York Labor News, 1918), p. 12.

16. For some examples, see Georg Gärtner, *Die nürnberger Arbeiterbewegung, 1868–1908* (1908; reprint, Berlin: Dietz, 1977). See also Hartmann Wunderer, *Arbeitervereine und Arbeiterparteien: Kultur- und Massenorganisationen in der Arbeiterbewegung, 1890–1933* (Frankfurt: Campus Verlag, 1980), esp. pp. 29–37, who suggests that socialist cultural organizations were especially prone to denouncing the bourgeoisie as vulgar and philistine.

17. Liebknecht, *Socialism,* p. 4, emphasis added. A similar appeal to science is evident in Kautsky's defense of the Erfurt Program when he asserts: "Modern science shows that nothing is stationary, that in society, just as in external nature, a continuous development is discoverable"; Karl Kautsky, *The Class Struggle* (Chicago: Charles H. Kerr, 1910), pp. 8–9.

18. One form of these debates that merits mention in passing involved the deliberate intermingling of terms from each end of this discursive speech. Much of the irony in socialist literature, in fact, is generated in this manner. Once a basic polarity between two sets of concepts has been established, it then becomes possible to point out some of the disturbing possibilities by moving an element from one set into the other. In the pamphlet *Socialism,* for example, Liebknecht asserts: "Poverty is the share of labor, riches the portion of the idle" (p. 10). In this case the irony of linking poverty with work and riches with idleness also suggests a sense of injustice. The way in which the contrast is presented associates the wrong reward with the right action. In other instances a similar mixing of categories provides a way of turning the tables, as it were—a turning that suggests the possibility of engaging in effective action. A favorite Marxist phrase such as "expropriating the expropriators," for example, suggests not only an avenue of change but one that returns things to their proper place, thereby restoring a sense of justice.

19. Marx, *Selected Works,* p. 429.

20. Ibid.

21. Steven Lukes, *Marxism and Morality* (Oxford: Clarendon Press, 1985), p. 37.

22. V. I. Lenin, *The State and Revolution* (1917; reprint, Moscow: Foreign Languages Publishing House, 1962), p. 458.

23. One of the things that most impressed John Dewey after listening to Leon Trotsky for nearly two weeks at his fortified villa in Mexico City was the latter's certainty in what to Dewey seemed little more than speculative conjectures. Dewey attributed much of this certainty to Trotsky's

belief in historical determinism. See, for example, John Dewey, *The Case of Leon Trotsky* (New York: Merit Press, 1969), pp. 432–433; and on the role of historical determinism as a means-ends schema, John Dewey, *Their Morals and Ours: Marxist versus Liberal Views on Morality* (1938; reprint, New York: Pathfinder Press, 1969), esp. pp. 52–53.

24. Jean Jaurès, *Studies in Socialism* (New York: G. P. Putnam's Sons, 1906), pp. 34–35.

25. Karl Kautsky, *Ethik und materialistische Geschichtsauffassung* (Stuttgart: Dietz, 1906), p. 99; partially reprinted as "Marxism and Ethics," in *Karl Kautsky: Selected Political Writings,* ed. Patrick Goode (New York: St. Martin's, 1983), pp. 32–52.

26. Indeed, Kautsky proceeds to debunk other ideologies that had provided more specific answers by showing that these answers had now become outdated and unworkable.

27. In *The Communist Manifesto,* Marx and Engels had written mainly of the proletariat and bourgeoisie as two clearly defined social categories but had also conceded that the "lower middle class" was on the verge of becoming part of the proletariat. Later, when the unity platform was forged at Gotha, a distinction was drawn between the "working class" and all other classes which were said to form "one reactionary mass." In his *Critique of the Gotha Programma,* Marx took strong exception to this characterization, arguing that artisans, small manufacturers, and peasants could scarcely be considered a reactionary mass. See especially Marx and Engels, *Selected Works,* p. 326.

28. Kautsky, *The Class Struggle,* p. 43.

29. Lafargue, *Economic Evolution,* pp. 22–23, 25.

30. Klönne, *Die deutsche Arbeiterbewegung,* pp. 35–44, argues that it is an error to see the ultimate split between proletarian and bourgeois democracy as an inevitable historical outcome, given the complex and often cooperative relations existing between workers and other social strata.

31. Quoted in August Bebel, *My Life* (London: T. Fisher Unwin, 1912), pp. 113–114. For background on Bebel's and Liebknecht's reasons for taking a broad view of the working class, see Detlef Lehnert, *Sozialdemokratie zwischen Protestbewegung und Regierungspartei, 1848–1983* (Frankfurt am Main: Suhrkamp, 1983), pp. 44–77.

32. Jaurès, *Studies in Socialism,* pp. 18–19.

33. For example, see Robert Tucker, *Philosophy and Myth in Karl Marx,* 2d ed. (Cambridge: Cambridge University Press, 1972).

34. And yet socialist theoreticians recognized that if the movement was to have any strength, it would have to transcend local and regional differences; thus an abstracted, figural conception of the proletariat came into play, a conception that took only part of its reality from the diverse experiences of the working class itself. For example, on the difficulties of

relating common theoretical concepts to the French and German contexts, see Jutta Seidel, *Deutsche Sozialdemokratie und Parti ouvrier, 1876–1889: Politische Beziehungen und theoretische Zusammenarbeit* (Berlin: Akademie-Verlag, 1982), and on the contrasts between concepts generated in the south German and north Germany contexts, see Heinrich Hirschfelder, *Die bayerische Sozialdemokratie, 1864–1914,* 2 vols. (Erlangen: Verlag Palm and Enke, 1979).

35. Quoted in Henderson, *The Life of Friedrich Engels,* vol. 1, pp. 94–95.

36. Perry Anderson has usefully sought to answer these questions by distinguishing between "moral consciousness" and "moralism" in Marxist discourse: "Moral consciousness is certainly indispensable to the very idea of socialism . . . Moralism, on the other hand, denotes the vain intrusion of moral judgments in lieu of causal understanding—typically, in everyday life and in political evaluations alike, leading to an 'inflation' of ethical terms themselves into a false rhetoric, which lacks the exacting sense of material care and measure that is inseparable from true moral awareness." See Perry Anderson, *Arguments within English Marxism* (London: Verso, 1980), pp. 97–98.

37. Temporal differentiation sometimes combined with physical separation to provide for theoretical reflection over against practical involvements; for example, August Bebel's imprisonment from July 1872 to April 1874 allowed him to reread Marx's *Capital,* to read Engels's *Condition of the Working Class in England* and Lassalle's *System of Acquired Rights,* to learn French and English, and to ponder the writings of Darwin, Mill, Machiavelli, and Plato.

38. Marx and Engels, *The Communist Manifesto,* p. 95.

39. Emile Durkheim, *Elementary Forms of the Religious Life* (New York: Free Press, 1915).

40. Max Adler, *Der Sozialismus und die Intellektuellen* (Vienna: Wiener Volksbuchhandlung Ignaz Brand, 1910), p. 52.

41. Althusser, *Reading Capital;* see esp. pp. 22–28.

42. Althusser writes: "Any object or problem situated on the terrain and within the horizon, i.e., in the definite structured field of the theoretical problematic of a given theoretical discipline, is visible. We must take these words literally. The sighting is thus no longer the act of an individual subject, endowed with the faculty of 'vision' which he exercises either attentively or distractedly; the sighting is the act of its structural conditions, it is the relation of immanent reflection between the field of the problematic and *its* objects and *its problems*." Ibid., p. 25.

43. "Marx's arguments for certain social arrangements are based partly on an appeal to a diverse assortment of goods . . . However, the catalog of

general goods does not entirely determine that socialism be chosen . . . The specific scale of values entailing the choice of socialism cannot be defined or justified in a non–question-begging way." Richard W. Miller, *Analyzing Marx: Morality, Power, and History* (Princeton: Princeton University Press, 1984), p. 52.

44. Liebknecht, *Socialism,* p. 14.

45. Karl Marx and Frederick Engels, *The German Ideology* (1846; reprint, New York: International Publishers, 1947), p. 74.

46. Kautsky, *Ethik und materialistische Geschichtsauffassung,* p. 135.

47. Ibid., p. 128.

48. In this sense, socialism was a self-referential system—that is, one in which specific moral arguments pointed the reader or listener back to the broader framework of the ideology itself. The contrast between a self-referential system and one rooted in more universalistic conceptions of absolute morality is especially evident in Kautsky's critique of Kantian ethics, which, he asserts, "derives its binding force from the fact that it is above and beyond all experience"; Kautsky, "Leben, Wissenschaft, und Ethik," *Neue Zeit* 24 (1906), 517.

49. Kautsky, *Ethik und materialistische Geschichtsauffassung,* p. 131.

50. As the prospect of an immediate attainment of the classless society receded into the distance, the idea of the proletariat developing a heightened moral consciousness in fact became an even stronger symbol in Marxist discourse. Writing in 1921, for example, Kautsky asserted: "The construction of a socialist system of production is now neither the only, nor, in this period, the first task of socialists . . . Thei task . . . is the elevation and the strengthening of the proletariat, heightening its insight into the economic process and its goals and extending the productivity of labour." Kautsky, *Georgien: Eine sozialdemokratische Bauernrepublik* (Vienna: Wiener Volksbuchhandlung, 1921), p. 43.

16. The Legacy of Classical Theory

1. Cf. Marshall D. Sahlins and Elman R. Service, *Evolution and Culture* (Ann Arbor: University of Michigan Press, 1960), p. 12.

2. Emile Durkheim, *The Division of Labor in Society* (1893; reprint, New York: Free Press, 1933).

3. Ibid., p. 287.

4. Talcott Parsons, *Societies: Evolutionary and Comparative Perspectives* (Englewood Cliffs, N.J.: Prentice-Hall, 1971), p. 27.

5. Ibid., p. 15.

6. Niklas Luhmann, *The Differentiation of Society* (New York: Columbia University Press, 1982), p. 101.

7. Robert N. Bellah, *Beyond Belief: Essays on Religion in a Post-Tra-*

ditional World (New York: Harper and Row, 1970), chap. 4; Jürgen Habermas, *Communication and the Evolution of Society* (Boston: Beacon Press, 1979).

8. Pierre Bourdieu, "The Market of Symbolic Goods," *Poetics* 14 (1985), 13–44.

9. Durkheim, *Division of Labor,* pp. 354–355.

10. Ibid., pp. 355–357.

11. Ibid., p. 297.

12. Parsons, *Societies,* p. 48.

13. Ibid., p. 97.

14. Karl Marx and Frederick Engels, *The German Ideology* (1846; reprint, New York: International Publishers, 1947), pp. 40–41.

15. Ibid., p. 39.

16. Max Weber, *Economy and Society* (Berkeley: University of California Press, 1978), p. 1197.

17. Ibid., p. 1209.

18. Ibid.

19. Ibid., p. 1400.

20. These quotes are from *The Eighteenth Brumaire of Louis Napoleon* and from Engels's letter to Ernst Bloch; both are discussed in Raymond Williams, *Marxism and Literature* (Oxford: Oxford University Press, 1977), pp. 75–86.

21. Ibid., p. 491.

22. Ibid. Or to take a different example, Lukács made it clear that subjectivity was a crucial aspect of his formulation of class consciousness when he wrote that class existence "is *subjectively* justified in the social and historical situation, as something which can and should be understood, i.e. as 'right.' " Georg Lukács, *History and Class Consciousness: Studies in Marxist Dialectics* (1922; reprint, Cambridge, Mass.: MIT Press, 1971), p. 50. And he noted that class consciousness consists of what people "thought, felt and wanted at any moment in history" and that it manifests itself essentially as the "psychological thoughts of men about their lives" (p. 50).

23. This emphasis is especially apparent in Marxist studies that have borrowed Freudian notions of the unconscious as a key to the taken-for-grantedness, and therefore power, of capitalist ideology. For instance, see Louis Althusser, *For Marx* (London: New Left Books, 1969), esp. pp. 233–235; and Frederic Jameson, *The Political Unconscious: Narrative as a Socially Symbolic Act* (Ithaca: Cornell University Press, 1981), esp. pp. 17–103, for two examples of the retention of subjectivist notions of culture in studies that have otherwise largely transcended these limitations. For a useful criticism of the subjectivity and individualism in Althusser, see Richard Harland, *Superstructuralism: The Philosophy of Structuralism and Post-Structuralism* (London: Methuen, 1987), esp. pp. 42–51.

24. Göran Therborn, *The Ideology of Power and the Power of Ideology* (London: Verso, 1980), pp. 101–102. For a more extensive discussion of the ways in which culture has been conceptualized in sociological theory, see Robert Wuthnow, *Meaning and Moral Order: Explorations in Cultural Analysis* (Berkeley: University of California Press, 1987), chap. 2.

25. In some formulations of the cultural adaptation model, the logic of explanation also exemplifies the fallacy of teleological reasoning. Cultural adaptation, it is argued, is necessary for further societal development; therefore, the logic of some formulations implies, cultural change occurs *because* it facilitates development. A variant of this problematic form of argumentation is evident in Durkheim's discussion of cultural change. Although Durkheim attempted to avoid a purely teleological form of functionalist reasoning, he ran into difficulty in actually formulating a causal argument about the sources of cultural change. Durkheim specifically argued against a teleological explanation. He stated that the development of culture is generally found to be societally functional, but argued that "it is not the services that it renders that make it progress" (Durkheim, *Division of Labor*, p. 337). Again, he observed that it is false "to make civilization the function of the division of labor"; instead, he insisted that the correct wording is to say that civilization is strictly a "consequence" of the division of labor. But he was somewhat at a loss, if a functionalist argument is disallowed, to say how this connection comes about. Having argued that cultural innovations should not be attributed to hereditary factors such as genius or innate creativity, he nevertheless fell back on an essentially physiological explanation of a different kind. Increases in social complexity lead to new ideas, he suggested, "because this superactivity of general life fatigues and weakens our nervous system [so] that it needs reparations proportionate to its expenditures, that is to say, more varied and complex satisfactions" (p. 337). This argument, of course, clearly exemplifies the tendency toward individualistic, psychological interpretations.

26. Karl Marx and Frederick Engels, *Selected Works* (New York: International Publishers, 1968), pp. 387–388. A similar difficulty is evident in Mannheim's discussion of the proletariat: despite a common class position, the proletariat adopted a variety of internally conflicting ideologies because of different relations to the state. Indeed, Mannheim at one point goes so far as to assert that "the investigator who, in the face of the variety of types of thought, attempts to place them correctly can no longer be content with the undifferentiated class concept, but must reckon with the existing social units and factors that condition social position, aside from those of class." Karl Mannheim, *Ideology and Utopia: An Introduction to the Sociology of Knowledge* (New York: Harcourt, Brace, and World, 1936), p. 276. Mannheim himself does not pursue the matter, however, and others in the Marxist tradition who have recognized similar empirical difficulties

have often been content to regard them simply as inevitable class contradictions. For example, see the remarks about Rousseau in Lukács, *History
and Class Consciousness,* p. 136.

27. Jürgen Habermas, *The Theory of Communicative Action,* vol. 1, *Reason and the Rationalization of Society* (Boston: Beacon Press, 1984), pp. 161–
162.

28. C. B. A. Behrens, *Society, Government, and the Enlightenment: The
Experiences of Eighteenth-Century France and Prussia* (New York: Harper and
Row, 1985), p. 9.

29. Lukács, *History and Class Consciousness,* p. 150.

30. Ibid., pp. 82–83.

31. Durkheim, for example, was particularly adamant about the deterministic connection between social change and cultural development.
"Civilization," he asserted, "is itself the necessary consequence of the
changes which are produced in the volume and density of societies." Durkheim, *Division of Labor,* p. 336.

32. Ibid., p. 337.

33. Bourdieu, "The Market of Symbolic Goods."

34. This line of reasoning also avoids the problem of subjectivity, it
should be noted, insofar as the mediating linkages between societal complexity and ideological change become an institutionalized aggregation of
artists and writers rather than the mental and emotional states of undifferentiated culture consumers.

35. Therborn, *The Ideology of Power and the Power of Ideology,* pp. vii,
115–123.

36. Even theoretical contributions that have tried to bridge the chasm
separating broad deductive generalizations from actual historical analyses
have often shown a remarkable inclination to rely on thematic assertions
rather than looking for the actual mechanisms of change. Karl Mannheim's
otherwise magnificent treatise on ideology and utopia, for example, provides
an illustration of this inclination. In following the class legitimation perspective, it is especially important to him to trace the development of a
class-conscious ideology among the proletariat. Yet, instead of considering
any of the concrete mechanisms (movements, parties, state officials, firms,
associations) linking the rise of this ideology with the growth of industry
in the nineteenth century, Mannheim merely emphasizes the long-term,
incremental appearance of this ideology between the sixteenth and the
nineteenth centuries. Indeed, he states specifically that the lower classes
"only very gradually" and "only bit by bit" arrived at a point where their
ideology became a distinct expression of opposition to the dominant strata.
Mannheim, *Ideology and Utopia,* p. 212; see also p. 240.

37. Even as much as a half century ago, for example, Lukács categor-
ically asserted that it is "not possible to reach an understanding of particular

[historical] forms by studying their successive appearances in an empirical and historical manner." Lukács, *History and Class Consciousness*, p. 186. Among more recent theorists, Habermas, Therborn, and Mark Seliger have in various ways espoused a version of this argument. Therborn, *The Ideology of Power and the Power of Ideology*, p. 54, asserts, for instance, that "it must be theoretically determined which ideologies are feudal, bourgeois, proletarian, petty-bourgeois or whatever; this question is not answerable by historical or sociological induction alone." Habermas, *Toward a Theory of Communicative Action*, p. 197, distinguishes sharply between two levels of inquiry: (1) "the work of rational reconstruction [which] concerns itself with internal relations of meaning and validity, with the aim of placing the structures of worldviews in a developmental-logical order and of arranging the contents in a typology" and (2) "empirical—that is, sociological—analysis [which] is directed to the external determinants of the contents of worldviews and to questions concerning the dynamics of development." Habermas's own work appears to fall primarily in the former category; the present study would appear to fit into his second category.

17. Social Structure and Ideology

1. For an exceptionally useful survey of these developments in the anthropological literature, see Sherry B. Ortner, "Theory in Anthropology since the Sixties," *Comparative Studies in Society and History* 26 (1984), 126–166.

2. Some of these conceptual emphases are discussed in Robert Wuthnow et al., *Cultural Analysis: The Work of Peter L. Berger, Mary Douglas, Michel Foucault, and Jürgen Habermas* (London: Routledge and Kegan Paul, 1984).

3. Karl Marx and Friedrich Engels, *The Communist Manifesto* (1848; reprint, Baltimore: Penguin, 1967), p. 84.

4. Ibid., p. 102.

5. Richard Ashcraft, *Revolutionary Politics and Locke's Two Treatises of Government* (Princeton: Princeton University Press, 1986).

6. Ibid., p. 5.

7. Ibid., p. 7.

8. Ibid., p. 11.

9. David Zaret, *The Heavenly Contract: Ideology and Organization in Pre-Revolutionary Puritanism* (Chicago: University of Chicago Press, 1985); see esp. pp. 3–21.

10. For example, a comparative study of Puritanism in seventeenth-century England and Pietism in Prussia and Württemberg has examined the ways in which broad institutional configurations influenced the likelihood of doctrinally similar religious teachings coming to include arguments about political dissent. Relations between established churches, dissenting move-

ments, landed aristocrats, and state officials turned out to be particularly important in accounting for the variations observed. Mary Fulbrook, *Piety and Politics: Religion and the Rise of Absolutism in England, Württemberg, and Prussia* (Cambridge: Cambridge University Press, 1983).

11. Terry Eagleton, *Criticism and Ideology* (London: NLB, 1976), esp. pp. 44–63.

12. Ibid., p. 48.

13. Ibid., pp. 62–63.

14. See, for example, Raymond Williams, *The Sociology of Culture* (New York: Schocken, 1981); Göran Therborn, *The Ideology of Power and the Power of Ideology* (London: Verso, 1980); and Fredric Jameson, *The Political Unconscious: Narrative as a Socially Symbolic Act* (Ithaca: Cornell University Press, 1981).

15. Several discussions of literary method that bear a close affinity with my own discussion include William C. Dowling, *Jameson, Althusser, Marx: An Introduction to the Political Unconscious* (Ithaca: Cornell University Press, 1984), esp. pp. 114–142; Tzvetan Todorov, *Mikhail Bakhtin: The Dialogic Principle* (Minneapolis: University of Minnesota Press, 1984), esp. pp. 41–59; and M. M. Bakhtin, *The Dialogic Imagination: Four Essays* (Austin: University of Texas Press, 1981), esp. pp. 259–422.

Index